World Dictionary of
Awards and Prizes

World Dictionary of Awards and Prizes

London

Europa Publications Limited

Europa Publications Limited
18 Bedford Square, London, WC1B 3JN

© Europa Publications Limited, 1979

British Library Cataloguing in Publication Data
World Dictionary of Awards and Prizes
1. Rewards (Prizes, etc.) – Directories
001.4'4   AS8
ISBN 0-905118-32-4

Printed and bound in England by
Staples Printers Rochester Limited
at the Stanhope Press

Contents

Foreword

This book contains information on over 2,000 international and national awards from 62 countries. The emphasis in our selection of awards is on achievement of an intellectual nature and of truly national and international standing. For this reason prestigious lectureships are also included, since these are regarded as honours (often accompanied by a medal or similar award) and offered in recognition of the lecturers' status in their field. Prizes for heroism, voluntary service and sport are excluded; so are grants, fellowships, scholarships and study awards for students and academic staff as these are amply described in other publications.

In nearly every case, the name and address of the awarding body has been printed; where it has not, it is at the express wish of the organization concerned. Prize-winners listed are generally the most recent recipients; however, in some cases, where an historical figure has received the prize, we have included this fact as an item of interest.

Most of the information in the book has been obtained direct from the awarding bodies. This is augmented by secondary sources such as embassies, international organizations, the press, and other relevant bodies. Where we knew of the existence of an important prize but could obtain no direct information, we have included an entry for it, using other sources. We are conscious of inevitable omissions, and we welcome suggestions and further information. These will be carefully considered in preparing a future edition.

We are most grateful to the organizations which replied to our questionnaire, and especially to those embassies, foundations and national and international bodies which responded to our requests for information on prizes in their respective countries and fields of activity.

We should like to mention especially Dr. Frits Hondius of the Council of Europe Secretariat, whose co-operation on the international level is greatly appreciated, and who brought to our notice many of the prizes in the book; Señora Isabel Forero de Moreno of Colciencias, Colombia, who provided the information on the Colombian prizes; and Mr. Aleksander Kwiatkowski of the Swedish Film Institute who provided information on Swedish and Polish film prizes.

How to Use the Book

The entries are arranged in alphabetical order. Where possible, titles of national prizes are given in their original language with an English translation where appropriate. International prizes are generally given their English title.

As is the accepted practice in most countries, prizes distinguished by a proper name are listed according to the surname (family name); e.g. the Jane Addams Children's Book Award is listed under A. Where the proper name starts with a preposition or an article (e.g. von, van der, de la) we have consulted the appropriate authorities and followed the usage of the country concerned (see also below). Hungarian 'name' prizes are listed surname first. Titles in languages where the word for prize precedes the rest of the title (e.g. Premio, Prix) are listed alphabetically under the first word (e.g. Prix des Deux Magots under P).

Three indexes are provided. An alphabetical index is included because many awards whose 'key' word is not immediately obvious are indexed in more than one way. The intention is to obviate cross-references and facilitate the reader's immediate access to the page he wants (e.g. Prix Littéraire de la Résistance is indexed under P, L and R). Prizes distinguished by a compound name are indexed following usage in the country concerned but also in a second or third way (e.g. Balthasar van der Pol Gold Medal is indexed under V and P). German 'name' awards are listed in two ways: under the surname and under the first word (forename).

The subject index provides immediate access to information on prizes in a specific field. Many prizes are given for more than one subject, and these are indexed under all relevant headings.

The geographical index is arranged in alphabetical order of country. International awards are indexed here under the country where the awarding body has its headquarters.

A

ACUM Prizes

Established in 1956 by ACUM (Israel Society of Authors, Composers and Music Publishers), the prizes are for music and literature. The awards (cash prizes to a total of I£18,000) are presented annually at the start of the Jewish New Year. There are two categories: for new works submitted anonymously, and for existing works for which publication is sought. One of the prizes for a popular song is awarded in memory of the late Mordechai Zeira (1903–68), a notable composer of popular songs and for many years Secretary to the Board of Directors of ACUM. The prizes are open to all Israeli citizens.

Awarding body: ACUM Ltd., ACUM House, 118 Rothschild Blvd., P.O.B. 11201, Tel-Aviv 61110, Israel.

Recipients include: Uri Zvi Greenberg (author, 1975); Esther Rab (author, 1975); Paul Ben-Haim (composer, 1975); Oeden Partos (composer, 1975).

ANZAAS Medal

The Australian and New Zealand Association for the Advancement of Science founded this medal in 1965. It is awarded for services in the advancement of science in Australia or New Zealand; for this purpose the word 'science' includes all the subjects included in the various sections of ANZAAS. The annual award is open only to persons normally resident in Australia or New Zealand, and nominations are made by Members or Fellows of ANZAAS.

Awarding body: Australian and New Zealand Association for the Advancement of Science, 157 Gloucester St., Sydney, N.S.W. 2000, Australia.

Recipients include: Dr. C. A. Fleming (1972); Sir Ian Wark (1973); Sir Frederick White (1975); Prof. E. J. Underwood (1976); Dr. Herbert Cole Coombs (1977).

John J. Abel Award in Pharmacology

Eli Lilly & Co., Indianapolis, donated to the American Society for Pharmacology and Experimental Therapeutics the annual John J. Abel Award of $2,000 and a bronze medal, for the purpose of stimulating fundamental research in pharmacology and experimental therapeutics by young investigators. Candidates should be under 36 on 30 April of the year of the award, and must be nominated by a member of ASPET. The award is made for original, outstanding research in the above field. Independence of thought, originality of approach, and clarity and excellence of data presentation are important criteria.

Awarding body: American Society for Pharmacology and Experimental Therapeutics, Inc., 9650 Rockville Pike, Bethesda, Md. 20014, U.S.A.

Sir Patrick Abercrombie Award

This award takes the form of a diploma conferred every two years for a remarkable work in the field of town planning or territorial development. The award was founded in 1974 by the International Union of Architects (UIA). It is not intended for personalities whose world-wide repute is already established. The award is a tribute to the memory of Sir Patrick Abercrombie, one of the first Presidents of the UIA.

Awarding body: International Union of Architects, 1 rue d'Ulm, 75005 Paris, France.

Academy Awards of Merit

These awards, better known as Oscars, were founded in 1927 by the American Academy of Motion Picture Arts and Sciences. Gold statuettes are presented annually in the spring in recognition of outstanding achievements in connection with motion pictures in various categories. Films should have been shown publicly in the Los Angeles area during the preceding calendar year. Academy members make nominations (up to five) in each category, and voting is by secret ballot. The main categories are: best actor; best actress; best supporting actor; best supporting actress; best director; best picture. Other awards are given for work in every field of motion picture making. The presentation ceremony in Los Angeles has become one of the most publicised events of the year; it began as a private dinner with less than 250 people present, and is now watched by TV viewers all over the world.

Awarding body: Academy of Motion Picture Arts and Sciences, 8949 Wilshire Blvd., Beverly Hills, Calif. 90211, U.S.A.

Recipients include: Richard Dreyfuss (best actor, *The Goodbye Girl*), Diane Keaton (best actress, *Annie Hall*), Jason Robards (best supporting actor, *Julia*), Vanessa Redgrave (best supporting actress, *Julia*), Woody Allen (best director, *Annie Hall*), 1978.

Acadia Science Seminars

These lectures are delivered annually at Acadia University by internationally renowned scientists.

They were established in 1972 on the initiative of Charles B. Huggins, Nobel Laureate and Chancellor of Acadia University.
Awarding body: Acadia University, Canada.
Lecturers include: Dr. Floyd Ratliff (U.S.A., 1974–75); Dr. Choh Hao Li (U.S.A., 1975–76); Dr. Victor A. McKusick (U.S.A., 1976–77).

Acoustical Society of America Gold Medal

The medal is presented in the spring of odd-numbered years to a member of the Society for outstanding contributions to acoustics. The first medal was presented in 1954 to mark the 25th anniversary of the Society's foundation.
Awarding body: Acoustical Society of America, 335 East 45th St., New York, N.Y. 10017, U.S.A.
Recipients include: Frederick V. Hunt (1969); Warren P. Mason (1971); Philip M. Morse (1973); Leo L. Beranek (1975); Raymond W. B. Stephens (1977).

Acoustical Society of America Silver Medal

The medal is presented for contributions to the advancement of science, engineering or human welfare through the application of acoustic principles or through research accomplishments in acoustics.
Awarding body: Acoustical Society of America, 335 East 45th St., New York, N.Y. 10017, U.S.A.
Recipients include: Harry F. Olson (1974); Franklin S. Cooper (1975); Isadore Rudnick (1975); Hugh S. Knowles (1976); Theodore J. Schultz (1976).

Acta Metallurgica Gold Medal

This award was established in 1973 by Acta Metallurgica Inc. and is given annually, provided that a suitable candidate is found, for proven ability and leadership in the field of materials research. The gold medal is accompanied by a certificate. Candidates must be proposed by sponsoring or co-operating societies of Acta Metallurgica, which is devoted to the advancement and dissemination of knowledge of materials science. Each society may propose one candidate each year.
Awarding body: Acta Metallurgica Inc., P.O.B. 8, Schenectady, N.Y. 12301, U.S.A.
Recipients include: Prof. Bruce Chalmers (U.S.A., 1974); Prof. Dr. W. G. Burgers (Netherlands, 1975); Sir Alan Cottrell (U.K., 1976); Prof. John W. Cahn (U.S.A., 1977).

Actonian Prize

By a Declaration of Trust in 1838 Mrs. Hannah Acton placed in the hands of trustees securities to the value of £1,070 19s. 0d. upon trust to award every seventh year in memory of her husband, Samuel Acton, a prize of £105 to the person 'who shall, in the judgment of the Committee of Managers of the Royal Institution for the time being, be the Author of the best Essay illustrative of the Wisdom and Beneficence of the Almighty in some department of Science selected by the Managers'.

Awarding body: The Royal Institution of Great Britain, 21 Albemarle St., London W1X 4BS, England.
Recipients include: Sir Alexander Fleming ('Penicillin: Its Discovery, Development and Uses', 1949); A. C. B. Lovell and Martin Ryle ('Researches on Radio Astronomy', 1956); J. Z. Young ('The Nervous System and Comparative Anatomy', 1963); Dame Kathleen Lonsdale ('X-ray Crystallography', 1970); Prof. R. L. Wain ('The Chemical Control of Plant Growth and the Chemical Basis of disease resistance in Plants', 1977).

Actors' Fund of America Award of Merit

This award, which was established in 1910 and revived in 1958, is given for activities contributing to the theatre and/or achievement in the theatre. It takes the form of a framed certificate, and is awarded whenever the occasion arises. Occasionally the Fund may present an individual with a medal and citation, in recognition of services to the theatre in general.
Awarding body: Actors' Fund of America, 1501 Broadway (2600), New York, N.Y. 10036, U.S.A.
Recipients include: Ethel Merman; Richard Rodgers; Alfred Lunt and Lynn Fontaine; Neil Simon; Clive Barnes.

Roger Adams Award in Organic Chemistry

Established in 1959 by Organic Syntheses, Inc. and Organic Reactions, Inc., the award is sponsored by those organizations and the Division of Organic Chemistry of the American Chemical Society. The award is presented biennially to recognize and encourage outstanding contributions to research in organic chemistry defined in its broadest sense. Candidates may be of any nationality. The award consists of a gold medal, a sterling silver replica, and $10,000. The recipient shall deliver a lecture at the Biennial National Organic Chemistry Symposium of the American Chemical Society, at which time the award will be presented; travelling expenses will be paid.
Awarding body: American Chemical Society, 1155 Sixteenth St., N.W., Washington, D.C. 20036, U.S.A.
Recipients include: Vladimir Prelog (1969); Herbert C. Brown (1971); George Wittig (1973); Rolf Huisgen (1975); William S. Johnson (1977).

Adamson Lectureship

The lectureship was founded in 1903 by friends and former colleagues of the late Professor Adamson, who held the Chair of Logic in Owens College (since incorporated in Manchester University) from 1876 to 1893. The lecture is usually delivered every two years by some person of distinction in philosophy, literature or science.
Awarding body: University of Manchester, Manchester M13 9PL, England.
Lecturers include: Prof. James Ward ('Mechanism and Morals: The World of Science and the World of History', 1905); Prof. A. Einstein ('Relativity', 1921); Prof. C. M. Bowra ('The Classical Back-

ground of English Poetry', 1947); Prof. B. Blanshard ('Philosophical Styles', 1953); Dame Helen Gardner ('T. S. Eliot's *The Waste Land*', 1972).

Jane Addams Children's Book Award

The award is presented to the author of a book for children that most effectively promotes the cause of social justice, peace and world community, combined with literary merit. The award was established in 1953 by the Jane Addams Peace Association which was founded in 1948 to foster better understanding between the peoples of the world in order to avoid war. The Association is the educational affiliate of the Women's International League for Peace and Freedom, founded in 1915 with Jane Addams as its first President. The award is made annually, for a book published the previous year. Books submitted may be translations or published in English outside the U.S.A. The winner receives a hand illuminated scroll, and silver seals are placed on the book jacket by the publisher.

Awarding body: Jane Addams Children's Book Award Committee, c/o Bertha Jenkinson, 940 Hayes St., San Francisco, Calif. 94117, U.S.A.

Recipients include: Betty Underwood (*The Tamarak Tree*, 1972); S. Carl Hirsch (*The Riddle of Racism*, 1973); Nicholasa Mohr (*Nilda*, 1974); Charlotte Pomerantz (*The Princess and the Admiral*, 1975); Eloise Greenfield (*Paul Robeson*, 1976).

Aeroacoustics Award

Established by the AIAA in 1973, this annual award is given for outstanding technical or scientific achievement by an individual in the field of aircraft community noise reduction. It comprises a medal and certificate of citation and is presented at the AIAA Aeroacoustics Conference.

Awarding body: American Institute of Aeronautics and Astronautics, 1290 Avenue of the Americas, New York, N.Y. 10019, U.S.A.

Recipients include: Michael J. Lighthill (1975); Herbert Ribner (1976).

Aerodynamic Deceleration Systems Award

Established by the AIAA in 1976, the award recognizes significant contributions to the effectiveness and/or safety of aeronautical or aerospace systems through the development or application of aerodynamic decelerator technology. The award comprises a medal and certificate of citation, and is presented every two years at the Aerodynamic Deceleration Conference.

Awarding body: American Institute of Aeronautics and Astronautics, 1290 Avenue of the Americas, New York, N.Y. 10019, U.S.A.

Aerospace Communications Award

Established by the AIAA in 1967, the award recognizes an outstanding contribution by an individual in the field of aerospace communications. This is held to include, but not be limited to, satellite communication between points on the earth, communication with spacecraft in earth orbit or in interplanetary journey, and communications between spacecraft and aircraft. The award comprises a medal and certificate of citation, and is presented biennially, alternating with the Information Systems Award (*q.v.*), at the Satellite Systems Conference.

Awarding body: American Institute of Aeronautics and Astronautics, 1290 Avenue of the Americas, New York, N.Y. 10019, U.S.A.

Recipients include: Edmund J. Habib (1970); Siegfried H. Reiger (1971); Wilbur Pritchard (1972); Arthur C. Clark (1974); Robert F. Garbarini (1976).

Aerospace Contribution to Society Award

In 1977 the AIAA established this award to recognize a notable contribution to society through the application of aerospace technology to society's needs. The award comprises a medal and certificate of citation, and is presented at either the Aerospace Sciences Meeting or a meeting appropriate to the technology of the primary interest.

Awarding body: American Institute of Aeronautics and Astronautics, 1290 Avenue of the Americas, New York, N.Y. 10019, U.S.A.

African Cultural Institute Grand Prize

The African Cultural Institute, established in 1971, organizes an annual competition for which three main prizes are given in the following categories: literature, art, and science (social science). The first prize in each section is 250,000 francs CFA, a gold medal and a diploma; second and third prizes are awarded of 150,000 francs CFA, a silver medal and diploma, and 100,000 francs CFA, a bronze medal and diploma respectively. Competitors must be citizens of ACI 'member countries.

Awarding body: Institut Culturel Africain, B.P. 01, Dakar, Senegal.

Recipients include: Agbeve Kossi Gam (sculpture, 1976); Mbaye Gana Kebe (poetry, 1976).

'The Age' Book of the Year Award

The award was established in 1974 by Stuart Sayers, then Literary Editor of 'The Age', to encourage and promote Australian writing. It is worth A$3,000, and is offered annually to the author of the book which, in the judges' opinion, is of outstanding literary merit and best expresses Australia's identity and character. Entrants should be Australian by birth or naturalization. Novels, collections of short stories, biographies, poetry, historical and scholarly works are all eligible but must have been published during the year prior to the award.

Awarding body: 'The Age', 250 Spencer Street, Melbourne, Victoria 3000, Australia.

Recipients include: Thea Astley (*The Kindness Cup*, 1975); Hugh Stretton (*Capitalism, Socialism and the Environment*, 1976); A. D. Hope (*A Late Picking*, 1976).

Agfa-Gevaert Gold Medal Award

The award takes the form of a gold medal and is given annually by the Society of Motion Picture and Television Engineers. The recipient will be a person who has shown outstanding leadership, inventiveness and/or other achievement in the research, development, or engineering of new techniques and/or equipment which result in a significant improvement to the interface between motion-picture film and television imaging systems, whereby the combined advantages of both contribute to the further development of visual communications systems.

Awarding body: Society of Motion Picture and Television Engineers, 862 Scarsdale Ave., Scarsdale, N.Y. 10583, U.S.A.

Georg Agricola Denkmünze (*Georg Agricola Medallion*)

Founded in 1924 by the Society of German Foundries and Mines (GDMB), the award is for outstanding achievements in foundry and mining work which have led to progress in technical, practical or economic aspects of these industries. It is awarded annually or every two years in memory of Georg Agricola (1494–1555), originator of the scientific basis of mineralogy, and the technology of mining and foundries. The recipient is selected by decision of the executive and administrative councils of the Society with no restrictions of age, sex or nationality. The award consists of a silver medal and chain and a certificate.

Awarding body: Gesellschaft deutscher Metallhütten- und Bergleute, D-3392 Clausthal-Zellerfeld, Paul-Ernst-Strasse 10, Postfach 210, Federal Republic of Germany.

Recipients include: Dr. Hellmut Ley (1972); Dr. Friedrich-Wilhelm Wrigge (1972); Dr. Hans Fritzsche (1973); Prof. Günter Dorstwilz (1975); Dr. Boris Tougarinoff (Belgium, 1976).

August Ahlqvist, Yrjö Wichmann, Artturi Kannisto and Kai Donner Prize

This annual prize was inaugurated in 1897 by pupils and friends of the late Professor August Ahlqvist. The award is paid from the interest on a fund established in memory of the following persons: August Ahlqvist (1826–89), professor of Finnish language and literature at the University of Helsinki; Yrjö Wichmann (1868–1932), professor of Finno-Ugric languages at the University of Helsinki; Artturi Kannisto (1874–1943), professor of Finno-Ugric languages at the University of Helsinki; Kai Donner (1888–1935), well-known researcher in the field of Uralic languages. The founders of the fund were affiliated to the Finno-Ugric Society. The prize is given for a notable research publication in Finnish or Finno-Ugric linguistics. It is awarded each March, and varies in value between 700 and 3,000 Fmk.

Awarding bodies: Kotikielen Seura, Castrenianum, Fabianinkatu 33, 00170 Helsinki 17; and Suomalais-ugrilainen Seura, Snellmaninkatu 9–11, 00170 Helsinki 17, Finland.

Recipients include: Lauri Posti (1943); Pertti Virtaranta (1947); Osmo Ikola (1951); Matti Sadeniemi (1951); Terho Itkonen (1958).

Air Breathing Propulsion Award

Established by the AIAA in 1975, the award is presented annually for meritorious accomplishment in the science or art of air breathing propulsion, including turbo-machinery or any other technical approach dependent upon atmospheric air to develop thrust or other aerodynamic forces for propulsion or other purposes for aircraft or other vehicles in the atmosphere or on land or sea. The award comprises a medal and certificate of citation, and is usually presented at the Annual Propulsion Conference.

Awarding body: American Institute of Aeronautics and Astronautics, 1290 Avenue of the Americas, New York, N.Y. 10019, U.S.A.

Recipients include: Frederick T. Rall, Jr. (1976).

Aircraft Design Award

Established by the AIAA in 1968, the award is given to a design engineer who conceives, defines or develops an original concept leading to a significant advance in aircraft design or design technology. It comprises a medal and certificate of citation, and is usually presented at the annual Aircraft Systems and Technology Conference.

Awarding body: American Institute of Aeronautics and Astronautics, 1290 Avenue of the Americas, New York, N.Y. 10019, U.S.A.

Recipients include: Ben R. Rich (1972); Herman D. Barkey (1973); Richard T. Whitcomb (1974); Walter E. Fellers (1975); Kendall Perkins (1976).

H. T. Airey Award

This award is made annually by the Metallurgical Society of the Canadian Institute of Mining and Metallurgy in recognition of significant contributions to the advancement of metallurgy in Canada. It was instituted in memory of H. T. Airey, who was instrumental in establishing the Society's Annual Conference of Metallurgists, and it is supported by the Noranda Group of companies. The recipient must be resident in Canada and a member of the Institute. Nominations must be endorsed by not fewer than five members of the Institute. The recipient may be invited to deliver a lecture.

Awarding body: The Metallurgical Society of the Canadian Institute of Mining and Metallurgy, 400-1130 Sherbrooke St. West, Montreal H3A 2M8, Canada.

Recipients include: R. W. Fraser (1971); V. N. Mackie (1972); D. W. McLean (1973); Guy Savard and Robert Lee (1974); G. R. Heffernan (1975).

Akademie-Preis der Philologisch-Historischen Klasse (*Academy Award for History of Philology*)

This prize, established by the Academy of Sciences in Göttingen in 1958, is conferred every two years for outstanding research work in the history of philology. The award is made to philologists under the age of 45, and consists of a certificate and a cash prize.

Awarding body: Akademie der Wissenschaften in Göttingen, 34 Göttingen, Prinzenstr. 1, Fed. Repub. of Germany.
Recipients include: Prof. Dr. W. Barner (1972); Dr. Paul Kunitzsch (1974); Dr. Michael Frede (U.S.A., 1976).

Akademieprys vir vertaalde werk (*Academy przie for translated work*)

In 1948 the South African Academy Selection Committee for the Hertzog prize (*q.v.*) for drama wished to consider a translation into Afrikaans of Euripides' *Women of Troy*. The Academy refused on the grounds that it was not an original creation, and this led to the formation of a separate prize for translation. A cash prize (currently R150, and since 1971 donated by Nedbank) is awarded annually for a translation of prose, poetry or drama into Afrikaans from any other language. Criteria are the accuracy and general success of the translation, and also the esteem that the original work enjoys in its own country.
Awarding body: Suid-Afrikaanse Akademie vir Wetenskap en Kuns, Posbus 538, Pretoria 0001, South Africa.
Recipients include: Uys Krige (*Twaalfde Nag –* Shakespeare) and W. J. du P. Erlank (*Faust –* Goethe), 1969; André P. Brink (*Alice deur die spieël –* Lewis Carroll, 1970); Uys Krige (*Spaans-Amerikaanse ballades,* 1971); Uys Krige (*Koning Lear –* Shakespeare, and *Dokter Teen-wil-en-dank –* Molière, 1972); N. A. Blanckenberg (*Bucolica Georgica –* Vergil, 1977).

Akademischer Preis aus der Dr.-Josef-Schneider, Theresia-Stiftung (*Academic Award of the Dr. Josef Schneider, Theresia Foundation*)

This award was established in 1914 by Dr. Josef Schneider, an ophthalmologist from Milwaukee. It is given biennially in odd-dated years by the University of Würzburg for an outstanding piece of work in some area of medical science, particularly one dealing with endemic illnesses such as tuberculosis. It should have been published in the previous 10 years. There are no restrictions as to age or nationality. The award takes the form of a certificate, commemorative coin and cash prize of between DM700 and DM800.
Awarding body: Fachbereich Medizin der Universität Würzburg, 8700 Würzburg, Josef-Schneider-Strasse 2, Federal Republic of Germany.

Akutagawa Prize

This major Japanese literary award was established in 1935 by the late Kan Kikuchi, founder of the Bungei-Shunju publishing company which sponsors the Society for the Promotion of Japanese Literature. The prize is in memory of Ryunosuke Akutagawa (1872–1927), the well-known Japanese novelist. It is for the best literary work published in the previous six months by an unknown or new writer. The award is made twice a year, in February and August, and consists of 300,000 yen and an inscribed watch.
Awarding body: Society for the Promotion of Japanese Literature, Bungei-Shunju Building, 3 Kioi-cho, Chiyoda-ku, Tokyo 102, Japan.
Recipients include: Kimifusa Abe; Yoshie Hotta; Shotaro Yasuoka; Shintaro Ishihara; Ryu Murakami.

Akzo Prijs

This annual prize was established in 1969 for work in the exact and applied sciences. It consists of 10,000 Dutch guilders and a certificate. The award is open to Dutch scientists and to foreigners working in the Netherlands, and is offered under the auspices of the Dutch Society of Sciences. It is sponsored by Akzo, the chemical company.
Awarding body: Hollandsche Maatschappij der Wetenschappen, Spaarne 17, Haarlem, Netherlands.
Recipients include: Dr. H. C. Volger (organic chemistry, 1971–72); F. J. Zuiderweg (physical technology, 1972–73); Dr. P. Wirtz (entomology, 1973–74); Dr. A. J. Van der Eb (virology, 1974–75); Dr. G. 'tHooft (theoretical physics, 1975–76).

Albert Medal

The award was established in 1864 by the Royal Society of Arts in memory of Prince Albert (1819–61). A gold medal is awarded annually to reward distinction in promoting the arts, manufactures and commerce. There are no restrictions on eligibility but nominations are accepted only from Fellows of the Society.
Awarding body: Royal Society of Arts, John Adam St., Adelphi, London WC2N 6EZ, England.
Recipients include: Her Majesty Queen Elizabeth the Queen Mother (1974); Sir Nikolaus Pevsner (1975); Lord Olivier (1976); Lord Robens of Woldingham (1977); Sir John Charnley (1978).

Alcan Award

This award was established by the Aluminum Co. of Canada Ltd. for a highly significant contribution to the advancement of metallurgy in Canada. It is made annually by the Metallurgical Society of the Canadian Institute of Mining and Metallurgy. The recipient must be resident in Canada, and a member of the Institute. Nominations must be endorsed by not fewer than five members of the Institute. The recipient may be invited to deliver a lecture.
Awarding body: The Metallurgical Society of the Canadian Institute of Mining and Metallurgy, 400–1130 Sherbrooke St. West, Montreal H3A 2M8, Canada.
Recipients include: C. S. Samis (1971); John Convey (1972); Jan Leja (1973); W. M. Armstrong (1974); K. W. Downes (1975).

Alcoa of Australia Award for Architecture

The award was established in 1973 and is sponsored by Alcoa of Australia Ltd. It is administered by the Royal Australian Institute of Architects. The award is made biennially and consists of A$5,000 in cash, an aluminium sculpture, a diploma and a plaque on the building for which the award was made, at the owner's discretion. It is awarded for an executed architectural work of outstanding merit within a State or Territory of Australia. The building must also make a positive contribution to its environment, make use of aluminium in a way which advances the bounds of building technology, and consist of more than one storey used primarily for commercial purposes. Applicants must be corporate members of the Royal Australian Institute of Architects who are also recognized architects in one or more states of Australia.

Awarding body: Royal Australian Institute of Architects, 2A Mugga Way, Red Hill, A.C.T. 2603, Australia.

Alexander Prize

This prize, in the form of a silver medal, was established in 1897 by L. C. Alexander, F.R.Hist.S. It is given annually for an essay on an historical subject; this must be a genuine work of original research, not hitherto published, and one which has not been awarded any other prize. The essay must be in English and not exceed 6,000 words. Prize-winning essays are printed in the Society's *Transactions*.

Awarding body: Royal Historical Society, University College, Gower St., London WC1E 6BT, England.

Allerton Award

To honour Robert Allerton, one of the founding benefactors of the Pacific Tropical Botanical Garden, the Trustees of the Garden inaugurated in 1975 the Robert Allerton Medal, which is awarded biennially for excellence in the fields of tropical botany or horticulture. The bronze medal is accompanied by an honorarium of $1,000, and the recipient is asked to read a paper at the presentation ceremony. Members of the Pacific Garden's International Scientific Advisory Committee and other relevant scientists make recommendations for the award.

Awarding body: Pacific Tropical Botanical Garden, Hawaii, U.S.A.

Recipients include: R. E. Holttum (1975); C. G. G. J. van Steenis (1977).

Alpár Ignác Memorial Medal

The Hungarian Building Society established this award in 1958 in memory of Ignác Alpár (1855–1928), a famous architect. The medal is for outstanding technical, economic, scientific or teaching achievements in the building industry, or for exceptional work for the Society. Seven prizes of 10,000 forints each are awarded annually.

Awarding body: Epitőipari T.E., c/o Federation of Technical and Scientific Societies, 1055 Budapest, Kossuth Lajos tér 6–8, Hungary.

Alpha Chi Sigma Award for Chemical Engineering Research

This award is sponsored by the Alpha Chi Sigma Fraternity and presented by the American Institute of Chemical Engineers to an individual, who need not be a member of either body, who in the previous 10 years has conducted outstanding fundamental or applied research in the field of chemical engineering. This should normally have been carried out in North America. The award is generally made annually, and consists of a certificate and $1,000. The recipient is invited to present his work at a symposium arranged in his honour, or a meeting of the Institute.

Awarding body: American Institute of Chemical Engineers, 345 East 47th St., New York, N.Y. 10017, U.S.A.

R. P. Alston Medal

Founded as a prize in 1940 by Mrs. H. G. Alston in memory of her husband, Peter Alston, who was killed in a flying accident in 1939, this award was originally intended for work aimed at the improvement of the safety of aircraft, particularly in stability and control. Since 1948 it has been awarded for practical achievement associated with the flight testing of aircraft, and since 1957 has been given as a medal.

Awarding body: The Royal Aeronautical Society, 4 Hamilton Place, London, W1V 0BQ, England.

Recipients include: A. L. Blackman (1972); D. Lean (1973); J. F. Farley (1974); D. M. S. Simpson (1975); T. M. S. Ferguson (1976).

Alvarenga Prize

The prize was founded in 1883 by the Swedish Society of Medical Sciences. It is awarded every year for an unpublished paper on some aspect of medical research. Applicants should be Swedish citizens. The prize money is currently about 8,900 kronor. The prize is named after the Portuguese doctor, Pedro Francisco da Costa Alvarenga, who was famous for his work on heart disease.

Awarding body: Swedish Society of Medical Sciences, P.O.B. 558, S-101 27 Stockholm, Sweden.

Recipients include: Ole Eklöf and Hans Ringertz (for a method of kidney size assessment, 1976).

American Academy of Arts and Letters Award of Merit

The Award of Merit is given annually to an outstanding person in America, who is not a member of the Institute of Arts and Letters, representing one of the following arts, in the order named: painting, sculpture, the novel, poetry, and drama. The award consists of a medal and a cash prize.

Awarding body: American Academy and Institute of Arts and Letters, 633 West 155th St., New York, N.Y. 10032, U.S.A.

American Association for the Advancement of Science – Newcomb Cleveland Prize

This award is made annually for an outstanding paper published in the Reports section of the journal *Science* during the past year (October to September), which has not previously appeared in another publication. Nominations are submitted by readers. The award consists of a bronze medal and cash prize of $5,000. It was established in 1923 with a donation from the late Newcomb Cleveland; originally it was known as the AAAS Thousand Dollar Prize, then as the American Association Award, and in 1951, after the donor's death, was renamed the AAAS-Newcomb Cleveland Prize.

Awarding body: AAAS-Newcomb Cleveland Prize, American Association for the Advancement of Science, 1515 Massachusetts Ave., N.W., Washington, D.C. 20005, U.S.A.

Recipients include: Cornelia P. Channing (1969); James W. Truman (1970); Alan Gelperin (1971); Bruce M. Carlson (1972); Amos Nur (1974).

American Association for the Advancement of Science – Rosenstiel Award in Oceanographic Science

This award, consisting of $5,000 and a certificate, was established in 1975 with a donation from the Rosenstiel Foundation through the Rosenstiel School of Marine and Atmospheric Science of the University of Miami. It is presented annually for outstanding achievement in oceanographic science, including relevant aspects of ocean engineering, and atmospheric science. The prize is awarded annually in rotation in one of three broad categories: physics, chemistry of the water column and the atmosphere; geology, physics and chemistry of the seabed; biology and living resources.

Awarding body: American Association for the Advancement of Science, c/o Harris B. Stewart, Jr., Atlantic Oceanographic and Meteorological Labs., NOAA, 15 Rickenbacker Causeway, Miami, Fla. 33149, U.S.A.

Recipients include: Kenneth O. Emery (geology, physics, chemistry of the sea-bed, 1975); Gordon A. Riley (biology and living resources, 1976).

American Association for the Advancement of Science Socio-Psychological Prize

This prize, consisting of $1,000, is offered annually for a paper that furthers understanding of the psychological, social and cultural behaviour of human beings. All nationalities are eligible, and the works may be either unpublished or recently published, but they must be methodological in approach, not purely empirical or theoretical. The award was established in 1952 with a donation from Arthur F. Bentley.

Awarding body: American Association for the Advancement of Science Executive Office, 8th Floor, 1776 Massachusetts Ave., N.W., Washington, D.C. 20036, U.S.A.

Recipients include: David C. Glass and Jerome E. Singer (1971); Norman H. Anderson (1972); Lenora Greenbaum (1973); William E. McAuliffe and Robert A. Gordon (1974); R. B. Zajonc and Gregory B. Markus (1975).

American Association for the Advancement of Science – Westinghouse Science Writing Awards

These awards, sponsored by the Westinghouse Educational Foundation, are presented annually for outstanding writing on the natural sciences and their engineering and technological applications,

excluding the field of medicine. Awards are made in three categories: general magazines (the Association's own publications excluded); newspapers with a daily circulation of more than 10,000; and newspapers with a circulation of less than 10,000. The award in each category consists of a cash prize of $1,000. Entries must generally have been published during the preceding year (November to October).

Awarding body: American Association for the Advancement of Science, 1776 Massachusetts Ave., N.W., Washington, D.C. 20036, U.S.A.

Recipients include: David Perlman (San Francisco *Chronicle*), Elizabeth J. Maggio (Arizona *Daily Star*), Paul Brodeur (*The New Yorker*, 1975); Paul G. Hayes (*The Milwaukee Journal*), Don Alan Hall (*Corvallis (Oregon) Gazette-Times*), Jonathan Eberhart (*Science News*, 1976).

American Association for Clinical Chemistry Award for Outstanding Contributions to Clinical Chemistry

The award was established in 1952 by the Ames Company, a pharmaceutical and reagent company. A scroll, a bronze medal and an honorarium of $1,000 are offered annually for achievements in clinical chemistry.

Awarding body: American Association for Clinical Chemistry, 1725 K St., N.W., Suite 1402, Washington, D.C. 20006, U.S.A.

Recipients include: David Seligson (1971); Ralph E. Thiers (1972); Bernard Klein (1975); Norman Anderson (1976); Donald S. Young (1977).

American Association for Clinical Chemistry Award for Outstanding Contributions to Clinical Chemistry in a Selected Area

Established by Boehringer Mannheim Corporation, a laboratory reagents and equipment firm, to recognize those who have advanced the field of clinical chemistry by their work in a particular area. The prize of a plaque and an honorarium of $1,000 is awarded annually.

Awarding body: American Association for Clinical Chemistry, 1725 K St., N.W., Suite 1402, Washington, D.C. 20006, U.S.A.

Recipients include: George N. Bowers, Jr. (enzymology, 1973); Lena Armstrong Lewis (lipids and lipoproteins, 1974); Rosalyn S. Yalow (1975); Nathan O. Kaplan (1976); Theodore Peters, Jr. (1977).

American Association for Clinical Chemistry Award for Outstanding Contributions through Service to Clinical Chemistry as a Profession

The award was established in 1966 by the Fisher Scientific Company, a laboratory equipment and supplies firm. A plaque and an honorarium of $1,000 are offered annually to honour a clinical chemist whose outstanding services have benefited the profession.

Awarding body: American Association for Clinical Chemistry, 1725 K St., N.W., Suite 1402, Washington, D.C. 20006, U.S.A.

Recipients include: Kurt M. Dubowski (1973); Joseph Benotti (1974); Gerald R. Cooper (1975); Robert S. Melville (1976); Joseph H. Boutwell, Jr. (1977).

American Association for Clinical Chemistry Award for Outstanding Efforts in Education and Training

Established in 1971 by Smith Kline Clinical Laboratories, the award recognizes those who, by their efforts in the education and training of clinical chemists, have helped obtain recognition of clinical chemistry as an entity within the broad field of chemistry. The prize consists of an honorarium of $1,000 and is awarded annually.

Awarding body: American Association for Clinical Chemistry, 1725 K St., N.W., Suite 1402, Washington, D.C. 20006, U.S.A.

Recipients include: Joseph I. Routh (1973); Morton K. Schwartz (1974); Max E. Chilcote (1975); Norbert W. Tietz (1976); Hugh J. McDonald (1977).

American Chemical Society Award in Analytical Chemistry

Established in 1947 by the Fisher Scientific Company, the award is for the recognition and encouragement of outstanding contributions to the science of analytical chemistry, pure or applied, carried out in the U.S.A. or Canada. A nominee must be a resident of the U.S.A. or Canada. Special consideration will be given to the independence of thought and the originality shown, or to the importance of the work when applied to public welfare, economics or the needs and desires of humanity. This annual award consists of $2,000 and an etching; travelling expenses incidental to the conferring of the award are met.

Awarding body: American Chemical Society, 1155 Sixteenth St., N.W., Washington, D.C. 20036, U.S.A.

Recipients include: James D. Winefordner (1973); Philip W. West (1974); Sidney Siggia (1975); Howard V. Malmstadt (1976); George G. Guilbault (1977).

American Chemical Society Award in Chemical Education

The award was established in 1950 by the Scientific Apparatus Makers Association, and sponsorship was assumed by the Union Carbide Corporation in 1976. The award is presented annually to recognize outstanding contributions to chemical education; this is considered in its broadest meaning, including the training of professional chemists; the dissemination of reliable information about chemistry to prospective chemists, to members of the profession, to students in other fields and to the general public; and the integration of chemistry into the U.S. educational system. The activities recognized by the award may lie in the fields of teaching (at any level), organization and administration, influential writing, educational research, the methodology of instruction, establishment of standards of instruction and public

enlightenment. Preference shall be given to American citizens. The award consists of $2,000 and a suitably inscribed certificate. An allowance of $350 is provided for travelling expenses to the meeting at which the award is made.

Awarding body: American Chemical Society, 1155 Sixteenth St., N.W., Washington, D.C. 20036, U.S.A.

Recipients include: Robert C. Brasted (1973); George S. Hammond (1974); William T. Lippincott (1975); Leallyn B. Clapp (1976); Robert W. Parry (1977).

American Chemical Society Award in Chromatography

This annual award was established by Lab-Line Instruments, Inc. in 1959, and sponsorship was assumed by SUPELCO, Inc. in 1970. It is intended to recognize outstanding contributions to the fields of chromatography, with particular consideration given to the development of new methods. The award consists of $2,000 and a certificate. An allowance of up to $350 is provided for travelling expenses to the meeting at which the award is presented.

Awarding body: American Chemical Society, 1155 Sixteenth St., N.W., Washington, D.C. 20036, U.S.A.

Recipients include: Albert Zlatkis (1973); Lockhart B. Rogers (1974); Egon Stahl (1975); James S. Fritz (1976); Raymond P. W. Scott (1977).

American Chemical Society Award in Colloid or Surface Chemistry

The award was established in 1952 by the Kendall Company to recognize and encourage outstanding scientific contributions to colloid or surface chemistry in the U.S.A. and Canada. Special consideration will be given to the independence of thought and the originality shown. Nominees must be residents of the U.S.A. or Canada. The award consists of $2,000 and a certificate. An allowance of not more than $350 is provided for travelling expenses to the meeting at which the award will be presented.

Awarding body: American Chemical Society, 1155 Sixteenth St., N.W., Washington, D.C. 20036, U.S.A.

Recipients include: Robert L. Burwell, Jr. (1973); W. Keith Hall (1974); Robert Gomer (1975); Robert J. Good (1976); Michel Boudart (1977).

American Chemical Society Award for Creative Invention

Established in 1966 by the ACS, the award recognizes individual inventors for successful applications of research in chemistry and/or chemical engineering which contribute to the material prosperity and happiness of people. A nominee must be a resident of the U.S.A. or Canada. A patent must have been granted for the work to be recognized and it shall have been developed during the preceding seventeen years. The annual award consists of $2,000, a gold medal and bronze replica. Travelling expenses up to $350, incidental to the conferring of the award, are paid.

Awarding body: American Chemical Society, 1155 Sixteenth St., N.W., Washington, D.C. 20036, U.S.A.

Recipients include: Carl Djerassi (1973); Charles C. Price (1974); James D. Idol, Jr. (1975); Manuel M. Baizer (1976); Herman A. Bruson (1977).

American Chemical Society Award for Creative Work in Synthetic Organic Chemistry

The award was established in 1955 by Synthetic Organic Chemical Manufacturers Association; sponsorship was assumed by Aldrich Chemical Company, Inc. in 1976. It is intended to recognize and encourage creative work in synthetic organic chemistry. A nominee must have accomplished such work and had it published in an American journal during the five years prior to the year of the award. The award consists of $2,000 and a certificate; the recipient may claim up to $350 travelling expenses for attending the presentation ceremony.

Awarding body: American Chemical Society, 1155 Sixteenth St., N.W., Washington, D.C. 20036, U.S.A.

Recipients include: Bruce Merrifield (1972); George Buchi (1973); Edward C. Taylor (1974); Herbert O. House (1975); Franz Sondheimer (1976).

American Chemical Society Award for Distinguished Service in the Advancement of Inorganic Chemistry

Established in 1963, this annual award has been sponsored by Mallinckrodt, Inc. since 1965. Nominees must have demonstrated extensive contributions to the advancement of inorganic chemistry. Activities recognized by the award may include such fields as teaching, writing, research and administration. A nominee must be a member of the American Chemical Society. The award consists of $2,000, an appropriate certificate and an allowance of not more than $250 for travelling expenses to the meeting at which the award is presented.

Awarding body: American Chemical Society, 1155 Sixteenth St., N.W., Washington, D.C. 20036, U.S.A.

Recipients include: Ronald J. Gillespie (1973); F. Albert Cotton (1974); Fred Basolo (1975); Daryle H. Busch (1976); James L. Hoard (1977).

American Chemical Society Award in Inorganic Chemistry

The award was established in 1960 by Texas Instruments, Inc., and sponsorship was assumed by Monsanto Company in 1976. It is intended to recognize and encourage fundamental research in the field of inorganic chemistry. A nominee must have accomplished outstanding research in the preparation, properties, reactions or structure of inorganic substances. Special consideration shall

be given to the independence of thought and originality shown. There are no restrictions as to age, nationality or sex. The award consists of $2,000 and a certificate. An allowance of not more than $350 is provided for travelling expenses to the meeting at which the award will be presented.

Awarding body: American Chemical Society, 1155 Sixteenth St., N.W., Washington, D.C. 20036, U.S.A.

Recipients include: Theodore L. Brown (1972); M. F. Hawthorne (1973); Lawrence F. Dahl (1974); James P. Collman (1975); Richard H. Holm (1976).

American Chemical Society Award for Nuclear Applications in Chemistry

The award was established in 1953 by Nuclear-Chicago Corporation, a subsidiary of G. D. Searle & Co., its sponsors. Its purpose is to recognize, encourage and stimulate isotopic applications in the field of chemistry. There are no limits as to age or nationality. The annual award consists of $2,000 and a certificate. An allowance of not more than $300 is provided for travelling expenses to the meeting at which the award will be presented.

Awarding body: American Chemical Society, 1155 Sixteenth St., N.W., Washington, D.C. 20036, U.S.A.

Recipients include: Albert Ghiorso (1973); Lawrence E. Glendenin (1974); John R. Huizenga (1975); John O. Rasmussen (1976); Glen E. Gordon (1977).

American Chemical Society Award in Petroleum Chemistry

The award was sponsored by Precision Scientific Company from 1948 to 1973, when sponsorship was assumed by The Lubrizol Corporation. It is usually presented annually, but no awards were given in 1974 or 1975. It is intended to recognize, encourage and stimulate outstanding research achievements in the field of petroleum chemistry in the U.S.A. and Canada. A nominee must be a resident of one of these countries and have accomplished research in the chemistry of petroleum or fundamental research that contributes directly and materially to the knowledge of petroleum and its products. Special consideration shall be given to the independence of thought and the originality shown. The award consists of $5,000 and a certificate. An allowance of $350 is provided for travelling expenses to the meeting at which the award will be presented.

Awarding body: American Chemical Society, 1155 Sixteenth St., N.W., Washington, D.C. 20036, U.S.A.

Recipients include: Gerasimos J. Karabtsos (1971); Paul G. Gassman (1972); Joe W. Hightower (1973); John H. Sinfelt (1976); Sidney W. Benson (1977).

American Chemical Society Award in Polymer Chemistry

The award was established in 1962 by the Witco Chemical Corporation Foundation to recognize outstanding contributions to polymer chemistry. The award is granted without regard to age, nationality or sex. It consists of $2,000 and a certificate. An allowance of $300 is provided for travelling expenses to the meeting at which the award is made.

Awarding body: American Chemical Society, 1155 Sixteenth St., N.W., Washington, D.C. 20036, U.S.A.

Recipients include: Turner Alfrey, Jr. (1973); John D. Ferry (1974); Leo Mandelkern (1975); Paul W. Morgan (1976); William J. Bailey (1977).

American College of Physicians Award

This award was established in 1958 and is bestowed for outstanding contributions to science as related to medicine. It is presented annually, and takes the form of a medal.

Awarding body: American College of Physicians, 4200 Pine St., Philadelphia, Pa. 19104, U.S.A.

Recipients include: Solomon A. Berson, Rosalyn S. Yalow (1971); Robert A. Good (1972); H. Sherwood Lawrence (1973); George C. Cotzias (1974).

American College of Physicians Distinguished Teacher Award

This award was established in 1968 and is made to a physician who has shown outstanding qualities as a teacher, particularly by inspiring others to attainments in the field of medical education. It is presented annually, and takes the form of a medal.

Awarding body: American College of Physicians, 4200 Pine St., Philadelphia, Pa. 19104, U.S.A.

Recipients include: George C. Griffith (1971); Thomas M. Durant (1972); Thomas Hale Ham, Robert F. Loeb (1973); William S. Middleton (1974).

American Council on Education Book Award

The Borden Foundation established the prize in 1962. It is given for significant contributions to the knowledge and advancement of postsecondary education in the United States. It is a cash prize of $1,000, and is awarded annually at the ACE's Annual Meeting.

Awarding body: American Council on Education, 1 Dupont Circle, Washington, D.C. 20036, U.S.A.

Recipients include: Joseph Ben-David (*American Higher Education*, 1972); David Riesman and Verne Stadtman (*Academic Transformation: Seventeen Institutions under Pressure*, 1973); Arthur Levine and John Weingart (*Reform of Undergraduate Education*, 1974); K. Patricia Cross (*Accent on Learning*, 1976); Murray G. Ross (*The University: The Anatomy of Academe*, 1977).

American Film Festival

The first annual American Film Festival, sponsored by the Educational Film Library Association, was held in 1959. During the Festival a Blue Ribbon is awarded to the highest rated film in each category and a Red Ribbon to runners-up. No Blue Ribbon is awarded in a category if no film scores over 75 per cent; in this case a Red Ribbon is awarded to the top ranked film in that category.

The Emily prize is awarded to the film which receives the highest numerical value of all the Blue Ribbon winners. The Grierson Award is given to a new documentary film maker in the social documentary field. The Blue Ribbon consists of a certificate and a trophy, the Red Ribbon of a certificate, the Emily of a trophy and the Grierson Award of a cash sum of $500. The Emily was named in honour of Emily Jones who was the Educational Film Library Association's Administrative Director from 1946 to 1969. Films must have been released within a two-year period prior to the Festival.

Awarding body: American Film Festival, 43 West 61st St., New York, N.Y. 10023, U.S.A.

American Institute of Chemical Engineers Award in Chemical Engineering Practice

This award is sponsored by the Bechtel Corporation and presented to a member of the Institute who has made an outstanding contribution to the industrial practice of the profession. This may be in such areas as development, design, marketing, manufacturing, economic analysis and planning; it is likely to be as an innovator, in the implementation of a research development, or in a supervisory or managerial capacity concerned with such development. The award is usually made annually, and takes the form of a certificate and $1,000.

Awarding body: American Institute of Chemical Engineers, 345 East 47 St., New York, N.Y. 10017, U.S.A.

American Institute of Chemical Engineers Award for Service to Society

This award is sponsored by the Fluor Corporation and presented by the American Institute of Chemical Engineers to one of its members for achievements of benefit to the community, and the solution of socially orientated problems. It is generally made annually, and consists of a certificate and $1,000.

Awarding body: American Institute of Chemical Engineers, 345 East 47 St., New York, N.Y. 10017, U.S.A.

American Institute of Chemical Engineers Founders Award for Outstanding Contributions to Chemical Engineering

This award is presented by the Institute to a member whose achievements have helped to advance the profession. It takes the form of a certificate and commemorative pin.

Awarding body: American Institute of Chemical Engineers, 345 East 47 St., New York, N.Y. 10017, U.S.A.

American Institute of Food Technologists International Award

This award is made annually to a member of the Institute who has made outstanding efforts to promote the international exchange of ideas and understanding in the field of food technology. It consists of an engraved silver salver donated by the Australian Institute of Food Science and Technology and a $1,000 honorarium from the Institute. Candidates are nominated by members of the Institute.

Awarding body: Institute of Food Technologists, Suite 2120, 221 North La Salle St., Chicago, Ill. 60601, U.S.A.

Recipients include: Fritz H. Reuter (1972); Francis Aylward (1973); Hisateru Mitsuda (1974); Georg A. Borgstrom (1975); Clinton O. Chichester (1976).

American Institute of Physics – U.S. Steel Foundation Science-Writing Award in Physics and Astronomy

Established in 1968, this award is given in two categories: to a journalist and to a physicist. It is given to stimulate and recognize distinguished writing that improves public understanding of physics and astronomy. The awards are given annually and consist of a Moebius Strip and a cash sum of $1,500.

Awarding body: American Institute of Physics, 335 East 45th St., New York, N.Y. 10017, U.S.A.

Recipients include: (journalists) Patrick Young (1974); Tom Alexander (1975); Frederic Golden (1976); (physicists) R. D. Chapman (1974); Robert March (1975); Jeremy Bernstein (1976).

American Meteorological Society Award for Applied Meteorology

This award is made to an individual for outstanding contributions to the advance of applied meteorology. These may take the form either of direct application of meteorological or climatological knowledge to the fulfilment of industrial or agricultural needs, or of research and development of scientific knowledge which can meet such needs.

Awarding body: American Meteorological Society, 45 Beacon St., Boston, Mass. 02108, U.S.A.

Recipients include: Robert E. Munn (1973); Robert A. McCormick (1974); William H. Klein (1975); Don G. Friedman; Bernard Vonnegut (1976).

American Meteorological Society Award for Outstanding Achievement in Bioclimatology

This is an occasional award given to an individual who has made outstanding contributions in the field of bioclimatology. The recipient is nominated by the Society's Awards Committee from a list submitted by the Committee on Biometeorology.

Awarding body: American Meteorological Society, 45 Beacon St., Boston, Mass. 02108, U.S.A.

Recipients include: William G. Wellington (1969); David M. Gates (1971); Igho H. Kornblueh (1972); Harold D. Johnson (1973); G. LeRoy Hahn (1976).

American Meteorological Society Editor's Award

This award is made annually to an individual who has contributed a referee's report of outstanding merit on a manuscript submitted for publication in a journal of the Society, in recognition of the important role played by the reviewing process in scientific writing.

Awarding body: American Meteorological Society, 45 Beacon St., Boston, Mass. 02108, U.S.A.

Recipients include: George W. Platzman (1973); Norihiko Fukuta (1974); Gabriel T. Csanady (1975); Stanley L. Barnes; Robert E. Dickinson (1976).

American Meteorological Society Special Awards and Citations

These are made to individuals or organizations who have made important contributions either to the science or practice of meteorology or to the Society, where a specific existing award would not be appropriate. They are frequently made to individuals employed at other than professional level (such as co-operative observers) and to amateurs who have made important contributions to meteorology. Awards are made annually, in such number as the Council of the Society decides.

Awarding body: American Meteorological Society, 45 Beacon St., Boston, Mass. 02108, U.S.A.

Recipients include: Illinois State Water Survey (1974); Robert O. Reid; National Weather Service Office, Huntsville, Ala.; Det. 15, 15th Wea. Sq., 5th Wea. Wg., Air Weather Service, Wright-Patterson AFB, Ohio (1975); Albert W. Duckworth (1976).

American Nuclear Society Special Award

This award has been made annually since 1962 for an outstanding contribution in a particular area, which is determined each year. The topic for 1977 was 'The Fuel Cycle'. Candidates are selected on the basis of nomination, and the winner receives a certificate and cash award of $1,000.

Awarding body: American Nuclear Society, 555 N. Kensington, LaGrange Park, Ill. 60525, U.S.A.

American Oil Chemists' Society Award in Lipid Chemistry

This award is made annually for outstanding original research in lipid chemistry of fundamental and far-reaching importance, the results of which have been presented through publication of technical papers of high quality. The award was established in 1964, and consists of a plaque and honorarium of $2,500. The Society's membership consists of scientists working in the fields of chemistry, biochemistry, nutrition or the processing of fats, oils and lipids.

Awarding body: American Oil Chemists' Society, 508 South 6th St., Champaign, Ill. 61820, U.S.A.

Recipients include: A. T. James (1972); F. D. Gunstone (1973); P. F. Stumpf (1974); W. O. Lundberg (1975); George J. Popjak (1977).

American Pharmaceutical Association – Academy of Pharmaceutical Sciences Research Achievements Awards

Established in 1961 by the American Pharmaceutical Association Foundation through grants from various pharmaceutical firms, the Research Achievement Awards are presented in recognition of outstanding individual contributions in specific areas of pharmacy. Each award consists of an inscribed certificate, a cash sum and travel expenses to the Annual Meeting to accept the award. There were originally seven awards but one was discontinued. Not all awards are given every year.

Awarding body: American Pharmaceutical Association, 2215 Constitution Avenue, N.W., Washington, D.C. 20037, U.S.A.

Recipients include: Ernest G. Wollish (drug standards and assay, 1975); Erminio Costa (pharmacology, 1975); Heinz G. Floss (natural products, 1976); John L. Lach (pharmaceutics, 1975); Milo Gibaldi (stimulation of research, 1976); Everett May (pharmaceutical and medicinal chemistry, 1976).

American Physical Society High-Polymer Physics Prize

The Ford Motor Company established the prize in 1960 to recognize outstanding accomplishments and excellence of contributions in high-polymer physics research. Nominations are open to scientists of all nations; the prize may be awarded to more than one person on a shared basis. It is awarded annually and consists of $3,000 and a certificate citing the contributions made by the recipient.

Awarding body: American Physical Society, 335 East 45th St., New York, N.Y. 10017, U.S.A.

Recipients include: Frank A. Bovey (1974); Walter H. Stockmayer (1975); Richard S. Stein (1976); Samuel Krimm (1977).

American Physical Society International Prize for New Materials

Sponsored by the International Business Machines Corporation, the prize is given to recognize and encourage outstanding achievement in the science and application of new materials, including theoretical and experimental work contributing significantly to the understanding of such materials. Nominations are open to scientists of all nationalities; the prize may be awarded to more than one person on a shared basis although preferably to not more than three persons. It is awarded annually and consists of $5,000, a travel allowance to the meeting of the Society at which the prize is announced, and a certificate citing the contributions made by the recipient.

Awarding body: American Physical Society, 335 East 45th St., New York, N.Y. 10017, U.S.A.

Recipients include: William G. Pfann and Henry C. Theurer (1976); Francis Bundy, H. Tracy Hall, Herbert Strong and Robert H. Wentof, Jr. (1977).

American Society of Civil Engineers State-of-the-Art of Civil Engineering Award

Because the science and art of civil engineering can cope with the information expansion only if its most gifted practitioners will review and interpret the state-of-the-art for the benefit of their colleagues, in 1966 the professional associates of

John D. Winter, M.A.S.C.E., endowed this prize. It is anticipated that a direct benefit of this award will be the scholarly review, evaluation, and documentation of the scientific and technical information needed by the profession. Annually, each technical division of the ASCE encourages individuals or committees to prepare papers on the status of knowledge in special areas of interest. These papers are published in the Division Journals, and each Division then nominates one paper for judging on a Society-wide basis. The authors of winning papers receive a suitable plaque and certificate.

Awarding body: American Society of Civil Engineers (ASCE), 345 East 47th St., New York, N.Y. 10017, U.S.A.

Recipients include: Committee of Atmospheric Pollution of the Environmental Engineering Division ('NO_x Emissions from Stationary Sources', 1975); Richard Field and John A. Lager ('Urban Runoff Pollution Control – State-of-the-Art', 1976).

American Society for Engineering Education Aerospace Division – American Institute of Aeronautics and Astronautics Educational Achievement Award

This award is bestowed upon a distinguished contributor to aerospace engineering education to recognize a recent outstanding educational achievement and to encourage original, innovative improvements in aerospace engineering. It consists of $1,000 in cash. It is intended that this award shall be given to an aerospace engineering educator who, at the time of selection, will be a faculty member engaged in teaching and research in some field of aerospace engineering but it may, in exceptional circumstances, be awarded to others who have made a substantial contribution to this field. The award can be received only once by any individual. Nominations may be made by any member of ASEE and/or AIAA.

Awarding body: American Society for Engineering Education, Suite 400, One Dupont Circle, Washington, D.C. 20036, U.S.A.

American Society of International Law Certificate of Merit

Two certificates may be given each year, one (instituted in 1976) for a work in the international legal field which exhibits high technical craftsmanship and is of great use to lawyers and scholars, and the other (established 1963) for a work which makes an eminent contribution to creative scholarship. These must have been written or edited during the previous two or three years.

Awarding body: American Society of International Law, 2223 Massachusetts Ave., N.W., Washington, D.C. 20008, U.S.A.

Recipients include: Jerome Cohen and Hungdah Chiu (eds. *People's Republic of China and International Law: A Documentary Study*, 1976); Ian Brownlie (*Principles of International Law*, 1976); Peter Fischer (*Die Internationale Konzession* and *A Collection of International Concessions and Related Instruments,*

1977); Leo Gross (ed. *The Future of the International Court of Justice*, 1977).

American Society of Mechanical Engineers Medal
This award was established in 1920 by the Council of the Society. The medal is awarded annually for 'eminently distinguished engineering achievement', and the recipient is presented with a gold medal, an engrossed certificate, and an honorarium of $1,000.

Awarding body: American Society of Mechanical Engineers, United Engineering Center, 345 E. 47th St., New York, N.Y. 10017, U.S.A.

Recipients include: Waloddi Weibull (1972); Christopher C. Kraft, Jr. (1973); Nicholas J. Hoff (1974); Maxime A. Faget (1975); Raymond D. Mindlin (1976).

American Society of Mechanical Engineers Rail Transportation Award
This award was established in 1964 by the ASME Railroad Division (now ASME Rail Transportation Division). It is made in recognition of an outstanding original paper on a railroad mechanical engineering subject by a single author or multiple authors. The paper must be original, current and contribute to engineering literature in the railroad field. Thus the paper might (1) report new and basic technical discoveries or research findings, (2) contain outstanding original thinking in railway mechanical engineering beyond the scope of daily engineering routine, or (3) describe such work reduced to practice. The paper must have been presented at a meeting of ASME during the calendar year prior to the year of the award. Recipients may be non-members of the Society. The award is made annually if warranted, and takes the form of an engrossed certificate.

Awarding body: American Society of Mechanical Engineers, United Engineering Centre, 345 E. 47th St., New York, N.Y. 10017, U.S.A.

Recipients include: V. Terry Hawthorne (1975); M. R. Johnson, R. Edward Welch, Kin S. Yeung (1976).

American Society for Pharmacology and Experimental Therapeutics Award for Experimental Therapeutics
Hoffmann-La Roche, Inc., of Nutley, N.J., donated this annual award consisting of $2,000 and a bronze medal, for the purpose of recognizing and stimulating outstanding research in experimental therapeutics – laboratory or clinical research that has had major impact on the pharmacological treatment of disease. Candidates must be nominated by a member of ASPET. The award is made on the basis of published reprints, manuscripts ready for publication, and a two-page summary, which is judged by a special selection committee appointed by the president of ASPET.

Awarding body: American Society for Pharmacology and Experimental Therapeutics, Inc., 9650 Rockville Pike, Bethesda, Md. 20014, U.S.A.

Amsterdam Prizes
The Amsterdam Foundation for the Arts gives awards every two or three years under this general title; the individual prizes bear the names of great Dutch artists. The Matthijs Vermeulen Prize is given in recognition of a musical composition completed in the preceding year. The Herman Gorter Prize is for a collection of poetry published in Dutch. The Multatuli Prize is given for a literary work (belles-lettres) in Dutch. The Busken Huët Prize is given biennially for an essay or volume of essays. The Albert van Dalsum Prize is for an individual or group performance of a play in Dutch. The H. H. Werkman Prize is given for graphic design. The Merkelbach Prize is awarded every three years for a piece of architecture completed in the preceding three years within the Amsterdam city boundary. Prizewinners receive a diploma and a sum of money (currently 7,000 guilders).

Awarding body: Amsterdam Foundation for the Arts, Town Hall, Amsterdam, The Netherlands.

Hans Christian Andersen Award
Established in 1955 by the International Board on Books for Young People, the prize is given in memory of Hans Christian Andersen (1805–75), the Danish storyteller. The award is conferred on a living author and, since 1965, illustrator, who are adjudged from their complete works to have made a lasting contribution to literature for children and young people. It is given every two years and comprises a gold medal and a diploma.

Awarding body: International Board on Books for Young People (IBBY), Leonhardsgraben 38a, CH-4051 Basel, Switzerland.

Recipients include: Maria Gripe (author, Sweden, 1974); Farshid Mesghali (illustrator, Iran, 1974); Cecil Bødker (author, Denmark, 1976); Tatjana Mawrina (illustrator, U.S.S.R., 1976); Paula Fox (author, U.S.A., 1978); Svend Otto (illustrator, Denmark, 1978).

Ion Andreescu Prize
This prize for contributions in the field of fine arts was founded in 1948 by the Romanian Academy. It commemorates Ion Andreescu (1850–82), the Romanian landscape painter. The award is presented annually at a General Assembly of the Academy, and consists of 10,000 lei and a diploma.

Awarding body: Academy of the S.R. of Romania, 125 Calea Victoriei, Bucharest, Romania.

Recipients include: Barbu Brezianu (1974).

Andrews Lectureship
Dr. Andrew Ungar, founder and owner of Andrews Laboratories, Sydney, established this Lectureship in 1960 at the University of New South Wales. Lecturers are chosen for eminence in organic or biochemistry. A series of three or four lectures is given over a period of about ten days.

Awarding body: School of Chemistry, University of New South Wales, Kensington, N.S.W. 2033, Australia.

Recipients include: Ernest Wenkert (Rice Univ., U.S.A., 1974); Alan R. Battersby (Cambridge Univ., U.K., 1975); Sir Derek Barton (Imperial Coll. of Science and Technology, U.K., 1976).

Angelicum Prize

This is an international prize of 800,000 lire awarded for a chamber orchestra composition. It was established in 1969 by the Angelicum chamber orchestra and is awarded at a biennial competition in collaboration with the music publishers Sonzogno di Piero Ostali, who offer a second prize of 300,000 lire. The competition is open to composers of all nationalities and of any age; entries must be unpublished and as yet unperformed. The Gianluigi Colombo Foundation offers a prize of 500,000 lire for a composition of sacred music; the same rules apply, and the winning compositions are performed at a public concert during the Angelicum concert season.

Awarding body: The Secretariat, Angelicum Prize, Piazza San Angelo 2, 20121 Milan, Italy.

Recipients include: Fausto Razzi (Italy, 1969); Jorge Antunes (Brazil) and Azio Corghi (Italy), 1971; Francesco Hoch (Switzerland, 1975).

Angus and Robertson Writers' Fellowships

The awards were established in 1972 and are presented annually. They are offered for manuscripts in two categories: (1) written for adults, preferably by a new author, and (2) written for young readers. Winners receive a contract with Angus and Robertson Publishers, and a substantial advance. In 1977 the 'adult manuscript' advance amounted to A\$2,000, and the 'writers for the young' advances, in two categories, amounted to A\$1,500 and A\$750 respectively. The award is open to Australian and New Zealand writers, wherever they are resident, and to writers of any nationality permanently resident in Australia or New Zealand. Entries are submitted on the understanding that the author is free to offer full world rights to Angus and Robertson.

Awarding body: Angus and Robertson Publishers, 102 Glover St., Cremorne, N.S.W. 2090, Australia.

Recipients include: Elizabeth Riley (1973); Geoff Pike (1974); Louis Nowra (1975); Judith Worthy (1976).

Annecy International Animated Film Festival

The Festival was inaugurated in 1960, and is held every two years. Any original film, completed in the last two years, may be submitted. Both short and feature length films are accepted. The jury awards two Grand Prizes, one of which can be awarded to a feature length film; a Jury's Special Prize; a Prize for the Best Children's Film; and a Prize for a Director's First Work. The jury may also award optionally: a second and third Jury's Special Prize; a Prize for the Best Commercial Film; a Prize for the Best TV Film; and a Prize for the Best National Selection.

Awarding body: Journées Internationales du Cinéma d'Animation (Festival d'Annecy), 21 rue de la Cour d'Auvergne, 75009 Paris, France.

Recipients include: Piotr Kamler (France, *Le Pas*, First Prize); I. Norstein (U.S.S.R., *The Heron and the Stork*, Jury's Special Prize); Bohuslaw Sramek (Czechoslovakia, *Kasparek, Honza a Drak*, Best Children's Film); Jacques Cardon (France, *L'Empreinte*, Prize for a Director's First Work), 1975.

Anti-Fascist Council of the People's Liberation of Yugoslavia Award

This award, consisting of 50,000 dinars and a certificate, was established in 1964 and is made annually by the Assembly of the Socialist Federal Republic of Yugoslavia. Twelve to 15 awards are made each year. They are for publications and other achievements in science, arts and other creative fields, which contribute to the development of the Socialist Federal Republic of Yugoslavia. Both individual and community attainments are eligible.

Awarding body: ACPLY Award Committee, Assembly of the Socialist Federal Republic of Yugoslavia, 11070 Novi Beograd, Bulevar Lenjina 2, Yugoslavia.

Nicholas Appert Award

This award is made annually for pre-eminence in and contributions to the field of food technology. It consists of a \$1,000 honorarium from the American Institute of Food Technologists and a bronze medal donated by its Chicago section. Candidates are nominated by Institute members.

Awarding body: Institute of Food Technologists, Suite 2120, 221 North La Salle St., Chicago, Ill. 60601, U.S.A.

Recipients include: John C. Ayres (1972); Hans Lineweaver (1973); George F. Stewart (1974); Ernest J. Briskey (1975); Amihud Kramer (1976).

Appleton Prize

The prize consists of a cash award of £100, and is given triennially for outstanding contributions to studies in ionospheric physics. Candidates must be proposed by one of the 36 National Member Committees of the International Union of Radio Science. The prize was founded in 1969 by the Royal Society, London, and commemorates Sir Edward Appleton (1892–1965), the British physicist whose work on the ionosphere is well known.

Awarding body: International Union of Radio Science, rue de Nieuwenhove 81, B-1180 Brussels, Belgium.

Recipients: Prof. W. I. Axford (U.S.A., ionospheric and magnetospheric physics, 1969); Prof. R. A. Helliwell (U.S.A., radio wave propagation in the magnetosphere, 1972); Dr. J. V. Evans (U.S.A., ionospheric physics including application of the incoherent scatter technique, 1975); Prof. P. Banks (U.S.A., study of plasma flow between the ionosphere and magnetosphere, 1978).

Sir Edward Appleton Memorial Lecture

Instituted in 1966 on the initiative of the Edinburgh University Physical Society, the annual lecture is on some branch of natural science. It is named after Sir Edward Appleton (1892–1965), the physicist.

Awarding body: Edinburgh University, Edinburgh EH8 9YL, Scotland.

Lecturers include: Prof. Norman Feather (1975); Prof. R. V. Jones (1977).

Aquinas Medal

This medal is awarded annually by the American Catholic Philosophical Association to honour distinguished contributions to the field of philosophy. It was established in 1952 by the late James Cardinal Spellman, Archbishop of New York, in memory of the philosopher and theologian St. Thomas Aquinas (1225–75).

Awarding body: American Philosophical Association, The Catholic University of America, Washington, D.C. 20064, U.S.A.

Recipients include: Henry B. Veatch (1971); Joseph Owens, C.SS.R. (1972); A. Hilary Armstrong (1973); Cornelio Fabro, C.S.S. (1974); Mortimer J. Adler (1975).

Årets Film (*Film of the Year*)

This award was established in 1974 by the Swedish Film Critics Association. It is given annually for the best Swedish film of the year. It consists of a monolithic statuette, containing a piece of celluloid of the winning film.

Awarding body: Svenska Filmkritikerförbundet.

Recipients include: Vilgot Sjöman (*En Handfull Kärlek*); Tage Danielsson (*Släpp Fångarne Loss – det är Vår!*); Stellan Olsson (*Sven Klangs Kvintett*).

'Guido d'Arezzo' International Polyphonic Competition

Established in 1953 by the 'Amici della Musica' Association, this annual music competition takes place in August and attracts choirs from many countries. It is named after the 11th-century monk and musician Guido d'Arezzo, who invented the solfa system. Prizes are awarded in six categories: mixed choir; male-voice choir; female-voice choir; youth choir; folk song; Gregorian chant. The prizes are monetary, and donated by various Italian organizations.

Awarding body: Associazione Amici della Musica, Arezzo, Italy.

First prize-winners 1976: Vox Humana (Vàc, Hungary: mixed choir and folk song); Coro Antonio Illersberg (Trieste, Italy: male-voice choir); Martinsfinken (Kaufbeuren, Fed. Germany: female-voice choir); Canzone Fresca (Sciumen, Bulgaria: youth choir); Deurne Male-Voice Choir (Deurne, Netherlands: Gregorian chant).

Carina Ari Medaljen (*Carina Ari Medal of Merit*)

This annual gold medal was established in 1961 by Carina Ari (1893–1970), an eminent Swedish dancer. It is given for outstanding service to the art of dance in Sweden. The recipient need not be Swedish.

Awarding body: Carina Ari Foundation, Box 27 109, 102 52 Stockholm 27, Sweden.

Recipients include: Margot Fonteyn (1969); Erik Bruhn (1970); Mary Skeaping and Frederick Ashton (1972); Kurt Jooss and Antony Tudor (1973); Fleming Flindt (1975).

Armstrong Award

This award is given by the Armstrong Memorial Research Foundation for excellence and originality in FM broadcasting. It was established in 1964 in honour of Major Edwin Howard Armstrong (1890–1954), inventor of the wide band FM system. FM radio stations in the U.S.A. and Canada are eligible. The award is made annually in six categories: music; news; news documentary; public or community service; education; creative use of the medium. The winners in each section receive a bronze plaque, and the runners-up a framed merit certificate.

Awarding body: Armstrong Memorial Research Foundation, Inc., 510 S. W. Mudd Building, Columbia University, New York, N.Y. 10027, U.S.A.

Recipients include: WRFM, New York City (*Crime in the Streets*, news); WFMT, Chicago (*Chicago Radio Theatre: Edgar Allan Poe*, education/creative arts); WFMT, Chicago (*The Monteaux Centennial*, music); KING-FM, Seattle (*Recall: A Special Report*, community service), 1975.

A. M. Arnan Award

This award, founded in 1960 by the Central Committee of the Association of Engineers and Architects in Israel, is named after one of the founders of the Association who was also its Chairman, and who founded the Israel Standards Institute. The monetary award of I£1,500 is given annually for original research work, in the form of a book or a paper, in the fields of engineering or architecture. Work submitted should have been published not later than two years previously, and authors must be members of the Association and Israeli citizens.

Awarding body: Association of Engineers and Architects in Israel, 200 Dizengoff St., Tel Aviv, Israel.

Recipients include: Prof. Gabriel Kassif, Prof. Moshe Livneh and Prof. Gedalyahu Weissman (*Pavements on Expansive Clays*); Prof. Yochanan Alon and Arch. Yigael Zamir ('Concept of the built-up environment in public housing'); Dr. Shlomo Friedman ('An inquiry into the stress strain behaviour of particulate media'); Eng. Israel Alterman ('Interaction between a conduit and the surrounding soil').

H. H. Arnold Award

This is the highest award of the U.S. Air Force Association, and is given annually to 'Aerospace's Man of the Year' – an individual who has made outstanding contributions in the field of aerospace activity. The award takes the form of a plaque, and was instituted in 1948 in honour of H. H. Arnold (1886–1950), General of the U.S. Air Force.

Awarding body: Air Force Association National Awards Committee, 1750 Pennsylvania Ave., N.W., Washington, D.C. 20006, U.S.A.

Recipients include: Air Units of the Allied Forces in SEA (1972); Gen. John D. Ryan (1973); Gen. George S. Brown (1974); James R. Schlesinger (1975); Hon Barry M. Goldwater (1976).

Aronson-Preis

The award was established by the Aronson Foundation, named after the Berlin doctor and scientist, Hans Aronson. Two prizes are presented every two years for outstanding medical achievements by German scientists in the field of microbiology and experimental therapy. The West Berlin Senate awards the prizes, which consist of cash awards of DM5,000 each.

Awarding body: Der Senat von Berlin, Senatskanzlei, 1000 Berlin 62, John-F.-Kennedy-Platz, Fed. Repub. of Germany.

Recipients include: August von Wassermann; Friedrich Karl Kleine; Paul Uhlenhut; Josef Fortner; Richard Otto.

Art Libraries Society of North America Annual Art Publishing Award

This award is intended to encourage the publishing in North America of high quality art books, and every year since 1973 one or two such books have been presented with the calligraphic scrolls of commendation. The award is intended for works released initially in North America by U.S. or Canadian publishers.

Awarding body: Art Libraries Society of North America, P.O.B. 3692, Glendale, Calif. 91201, U.S.A.

Recipients include: University of Chicago Press (*The Prints of Rockwell Kent,* 1975); Harry N. Abrams, Inc. (*Monographic Series,* 1975); David Godine and International Museum of Photography (*The Spirit of Fact,* 1976); Edward Ruscha (Special Award for his books, 1976); Aperture Publishers (Special Award for its continued efforts in support of the field of photography, 1976).

Arts and Letters Awards

Twenty-one Arts and Letters Awards are given annually by the American Academy and Institute of Arts and Letters to honour and encourage distinguished artists, composers and writers who are not members of the Institute, and to help them to continue their creative work. Each award consists of a cash prize. The work of the recipients is included in the annual spring exhibition of art, manuscripts and books, while a recording is provided for each recipient of a music award.

Awarding body: American Academy and Institute of Arts and Letters, 633 West 155th St., New York, N.Y. 10032, U.S.A.

Asa Honorary Award

The award was established in 1968 by Mrs. Asa Gudmundsdottir Wright, in memory of her husband and close relatives. It is offered annually for a major achievement in science and the humanities, and all Icelanders are eligible. It comprises a certificate, a silver medal and approximately £800 in cash.

Awarding body: The Asa Wright Award Fund Committee, Vísindafélag Islendinga, Societas Scientiarum Islandica, Reykjavík, Iceland.

Recipients include: Dr. Jakob Benediktsson (studies in early Icelandic history, 1974); Prof. Jon Steffensen (anthropological studies, 1975); Dr. Pall A. Palsson (research on slow virus diseases, 1976).

Asahi Prize

This annual prize was established in 1929 to commemorate the 50th anniversary of the foundation of the Asahi Shimbun Publishing Company. The award is designed to recognize and encourage contributions to the development of Japanese society or culture through outstanding individual achievements. It comprises a certificate, a shield and one million yen in cash. Eligibility is irrespective of age, sex or nationality.

Awarding body: Asahi Shimbun, 2-6-1 Yuraku-cho, Chiyoda-ku, Tokyo, Japan.

Recipients include: Reona Esaki (invention of the Esaki diode, 1959); Shiko Munakata (wood engravings, 1964); Kenzo Tange (achievements in architecture, 1964); Akira Kurosawa (contributions to raising the world status of the Japanese cinema, 1965); Kanson Arahata (achievements in the social and literary fields, 1974).

Margaret Ashton Memorial Lectureship

Part of the fund subscribed in memory of the late Miss Margaret Ashton was applied to the establishment of a Memorial Lectureship at Manchester University. The lecture, which is concerned with some aspect of public and international affairs, is normally delivered in alternate years in the University and in the Manchester Central Library.

Awarding body: University of Manchester, Manchester M13 9PL, England.

Lecturers include: Lady Tweedsmuir ('Women in Public Life', 1958); Dame Mary Smieton ('Some Aspects of Education in the Commonwealth', 1962); Miss Mary Holland ('Londonderry or Derry – the Heart of the Ulster Crisis', 1969); Margaret Lane ('Frances Wright and the Great Experiment', 1970).

Associated American Artists Gallery Purchase Award

This award was established by the Society of American Graphic Artists (S.A.G.A.), and is made every two or three years for original graphic art (print). Both members and non-members of S.A.G.A. are eligible. There are no restrictions on the subject matter, provided that the works have never been offered for sale, and that the artist agrees to make for the A.A.A. an edition of 50 numbered impressions and five artist's proofs, after which the plates, stones or blocks shall be can-

celled. The winner receives a cash prize of between
$1,000 and $2,000.

Awarding body: Associated American Artists,
663 Fifth Ave., New York, N.Y., U.S.A.

Recipients include: Bruce McCombs (1968);
Robert Blackburn (1969); Seong Moy (1969);
Robert Broner (1969); Jack Sonenberg (1973).

Association of the Friends of History Award

This prize is awarded annually for a book which
has extended and deepened the knowledge of
history in Finland. It consists of a medal and a
certificate, and was founded by the Association in
1972.

Awarding body: Association of the Friends of
History, Museokatu 46, B 42, 00100 Helsinki 10,
Finland.

Recipients include: Jussi T. Lappalainen (*Kaarle X
Kustaan Venäjän sota 1656–58 Suomen suunnalla*,
1973); Juhani Suomi (*Talvisodan tausta*, 1974);
Kaarlo Wirilander (*Herrasväkeä – Suomen säätyläistö
1721–1880*, 1975); Martti Julkunen (*Talvisodan
kuva, ulkomaisten sotakirjeenvaihtajien kuvaukset Suo-
mesta 1939–1940*, 1976).

Association of Iron and Steel Engineers – Kelly Awards

The awards were established in 1943 and named
in honour of John F. Kelly, first Managing
Director of the Association from 1917 to 1934, to
perpetuate the memory of his achievements in the
advancement of the organization. Three cash
awards (first $500, second $300, third $200) and
a plaque each are presented annually to the
authors of the best papers published in the
Association's journal, *Iron and Steel Engineer*, during
the preceding year. Only papers prepared by
employees of steel producing companies are considered.

Awarding body: Association of Iron and Steel
Engineers, Suite 2350, Three Gateway Center,
Pittsburgh, Pa. 15222, U.S.A.

Recipients include: Colin N. Hammill, Leslie C.
McLean and Ahmed A. Ghobarah (Steel Co. of
Canada Ltd., 'Why did that Roll Break?', 1974);
Theodore Pajor and Allan Ostling (Inland Steel
Co., 'Mechanical Problems Associated with
Inland's 2-Strand Slab Caster – Start-up and
Operation', 1975).

Carl Auer von Welsbach-Medaille

This award is made by the Austrian Chemical
Society in memory of Carl Auer von Welsbach
(1858–1929), who was noted for his investigations
into the chemistry of rare earth metals. It is given
for the encouragement and development of the
Austrian chemical industry, takes the form of a
medal and certificate, and is awarded irregularly.

Awarding body: Verein Österreichischer Chemiker, 1010 Vienna, Eschenbachgasse 9, Austria.

Recipients include: Richard Kieffer (1952); Herbert Hönel (1960); Ernst Brandl (1966); Erwin
Plöckinger (1968); Friedrich Asinger (1972).

Petre Aurelian Prize

This prize for economics was founded by the
Romanian Academy in 1948. It commemorates

Petre Aurelian (1833–1909), agronomist and
economist, who was President of the Academy and
professor of agriculture and agrarian economy.
He contributed much to the economic development and industrialization of Romania. The
award is given annually at a General Assembly of
the Academy, and consists of 10,000 lei and a
diploma.

Awarding body: Academy of the S.R. of Romania,
125 Calea Victoriei, Bucharest, Romania.

Australasian Institute of Metals Lecture

Established in 1952 as the Australian Institute of
Metals Annual Lecture, this award is intended to
honour outstanding persons by inviting them to
deliver a lecture to members of the Institute at its
Annual Conference. The subject is chosen by the
lecturer and is usually to do with metallurgy.

Awarding body: The Australasian Institute of
Metals, 191 Royal Parade, Parkville, Victoria
3052, Australia.

Recipients include: W. Boas (1959); L. E.
Samuels (1964); Sir Ian McLennan (1968); C. W.
Court (1971); D. Dunstan (1974).

Australasian Institute of Metals Silver Medal

Established in 1956, this award is given for outstanding contributions to metallurgy in Australia.
There is no fixed period of time for its presentation.

Awarding body: The Australasian Institute of
Metals, 191 Royal Parade, Parkville, Vic. 3052,
Australia.

Recipients include: J. Neill Greenwood (1962);
J. G. Ritchie (1966); R. C. Gifkins (1968); L. E.
Samuels (1971); Howard K. Worner (1974).

Australasian Institute of Mining and Metallurgy Medal

The award is made annually at the discretion of
the Council of the Institute in recognition of
eminent services to mining or metallurgy. It is
given irrespective of nationality or of membership
of the Institute.

Awarding body: The Australasian Institute of
Mining and Metallurgy, Clunies Ross House, 191
Royal Parade, Parkville, Vic. 3052, Australia.

Australasian Institute of Mining and Metallurgy President's Award

This is made annually to one person, except that
two or more awards may be made for a joint
project. It is in recognition of notable achievement
within the industry in some specific sphere of
activity, e.g. exploration, production, construction, education, research, authorship, equipment
development, etc. The award is normally made to
a member of the Institute, but exceptions may be
made.

Awarding body: The Australasian Institute of
Mining and Metallurgy, Clunies Ross House, 191
Royal Parade, Parkville, Vic. 3052, Australia.

Australian Film Awards

These awards were established in 1958 by the
Australian Film Institute to provide a stimulus to

Australian film producers. Cash prizes are sponsored by various organizations and are awarded annually for the best film, actor and actress, supporting actor and actress, direction, screenplay, cinematography, editing and foreign film. The film must normally have been completed within the previous 18 months.

Awarding body: Australian Film Institute, P.O.B. 165, Carlton South, Vic. 3053, Australia.

Recipients include: Fred Schepisi (*The Devil's Playground*, best film and best director), Edward McQueen-Mason (*End Play*, best editor), 1976.

Australian Numismatic Society Gold Medal

Established in 1967 by the Australian Numismatic Society, the award is made when required, but no more than once every two years, for advancement of numismatics particularly in Australia. The award is in the form of a gold medal accompanied by a certificate and the recipient is known as a Fellow of the Society. Eligibility is usually limited to members of the Society.

Awarding body: Australian Numismatic Society, G.P.O. Box 3644, Sydney, N.S.W. 2001, Australia.

Awgie Awards

The initials A.W.G. of the award title represent the Australian Writers' Guild, which presents annual awards for the best scripts for screen, television, stage and radio. The awards are given in various categories: children's (best adaptation, best original work); documentary; comedy (best radio adaptation, best original work); television (best serial episode, best series episode, best adaptation, best original work); film (best feature film adaptation, best original feature film screenplay); stage. All scripts must have been professionally produced during the preceding year. Entrants must be financial members or associates of the Guild. The awards take the form of inscribed statuettes.

Awarding body: Australian Writers' Guild, 197 Blues Point Rd., North Sydney, N.S.W. 2060, Australia.

Recipients include: Shan Benson (*Family Occasions*, best radio script, 1975); John Dingwall (*Sunday Too Far Away*, best feature film, 1975); Cliff Green and Howard Griffiths (*Power Without Glory*, best TV script, 1976); Cliff Green (*Picnic at Hanging Rock*, best feature film, 1976).

Ayerst Award

Founded in 1966 by the Ayerst Laboratories, a pharmaceutical firm, this award is made annually for meritorious research in biochemistry in Canada, and thereby to stimulate fundamental research by younger biochemists in Canada. The award consists of $1,000 donated by the Ayerst Research Laboratories, and a commemorative tray from the Canadian Biochemical Society. Nominees must not be over 40, and need not be Canadian citizens, but the research work must have been done in Canada. Nominations are made by members of the Canadian Biochemical Society.

Awarding body: Canadian Biochemical Society, Dept. of Biochemistry, University of Alberta, Edmonton, Alb. T6G 2H7, Canada.

Recipients include: Dr. Jean Himms-Hagen (1973); Dr. D. H. Maclennan (1974); Dr. W. W.-C. Chan (1975); Dr. M. Clelia Ganoza-Becker (1976); Dr. Keith Dorrington (1977).

Matti Äyräpään Luento ja Palkinto (*Matti Äyräpää Lecture and Award*)

This annual award was established in 1969 by the Finnish Medical Society Duodecim, in memory of Matti Äyräpää (1852–1928), a co-founder of the Society. The award is given to a Finnish medical scientist for outstanding research. The winner has the honour of delivering a lecture, and also receives a cash prize of 15,000 Fmk.

Awarding body: Suomalainen Lääkäriseura Duodecim, Runeberginkatu 47 A, SF-00260, Helsinki 26, Finland.

Recipients include: Olavi Eränkö (histochemistry of the sympathetic nervous system, 1973); Kari Penttinen (prophylaxis of virus diseases, 1974); Lauri Saxén (control mechanisms of differentiation, 1975); Erkki Klemola (mononucleosis, 1976); Kari Kivirikko (collagen biosynthesis and its disorders, 1977).

B

BDH Award in Analytical Biochemistry

The award was established in 1968 by BDH Chemicals Ltd. A medal and a prize of £200 are awarded triennially for outstanding work carried out in a laboratory in the U.K. or Ireland, leading to advances in biochemistry related to the development and application of a new reagent or method.

Awarding body: The Biochemical Society, 7 Warwick Court, High Holborn, London WC1R 5DP, England.

Recipients: B. S. Hartley, F.R.S. ('Strategy and Tactics in Protein Chemistry', 1969); J. E. Scott ('Affinity, Competition and Specific Interactions in the Biochemistry and Histochemistry of Polyelectrolytes', 1972); J. Landon ('Recent Development in Non-Isotopic Immunoassay', 1975).

Babcock-Hart Award

This award is made annually to individuals who have distinguished themselves by contributions to food technology which have resulted in improved public health through more nutritious food. It consists of an engraved plaque from the American Institute of Food Technologists and a $1,000 honorarium donated by the Nutrition Foundation, Inc. Candidates are nominated by members of the Institute.

Awarding body: Institute of Food Technologists, Suite 2120, 221 North La Salle St., Chicago, Ill. 60601, U.S.A.

Recipients include: James W. Pence (1972); Clinton O. Chichester (1973); Bernard S. Schweigert (1974); Donald K. Tressler (1975); Harold S. Olcott (1976).

Victor Babeş Prize

The prize was founded by the Romanian Academy in 1948, and is for achievement in the field of medicine. It is named after Victor Babes (1854–1926), the famous physician and professor of medicine. He was one of the founders of modern microbiology, and contributed to the study of rabies on an international level; he also laid the foundations of serotherapy. The award is presented annually at a General Assembly of the Academy, and consists of 10,000 lei and a diploma.

Awarding body: Academy of the S.R. of Romania, 125 Calea Victoriei, Bucharest, Romania.

Bach-Preis für Musik

The prize was established by the city council and parliament of Hamburg in 1950, on the occasion of the 200th anniversary of the death of Johann Sebastian Bach (1685–1750). The prize is awarded to composers who belong to the German Cultural Circle, and whose works are of a sufficiently high standard to merit their association with the name of Bach. Exceptionally, in recognition of work of particular significance to Hamburg, the prize may be awarded to someone from outside the German Cultural Circle. The prize of DM15,000 is awarded every three years. It is presented if possible on 21 May, the anniversary of the birthday of J. S. Bach.

Awarding body: Senat der Freien und Hansestadt Hamburg, 2 Hamburg 1, Rathaus, Federal Republic of Germany.

Back Award

The award was established in 1882 as a result of a bequest of Admiral Sir George Back, F.R.S. (1796–1878), Arctic traveller and navigator and first recipient of the Royal Geographical Society's Founder's Medal. The award is for the advancement of scientific geography or discovery, or to help those actively engaged in discovery or exploration. It is not a regular award, but is usually made annually if a suitable candidate is forthcoming. It is presented at the Annual Meeting of the Royal Geographical Society in June, and is monetary, but may be taken in the form of survey instruments, books, etc. There is no application for the award. It is granted on the recommendation of a special committee, the criteria being the academic or other achievements of the recipient. Anyone of any nationality is eligible.

Awarding body: Royal Geographical Society, 1 Kensington Gore, London SW7 2AR, England.

Recipients include: Dr. Brian B. Roberts (1949); Dr. G. de Q. Robin (1953); Commander G. S. Ritchie, D.S.C., R.N. (1954); Prof. Sigurdur Thorarinsson (1967); Dr. Keith Miller (1976); Dr. Andrew Warren (1978).

Ida Bäckman Prize

This prize for Swedish literature and journalism is given every second year by the Swedish Academy. It was endowed in 1953 by Ida Bäckman in memory of the Swedish writers Gustaf Froding (1860–1911) and Selma Lagerlöf (1858–1940). It is a cash prize with a current value of 10,000 Swedish kronor. It cannot be applied for.

Awarding body: The Swedish Academy, Börshuset, Källargränd 4, S-111 29 Stockholm, Sweden.

Lode Baekelmansprijs

The prize was established in 1940 by the Belgian Royal Academy of Dutch Language and Literature in honour of Lode Baekelmans (1879–1965), writer, playwright and director of Antwerp Public Libraries. An award of 40,000 Belgian francs is made every three years for the best literary work in Dutch dealing with the sea, sailors, navigation or a related topic. Recipients must be Belgian nationals.

Awarding body: Koninklijke Academie voor Nederlandse Taal- en Letterkunde, Koningstraat 18, B-9000 Ghent, Belgium.

Recipients include: Karel Jonckheere (*Cargo*, 1942); L. B. Carlier (*Duel met de Tanker*, 1957); K. van Isacker (*De Antwerpse dokwerker 1830–1940*, 1963).

Adolf-von-Baeyer-Denkmünze

The medal was established by Carl Duisberg in 1910, in celebration of the 75th birthday and the 50th year as a university lecturer of his teacher Adolf von Baeyer (1835–1917). Von Baeyer was several times President of the German Chemical Society and won the Nobel Prize for Chemistry in 1905. The award was originally administered by the Association of German Chemists, which in 1912 created the Carl Duisberg Foundation for the award of both this medal and the Emil Fischer Medal (*q.v.*). The Society of German Chemists took over the award in 1949. The gold medal and a sum of money is given to the German chemist who is considered to have published during the preceding year the best work in the field of organic chemistry (particularly a work on experimental colour or pharmaceutical chemistry), or who has rendered particular service to the chemical industry by the production of organic or pharmaceutical preparations, important dyestuffs, perfumes, etc.

Awarding body: Gesellschaft Deutscher Chemiker, 6000 Frankfurt (Main) 90, Carl Bosch-Haus, Varrentrappstr. 40–42, Federal Republic of Germany.

Recipients include: Prof. Franz Sondheimer (1965); Prof. Siegfried Hünig (1967); Dr. Otto Scherer (1968); Prof. Eugen Müller (1971); Prof. Hans Albert Offe (1975).

Clyde H. Bailey Memorial Medal

The medal was created by the Executive Committee of the International Association for Cereal Chemistry (ICC) in 1969 at the suggestion of its President, Prof. Dr. J. A. Shellenberger. Dr. Clyde H. Bailey (1887–1968) was an outstanding cereal chemist who was Professor and Dean of Agriculture at the University of Minnesota and won international recognition in his field. The gold medal and a certificate are awarded irregularly to specialists who have made particularly important contributions to cereal research as well as to international co-operation in this field.

Awarding body: International Association for Cereal Chemistry (ICC), Schmidgasse 3–7, A-2320 Schwechat, Austria.

Recipients include: Dr. F. Schweitzer (Austria, 1970); Prof. Dr. J. A. Shellenberger (U.S.A., 1974); Prof. Dr. R. Schneeweiss (German Democratic Rep., 1974).

Bakerian Lecture

The lecture was founded in 1775 through a bequest by Mr. Henry Baker, F.R.S., of £100 for an oration or discourse which was to be spoken or read yearly by one of the Fellows of the Royal Society on such part of natural history or experimental philosophy, at such time and in such manner as the President and Council of the Society shall please to order and appoint. The gift for the lecturer is now £25. Since 1957 an additional Mr. and Mrs. John Jaffé Prize of £200 has been awarded and, if the lecturer as a Nobel Laureate has been precluded from receiving a Jaffé Prize, £200 has been provided from another source.

Awarding body: Royal Society of London, 6 Carlton House Terrace, London SW1Y 5AG, England.

Lecturers include: Prof. F. C. Frank ('Crystals Imperfect', 1973); Dr. D. G. King-Hele ('A View of Earth and Air', 1974); Prof. M. F. Atiyah ('Global Geometry', 1975); Prof. G. W. Kenner (1976).

Bakhuis Roozeboom Medal

The Royal Netherlands Academy of Arts and Sciences established this gold medal in 1911 in memory of Professor H. W. Bakhuis Roozeboom (1854–1907). It is awarded every eight years to a scientist of any nationality for outstanding research in the field of phase theory.

Awarding body: Koninklijke Nederlandse Akademie van Wetenschappen, Kloveniersburgwal 29, 1011 JV Amsterdam, The Netherlands.

Recipients include: J. L. Meijering (Netherlands, 1960); F. P. Bundy (U.S.A., 1969); M. H. Hillert (Sweden, 1978).

Balázs Béla Prize for Cinematographic Art

Instituted by the Hungarian Council of Ministers in 1953, the prize is awarded annually by the Minister of Culture. It is an honorary distinction, divided into three classes, and given for outstanding achievements in the field of cinema. It is named after Béla Balázs (1884–1949), the poet, novelist and film critic.

Awarding body: Committee for the Balázs Béla Prize, Ministry of Culture, Szalay-utca 10, Budapest V, Hungary.

Recipients include: János Dömölky (stage director, Hungarian TV), János Tóth (cameraman), 1976.

Nicolae Bălcescu Prize

This prize for contributions in the field of history was founded in 1948 by the Romanian Academy. It commemorates Nicolae Bălcescu (1819–52), historian, democratic revolutionary thinker and politician, who played an important part in the organization of the 1848 revolution in Wallachia. The award is presented annually at a General

Assembly of the Academy, and consists of 10,000 lei and a diploma.

Awarding body: Academy of the S.R. of Romania, 125 Calea Victoriei, Bucharest, Romania.

Recipients include: Răzvan Theodorescu (1974).

Edgardo Baldi Memorial Lecture

The Edgardo Baldi Memorial Foundation was set up with the aim of perpetuating the memory of Edgardo Baldi by stimulating research within the field of theoretical limnology to which he devoted his life work. The interest accruing from the Foundation is used to defray the honorarium and expenses for one Baldi Memorial Lecture on subjects within the realm of theoretical limnology, to be delivered at each triennial General Assembly (International Congress) of the International Association of Limnology. The Lecturer is selected by the Memorial Committee, and the nomination is announced at the preceding Congress.

Awarding body: International Association of Limnology, c/o Gen. Sec., Prof. R. G. Wetzel, W. K. Kellogg Biological Station, Michigan State University, Hickory Corners, Mich. 49060, U.S.A.

Lecturers include: H. B. N. Hynes ('The Stream and its Valley', 1974).

F. W. (Casey) Baldwin Award

This award is presented annually by the Canadian Aeronautics and Space Institute for the best article published in the *Canadian Aeronautics and Space Journal* during the preceding year. It was established in 1957, and consists of a silver medal.

Awarding body: Canadian Aeronautics and Space Institute, Suite 406, 77 Metcalfe St., Ottawa, Ont. K1P 5L6, Canada.

Recipients include: M. C. Eames ('Experimental Bodies for High-Speed Underwater Towing Research', 1968); D. C. Whittley ('The Augmentor-Wing Research Program: Past, Present and Future', 1969); L. Brown ('The Changing Face of Production – The Use of Numerical Control in Manufacturing', 1970); Dr. A. B. Bauer, A. M. O. Smith and J. L. Hess ('Potential Flow and Boundary Layer Theory as Design Tools in Aerodynamics', 1971); F. Mavriplis ('Aerodynamic Research on High Lift Systems', 1972).

Sidney Ball Lectureship

In 1919 a fund was established at the University of Oxford to endow a lecture on modern social, economic and political questions. It is in memory of the late Sidney Ball, M.A., Fellow of St. John's College. The lecturer must deliver his lecture, or a copy thereof, to the Vice-Chancellor for preservation in the Bodleian Library.

Awarding body: University of Oxford, Wellington Square, Oxford OX1 2JD, England.

Lecturers include: Sir Leslie Scarman ('Law and the Problem of Change', 1971); J. E. Meade ('Poverty in the Welfare State', 1972); Rt. Hon. R. H. S. Crossman ('The Role of the Volunteer in the Modern Social Service', 1973); T. Lynes ('Social Security and Inflation', 1974); E. Lipinski

('The Feasibility of a Socialist Society and Economy viewed from Experience', 1975).

Stuart Ballantine Medal

Charles Stuart Ballantine (1897–1944) made important contributions to science and technology in the field of radio science. In 1945 a group of his friends and business associates formed the Boonton Foundation, Inc. as a medium for charitable donations. A sum of money was given to the Franklin Institute to establish the gold medal, with the directive that it be awarded in recognition of outstanding achievement in the fields of Communication and Reconnaissance which employ electromagnetic radiation.

Awarding body: The Franklin Institute, Benjamin Franklin Parkway at 20th St., Philadelphia, Pa. 19103, U.S.A.

Recipients include: M. M. Atalla and Dawon Kahng (development of the insulated gate field-effect transistor (MOS), 1975); Bernard C. de Loach, Jr. (practical development of IMPATT, an extremely high-frequency oscillator, 1976); Dr. Charles Kuen Kao (conceptual studies of lightguide communications, 1977); Stewart E. Miller (development of lightwave communications systems, 1977).

Bampton Lectureship

In pursuance of the will of the Revd. John Bampton, M.A., sometime of Trinity College, Oxford, and Canon of Salisbury, eight Divinity Lecture Sermons are preached at Oxford University in alternate years on as many Sunday mornings in full Hilary and Trinity Terms, 'upon either of the following subjects: to confirm and establish the Christian Faith, and to confute all heretics and schismatics – upon the authority of the writings of the primitive Fathers as to the Faith and Practice of the primitive Church – upon the Divinity of our Lord and Saviour Jesus Christ – upon the Divinity of the Holy Ghost – upon the Articles of the Christian Faith, as comprehended in the Apostles' and Nicene Creeds'. The lecturer must be a graduate, and a clergyman of the Anglican Communion. He is chosen biennially by the heads of colleges.

Awarding body: Oxford University, Wellington Square, Oxford OX1 2JD, England.

Lecturers include: Revd. C. P. M. Jones ('Christ and Christianity: a study in origins in the light of St. Paul', 1970); Revd. H. E. Root ('The Limits of Radicalism', 1972); Revd. P. R. Baelz ('The Forgotten Dream (Experience, Hope and God)', 1974); Revd. Prof. G. W. H. Lampe (1976); Revd. A. R. Peacocke (1978).

Bancroft Award

The award is given every two years, if there is a suitable candidate, for publication, instruction and research in the geological and geophysical sciences that have conspicuously contributed to public understanding and appreciation of the subject. The prize consists of a presentation scroll and C$1,000. Canadian citizens or persons who have been Canadian residents for the five years preceding the award are eligible. The award was endowed in 1968 by Mrs. J. A. Bancroft to honour Joseph Austin Bancroft (1882–1957), former Dawson Professor at McGill University.

Awarding body: The Royal Society of Canada, 395 Wellington, Ottawa, Ont. K1A 0N4, Canada.

Recipients include: J. Tuzo Wilson (1968); D. M. Baird (1970); E. R. W. Neale (1975); Roger Blais (1976).

Bancroft Gold Medal

This award was established in 1904 by the actor-manager Sir Squire Bancroft. The medal is awarded for fine acting three times every two years: in April and December in odd years, and in August in even years. Persons attending the Royal Academy of Dramatic Art are eligible.

Awarding body: Royal Academy of Dramatic Art, 62 Gower St., London WC1E 6ED, England.

Recipients include: Rosemary Harris (1952); Sian Phillips (1957); Susan Fleetwood (1964); Anton Lesser (1977); Timothy Spall (1978).

Bangla Academy Literary Award

In 1960 the Academy instituted six annual awards to be made to outstanding writers for work in various categories: research/creative essay, poetry, novel, short story, drama, children's literature. In 1970 an additional award for translation was introduced. Winners receive a cash prize of 4,000 taka and a certificate. The awards are presented on 21 February in memory of the great language movement of 21 February 1952. Only Bangladeshi writers are eligible.

Awarding body: Bangla Academy, Burdwan House, Dacca 2, Bangladesh.

Recipients include: Motiul Islam (poetry); Dilara Hashem (novel); Sucharit Chowdhury (short story); Serajuddin Kasempuri (research); Momta-zuddin Ahmed (drama); Sardar Fazlul Karim (translation); Faiz Ahmed (children's literature), 1977.

Hermann-Bank-Senior-Medaille

The medal was established in 1969 by Prof. Hermann Bank, Junior, in memory of his father (1890–1969), a merchant of precious stones who contributed to the advance of gemmology as a science and as a field of professional training. A cash prize of DM1,000 and a certificate are awarded with each prize. A gold award is made for basic research papers in gemmology, and a silver award is made for the year's best performance in the examination (conducted by the German Gemmological Society) for the 'Gemmologe DGemG', a practical and technical qualification. Recipients of this qualification only are eligible for the award. The presentation is made at the Annual Meeting of the German Gemmological Society, which is normally in the last week of May, or on another occasion as may be necessary.

Awarding body: Deutsche Gemmologische Gesell-schaft, e.V., Gewerbehalle, D-6580 Idar-Oberstein 2, Federal Republic of Germany.

William Mitchell Banks Memorial Lecture-ship

The Lectureship was established in 1905 to commemorate the services to the City and University of Liverpool of Sir William Mitchell Banks, M.D., LL.D., F.R.C.S., Emeritus Professor of Anatomy, Consulting Surgeon to the Royal Infirmary, and formerly Lecturer in Clinical Surgery, who died in 1904. The lectureship was endowed with £1,500 from a sum raised by public subscription. The appointment is made by the University Council every two years. The lecturer delivers a lecture or course of lectures related to the study or practice of Surgery.

Awarding body: The University of Liverpool, P.O.B. 147, Liverpool L69 3BX, England.

Dr. Karel Barbierprijs

The prize was established in 1927 by the Belgian Royal Academy of Dutch Language and Literature in memory of Dr. Karel Barbier (1845–1924), doctor of medicine and patron of the Academy. An award of 5,000 Belgian francs is made every two years for the best published historical novel written in Dutch. Recipients must be Belgian nationals.

Awarding body: Koninklijke Academie voor Nederlandse Taal- en Letterkunde, Koningstraat 18, B-9000 Ghent, Belgium.

Recipients include: Paul Kennis (*Uit het Dagboek van Lieven de Myttenaere*, 1930); E. Rombauts (*Adriaan Poirters*, 1938); E. van Hemeldonck (*De cleyne Keyser*, 1948); L. P. Boon (*De zoon van Jan de Lichte*, 1962).

Laura Taber Barbour Award

This annual award was established in 1956 by Dr. Clifford E. Barbour and his son, Clifford E. Barbour, Jr., in memory of Mrs. Laura Taber Barbour, who was killed in an aeroplane accident. The award was created to recognize notable achievement in the field of aviation safety, civil or military, in method, design invention, study or other improvements. The award of a medallion, certificate and an honorarium of $500 is presented at the annual luncheon of the Aero Club of Washington.

Awarding body: Flight Safety Foundation, Inc., 1800 North Kent St., Arlington, Va. 22209, U.S.A.

Recipients include: Dr. John Swearingen, FAA (1972); Capt. Homer Mouden (1973); Dr. Ross A. McFarland (1974); Fred E. Weick (1975); George Wansbeek, KLM (1976).

Henry Barnes Lecture

A lecturer is appointed triennially to lecture on recent advances in clinical medicine and receives an honorarium. The lecture is open to general practitioners as well as to all members of the Royal Society of Medicine.

Awarding body: Royal Society of Medicine, 1 Wimpole St., London W1M 8AE, England.

Simion Bărnuţiu Prize

This prize for achievement in the field of law was founded by the Romanian Academy in 1948. It commemorates Simion Bărnuţiu (1808–64), professor of law and philosophy at Iaşi University, and one of the leaders of the Romanian revolution in Transylvania in 1848. The award is presented annually at a General Assembly of the Academy, and consists of 10,000 lei and a diploma.

Awarding body: Academy of the S.R. of Romania, 125 Calea Victoriei, Bucharest, Romania.

Harland Bartholomew Award

The award was established in 1968 by the Urban Planning and Development Division of the American Society of Civil Engineers, in recognition of the achievement of H. Bartholomew, Hon. M.A.S.C.E. The award consists of a wall plaque and certificate, and is made annually to the person who has made the most commendable contribution to the role of the civil engineer in urban planning and development, either in written or in practical form. The award is restricted to Fellows, Members and Associate Members of the Society.

Awarding body: American Society of Civil Engineers, 345 East 47th St., New York, N.Y. 10017, U.S.A.

Recipients include: Roger H. Gilman (1972); Jack R. Newville (1973); Ladislas Segoe (1974); George C. Bestor (1975); Albert A. Dorman (1976).

Alice Hunt Bartlett Prize

This award of £200 is made annually to the poet whom the Poetry Society most wishes to honour and encourage, for the production of a published collection of not less than 20 poems or 400 lines in English (either original or translated), in a book presented in duplicate to the Society's library in the year of publication. Special consideration will be given to newly emerged poets and to first published collections as far as merit warrants. If the poetry is translated into English, the prize is divided between the poet and the translator.

Awarding body: The Poetry Society, 21 Earls Court Square, London SW5, England.

Basanti Devi Amir Chand Prize

This prize was established with a donation from the late General Amir Chand in 1953. It is awarded annually to a senior research worker for published research work in any subject in the field of medical science, including clinical research. The prize consists of a cash sum of 1,000 rupees.

Awarding body: Indian Council of Medical Research, Ansari Nagar, Post Box 4508, New Delhi 110016, India.

Recipients include: Prof. Usha K. Luthra (1973); Dr. C. R. Krishnamurti (1974); Dr. S. Sriramachari (1975); Dr. K. M. Pavri (1976); Dr. S. G. Srikantia (1977).

von Basedow-Forschungspreis (Schilddruse)

(von Basedow Prize for Research into the Thyroid Gland)

This annual award was donated by the company E. Merck of Darmstadt to be awarded to young scientists for an exceptional work on the subject of the thyroid gland. Applicants must be no more than 40 years of age, and resident in the Federal Republic (including West Berlin), Austria or Switzerland. Scientists employed in industry or commerce are not eligible, nor those whose entries have previously appeared in print. A sum of DM15,000 is awarded annually, usually in the form of a first prize of DM10,000 and a second prize of DM5,000.

Awarding body: Deutsche Gesellschaft für Endokrinologie, Med. Hochschule, Dept. Innere Medizin, Abt. für klinische Endokrinologie, D-3000 Hannover-Kleefeld, Roderbruchstr., Federal Republic of Germany.

Bass Charrington Arts Award

This award consists of a principal prize of £400 and a second prize of £200, and is made to an individual or organization for activities in one or more of a variety of artistic fields. It is sponsored by the brewers Bass Charrington Ltd., and the Arts Council of Northern Ireland assists in its administration.

Awarding body: Arts Council of Northern Ireland, 181A Stranmillis Rd., Belfast BT9 5DU, Northern Ireland.

Recipients include: Octagon Gallery (1973); Colin Fleming (1975); Fr. Desmond Wilson (1976).

Arthur Batchelor Lecture

The benefaction given to the University of East Anglia in 1963 by Miss D. M. Batchelor constitutes a trust fund, the income from which is used to provide lectures on a subject concerning music or the visual arts. The lectures are subsequently published.

Awarding body: University of East Anglia, Norwich NR4 7TJ, England.

J. E. Batchelor Award

This annual award, named after a past President of the Society of Automotive Engineers – Australasia, takes the form of a certificate and a cash prize of A$150. It is given for an outstanding written paper presented to any Division or Group of the Society or published in the Society's journal in the previous calendar year, and is open to any person, whether or not a member of the Society, who is a resident of Australia, New Zealand or a territory administered by either country. Nominations are made by Divisions or independent Group Committees to the Society's Council.

Awarding body: Society of Automotive Engineers – Australasia, National Science Centre, 191 Royal Parade, Parkville, Vic. 3052, Australia.

Louis H. Bauer Founders Award

Established by the Aerospace Medical Association to honour Louis H. Bauer, M.D., its founder, this prize is awarded annually in May for the most significant contribution in space medicine. It is sponsored by the Eaton Laboratories Division of the Norwich Pharmacal Company, and consists of $500 and a certificate.

Awarding body: Aerospace Medical Association, Washington National Airport, Washington, D.C. 20001, U.S.A.

Recipients include: Capt. Ralph L. Christy (1972); Dr. Karl H. Houghton (1973); Dr. Willard R. Hawkins (1974); Col. John Pickering (1975); Dr. Lawrence F. Dietlein (1976).

Bavarian Academy of Fine Arts Prize for Literary Merit

The Academy has awarded a literary prize annually since 1950. This consists of a sum of money which by 1974 had been increased to DM8,000. The recipient is selected by the literary section of the Academy, on the basis of his entire work. The quality of the literary work is decisive.

Awarding body: Bayerische Akademie der Schönen Künste, Max-Joseph-Platz 3, 8000 München 22, Federal Republic of Germany.

Recipients include: Elias Canetti (1969); Manès Sperber (1971); Jean Améry (1972); Reiner Kunze (1973); Gershom Scholem (1974).

Samuel Baxter Prize

Up to £60 may be awarded annually at the discretion of the Council of the Royal Institution of Naval Architects, as a recognition of the best contribution during the year towards the safety and/or efficiency of sea-going vessels.

Awarding body: Royal Institution of Naval Architects, 10 Upper Belgrave St., London SW1X 8BQ, England.

Josef-Bayer-Medaille

This medal was established in 1957 by the Society of Friends of the Veterinary University of Vienna in memory of Josef Bayer, the outstanding veterinary surgeon and first Rector of the K. u. K. Militär-Thierarznei-Institut. The medal is awarded to Austrian – or in exceptional cases to foreign – practitioners, in recognition of outstanding achievements in veterinary science. Candidates are nominated by a commission consisting of lecturers and professors on the Board of the Society. Nominations are made primarily on the basis of published works, but with reference also to scientific activity. Alternatively nomination can be made on the basis of a candidate's discovery or invention of new techniques. Should the Board fail to select a candidate in any one year, the medal can be presented the following year as an additional award.

Awarding body: Gesellschaft der Freunde der Veterinärmedizinischen Universität Wien, 1130 Vienna, Hietzinger Kai 125, Austria.

Recipients include: Dr. Josef Pointner (1974); Dr. Robert Winkler (1974); Dr. Wilfried Lenz (1976).

Joseph Bech Prize

This international prize is one of many given by the F.V.S. Foundation of Hamburg. It was estab-lished in 1977 as an annual award for outstanding service and achievement in the European cause. It is named in memory of Dr. Joseph Bech (1887–1975), the Luxembourg statesman. It consists of a monetary prize of DM20,000 and a gold medal.

Awarding body: Stiftung F.V.S., Georgsplatz 10, 2 Hamburg 1, Federal Republic of Germany.

Recipients include: Mrs. Shirley Williams (U.K., Secretary of State for Education and Science), Prof. Henri Rieben (Switzerland, Dir. of Centre for European Studies, Univ. of Lausanne), Prof. Sir Heinz Koeppler (U.K., Dir. of Wilton Park), 1977.

Stephen D. Bechtel Pipeline Engineering Award

The Bechtel Foundation donated funds in honour of Stephen Bechtel's notable achievements in pipeline design and construction to establish this award in 1970. It is made annually to the member who has made the most definite contribution to pipeline engineering in research, planning, design, or construction, either in the form of papers or outstanding performance. The award consists of a plaque and certificate.

Awarding body: American Society of Civil Engineers, 345 East 47th St., New York, N.Y. 10017, U.S.A.

Recipients include: Nathaniel Clapp (1972); Eldon V. Hunt (1973); Maynard M. Anderson (1974); Joe E. Thompson (1975); Kenneth E. Britain (1976).

George Louis Beer Prize

This award is made annually for the best work in the field of European international history since 1895. It carries a cash award of $300.

Awarding body: American Historical Association, 400 A St., S.E., Washington, D.C. 20003, U.S.A.

August Beernaertprijs

The prize was established in 1912 by the Belgian Royal Academy of Dutch Language and Literature in memory of August Beernaert (1829–1912), Prime Minister of Belgium from 1884 to 1894, at whose instigation the Academy was founded. An award of 25,000 Belgian francs is made every two years for the best submitted literary work, irrespective of genre, written in Dutch. Recipients must be Belgian nationals.

Awarding body: Koninklijke Academie voor Nederlandse Taal- en Letterkunde, Koningstraat 18, B-9000 Ghent, Belgium.

Recipients include: André Demedts (*Het heeft geen belang,* 1945); J. Daisne (*De man die zijn haar kort liet knippen,* 1949); Dr. R. F. Lissens (*De Vlaamse Letterkunde van 1780 tot Heden,* 1953); Prof. Dr. H. Uyttersprot (*Het proza van Paul van Ostaijen,* 1959); Hugo Claus (*De verwondering,* 1963).

Clifford W. Beers Award

The award was established in 1976 by the Mental Health Association and the American Foundation for Mental Hygiene in memory of Clifford W. Beers, founder of the Association. The award is

presented annually for a nation-wide contribution to the relief of mental or emotional disorders. The recipient must share Mr. Beer's concern for improving conditions and public attitudes. The prize consists of a stipend and a medal.
Awarding body: Mental Health Association, 1800 N. Kent St., Arlington, Va. 22190, U.S.A.

Martin-Behaim-Plakette

This medal is awarded at irregular intervals by the Franconian Geographical Society to honour outstanding achievements in geographical research, particularly into the geography of Franconia. It was established in 1954 in honour of Martin Behaim (1459–1507), maritime explorer and cartographer.
Awarding body: Fränkische Geographische Gesellschaft (Sitz Erlangen), 8520 Erlangen, Kochstr. 4, Federal Republic of Germany.
Recipients include: Hermann Haack (G.D.R., 1962); Edouard Imhof (Switzerland, 1969); Hermann von Wissmann (F.R.G., 1969); Hans Bobek (Austria, 1973); Erich Otremba (F.R.G., 1975).

M. W. Beijerinck-Virologie-Medaille

This gold medal was founded in 1965 by Dr. Ir. L. E. den Dooren de Jong and Mrs. Ir. A. P. den Dooren de Jong-Ris, to commemorate Dr. M. W. Beijerinck (1851–1931), founder of virology. The medal is awarded every three years by the Royal Netherlands Academy of Arts and Sciences to scientists (preferably Dutch) who have made outstanding contributions in the field of virology.
Awarding body: Koninklijke Nederlandse Akademie van Wetenschappen, Kloveniersburgwal 29, 1011 JV Amsterdam, The Netherlands.
Recipients include: Prof. W. Berends (1972); Dr. E. M. J. Jaspars and Prof. Dr. A. van Kammen (1975); Prof. Dr. A. J. van der Eb (1978).

Beilby Memorial Award

This award was founded by three British scientific societies: the Society of Chemical Industry, the Royal Institute of Chemistry, and the Institute of Metals (now the Metals Society). Sir George Beilby had been President of each of the three bodies and after his death in 1924 they jointly sponsored an appeal for funds to commemorate his services. Throughout his career Sir George was greatly interested in fuel, and was Chairman of the Fuel Research Board and Director of Fuel Research in the Department of Scientific and Industrial Research from 1917 to 1923. The award, a bronze medal and a sum of money (currently £200), is made to British investigators for advancement in science and practice, in recognition of individual work of exceptional merit, carried out continuously over a period of years and involving the development and application of scientific principles in the fields of chemical engineering, fuel technology and metallurgy. The recipient is usually under 40 years of age.
Awarding body: Sir George Beilby Memorial Fund, c/o Royal Institute of Chemistry, 30 Russell Square, London WC1B 5DT, England.
Recipients include: J. Szekely and G. C. Wood (1973); P. R. Swann (1975); I. Fells (1976); J. E. Castle (1977); Dr. J. C. Scully (1978).

Beke Manó Memorial Prize

The Hungarian 'Bolyai János' Mathematical Society established this prize in 1951 in memory of Manó Beke (1862–1946), a professor at Budapest University, who worked in the field of differential and integral calculus. The prize is for successful teaching or popularizing activity in mathematics. Awards amounting to 20,000 forints are made annually in two grades; the number of awards varies.
Awarding body: 'Bolyai János' Matematikai Társulat, Budapest VI, Anker-köz 1, Hungary.

Békésy Prize

Founded in 1976 by the Hungarian Society for Optics, Acoustics and Cinematography, the award is given to members of the Society who have made outstanding contributions to the physical, technical, medical or other fields of acoustics. A cash prize of 5,000 forints is awarded every two years.
Awarding body: Optikai, Akuzstikai és Filmtechnikai Egyesület, Budapest VI, Anker-köz 1, Hungary.

Belgica Prize

A gold medal is awarded by the Belgian Royal Academy to a scientist or group of scientists who have most successfully carried out research within the Antarctic Circle. The prize-winner(s) may be of any nationality. The prize, instituted in 1901 and originally triennial, is now awarded every five years. Any surplus income from the Foundation may be used to finance oceanographic research by Belgians.
Awarding body: Académie Royale de Belgique, Palais des Académies, rue Ducale 1, 1000 Brussels, Belgium.
Recipients include: E. Picciotto (1968); Mlle P. Doyen (1973).

Bellman Prize

This prize was established in 1920 by the painter Anders Zorn in memory of Carl Michael Bellman, the Swedish poet (1740–95), and is administered by the Swedish Academy. It consists of an annual cash prize with a current value of 50,000 Swedish kronor, presented to a poet writing in Swedish, not necessarily of Swedish nationality. The prize cannot be applied for.
Awarding body: The Swedish Academy, Börshuset, Källargränd 4, S-111 29 Stockholm, Sweden.

Vincent Bendix Award

This annual award was established in 1956 in memory of Vincent Bendix (1882–1945), the distinguished engineer, inventor and industrialist. It is conferred for outstanding and sustained research contributions, either in original thought or administrative leadership, on a staff member of the colleges of engineering in the United States. The award consists of a gold medal, bronze replica and a certificate.

Awarding body: American Society for Engineering Education, Suite 400, One Dupont Circle, Washington, D.C. 20036, U.S.A.

Recipients include: Ernst R. G. Eckert (1972); John R. Low, Jr. (1973); James W. Westwater (1974); Aldert van der Ziel (1975); Harry Bolton Seed (1976).

Stephen Vincent Benet Narrative Poem Awards

The awards were established by John William Andrews in memory of the American poet Stephen Vincent Benet, author of *John Brown's Body* and other classics. Prizes of $100, $50 and $25 are awarded annually for the three best narrative poems published in *Poet Lore* during the previous year. Entries must not exceed 200 lines.

Awarding body: Poet Lore, 4000 Albemarle St., Suite 510, Washington, D.C. 20016, U.S.A.

Adolphe Bentinck Prize

Awarded annually since 1973, this prize of 20,000 French francs is for a book contributing to European unity, the cause of peace or the struggle against fanaticism. It is named after a former French ambassador to the Netherlands. Publishers are invited to submit suitable entries, written for the general reader, which are judged by an international jury.

Awarding body: Monsieur Robert Lange, Secretary, Adolphe Bentinck Prize, 33 rue Poissonnière, 75002 Paris, France.

Recipients include: Giovanni Magnifico (Italy, 1974); Hendryck Brugmans (Netherlands, 1975); Jean Monnet (France, 1976); Raymond Aron (France, 1977).

Ernst von Bergmann-Gedenkmünze (*Ernst von Bergmann Commemorative Coin*)

This award, consisting of a gold coin and certificate, was founded in 1957, and is given occasionally by the German ·Surgical Society to a surgeon from a German-speaking country who has contributed substantially to the cause of German surgery.

Awarding body: Deutsche Gesellschaft für Chirurgie, 1000 Berlin 15, Kurfürstendamm 179, Federal Republic of Germany.

Recipients include: Prof. Emil K. Frey (Fed. Rep. of Germany, 1959); Prof. K. H. Bauer (Fed. Rep. of Germany, 1962); Prof. E. Rehn (Fed. Rep. of Germany, 1966); Prof. H. Bürkle de la Camp (Fed. Rep. of Germany, 1971); Prof. R. Nissen (Switzerland, 1974).

Vitus Bering medaljen

This medal was established in 1941 by Crown Prince Frederik of Denmark, Prime Minister Th. Stauning, and Professor Niels Bohr. It commemorates the discovery by Vitus Jonassen Bering (1681–1741) of the North-east corner of Asia and the Bering Strait during the Great Nordic Expedition of 1734–41 undertaken for Tsar Peter the Great of Russia. The medal is awarded occasionally for outstanding contributions in the field of scientific geography.

Awarding body: Det Kongelige Danske Geografiske Selskab, Haraldsgade 68, DK-2100 Copenhagen O, Denmark.

Recipients include: Prof. dr. T. Hägerstrand (1970); Admiral dr. A. H. Vedel (1974); Prof. dr. S. Thorarinsson (1976).

Berliner Kunstpreis/Fontanepreis (*Berlin Arts Prize/Fontane Prize*)

The Berlin Academy of Arts awards prizes annually in rotation in two of the following categories: fine arts; music; literature (Fontane Prize); dramatic arts; film, radio and television; architecture. They take the form of cash awards of DM15,000 each.

Awarding body: Akademie der Künste, 1000 Berlin 21, Hanseatenweg 21, Federal Republic of Germany.

Recipients include: Bernhard Minetti.

Bernal Lecture

A Fund was established in 1969 by means of an endowment of £2,000 by Professor J. D. Bernal, F.R.S. Its purpose is to provide a lectureship on some aspect of the social function of science. The lecture is given every three years, the first in 1971. A gift of £200 is paid to the lecturer.

Awarding body: Royal Society of London, 6 Carlton House Terrace, London SW1Y 5AG, England.

Lecturers include: Lord Ashby ('Science and Antiscience', 1971).

Claude Bernard Lectureship

The lectureship, with a medal and a cash prize of 2,000 French francs, is awarded annually to a person who has made a significant contribution to the advancement of knowledge about *diabetes mellitus*. The lectureship was founded in 1969 by the European Association for the Study of Diabetes, sponsored by the Paul Neumann Foundation. It commemorates the research of Claude Bernard (1813–78) into metabolism, the way in which the body deals with carbohydrates.

Awarding body: European Association for the Study of Diabetes, 3/6 Alfred Place, London, WC1E 7EE, England.

Recipients include: K. Lundbaek (Denmark, 1972); A. E. Renold (Switzerland, 1973); T. R. Fraser (U.K., 1974); R. G. Spiro (U.S.A., 1975); H. G. Hers (Belgium, 1976).

Claude Bernard Science Journalism Awards

These awards, established in 1967 by the National Society for Medical Research, commemorate Claude Bernard, the 19th-century French physiologist and 'founder of modern experimental medicine'. They are made in recognition of responsible science reporting which has made a significant contribution to public understanding of basic research in the life sciences, including experimental medicine. The awards are made annually, and consist of a $1,000 cash prize and certificate in each of two categories: magazines of general interest, and newspapers (daily, weekly or monthly). Articles published in medical or scientific journals or whose authors are employees of the Society are not eligible. Entries must have been published during the previous calendar year.

Awarding body: National Society for Medical Research, Suite 1100, 1000 Vermont Ave., N.W., Washington, D.C. 20005, U.S.A.

Recipients include: Arthur J. Snider (newspaper, 1973); Gene Bylinski (magazine, 1974); Lawrence K. Altman (newspaper, 1974); Albert Rosenfeld *et al.* (magazine, 1975); Alton Blakeslee (newspaper, 1975).

Léon Bernard Foundation Prize
The prize is awarded for outstanding service in the field of social medicine, and consists of a bronze medal and the sum of 1,000 Swiss francs. The award is made periodically, whenever the accumulated interest on the Foundation's capital amounts to a net sum of not less than 1,000 Swiss francs. Anyone is eligible to receive the prize and may be nominated by any national health administration or former recipient of the prize. The Léon Bernard Foundation was established by the (then) League of Nations Health Organization in memory of Professor Léon Bernard, one of the Organization's founders.

Awarding body: World Health Organization, Avenue Appia, 1211 Geneva 27, Switzerland.

Recipients include: Prof. F. J. C. Cambournac (Portugal, 1978).

Ernst W. Bertner Memorial Award
Established in 1950 by the University of Texas System Cancer Center, the award is in honour of the late Ernst W. Bertner, M.D., who was the first director of the M. D. Anderson Hospital and Tumor Institute and first president of the Texas Medical Center. The prize is given to a physician or scientist in recognition of an outstanding contribution to the field of cancer research. It is awarded annually at the Symposium on Fundamental Cancer Research held in Houston, and consists of a bronze medallion and an honorarium.

Awarding body: The University of Texas System Cancer Center, M. D. Anderson Hospital and Tumor Institute, Texas Medical Center, Houston, Tex. 77030, U.S.A.

Recipients include: Dr. Howard M. Temin (U.S.A., 1972); Dr. George Klein (Sweden, 1973); Dr. George H. Hitchings (U.S.A., 1974); Michael Abercrombie (U.K., 1975); Dr. Howard E. Skipper (U.S.A., 1976).

Berzelius Medal
The Swedish Society of Medical Sciences founded this gold medal in 1898 to commemorate Jacob Berzelius (1779–1848), the Swedish chemist who was one of the founders of the Society. The medal is awarded every ten years to a scientist of any nationality who has contributed to the progress of medical chemistry.

Awarding body: Swedish Society of Medical Sciences, P.O.B. 558, S-101 27 Stockholm, Sweden.

Recipients include: Prof. The Svedberg (Sweden, 1941); Prof. A. J. P. Martin (U.K., 1951); Prof. Erik Jorpes (Sweden, 1961); Prof. Pehr Edman (Australia, 1971).

Beskow Prize
This prize was established in 1873 by Bernhard von Beskow. It is administered by the Swedish Academy, and awarded every second year to a Swedish writer. The prize consists of cash, at present to the value of 6,000 Swedish kronor, to be spent only on travel. It cannot be applied for.

Awarding body: The Swedish Academy, Börshuset, Källargränd 4, S-111 29 Stockholm, Sweden.

Bessemer Gold Medal
The award was established in 1873 by Sir Henry Bessemer and the Council of the Iron and Steel Institute (merged with the Institute of Metals to form the Metals Society in 1974). The medal is awarded annually in recognition of outstanding services to the iron and steel industry, whether on the industrial or scientific side. It is presented at the Society's Annual General Meeting in May. Anyone who is associated with the science or technology of iron and steel is eligible.

Awarding body: The Metals Society, 1 Carlton House Terrace, London SW1Y 5DB, England.

Recipients include: Sir Montague Finniston, F.R.S. (1974); Dr. R. Weck, C.B.E. (1975); J. D. Joy (1976).

Elsdon Best Memorial Award
This award is presented for outstanding ethnographic work on the Maori. It was established in 1970 by the Polynesian Society in memory of Elsdon Best (1856–1931), a foundation member and prolific contributor to the Society's journal. He was noted as an ethnographer and author of *Tuhoe* and *The Maori as he was*. The Polynesian Society, founded in 1892, aims to promote the study of Pacific history, anthropology, linguistics, etc. The award consists of a medal and a cash prize of NZ$20. While there are no restrictions governing the nationality of those eligible, all previous recipients have been New Zealanders. The awards are usually made annually at the Society's A.G.M.

Awarding body: Polynesian Society (Inc.), P.O.B. 10323, Wellington, New Zealand.

Recipients include: Don Stafford (author of *Te Arawa*, 1970); Prof. Roger Green (for outstanding contribution to knowledge of Polynesian prehistory, 1973); Dr. Ann Salmond (author of *Hui*, 1976).

Besterman Medal
The Library Association founded the medal in 1970 in honour of Dr. Theodore Besterman (died

1976), internationally known as a bibliographer. The annual award is for an outstanding bibliography or guide to the literature first published in the U.K. during the preceding year. Recommendations are made by members of the Library Association.

Awarding body: The Library Association, 7 Ridgmount St., London WC1E 7AE, England.

Recipients include: E. A. R. Bush (*Agriculture: a bibliographical guide*, 1974); Ralph Hyde (*Printed maps of Victorian London*, 1975); Central Statistical Office (*Guide to official statistics, No. 1, 1976*, 1976).

Albert J. Beveridge Award

This award is made annually for the best book in English on American history (United States, Canada, or Latin America). The prize carries a cash award of $1,000.

Awarding body: American Historical Association, 400 A St., S.E., Washington, D.C. 20003, U.S.A.

Homi J. Bhabha Medal

This medal was established in 1975 by the Indian National Science Academy. It is awarded every three years for outstanding contributions in the fields of physics, chemistry and mathematics.

Awarding body: Indian National Science Academy, Bahadur Shah Zafar Marg, New Delhi 110001, India.

Shanti Swarup Bhatnagar Medal

This medal was established in 1957 by the Indian National Science Academy. It is awarded every three years for outstanding contributions in the field of engineering and technology.

Awarding body: Indian National Science Academy, Bahadur Shah Zafar Marg, New Delhi 110001, India.

Recipients include: T. R. Seshadri (1964); D. S. Kothari (1966); P. Ray (1968); S. Bhagavantam (1970); A. N. Khosla (1974).

Bibliographical Society Gold Medal

Established by the Bibliographical Society in 1929, the award is made from time to time for services to bibliography.

Awarding body: Bibliographical Society, at the Rooms of the British Academy, Burlington House, Piccadilly, London W1V 0NS, England.

Recipients include: W. A. Jackson, Fredson Bowers, Graham Pollard, John Carter, Neil Ker.

Bibliography Prize

The International League of Antiquarian Booksellers established in 1962 a triennial prize worth $1,000 which is awarded to the author of the best work, published or unpublished, of learned bibliography or of research into the history of the book or of typography, and books of general interest on the subject. Entries must be submitted in a language which is universally used. A work already published is eligible only if it was published in the preceding three years.

Awarding body: International League of Antiquarian Booksellers, c/o Secretary, Dr. F. Kocher-Benzing, Rathenaustr. 21, 7000 Stuttgart 1, Federal Republic of Germany.

Recipients include: Claus Nissen (*Die zoologische Buchillustration*, 1971); William C. Miller (*Benjamin Franklin's Philadelphia Printing*, 1974).

Dr. Josef-Bick-Ehrenmedaille

This medal was established in 1967 by the Association of Austrian Librarians in memory of Dr. Josef Bick (1880–1952), former General Director of the Austrian National Library and General Inspector of Austrian libraries. It is awarded for scientific and organizational services to Austrian librarianship and libraries. The medal is conferred in two grades: silver, as an honour to persons over 40 years of age, and bronze, as an encouragement to persons under 40 years of age. It is awarded irregularly.

Awarding body: Vereinigung Österreichischer Bibliothekare, Josefsplatz 1, 1014 Vienna, Austria.

Recipients include: Dr. Ludwig Otruba (1970); Dr. Breycha-Vauthier (1973); Dr. Rudolf Fiedler, Dr. Walter Ritzer (1977).

Biennial International Art Book Prize

The prize was established by the Israel Museum in 1967. Illustrated books on archaeology, fine arts, architecture and applied arts, including photography, are judged by an international jury of designers and art historians, with special attention paid to the fully integrated book. The prize, an original work of art by an Israeli artist, is presented to the publisher and designer of the winning entry at the Biennial Jerusalem International Book Fair, where all entries are exhibited. Three or four other books are cited for honourable mention and awarded silver medals. Publishers may submit up to three titles published during the preceding two years.

Awarding body: The Israel Museum, P.O.B. 1299, Jerusalem 91000, Israel.

Recipients include: Mack: Imaginationen 1953–1973 (Kurt Weidemann and Verlag Ullstein GmbH-Propylaen Verläg, Fed. Rep. of Germany, 1973/74).

Bilim Ödülü (*Science Award*)

This award was founded in 1965 and is presented annually for a contribution to science on an international level, or for an important contribution to the development of science in Turkey. It consists of a gold plaque, a certificate, and 10,000 liras, and is open to Turkish scientists only. It may be given to more than one person at a time.

Awarding body: Scientific and Technical Research Council of Turkey, 221 Atatürk Boulevar, Kavaklidere, Ankara, Turkey.

Robert Bing Prize

This award is made by the Swiss Academy of Medical Sciences for outstanding work in the recognition, treatment and cure of neurological diseases by Swiss, Belgian, British, French, Dutch or U.S. citizens of about 40 years of age. It is normally given every two years, and is financed by a fund established in 1956 by Professor Robert Bing, M.D. (1878–1956), a prominent Swiss neurologist. The award takes the form of a certificate and cash prizes.

Awarding body: Schweizerische Akademie der Medizinischen Wissenschaften, Petersplatz 13, 4051 Basel, Switzerland.

Recipients include: Prof. Dr. Michel Cuénod (Switzerland), Prof. Dr. Leonhard Hösli (Switzerland), Dr. Hans Rudolf Müller (Switzerland) (1973); Dr. Gilbert Assal (Switzerland), Dr. Colin Brian Blakemore (U.K.), Dr. François de Ribaupierre (Switzerland) (1975).

Bingham Medal

Established in 1948 by the U.S. Society of Rheology, the medal is awarded annually to a resident of North America who has made an outstanding contribution to the science of rheology or has performed particularly meritorious service to the Society.

Awarding body: Society of Rheology, American Institute of Physics, 335 East 45th St., New York, N.Y. 10017, U.S.A.

Recipients include: Arthur S. Lodge (1971); Richard Stein (1972); Robert Simha (1973); R. Byron Bird (1974); Alan N. Gent (1975).

Binkley-Stephenson Award

This prize is given by the Organization of American Historians for the best scholarly article published in *The Journal of American History* during the preceding year. It is awarded annually, in memory of two past editors, and consists of a cash prize of $500.

Awarding body: Organization of American Historians, 112 North Bryan St., Bloomington, Ind. 47401, U.S.A.

Biochemical Society Jubilee Lectureship

In 1961 a lecture was established to commemorate the 50th anniversary of the Biochemical Society. It is given every two years by a distinguished biochemist of any nationality, who is expected to talk on his chosen field of research. An award in the form of a cash prize is made to the lecturer.

Awarding body: The Biochemical Society, 7 Warwick Court, London WC1R 5DP, England.

Lecturers include: H. G. Khorana ('Synthesis of the Nucleic Acids', 1968); A. L. Lehninger ('Mitochondria and Calcium Transport', 1970); C. B. Anfinsen ('Studies on the Co-operativity of Protein Folding', 1972); J. H. Quastel, C.C., F.R.S. ('Amino Acids and the Brain', 1974); A. Kornberg ('Multienzyme Systems Deoxyribonucleic Acid Replication', 1976).

George David Birkhoff Prize

This prize is awarded jointly by the American Mathematical Society and the Society for Industrial and Applied Mathematics and is endowed by the Birkhoff family. It is awarded every five years for an outstanding contribution to applied mathematics in the highest and broadest sense. It consists of a cash sum of $300.

Awarding body: Society for Industrial and Applied Mathematics, U.S.A.

Recipient: Jurgen K. Moser (1968).

James Tait Black Memorial Prizes

These prizes were inaugurated in 1918 by the late Mrs. Black in memory of her husband, James Tait Black, ·a partner in the publishing house of A. & C. Black Ltd. The prizes are now administered by a trust fund at Edinburgh University. One prize is given for the best biography published in English in Britain during the previous calendar year, and one prize for the best novel. The choice is made by the Professor of English Literature at Edinburgh University, or, failing him, the Professor of Literature at Glasgow University. The amount of the cash prizes is currently about £450 each, and awards are generally made in the first months of the year following publication of the books selected.

Awarding body: University of Edinburgh, Old College, South Bridge, Edinburgh EH8 9YL, Scotland.

Recipients include: Prof. Karl Miller (*Cockburn's Millenium*, biography) and Brian Moore (*The Great Victorian Collection*, novel), 1975; Ronald Hingley (*A New Life of Anton Chekhov*, biography) and John Banville (*Dr. Copernicus*, novel), 1976; George Painter (*Châteaubriand: The Longed-for Tempests*, biography) and John Le Carré (*The Honourable Schoolboy*, novel), 1977.

Blackall Machine Tool and Gage Award

This award was established in 1954 by Frederick S. Blackall, Jr., Fellow and seventy-second President of the American Society of Mechanical Engineers. The award is given for the best paper or papers clearly concerned with or related to the design or application of machine tools, gages or dimensional measuring instruments, submitted to ASME for presentation and publication. Papers by more than one author are eligible. Authors are not restricted by nationality, age or society membership. The award is made annually if warranted. A bronze plaque and an honorarium of $100 for each author are given.

Awarding body: American Society of Mechanical Engineers, United Engineering Centre, 345 E. 47th St., New York, N.Y. 10017, U.S.A.

Recipients include: S. P. Loutrel, N. H. Cook (1974); Sindre Holøyen, Clayton D. Mote, Jr. (1975).

Blackstone Lecture

The lecture was established in 1976 by Mr. Reginald Graham, a former member of Pembroke College, Oxford. The annual lecture is in memory of the association of Sir William Blackstone (first Vinerian Professor of English Law, who entered Pembroke in 1738) with Pembroke College. The lecturer is required to be an eminent legal scholar. An honorarium is awarded.

Awarding body: Pembroke College, Oxford, England.
Lecturers include: Prof. Sir Rupert Cross (Vinerian Prof. of English Law, Univ. of Oxford, 1976).

Blair-Bell Medal

The medal is awarded every five years by the Royal Society of Medicine for work in the science of gynaecology and obstetrics. It commemorates William Blair-Bell, pioneer in this branch of medicine, and founder of the Royal College of Obstetricians and Gynaecologists.
Awarding body: Royal Society of Medicine, 1 Wimpole St., London W1M 8AE, England.

William Blair-Bell Memorial Lectureships

The Lectureships were established under the bequest of William Blair-Bell, founder of the Royal College of Obstetricians and Gynaecologists. Two lecturers are appointed each year to speak on obstetrics, gynaecology or another closely related subject, preference being given to lectures based on original work. The honorarium for each is £40. The lecturers must be either Members of the College or Fellows of not more than two years' standing.
Awarding body: Royal College of Obstetricians and Gynaecologists, 27 Sussex Place, Regent's Park, London NW1 4RG, England.
Lecturers include: J. F. Murphy (1975); D. A. Abell, N. M. Duignan (1976); Dr. A. Alaily, A. A. Calder (1977).

Bláthy Award

This award is presented annually by the Hungarian Electrotechnical Association to members who, over a period of time, have achieved outstanding results in heavy-current electronics and have furthered both the activities of the Association and the progress of heavy-current engineering. It takes the form of a medal and 5,000 forints cash prize. Established in 1958, it commemorates Ottó Titusz Bláthy, distinguished inventor and pioneer in the field of applied electrical engineering.
Awarding body: Magyar Elektrotechnikai Egyesület, 1055 Budapest, Kossuth Lajos tér 6–8, Hungary.
Recipients include: Aladár Gregor (1970); Aba Kádár (1971); István Géczy (1973); István Futó (1974); László Viosz (1976).

Selwyn G. Blaylock Medal

This award, which was established in 1948, is administered by the Canadian Institute of Mining and Metallurgy. It takes the form of a gold medal, which is awarded annually to a member of the Institute for distinguished service to Canada through exceptional achievement in the field of mining, metallurgy or geology. Nominations must be endorsed by not fewer than five members of the Institute.
Awarding body: The Canadian Institute of Mining and Metallurgy, 400-1130 Sherbrooke St. West, Montreal H3A 2M8, Canada.

Recipients include: Alexis Ignatieff (1972); Walter J. Riva (1973); Duncan R. Derry (1974); R. V. Porritt (1975); Kenneth M. Dewar (1976).

Louis Blériot Medal

This award is made annually to holders of the highest records for speed, altitude and distance achieved during the previous year, by light aircraft of the first two categories.
Awarding body: Fédération Aéronautique Internationale, 6 rue Galilée, 75016 Paris, France.
Recipients include: Edgar J. Lesher (U.S.A., 1975).

Marc Blitzstein Award for the Musical Theatre

In 1965 the friends of Marc Blitzstein, a member of the National Institute of Arts and Letters, set up a fund in his memory for an award of $2,500 to a composer, lyricist or librettist, to encourage the creation of works of merit for the musical theatre.
Awarding body: American Academy and Institute of Arts and Letters, 633 West 155th St., New York, N.Y. 10032, U.S.A.

Maurice Bloch Lectureship

The Lectureship was founded in 1956 and endowed from a trust established by Sir Maurice Bloch, distiller in Glasgow. The endowment provides for an annual lecture on the general subject 'Medicine in Relation to the Community'. The lecture is subsequently published.
Awarding body: University of Glasgow, Glasgow G12 8QQ, Scotland.
Lecturers include: Rt. Hon. R. H. S. Crossman (1972); Sir Charles Stuart-Harris (1972); Sir Dugald Baird (1975); Sir George Godber (1975); David Steel (1976).

Blom Prize

This prize is given by the Swedish Academy for scientific work on the Swedish language. It was endowed in 1945 by Edward and Eva Blom. It is a cash prize (current value is 4,000 Swedish kronor), presented annually to a Swedish expert in linguistics. It cannot be applied for.
Awarding body: The Swedish Academy, Börshuset, Källargränd 4, S-111 29 Stockholm, Sweden.

Niels Bohr International Gold Medal

The medal was established in 1955 by the Danish Engineering Society on the occasion of Prof. Niels Bohr's 70th birthday. Prof. Bohr (1885–1962) was Director of the Institute for Theoretical Physics, University of Copenhagen, and winner of the Nobel Prize for Physics in 1922. A gold medal is awarded every three years to an engineer or physicist in recognition of outstanding work for the peaceful utilization of atomic energy, interpreted in a wider sense as a symbol of achievement in the field of modern atomic physics.
Awarding body: Dansk Ingeniørforening, Vester Farimagsgade 31, DK 1606 Copenhagen V, Denmark.

Recipients include: Prof. George de Hevesy (1961); Prof. P. L. Kapitza (1965); Prof. Isidor Isaac Rabi (1967); Prof. Werner Karl Heisenberg (1970); Prof. Richard P. Feynman (1973).

Herbert Eugene Bolton Memorial Prize

Established in 1956 by the Conference on Latin American History, the prize is awarded annually to the author of a book in English on any significant aspect of Latin American history. The book must have been published during the preceding year; translations, anthologies, reprints, new editions and works not primarily historiographical in content are not normally eligible. Sound scholarship, grace of style and the importance of the contribution are among the criteria for the award, which carries a stipend of $300.

Awarding body: Conference on Latin American History, University of Wisconsin-Milwaukee, College of Letters and Science, Center for Latin America, P.O.B. 413, Milwaukee, Wis. 53201, U.S.A.

Recipients include: Warren L. Cook (*Flood Tide of Empire: Spain and the Pacific Northwest, 1543–1819,* 1974); Frederick P. Bowser (*The African Slave in Colonial Peru, 1524–1650,* 1975); David Rock (*Politics in Argentina, 1890–1930, the Rise and Fall of Radicalism,* 1976).

Boltzmann Medal

This gold medal is awarded for outstanding achievements in thermodynamics or statistical mechanics. The award was founded in 1973 by the International Commission on Thermodynamics and Statistical Mechanics of the International Union of Pure and Applied Physics (IUPAP), in memory of the Austrian physicist Ludwig Boltzmann (1844–1906). The medal is awarded at every IUPAP International Conference on Statistical Mechanics.

Awarding body: IUPAP International Commission on Thermodynamics and Statistical Mechanics, c/o The Secretary, Institute of Physics, Norges Tekniske Högskole, N-7034 Trondheim, Norway.

Recipients include: Prof. K. G. Wilson (U.S.A., introducing the renormalization group methods for the study of critical phenomena and phase transitions, 1975).

Tom W. Bonner Prize in Nuclear Physics

Established in 1964 as a memorial to Tom W. Bonner by his friends, students and associates, the prize is awarded annually to recognize and encourage outstanding experimental research in nuclear physics, including the development of a method, technique or device that contributes significantly in a general way to nuclear physics research. Nominations are open to physicists whose work in nuclear physics is primarily experimental, but a particularly outstanding piece of theoretical work will take precedence over experimental work. There is no time limit on work described.

The prize consists of $1,000 and a certificate citing the contributions made by the recipient.

Awarding body: American Physical Society, 335 East 45th St., New York, N.Y. 10017, U.S.A.

Recipients include: Denys Wilkinson (1974); Chien-Shiung Wu (1975); John P. Schiffer (1976); Stuart T. Butler and G. Raymond Satchler (1977).

R. H. G. Bonnycastle Foundation Lectures

The lectureship was established in 1970 in memory of R. H. G. Bonnycastle, the first Chairman of the Metropolitan Corporation of Greater Winnipeg and first Chancellor of the University of Winnipeg (1967–68). The lectures are designed to bring outstanding leaders in the fields of urban affairs and municipal government to Winnipeg every year. Two lectures are held annually.

Awarding body: University of Winnipeg, 515 Portage Avenue, Winnipeg, Man. R3B 2E9, Canada.

Lecturers include: Arthur Phillips (fmr. Mayor of Vancouver, 1975); William Terron (Pres., Central Mortgage and Housing Corpn., Ottawa, 1975); Dr. Edwin Mills (Prof. of Economics, Princeton Univ., 1976); Lady Jackson (Barbara Ward) (British economist and writer, 1976); Dr. George Sternlieb (Center for Urban Policy Research, Rutgers Univ., 1977).

Book Centre of Rhodesia Annual Literary Awards

Established in 1971 and awarded for the first time in 1972, two prizes of R$300 each are given annually, one for a published work in English and one for a published work in an African language. The work may be a book, a series of published articles, a collection of published poems, broadcast radio scripts, a play which has been performed or published, or a piece of creative writing in recorded form. Rhodesians by birth, domicile or by long association, irrespective of age or sex, are eligible. The prizes are administered by the P.E.N. Centre of Rhodesia.

Awarding body: Book Centre and Textbook Sales of Rhodesia, P.O.B. 1900, Salisbury, Rhodesia.

Recipients: Noel Brettell (poetry, 1972); Dr. Oliver Ransford (historical work, 1973); Tony Tanser (books on Rhodesia, 1975); Charles Mungoshi (works in English and Shona, 1976).

Book Design Award

This award is made annually for the design of a book published within the previous 12 months. It was established in 1952 and takes the form of a certificate. It is open only to members of the Australian Book Publishers' Association.

Awarding body: Australian Book Publishers' Association, 163 Clarence St., Sydney, N.S.W., Australia.

Booker Prize for Fiction

One of the most important literary awards in the U.K., this annual prize is sponsored by Booker McConnell Ltd. and administered by the National Book League. It is for the best full-length novel written in English by a citizen of the U.K., the Commonwealth, Eire or South Africa. Publishers are invited to submit entries with scheduled publication dates between January and November of the award year. A short-list is announced in October, and the prize is awarded at the end of November. The prize was established in 1968 for a seven-year period; in 1975 Booker McConnell announced that it would be renewed for a further seven years. In 1978 the prize money was doubled from £5,000 to £10,000.

Awarding body: National Book League, 7 Albemarle St., London W1, England.

Recipients include: Nadine Gordimer (*The Conservationist*) and Stanley Middleton (*Holiday*), 1974; Ruth Prawer Jhabvala (*Heat and Dust*, 1975); David Storey (*Saville*, 1976); Paul Scott (*Staying On*, 1977); Iris Murdock (*The Sea, The Sea*, 1978).

Walter M. Boothby Award

This prize was established by the Aerospace Medical Association in memory of Walter M. Boothby, M.D. It is awarded in alternate years in May for outstanding research directed at the promotion of health and prevention of disease in professional airline pilots. Sponsored by the Aviation Insurance Agency, it consists of $1,000 and a certificate.

Awarding body: Aerospace Medical Association, Washington National Airport, Washington, D.C. 20001, U.S.A.

Recipients include: Dr. Michael T. Lategola (1970); Dr. Kenneth G. Bergin (1971); Dr. George F. Catlett (1972); Dr. Charles E. Billings (1973); Dr. Karl E. Klein (1975).

Borden Award in Nutrition

This annual award, presented by the American Institute of Nutrition, was established by the Borden Foundation, Inc., and is given for distinctive research in the U.S. and Canada which has emphasized the nutritional significance of any food or food component. The award is made primarily for work published during the previous two years. It consists of $1,000 and an engraved wall plaque.

Awarding body: American Institute of Nutrition. (Nominations to Dr. D. B. Zilversmit, Division of Nutrition Science, Cornell University, Ithaca, N.Y. 14853, U.S.A.)

Recipients include: S. J. Gershoff (1972); A. L. Tappel (1973); David Kritchevsky (1974); W. G. Hoekstra (1975); D. B. Zilversmit (1976).

Max Born Medal and Prize

A silver medal, a certificate and a prize of £150 are awarded for outstanding contributions to physics. The award was established in 1972 by the Institute of Physics and the German Physical Society to commemorate Max Born who died in 1970. He was born in Germany in 1882, and later naturalized British. He won the Nobel prize for Physics in 1954. In even dated years the award is presented in England to a German physicist and in odd dated years in Germany to a British physicist.

Awarding body: The Institute of Physics, 47 Belgrave Square, London SW1X 8QX, England.

Recipients include: Roger A. Cowley (1973); Walter Greiner (1974); Trevor S. Moss (1975); Hermann Haken (1976); Walter E. Spear (1977).

Jagdish Chandra Bose Medal

This medal was established in 1975 by the Indian National Science Academy. It is awarded every three years for outstanding contributions in the field of life sciences.

Awarding body: Indian National Science Academy, Bahadur Shah Zafar Marg, New Delhi 110001, India.

S. N. Bose Medal

Established in 1975 by the Indian National Science Academy, this medal is awarded for outstanding contributions in the fields of physics, chemistry and mathematics. It is awarded every three years.

Awarding body: Indian National Science Academy, Bahadur Shah Zafar Marg, New Delhi 110001, India.

Recipients include: E. C. G. Sudarshan (1977).

Bourke Lectures

These lectures were instituted by the Council of the Faraday Society in 1954 to commemorate the name of Lieut.-Col. Bourke, one of the Society's benefactors, with the purpose of enabling distinguished scientists from overseas to lecture in Great Britain. The lecturer gives a series of lectures in different parts of the country. He receives a silver medal and an honorarium of £100.

Awarding body: The Chemical Society, Burlington House, London W1V 0BN, England.

Recipients include: Prof. B. Baranowski (Poland, 1973); Prof. J. Jortner (Israel, 1974); Prof. G. C. Pimentel (U.S.A., 1975); Prof. P.-G. de Gennes (France, 1976); Prof. R. G. Gordon (U.S.A., 1977).

Karel Bouryprijs

The prize was established in 1909 by the Belgian Royal Academy of Dutch Language and Literature in memory of Karel Boury (1824–95), the Flemish literature enthusiast. An award of 3,000 Belgian francs is made every four years for the best submitted unpublished Flemish school-songs or folk-songs (collections of two or more). Recipients must be Belgian nationals.

Awarding body: Koninklijke Academie voor Nederlandse Taal- en Letterkunde, Koningstraat 18, B-9000 Ghent, Belgium.

Recipients include: Arthur Meulemans (1914); Jan Broeckx (1940).

Boutwood Lectures

A bequest of £1,000 was originally made to Corpus Christi College, Cambridge, in 1932 by Mary Boutwood, to endow a College Essay Prize, and, with the balance of income available, a short course of public lectures on some religious, philosophic or political theme, to be given annually or biennially. The practice has been to invite every other year lecturers, usually from outside the College and University, to give a course of two public lectures on a subject of their own choice (falling within the above broad categories) in one of the main University lecture rooms.

Awarding body: Corpus Christi College, Cambridge CB2 1RH, England.

Lecturers include: Chancellor the Revd. Garth Moore (1969); Lord Boyle of Handsworth (1971); The Very Revd. Henry Chadwick (1973); The Most Revd. Lord Ramsey of Canterbury (1975); Dr. E. F. Schumacher (1977).

Johann-Maria-Boykow-Preis

The prize was established in 1964 by the German Society for Aeronautics, the predecessor of the German Aerospace Research and Experimental Establishment (DFVLR) in Cologne. The prize commemorates Johann Maria Boykow (1879–1935), pioneer of gyroplanes. Persons working with the DFVLR are eligible to receive the prize for works they have published or lectures they have given about their scientific achievements. The prize consists of a certificate and a sum of money of up to DM5,000, and is awarded every two years.

Awarding body: Deutsche Forschungs- und Versuchsanstalt für Luft- und Raumfahrt e.V., Postfach 90 60 58, D-5000 Cologne 90, Federal Republic of Germany.

Charles Vernon Boys Prize

The prize was established in 1944 by a bequest of Sir Charles Vernon Boys who was President of the Physical Society from 1916 to 1918. A cash prize of £150 is awarded annually for distinguished research in experimental physics; the work should either be still in progress or have been carried out within the preceding ten years. Candidates should normally be not more than 35 years old and are considered on the recommendation of members of the Institute of Physics and of its Awards Committee.

Awarding body: The Institute of Physics, 47 Belgrave Square, London SW1X 8QX, England.

Recipients include: Michael Hart (1971); Michael Warwick Thompson (1972); John William Charles Gates (1973); Patrick George Henry Sandars (1974); Richard Anthony Stradling (1975).

Bragg Medal and Prize

A bronze medal and a prize of £150 are awarded in odd dated years by the Council of the Institute of Physics for distinguished contributions to the teaching of physics. The award was established in 1965 in memory of Sir Lawrence Bragg, who had an international reputation for the popularization and teaching of physics. Candidates are considered on the recommendation of members of the Institute and of its Awards Committee.

Awarding body: The Institute of Physics, 47 Belgrave Square, London SW1X 8QX, England.

Recipients: Donald McGill (posthumously 1967); John Logan Lewis (1969); George Robert Noakes (1971); Jon Michael Ogborn and Paul Joseph Black (1973); William Albert Coates (1975).

Johannes-Brahms-Medaille

The medal was established in 1928 by the city council of Hamburg for outstanding achievements in music, especially where these contribute to the cultivation of the music of Brahms (1833–97), who was born in Hamburg.

Awarding body: Senat der Freien und Hansestadt Hamburg, 2 Hamburg 1, Rathaus, Federal Republic of Germany.

Walter-Brecht-Denkmünze

This award is given by the West German Association of Pulp and Paper Chemists and Engineers (Zellcheming) for outstanding technical and scientific achievements in the paper industry. Nominations must be made by members of Zellcheming. The award was instituted in 1976 in honour of Prof. Dr.-Ing. Walter Brecht's distinguished career in paper technology.

Awarding body: Verein der Zellstoff- und Papier-Chemiker und Ingenieure, 6100 Darmstadt, Berliner Allee 56, Federal Republic of Germany.

Bretey Memorial Lectureship

The Lectureship is provided from the bequest made to Manchester University under the will of Miss Anne Jeanne Bretey in memory of her brother, Elie Auguste Bretey. The income from the bequest is applied in such manner as Council may decide for the promotion of the study of French Literature and Thought and for the advancement of peace.

Awarding body: University of Manchester, Manchester M13 9PL, England.

Lecturers include: Henri Michel ('L'Evolution politique de la Résistance Française', 1970); Michel Butor ('Le Livre et la Civilisation d'Aujourd'hui', 1971); Prof. Albert Soboul ('Robespierre ou les Contradictions du Jacobinisme', 1972); Prof. Louis Grodecki ('Les Vitraux de St. Denis; Abbé Suger et les Débuts de l'Art Gothique en France', 1974); Prof. Georges Duby ('Le Réel et l'Imaginaire dans la Société Féodale', 1976).

Brewster Memorial Award

This award was established in 1919 by friends and colleagues of William Brewster (1851–1919), an important Massachusetts ornithologist and one of the founders of the American Ornithologists' Union. It consists of a medal and honorarium, given annually for the most meritorious work on birds of the Western Hemisphere published during the previous ten years.

Awarding body: American Ornithologists' Union, National Museum of Natural History, Smithsonian Institution, Washington, D.C. 20560, U.S.A.

Recipients include: David W. and Barbara K. Snow (biological studies of neotropical birds,

1972); Rudolfo Phillipi B., Alfred W. Johnson and J. D. Goodall (research on birds of Chile, 1973); James King (physiological studies on Zonotrichia finches, 1974); Jurgen Haffer (Avian speciation in tropical South America with systematic survey of toucans and jacamars, 1975); Gordon Orians (evolutionary ecology of birds, 1976).

British Film Institute Award

This annual award was established in 1958 and originally called the Sutherland Award, after its donor, the Duke of Sutherland. It takes the form of a silver statue of abstract design, and is given to the director of the most original and imaginative film of the year, introduced to Britain at the National Film Theatre, London. The British Film Institute, a government-sponsored organization, was founded in 1933 to encourage the art of the film.

Awarding body: British Film Institute, 81 Dean St., London W1, England.

Recipients include: Bernardo Bertolucci (*Il Conformista*, Italy, 1970); Robert Bresson (*Quatre Nuits d'un Reveur*, France, 1971); Hans-Jurgen Syberberg (*Hitler – A Film from Germany*, Fed. Rep. of Germany, 1977); John Carpenter (*Dark Star* and *Assault on Precinct 13*, U.S.A., 1978); Mark Rappaport (*The Scenic Route*, U.S.A., 1979).

British Gold Medal for Aeronautics

This medal is awarded annually for outstanding practical achievement leading to advancement in aeronautics. The award was founded by the Royal Aeronautical Society in 1933 at the request of the Secretary of State for Air, Lord Amulree. The medal commemorates Sir George Cayley and his first model aeroplane of 1804.

Awarding body: The Royal Aeronautical Society, 4 Hamilton Place, London W1V 0BQ, England.

Recipients include: Dr. G. S. Hislop (1972); F. W. W. Morley (1973); P. F. Foreman (1974); R. P. Probert (1975); J. T. Stamper (1976).

British Press Awards

The International Publishing Corporation (IPC) established these annual awards for journalism in 1962 in memory of Hannen Swaffer, a distinguished journalist and notable editor of *The People* in the 1920s. The major British newspaper groups join to organize the awards, which are made to British professional journalists whose writings appear in any morning, evening, Sunday or weekly newspaper published in Britain. Prizes are given in the following categories: (1) Journalist of the Year (premier award – £1,000); (2) International Reporter of the Year (to a British correspondent stationed abroad or a journalist who has carried out a major assignment abroad); (3) Young Journalist of the Year (age limit 25 years of age – £500); (4) Provincial Journalist of the Year); (5) News Reporter of the Year; (6) Critic of the Year; (7) Specialist Writer of the Year; (8) Sports Writer of the Year; (9) Columnist of the Year; (10) Press Photographer of the Year;

(11) Provincial Press Photographer of the Year. The cash prize for each award, unless otherwise indicated, is £250. The judges may make additional awards from year to year.

Awarding body: British Press Awards, Holborn Circus, London EC1P 1DQ, England.

Recipients include: Peter Niesewand (International Reporter, *Guardian*, 1976); Barry Askew, Robert Satchwell, David Graham (Journalists of the Year, *Lancashire Evening Post*, 1977).

British Silver Medal for Aeronautics

This medal is awarded annually for practical achievement leading to advancement in aeronautics. The award was founded by the Royal Aeronautical Society in 1933. It commemorates the Henson machine of 1842 and the Stringfellow model of 1848.

Awarding body: The Royal Aeronautical Society, 4 Hamilton Place, London W1V 0BQ, England.

Recipients include: Mallinson Powley (1972); R. S. Hooper (1973); R. F. Creasey (1974); G. A. Whitehead (1975); Dr. P. H. Calder (1976).

British Society of Rheology Gold Medal

Founded in 1966 by the Society, the medal is awarded at irregular intervals for an outstanding contribution to rheology. There are no restrictions on eligibility.

Awarding body: British Society of Rheology, 67 Daniells, Welwyn Garden City, Herts. AL7 1QT, England.

Recipients include: Prof. D. M. Dowson; Prof. G. R. Higginson; Dr. G. W. Scott Blair; Dr. V. G. W. Harrison; Prof. L. R. G. Treloar.

British Sponsored Film Festival

This annual festival was established in 1957 by the British Industrial and Scientific Film Association. Awards of trophies and certificates are made for British sponsored films which best achieve the sponsor's purpose, taking into consideration the intended audience. They are given in 10 categories: education; careers; training; safety; public welfare and social questions; medical; technical, scientific and research; sales; public relations and prestige; ecology and the environment. In addition, there are three special awards: the *Financial Times* Export Award for the film considered most suitable for the promotion of British exports; *The Times* Newcomer Award for the best film entered by a sponsor who has produced a film for the first time; and the Clifford Wheeler Memorial Award which is offered by the Film and Video Press Group to the sponsor who has shown most enterprise and initiative in securing effective distribution of his film, based on the previous year's BISFA Award winners (this award is in memory of Clifford Wheeler, who handled British film distribution at the Central Office of Information).

Awarding body: British Industrial and Scientific Film Association, 26 D'Arblay St., London W1V 3FH, England.

Broadcast Media Award

This award is made for outstanding reportage on reading or related subjects by broadcast journalists, or contributions to literacy education or understanding of literacy in the fields of radio, television and other broadcast media. It is presented annually, when merited, for work done in the previous calendar year. Established in 1973, the award takes the form of a citation. There are no limitations as to eligibility.

Awarding body: International Reading Association, 800 Barksdale Rd., Newark, Dela. 19711, U.S.A.

Brock Gold Medal Award

The medal is presented at quadrennial Congresses of the International Society for Photogrammetry to a person who is responsible for an outstanding landmark in the evolution of photogrammetry. The award-winning work should have been carried out between two and 12 years before the Congress. The award was founded by the Society in 1952 to encourage the advancement of photogrammetry. The funds for the provision of medals were given in memory of Arthur and Norman Brock.

Awarding body: International Society for Photogrammetry, U.S. Geological Survey 516, Reston, Va. 22092, U.S.A.

Recipients: Dr. L. Bertele (1956); Prof. W. Schermerhorn (1960); Dr. H. Schmid (1968); U. V. Helava (1972); Prof. F. Ackermann (1976).

John A. Brodie Medal

In 1977 this medal replaced the Chemical Engineering Prize, established in 1963, of the Institution of Engineers, Australia. The medal is named in honour of Mr. J. A. Brodie, who was Chief Engineer with Union Carbide. He established a reputation as a leading industrial innovator in Australia, having been responsible for the design and construction of polyethylene film extrusion units, the manufacture of bakelite and a continuous crystallization plant known as the Brodie Purifier. He was a Councillor of the Institution of Engineers, Australia, from 1967 to 1971. The medal is awarded for the best paper in chemical engineering selected by the Board of the College of Chemical Engineers (a foundation College of the Institution of Engineers, Australia). The award is open to members of the Institution only.

Awarding body: Institution of Engineers, Australia, 11 National Circuit, Barton, A.C.T. 2600, Australia.

Recipients include: P. B. Linkson (1969); J. S. Ratcliffe (1970); J. A. Brodie (1971); J. S. Ratcliffe (1974).

Brødy Imre Prize

The 'Eötvös Loránd' Physical Society of Hungary established this prize in 1950 in memory of Imre Bródy (1891–1944), the famous physicist and inventor of the crypton bulb, who was killed in the war. The prize is awarded to young research workers for outstanding results in experimental physics. It is an annual prize of 5,000 forints.

Awarding body: Eötvös Loránd Fizikai Társulat, 1061 Budapest VI, Anker-köz 1, Hungary.

Brohee Medal in World Gastroenterology

The medal, with a cash prize of U.S.$100, is awarded every four years at each World Congress of Gastroenterology. The host country chooses its most outstanding gastroenterologist to lecture to the Congress and receive the medal. The award was first established in 1966 by the Governing Council of the World Organisation of Gastroenterology, in memory of Dr. George Brohee, a famous Belgian gastroenterologist.

Awarding body: World Organisation of Gastroenterology.

Recipients include: Prof. Kawashima (Japan, 1966); Prof. Blank (Sweden, 1970), Dr. H. Bochus (U.S.A., 1974).

Heywood Broun Award

Founded by the Newspaper Guild in 1941, this award seeks to recognize outstanding journalistic achievement 'in the spirit of Heywood Broun' (1888–1939), the founder of the Guild who was distinguished by an unceasing devotion to the public interest, especially to the poor, the weak and the oppressed. The award is open to individual employees in the Guild's jurisdiction on newspapers, news services, news magazines, and radio and TV services in the U.S., Canada and Puerto Rico, whether or not they are Guild members. Both written and illustrative work (such as cartoons or advertisements) is considered. The award consists of a cash prize of $1,000 and a Guild citation.

Awarding body: The Newspaper Guild, 1125 15th Street, N.W., Washington, D.C. 20005, U.S.A.

Recipients include: Carl Bernstein and Bob Woodward (*Washington Post*, series exposing Watergate ramifications, 1972); Donald L. Barlett and James B. Steele (*Philadelphia Inquirer*, series exposing judicial discrimination, 1973); Selwyn Raab (*New York Times*, article with new evidence questioning two murder convictions, 1974); Kent Pollock (*Philadelphia Inquirer*, series on police brutality in Philadelphia, 1975); Acel Moore and Wendell Rawls, Jr. (series exposing brutality, corruption and murder at hospital for the criminally insane, 1976).

Frank P. Brown Medal

Frank Pierce Brown (1856–1935) bequeathed 'five thousand dollars to be paid to the Franklin Institute . . . for the purpose of a fund, to be invested, so as to produce an interest or income, which is to be used to pay for Silver Medals, to be awarded and given to inventors, as the Institute may think deserving for meritorious inventions or discoveries'. The Institute subsequently further defined the award as being for inventions and discoveries involving meritorious improvements in the building and allied industries.

Awarding body: The Franklin Institute, Benjamin Franklin Parkway at 20th St., Philadelphia, Pa. 19103, U.S.A.

Recipients include: Hans Liebherr (portable, self-erecting, tower climbing, slewing cranes, 1974); Public Building Services of the General Services Administration of the U.S. Government (systems approach for designing, specifying and constructing large federal office buildings, 1975); E. Dale Waters (development of heat pipes applied to the stabilization of foundations in Arctic regions, 1976).

S. G. Brown Award and Medal

The award and medal were instituted in 1963 following a bequest to the Royal Society by S. G. Brown, F.R.S., inventor and electrical engineer, to create a trust fund, the income from which provides for a medal, and the balance of the income paid as a cash award annually to a person, preferably not more than 40 years of age, who, in any one year, or during the preceding five years, has made an outstanding contribution to the promotion and development of mechanical inventions. The awards are granted by the Royal Society on the recommendation of the Councils of the Institution of Civil Engineers, the Institution of Mechanical Engineers and the Institution of Electrical Engineers respectively in rotation.

Awarding body: The Royal Society, 6 Carlton House Terrace, London SW1Y 5AG, England.

Recipients include: G. Auton (development of vacuum breakers in metal-clad distribution equipment, 1975); F. R. Mackley (innovation and development of the Hover platform, 1976).

Edward W. Browning Award for Improvement of World Food Resources

This award is given by the American Society of Agronomy for achievements within the previous ten years in the improvement of world food resources by research, education, administration, government, or private enterprise in any country. The award is $5,000 and a gold medal.

Awarding body: American Society of Agronomy, 677 South Segoe Rd., Madison, Wis. 53711, U.S.A.

James D. Bruce Memorial Award

This award was established in 1946 and is made for distinguished contributions in preventive medicine. It is presented annually, and takes the form of a medal.

Awarding body: American College of Physicians, 4200 Pine St., Philadelphia, Pa. 19104, U.S.A.

Recipients include: Theodore E. Woodward (1970); Lowell T. Coggeshall (1971); Saul Krugman (1972); Alexander D. Langmuir (1973); Vincent P. Dole (1974).

Arnold W. Brunner Memorial Prize in Architecture

This prize of $1,000 was established through a bequest from Emma Beatrice Brunner, widow of Arnold W. Brunner, a former treasurer of the National Institute of Arts and Letters. It is given annually to a person who shows promise of contributing to architecture as an art.

Awarding body: American Academy and Institute of Arts and Letters, 633 West 155th St., New York, N.Y. 10032, U.S.A.

Serge-von-Bubnoff-Medaille

The award was instituted in 1958 by the East German Society for Geological Science in honour of Serge von Bubnoff (1888–1957), the eminent geologist. It honours outstanding achievements in the geosciences, and may be awarded to citizens of the GDR and others. It consists of a silver medal and diploma, and is generally awarded at about two-yearly intervals.

Awarding body: Gesellschaft für Geologische Wissenschaften der DDR, 104 Berlin, Invalidenstr. 43, German Democratic Republic.

Recipients include: Prof. Dr. Alexander P. Vinogradov (U.S.S.R., 1967); Prof. Dr. Alexander V. Sidorenko (U.S.S.R., 1969); Prof. Dr. Robert Lauterbach (G.D.R., 1974); Prof. Dr. Vasili V. Gluschko (U.S.S.R., 1974); Prof. Dr. Alexander L. Yanschin (U.S.S.R., 1975).

Buccheri La Ferla International Prizes

These three biennial prizes are awarded in even dated years for research work in the following sciences: labour medicine, legal and insurance medicine, traumatology. They were established in 1970 in fulfilment of the will of Mrs. Anna Buccheri La Ferla, and the prize money is the accrued interest from her legacy during the two years preceding the award of the prize. The National Employment Accident Insurance Institute of Italy (I.N.A.I.L.) administers the fund. The founder devoted her life to the fight against poverty and suffering, and the prizes are in memory of her father, Professor Rosario Buccheri, and her husband, Professor Luigi La Ferla, both phthisiologists. Nominations for the prizes are made by various national institutions.

Awarding body: I.N.A.I.L., 144 Via 4 Novembre, Rome, Italy.

Recipients include: Prof. Jaroslaw Teisinger (Czechoslovakia, labour medicine, 1970); Prof. Etienne Grandjean (Switzerland, legal medicine, 1972); Prof. Oscar Scaglietti (Italy, traumatology, 1974); Prof. Enrico Carlo Vigliani (Italy, labour medicine, 1976).

Buchanan Medal

In 1894 £276 12s. and a die for a medal was presented to the Royal Society in honour of Sir George Buchanan, F.R.S. A silver gilt medal is awarded every five years in respect of distinguished services to Hygienic Science or Practice in the direction either of original research or of professional, administrative, or constructive work, without limit of nationality or sex. A gift of £200 accompanies the medal.

Awarding body: Royal Society of London, 6 Carlton House Terrace, London SW1Y 5AG, England.

Recipients include: G. S. Wilson (1967); Sir Richard Doll (1972); Sir David Evans (1977).

Georg-Büchner-Preis

This prize was established in 1923 by the State of Hesse, and was awarded annually until 1932. After the second world war the prize was re-established by the town of Darmstadt, and in 1951 it was finally transferred to the German Academy for Language and Poetry as a literary prize. The award of DM10,000 is made annually to German-speaking authors and poets who have made significant contributions to contemporary cultural life in Germany. The prize is named after Georg Büchner (1813–37), the German poet.

Awarding body: Deutsche Akademie für Sprache und Dichtung, Alexandraweg 23 (Glückert-Haus), 6100 Darmstadt, Federal Republic of Germany.

Recipients include: Elias Canetti (1972); Peter Handke (1973); Hermann Kesten (1974); Manès Sperber (1975); Heinz Piontek (1976).

L. Ray Buckendale Lectures

The annual lectures were established in 1953 to commemorate L. Ray Buckendale, an authority on the theory and practice of gearing, particularly as applied to automotive vehicles. The lectures are intended to provide procedures and data useful in the solution of problems of design, manufacture, application, operation and maintenance of commercial vehicles. The lectures should be directed to the needs of young engineers and students, with emphasis on related practical aspects of the topic. The lecturer, who is selected by a committee, is distinguished in the field of the selected subject and must prepare a monograph of his lecture suitable for publication. He receives an honorarium of $500 and a certificate, and a reception in his honour is held after the lecture. This is presented during the Automotive Engineering Congress and Exposition in February each year.

Awarding body: Society of Automotive Engineers, Inc., 400 Commonwealth Drive, Warrendale, Pa. 15096, U.S.A.

Recipients include: Ernest R. Sternberg (White Motor Corporation, 'Heavy Duty Truck Suspensions', 1976).

Buckland Literary Award

This award is presented to a New Zealand author who has produced, during the preceding year, a literary work (novel, poem, article, essay, biography or play) of the highest standard. It is awarded annually; however, no award need be made in a particular year if the standard of entries is not sufficiently high. The award was first made in 1967 under the provisions of the will of the late Freda Mary Buckland who died in 1966. The winner receives a cash prize of the total income received from a capital sum of N.Z.$5,000.

Awarding body: The Trustees, Executors & Agency Co. of New Zealand Ltd., P.O.B. 760, Dunedin, New Zealand.

Recipients include: Maurice Duggan (*O'Leary's Orchard and Other Stories*, 1970); Joy Cowley (*Man of Straw*, 1971); Janet Frame (*Intensive Care*, 1972); Witi Ihimaera (*Pounamu Pounamu*, 1973); Margaret Sutherland (*The Fledgling*, 1975).

Oliver E. Buckley Solid State Physics Prize

The prize was established in 1952 by Bell Laboratories to recognize and encourage outstanding theoretical or experimental contributions to solid-state physics in the U.S.A. It is awarded annually and consists of $5,000 and a certificate citing the contributions made by the recipient.

Awarding body: American Physical Society, 335 East 45th St., New York, N.Y. 10017, U.S.A.

Recipients include: Gen Shirane (1973); Michael Tinkham (1974); Albert W. Overhauser (1975); George Feher (1976); Leo P. Kadanoff (1977).

Alexander Buist Memorial Lecture

This annual lecture, founded in memory of Alexander Buist, was instituted in 1973. It carries an honorarium, and is intended to encourage interest in and knowledge of the craft of poetry.

Awarding body: University of Edinburgh, Old College, South Bridge, Edinburgh EH8 9YL, Scotland.

Lecturers: Stephen Spender (1973); Michael Hamburger (1974); Christopher Ricks (1975); Magnus Magnusson (1976); Peter Levi (1977).

Titia Buning-Brongers Prijs

The award was established in 1962 as a memorial to Titia Buning-Brongers (1904–61) by her husband, the artist Johan Buning, and her sister, Jeanette Brongers. A cash prize of about 2,500 Dutch guilders is awarded annually to a young Dutch painter for work in oils or water colour.

Awarding body: Titia Buning-Brongers Stichting, Leidse Gracht 110–3, Amsterdam C, The Netherlands.

Recipients include: B. B. J. Maynard (1974); Chris de Bueger (1975).

Burnet Lecture

The Lecture was established in 1969 by the Council of the Australian Academy of Science to mark the outstanding contribution to science in Australia by Sir Macfarlane Burnet, O.M., K.B.E., F.R.S., F.A.A. The Council chooses as Lecturer the scientist deemed most deserving of such honour. He receives a bronze medallion and an honorarium of A$200. The Lecture is usually biennial, and alternates with the Matthew Flinders Lecture (*q.v.*). It is given at the A.G.M. of the Academy, normally held in April.

Awarding body: Australian Academy of Science, P.O.B. 783, Canberra City, A.C.T. 2601, Australia.

Recipients include: J. F. A. P. Miller (1971); E. J. Underwood (1973); R. N. Robertson (1975); W. Hayes (1977).

Franklin L. Burr Prize for Science

The prize was established in 1930 following a bequest to the National Geographic Society by Mary C. Burr in memory of her father. Cash prizes are awarded as and when merited to leaders in the Society's expeditions and researches, for especially meritorious work in the field of geographic science.

Awarding body: National Geographic Society, 17th and M Streets, N.W., Washington, D.C. 20036, U.S.A.

Recipients include: Norman G. Dyhrenfurth (1965); Maynard M. Miller (1967); Richard E. Leakey (1973); Dr. Kenan T. Erim (1973); Dian Fossey (1973).

Busk Medal

This is an annual award for fieldwork abroad in geography or in a geographical aspect of an allied science. The medal was established in 1975 by Sir Douglas and Lady Busk. Sir Douglas Busk is an active member of the Royal Geographical Society who is keen on the support and encouragement of scientific exploration. There is no application for the award; it is granted on the recommendation of a special committee, and presented at the Annual Meeting of the Society in June.

Awarding body: Royal Geographical Society, 1 Kensington Gore, London SW7 2AR, England.

Recipients: Prof. N. N. Ambraseys (1975); Dr. A. H. B. Stride (1976); Dr. William O. Field (1978).

'F. Busoni' International Piano Competition

This annual competition, named after the Italian composer, was established by a founding committee of 18 internationally known musicians and first held in 1952. It takes place in Bolzano under the auspices of the Italian Ministries of Tourism and Entertainment and Education, and the Municipality of Bolzano. Candidates must be between the ages of 15 and 32. The first prize, known as the Busoni Prize, consists of 1,500,000 lire, contracts for concerts with various orchestras, and recitals. A second prize of 500,000 lire, third prize of 400,000 lire, fourth prize of 300,000 lire and fifth prize of 200,000 lire are also awarded.

Awarding body: 'F. Busoni' International Piano Competition, Conservatorio statale di musica 'C. Monteverdi', Piazza Domenicani 19, 39100 Bolzano, Italy.

Recipients include: Arnaldo Cohen (Brazil, 1972); Robert Benz (Fed. Rep. of Germany, 1974); Roberto Cappello (Italy, 1976).

Buxtehudepreis

The prize was established in 1951 by the council of the Hanseatic city of Lübeck, on the occasion of the 700th anniversary of the Church of St. Mary in Lübeck (Marienkirche zu Lübeck). The prize is named after the composer and organist, Dietrich Buxtehude (1637–1707), who was organist at the Marienkirche from 1668 to 1707. The prize is for distinction in music, especially in interpreting Buxtehude's work. It is usually awarded every three years, and consists of DM5,000 and a certificate.

Awarding body: Senat der Hansestadt Lübeck, Rathaus, 2400 Lübeck, Federal Republic of Germany.

Recipients include: Dr. Oskar Söhngen (Berlin, 1963); Bruno Grusnick (Lübeck, director of church music, 1969); Walter Kraft (Lübeck, organist, 1969); Søren Sørensen (Denmark, 1972); Marie-Claire Alain (France, organist, 1975).

Buys Ballot Medal

This gold medal was founded in 1888 by the Royal Netherlands Academy of Arts and Sciences in honour of Professor C. H. D. Buys Ballot (1817–90), who was the first Director of the Royal Netherlands Meteorological Institute and first President of the International Meteorological Institute. The medal is awarded every ten years for research in meteorology; scientists of any nationality are eligible.

Awarding body: Koninklijke Nederlandse Akademie van Wetenschappen, Kloveniersburgwal 29, 1011 JV Amsterdam, The Netherlands.

Recipients include: G. J. H. Swoboda (Switzerland, 1953); E. H. Palmén (Finland, 1963); J. Smagorinsky (U.S.A., 1973).

C

CIBA Medal

The medal was endowed in 1964 by CIBA Laboratories, manufacturers of pharmaceutical products. It is awarded annually in recognition of outstanding contributions to the development of any branch of biochemistry. The recipient is also awarded a cash prize of £100. The selected biochemist may be of any nationality, but the work in question must have been carried out in Great Britain or Northern Ireland. The medal is bestowed after the delivery of a lecture at a meeting of the Biochemical Society.

Awarding body: The Biochemical Society, 7 Warwick Court, High Holborn, London WC1R 5DP, England.

Recipients include: D. H. Northcote, F.R.S. ('Cellular Organization During Wall Synthesis', 1971); R. T. Williams, F.R.S. ('Inter-Species Variations in the Metabolism of Xenobiotics', 1972); P. D. Mitchell, F.R.S. ('Vectorial Chemistry and the Molecular Mechanics of Chemiosmotic Coupling: Power Transmission by Proticity', 1973); E. Kodicek, C.B.E., F.R.S. ('The Metabolism and Function of Vitamin D', 1974); E. F. Hartree ('Spermatozoa, Eggs and Proteinases', 1975).

CNA Literary Award/CNA Letterkunde-Toekenning

This annual literary award, the largest in South Africa, was established in 1961 by Mr. F. A. Berrill, former chairman of Central News Agency Ltd., a newsagents, booksellers and stationery company, with the aim of fostering good creative writing by South African authors. Two prizes of R2,500 each and a bronze plaque are awarded in March/April for the best books published in the previous calendar year – one in English, one in Afrikaans. Books by South African citizens or residents may be submitted in any of the following categories: novel, poetry, biography, drama, history, travel.

Awarding body: Central News Agency Ltd., P.O.B. 9380, Johannesburg, South Africa.

Recipients include: Prof. Guy Butler (*Selected Poems*) and Anna M. Louw (*Kroniek van Perdepoort*), 1975; Anthony Delius (*Border*) and Etienne Leroux (*Magersfontein, O Magersfontein!*), 1976; J. M. Coetzee (*In the Heart of the Country*), 1977.

Bernard-Joseph Cabanes International Journalism Prize

Bernard-Joseph Cabanes, Editor-in-Chief of Agence France-Presse, died in 1975 as the result of a bomb attack (later thought to be a case of mistaken identity). In 1977 the Association of Friends of Bernard-J. Cabanes announced the creation of an annual international prize in his memory. It is intended to recognize the professional qualities of a journalist, or a team of journalists, working for a telegraphic news agency. It is awarded to a news story or a series of stories providing coverage of a current event, distributed by a news agency during the preceding 12 months. Submissions may be in the form of a straight story, a feature-type story, or an investigation. The award is announced on 14 June, anniversary of Cabanes' death. It takes the form of a symbolic gold pen.

Awarding body: Association des Amis de Bernard-J. Cabanes, 33 rue Chardon-Lagache, 75016 Paris, France.

Recipients include: Maureen Johnson (U.K., working for Associated Press (U.S.A.) in Johannesburg, for her report on the treatment of Mrs. Winnie Mandela, 1977); Hazem Foda (Egypt, Middle East News Agency, for his report on the assassination of Youssef El-Sebai in Nicosia, 1978).

Bradford Cadmus Memorial Award

This award was established in 1966 by the American Institute of Internal Auditors to recognize outstanding contributions to the advancement of the profession, primarily in the fields of education, publications and research, by members of the Institute. It is presented annually, and consists of a plaque and scroll. It was instituted in memory of Bradford Cadmus (1902–64), first managing director of the Institute.

Awarding body: The Institute of Internal Auditors, Inc., 249 Maitland Ave., Altamonte Springs, Fla. 32701, U.S.A.

Recipients include: William S. Smith (1971); Frank W. Lennon (1972); Lawrence B. Sawyer (1973); Odd Hunsbedt (1974); F. Arnold Beale (1975).

California Gold Medal

The medal was established in the 19th century from the California Fund (begun in San Francisco) for the purpose of encouraging Irish artists.

The medal is now awarded annually for work of outstanding merit in the National Crafts Competition of the Royal Dublin Society. All craftworkers, irrespective of age, sex or nationality, who have entered work in the Competition are eligible.

Awarding body: Royal Dublin Society, Ballsbridge, Dublin 4, Ireland.

Recipients include: Rudolf Heltzel (gold ring, 1973); Kathleen Flanagan (Carrickmacross lace veil, 1974); Leonora Fowler (woven vestment, 1975); Evelyn Lyndsay (woven chasuble, 1976).

Callendar Medal

This silver medal is awarded annually by the British Institute of Measurement and Control for outstanding practical or theoretical achievement in the field of instruments or measurement. It was instituted in 1969 in honour of the late Prof. H. L. Callendar, F.R.S. (1863–1930), who carried out distinguished work in the development of platinum thermometry and continuous flow colorimetry.

Awarding body: The Institute of Measurement and Control, 20 Peel St., London W8 7PD, England.

Recipients include: Dr. L. Essen (1972); Dr. R. E. Reason (1973); Dr. W. Jasper Clark (1974); Prof. J. D. McGee (1975); Dr. D. Ambrose (1976).

Cameron Prize and Lectureship

The prize was founded in 1878 by Dr. Andrew R. Cameron of Richmond, New South Wales, a medical graduate of Edinburgh University. It is awarded biennially to a person who in the five preceding years has made an important and valuable addition to practical therapeutics.

Awarding body: Edinburgh University, Edinburgh EH8 9YL, Scotland.

Lecturers include: Prof. John Charnley (1974); Norman E. Shumway (1976).

Campion Award

This award, consisting of an enamel medallion and a scroll, was instituted in memory of the Jesuit martyr St. Edmund Campion, who was noted for his literary abilities. It is made periodically for longstanding work and eminence in the field of Christian letters, and recipients have generally been Catholic writers of any nationality.

Awarding body: Catholic Book Club, Division of America Press, 106 West 56th St., New York, N.Y. 10019, U.S.A.

Recipients include: Jacques Maritain; T. S. Eliot; Karl Rahner; Walter and Jean Kerr; Frank Sheed and Maisie Ward; Paul Horgan.

Can-Am Civil Engineering Amity Award

This award was established by the American Society of Civil Engineers in 1972 by the endowment of James A. Vance, Hon. M.A.S.C.E., in order to recognize those civil engineers who have made outstanding and unusual contributions to the advancement of relationships between civil engineers in Canada and the United States of America. The award is made for either a specific instance that has had continuing benefit in under-

standing and good will, or a career of exemplary professional activity that has contributed to the amity between the two nations. The recipient must be a member of the ASCE. The Engineering Institute of Canada is invited to nominate one candidate. The award consists of a plaque and a certificate.

Awarding body: American Society of Civil Engineers, 345 East 47th St., New York, N.Y. 10017, U.S.A.

Recipients include: L. Austin Wright (1973); Eugene Weber (1974); John B. Stirling (1975); John R. Kiely (long service in the study, practice, design and management of construction projects in the U.S.A., Canada and all over the world, 1976).

Canada-Australia Literary Prize

This award is made annually to honour an English-language Canadian writer and (in alternate years) an Australian writer, on the basis of his/her entire works. The prize of C$2,500 was established in 1976 by an agreement between the Australian and Canadian governments, who are co-sponsors of the award. It is intended to help make better known in Australia and Canada the work of writers of the other country, and was established following the success of the Canada-Belgium Literary Prize (*q.v.*) for French-language authors.

Awarding body: Canada Council, P.O.B. 1047, Ottawa, Ont. K1P 5V8, Canada.

Recipients include: John Romeril (Australia, author of three plays: *Chicago, Chicago; I Don't Know Who to Feel Sorry For; The Floating World,* 1976).

Canada Council Translation Prizes

These awards are made annually for the two best translations, one in English and one in French, published during the previous calendar year. The two winners, who must be Canadian citizens or immigrants who have been resident in Canada for at least 12 months, receive a cash prize of $5,000 each. The awards were instituted in 1974.

Awarding body: The Canada Council, P.O.B. 1047, Ottawa, Ont. K1P 5V8, Canada.

Recipients include: John Glassco (English version of the *Complete Poems of Saint-Denys Garneau,* 1976); Jean Simard (*Mon père, ce héros,* translation of *Son of a Smaller Hero* by Mordecai Richler, 1976); Joyce Marshall (*Enchanted Summer,* translation of *Cet été qui chantait* by Gabrielle Roy, 1977).

Canadian Authors Association Awards

Originally established in 1937, these awards were reinstituted in 1975 and are now funded by Harlequin Enterprises Ltd. of Toronto. They honour writing that achieves literary excellence without sacrificing popular appeal. These annual awards are in four categories: prose fiction, prose non-fiction; poetry; drama (for any medium). Nominations may be made by anyone, but the awards may only be won once by an individual writer in any category. They each comprise a silver medal and $1,000.

Awarding body: Canadian Authors Association, 22 Yorkville Avenue, Toronto, Ont. M4W 1L4, Canada.

Recipients include: John Mellor (*Forgotten Heroes*, prose non-fiction); Jim Green (*North Book*, poetry); John Hirsch (*The Dybbuck*, drama), 1976.

Canadian Booksellers Association Book Award

Established in 1972, the award of $500 is given annually to the author of the book which, in the opinion of CBA members, is the most outstanding Canadian book published during the previous year. The prize is presented at the CBA Convention in June for a book published the previous calendar year.

Awarding body: Canadian Booksellers Association, 56 The Esplanade, Suite 400, Toronto, Ont. M5E 1A7, Canada.

Recipients include: Blanche Howard (*The Manipulator*, 1973); Constance Beresford-Howe (*The Book of Eve*, 1974); Adele Wiseman (*Crackpot*, 1975); Peter Newman (*The Canadian Establishment*, Vol. 1, 1976); Margaret Atwood (*Lady Oracle*, 1977).

Canadian Institute of Mining and Metallurgy Distinguished Lectureships

CIM Distinguished Lecturers are selected annually on the basis of their distinguished services and accomplishments in scientific, technical or administrative activities related to the mineral industries. Not more than five are selected each year. They are presented with a certificate and award of $500, and, if necessary, their travelling expenses during the course of the lectureship will be defrayed.

Awarding body: The Canadian Institute of Mining and Metallurgy, 400-1130 Sherbrooke St. West, Montreal H3A 2M8, Canada.

Recipients include: P. J. Benn; G. R. Guillet; A. R. MacLean; J. M. Michaud; L. S. Renzoni (1976).

Canadian Society for Chemical Engineering Award in Industrial Practice

Established in 1975 by the Canadian Society for Chemical Engineering, a constituent society of The Chemical Institute of Canada, the annual award is made to persons residing in Canada or to Canadian citizens for the application of chemical engineering or industrial chemistry to the industrial sphere. Nominations are made by members of the Institute. Preference is given to those whose achievements in chemical engineering or industrial chemistry have been relevant specifically to Canadian industry. The award-winning work should have an element of innovation. The presentation takes place at the Annual Meeting of the Canadian Society for Chemical Engineering. The award consists of a plaque and $300.

Awarding body: The Chemical Institute of Canada, 151 Slater St., Ottawa, Ont. K1P 5H3, Canada.

Canadian Society of Microbiologists Award/Prix de la Société canadienne des Microbiologistes

Founded in 1962, the award is for outstanding contributions to microbiology. It is awarded at the Annual Meeting of the Society and consists of $500 and a plaque. Any Canadian citizen or resident of Canada is eligible, provided he/she is able and willing to give an address at the Annual Meeting. The award may be for an accumulation of accomplishments or for one outstanding contribution.

Awarding body: Canadian Society of Microbiologists/Société canadienne des Microbiologistes.

Recipients include: A. Frappier (1972); R. A. MacLeod (1973); A. J. Rhodes (1975); L. C. Vining (1976); P. C. Fitz-James (1977).

Melville Cane Award

This annual award of $500 was established in 1960 by Harcourt Brace Jovanovich, Inc., in honour of the poet and lawyer Melville Cane, and is awarded by the Poetry Society of America. It is given for a book of poems (published in odd-numbered years), or a prose work on poetry or one or more poets (published in even-numbered years). The recipient is selected on the basis of works submitted to the Society by publishers.

Awarding body: The Poetry Society of America, 15 Gramercy Park, New York, N.Y. 10003, U.S.A.

Recipients include: William Stafford; Richard B. Sewall; Harold Bloom; Ruth Miller; Jean Garrigue.

Cannes International Film Festival

Established in 1939 by the French Government, the first festival was not held until 1946. It takes place annually at Cannes. Prizes vary from year to year; those which are awarded every year include the major prize – the Gold Palm (until 1975 the Grand Prix) for the best film, the Special Jury Prize for the most original film, and prizes for the best actor and actress. Films must have been made during the previous 12 months.

Awarding body: Association Française du Festival International du Film, 71 rue du Faubourg Saint Honoré, 75008 Paris, France.

Recipients of the Gold Palm include: Francis Ford Coppola (U.S.A., *The Conversation*) 1974; M. Lakhdar Hamina (Algeria, *Chronique des Années de Braise*) 1975; Martin Scorsese (U.S.A., *Taxi Driver*) 1976; Paolo and Vittorio Taviani (Italy, *Padre Padrone*) 1977; Ermanno Olmi (Italy, *L'Albero degli Zoccoli*) 1978.

'Stanislao Cannizzaro' Foundation International Prize

Established in 1957, this award of a gold medal is made by the Italian Academy of Sciences. It is awarded every five years for research work in the field of chemistry. Applications are not submitted; nominations are made by Academy members.

Awarding body: Accademia Nazionale dei Lincei, Palazzo Corsini, Via della Lungara 10, Rome, Italy.

Recipients include: Prof. Emilio Segre (U.S.A., 1957); Prof. Duilio Arigoni (Italy, 1971); Prof. Hermann Hartmann (Fed. Rep. of Germany, 1976).

Capezio Dance Award

The award was established in 1950 by Anatole Chujoy, Editor and Critic of *Dance News* and *Dance Encyclopedia*, Martha Hill, Director of the Dance Department, Juilliard School of Music, John Martin, Editor and Critic, *New York Times*, and Walter Terry, Editor and Critic, *New York Herald Tribune*. It was established to express Capezio's commitment to the world of dance and to contribute to public awareness of the progress of the dance in the United States. The award comprises $1,000 in cash, a plaque, a souvenir booklet and a presentation party, and is given for a life-time contribution to dance by an individual. It is awarded annually.

Awarding body: Capezio Foundation, U.S.A.

Recipients include: Isadora Bennett (1973); Robert Joffrey (1974); Robert Irving (1975); Jerome Robbins (1976); Merce Cunningham (1977).

Ion Luca Caragiale Prize

This prize for the best published dramatic work of the year was founded in 1948 by the Romanian Academy. It is named after Ion Caragiale (1852–1912), dramatist, writer and publicist, whose comedies have been translated into many languages. The award is presented at an annual General Assembly of the Academy, and consists of 10,000 lei and a diploma.

Awarding body: Academy of the S.R. of Romania, 125 Calea Victoriei, Bucharest, Romania.

Carey-Thomas Award

This award was established in 1942 by Frederic G. Melcher, president of the R. R. Bowker Co. and editor of *Publishers Weekly*, and is designed to honour 'creative book publishing at its best'. It takes the form of a printed certificate, and is presented annually in the spring. Any book published within the award year by an American publisher is eligible, and books are nominated by the Bowker book review staff. The award was instituted in memory of Isaiah Thomas and Mathew Carey, two pioneers of American publishing.

Awarding body: Publishers Weekly, R. R. Bowker Co., 1180 Avenue of the Americas, New York, N.Y. 10036, U.S.A.

Recipients include: Yale University Press (*The Children of Pride: A True Story of Georgia and the Civil War*, 1972); Princeton University Press (*The Bollingen Series*, 1973); McGraw-Hill Book Co. (*Madrid Codices of Leonardo da Vinci* and *The Unknown Leonardo*, 1974); Morgan Library/David R. Godine, Publisher (*Early Children's Books and Their Illustration*, 1975).

W. A. Cargill Memorial Lectureship

Endowed anonymously in 1964, the foundation provides for a public lecture, to be delivered in Glasgow University biennially or as funds permit, on a subject related to fine art. The lecturer shall, at the discretion of the Professor of Fine Art, conduct a discussion with a class or classes in Fine Art on the day following the lecture. The lecture is subsequently published.

Awarding body: University of Glasgow, Glasgow G12 8QQ, Scotland.

Lecturers include: Kenneth Clark (Lord Clark of Saltwood) (1969); Rudolf Wittkower (1971); E. K. Waterhouse (1973); Sir John Summerson (1975).

Chester F. Carlson Award

This annual award, in honour of the inventor of xerography, is sponsored by the Xerox Corporation and consists of $1,000 in cash and a certificate. It is presented to an innovator in engineering education who has made a significant contribution by applying creative talents in the design and implementation of new instructional technique, methodology or concept.

Awarding body: American Society for Engineering Education, Suite 400, One Dupont Circle, Washington, D.C. 20036, U.S.A.

Recipients include: Henry O. Fuchs (1974); Robert Steidel, Jr. (1974); Robert W. Dunlap (1975); Gordon H. Lewis (1975); James E. Shamblin (1976).

Carnegie Medal

The Library Association established this annual medal in 1936 in honour of Andrew Carnegie (1835–1919), benefactor of public library buildings. The medal is given for an outstanding book for children written in English and first published in the U.K. during the preceding year.

Awarding body: The Library Association, 7 Ridgmount St., London WC1E 7AE, U.K.

Recipients include: Penelope Lively (*The Ghost of Thomas Kempe*, 1973); Mollie Hunter (*The Stronghold*, 1974); Robert Westall (*The Machine Gunners*, 1975); Jan Mark (*Thunders and Lightnings*, 1976); Gene Kemp (*The Turbulent Term of Tyke Tyler*, 1977).

Cartwright Prize and Medal

Founded in 1884 by the 'Association of Surgeons practising Dental Surgery', the prize of £200 and a bronze medal is awarded quinquennially to the author of the best essay on a subject relating to dental surgery. Candidates must be engaged in the study or practice of dental surgery and possess qualifications capable of registration under the Medical Acts of the United Kingdom. The prize commemorates the services of Samuel Cartwright, F.R.C.S., in improving the status of the dental profession.

Awarding body: The Royal College of Surgeons of England, 35–43 Lincoln's Inn Fields, London WC2A 3PN, England.

Recipients include: Brian Ernest Dudley Cooke ('The diagnosis and treatment of fibro-osseous enlargement of the jaws', 1951–55); Geoffrey Leslie Howe ('The role of surgical procedure in relation to dental prosthetic problems', 1956–60); Donald Winstock ('The dental management of the haemophiliae and allied blood conditions', 1961–65); John Francis Towers ('The management of congenital and acquired deformity of the mandibular condyle in children', 1971–75).

Carus-Medaille
This prize was founded in 1864 by the members and Friends of the Leopoldina German Academy of Researchers in Natural Sciences on the occasion of the 50th year as a Professor of Carl Gustav Carus (1789–1869), the 13th President of the Academy. Originally known as the Carus-Preis, the name was changed in 1937. Since 1961 the Carus-Medaille has been allied with the Carus-Preis (*q.v.*) of the city of Schweinfurt in the Federal Republic, where the Academy was founded. The medal is awarded for important research in the field of natural sciences and medicine.
Awarding body: Deutsche Akademie der Naturforscher Leopoldina, 401 Halle/Saale, August-Bebel-Strasse 50A, German Democratic Republic.
Recipients include: Prof. Dr. Günter Bruns and Prof. Dr. Horst Hanson (G.D.R., 1969); Prof. Dr. Heinz Maier-Leibnitz (Fed. Rep. of Germany, 1971); Prof. Dr. Heinz Bethge and Prof. Dr. Rudolf Kippenhahn (Fed. Rep. of Germany, 1973); Prof. Dr. Norbert Hilschmann (Fed. Rep. of Germany, 1975).

Carus-Preis
Established in 1961 by the city of Schweinfurt, this prize is awarded in conjunction with the Carus-Medaille (*q.v.*) of the Leopoldina German Academy of Researchers in Natural Sciences in the German Democratic Republic. The prize consists of a certificate and a cash sum of DM10,000.
Awarding body: Oberbürgermeister der Stadt Schweinfurt, Stadtrat, Schweinfurt, Federal Republic of Germany.
Recipients: see the Carus-Medaille.

'Alessandro Casagrande' International Piano Competition
The competition was founded in 1966 by Adriana Casagrande and Carla Rinaldi in memory of Alessandro Casagrande (1922–64) who was born in Terni and was director of the G. Briccialdi Musical Institute in that town. The competition is held annually; pianists of any nationality under the age of 32 and who have not previously won first prize at the competition are eligible. The first, second and third prizes are worth 1,500,000 lire, 700,000 lire and 350,000 lire respectively; the winners also receive engagements to play at various concerts in Italy.
Awarding body: 'Alessandro Casagrande' International Piano Competition, Comune di Terni, 05100 Terni, Italy.

Recipients include: Robert Groslot (Belgium, 1974); Boris Petrushansky (U.S.S.R., 1975); Takeda Makiko (Japan, 1976); Alexander Lonquich (1977).

Castner Lecture and Medal
In 1949 ICI donated a sum of money to the Society of Chemical Industry for the endowment of a lecture in memory of Hamilton Young Castner (1858–98), a pioneer in the field of industrial electrochemistry. The lecture is delivered not less than ten times at intervals of two or three years by a person of outstanding ability in science and chemistry on a subject connected with chemical research. Each lecturer is awarded the Castner Medal and receives an honorarium.
Awarding body: Society of Chemical Industry, 14 Belgrave Square, London SW1X 8PS, England.
Lecturers include: Dr. W. J. Kroll ('The Fusion Electrolysis of Titanium', 1960); Dr. H. M. Stanley ('Some Achievements in Petroleum Chemicals', 1965); Dr. D. S. Davies ('Ion Radicals – a Link between the Past and the Future', 1967); Prof. B. Timm ('The Fertiliser Industry', 1970).

Catalysis Award/Prix de Catalyse
Established in 1975 by The Chemical Institute of Canada, the award is made every two years to a person who, while resident in Canada, has made a distinguished contribution in the field of catalysis. The recipient is normally required to present a lecture about that contribution at the Annual Conference of either The Chemical Institute of Canada or its constituent society, the Canadian Society for Chemical Engineering. He is known as the 'Catalysis Award Lecturer' and' receives a rhodium-plated silver medal donated by Johnson, Matthey and Mallory Ltd., as well as travelling expenses for the presentation of the award lecture. The award may be given to two or three persons working as a team, in which case each member of the team receives a medal. Nominations for the award are made by members of The Chemical Institute of Canada.
Awarding body: The Chemical Institute of Canada, 151 Slater St., Ottawa, Ont. K1P 5H3, Canada.

Certamén Literario (*Literary Competition*)
The University of Sinaloa organizes an annual literary competition. A prize of 40,000 pesos is given for the best unpublished work entered in any one of the following fields: short stories, poetry, novel, play. Any Spanish-speaking writer can enter, whatever his nationality and place of residence.
Awarding body: Dirección de Difusión Cultural, Universidad Autónoma de Sinaloa, Apdo. Postal 919, Culiacán, Sinaloa, Mexico.

Certamén Nacional de Pintura 'Arturo Martínez' (*Arturo Martínez National Painting Competition*)
A competition is held annually in October, for which the first prize consists of the dollar equiva-

lent of 300 quetzales and a certificate, and the second prize the dollar equivalent of 200 quetzales and a certificate. The competition was established in 1969 by Professor Rafael Mora and Julio César de la Roca (Executive Director of the Casa de la Cultura) in memory of the Guatemalan painter, Arturo Martínez. Any Guatemalan painter, or foreign painter either naturalized or resident in Guatemala, is eligible for the prize.

Awarding body: Casa de la Cultura de Occidente 'Julio César de la Roca', 7a Calle 11-35, Zona 1, Quezaltenango, Guatemala.

Challenge Trophy

The trophy is awarded approximately every four years for the most effective film presentation to the general public of housing, planning and environmental problems, their remedies and related issues. The competition was established in 1956 and the trophy was donated by the City of Vienna on the occasion of the 23rd World Congress of the I.F.H.P. held in that city. A certificate is also awarded and the winning film is given wide publicity. Films submitted must have been produced in the four years preceding the competition and there is national preselection, where necessary, to limit submissions from any single country to a maximum of two films and 60 minutes per country.

Awarding body: International Federation for Housing and Planning (I.F.H.P.), 43 Wassenaarseweg, The Hague, Netherlands.

Recipients: International Cooperation Administration, Philadelphia, U.S.A. (1956); Ministère de la Construction, Paris, France (1960); City of Copenhagen, Denmark (1964); Regional Planning Office, Province of Örebro, Sweden (1968); K. Gloor, Zürich, Switzerland (1974).

Chalmers Medal

This silver gilt medal is awarded annually in recognition of research contributing to the knowledge of tropical medicine or tropical hygiene. It was established in 1921 when the widow of Dr. Albert John Chalmers, M.D., F.R.C.S., D.P.H., gave £500 to the Royal Society of Tropical Medicine and Hygiene in memory of her husband. Dr. Chalmers was well known for his work on tropical medicine; he was an investigator who took a great interest in the work of younger men, being always ready to give them help and encouragement; for this reason the Chalmers Medal is awarded only to those under 45 years of age.

Awarding body: Royal Society of Tropical Medicine and Hygiene, Manson House, 26 Portland Place, London W1N 4EY, England.

Recipients include: William Weir MacDonald (1972); Philip D. Marsden (1973); Alister Voller (1974); David I. H. Simpson (1975); A. R. Gray (1976).

Chambers Awards to Encourage Scottish Writing

The awards were established in 1976 by W. & R. Chambers Ltd., book publishers. Three annual awards of £1,000 each are given for: a work of fiction; a work of non-fiction; and an illustrated book for young children. The awards are open to writers who were born in Scotland, are of Scottish parentage, are resident in Scotland or are writing on a distinctively Scottish theme.

Awarding body: W. & R. Chambers Ltd., 11 Thistle St., Edinburgh EH2 1DG, Scotland.

Recipients include: Frank Wordsall (non-fiction), Jeremy Bruce-Watt and Stewart Hutchison (fiction), 1976.

James T. Y. Chan Medal

The medal was established by the Chinese Institute of Engineers in 1961. It is awarded annually for significant research work in the field of engineering.

Awarding body: Chinese Institute of Engineers, 2nd Floor, 4 Lane, 180 Kwangfu Rd., South Taipei, Taiwan.

The Chancellor's Lectures

The Council of the Victoria University of Wellington established these lectures in 1962. They are designed to 'bring to New Zealand a distinguished lecturer who might not otherwise visit New Zealand'. A lecturer is appointed annually; four lectures are required to be given. All expenses are met.

Awarding body: Victoria University of Wellington, Private Bag, Wellington, New Zealand.

Lecturers include: Dr. R., O. Laing (psychiatry, 1973); Miss Juliet Mitchell (feminism, 1974); Sir Geoffrey Cox (television, 1975); Rt. Hon. Lord Redcliffe-Maud (arts administration, 1976).

Chant Medal

The medal was established in 1940 in appreciation of the great work of the late Professor C. A. Chant in furthering the interests of astronomy in Canada. The medal is awarded, not oftener than once a year, to an amateur astronomer, resident in Canada, on the basis of the value of the work which he has carried out in astronomy and closely allied fields of original investigation.

Awarding body: The Royal Astronomical Society of Canada, 124 Merton St., Toronto, Ont. M4S 2Z2, Canada.

Recipients include: P. G. Martin (1968); J. Kormendy (1970); Blake F. Kinahan (1971); M. J. McCutcheon (1972); Chris Rodgers (1976).

Chanute Flight Award

Originally the Octave Chanute Award, one of the earliest in aeronautics, the award honours the memory of the pioneer U.S. aeronautical investigator. It is given for an outstanding contribution by a pilot or test personnel to the advancement of the art, science and technology of aeronautics. The award comprises a medal and certificate of citation and is now given biennially at the Aircraft Systems and Technology Conference, and alternates with the Haley Space Flight Award (*q.v.*).

Awarding body: American Institute of Aeronautics and Astronautics, 1290 Avenue of the Americas, New York, N.Y. 10019, U.S.A.

Recipients include: Charles A. Sewell (1974); Alan L. Bean, Owen K. Garriott, Jack R. Lousma (1975); Thomas Stafford (1976).

Chaplinpriset
This award is made annually by the Swedish film magazine *Chaplin* (named as a tribute to Sir Charles Chaplin, who at the time of the magazine's foundation in 1959 was 70 years old). The award was founded in 1961 by Bengt Forslund, the magazine's first editor. The prizes consist of works of art, and are for distinguished accomplishment in Swedish films (director, actor, actress, cameraman, etc.). The magazine's editorial board act as judges.
Awarding body: Chaplin Magazine, P.O.B. 27 126, 102 52 Stockholm, Sweden.
Recipients include: Agneta Ekmanner, Gösta Ekman, Mats Arehn, Ingemar Ejve (1976); Gunn Wållgren, Håkan Serner, Stellan Olsson, music group 'Oktober' (1977).

R. W. Chapman Medal
This bronze medal was first awarded in 1935 following a donation for this purpose from Mr. M. S. Stanley to the Institution of Engineers, Australia. The medal is given in memory of Sir Robert Chapman, a former Professor of Engineering at the University of Adelaide. He was a Councillor of the Institution, and its President in 1922. The award is made for the best paper on structural engineering selected by the Board of the College of Civil Engineers (a foundation College of the Institution). The award is open to members of the Institution only.
Awarding body: Institution of Engineers, Australia, 11 National Circuit, Barton, A.C.T. 2600, Australia.
Recipients include: F. J. Carter (1970); B. J. Vickery (1971); D. C. Knight (1973); A. Fried (1974); N. S. Trahair (1977).

Charlton Memorial Lecture
The William Henry Charlton Lecture, given at Newcastle University to commemorate a benefactor of the King Edward VII University School of Fine Art, is devoted to aspects of the history and practice of the Fine Arts. It has not been given regularly recently, but it is hoped to resume it in the future. The lecture is published.
Awarding body: University of Newcastle upon Tyne, 6 Kensington Terrace, Newcastle upon Tyne NE1 7RU, England.
Lecturers include: J. K. J. Shearman (Courtauld Inst., 1968); Sir Roland Penrose (Chairman, Inst. of Contemporary Arts, 1969); Prof. P. Murray (Birkbeck Coll., Univ. of London, 1970); H. J. Golding (Courtauld Inst., 1972).

Chauveau Medal
The prize is awarded for a distinguished contribution to knowledge in the humanities other than Canadian literature and Canadian history, and consists of a silver medal and C$1,000. The award is made every two years if there is a suitable

candidate, who must be a Canadian citizen or have been resident in Canada for the preceding five years. The award was established in 1951 in memory of Pierre J. O. Chauveau (1820–90), writer, orator, educator and Canadian statesman.
Awarding body: The Royal Society of Canada, 395 Wellington, Ottawa, Ont. K1A 0N4, Canada.
Recipients include: B. Wilkinson (1968); Northrop Frye (1970); Louis-Edmond Hamelin (1972); Wilfred Cantwell Smith (1974); Edward Togo Salmon (1976).

Chemical Engineering Division Lectureship Award
Established in 1963, this annual award is bestowed upon a distinguished engineering educator to recognize and encourage outstanding achievement in an important field of fundamental chemical engineering theory or practice. The recipient will deliver the Annual Lecture of the Chemical Engineering Division at the ASEE's Annual Conference and at a few departments of chemical engineering selected by the recipient in consultation with the Award Committee. The award of $1,000 in cash and a certificate is sponsored by the Minnesota Mining and Manufacturing Company.
Awarding body: American Society for Engineering Education, Suite 400, One Dupont Circle, Washington, D.C. 20036, U.S.A.
Recipients include: Dale F. Rudd (1972); Rutherford Aris (1973); Elmer L. Gaden, Jr. (1974); John M. Prausnitz (1975); Abraham E. Dukler (1976).

Chemical Industry (America) Medal
The medal was instituted in 1933 by the American Section of the Society of Chemical Industry. It is awarded annually to a person who has rendered conspicuous service to applied chemistry as an active guiding force in the management of his company during periods of maximum growth or developing of new chemical or allied fields.
Awarding body: Society of Chemical Industry (American Section), 50 East 41st St., Suite 92, New York, N.Y. 10017, U.S.A.
Recipients include: Jesse Werner (1972); Ralph Landau (1973); Carl A. Gerstacker (1974); Leonard P. Pool (1975).

Chemical Institute of Canada Environmental Improvement Award
Established in 1975 by The Chemical Institute of Canada and sponsored by Beak Consultants Ltd., the award is made, normally each year, to an organization operating within Canada, which has made a significant contribution to the improvement of environmental quality. The magnitude of the environmental problem solved, the novelty of the approach and the capacity of the work of improvement to conserve resources are the major features by which works are judged. The work of improvement should have been continuously implemented on a practical basis in Canada within the preceding three years, and should have a 'major chemical or chemical engineering com-

ponent, and not rely entirely on physical principles for its effect'. The award consists of an artifact for the organization and certificates for the individuals responsible, and these are presented at an occasion designed to lend publicity to the recipient. If the winning submission is a joint one on behalf of two or more organizations, replicate artifacts up to a maximum of three are provided.

Awarding body: The Chemical Institute of Canada, 151 Slater St., Ottawa, Ont. K1P 5H3, Canada.

Recipients: B. & W. Heat Treating (1967) Ltd. and University of Waterloo (1975).

Chemical Institute of Canada Medal

Established in 1951, the medal is awarded in recognition of outstanding contributions to the science of chemistry or chemical engineering in Canada. The six-sided medal is made of palladium and is provided by the International Nickel Company of Canada Ltd. It is presented, if possible, at the first Annual General Meeting of the Chemical Institute after the announcement of the award. Nominations are made by members of the Institute.

Awarding body: The Chemical Institute of Canada, 151 Slater St., Ottawa, Ont. K1P 5H3, Canada.

Recipients include: G. Herzberg ('Spectra of Simple Free Radicals', 1972); S. G. Mason ('The Micro-rheology of Disperse Systems', 1973); H. J. Bernstein ('Resonance Raman Spectroscopy', 1974); B. E. Conway ('Electrochemical Studies in Surface Science', 1975); Ronald J. Gillespie (for inorganic chemical research, 1977).

Chemical Institute of Canada Protective Coatings Award

The Institute established the annual award of $500 in 1976 with the aim of stimulating research and development work in coatings generally, and with particular reference to Canada. The award is given primarily for a significant contribution, in English or French, in one of the following forms: either expositions of new, previously unpublished work submitted in a form suitable for publication to established journals; or unpublished reviews of published work (preferably including the author's work or the necessary linking material or contributions made by him/her). In the absence of suitable material in the above form the award may be given in recognition of important practical contributions to the coatings industry in Canada. Alternatively it may be given for graduate research work or as seed money for new programmes. Canadian citizens, or those resident in Canada, are eligible; members of the CIC are given preference. The author of the winning work retains the right of publication, but the CIC reserves the right to publish work in resumé form in its journal, *Chemistry in Canada*.

Awarding body: The Chemical Institute of Canada, 151 Slater St., Ottawa, Ont. K1P 5H3, Canada.

Chemical Society Centenary Lectureship

The Centenary Fund was formed by the contributions of the British Chemical Industry to commemorate the centenary of the Society (1941) which was formally celebrated in 1947. The purpose of the fund is to promote the interchange of chemists between Britain and overseas countries. One activity financed by the Fund is the appointment each year of one or more Centenary Lecturers, who have normally visited a number of centres in the United Kingdom. No precise terms of reference are laid down for the appointment, and any person normally working overseas is eligible for consideration. Lecturers receive a silver medal and £100.

Awarding body: The Chemical Society, Burlington House, London W1V 0BN, England.

Recipients include: D. J. Cram (U.S.A.), W. H. Flygare (U.S.A.), J. B. Goodenough (U.S.A.), 1975–76; D. Herschbach (U.S.A.), A. E. Ringwood (Australia), K. Wiesner (Canada), 1976–77; J. D. Dunitz, G. A. Olah (U.S.A.), K. S. Pitzer (U.S.A.), 1977–78.

Cherwell-Simon Memorial Lectureship

In 1959 a fund was set up at the University of Oxford to establish an annual lecture in memory of Professor Lord Cherwell and Professor Sir Francis Simon. The lecture should be on a subject in some branch of physics of general interest. The lecturer's stipend is paid from the fund.

Awarding body: University of Oxford, Wellington Square, Oxford OX1 2JD, England.

Lecturers include: P. V. Auger (Faculty of Sciences, Univ. of Paris, 1972–73); N. F. Ramsey (Fellow of Balliol Coll., 1973–74); E. W. Montroll (Einstein Prof. of Physics, Univ. of Rochester, N.Y., 1974–75); Abdus Salam, F.R.S. (Prof. of Theoretical Physics, Univ. Coll., London, 1975–76).

Chia Hsin Prize

The Chia Hsin Cement Corporation established the Chia Hsin Foundation to encourage and finance cultural activities. Various prizes, established in 1963, are given under its aegis. Distinguished Contributions Awards are given every two years to scholars for outstanding academic achievements in all fields; the awards consist of a medal, certificate, and a cash prize of N.T.$400,000 each. Literary Awards are given annually to scholars and writers for outstanding academic and literary works; these awards consist of a certificate and a cash prize of N.T.$40,000, N.T.$60,000 or N.T.$80,000 each. Fifteen awards were made in 1976.

Awarding body: Chia Hsin Foundation, 96 Chung Shan Rd. N. Sec. 2, Taipei, Taiwan.

Children's Book of the Year Award

This award was established in 1946 by a group of interested librarians, authors and publishers concerned at the lack of good literature for children after the second world war. A medal is presented annually in July (during Children's Book Week in

Australia) for the best literary composition published in the current year. A grant from the Literature Board of the Australia Council (A\$1,500 in 1977) is also awarded. Winners must be Australian nationals or resident in Australia for at least five years.

Awarding body: Children's Book Council of Australia.

Recipients include: Hesba Brinsmead (*Long Time Passing*, 1972); Noreen Shelley (*Family at the Lookout*, 1973); Patricia Wrightson (*The Nargun and the Stars*, 1974); Ivan Southall (*Fly West*, 1976); Eleanor Spence (*The October Child*, 1977).

Children's Literature Prizes

Instituted in 1976 by the Canada Council, these awards are made annually for the two best books for young people, one in English and one in French, written by Canadians during the preceding year. A cash prize of \$5,000 is awarded to each winner.

Awarding body: Canada Council, P.O.B. 1047, Ottawa, Ont. K1P 4V8, Canada.

Recipients include: Bill Freeman (*Shantymen of Cache Lake*, 1976); Louise Aylwin (*Raminagradu*, 1976); Bernadette Renaud (*Emilie, la baignoire à pattes*, 1977); Myra Paperny (*The Wooden People*, 1977).

Chopin International Piano Competition

This competition is held every five years (next in 1980) and is sponsored by the Polish Ministry of Culture and Art and the Frederic Chopin Association. There are six cash prizes for the interpretation of Chopin's music, as well as a Frederic Chopin Association Prize and a Polish Radio Prize for the best polonaise performances.

Awarding body: Frederic Chopin Association, ul. Okulnik 1, 00-368 Warsaw, Poland.

Bashambar Nath Chopra Lecture

This lecture was established in 1968 by the Indian National Science Academy. It is awarded for distinguished contributions to any branch of biological science. The lectureship is awarded every three years and the lecturer receives an honorarium.

Awarding body: Indian National Science Academy, Bahadur Shah Zafar Marg, New Delhi 110001, India.

Recipients include: P. N. Wahi (1971); J. Venkateswarlu (1974); B. K. Bachhawat (1977).

Charles Chree Medal and Prize

Established in 1939 in memory of Dr. Charles Chree (President of the Physical Society 1908–10) by his sister, the award is for distinguished research in branches of physics in which Dr. Chree was particularly interested, namely: terrestrial magnetism, atmospheric electricity and related subjects, such as other aspects of geophysics comprising the earth, oceans, atmosphere and solar-terrestrial problems. The award consists of a silver medal, a prize of £150 and a parchment certificate, and is made in odd-dated years by the Council of

the Institute of Physics. Candidates are considered on the recommendation of members of the Institute and of its Awards Committee.

Awarding body: The Institute of Physics, 47 Belgrave Square, London SW1Z 8QX, England.

Recipients include: John Herbert Chapman (1967); Stanley Keith Runcorn (1969); Desmond George King-Hele (1971); David Robert Bates (1973); Raymond Hide (1975).

Chungshan Cultural Foundation Prizes

The Foundation was set up in 1965 in memory of Dr. Sun Yat-Sen, the founder of the Republic of China. Annual awards are offered for outstanding academic and literary publications and inventions. Winners receive a citation, a plaque, and N.T.\$50,000 each. In 1976 there were 18 prize-winners.

Awarding body: Chungshan Cultural Foundation, Taipei, Taiwan.

Edwin F. Church Medal

The Church Award was established in 1972 by the Council of the American Society of Mechanical Engineers, with funds from a bequest of Edwin F. Church, Jr. (1879–1964), loyal member of ASME and professor of mechanical engineering at the Polytechnic Institute of Brooklyn. The medal is awarded annually, if warranted, to the individual who has rendered eminent service in increasing the value, importance and attractiveness of mechanical engineering education. Mechanical engineering is used here in its broadest sense of preparation for any aspect or level of mechanical engineering through any appropriate mechanism. The award may be made to one recipient of any age who need not be a member of ASME. It consists of an honorarium of \$1,000, a bronze medal embedded in lucite, and a certificate.

Awarding body: American Society of Mechanical Engineers, United Engineering Center, 345 East 47th St., New York, N.Y. 10017, U.S.A.

Recipients include: Wilbur Richard Leopold (1973); Hobart A. Weaver (1974); Harry Conn (1975); Frank W. Von Flue (1976).

Churchill Gold Medal

Sir Winston Churchill, an Honorary Fellow of the Society of Engineers, founded this medal in 1951 for outstanding contributions to contemporary engineering or science within the British Commonwealth. It is awarded every two years.

Awarding body: The Society of Engineers, 21/23 Mossop St., London SW3 2LW, England.

Recipients include: Dr. S. C. Hooker (jet engines, 1968); Sir Gilbert Roberts (bridge design, 1970); Francis T. Bacon (fuel cells, 1972); F. R. Farmer (nuclear safety, 1974); Godfrey Hounsfield (brain and body scanner, 1976).

'Cîntarea Romaniei' Prize ('*Singing Romania*' Prize)

The prize was established in 1976 at the suggestion of President Nicolae Ceausescu of Romania, and first awarded in 1977, the centenary of Romania's independence. A musical competition is held every two years at local and national level, and every branch of music is represented, with sections for amateur and professional performance. Prizes (diplomas and medals) are given in various categories for solo and group performance.

Awarding body: Council of Socialist Education and Culture, 1 Piaţa Scînteii, Bucharest, Romania.

Timotei Cipariu Prize

This prize for contributions in the field of philology was founded by the Romanian Academy in 1948. It is named after Timotei Cipariu (1805–87), linguist and philologist, who was a leading figure in the movement for Latinizing the language, and founded the historical grammar of the Romanian language. The award is presented annually at a General Assembly of the Academy, and consists of 10,000 lei and a diploma.

Awarding body: Academy of the S.R. of Romania, 125 Calea Victoriei, Bucharest, Romania.

Civil Engineering History and Heritage Award

A former President of the American Society of Civil Engineers, Trent R. Dames, and his wife, Phoebe L. Dames, contributed the funds for this award, which is made annually to encourage an appreciation of civil engineering history. The award was established in 1966, and consists of a plaque and certificate. Non-members of the Society are eligible; nobody may receive the prize more than once, and it may not be awarded posthumously unless the person was alive at the time of nomination. The Committee on History and Heritage of American Civil Engineering and local Section committees recommend the nominees for the award.

Awarding body: American Society of Civil Engineers, 345 East 46th St., New York, N.Y. 10017, U.S.A.

Recipients include: Charles J. Merdinger (1972); Sarah Ruth Watson (1973); Clifford A. Betts (1975); Neal Fitzsimons (1976).

Francis J. Clamer Medal

Francis J. Clamer (1841–1927) was a member o the Franklin Institute for many years. In his wil he left $1,000 to the Philadelphia Technical Society to 'establish a medal and premium fund. ... Each year a medal is to be awarded together with a premium in cash ... for the most meritorious invention, discovery or research work in the field of metallurgy...'. The Philadelphia Technical Society having been dissolved, the money was awarded to the Franklin Institute in 1943. The medal was struck in silver from 1943 to 1962 when Mr. Cramer's son added $1,500 to the fund with the request that the medal thereafter be struck in gold.

Awarding body: The Franklin Institute, Benjamin Franklin Parkway at 20th St., Philadelphia, Pa. 19103, U.S.A.

Recipients include: F. H. Spedding (constributions to extractive and rare earth metallurgy, 1969);

Robert D. Heidenreich and Peter B. Hirsch (thin film transmission electron microscopy, 1970); Francis L. Versnyder (directional solidification process, 1973).

John Bates Clark Medal

This bronze medal, awarded every two years, is given in recognition of a significant contribution to economic thought and knowledge. It was instituted in 1947 by the Executive Committee of the American Economic Association, in memory of the American economist John Bates Clark who, together with von Thumen, was responsible for developing the marginal productivity theory of wages and interest. The award is restricted to American economists under the age of 40 who are members of the American Economic Association.

Awarding body: American Economic Association, 1313 21st Ave. South, Nashville, Tenn. 37212, U.S.A.

Recipients include: Gary S. Becker (1967); Marc Leon Nerlove (1969); Dale W. Jorgenson (1971); Franklin M. Fisher (1973); Daniel McFadden (1975).

Walton Clark Medal

Dr. Walton Clark (1856–1934), consulting engineer and former Vice-President of the United Gas Improvement Company, received from the Franklin Institute in 1926 the first Walton Clark Medal, endowed by the Company in his honour. The gold medal is awarded annually to one person for original or notable work in the gas industry, or in any of the mechanic arts.

Awarding body: The Franklin Institute, Benjamin Franklin Parkway at 20th St., Philadelphia, Pa. 19103, U.S.A.

Recipients include: Earl R. Thomas (leak detection device for gas mains, 1964); Frederick J. Dent (fuel-gas research, 1965); Henry R. Linden (gasification of coal, 1972).

Clarke Medal

The Clark Medal is awarded for distinguished work in the natural sciences carried out in, or on the subject of, the Australian Commonwealth and its Territories. It was established in 1878 in memory of Rev. W. B. Clarke (1798–1878), clergyman, educator and geologist.

Awarding body: The Royal Society of New South Wales, Australia.

Recipients include: N. T. Burbridge (1971); H. King (1972); M. D. Hatch (1973); C. H. Tyndale-Biscoe (1974); J. N. Jennings (1975).

F. W. Clarke Medal

A medal and certificate are awarded annually or at the discretion of the Geochemical Society's Council for a single outstanding contribution to geochemistry or cosmochemistry by a young scientist. Work must have been published within five years of the recipient's completion of formal studies.

Awarding body: Geochemical Society, c/o Dr. Peter R. Buseck, Chemistry Dept., Arizona State University, Tempe, Ariz. 85281, U.S.A.

Clements Memorial Prize

This award was established in 1938 by the South Place Sunday Concert Society in memory of Alfred J. Clements, Organizer and Honorary Secretary of the Society from its inception in 1887 till his death in 1938. The award is given for a chamber music work for three to six instruments, and 15 to 30 minutes in length. The composer must be a British subject, and the work should not have been publicly performed, nor have won a prize in any other competition. The prize is awarded every two years, and at present consists of £250 in cash.
Awarding body: South Place Sunday Concerts, Conway Hall, Red Lion Square, London WC1R 4RL, England.
Recipients include: Hugo Cole (1951); Reginald Smith Brindle (1953); Sebastian Forbes (1963); Justin Connolly (1967); David Nevens (1975).

Hans-Clemm-Denkmünze

This medal, instituted in 1936, is presented by the West German Association of Pulp and Paper Chemists and Engineers (Zellcheming), usually in conjunction with a cash prize donated by the Hans Clemm Foundation (established in 1927). The awards are made in recognition of achievements in the field of paper and cellulose technology or in the service of Zellcheming. Nominations must be made by members of Zellcheming. The award commemorates Hans Clemm (1872–1927), and is usually made annually.
Awarding body: Verein der Zellstoff- und Papier-Chemiker und Ingenieure, 6100 Darmstadt, Berliner Allee 56, Federal Republic of Germany.
Recipients include: Dir. Dr.-Ing. Wilhelm Kilpper (1972); Prof. Dr. Otto Huber (1973); Dr. phil. nat. Hermann F. J. Wenzl (1974); Dipl.-Ing. Dieter Pothmann (1975); Prof. Dr. Theodor Ploetz (posthum., 1976).

Howard Francis Cline Memorial Prize

Established in 1976 by the Conference on Latin American History, a stipend of $100 is awarded annually for the best article on Latin American ethnohistory published in the preceding year.
Awarding body: Conference on Latin American History, University of Wisconsin-Milwaukee, College of Letters and Science, Center for Latin America, P.O.B. 413, Milwaukee, Wis. 53201, U.S.A.

Grigore Cobălcescu Prize

The Romanian Academy founded this prize for geography or geology in 1948. It is presented annually at a General Assembly of the Academy, and consists of 10,000 lei and a diploma. It is named after Grigore Cobălcescu (1831–92), geologist and palaeontologist, and the author of the first Romanian work on geology (1882).
Awarding body: Academy of the S.R. of Romania, 125 Calea Victoriei, Bucharest, Romania.

Henry Cohen History of Medicine Lectureship

Founded in 1972 by E. R. Squib & Sons Ltd., the lectureship is in recognition of the distinguished contributions to the history of medicine made by Lord Cohen of Birkenhead. The appointment is made annually by the Council of Liverpool University. The lecture is delivered alternately in Liverpool University and the Liverpool Medical Institution. The remuneration is £100.
Awarding body: University of Liverpool, P.O.B. 147, Liverpool L69 3BX, England.

Allan P. Colburn Award for Excellence in Publications by a Young Member of the American Institute of Chemical Engineers

This award is generally presented annually, and consists of a certificate, plaque and $1,000. It is awarded for publications of outstanding influence on the theory, practice and teaching of chemical engineering. Applicants should have been under 35 years of age at the time the last paper under consideration was submitted for publication.
Awarding body: American Institute of Chemical Engineers, 345 East 47th St., New York, N.Y. 10017, U.S.A.

Willink van Collen Prijs

This award for painting is given every two years to a young Dutch artist (under 30) for recent work. It consists of a first prize of 2,000 Dutch guilders, and second and third prizes of 1,500 and 1,000 guilders respectively. The prize is named after the 19th-century Dutch artist. It was established in 1880.
Awarding body: Maatschappij Arti et Amicitiae, Rokin 112, Amsterdam, The Netherlands.
Recipients include: Jacob Hillenius (1967).

Robert J. Collier Trophy Award

The award was established in 1912 by Robert J. Collier, publisher and pioneer aviation enthusiast, as the Aero Club of America Trophy. In 1922 the Aero Club of America was incorporated as the National Aeronautic Association; in 1944 the Association renamed the award the Robert J. Collier Trophy. It is presented annually for the greatest achievement in aeronautics or astronautics in America, with respect to improving the performance, efficiency or safety of air or space vehicles, the value of which has been thoroughly demonstrated by actual use during the preceding year.
Awarding body: National Aeronautic Association, 806 Fifteenth St., N.W., Washington, D.C. 20005, U.S.A.
Recipients include: The Skylab Program, with special recognition to William C. Schneider, Program Director, and three Skylab astronaut crews (1973); John F. Clark and Daniel J. Fink (1974); David S. Lewis (1975).

Collins Biennial Religious Book Award

This £1,000 prize was established in 1969 to commemorate the 150th anniversary of the founding of William Collins Sons & Co. Ltd. The prize is awarded to the book which, in the opinion of the judges, has made the most distinguished contribution to the relevance of Christianity in the modern world, on one of the following subjects: Science, Ethics, Sociology, Philosophy, Psychology and Other Religions. The subject should be specific enough to preclude purely academic and historical writing, wide enough to allow scholars' ideas to mature over a long period, and provocative enough for the winning book to be a notable contribution to the continuing debate about God. The award is open to living citizens of the U.K., the Commonwealth, the Republic of Ireland, and South Africa.

Awarding body: Collins Publishers, 14 St. James's Place, London SW1A 1PS, England.

Recipients: Prof. T. F. Torrance (*Theological Science*, 1969); Prof. C. H. Dodd (*The Founder of Christianity*, 1971); Bishop John V. Taylor (*The Go-Between God*, 1973); Rev. Alan Ecclestone (*Yes To God*, 1975); Prof. C. F. D. Moule (*Origin of Christology*, 1977).

Arch T. Colwell Merit Award

Established in 1965 by the Society of Automotive Engineers, the award is made annually to the authors of papers of outstanding technical or professional merit, presented at a Society meeting during the previous calendar year. Papers are judged primarily for their value as new contributions to the knowledge of automotive engineering. Entries are nominated by the Engineering Activity Board. The award comprises a certificate and a citation; recipients are cited in the annual *Transactions* of the Society.

Awarding body: Society of Automotive Engineers, Inc., 400 Commonwealth Drive, Warrendale, Pa. 15096, U.S.A.

Colworth Medal

The medal was endowed by the Unilever Research Laboratory in 1963, and is awarded annually to a young British biochemist for work of an outstanding nature. The recipient must normally not have reached the age of 35 at the end of the year of the award. The medal is bestowed after delivery of a lecture given at a meeting of the Biochemical Society, and later at one of the Unilever Research Laboratories.

Awarding body: The Biochemical Society, 7 Warwick Court, High Holborn, London WC1R 5DP, England.

Recipients include: A. R. Williamson ('Extent and Control of Antibody Synthesis', 1971); J. M. Ashworth ('Studies on Cell Differentiation in Cellular Slime Mould *Dictyostelium discoideum*', 1972); J. C. Metcalfe ('The Role of Phospholipids in a Calcium Pump Reconstituted from Defined Membrane Compounds', 1973); D. R. Trentham ('The Adenosine Triphosphatase Reactions of Myosin and Actomyosin and their Relation to Energy Transduction in Muscle', 1974); W. J. Brammar ('The *in vitro* Construction and Exploita-

tion of Specialized Transducing Derivatives of Bacteriophage Lambda', 1975).

Colwyn Medal

This medal, first awarded in 1928, was founded by the Institution of the Rubber Industry which in 1975 amalgamated with the Plastics Institute to become the Plastics and Rubber Institute. The award is for outstanding services to the rubber and plastics industry of a scientific, technical or engineering nature. It is open to members and non-members, and is usually awarded annually.

Awarding body: The Plastics and Rubber Institute, 11 Hobart Place, London SW1W 0HL, England.

Recipients include: A. R. Payne (1972); C. E. H. Bawn (1973); J. I. Cuneen (1974); J. Furukawa (1975); J. M. Massoubre (1976).

Colyer Gold Medal

The medal was established in 1951 and is awarded chiefly for liberal acts or distinguished labours, researches and discoveries eminently conducive to the improvement of natural knowledge and to dental surgery. It was founded by the Faculty of Dentistry of the Royal College of Surgeons to commemorate the long and distinguished service of Sir Frank Colyer, especially as Honorary Curator of the Odontological Museum.

Awarding body: The Royal College of Surgeons of England, 35–43 Lincoln's Inn Fields, London WC2A 3PN, England.

Recipients include: Sir Robert Vivian Bradlaw and Martin Amsler Rushton (1968); Sir Terence George Ward (1971); Gerald Hubert Leatherman (1972); Clifford Frederick Ballard (1975).

Commonwealth Poetry Prize

This award is made annually for a first book of poetry in English published by an author from a Commonwealth country other than Britain. The prize is awarded by the Commonwealth Institute in conjunction with the National Book League, and consists of £500. Applications are submitted primarily by publishers.

Awarding body: Commonwealth Institute, Kensington High St., London W8 6NQ, England.

Recipients include: Timoshenko Aslanides (Australia, *The Greek Connection*, 1978).

Arthur Holly Compton Award

This award is made by the American Nuclear Society for an outstanding contribution to education in the fields of nuclear science and engineering. It takes the form of a certificate and a cash prize of $1,000. It is made on the basis of nominations. The award was established in 1966 through an endowment by Mrs. Edward Mallinckrodt, Jr. and George E. Mallinckrodt, in memory of Dr. Arthur Holly Compton.

Awarding body: American Nuclear Society, 555 N. Kensington, LaGrange Park, Ill. 60525, U.S.A.

Karl Taylor Compton Medal

Established in 1957 by the American Institute of Physics, this medal is given in recognition of the outstanding statesmanship in science of distinguished physicists. It is awarded at infrequent intervals of three to five years, whenever suitable candidates are found, and consists of a gold medal and a cash sum of $1,000. It is intended primarily for U.S. nationals.

Awarding body: American Institute of Physics, 335 East 45th St., New York, N.Y. 10017, U.S.A.

Recipients include: Alan T. Waterman (1967); Frederick Seitz (1970); Ralph A. Sawyer (1971); S. A. Goudsmit (1974).

'Comte Daniel le Grelle' Maritime Award

The European Shipping Press Association established this award in 1968. It is given annually for the best paper on a port or shipping problem in a Benelux or an EEC country. The monetary prize of 35,000 Belgian francs is donated by the Continental Bank in Antwerp. Anyone under the age of 40 may participate, and works may be in Dutch, French, German or English; they should be unpublished.

Awarding body: European Shipping Press Association, Ter Rivierenlaan 10 bus 7, B-2100 Deurne, Belgium.

Recipients include: G. de Monnie; J. Keereman; W. Winkelmans; J. L. Marchal.

Concours Littéraire (*Literary Competition*)

An annual competition is held under the auspices of the Royal Association of Walloon Writers, one year for literature in French, the next year for literature in a Walloon dialect. The prize is a cash award (variable) and a diploma. The competition is open to all writers.

Awarding body: Association Royale des Ecrivains Wallons, Maison de la Francité, Brussels, Belgium.

Recipients include: Louis Merlan (short story in dialect, 1976).

Concurso Nacional de Novela (*National Short Story Competition*)

This literary competition was established in 1973 to encourage Colombian writers. A cash prize of $10,000 is awarded every two years by the magazine *Vivencias*.

Awarding body: Vivencias, Cali, Colombia.

Margaret Condliffe Memorial Prize

This prize is awarded irregularly to recognize and encourage creative achievement by New Zealanders who show promise of marked distinction in the fields of letters, fine arts or the service of humanity. It was established in 1945 by Professor and Mrs. J. B. Condliffe; Professor Condliffe is a distinguished graduate of the University of Canterbury, and its first professor of economics (now retired). The award – a medal – is named after Prof. Condliffe's mother. Only New Zealanders are eligible for the prize.

Awarding body: University of Canterbury, Christchurch 1, New Zealand.

Recipients include: Dr. D. W. Beaven (Dir., Medical Research Unit, Princess Margaret Hospital, Christchurch, specialist in endocrine and metabolic medicine, 1970); M. G. Thomson (Dir. of Downstage Theatre, Wellington, producer and playwright, 1976).

Conference on Christianity and Literature Book Award

This award was established in 1967. It is given for the book which has done most to further dialogue between literature and the Christian faith. Both the author and the publisher receive a certificate. The book must have been published during the preceding year. The award is made annually in December at the Modern Language Association's meeting.

Awarding body: Conference on Christianity and Literature, c/o Calvin College, Grand Rapids, Mich. 49506, U.S.A.

Recipients include: William F. Lynch, S.J. (*Christ and Prometheus*, 1971); Owen Barfield (*What Coleridge Thought*, 1972); C. A. Patrides (*The Grand Design of God*, 1973); Barbara Kiefer Lewalski (*Donne's Anniversaries and the Poetry of Praise*, 1974); David L. Jeffrey (*The Early English Lyric and Franciscan Spirituality*, 1975).

Conference on Latin American History Award for Distinguished Service to the Profession

Established in 1969, the award is conferred upon a person whose career in scholarship, teaching, publishing, librarianship, institutional development or other fields has made a significant contribution to the advancement of the study of Latin American history in the U.S.A. It is awarded not oftener than every other year and nominations must be made by members of the Conference. The award comprises a plaque and stipend of $500, which are presented at the annual Conference luncheon in December of the award year.

Awarding body: Conference on Latin American History, University of Wisconsin-Milwaukee, Center for Latin America, Milwaukee, Wis. 53201, U.S.A.

Recipients include: Charles C. Griffin (1970); Howard F. Cline (1972); Lewis U. Hanke (1974); Nettie Lee Benson (1976).

Conference on Latin American History Prize

Established in 1961, the prize is awarded annually for a distinguished article on any significant aspect of Latin American history in journals published in the U.S.A. (including Puerto Rico) during the preceding year, but not in the *Hispanic American History Review*. The award carries a stipend of $100.

Awarding body: Conference on Latin American History, University of Wisconsin-Milwaukee, Center for Latin America, Milwaukee, Wis. 53201, U.S.A.

Recipients include: Charles A. Hale ('Reconstruction of Nineteenth Century Politics in South America. A Case for the History of Ideas', 1974); John M. Hart ('Nineteenth Century Urban Labor Precursors of the Mexican Revolution: the Development of an Ideology', 1975); Leon G. Campbell ('The Changing Racial and Administrative Structure of the Peruvian Military under the Later Bourbons', 1976).

G. Miles Conrad Award

This award was instituted in 1965 by the National Federation of Abstracting and Indexing Services, in honour of G. Miles Conrad (1911–64), biologist and world-recognized expert in the communication of science information. It takes the form of a cash honorarium presented annually to a person outstanding in the field of abstracting and indexing, on the occasion of his delivery of the Memorial Lecture.

Awarding body: National Federation of Abstracting and Indexing Services, U.S.A.

Recipients include: Jack E. Brown (Nat. Research Ccl., 1972); Phyllis V. Parkins (BIOSIS, 1973); Dale B. Baker (Chemical Abstracts Service, 1974); Melvin S. Day (Nat. Library of Medicine, 1975); Frederick G. Kilgour (Ohio Coll. Library Center, 1976).

Construction Management Award

The award was instituted and endowed by Marvin Gates and Amerigo Scarpa, Fellows, ASCE, in 1973. It is made annually to a member of the American Society of Civil Engineers who has made definite contributions in the field of construction management in general and, more particularly, in the application of the theoretical aspects of engineering economics, statistics, probability theory, operations research and related mathematically oriented disciplines to problems of construction management, estimating, cost accounting, planning, scheduling and financing. These contributions may be made in the form of written presentations, or notable performance. The award consists of a suitable plaque and certificate; no one may receive it more than once.

Awarding body: American Society of Civil Engineers, 345 East 47th St., New York, N.Y. 10017, U.S.A.

Recipients include: Joseph C. Kellogg (1974); James Douglas (1975); James J. O'Brien (1976).

Vasile Conta Prize

This prize for philosophy or psychology was founded by the Romanian Academy in 1948. It is named after Vasile Conta (1845–82), professor and materialistic philosopher, and author of an original theory of evolution, 'The theory of the Universal Undulation'. The award is presented annually at a General Assembly of the Academy, and consists of 10,000 lei and a diploma.

Awarding body: Academy of the S.R. of Romania, 125 Calea Victoriei, Bucharest, Romania.

James Cook Medal

This medal is awarded for outstanding contributions to science and human welfare in and for the benefit of the Southern Hemisphere. It was established in 1947 with a gift from Henry F. Halloran in memory of the navigator and explorer, Captain James Cook (1728–79).

Awarding body: The Royal Society of New South Wales, Australia.

Recipients include: Dr. M. R. Lemberg (1964); Dr. John Gunther (1965); Sir William Hudson (1966); Lord Casey of Berwick (1969); Sir Mark Oliphant (1974).

Duff Cooper Memorial Prize

The prize was established in 1954 by the friends of Duff Cooper, first Viscount Norwich (1890–1954), statesman, writer and ambassador. The award is a specially bound copy of Duff Cooper's autobiography, *Old Men Forget*, together with a cheque representing the interest on the sum subscribed by his friends on his death. The prize is awarded annually for any book published in the past two years in English or in French on a subject of history, biography, politics or poetry, which, in the judges' opinion, Duff Cooper would have most enjoyed reading.

Awarding body: Duff Cooper Memorial Prize Panel of Judges, c/o The Viscount Norwich, 24 Blomfield Road, London W9, England.

Recipients include: Seamus Heaney (*North*, 1975); Dennis Mack Smith (*Mussolini's Roman Empire*, 1976); E. R. Dodds (*Missing Persons*, 1777); Mark Girouard (*Life in the English Country House*, 1978).

Arthur C. Cope Award

The award was established in 1972 by the American Chemical Society, under the terms of the will of Arthur C. Cope. It is intended to recognize outstanding achievement in the field of organic chemistry, the significance of which has become apparent within the preceding five years. The award is presented biennially in even-numbered years, and consists of a gold medal, a bronze replica and $10,000. Travelling expenses incidental to the conferring of the award will be paid. In addition, an unrestricted grant-in-aid of $10,000 for research in organic chemistry under the direction of the recipient, designated as an Arthur C. Cope Fund Grant, will be made to any university or non-profit-making institution selected by the recipient. He or she may choose to assign the Arthur C. Cope Fund Grant to an institution for use by others than the recipient for research or education in organic chemistry.

Awarding body: American Chemical Society, 1155 Sixteenth St., N.W., Washington, D.C. 20036, U.S.A.

Recipients include: Robert B. Woodward and Roald Hoffmann (1973); Donald J. Cram (1974); Elias J. Corey (1976).

Copernicus Award

The Academy of American Poets was founded in 1934 to assist the careers of American poets; since 1974 it has presented a group of annual awards, sponsored by the Copernicus Society of America, spanning the full range of American poetic accomplishment. The Copernicus Award of $10,000 is made in recognition of the lifetime achievement of a poet over 45 years of age.

Awarding body: The Academy of American Poets, 1078 Madison Ave., New York, N.Y. 10028, U.S.A.
Recipients include: Robert Lowell (1974); Kenneth Rexroth (1975).

Copley Medal

The silver gilt medal was endowed in 1731 as the legacy of Sir Godfrey Copley, Bart., F.R.S. It is awarded annually to the living author of such philosophical research, either published or communicated to the Royal Society, as may appear to the Society's Council to be deserving of that honour. The subject(s) of research must be specified in making the award. No limitation is imposed either as to the period of time within which the research was made, or to the particular country to which its author may belong. The medal may not be awarded to anyone who is a member of Council of the Royal Society at the time of the award; it may be given more than once to the same person. A gift of £100 accompanies the medal. Since 1957 a Mr. and Mrs. John Jaffé Prize of £1,000 has accompanied the medal and gift; if the medallist as a Nobel Laureate has been precluding from receiving a Jaffé prize, £1,000 has been provided from another source.
Awarding body: Royal Society of London, 6 Carlton House Terrace, London SW1Y 5AG, England.
Recipients include: Sir Andrew Huxley (1973); W. V. D. Hodge (1974); Dr. F. H. C. Crick (1975); Prof. Dorothy Hodgkin (1976); Dr. F. Sanger (1977).

Corday-Morgan Medal and Prize

The Chemical Society makes three annual awards in different branches of chemistry. They each consist of a silver medal and a monetary prize of 250 guineas, and are made to the British chemists of either sex who have published in the preceding five years the most meritorious contribution to experimental chemistry. The awards are restricted to those under 36 years of age.
Awarding body: The Chemical Society, Burlington House, London W1V 0BN, England.
Recipients include: L. D. Hall, B. F. G. Johnson, A. McKillop (1974); R. J. Donovan, J. A. Osborn, G. Pattenden (1975); Laurance D. Hall (1976).

R. A. Cordingley Lectureship

The lectureship was founded in 1964 by the colleagues, pupils and friends of the late Professor R. A. Cordingley who held the Chair of Architecture in Manchester University from 1933 to 1962. The lecture is normally delivered biennially by a person of distinction in architecture or a related subject.
Awarding body: University of Manchester, Manchester M13 9PL, England.
Lecturers include: P. Shepheard ('What Future for Architecture?', 1970); J. H. Harvey ('Architectural Design in Medieval Carpentry', 1972); B. M. Feilden ('The Need for a New History of Architecture', 1974); Sir Denys Lasdun ('The National Theatre – an architecture of urban landscape', 1977).

Albert B. Corey Prize in Canadian-American Relations

This award was established in 1967, for the best book on the history of Canadian-American relations, or on the history of both countries. It consists of a cash award of $2,000.
Awarding body: American Historical Association, 400 A St., Southeast, Washington, D.C. 20003, U.S.A.

Lovis Corinth-Preis

This award, which commemorates the Impressionist painter Lovis Corinth (1858–1925), who was born in East Prussia, is given to individuals who have distinguished themselves in painting and the graphic or plastic arts, and whose life and works are linked with Germany's eastern regions. German artists who were born in these regions or whose careers are connected with them are eligible. This annual prize, first awarded in 1974, is funded by the West German Ministry of the Interior (DM10,000) and all the Länder (DM8,000). The principal prize is worth DM10,000, and there are two secondary prizes of DM4,000 each.
Awarding body: Die Künstlergilde, e.V., 7300 Esslingen/N., Webergasse 1, Federal Republic of Germany.
Recipients include: Prof. Karl Schmidt-Rottluff (1974); Prof. Bernhard Heiliger (1975); Prof. Oskar Kokoschka (1976).

Cork Film International

This annual film festival held in June was established in 1956 by Dermot Breen to promote popular interest in the short film. Entries are accepted from all countries. A bronze statuette of St. Finbarr is presented to the outstanding film in each category of the festival. Four certificates of merit are awarded at the discretion of the jury to particular films for outstanding aspects. For the first time in 1976 the Commission of the European Communities presented a special prize for the film which, in the opinion of an international jury, contributed most to mutual understanding between people of different European countries and of the common problems of contemporary society.
Awarding body: Cork Film International, 15 Bridge St., Cork, Ireland.

Arthur H. Cornetteprijs

The prize was established in 1950 by the Belgian Royal Academy of Dutch Language and Literature in memory of Arthur Hendrik Cornette (1880–1945), Flemish author and university professor. An award of 50,000 Belgian francs is made every five years for the best essay in Dutch. Recipients must be Belgian nationals.
Awarding body: Koninklijke Academie voor Nederlandse Taal- en Letterkunde, Koningstraat 18, B-9000 Ghent, Belgium.

Laurens Janszoon Coster Prijs

An annual prize was established in 1977 to reward a substantial contribution to the world of books in the Netherlands. Laurens Janszoon Coster (*c.* 1436–83) is considered to be the inventor of printing in the Netherlands. The prize consists of 5,000 Dutch guilders and a statue, and may be awarded to a person or an institution.

Awarding body: Stichting Laurens Janszoon Coster Prijs, Jacobijnestraat 3, P.O.B. 274, 2000 AG Haarlem, The Netherlands.

Recipients include: Geert van Oorschot (1977); Jan de Slegte (1978).

Cothenius-Medaille

This prize was established with a bequest of 1,000 gold Thaler to the Leopoldina German Academy of Researchers in Natural Sciences by Christian Andreas von Cothenius (1708–89), a member and director of the Academy. He asked that the interest should be used for a commemorative gold medal, engraved with his picture, to be awarded every two years for the best treatment of a set question in the field of practical medicine. Since 1954 the medal has been awarded to outstanding researchers for a completed life-work.

Awarding body: Deutsche Akademie der Naturforscher Leopoldina, 401 Halle/Saale, August-Benel-Strasse 50A, German Democratic Republic.

Recipients include: Prof. Dr. Friedrich Hund (Fed. Rep. of Germany, 1971); Prof. Dr. Otto Kratky (Austria, 1971); Prof. Dr. Albrecht Unsöld (Fed. Rep. of Germany, 1973); Prof. Dr. Viktor A. Ambartsumyan (U.S.S.R., 1974); Prof. Dr. Ilja Prigogine (Belgium, 1975); Prof. Dr. Ernst Ruska (Fed. Rep. of Germany, 1975).

Elliott Coues Award

This award was established by the Council of the American Ornithologists' Union in 1972, in memory of Elliott Coues (1842–99), a scholarly and innovative ornithologist who made great contributions to the study of North American birds. It consists of a certificate or plaque, and is awarded for a work which has had an important impact on the study of birds within the Western Hemisphere but may not be eligible for the Brewster Award (*q.v.*).

Awarding body: American Ornithologists' Union, National Museum of Natural History, Smithsonian Institution, Washington, D.C. 20560, U.S.A.

Crafts Council of Ireland Medal

The silver medal, established in 1976, is presented each year at the Royal Dublin Society's National Crafts Competition in recognition of the work which the Society has carried out for the benefit of craftsmanship since its foundation in 1731 and also in appreciation of the help which the Society has given to the Crafts Council of Ireland since its establishment in 1971. The medal is for work of outstanding merit in the National Crafts Competition.

Awarding body: Crafts Council of Ireland Ltd., Thomas Prior House, Merrion Rd., Dublin 4, Ireland.

Recipients include: Teresa Bradley (Irish crochet lace, 1976).

Kenneth Craik Award

The award was established by St. John's College, Cambridge, in 1946 in memory of Kenneth Craik (1914–45), a research Fellow of St. John's and first Director of a Unit for Applied Psychology of the Medical Research Council. The award of £300 is made annually for distinguished work in physiological psychology. It is hoped that the recipient will spend a few days in Cambridge to meet those interested in his work and to give a lecture.

Awarding body: St. John's College, Cambridge CB2 1TP, England.

Recipients include: Prof. Hans-Lukas Teuber (Psychophysiological Laboratory, M.I.T., 1971); Prof. Frank A. Beach (Dept. of Psychology, Univ. of California, Berkeley, 1972); Prof. Paul E. Polani (Prince Philip Prof. of Paediatric Research, Univ. of London, 1974); Prof. W. A. H. Rushton (Emer. Prof. of Visual Physiology, 1975); Prof. L. Weiskrantz (Prof. of Psychology, Univ. of Oxford, 1976).

Rose Mary Crawshay Prizes

In 1888 Mrs. Rose Mary Crawshay established the 'Byron, Shelley, Keats In Memoriam Yearly Prize Fund'. In 1914, some years after her death, the Charity Commissioners transferred the administration of the prize fund to the British Academy. Mrs. Crawshay was the wife of a wealthy Welsh industrialist. She encouraged the establishment of libraries and other cultural institutions in Wales, and was interested in the education and position of women, particularly 'impecunious gentlewomen'. Until 1976 a single annual prize was awarded; since then a second prize has been introduced. They are given 'to women of any nationality who, in the judgement of the Council of the British Academy, have written or published within three years next preceding the year of the award an historical or critical work of sufficient value on any subject connected with English literature, preference being given to a work regarding Byron, Shelley or Keats'.

Awarding body: The British Academy, Burlington House, Piccadilly, London W1V 0NS, England.

Recipients include: Jean Bromley (ed. *Old Arcadia* by Sir Philip Sidney, 1974); Doris Langley Moore (*Lord Byron – Accounts Rendered*, 1975); Hilary Spurling (*Ivy When Young*, 1976).

Ion Creangă Prize

The prize is awarded for the best published prose work of the year, and was founded in 1948 by the Romanian Academy. It commemorates Ion Creangă (1837–89), the famous story-teller and writer whose works have been translated into many languages. The award is presented annually at a

General Assembly of the Academy, and consists of 10,000 lei and a diploma.

Awarding body: Academy of the S.R. of Romania, 125 Calea Victoriei, Bucharest, Romania.

Elliott Cresson Medal

This gold medal is awarded for discovery or original research adding to the sum of human knowledge, irrespective of commercial value; leading and practical utilizations of discovery; and invention, methods or products embodying substantial elements of leadership in their respective classes, or unusual skill or perfection in workmanship. It was established in 1848 by Elliott Cresson (1796–1854), a philanthropist from Philadelphia, who was a life member of the Franklin Institute.

Awarding body: The Franklin Institute, Benjamin Franklin Parkway at 20th St., Philadelphia, Pa. 19103, U.S.A.

Recipients include: Mildred Cohn (pioneering application of nuclear magnetic resonance to determine structure and function of enzyme complexes) and Michael James Lighthill (acoustic quadruple theory of aerodynamic noise generation), 1975; Leon M. Lederman (experimental work in nuclear and particle physics), 1976.

James R. Croes Medal

This prize was established in 1912 by the American Society of Civil Engineers in honour of the first recipient of the Norman Medal (*q.v.*), John James Robertson Croes, Past President of ASCE. The award consists of a gold medal, bronze duplicate and certificate, and is given annually to the author of the paper next in merit to that awarded the Norman Medal, or, if the Norman Medal is not awarded, to any paper which is considered worthy of the prize, for its merit as a contribution to engineering science.

Awarding body: American Society of Civil Engineers, 345 East 47th St., New York, N.Y. 10017, U.S.A.

Recipients include: Subrata K. Chakrabarti ('Wave Forces on Submerged Objects of Symmetry', 1974); G. E. Blight ('Fracture of Pavement Materials', 1975); Frank H. Pearson and Archie J. McDonnell ('Limestone Barriers to Neutralize Acidic Streams', 1976).

Croonian Lecture

Dr. Croone, one of the original members of the Royal Society, left on his death in 1684 a scheme for two lectureships, one at the Royal Society and the other at the Royal College of Physicians. His widow, in 1701, provided the means for carrying out this scheme and indicated that the bequest was 'for the support of a lecture and illustrative experiment for the advancement of natural knowledge on local motion, or of such other subjects as, in the opinion of the President, should be most useful in promoting the objects for which the Royal Society was instituted'. The income of the fund is received from the Charity Commissioners and the gift to the lecturer is about £45. Since

1957 an additional Mr. and Mrs. John Jaffé Prize of £200 has been awarded and, if the lecturer as a Nobel Laureate has been precluded from receiving a Jaffé Prize, £200 has been provided from another source.

Awarding body: Royal Society of London, 6 Carlton House Terrace, London SW1Y 5AG, England.

Lecturers include: Dr. E. J. Denton ('On Buoyancy and the Lives of Modern and Fossil Cephalopods', 1973); Dr. J. Heslop-Harrison ('The Physiology of the Spore Surface', 1974); Dr. F. Sanger ('Nucleotide Sequences in DNA', 1975).

Louise du Pont Crowninshield Award

This award was established in 1960 by the U.S. National Trust in honour of Mrs. Louise du Pont Crowninshield, a founding member of the National Trust. The prize is awarded annually for superlative achievement in the preservation and interpretation of sites, buildings, architecture, districts and objects of national significance in the history and culture of the United States and its territories. It may be awarded to an organization, individual or several entities jointly. It consists of a trophy, certificate and a stipend of $1,000.

Awarding body: The National Trust for Historic Preservation, 740–748 Jackson Place, N.W., Washington, D.C. 20006, U.S.A.

Recipients include: Frank L. Horton (1970); Mrs. Henry Edmunds (1971); Miss Alice Winchester (1972); Dr. Ricardo E. Alegria (1973); Mrs. George Henry Warren and the Preservation Society of Newport County, R.I. (1976).

William V. Cruess Award

This award is made annually by the American Institute of Food Technologists to teachers of food science and technology who have distinguished themselves in their professions. It consist of a $1,000 honorarium and a bronze medal donated by the Northern California Section of the Institute. Candidates are nominated by members of the Institute.

Awarding body: Institute of Food Technologists, Suite 2120, 221 North La Salle St., Chicago, Ill. 60601, U.S.A.

Recipients include: Edward E. Burns (1972); John R. Whitaker (1973); Elizabeth F. Stier (1974); Charles M. Stine (1975); Fergus M. Clydesdale (1976).

Cullum Geographical Medal

This award was established in 1896. A gold medal is given intermittently 'to those who distinguish themselves by geographical discoveries, or in the advancement of geographical science'.

Awarding body: American Geographical Society, Broadway at 156th St., New York, N.Y. 10032, U.S.A.

Recipients include: Peter Haggett (1967); Luna B. Leopold (1968); Neil A. Armstrong, Edwin E. Aldrin, Jr., Michael Collins (1969); Bruce Heezen (1973); René Dubos (1975).

'A. Curci' International Violin Competition
Maestro Alberto Curci (1886–1973), the internationally famous violinist, founded the competition in Naples, his home town, in 1966. It is held every three years in November, and is open to violinists of every nationality under the age of 35. First, second and third prizes of 2,000,000 lire, 1,000,000 lire and 500,000 lire respectively are awarded.
Awarding body: Fondazione 'A. Curci', Via Nardones 8, 80132 Naples, Italy.
Recipients include: Isabella Petrosjan (U.S.S.R., 1971); Bernhard Hartog (Fed. Rep. of Germany, 1974); Eugen Sarbu (Romania, 1976).

Curl Lecture
Instituted in 1963, in memory of Samuel Matthias Curl, this lecture is delivered every two years (alternating with the Henry Myers Lecture). The lecturer, who must be under 40 years old, is elected by the Council of the Royal Anthropological Institute and preference is given to a topic from the fields of physical anthropology, archaeology, material culture and linguistics. The lecturer receives 50 guineas.
Awarding body: Royal Anthropological Institute of Great Britain and Ireland, 36 Craven St., London WC2N 5NG, England.
Lecturers include: Dr. Peter Ucko (1969); Dr. Warwick Bray (1971); Mrs. Caroline Humphrey (1973); Dr. A. J. Boyce (1975); Richard E. Leakey (1977).

Merle Curti Award
This award, first presented in 1977, is given to the author of a book in the field of American intellectual history published during the preceding two years. It consists of a cash prize of $500, a medal and certificate, and is made every two years. Books are nominated and selected by the Organization of American Historians.

Awarding body: Organization of American Historians, 112 North Bryan St., Bloomington, Ind. 47401, U.S.A.

Cymmrodorion Medal (Medal of the Honourable Society of Cymmrodorion)
This bronze medal is awarded for distinguished services to Wales, and was established by resolution of the Council of the Honourable Society in 1877. It is conferred by the Society from time to time; it is considered a high and rare honour and conferred only in cases of real merit. It has been conferred only 42 times since its inception.
Awarding body: The Honourable Society of Cymmrodorion, 118 Newgate St., London EC1A 7AE, England.
Recipients include: Dr. Llewelyn Wyn Griffith (1970); Sir Goronwy Edwards (1970); Sir Ben Bowen Thomas (1976); Dr. Thomas Parry (1976); Dr. I. C. Peate (1978); Dr. J. G. Jones (1978).

Adalbert-Czerny-Preis
This award is given annually by the German Society of Paediatrics to mark particular scientific achievements in that field. It was instituted in 1961, anticipating the centenary in 1963 of Adalbert Czerny's birth, and consists of a medal depicting Czerny and a cash prize of DM3,000. This award replaced the Moro Prize, which was sponsored by the company Joh. A. Benckiser of Ludwigshafen, but discontinued in 1961 when the company changed production. Eligibility for the Czerny Prize is restricted to paediatricians from German-speaking countries, and preference is given to practising paediatricians and young researchers; professors are excluded. Applicants must submit five examples of their work, which should not be entered simultaneously for any other contest. The prize may not be shared.
Awarding body: Deutsche Gesellschaft für Kinderheilkunde e.V., D-5000 Cologne 60, Amsterdamer Str. 59, Federal Republic of Germany.

D

Dairy and Food Industries Supply Association – American Society of Agricultural Engineers Food Engineering Award

This biennial award is presented each even-numbered year to honour those who have made original contributions in research, development, or design, or in the management of food processing equipment or techniques of significant economic value to the food industry and the consumer. The award consists of a gold medal, a certificate and a cash sum of $2,000.

Awarding body: American Society of Agricultural Engineers, 2950 Niles Rd., St. Joseph, Mich. 49085, U.S.A.

Dalrymple Lectureship in Archaeology

The lectureship was established in the years 1907–12 by the annual covenant of James D. G. Dalrymple of Woodhead, formerly James Dalrymple Duncan, writer, of Glasgow, secretary of the Glasgow Archaeological Society, and subsequently endowed by his bequest. It is now biennial, and the lecturer is chosen by a Board of Curators, four appointed by Glasgow University Court, and three by the Council of the Glasgow Archaeological Society.

Awarding body: University of Glasgow, Glasgow G12 8QQ, Scotland.

Lecturers include: Eric Burley (fmr. Prof. of Roman British History and Archaeology, Durham Univ., 1972–73); A. Colin Renfrew (Prof. of Archaeology, Southampton Univ., 1975); R. B. K. Stevenson (Keeper of the Nat. Museum of Antiquities of Scotland, 1977).

Charles P. Daly Medal

The Charles P. Daly Medal is awarded intermittently 'for valuable or distinguished geographical services or labors'. The award was founded in 1902, and the winner receives a gold medal.

Awarding body: American Geographical Society, Broadway at 156th St., New York, N.Y. 10032, U.S.A.

Recipients include: O. H. K. Spate (1968); Paul B. Sears, William O. Field (1969); Gilbert F. White (1971); Walter Sullivan (1973); Walter Wood (1974).

Dance Magazine Award

This silver cup has been awarded annually since 1954 in recognition of achievements in the world of dance. *Dance Magazine* is published monthly, and highlights performers, events and other aspects of dancing.

Awarding body: Dance Magazine, 10 Columbus Circle, New York, N.Y. 10019, U.S.A.

Recipients include: Fred Astaire, Dorothy Alexander, George Balanchine (1959); Judith Jamison, Anthony Dowell (1972).

Danube Prize

Czechoslovak Television founded the International Festival of Television Programmes for Children and Youth in 1971. It is held every two years in the last week of September in Bratislava. The aim of the Festival is to further a progressive relationship of children and youth to life. There are four categories: (1) documentary and informative programmes; (2) musical, entertainment and competitive programmes (no classical music); (3) dramatic programmes up to 60 minutes (all forms); (4) dramatic programmes up to 16 minutes (all forms). Each participating television organization may enter for the competition in all four categories. Programmes must express the basic idea of the Festival, by featuring in a creative manner the life, problems and aspirations of contemporary children and youth. 'Only original, recent television programmes are eligible. The main prize – the Danube Prize (a bronze sculpture) – is awarded in each category. Other prizes and honourable mentions are also given.

Awarding body: Czechoslovak Television in Bratislava, Osmolovova 24, 893 19 Bratislava, Czechoslovakia.

Recipients include: Oy Yleisradio AB, Finland (drama, *Vinski and Vincenti*, 1971); Czechoslovak Television (drama, *Nobody Tells Me Anything*, 1973); Czechoslovak Television (drama feature, *The Robinson Girl*, 1975); Polish Television (drama, *Reksio the Tamer*, 1975).

Darbaker Prize in Phycology

The Darbaker family established this annual cash prize (currently $425) and a certificate to be given for meritorious work in the study of microscopical algae in all its facets. It is based on papers published during the preceding two years.

Awarding body: Botanical Society of America, New York Botanical Garden, Bronx, N.Y. 10458, U.S.A.

Recipients include: Kenneth Stewart; Karl Mattox; Sarah P. Gibbs; Larry R. Hoffman; Jeremy D. Pickett-Heaps.

Darling Foundation Prize

The prize is awarded for outstanding achievements in the pathology, etiology, epidemiology, therapy, prophylaxis or control of malaria. It consists of a bronze medal and 1,000 Swiss francs, and is awarded periodically whenever the accumulated interest on the Foundation's capital amounts to a net sum of not less than 1,000 Swiss francs. The administrator invites member states and associate members of the World Health Organization, and the members of the Expert Advisory Panel who have already served on an Expert Committee on Malaria, to nominate candidates. The candidature must be in respect of a work published or accomplished not more than ten years before its submission. The Darling Foundation was created by private funds in memory of Dr. S. T. Darling, accidentally killed during a study mission of the League of Nations' Malaria Commission.

Awarding body: World Health Organization, Avenue Appia, 1211 Geneva 27, Switzerland.

Darwin Medal

Established in 1890, this silver medal is given biennially in reward of work of acknowledged distinction (especially in biology) in the field in which Charles Darwin himself laboured. The award may be made either to a British subject or a foreigner. A gift of £200 accompanies the medal.

Awarding body: Royal Society of London, 6 Carlton House Terrace, London SW1Y 5AG, England.

Recipients include: C. S. Elton (1970); David Lack (1972); Prof. P. M. Sheppard (1974); Prof. Charlotte Auerbach (1976).

Chaturvedi Kalawati Jagmohan Das Memorial Award

This prize is awarded to an eminent scientist for valuable contributions in the field of cardiovascular diseases. The winner receives a gold medal and a cash sum of 1,000 rupees.

Awarding body: Indian Council of Medical Research, Ansari Nagar, Post Box 4508, New Delhi 110016, India.

Recipients include: Dr. K. S. Mathur (1975).

David Memorial Lectureship

The Australian National Research Council established the lecture in 1932 in honour of Sir Tannath William Edgeworth David (1859–1934), geologist, explorer, teacher and investigator of the first rank. The lecture is given every fourth year at a Congress of the Australian and New Zealand Association for the Advancement of Science, and subsequently published in the Association's journal *Search* as part of the Report of the Congress at which the lecture is given. The person appointed is chosen for his distinguished contributions to one of the following: anthropology, agriculture, botany, forestry, geology, geography, mental science and education, pathology, physiology, veterinary science or zoology. The lecturer receives a fee of $50 from the Lectureship Fund held by ANZAAS.

Awarding body: Australian and New Zealand Association for the Advancement of Science, 157 Gloucester St., Sydney, N.S.W. 2000, Australia.

Recipients include: S. W. Carey ('Fifty Years since Wegener', 1965); F. C. Courtice ('Biology of Organ Transplantation in Man and Animals', 1969); F. Fenner ('The Evolution of Viruses', 1973).

Davidson Medal

This medal is awarded biennially for outstanding scientific accomplishment in ship research. It was established in 1959 by the Society of Naval Architects and Marine Engineers in honour of Kenneth S. M. Davidson (1898–1958), a former Vice-President of the Society and Director of the Experimental Towing Tank at the Stevens Institute in New Jersey.

Awarding body: Society of Naval Architects and Marine Engineers, Suite 1369, One World Trade Center, New York, N.Y. 10048, U.S.A.

George Davidson Medal

This gold medal is awarded occasionally, for exceptional achievement in research or exploration in the Pacific Ocean or the lands bordering thereon. The award was established in 1946.

Awarding body: American Geographical Society, Broadway at 156th St., New York, N.Y. 10032, U.S.A.

Recipients include: George B. Cressey (1952); F. Raymond Fosberg (1972); Joseph Spencer (1974); Shinzo Kiuchi (1975).

Sir Stanley Davidson Lectureship

The lectureship was endowed by Professor Emeritus Sir Stanley Davidson, former Regius Professor of Medicine, University of Edinburgh, and is awarded biennially.

Awarding body: Edinburgh University, Edinburgh EH8 9YL, Scotland.

Lecturers include: Prof. W. S. Peart (1972); Prof. N. A. Mitchison (1977).

Davisson-Germer Prize

The prize was established in 1965 by Bell Laboratories to recognize and encourage outstanding work in atomic physics or surface physics in the U.S.A. It is normally awarded alternately for outstanding work in atomic physics one year and for outstanding work in surface physics in the next year. It consists of $2,500 and a certificate.

Awarding body: American Physical Society, 335 East 45th St., New York, N.Y. 10017, U.S.A.

Recipients include: James J. Lander and Homer D. Hagstrum (1975); Ufo Fano (1976); Walter Kohn and Norton Lang (1977).

Davy Medal

By the will of Dr. John Davy, F.R.S., the service of plate presented to Sir Humphrey Davy for the invention of the miner's safety lamp was bequeathed to the Royal Society. Through this benefaction the Davy Medal was established in 1877. The bronze medal is awarded annually for the most important discovery in chemistry made in Europe or in Anglo-America. A gift of £200 accompanies the medal.

Awarding body: Royal Society of London, 6 Carlton House Terrace, London SW1Y 5AG, England.

Recipients include: Prof. J. S. Anderson (1973); Prof. James Baddiley (1974); Prof. T. M. Sugden (1975); Dr. R. E. Richards (1976); Prof. A. R. Battersby (1977).

Arthur L. Day Medal

Mr. Arthur L. Day donated a sum of money in 1948 to the Geological Society of America to establish a permanent fund from the income of which a gold medal is awarded 'for outstanding distinction in contributing to geologic knowledge through the application of physics and chemistry to the solution of geologic problems'. The donor wished to provide a token which would recognize outstanding achievement and inspire further effort, rather than to reward a distinguished career.

Awarding body: Geological Society of America, Inc., 3300 Penrose Place, Boulder, Colo. 80301, U.S.A.

Recipients include: Frank Press (1972); David T. Griggs (1973); A. E. Ringwood (1974); Allan Cox (1975); Hans Ramberg (1976).

H. Trendley Dean Memorial Award

This award for meritorious research in epidemiology and dental caries was established and is supported by Frank J. McClure in memory of the late H. Trendley Dean. The award, consisting of a bronze plaque and a cash stipend of $200, is presented annually.

Awarding body: International Association for Dental Research, 211 East Chicago Ave., Chicago, Ill. 60611, U.S.A.

Dechema-Preis der Max-Buchner-Forschungsstiftung (*Dechema Prize of the Max Buchner Research Foundation*)

This prize was established in honour of Max Buchner (1866–1934), the founder of DECHEMA (Deutsche Gesellschaft für chemisches Apparatewesen e.V.) which administers the Research Foundation. It is for research and development work of significance in various fields of chemical engineering, particularly that carried out by young scientists and from which further development can be expected. Established in 1950, the prize is given annually, and consists of a gold medal, certificate, and cash prize of DM15,000. It is a requirement that the work must have been carried out in Germany (with the exception of 1975, when, in commemoration of DECHEMA's 50th anniversary, a European Dechema Prize to the value of DM25,000 was awarded at international level).

Awarding body: Max-Buchner-Forschungsstiftung, Dechema-Haus, Theodor-Heuss-Allee 25, Postfach 97 01 46, D-6000 Frankfurt/Main 97, Federal Republic of Germany.

Recipients include: Dr.-Ing. Lothar Reh (1971); Dr.rer.nat. Ulrich Wagner and Dr.rer.nat. Hans Martin Weitz (1972); Prof. Dr.phil. Walter Nitsch (1973); Prof. Dr.-Ing. Gerhard Luft and Prof. Dr.-Ing. Rudolf Steiner (1974); Prof. Dr. Cornelis van Heerden (Netherlands, Europa Dechema Prize 1975).

John Deere Medal

This medal is awarded by the American Society of Agricultural Engineers for distinguished achievement in the application of science and art to the soil. It is intended to honour achievement in connection with engineering ways and means for both soil and water manipulation, conservation and management. Only ASAE members in good standing may sponsor candidates for the medal.

Awarding body: American Society of Agricultural Engineers, 2950 Niles Rd., St. Joseph, Mich. 49085, U.S.A.

Admiral Luis De Florez Flight Safety Award

The award was established in 1966 by the Flight Safety Foundation. A plaque, accompanied by a certificate and cash honorarium, is awarded annually to recognize outstanding individual contributions to aviation safety made through basic design, device or practice.

Awarding body: Flight Safety Foundation Inc., 1800 North Kent St., Arlington, Va. 22209, U.S.A.

Recipients include: Capt. Victor Hewes (ALPA, 1970); Dr. John T. Dailey (FAA, 1972); Kenneth B. Olsen (American Airlines, 1974); C. D. Bateman (Sundstrand Data Control, 1975); Daniel F. Sowa (Northwest Airlines, 1976).

De Florez Training Award

This annual award was established in honour of the late Admiral De Florez, who did much to advance the use of simulators in the training of pilots. It is given to an individual responsible for outstanding improvement in aerospace training. It comprises a medal and certificate of citation, and is usually presented at the Annual Meeting.

Awarding body: American Institute of Aeronautics and Astronautics, 1290 Avenue of the Americas, New York, N.Y. 10019, U.S.A.

Recipients include: James W. Campbell (1972); Carroll H. Woodling (1973); Hugh Harrison Hurt, Jr. (1974); John C. Dusterberry (1975); John E. Duberg (1977).

Georg Dehio-Preis

This annual award was first made in 1964, and commemorates Georg Dehio (1850–1932), an art historian born in Reval. It is intended primarily for those from the German eastern regions, and the prize is given for publications dealing with the history of art, literature, culture or ideas, which concern the east of Germany, middle Germany or contacts between Germans and the peoples of neighbouring countries. It can also be made for outstanding achievements in these fields of study, or for collections of works. There are two principal prizes of DM5,000 each and two secondary prizes of DM2,000 each. The award is financed by the Ministry of the Interior (DM9,250), the Länder of Baden-Württemberg, Bavaria, Hessen, Lower Saxony and North Rhine-Westphalia (DM3,750), and the Cultural Association of Württemberg (DM1,000).

Awarding body: Dir Künstlergilde, e.V., 7300 Esslingen/N., Webergasse 1, Federal Republic of Germany.

Recipients include: Prof. Dr. Dr. Ernst Scheyer (1972); Prof. Dr. Bruno Schier (1973); Hans Diplich (1974); Prof. Dr. Karl Heinz Clasen (1975); Prof. Dr. Erich Bachmann (1976).

Thomas-Dehler-Preis

This prize is offered by the West German Ministry for Intra-German Relations for a literary work relating to some aspect of Germany (East and West). It was established in 1967 and dedicated to the memory of the politician Thomas Dehler (1897–1967). Prize-winners are elected every two years and receive a certificate and DM20,000.

Awarding body: Bundesminister für inner-deutsche Beziehungen, Godesberger Allee 140, Postfach 120250, D-5300 Bonn 2, Federal Republic of Germany.

Recipients include: Horst Krüger (1970); Loachim Fest (1973); Peter Weiss (1977).

De la Vaulx Medal

This award is made to holders of world records in the areas of aeronautics and spaceflight achieved during the year.

Awarding body: Fédération Aéronautique Internationale, 6 rue Galilée, Paris 16, France.

Recipients include: T. P. Stafford (U.S.A.), V. Grand (U.S.A.), D. Slayton (U.S.A.), A. A. Leonov (U.S.S.R.), V. N. Kubasov (U.S.S.R.) (Apollo-Soyuz mission), 1975.

J. H. Dellinger Gold Medal

This medal is awarded by the International Union of Radio Science (URSI) for achievements which have been particularly valuable in any of the branches of science covered by the Commissions of URSI. The award is triennial. Candidates must be proposed by one of the 36 National Member Committees of URSI, and the work for which the medal is awarded must have been carried out mainly during the six-year period preceding the award. The medal was established by the United States National Committee of URSI in 1966, in memory of Dr. J. H. Dellinger (1886–1962), an American physicist renowned for his work on solar-terrestrial relations and the ionosphere.

Awarding body: International Union of Radio Science (URSI), Rue de Nieuwenhove 81, B-1180 Brussels, Belgium.

Recipients include: Dr. J. H. Chapman (Canada, radio wave propagation and the Alouette 1 top-side ionosphere sounder, 1966); Prof. H. M. Barlow (U.K., development of waveguides; the characteristics of surface waves, 1969); Prof. A.

Hewish (U.K., advances in radio astronomy, 1972); Prof. N. M. Brice (U.S.A., theory of the Earth's plasmapause and theoretical investigations of the physics of Jupiter's magnetosphere, 1975).

Dent Medal

This award is made for an outstanding contribution to musical scholarship. It was established in 1961 by the Royal Musical Association to honour the musicologist Edward J. Dent (b. 1876), and is awarded annually, usually in July. It is given for a particular work, or a closely related group of works, published within the last five years, and the recipient should normally be under 40 years of age.

Awarding body: Royal Musical Association, c/o Music Library, British Library, Great Russell St., London WC1B 3DG, England.

Recipients include: William W. Austin (1967); Daniel Heartz (1970); Jozef Robijns (1972); Max Lütolf (1973); Martin Staehelin (1975).

Déri Award

This award is made annually by the Hungarian Electrotechnical Association for a paper by a member published that year in one of the Association's technical reviews, illustrating the author's practical creative work. It takes the form of a medal and 4,000 forints in cash. It was established in 1960, in memory of Miksa Déri, distinguished inventor and pioneer in the field of applied electrotechnology.

Awarding body: Magyar Elektrotechnikai Egyesület, 1055 Budapest, Kossuth Lajos tér 6–8, Hungary.

Recipients include: Dr. Iván Bach (1969); Imre Gombos (1970); A. Ödön Kerényi (1971); Ferenc Kovács (1973); Dr. Róbert Szabó Bakoss (1974).

Design Council Awards

These awards were established in 1957 by the Council of Industrial Design, since renamed the Design Council. A certificate is awarded for the highest standards of design and manufacture in each of the following categories: (i) consumer and contract goods; (ii) engineering products and components; (iii) motor vehicles; (iv) medical equipment. The certificates are awarded annually in June. Any manufacturer in the United Kingdom is eligible.

Awarding body: The Design Council, 28 Haymarket, London SW1Y 4SU, England.

Nestor De Tièreprijs

The prize was established in 1931 by the Belgian Royal Academy of Dutch Language and Literature in memory of Nestor De Tière (1856–1920), Flemish playwright and pioneer of realism on the Flemish stage. An award of 7,500 Belgian francs is made every two years for the best unpublished Flemish stage-play submitted. Recipients must be Belgian nationals.

Awarding body: Koninklijke Academie voor Nederlandse Taal- en Letterkunde, Koningstraat 18, B-9000 Ghent, Belgium.

Recipients include: Raymond Brulez (*De Schone Slaapster*, 1933); Marcel Coole (*Dit Moellijk Leven*, 1953); A. Mussche (*Christoffel Marlowe*, 1955); J. van Hoeck (for his collected works, 1959).

Detre László Prize

The award was established in 1976 by the Hungarian Physical Society in honour of László Detre (b. 1906), the astronomer. An annual cash prize of 5,000 forints is awarded annually for outstanding research in astronomy.

Awarding body: 'Eötvös Loránd' Fizikai Társulat, 1061 Budapest VI, Anker-köz 1, Hungary.

Deutscher Filmpreis (*German Prize for Cinema*)

This award is made annually by the West German Ministry of the Interior in recognition and encouragement of cinematic excellence, and is intended to raise the cultural standard of German films. Instituted in 1951, it takes the form of a Golden Bowl (Wanderpreis), and gold and silver circlets for films and individual achievements. The awards for films also carry cash prizes from DM30,000 to DM500,000. Films should have been completed in the award year or the preceding calendar year. Producers and directors of German films are eligible, also foreigners permanently resident in the Federal Republic. The award may also be given to scriptwriters, actors, cameramen, designers, etc.

Awarding body: Bundesminister des Innern, 5300 Bonn, Rheindorfer Strasse 198, Federal Republic of Germany.

Recipients include: Independent Film Heinz Angermeyer and Johannes Schaaf (*Trotta*, 1972); Peter Schamoni (*Hundertwassers Regentag*, 1972); Maximilian Schell (*Der Fussganger*, 1974); Werner Herzog (*Jeder für sich und Gott gegen alle*, 1975); Peter Lilienthal (*Es herrscht Ruhe im Land*, 1976).

Deutscher Jugendbuchpreis (*German Juvenile Book Prize*)

The prize was established in 1956 by the Federal German Ministry for Youth and the Family. Awards are made annually for four types of book: picture-book; children's book; young people's book; non-fiction book. The winners receive a certificate and a cash prize of DM7,500. The books must have been published in the previous year and be in German.

Awarding body: Arbeitskreis für Jugendliteratur e.V., 8000 Munich 40, Elisabethstr. 15, Federal Republic of Germany.

Recipients include: Wilhelm Schlote (picture book: *Heute wünsch ich mir ein Nilpferd*); Peter Härtling (children's book: *Oma*); John Christopher (young people's book: *Die Wächter*); Theodor Dolezol (non-fiction: *Planet des Menschen*), 1976.

Isaac Deutscher Memorial Prize

The prize was established in 1968 by British, American and European scholars in commemoration of Isaac Deutscher, the distinguished Marxist historian and theorist, who died in 1967. A cash prize of £100 is awarded to the author of a work which, in the opinion of the jury, contributes to Marxist thought. Whenever possible a lecture is delivered by the prize-winner at the presentation; this usually takes place in the autumn. Published or unpublished works should be submitted before 1 May.

Awarding body: The Isaac Deutscher Memorial Prize, c/o Lloyd's Bank, 68 Warwick Square, London SW1V 2AS, England.

Recipients include: Prof. L. Colletti (Univ. of Rome, 1973); Prof. M. Rodinson (Univ. of Paris, 1974); Prof. M. Liebman (Univ. of Brussels, 1975); Prof. W. Brus (Wolfson Coll., Oxford, 1976); Prof. S. S. Prawer (Univ. of Oxford, 1977).

Denis Devlin Memorial Award for Poetry

This award, a cash prize of £600, is made every three years in memory of Denis Devlin, poet and diplomat. Born in Scotland in 1908, he was educated in Dublin and entered the Irish Diplomatic Service in 1935. He became Ambassador to Italy in 1958 and died in 1959. The award was established in 1959 by his friends and admirers; it is for a book of poetry in English published in the three years prior to the award. It is restricted to Irish citizens.

Awarding body: Irish Arts Council, 70 Merrion Square, Dublin 2, Ireland.

Recipients include: Austin Clarke (1964); Thomas Kinsella (1967 and 1970); Seamus Heaney (1973); Derek Mahon (1976).

Dexter Prize

This cash prize of $1,000 and a plaque was established by the Dexter Chemical Corporation of New York City. It is given to the author of an outstanding book on the history of technology published during the preceding three years. It is presented annually at the banquet of the Society for the History of Technology.

Awarding body: Society for the History of Technology, c/o Dr. Carroll Pursell, Jr., Secretary, Dept. of History, University of California, Santa Barbara, Calif. 93106, U.S.A.

Recipients include: Thomas Park Hughes (1972); Donald S. L. Cardwell (1973); Daniel J. Boorstin and Donald R. Hill (1974); Bruce Sinclair (1975); Hugh G. J. Aitkin (1976).

Shree Dhanwantari Prize

This prize was established in 1969 by the Indian National Science Academy, and takes the form of a medal. It is awarded every five years for outstanding work in India in any branch of medicine including research in drugs and the methodology of Ayurveda.

Awarding body: Indian National Science Academy, Bahadur Shah Zafar Marg, New Delhi 110001, India.

Recipients include: R. Vishwanathan (1971); B. Mukerji (1976).

Diesel and Gas Engine Power Award

The Diesel and Gas Engine Power Division of the American Society of Mechanical Engineers established this award in 1966. It takes the form of a bronze plaque. It is given in recognition of eminent achievement or distinguished contribution over a substantial period of time, which may result from research, innovation or education in advancing the art of engineering in the field of internal-combustion engines; or in directing the efforts and accomplishments of those engaged in engineering practice in the design, development, application and operation of internal-combustion engines. The recipient need not be a member of ASME. Candidates for the award should be living citizens of the U.S.A.

Awarding body: American Society of Mechanical Engineers, United Engineering Center, 345 East 47th St., New York, N.Y. 10017, U.S.A.

Recipients include: Melvin J. Helmich (1971); R. Rex Robinson (1972); Warren A. Rhoades (1973); Warren J. Severin (1974); William Speicher (1975).

Dinabot Award

This is an annual prize established by the Japanese Society of Nuclear Medicine in 1962 for distinguished original work in the field of nuclear medicine. It consists of U.S.$3,000, divided equally between two awardees who must be scientists of Japanese nationality under 45 years of age and have been members of the Society for more than four years. The cash award is intended to cover the costs of travelling to the U.S.A., especially to attend the Annual Meeting of the Society of Nuclear Medicine.

Awarding body: Japanese Society of Nuclear Medicine, c/o Japanese Radioisotope Association, 2-28-45, Honkomagome, Bunkyo-ku, Tokyo 113, Japan.

Recipients include: Kazuo Uemura, M.D., and Kengo Matsui, M.D. (1975); Rikushi Morita, M.D., and Yukio Tateno, M.D. (1976); Akira Kohono, Ph.D., and Kikuo Machida, M.D. (1977).

Diplôme d'Honneur

This award is presented annually to one or more people who have rendered distinguished service to the arts in Canada. It consists of a diploma and a silver medal. Candidates are nominated by members of the Canadian Conference of the Arts (CCA), which founded the award in 1954.

Awarding body: Canadian Conference of the Arts, 3 Church Street, Suite 47, Toronto, Ont. M5E 1M2, Canada.

Recipients include: Ernest Lindner, Alfred Pellan, Barbara Pentland (1977).

Dischinger-Preis

This prize was established in 1953 by the German Concrete Association in honour of Professor Dr.-ing. Franz Dischinger, who widened the use of ferro-concrete in building construction. It is intended for graduates of the Technische Universität Berlin whose principal subject was ferro-concrete. A winner is selected each year and the prizes are presented every two years on a given day. The winner receives a certificate and a cash sum of DM3,000.

Awarding body: Deutscher Beton-Verein e.V., 6200 Wiesbaden 1, Postfach 21 26, Federal Republic of Germany.

Recipients include: Dipl.-Ing. Georg Stülken, Dipl.-Ing. Spyridon Samaras (1970); Dipl.-Ing. Herbert Grill (1971); Dipl.-Ing. Michael Cowalsky (1973); Dipl.-Ing. Günter Schmidt-Gönner (1974).

Distinguished Service Award for Excellence in Medicine and Surgery

This award, consisting of an inscribed plaque, is presented at irregular intervals by the American Society of Contemporary Medicine and Surgery for excellence in these fields. It was instituted in 1973 by John G. Bellows, M.D., Ph.D., Director of the Society.

Awarding body: American Society of Contemporary Medicine and Surgery, 6 North Michigan Ave., Suite 1110, Chicago, Ill. 60602, U.S.A.

Recipients include: Morris Fishbein, M.D. (1972); Michael DeBakey, M.D. (1973); Renee Bubos, M.D. (1974); Louis Weinstein, M.D. (1975).

Distinguished Service Award for Excellence in Ophthalmology

This award, consisting of a gold medal, is presented at irregular intervals by the American Society of Contemporary Ophthalmology for excellence in this field. It was instituted in 1973 by Dr. John Bellows, M.D., Ph.D., Director of the Society.

Awarding body: American Society of Contemporary Ophthalmology, 6 North Michigan Ave., Chicago, Ill. 60602, U.S.A.

Recipients include: Prof. James Allen (U.S.A., 1972); Prof. Charles Schepens (U.S.A., 1973); Prof. Harold Scheie (U.S.A., 1974); Prof. Fritz Hollwich (Fed. Rep. of Germany, 1975); Prof. Jules François (Belgium, 1976).

W. E. Dixon Memorial Lecture in Therapeutics and Pharmacology

A lecturer is appointed every three years and receives an honorarium.

Awarding body: Royal Society of Medicine, 1 Wimpole St., London W1M 8AE, England.

Dobloug Prize

This prize is given annually for Swedish literature and history of literature. It was endowed in 1955 by Birger Dobloug, and is the counterpart of a similar prize given in Norway for Norwegian literature. The prize is a sum of money, at present 25,000 Swedish kronor, and any Swedish writer or scientist is eligible. The prize cannot be applied for.

Awarding body: The Swedish Academy, Börshuset, Källargränd 4, S-111 29, Stockholm, Sweden.

Doubleday Lecture
A lecturer is appointed every five years to deliver a lecture to the Section of Odontology of the Royal Society of Medicine. He receives an honorarium.
Awarding body: Royal Society of Medicine, 1 Wimpole St., London W1M 8AE, England.

James Douglas Gold Medal
This award is made annually by the American Institute of Mining, Metallurgical, and Petroleum Engineers for distinguished achievement in the field of non-ferrous metallurgy. Candidates of all nationalities are eligible, provided they are proposed by a member of the Institute and have not previously received an Institute award. The Award Fund was established by anonymous donation in 1922, in memory of James Douglas, industrialist, mining and metallurgical engineer and founder of the Phelps Dodge Corporation, which in 1953 made a substantial gift to the Fund.
Awarding body: American Institute of Mining, Metallurgical and Petroleum Engineers, Inc., 345 East 47th St., New York, N.Y. 10017, U.S.A.
Recipients include: Herbert Humphrey Kellogg (1973); Sir Alan Howard Cottrell (1974); Petri B. Bryk (1975); John F. Elliott (1976); Carleton C. Long (1977).

Joseph-E.-Drexel-Preis
The prize was founded in 1956 by Verlag Nürnberg Presse and the Olympia-Verlag in Nuremberg, in honour of Joseph E. Drexel (1896–1976), founder of the newspaper *Nürnberger Nachrichten* and the associated publishing company. It is awarded annually for achievements in the press in its widest sense, including publishing, all aspects of journalism, translating and pictorial contributions to any publication. The two firms contribute to a foundation from which a cash prize is made each year to more than one recipient, amounting to up to DM16,000. Nominations may be made to the board of the foundation by chief editors, professors of journalism or members of the board itself.
Awarding body: Joseph E. Drexel Stiftung, 8500 Nuremberg, Marienplatz 5, Federal Republic of Germany.
Recipients include: Dr. Anton Dieterich (Madrid), Hidde Fürstenberg (Mölln), Gustav Peichl (Vienna), 1974; Dr. Bohne (Hanover), Prof. Fink (Strasbourg), Dr. Hans Dahmen, 1975; no awards in 1976 on account of the death of Dr. Drexel.

Dryden Lectureship in Research
The Dryden Research Lecture was named in honour of Dr. Hugh L. Dryden in 1967, and its name changed in 1975. This annual award is intended to emphasize the importance of basic research to advancement in aeronautics and astronautics and to honour research scientists and engineers. However, it not only honours a particular person but, by means of the lecture, enables the recipient to share his technological gifts with AIAA membership and the public at large. The award consists of a medal and a certificate of citation; the lecture is usually presented at the annual Aerospace Sciences Meeting.
Awarding body: American Institute of Aeronautics and Astronautics, 1290 Avenue of the Americas, New York, N.Y. 10019, U.S.A.
Recipients include: Abraham Hertzberg (1977); Gerald A. Soffen (1978).

Alexander Duckham Memorial Award
This award is made annually to two corporate members of The Institution of Plant Engineers for papers which contribute substantially to the advancement of plant and works engineering. The prize-winners receive from Alexander Duckham & Co. Ltd. a silver and bronze medal, as first and second prizes respectively. If they are present at the Conference at which the medals are presented, a cash grant of £10 each is available. In addition, cash prizes of £150 and £75 respectively are awarded by the Institution.
Awarding body: The Institution of Plant Engineers, 138 Buckingham Palace Rd., London SW1W 9SG, England.

Duddell Medal and Prize
A bronze medal and a prize of £150 are awarded annually to a person who has contributed to the advancement of knowledge by the invention or design of scientific instruments or by the discovery of materials used in their construction or has made outstanding contributions to the application of physics. The award was established by the Council of the Physical Society in 1923 as a memorial to William du Bois Duddell, inventor of the electromagnetic oscillograph. Candidates are considered on the recommendation of members of the Institute of Physics and its Awards Committee.
Awarding body: The Institute of Physics, 47 Belgrave Square, London SW1X 8QX, England.
Recipients include: Keith Davy Froome and Robert Howard Bradsell (1967); Charles William Oatley (1969); Vernon Ellis Cosslett and Kenneth Charles Arthur Smith (1971); Albert Franks (1973); Ernst Ruska (1975).

Konrad-Duden-Preis der Stadt Mannheim
(*Konrad Duden Prize of the City of Mannheim*)
This award was established in 1960 by the West German town of Mannheim in memory of Konrad Duden (1829–1911), who was instrumental in the establishment of modern German orthography. The award, which is non-competitive, is made for exceptional services to the German language. It is given every two years, and takes the form of a certificate and DM10,000, provided equally by the town of Mannheim and the Bibliographical Institute of Mannheim (seat of publication of the *Duden* reference books).
Awarding body: Gemeinderat der Stadt Mannheim, Rathaus E 5, 6800 Mannheim 1, Federal Republic of Germany.
Recipients include: Prof. Dr. Jost Trier (Fed. Rep.

of Germany) and Prof. Dr. Gustav Korlén (Sweden), 1967; Prof. Dr. Johannes Erben (Austria, 1969); Prof. Dr. Hans Eggers (Fed. Rep. of Germany, 1971); Prof. Dr. Jean Fourquet (France, 1973); Prof. Dr. Ludwik Zabrocki (Poland, 1975).

Carl-Duisberg-Gedächtnispreis *(Carl Duisberg Memorial Prize)*

The prize was established in 1935 by the dye manufacturers I. G. Farbenindustrie AG, in commemoration of Carl Duisberg (died 1935), honorary member of the Association of German Chemists. The award lapsed after the second world war until 1969 when, at the request of the Society of German Chemists, the dye manufacturers Farbenfabriken Bayer AG of Leverkusen contributed the money to revive the Carl Duisberg Foundation.

Awarding body: Gesellschaft Deutscher Chemiker, 6000 Frankfurt (Main) 90, Carl Bosch-Haus, Varrentrappstr. 40–42, Federal Republic of Germany.

Recipients include: Dr. Werner Kutzelnigg (1971); Dr. Fritz Eckstein (1972); Dr. Richard Schmidt (1974); Dr. Dieter Sellmann (1975); Dr. Konrad Sandhoff (1976).

Carl-Duisberg-Plakette *(Carl Duisberg Medal)*

Established in 1953 by the dye manufacturers Bayer, Leverkusen-Bayerwerk, the medal is in memory of Carl Duisberg (died 1935). It is awarded at irregular intervals to German chemists in recognition of contributions to the advance of chemistry and the fulfilment of the aims of the Society of German Chemists.

Awarding body: Gesellschaft Deutscher Chemiker, 6000 Frankfurt (Main) 90, Carl Bosch-Haus, Varrentrappstr. 40–42, Federal Republic of Germany.

Recipients include: Prof. Karl Winnacker (1968); Prof. Heinrich Schackmann (1970); Dr. Rudolf Wolf (1972); Prof. Adolf Steinhofer (1973); Prof. Rolf Sammet (1976).

Dunlop Lecture Award

The award was established in 1971 by The Chemical Institute of Canada and is sponsored by the Dunlop Research Centre, Sheridan Park, Ontario. It is given to an individual who, while resident in Canada, has made a distinguished contribution to macromolecular science or technology. The recipient delivers the Dunlop Lecture at the Annual Conference of The Chemical Institute of Canada or at an Annual Symposium of the Macromolecular Science Division. He receives the title of 'Dunlop Lecturer', an honorarium of $500 and a framed scroll provided by the Dunlop Research Centre. The award is made every two years. Nominations are made by members of The Chemical Institute.

Awarding body: The Chemical Institute of Canada, 151 Slater St., Ottawa, Ont. K1P 5H3, Canada.

Recipients include: G. S. Whitby ('Reflections on the Early Days of Canadian Polymer Chemistry', 1971); S. Bywater ('Recent Advances in Ionic Polymerization', 1973); S. G. Mason ('Some New Aspects of Wetting Solids by Liquids', 1975).

John H. Dunning Prize

This prize is awarded in even-numbered years for a book on any subject relating to American history and carries a cash award of $300.

Awarding body: American Historical Association, 400 A St., S.E., Washington, D.C. 20003, U.S.A.

F. J. Duparc-prijs

This award is given every three years by the Dutch Ministry of Culture, Recreation and Social Work for study in the field of archives. It is a cash award of 2,000 guilders.

Awarding body: Ministerie van Cultuur, Recreatie en Maatschappelijk Werk, Steenvoordelaan 370, Rijswijk (ZH), The Netherlands.

Frans du Toit-medalje vir bedryfsleiding *(Frans du Toit Medal for Business Management)*

This prize was established in 1961 by the South African Academy for Science and Arts, and is named after Dr. F. J. du Toit (1897–1961), leader of industry and Academy member. It was formerly a cash prize, donated by Shell (S.A.); since 1969 it has been a gold medal inscribed with the image of Dr. du Toit. In selecting the prize-winner the following criteria are used: his creative contribution to South African industrial life; his continued development over a long period in the area to which he has devoted himself; his leadership in particular fields and the inspiration he has given to further develop those fields. The prize is intended to crown a life's work and can only be awarded to any person once. Since 1975 it has been awarded every three years.

Awarding body: Suid-Afrikaanse Akademie vir Wetenskap en Kuns, Posbus 538, Pretoria 0001, South Africa.

Recipients include: Dr. J. A. Hurter (1970); Dr. A. D. Wassenaar (1971); Prof. S. P. du T. Viljoen (1972); Dr. W. B. Coetzer (1973); Dr. F. C. J. Cronjé (1975).

Dutton Animal Book Award

This annual award, established in 1962 by E. P. Dutton & Co., is the largest in this field offered by a publisher for a work of adult fiction or nonfiction relating to animals. Dutton guarantee a minimum of $15,000 as an advance against all earnings to the author of the winning manuscript. Entries are judged by the editors of E. P. Dutton & Co. Both American and overseas authors are eligible, but entries must be submitted in English. Books written primarily for children are ineligible, as are works previously published in book form in the U.S.A., and those less than 35,000 words in length.

Awarding body: E. P. Dutton & Co., Inc., 201 Park Ave. South, New York, N.Y. 10003, U.S.A.

Recipients include: Robert Murphy (*The Pond*, 1964); Faith McNulty (*The Whooping Crane*, 1966); Daniel P. Mannix (*The Fox and the Hound*, 1967); Sterling North (*The Wolfling*, 1969); Dayton O. Hyde (*Strange Companion*, 1975).

Philip and Florence Dworsky Prize for Design

A prize of I£3,000 is awarded annually at the International Council meetings of the Israel Museum for excellence in the field of design.

Awarding body: The Israel Museum, P.O.B. 1299, Jerusalem 91000, Israel.

Recipients include: Peret Co.; Amiram Steinberg and Snapir Co.; Israel Digitronics Ltd.

Dwyer Memorial Lectureship

Founded in 1962 by the University of New South Wales Chemical Society, the lectureship is named after Francis Patrick Dwyer (1910–62) in recognition of his contributions in the field of coordination chemistry. The lecture is given irregularly, at the discretion of the Dwyer Memorial Committee, and the lecturer receives a medal and honorarium.

Awarding body: University of New South Wales Chemical Society, Kensington, N.S.W. 2033, Australia.

Recipients include: H. Taube (1973); G. Schwarzenbach (1975); Fred Basolo (1976); G. Wilkinson (1977); L. Sacconi (1977).

E

Eadie Medal

Awarded annually in recognition of major contributions to any field of engineering or applied science, the prize consists of a silver medal and C$1,000. It is open to Canadian citizens or persons who have been resident in Canada for the preceding five years. The award was established by Bell Canada in appreciation of its past president, Thomas Wardrope Eadie, and in recognition of the increasingly important role of applied science to the standard of life in Canada.

Awarding body: The Royal Society of Canada, 395 Wellington, Ottawa, Ont. K1A 0N4, Canada.

Recipients include: Marshall Kulka (1975); John W. Hilborn (1976).

Earl Grey Memorial Lecture

Founded in 1918 at the University of Newcastle upon Tyne, the lecture is in memory of Albert, Fourth Earl Grey (1851–1917), who was President of Armstrong College from 1911 to 1917. The lecture is delivered annually on some subject of educational or social importance, and is subsequently published.

Awarding body: University of Newcastle upon Tyne, 6 Kensington Terrace, Newcastle upon Tyne, NE1 7RU, England.

Lecturers include: R. W. Southern (Pres., St. John's Coll., Oxford, 1973); Prof. Sir Michael Swann (Principal and Vice-Chancellor, Edinburgh Univ., 1974); Sir Frederick Dainton (Chairman, Univ. Grants Cttee., 1975); A. W. Merrison (Vice-Chancellor, Bristol Univ., 1976); Roy Shaw (Sec.-Gen., Arts Council of Great Britain, 1977).

Eastman Kodak Gold Medal Award

Established in 1966 by the Society of Motion Picture and Television Engineers, the medal is awarded annually in recognition of outstanding contributions which lead to new or unique educational programmes utilizing motion pictures, television, high-speed and instrumentation photography or other photographic sciences.

Awarding body: Society of Motion Picture and Television Engineers, 862 Scarsdale Ave., Scarsdale, N.Y. 10583, U.S.A.

Ebert Prize

This prize was established in 1873 by the retiring President of the American Pharmaceutical Association, Albert E. Ebert. The prize is awarded each year to the author (and co-authors) of the best original research paper published in the *Journal of Pharmaceutical Sciences* during the previous year. The author receives a medal and certificate while the co-author(s) receives an honourable mention certificate.

Awarding body: American Pharmaceutical Association, 2215 Constitution Ave., N.W., Washington, D.C. 20037, U.S.A.

Recipients include: Kenneth B. Bischoff with Robert L. Dedrick, Daniel S. Zaharko and James A. Longstreth (1972); Gordon L. Flynn with Samuel Yalkowsky (1973); Jacob L. Varsano with Seymour G. Gilbert (1974); Gordon L. Amidon with Samuel Yalkowsky (1975); J. T. Carstensen with Pakdee Pothisiri (1976).

Eckersberg Medal

The medal was established in 1883 by the Danish Academy of Fine Arts in memory of Christoffer Vilhelm Eckersberg (1783–1853), the artist and sometime president of the Academy. A medal is awarded annually to honour an achievement of high artistic value in the free arts or architectural art. Recipients must be of Danish nationality save in exceptional cases.

Awarding body: Akademiet for de skønne Kunster, Akademiraadet, Kgs. Nytorv 1, 1050 Copenhagen K, Denmark.

Edgar Gentilli Prize

The annual award of £100, established by Mr. and Mrs. Gilbert Edgar, is made in recognition of original work on the cause, nature, recognition and treatment of any form of cancer of the female genital tract, including chorion carcinoma. Candidature is not restricted to Fellows and Members of the Royal College of Obstetricians and Gynaecologists. Candidates should submit results of their researches in the form of a previously unpublished essay or article in English. It is a condition of the award that the successful essay shall remain the property of the College.

Awarding body: Royal College of Obstetricians and Gynaecologists, 27 Sussex Place, Regent's Park, London NW1 4RG, England.

Recipients include: Dr. M. Y. Dawood, Dr. E. S. Teoh (jointly, 1974); A. Singer (1975); L. Levin, C. Hudson (jointly, 1977).

Howard K. Edwards Award

Awarded every two years in May, this prize is in memory of Howard K. Edwards, M.D. It is given for outstanding achievement in the practice of clinical aviation medicine pertaining to professional airline pilots. It is sponsored by the Aviation Insurance Agency, and consists of $1,000 and a certificate.

Awarding body: Aerospace Medical Association, Washington National Airport, Washington, D.C. 20001, U.S.A.

Recipients include: Ian Anderson (1974); Eugene Lafontaine (1976).

Joris Eeckhoutprijs

The prize was established in 1937 by the Belgian Royal Academy of Dutch Language and Literature in honour of Joris Eeckhout (1887–1951), Flemish author and priest. An award of 15,000 Belgian francs is made every two years for the best literary essay about an author, written in Dutch (minimum 100 pages). Recipients must be Belgian nationals.

Awarding body: Koninklijke Academie voor Nederlandse Taal- en Letterkunde, Koningstraat 18, B-9000 Ghent, Belgium.

Recipients include: Dr. Lieven Rens ('Het Priester-Koning-conflict in Vondels Drama', 1965); Dr. Louis Gillet ('Jan Greshoff, zijn poëzie en poëtiek', 1969); Prof. Dr. Marcel Janssens ('Max Havelaar, de held van lebak', 1971); Prof. Dr. M. Rutten ('De "interludiën" van Karel van de Woestijne', 1973); Dr. J. van Schoor ('Herman Teirlinck en het toneel', 1975).

Egede medaljen

This medal is awarded occasionally by the Royal Danish Geographical Society. It was established in 1916 in memory of the Revd. Hans Poulsen Egede (1686–1758) who discovered the Norsemen in Greenland in 1721 and became a missionary among the Eskimos. The award is given to outstanding scientists for geographical research in the Arctic.

Awarding body: Det Kongelige Danske Geografiske Selskab, Haraldsgade 68, DK-2100 Copenhagen Ø, Denmark.

Recipients include: Prof. dr. W. Dansgaard (studies of the Greenland icecap in relation to climatic fluctuations, 1971); B. Fristrup (glaciological studies in Greenland, Pearyland and EGIG (*Expédition glaciologique au Groenland*), 1971); Dir. K. Ellitsgaard-Rasmussen (expedition to Pearyland, Dir. of Geological Survey of Greenland, 1976); Jørgen Meldgaard (expeditions to Greenland and N.W. territories; discovered the paleo-Eskimo culture Sarqaq in West Greenland, 1976).

Sir Alfred Egerton Medal

Established in 1958 by the Combustion Institute, this biennial award is given for distinguished, continuing and encouraging contributions to the field of combustion. It is presented at the Institute's International Symposium.

Awarding body: The Combustion Institute, 986 Union Trust Bldg., Pittsburgh, Pa. 15219, U.S.A.

Recipients include: Dr. T. M. Sugden (U.K., 1976).

Ehrenring der Stadt Salzburg (*City of Salzburg Ring of Honour*)

This gold ring was established in 1950 to honour outstanding achievements of significance to Salzburg. It is given in one of two forms: the *Paracelsusring* for scientific achievements (commemorating Theophrastus Paracelsus (1493–1541), the Swiss alchemist and father of hermetic medicine); or the *Wappenring* (heraldic ring) for achievements in the arts (excluding music, for which there is a separate award – see *Medaille der Mozartstadt Salzburg*). The awards are made irregularly, and at any one time neither ring may be held by more than ten people.

Awarding body: Landeshauptstadt Salzburg, A-5024 Salzburg, Austria.

Recipients include: Friedrich Welz (Wappenring, 1968); Friedrich Gehmacher (Wappenring, 1976); Dr. Kurt Goldammer (Paracelsusring, 1976).

Ehrenring der Wiener Beethoven Gesellschaft (*Vienna Beethoven Society Ring of Honour*)

This award, a gold ring, was instituted in 1959 by the Vienna Beethoven Society and is given for services to the interpretation of the music of Beethoven.

Awarding body: Wiener Beethoven Gesellschaft, 1190 Vienna, Probusgasse 6, Austria.

Recipients include: Dr. Volkmar Andreae; Prof. Elly Ney.

Paul-Ehrlich-Ludwig-Darmstaedter-Preis

The Paul Ehrlich Foundation was established in 1929 by Frau Hedwig Ehrlich in memory of her husband (1854–1915), the Nobel prize-winning pioneer of modern chemotherapy. In 1952 the prize instituted in his honour was combined with the *Ludwig Darmstaedter Preis*, which commemorates Paul Ehrlich's friend, a notable chemist. Awards are made annually for outstanding achievements in such fields as chemotherapy, bacteriology, immunology, haematology and cancer research. The principal prize is awarded in even-dated years, and consists of a gold medal and cash prize of DM50,000. In odd-dated years subsidiary awards are made, between two and four in number, and preferably to younger scientists. Prizewinners receive a silver medal and share a further DM50,000. The West German Ministry for Public Health is responsible for these cash awards.

Awarding body: Paul Ehrlich-Stiftung, c/o Vereinigung von Freunden und Förderern der Johann Wolfgang Goethe-Universität Frankfurt am Main e.V., 6000 Frankfurt am Main, Frauenlobstr. 8, Federal Republic of Germany.

Recipients include: Prof. Dr. Georges Barski, Prof. Dr. Boris Ephrussi (France, 1976); Prof. Dr. T. Caspersson (Sweden), Prof. Dr. J. B. Gurdon (U.K.), 1977.

Eichendorff-Medaille

A medal and certificate are awarded for research on Joseph von Eichendorff, his work and his time; for research on the German romantics; or for any activity of distinction connected with Eichendorff.

The award was created in 1974 by the Eichendorff Society and commemorates Joseph von Eichendorff (1788–1857), one of the most important German romantic poets. It is presented to two people on the occasion of the Society's General Meeting. Researchers, writers, artists, as well as patrons and others who are of service to the poetic heritage and the Society itself, are eligible.

Awarding body: Eichendorff-Gesellschaft, Schönleinstr. 3, Postfach 55 03, D-8700 Würzburg 1, Federal Republic of Germany.

Recipients: Prof. Oskar Seidlin (literary historian, Indiana Univ., U.S.A., 1974); Karl Schodrock (Hon. Pres. of the Eichendorff Society, 1974); Prof. Paul Stöcklein (literary historian, Univs. of Framkfurt am Main and Salzburg, 1976); Heinrich G. Merkel (publisher, 1976).

Alfred Einstein Award

This award is presented to a young scholar for the best article on a musicological subject published in the preceding year. It was established in 1967 in memory of Alfred Einstein (1880–1952), the renowned musicologist, editor, teacher and critic, and former member of the American Musicological Society. The award is made annually and consists of a cash prize of U.S.$400 given by Eva H. Einstein. Only U.S. or Canadian nationals under 35 are eligible.

Awarding body: American Musicological Society.

Recipients include: Sarah Fuller ('Hidden Polyphony – a Reappraisal', 1972); Rebecca A. Baltzer ('Thirteenth-Century Illuminated Miniatures and the Date of the Florence Manuscript', 1973); Lawrence F. Bernstein ('*La Courone et fleur des chansons a troys:* A Mirror of the French Chanson in Italy in the Years between Ottaviano Petrucci and Antonio Gardano', 1974); Eugene K. Wolf and Jean K. Wolf ('A Newly Identified Complex of Manuscripts from Mannheim', 1975); Craig Wright ('Dufay at Cambrai: Discoveries and Revisions', 1976).

Signe Ekblad-Eldh Prize

This prize is given by the Swedish Academy for prose or poetry. It was endowed in 1960 by Signe Ekblad-Eldh, and is given annually to a Swedish writer. It is a monetary prize (at present 25,000 Swedish kronor) and it cannot be applied for.

Awarding body: The Swedish Academy, Börshuset, Källargränd 4, S-111 29 Stockholm, Sweden.

Electrotechnical Award

This award is presented annually by the Hungarian Electrotechnical Association to honour a career of outstanding achievement of national importance in the field of applied heavy-current electrical engineering. The award consists of a medal and cash prize of 10,000 forints, and is made to members of the Association only. It was established in 1969.

Awarding body: Magyar Elektrotechnikai Egyesület, 1055 Budapest, Kossuth Lajos tér 6–8, Hungary.

Recipients include: Pál Gergely (1972); Dr. Endre Szepesi (1973); Dr. János Eisler (1974); Sándor Szepessy (1974); Dr. Károly Karsay (1975).

Ida and George Eliot Prize Essay Award

This prize of $100 is awarded for the essay published in any journal during the past year which, in the opinion of the American Medical Library Association, has done most to further medical librarianship.

Awarding body: Medical Library Association, 919 North Michigan Ave., Chicago, Ill. 60611, U.S.A.

Phillip Ellman Lecture

A lecturer is appointed every three years to lecture on some aspect of the preventive and curative treatment of diseases of the chest or of the rheumatic diseases. He receives an honorarium.

Awarding body: Royal Society of Medicine, 1 Wimpole St., London W1M 8AE, England.

Conrad A. Elvehjem Award for Public Service in Nutrition

This award, presented annually by the American Institute of Nutrition, was established by the WARF Institute, Inc., and is bestowed in recognition of specific and distinguished service to the public through the science of nutrition. It is intended primarily for work in governmental, industrial, private or international institutions. The award consists of $1,000 and an inscribed scroll.

Awarding body: American Institute of Nutrition. (Nominations to Dr. R. M. Leverton, 3900 16th St., N.W., Apartment 240, Washington, D.C. 20011, U.S.A.)

Recipients include: W. J. Darby (1972); R. M. Leverton (1973); R. W. Engel (1974); R. H. Barnes (1975); N. S. Scrimshaw (1976).

Eminent Artist of the Hungarian People's Republic

Instituted by the Hungarian Presidential Council in 1950, the award is made annually by the Council of Ministers. It is given to an artist with an outstanding record of contributions to the fostering of socialist culture. The distinction carries a pension of 4,000 forints a month.

Awarding body: Council of Ministers, Kossuth Lajos tér 1, Budapest V, Hungary.

Recipients include: Erzsébet Házy (singer, State Opera House), György Kádár (painter), Adél Orosz (dancer, State Opera House), Viktor Róna (dancer, State Opera House), Ferenc Szécsényi (cameraman), 1976.

Eminent Ecologist Award

The award was established in 1954 by the Ecological Society of America. A certificate is awarded annually in recognition of outstanding contributions to the field of ecology.

Awarding body: Ecological Society of America, c/o Secretary, Edward J. Kormondy, The Evergreen State College, Olympia, Wash. 98505, U.S.A.

Recipients include: Paul Sears (1965); A. Redfield (1966); A. E. Emerson (1967); Victor Shelford (1968); Eugene Odam (1974).

Mihai Eminescu Prize

The prize was founded in 1948 by the Romanian Academy. It is awarded for a published volume of poetry, and is named after Mihai Eminescu (1850–89), the famous lyric poet whose work has been translated into over 30 languages. The award is presented annually at a General Assembly of the Academy, and consists of 10,000 lei and a diploma.

Awarding body: Academy of the S.R. of Romania, 125 Calea Victoriei, Bucharest, Romania.

Recipients include: Emil Botta (1971).

George Enescu Prize

Founded by the Romanian Academy in 1956, the prize is for outstanding achievement in musical composition. It is named in memory of George Enescu (1881–1955), the brilliant composer and interpreter (violinist, pianist, conductor) of international fame. The prize consists of 10,000 lei and a diploma, and is awarded retroactively every other year.

Awarding body: Romanian Academy, Calea Victoriei 125, Bucharest, Romania.

Recipients include: Pascal Bentoiu (opera 'Hamlet', 1971).

Engineering Concept of the Year Award

This award is sponsored by the Doerfer Corporation of Cedar Falls, Iowa and administered by the American Society of Agricultural Engineers. It is given annually to recognize the engineer(s) making the most outstanding contribution to the development or advancement of a new engineering concept having a wide or significant impact on the profession or the industries it serves. The concept must have been presented in *Agricultural Engineering, Transactions* of the ASAE or another regular publication of the ASAE. The award consists of an engraved plaque.

Awarding body: American Society of Agricultural Engineers, 2950 Niles Rd., St. Joseph, Mich. 49085, U.S.A.

Carl-Engler-Medaille

The medal is awarded for outstanding services of lasting importance in petroleum science and coal chemistry as well as related aspects of subjects such as drilling technology, geology and geophysics. It consists of a medal and certificate and is normally awarded once a year, to one person. It was established in 1935 by the German Society for Petroleum Science and Coal Chemistry (DGMK) in memory of Prof. Carl Engler (1842–1925), a founder of the modern discipline of petroleum research. The recipient is selected by decision of the Executive and the Advisory Council of the Society.

Awarding body: Deutsche Gesellschaft für Mineralöl- und Kohlechemie e.V., 2000 Hamburg 1, Nordkanalstr. 28, Federal Republic of Germany.

Recipients include: Prof. Friedrich Asinger (Head of Dept. of Chemical Engineering and Petroleum Chemistry, Rhein.-Westfal. Technical Univ., Aachen, 1972); Prof. Alfred Mayer-Gürr (Brigitta and Elwenrath Trade Unions, Hanover, 1973); Prof. Wilhelm Reerink (founder of the Mining Research Inst., Essen-Kray, 1974); Dr. Hans Walter Krekeler (development of modern techniques in manufacture of petroleum byproducts, 1975); Prof. Frederick D. Rossini (U.S.A., fmr. Pres. of World Petroleum Congresses, for contributions to physical chemistry of hydrocarbons and mineral oils, 1976).

English Folk Dance and Song Society Gold Badge

The Society has awarded Gold Badges since 1922. They are awarded at irregular intervals to persons who have made a unique contribution to the art and science of folk song and dance, to those who have rendered distinguished service to the Society, and to those who have made exceptional contributions to the Society's work. When the badge is given for distinguished service to the Society, the award is usually made on the retirement of the recipient or more rarely on some special occasion such as a jubilee.

Awarding body: The English Folk Dance and Song Society, Cecil Sharp House, 2 Regent's Park Road, London NW1 7AY, England.

Recipients include: William Ganiford (1974); A. L. Lloyd (1975); Johnson Ellwood (1976); Kenneth Clark (posthumously, 1976).

Axel Enströmmedalj

The gold medal was established by the Swedish Academy of Engineering Sciences in 1958 in memory of Axel Fredrik Enström (1875–1948), its first President. It is the Academy's highest honour and is therefore only awarded at irregular intervals. It is given to those who, without necessarily being scientists or engineers themselves, have contributed to the successful promotion of technical research and development.

Awarding body: Ingenjörsvetenskapsakademien, Box 5073, S-102 42 Stockholm, Sweden.

Recipients include: University Chancellor Nils Gustav Rosén (for his work with the Nat. Technical Research Council, 1970); Tekn. Dr. Martin Fehrm (contributions to technical and scientific research, 1972).

Environmental Award in Chemical Engineering

This award is made by the Environmental Division of the American Institute of Chemical Engineers to a member of the Institute who has made an outstanding contribution in this field toward the preservation or improvement of Man's natural environment. Criteria for selection include research, discovery or development of new processes or equipment; outstanding contributions to the design, construction, operation or management of environmental protection facilities and enterprises; or distinguished service as a professional engineer, industrial leader or educator. The award, which consists of a certificate and $1,000, is normally made annually, on which occasion the recipient is invited to deliver an address.

Awarding body: Environmental Division of the American Institute of Chemical Engineers, 345 East 47th St., New York, N.Y. 10017, U.S.A.

Eötvös Loránd Memorial Medal

This medal is presented every three years to a member of the Association of Hungarian Geophysicists for achievements in geophysics, which may represent either a single outstanding contribution or a lifetime's work. It was established in 1957 in honour of Prof. Loránd Eötvös (1848–1918), physicist and inventor of the Eötvös balance.

Awarding body: Magyar Geofizikusok Egyesülete, 1368 Budapest VI, Anker köz 1, P.O.B. 240, Hungary.

Recipients include: Prof. L. Egyed; Prof. G. Barta; Dr. R. Renner.

Eötvös Loránd Physical Society Medal

Established in 1968, the medal is awarded to members (including Honorary Members) of the Society who have contributed to the development of physics by outstanding research or teaching activity. The Society is named after Loránd Eötvös (1848–1918), the greatest Hungarian physicist, who was head of the faculty of experimental physics at Budapest University.

Awarding body: Eötvös Loránd Fizikai Társulat, 1061 Budapest VI, Anker-köz 1, Hungary.

Erasmus Prize

Established in 1958 by His Royal Highness, the Prince of the Netherlands, and awarded by the European Cultural Foundation, this annual prize is named after the great Dutch humanist, Erasmus (1467–1536). It is awarded to individuals or institutions who have made a contribution of particular importance to Europe in the cultural, social or social-scientific sphere. The prize is worth 100,000 Dutch guilders. Half the prize money must be spent on the furtherance of suitable projects. Applications and nominations are not accepted.

Awarding body: Stichting Praemium Erasmianum (Erasmus Prize Foundation), Jan van Goyenkade 5, Amsterdam, Netherlands.

Recipients include: Sir Ernst Gombrich (U.K.) and Dr. Willem Sandberg (Netherlands), for contributions to the appreciation of art, 1975; Amnesty International and René David (France), 1976; Werner Kaegi (Switzerland), 1977; *Die Zeit* (Fed. Rep. of Germany) and *Neue Zürcher Zeitung* (Switzerland), for high journalistic standards, 1978.

ERCO Award of the Canadian Society for Chemical Engineering

The award was established in 1970 by the Canadian Society for Chemical Engineering, which is a constituent society of The Chemical Institute of Canada. The award is given annually to a resident of Canada who has made a distinguished contribution in the field of chemical engineering while working in Canada. The award consists of the title 'ERCO Award Winner', $500 cash and an engraved silver medallion provided by ERCO Industries Ltd. It is presented at the Annual Meeting of the Society, and the recipient is invited to give a lecture at the Canadian Chemical Engineering Conference. Nominations, signed by at least three professional members of the Canadian Society for Chemical Engineering, must reach the General Manager of The Chemical Institute of Canada by 1 January of each year, and they remain valid for three years. Nominees must be under the age of 40.

Awarding body: The Chemical Institute of Canada, 151 Slater St., Ottawa, Ont. K1P 5H3, Canada.

Recipients include: N. J. Themelis ('Development of a New Process: a Case History', 1971); I. S. Pasternak ('I Think I Can – I Knew I Could (The Technology Challenge)', 1972); M. Moo-Young ('Food Production from Unconventional Sources', 1973); A. E. Hamielec ('Polymer Reaction Engineering – An Overview', 1974); C. E. Capes ('Basic Studies in Particle Technology and Some Novel Applications', 1975).

Erdös Prize

The prize was established in 1976 with a donation from Professor Paul Erdös. A monetary award of about $1,000 is presented annually for outstanding work by an Israeli mathematician. Preference is given to entrants under the age of 40.

Awarding body: Israel Mathematical Union.

Professor Gunnar Erdtman International Medal for Palynology

The gold medal was established in 1968 to honour Professor Erdtman, Director of the Palynology Laboratory in Sweden, in recognition of his pioneering work in establishing palynology as a science. (Professor Erdtman died in 1974.) The annual award is made to a scientist of any nationality who has made a significant contribution to the growth of palynological knowledge.

Awarding body: Palynological Society of India, National Botanic Gardens, Lucknow, India.

Recipients include: Prof. J. Heslop-Harrison (U.K.); Prof. C. R. Wilson (U.S.A.); Prof. F. P. Jonker (Netherlands); Prof. P. N. Mehra (India); Prof. M. Van Campo (France).

Erkel Ferenc Prize for Musical Composition

Instituted by the Hungarian Council of Ministers in 1953, the prize is awarded by the Minister of Culture. It is given annually to a composer or musicologist for outstanding work. It is an honorary distinction, and is divided into three classes. It is named in honour of Ferenc Erkel (1810–93), the famous pianist and composer, who was orchestra conductor of the National Theatre and the first director and professor of piano at the Academy of Music.

Awarding body: Committee for the Erkel Ferenc Prize, Ministry of Culture, Szalay-utca 10, Budapest V, Hungary.
Recipients include: László Bánki (editor, Hungarian TV), István Kecskeméti (music historian), Antal Kricskovics (choreographer, art director), Hungarian National Dance Ensemble, Bálint Sárosi (musicologist), István Vántus (composer), 1976.

Esso Award

The Royal Society Esso Award for the Conservation of Energy, which consists of a gold medal and a prize of £1,000, was instituted in 1974 following agreement reached between the Royal Society and Esso Petroleum Co. Ltd. for a special award for outstanding contributions to the advancement of science or engineering or technology leading to the more efficient conversion or use of energy.
Awarding body: Royal Society of London, 6 Carlton House Terrace, London SW1Y 5AG, England.
Recipients include: Prof. H. C. Hottel and Prof. Harry Tabor (1975); T. B. Jackson (1976).

Eternit International Prize for Architecture

The purpose of this prize is to select and draw attention to architectural works which are outstanding for their human, functional, aesthetic or technical qualities. It is organized in conjunction with the International Union of Architects, and in consultation with the professional architectural bodies in the participating countries – U.K., Belgium, Netherlands and Luxembourg. Entries are restricted to architects from these countries. The biennial competition is organized in turn by the members of the Eternit Group in each of the four countries. Various prizes (amounting to one million Belgian francs in 1978) are awarded: the two main prizes (250,000 francs each) are for housing developments, and buildings other than dwellings.
Awarding body: Speakers Eternit, Eternit House, 56–70 High St., Putney, London SW15 1SF, England.
Recipients include: Nigel Lane in association with Timothy Young (U.K.), Jean Potvin (Belgium), Andrew Sebire and Kit Allsopp (U.K.), Renato Baldi (Italy), housing (*ex aequo*), 1978; Romano Boico (Italy, Resistenza Museum, Trieste), other buildings, 1978.

Etna-Taormina International Poetry Prize

This is an annual prize of 3,000,000 lire awarded to one Italian and two foreign poets. It was established in 1951 by the Tourist Board of Catania. Those eligible are poets who have published a volume of poetry in the two years preceding the award.
Awarding body: Ente Provinciale per il Turismo Catania, Largo Paisiello 5, 95124 Catania, Italy.
Recipients include: Attilio Bartolucci (Italy), Murilo Mendes (Brazil), 1972; Biagio Marin (Italy), Ghiannis Ritsos (Greece), 1976; Jorge de Sena (Portugal), 1977.

Etoile de Cristal de l'Académie du Cinéma
(*Crystal Star of the Academy of Cinema*)

This is the title given to the six annual prizes awarded by the Academy. They were established in 1955 by Georges Franju and Dominique Johansen, Secretary-General and Directress of the Academy. Prizes are given for the best foreign film (*Prix International*), and the best French film (*Grand Prix*) released in the preceding year, and for the best French actor and actress and the best foreign actor and actress (*Prix d'Interprétation*). Crystal stars made at the Daum glass-works in Nancy are presented to each winner, and the directors of the two best films also receive diplomas. No one may win a prize more than once.
Awarding body: Académie du Cinéma, 13 quai des Grands-Augustins, 75006 Paris, France.
Recipients include: Aguirre, Wrath of God (Werner Herzog, *Prix International*); *India Song* (Marguerite Duras, *Grand Prix*); Jeanne Goupil, Carol Kane, Al Pacino, Patrick Dewaere and Patrick Bouchitey (*Prix d'Interprétation*), 1976.

Europa Nostra Conservation Awards

Europa Nostra, founded in 1963, is an international federation of associations whose aim is to protect Europe's cultural and natural heritage. The awards were established in 1978 to draw attention to the threats to this heritage, and to stimulate interest and action for its conservation. Five silver medals, donated and designed by Franklin Mint Ltd. of London, are given annually for projects which make an outstanding contribution to the conservation and enhancement of Europe's architectural and natural heritage. The medals are accompanied by engraved silver plaques. Ten commended entries receive framed Diplomas of Merit. Submissions from individuals or organizations may be entered in the following categories: restoration of old buildings; new construction in areas of historic or architectural interest; adaptation of old buildings to new uses; modern buildings of distinction; new shop fronts in old quarters; removal of ugly features; floodlighting of buildings, parks, etc.; discreetly sited car parks in areas of beauty; pedestrian areas; urban landscaping in old towns; use of paint to improve the urban scene; action to protect areas of natural beauty against excessive or incongruous development. Projects should have been completed within the previous ten years.
Awarding body: Europa Nostra, 86 Vincent Square, London SW1P 2PG, England.

Europa Prize for Folk Art

This award of DM20,000 was established in 1973 to recognize services towards folk art, particularly dance, music and drama. It is intended chiefly to mark the efforts of amateur groups.
Awarding body: Stiftung FVS, Georgsplatz 10, 2 Hamburg 1, Federal Republic of Germany.
Recipients include: Siamsa Tire theatre group (Ireland), Leksands Spelmanslag folk dance group (Sweden), France Marolt academic folklore group (Yugoslavia), Plana folk song group (Bulgaria),

Alois Senti (Switzerland, folklorist), 1974; Edinburgh Piobaireachd Society (U.K., 1976).

Europa Prize for the Preservation of Historic Monuments

This award was established in 1973 and is worth DM25,000. It is designed to honour outstanding work by European individuals or groups concerned with the preservation of monuments. A gold medal is also awarded, which is principally intended to recognize a community's exemplary care of its architectural heritage.

Awarding body: Stiftung FVS, Georgsplatz 10, 2 Hamburg 1, Federal Republic of Germany.

Recipients include: National Trust for Scotland (U.K., 1976).

Europe Prize

Instituted in 1953 by the Parliamentary Assembly of the Council of Europe, the prize is awarded annually by the Committee on Regional Planning and Local Authorities of the Parliamentary Assembly to the municipality considered to have made outstanding efforts to propagate the idea of European unity. The prize consists of a trophy to be held by the winner for one year, a bronze medal, a parchment, a Council of Europe flag of honour, and a scholarship to be spent on arranging travel in Europe for a young person (or persons) resident in the winning town. A Council of Europe flag of honour is also presented to certain towns which, though not prize-winners, are considered to be deserving of an award. The Europe Prize is officially presented during a 'Europe Day' arranged by the winning town.

Awarding body: Council of Europe, Avenue de l'Europe, 67006 Strasbourg, France.

Recipients include: Würzburg (Fed. Rep. of Germany, 1973); Cesenatico (Italy) and Mâcon (France), 1974; Darmstadt (Fed. Rep. of Germany, 1975); Devon County Council (U.K., 1976).

European Cortina Ulisse Prize

The prize was established in 1949 by the Italian magazine *Ulisse*, in the belief that culture ought to be a common instrument of civilization and not the privilege of a few. It consists of one million lire and is awarded annually for a work of popular science. It is presented in Cortina and the jury consists of representatives of relevant Italian and international organizations. If the winning work is not by an Italian, the jury recommends its translation and publication by an Italian publisher.

Awarding body: Rivista *Ulisse*, Via Po 11, 00198 Rome, Italy.

Recipients include: Max Nicholson (*The Environmental Revolution*, 1971); George Steiner (*Language and Silence*) and Ezio Raimondi (*Tecniche della Critica letteraria*), 1973; Andrew Shonfield (*Europe: Journey to an Unknown Destination*, 1974); Paul Bairoch (*Le Tiers-Monde dans l'Impasse*, 1976).

European Essay Award

The award is given annually for an essay offering a constructive critique of contemporary social problems. The prize of 10,000 Swiss francs was established in 1974 by the Veillon Foundation, in memory of Charles Veillon, a philanthropic supporter of numerous artistic and scientific ventures. Any author or publisher in Europe may submit an entry. The essay must be written in one of the main European languages and must be submitted at least three months before the presentation of the award, which usually takes place in December.

Awarding body: Fondation Veillon, Route de Crissier, 1030-Bussigny, Lausanne, Switzerland.

Recipients include: Prof. Jacques Ellul (France, *Trahison de l'Occident*, 1975); Ernst F. Schumacher (U.K., *Small is Beautiful*, 1976).

James Alfred Ewing Medal

The medal was founded in 1936 in memory of Sir Alfred Ewing (1855–1935), an Honorary Member of the Institution of Civil Engineers. It is given to a person, whether a member of the Institution or not, for specially meritorious contributions to the science of engineering in the field of research. Recommendations are made by the Institution of Civil Engineers, the Institution of Mechanical Engineers, the Royal Institution of Naval Architects, and the Institution of Electrical Engineers.

Awarding body: The Institution of Civil Engineers, Great George St., London SW1P 3AA, England.

Recipients include: Sir Eric Eastwood (contributions to radar, 1976); Sir Christopher Cockerell (contributions to the development of hovercraft, 1977).

F

FIPRESCI Prize

The International Federation of the Cinematographic Press (FIPRESCI) awards a prize each year at the various international film festivals (Oberhausen, Cannes, Cracow, Berlin, Grenoble, Moscow, Locarno, Mannheim, Leipzig) for the artistic quality of a film and its human and social interest. The prize, in the form of a certificate, was established in 1930 by a group of film critics. FIPRESCI consists of 25 national associations of film critics.

Awarding body: Fédération Internationale de la Presse Cinématographique (FIPRESCI), c/o Marcel Martin, 2 rue Léopold Robert, 75014 Paris, France.

Recipients include: Theo Angelopoulos (*O Thiassos*, Cannes, 1975); Akira Kurosawa (*Dersou Ouzala*, Moscow, 1975); Alexander Kluge (*Ferdinand der Starke*, Cannes, 1976); Alain Tanner (*Jonas qui aura 25 ans en l'an 2000*, Locarno, 1976); Wim Wenders (*Im Lauf der Zeit*, Cannes, 1976).

Geoffrey Faber Memorial Prize

Established in 1964 by Faber and Faber Ltd., the prize is in memory of Sir Geoffrey Faber, founder of the publishing company. The prize of £250 is awarded annually, alternately for a volume of verse and for a volume of prose fiction. It may be awarded to any novelist or poet who is (a) not more than 40 years old at the publication of the book, and (b) a citizen of the United Kingdom and Colonies, of any other Commonwealth state, of the Republic of Ireland or of the Republic of South Africa. The ·prize-winning volume must have been published originally in the U.K. during the preceding two years. There are three judges, who are reviewers of poetry or of fiction as the case may be. They are nominated each year by the editors or literary editors of newspapers and magazines which regularly publish such reviews.

Awarding body: Faber & Faber Ltd., 3 Queen Square, London WC1N 3AU, England.

Recipients include: John Fuller (*Cannibals and Missionaries, Epistles to Several Persons*, poetry, 1974); Richard Wright (*In the Middle of a Life*, novel, 1975); Douglas Dunn (*Love or Nothing*, poetry, 1976); Carolyn Slaughter (*The Story of the Weasel*, novel, 1977); David Harsent (*Dreams of the Dead*) and Kit Wright (*The Bear Looked Over the Mountain*), poetry, jointly, 1978.

John K. Fairbank Prize in East Asian History

This award was established in 1968 by the friends of John K. Fairbank, and first presented in 1969. It is awarded in odd-numbered years for an outstanding book on the history of China proper, Vietnam, Chinese Central Asia, Mongolia, Manchuria, Korea, or Japan since 1800. The prize carries a cash award of $500.

Awarding body: American Historical Association, 400 A St., Southeast, Washington, D.C. 20003, U.S.A.

Benjamin F. Fairless Award

This award is made annually by the American Institute of Mining, Metallurgical, and Petroleum Engineers for distinguished achievement in iron and steel production and ferrous metallurgy. Candidates of all nationalities are eligible, provided they are proposed by a member of the Institute and have not previously received an Institute award. The award consists of a copper and silver-finished plaque, and was instituted in 1954 by the U.S. Steel Corporation, in honour of their Chairman, Benjamin F. Fairless.

Awarding body: American Institute of Mining, Metallurgical, and Petroleum Engineers, Inc., 345 East 47th St., New York, N.Y. 10017, U.S.A.

Recipients include: John Hugh Chesters (1973); Theodore F. Olt (1974); Michael Tenenbaum (1975); David S. Holbrook (1976); Edgar B. Speer (1977).

Faraday Medal

The medal was founded in 1922 to commemorate the 50th anniversary of the first ordinary meeting of the Society of Telegraph Engineers (now the Institution of Electrical Engineers). It is given either for notable scientific or industrial achievement in electrical engineering or for conspicuous service rendered to the advancement of electrical science without restriction as regards nationality, country of residence or membership of the institution. The medal is named after Michael Faraday (1791–1867), the famous pioneer in electrical engineering.

Awarding body: Institution of Electrical Engineers, Savoy Place, London WC2R 0BL, England.

Recipients include: G. Millington (theoretical studies of radio-wave propagation, 1974); Prof. J. M. Meek (research on electrical discharges in gases, 1975); Dr. T. O. Paine (leadership of Apollo manned space flight programme, and creative thinking on the technology and future activity of the electrical and electronic industries, 1976); J. B. Adams (contributions to design and construction of high-energy particle accelerators, 1977); Dr. E. Friedlander (work in the field of power transmission and stabilization of power transmission systems, 1978).

Faraday Medal and Lectureship

This award was founded in 1867 to commemorate the name of Michael Faraday, who was elected a Fellow of the Chemical Society in 1842 and who died in 1867. The Faraday Lecture is usually delivered every three years. Lecturers receive a bronze medal and £100.

Awarding body: The Chemical Society, Burlington House, London W1V 0BN, England.

Recipients include: G. Herzberg (1970); Sir Frederick Dainton (1974); M. Eigen (1977).

Eleanor Farjeon Award

Established in 1965 by the Children's Book Circle, the award is in memory of Eleanor Farjeon (1881–1965), the distinguished children's writer. A cash prize of £50 and an appropriate gift are awarded annually for distinguished services in the field of children's books. The award may be made to anyone working with or for children through books (e.g. librarians, teachers, authors, artists, publishers, reviewers, television producers, booksellers).

Awarding body: The Children's Book Circle, England.

Recipients include: Leila Berg (1973); Naomi Lewis (1974); Joyce and Court Oldmeadow (1975); Elaine Moss (1976); Peter Kennerley (1977).

Prudence Farmer Poetry Prize

The prize was established in 1975 under the terms of Prudence Farmer's will. £100 is awarded annually for the best poem published in English in the *New Statesman* during the preceding twelve months.

Awarding body: The Statesman and Nation Publishing Co. Ltd., Great Turnstile, London WC1V 7HJ, England.

Recipients: John Fuller (*Wild Raspberries*) and Laurence Lerner (*Raspberries*), jointly, 1975; Roy Fuller (*Crisis*), 1976.

Federation of American Societies for Experimental Biology Award for Research in the Life Sciences

This award, which is sponsored by the 3M Co., was established in 1976. It is given for research studies which have significantly contributed to the health and welfare of mankind. The recipient must be a member of one of FASEB's constituent societies, and nominated by two other members. The award is given annually, and consists of a $5,000 cash prize and a further $10,000 to the recipient's parent institution to assist his research and travel.

Awarding body: Federation of American Societies for Experimental Biology, 9650 Rockville Pike, Bethesda, Md. 20014, U.S.A.

Recipients include: Bruce N. Ames, Ph.D. (development of tests for chemical carcinogenesis, 1976).

Federation of Danish Architects Medal of Honour

This silver or silver gilt medal was established in 1932 at the general meeting of the Federation. It is awarded irregularly for special merit in the field of the Federation's work, or as a special honour. It is given to members of DAL/AA or members of similar institutions.

Awarding body: Danske Arkitekters Landsforbund/Akademisk Arkitektforening, 66 Bredgade, 1260 Copenhagen K, Denmark.

Recipients include: Kenzo Tange (Japan, 1968); Kaj Gottlob (Denmark, 1975); Edmund Hansen (Denmark, 1976); Vridsløselille Andelsboligforening (Denmark, 1976); Albertslund County (Denmark, 1976).

Feldberg-Preis

This award, established in 1960 by Professor Wilhelm Feldberg, is designed to encourage contact between eminent German and English scientists within the sphere of experimental medical research, particularly in physiology and related fields, by the institution of exchange lectures. Candidates are selected from nominations by the awarding body only. The award is made annually, and consists of DM8,000.

Awarding body: Feldberg Foundation, Federal Republic of Germany.

Recipients include: Prof. W. A. H. Rushton (1967); Prof. H. T. Witt (1970); Prof. H. Harris (1972); Prof. P. Karlson (1974); Prof. H. G. Wittmann (1975).

Fellowship of The Academy of American Poets

The Academy was founded in 1934 to assist the careers of American poets; since 1946 annual Fellowship awards have been made for distinguished poetic achievement. A trust fund was established for this purpose, and at present the amount of each award is $10,000.

Awarding body: The Academy of American Poets, 1078 Madison Ave., New York, N.Y. 10028, U.S.A.

Recipients include: James Wright (1971); W. D. Snodgrass (1972); W. S. Merwin (1973); Léonie Adams (1974); Robert Hayden (1975).

Fennia Gold Medal

This award was founded by the Geographical Society of Finland in 1941. It is given to explorers and scientists of any nationality for expeditions and studies of importance in the field of Finnish geographical research. It is awarded irregularly on special occasions. There is also a Fennia Silver Medal, founded in 1962, for important geographical studies or valuable work for the Society.

Awarding body: Geographical Society of Finland, Snellmanink. 9–11, 00170 Helsinki 17, Finland.

Recipients include: Prof. Väinö Auer; Prof. Gabriel Granö; Baron Carl Gustav Mannerheim.

Enrico Fermi Award

This international award, established in 1956, is given not more frequently than once a year for exceptional and outstanding scientific and technical achievements in the development, use, or control of atomic energy. It is not awarded for a single prominent contribution but for a career marked by such achievements. The prize consists of $25,000, a citation and a gold medal. In the event that the award is granted to more than one individual, the recipients share $50,000. The award is made with the approval of the President of the U.S.A. Nominations are invited from members of the National Academy of Sciences, officers of scientific and technical societies and other individuals with special knowledge and competence, including heads of foreign government agencies with scientific missions. The award is named after Enrico Fermi (1901–54), the famous Italian physicist and Nobel prize-winner.

Awarding body: Energy Research and Development Administration, 20 Massachusetts Ave., N.W., Washington, D.C. 20545, U.S.A.

Recipients include: Dr. Shields Warren and Dr. Stafford L. Warren (U.S.A., early development of atomic energy to assure the protection of man and the environment, and establishment of a biomedical research programme, 1972); Dr. Manson Benedict (U.S.A., leadership in the development of the nation's first gaseous diffusion plant, 1972); Dr. William L. Russell (U.S.A., evaluation of genetic effects of radiation in mammals, 1976).

Bernhard Eduard Fernow Award

This annual award of a medal is presented in alternate years by the American Forestry Association and the German Forestry Association for exceptional contributions in the field of international forestry and assistance to other countries. Established in 1965, it commemorates Bernhard Eduard Fernow's outstanding work in this field.

Awarding body: The American Forestry Association, 1319 18th St., N.W., Washington, D.C. 20036, U.S.A., and Deutscher Forstverein, 771 Donaueschingen, Josefstrasse 10, Federal Republic of Germany.

Recipients include: Dr. Frank H. Wadsworth (U.S.A., 1973); Dr. Herbert Hesmer (Fed. Rep. of Germany, 1974); Dr. Douglas R. Redmond (Canada, 1975); Prof. Jvar Samset (Norway, 1976); Flavio Bazan (Peru, 1977).

Ferrier Lecture

At the request of the contributors to a Fund to perpetuate the memory of Sir David Ferrier and his pioneer work on the functions of the brain, the Royal Society in 1928 accepted the sum of £1,000 in trust for the institution of a David Ferrier lecture which is given triennially on a subject related to the advancement of natural knowledge on the structure and function of the nervous system. The lecturer's gift is £150.

Awarding body: Royal Society of London, 6 Carlton House Terrace, London SW1Y 5AG, England.

Lecturers include: D. H. Hubel and T. N. Wiesel ('The Function and Architecture of the Visual Cortex', 1971); Prof. W. S. Feldberg ('Body Temperature and Fever: Changes in our Views during the last Decade', 1974).

Festival of the Americas

This festival, established in 1967 by J. Hunter Todd, its current president and director, is held annually. Various awards are made for outstanding creative excellence in motion pictures; they consist of 'Gold Venus' and 'Silver Venus' statuettes, and gold, silver and bronze medals, equipment grants and cash awards of $1,000. Films must have been completed or released in the year of the festival or the previous year.

Awarding body: Festival of the Americas, Box 7789, St. Thomas, U.S. Virgin Islands 00801.

Recipients include: John Frankenheimer; Joshua Logan; Carl Foreman; William Wyler; Samuel Bronston.

Festival de Teatro Nacional (*National Drama Festival*)

The festival was established in 1971, with the intention of encouraging social and cultural events throughout Colombia. It is held irregularly, and medals are awarded in three categories: classical; regional customs; and modern.

Awarding body: Controlaría General de la República, Bogotá, Colombia.

Lion-Feuchtwanger-Preis

This prize was established by Marta Feuchtwanger in 1971 in memory of Lion Feuchtwanger (1884–1956), the German dramatist and novelist. The award is made annually either to an individual or to a group of writers in recognition of literary work which deals with the problems of history in the progressive and humanistic spirit of Feuchtwanger. The prize consists of a cash award and a certificate. (Alternatively the prize can be given in the form of a grant to young writers who have published their first works, to enable them to undertake further education of some sort.) German-speaking authors of prose and dramatic works in the field of theatre, film or television, are eligible.

Awarding body: Akademie der Künste der D.D.R., 104 Berlin, Hermann-Matern-Strasse 58/59, German Democratic Republic.

Recipients include: Hedda Zinner (1973); Dr. Christa Johannsen (1974); Prof. Dr. Heinz Kamnitzer (1975); Rosemarie Schuder (1976); Waldtraut Lewin (1978).

Adolf-Fick-Preis

This award is made every five years by the Würzburg Society for Physical Medicine for outstanding publications in the field of physiology, or a related area. Preference is given to works on physical physiology. The researcher's mother tongue must be German. The award consists of a silver commemorative coin and cash prize of DM1,000. It was instituted by Drs. Friedrich and Rudolf Fick in 1928, to commemorate the centenary of the birth of Dr. Adolf Fick (1829–1901), sometime Professor of Physiology at Würzburg.

Awarding body: Physikalisch-medizinische Gesellschaft Würzburg, 8700 Würzburg, Röntgenring 9, Federal Republic of Germany.

David E. Finley Award

Formerly known as the David E. Finley Citation, this award was established in 1968 by the U.S. National Trust in honour of David E. Finley, founder and first Chairman of the National Trust and first Director of the National Gallery of Art. The award is given annually for outstanding achievement, specifically in the preservation, restoration and interpretation of sites, buildings, architecture, districts and objects significant in American history and culture at the regional level. It may be given to an organization, an individual or several entities jointly, and consists of a trophy or a scroll or both.

Awarding body: The National Trust for Historic Preservation, 740–748 Jackson Place, N.W., Washington, D.C. 20006, U.S.A.

Recipients include: Pittsburgh History and Landmarks Foundation and Old Santa Fe Asscn. (1972); Bishop Hill Heritage Asscn., Ill., and Dr. Pearl Chase, Calif. (1973); Community Design Commission, Medina, Ohio, and Utah Heritage Foundation (1975); Junior League of Louisville, Ky., and New Mexico and Colorado Railroad Authority (1976).

Finsen Award

This award is made every four years to scientists or groups of scientists who are distinguished for their research in photobiology or in the pure and applied sciences directly related to photobiology. The award consists of a gold medal, although monetary prizes and grants may also be awarded. It was established in 1937 by the Comité International de la Lumière, in honour and memory of Niels Finsen (1860–1904) who received the Nobel Prize in Medicine and Physiology in 1903 for his work on the healing and damaging effects of sunlight on human skin.

Awarding body: Niels Finsen Foundation of the International Photobiology Association (AIP), Secretary-General Prof. L. O. Björn, Dept. of Plant Physiology, University of Lund, Fack S-220-07 Lund, Sweden.

Recipients include: Th. Förster (Fed. Rep. of Germany), R. Hill (U.K.), R. Latarjet (France), 1972; H. F. Blum (U.S.A.), S. B. Hendricks (U.S.A.), D. Shugar (Poland), 1976.

Emil-Fischer-Medaille

The medal was established by Carl Duisberg in 1912, in celebration of the 60th birthday of Emil Fischer (1852–1919), honorary member of the Association of German Chemists, several times president of the German Chemical Society and winner of the Nobel Prize for Chemistry in 1902. The award was originally administered by the Association of German Chemists, which in 1912 created the Carl Duisberg Foundation for the award of both this medal and the Adolf von Baeyer Commemorative Medal (*q.v.*). The Society of German Chemists took over the award in 1950. The gold medal and a sum of money are awarded to the German chemist who is considered to have published during the preceding year the best work in the field of organic chemistry (particularly on experimental colour or pharmaceutical chemistry), or who has rendered particular service to the chemical industry by the production of organic or pharmaceutical preparations, important dyestuffs, perfumes, etc.

Awarding body: Gesellschaft Deutscher Chemiker, 6000 Frankfurt (Main) 90, Carl Bosch-Haus, Varrentrappstr. 40–42, Federal Republic of Germany.

Recipients include: Prof. Hellmut Bredereck (1966); Prof. Arthur Lüttringhaus (1967); Prof. Theodor Wieland (1969); Prof. Günther Wilke (1970); Prof. Emmanuel Vogel (1975).

Fisher Scientific Lecture Award

Established in 1968 by The Chemical Institute of Canada, the award is sponsored by the Fisher Scientific Company Ltd. It is given annually to a scientist resident in Canada who has made a distinguished contribution, while working in Canada, in the field of analytical chemistry. Nominations are made by members of the Institute. The recipient is given the title 'Fisher Scientific Lecturer', $500 cash and a framed scroll. The presentation is made at the Annual Conference of The Chemical Institute of Canada, to which the recipient's travelling expenses may be provided. The award lecture must be delivered either at the Annual Conference or at the Annual Symposium. The recipient of the Fisher Scientific Lecture Award may not receive the Noranda Lecture Award (*q.v.*) of the same year.

Awarding body: The Chemical Institute of Canada, 151 Slater St., Ottawa, Ont. K1P 5H3, Canada.

Recipients include: R. N. Jones ('Data Banking for Science and Technology', 1971); D. E. Ryan ('Trace Analysis by Solution Spectroscopy', 1972); W. A. E. McBryde ('Solution Chemistry – An Analyst's Playground', 1973); G. C. B. Cave ('Solvates and Aggregates of Solvent-Extraction Systems', 1974); S. Barabas ('Water Quality – A Global Problem of Many Common Denominators', 1975).

Flavelle Medal

The medal is awarded every two years, if there is a suitable candidate, for an outstanding contribution to biological science during the preceding ten years or for significant additions to a previous outstanding contribution to biological science. The prize takes the form of a gold medal and C$1,000.

Canadian citizens or persons who have been Canadian residents for five years are eligible. The award was endowed by Sir Joseph Wesley Flavelle (1858–1939), a financier and businessman.

Awarding body: The Royal Society of Canada, 395 Wellington, Ottawa, Ont. K1A 0N4, Canada.

Recipients include: W. E. Ricker (1970); D. Harold Copp (1972); J. H. Quastel (1974); Michael Shaw (1976); Louis Siminovitch (1978).

Carl Flesch International Violin Competition

The first Carl Flesch Medal was awarded in 1945 for 'excellence in violin playing' as a result of a competition held at the Guildhall School of Music and Drama and open to violinists of any nationality. The award of the medal was instituted by Professor Max Rostal, the late Edric Cundell and Mr. C. F. Flesch, to commemorate the work and residence in London during the 1930s of the latter's father, Carl Flesch, one of the major figures in the development of violin playing and teaching in the 20th century. The Carl Flesch International Violin Competition developed from the award of this medal and has been held in its present form biennially since 1968. Six prizes are awarded at each competition. The first prize consists of £1,250, the Carl Flesch medal, a certificate and concert engagements. The other prizes are £1,000, £750, £400, £250 and £100 respectively, donated by various organizations and individuals. In addition special prizes are awarded, such as the audience prize, for which the winner is chosen by members of the public. The competition is open to violinists of any nationality under the age of 30. All stages of the competition are held in public.

Awarding body: City Arts Trust, c/o Corporation of London, Guildhall, London EC2P 2EJ, England.

Recipients of First Prize include: Stoika Milanova (Bulgaria, 1970); Csaba Erdelyi (Hungary, 1972); Mincho Minchev (Bulgaria, 1974); Dora Schwarzberg (Israel, 1976); Eugene Sarbu (Romania, 1978).

Ernest Fletcher Memorial Lecture

A lecturer is appointed every three years to lecture upon a rheumatological subject. He receives an honorarium.

Awarding body: The Royal Society of Medicine, 1 Wimpole St., London W1M 8AE, England.

Flight Safety Foundation – Aviation Week & Space Technology/Distinguished Service Award

The award was established in 1949 by *Aviation Week & Space Technology Magazine* and is administered by the Flight Safety Foundation. The award is made annually for distinguished service in achieving safer utilization of aircraft and consists of a certificate stating the specific achievement for which the award is made, accompanied by a plaque.

Awarding body: Flight Safety Foundation Inc., 1800 North Kent St., Arlington, Va. 22209, U.S.A.

Recipients include: Ralph Nelson (AOPA, 1973); General Aviation Manufacturers Asscn. and its Safe Pilot Program (1974); George Wansbeek (KLM, 1975); Joseph Tymczyszyn (FAA, 1976).

Flight Safety Foundation – Publications Award

Established in 1968, a $100 cash honorarium and a certificate are awarded annually to recognize significant contributions to aviation safety through outstanding articles, books or other communication media.

Awarding body: Flight Safety Foundation Inc., 1800 North Kent St., Arlington, Va. 22209, U.S.A.

Recipients include: Douglas Aircraft Co., McDonnel Douglas Corpn. and *Flight International* (1974); Richard Witkin (*New York Times*) and *Shell Aviation News* (1975); NTSB and *Airwork* (1976).

Matthew Flinders Lecture

Established in 1956 by the Australian Academy of Science, the lecture takes its name from Matthew Flinders (1774–1814), the navigator, who explored the coast of Australia; the title identifies the lecture with the early scientific work carried out in Australia. The Council of the Academy chooses as lecturer the scientist deemed most worthy of such an honour. He receives a bronze medal and an honorarium of A$200. The lecture is usually biennial, and alternates with the Burnet Lecture (*q.v.*). It is delivered at the AGM of the Academy, normally held in April.

Awarding body: Australian Academy of Science, P.O.B. 783, Canberra City, A.C.T. 2601, Australia.

Recipients include: K. E. Bullen (1969); A. J. Birch (1972); J. P. Wild (1974); C. H. B. Priestley (1976); A. E. Ringwood (1978).

Flintoff Medal and Prize

This award originated from a bequest to the Chemical Society by the late Mr. Robert Flintoff. A silver medal and a monetary prize of £100 are awarded usually every three years to the Fellow of the Society of either sex who has made the most meritorious contribution to the knowledge of the relations between chemistry and botany.

Awarding body: The Chemical Society, Burlington House, London W1V 0BN, England.

Recipients include: R. L. Wain (1969); A. J. Birch (1972); A. R. Battersby (1975).

John Florio Prize (Contemporary)

This cash award (£400 in 1977) is made annually in the autumn for the best translation of a 20th-century Italian literary work published in the U.K. by a British publisher during the previous year. Entries are submitted by publishers. The award was established in 1963 by G. D. Astley, Secretary of the Association, under the auspices of the Italian Institute and the British Italian Society.

Awarding body: The Translators Association, 84 Drayton Gardens, London SW10 9SD, England.

Recipients include: Isabel Quigly (*The Transfer* by Silvano Ceccherini, 1967); Frances Frenay (*Paese d'Ombre* by Giuseppe Dessi, 1976); Ruth Feldman and Brian Swann (*Shema, the Collected Poems of Primo Levi*, 1977).

Flückiger-Medaille/Médaille d'Or Flückiger

The Flückiger Foundation and Medal were established in 1892 with contributions from societies and individuals in 18 countries, for the advancement of the science of pharmacy, and to mark the retirement of Dr. Friedrich August Flückiger (1828–94), President of the Swiss Association of Pharmacists, professor at the Pharmaceutical Institute at Strasbourg, and considered the father of pharmacognosy. A gold medal is awarded every five years to distinguished scientists of any nationality in the field of pharmacy. It is presented alternately by the German Pharmacists' Representative Group (ABDA) and the Swiss Association of Pharmacists at their respective general meetings. The interest on the capital of the Foundation is used for research grants and bursaries; the Foundation is directed by a board of German and Swiss membership.

Awarding bodies: Arbeitsgemeinschaft der Berufsvertretungen Deutscher Apotheker (ABDA), 6000 Frankfurt am Main, Beethovenplatz 1, Federal Republic of Germany; Société Suisse de Pharmacie, Marktgasse 52, 3011 Berne, Switzerland.

Recipients include: Prof. Karl Winterfeld (Fed. Rep. of Germany, 1962); Prof. Karl Stainier (Belgium, 1966); Prof. Egon Stahl (Fed. Rep. of Germany, 1971); Prof. Hegnauer (Netherlands, 1976).

Fluid and Plasmadynamics Award

This award, established by the AIAA in 1975, is presented for outstanding contributions to the understanding of the behaviour of liquids and gases in motion or of the physical properties and dynamical behaviour of matter in the plasma state as related to needs in aeronautics and astronautics. It comprises a medal and certificate of citation, and is usually presented at the Fluid and Plasmadynamics Conference.

Awarding body: American Institute of Aeronautics and Astronautics, 1290 Avenue of the Americas, New York, N.Y. 10019, U.S.A.

Recipients include: Mark Morkovin (1976); Harvard Lomax (1977).

Food, Pharmaceutical and Bioengineering Division Award in Chemical Engineering

This award is sponsored by CPC International, Inc. It honours outstanding achievements by an individual (not necessarily a member of AIChE) in those industries involved in food, pharmaceutical and bioengineering activities. These may have occurred in industrial, governmental, academic or other organizations. The award is normally made annually, and consists of a certificate and $1,000.

Awarding body: Food, Pharmaceutical and Bioengineering Division of the American Institute of Chemical Engineers, 345 East 47th St., New York, N.Y. 10017, U.S.A.

Förderungspreis der Landeshauptstadt Stuttgart zur Förderung junger Komponisten ernster Musik (*City of Stuttgart prize to encourage young composers of serious music*)

This annual prize for contemporary compositions was instituted by the West German city of Stuttgart at the suggestion of the Association of German Composers. Composers of up to 35 years of age resident in the Federal Republic are eligible, with the exception of schoolchildren and music students. Both performed and unperformed works may be entered. The prize takes the form of DM10,000 and certificates, and may be shared among a maximum of five people.

Awarding body: Kultur- und Schulreferat der Stadt Stuttgart, 7000 Stuttgart 1, Rathaus, Postfach 161, Federal Republic of Germany.

Recipients include: Jens-Peter Ostendorf (*Chor für Orchester*), Peter Michael Hamel (*Diaphainon*), Berthold Paul (*Réaction pour Orchestre*, op. 16) (1975); Wolfgang-Andreas Schultz (*Flötenkonzert*), Wolfgang von Schweinitz (*Variationen über ein Thema von Mozart für grosses Orchester*, op. 12), Frank Michael (*Veränderungen einer Landschaft*) (1976).

Förderungspreise des Bundesministerium für Unterricht und Kunst (*Austrian Ministry of Education and Arts Prizes*)

The prizes are awarded to encourage work in the fields of literature, music, fine arts and cinema. One prize is normally awarded annually in each category, and the winner is chosen in open competition. Each prize is worth 25,000 Schillings.

Awarding body: Bundesministerium für Unterricht und Kunst, 1014 Vienna, Minoritenplatz 5, Austria.

Recipients include: Otto Volkmar Deisenhammer, Michael Rössner (literature), Traudi Pichler, Reimo Wukounig (fine arts), Carl Colman (music), 1975.

Förderungspreise für Erwachsenenbildung (*Adult Education Prizes*)

The awards are made by the Austrian Ministry of Education and Arts for work dealing with the theory, practice or history of adult education. Only Austrian citizens are eligible, and the work must have been completed during the past three years. Each prize is worth 20,000 Schillings. Occasionally an additional prize of 5,000 Schillings may be awarded, which honours an individual's life's work in this area.

Awarding body: Bundesministerium für Unterricht und Kunst, 1014 Vienna, Minoritenplatz 5, Austria.

E. M. Forster Award

The writer E. M. Forster bequeathed the American publication rights and royalties of his posthumous novel *Maurice* to Christopher Isherwood, who transferred them in 1972 to the National Institute of Arts and Letters for the establishment of an E. M. Forster Award of $5,000, to be given periodically to a young English writer for a stay in the United States.

Awarding body: American Academy and Institute of Arts and Letters, 633 West 155th St., New York, N.Y. 10032, U.S.A.

Recipients include: Paul Bailey (1975); Jon Stallworthy (1976).

Forwood Lectureship in the Philosophy and History of Religion

In 1928 Sir William Forwood bequeathed £1,000 to Liverpool University for the endowment of a lectureship in non-sectarian Divinity, and an annual short course of lectures on the 'Philosophy of Religion' was established. The title of the lectureship was revised in 1949; and since 1952 the lectures have been delivered every two years.

Awarding body: The University of Liverpool, P.O.B. 147, Liverpool L69 3BX, England.

Cyril Foster Lectureship

In 1958 the University of Oxford accepted a bequest from the late C. A. Foster 'for such purposes as will ... best serve the promotion of international peace and the prevention of future wars'. An annual lectureship was consequently established; it may take the form of a single lecture or a course of several.

Awarding body: University of Oxford, Wellington Square, Oxford OX1 2JD, England.

Lecturers include: Rt. Hon. Denis Healey ('European Security in the Seventies', 1971–72); Brian Urquhart ('The United Nations: responsibility without power', 1972–73); Egon Bahr ('The Future of European Security', 1973–74); Elliott Richardson ('The Dynamics of Stability in East-West Relations', 1974–75); Roy Jenkins ('Europe and the Third World: the political economy of interdependence', 1977–78).

Foundation for Australian Literary Studies Award

The award was established in 1967 by the Foundation for Australian Literary Studies within the Department of English at the James Cook University of North Queensland. A cash prize of A$750 is given annually for the best book first published during the year in Australia and dealing with any aspect of Australian life, fiction or non-fiction.

Awarding body: James Cook University of North Queensland, Post Office, James Cook University, Qld. 4811, Australia.

Recipients include: Geoffrey Serle (*The Rush to be Rich*), 1971; Sir Keith Hancock (*Discovering Monaro*), 1972; Mrs. Dorothy Green (*Ulysses Bound*), 1973; David Malouf (*Neighbours in a Thicket*), 1974; Dr. D. J. Murphy (Biography *T. J. Ryan*), 1975.

Foundation Lecture

This annual lecture was founded by the Institution of the Rubber Industry which in 1975 amalgamated with the Plastics Institute to become the Plastics and Rubber Institute. The lecturer is invited by the Medals Selection Committee to speak on a topic within the scope of the Institute.

Awarding body: The Plastics and Rubber Institute, 11 Hobart Place, London SW1W 0HL, England.

Recipients include: W. C. Wake ('Adhesion science and tyres', 1973); W. F. Watson ('Science of rubber processing and its applications', 1974); G. Allen ('Two worlds of rubber technology: new products, new properties for industry', 1975); E. R. Gardner ('Hovercraft and their skirts', 1977).

Franklin Medal

This gold medal is the highest honour of the Franklin Institute. It is awarded annually to those workers in physical science or technology, without regard to nationality, whose efforts have done most to advance a knowledge of physical science or its applications. It was founded in 1914 by Samuel Insull (1859–1938) who was private secretary to Thomas Edison, and later Vice-President of the General Electric Company, and President and Chairman of the Commonwealth Edison Company. The Franklin Institute, named after Benjamin Franklin, was founded in 1824; it is a science education and research institution devoted to the physical sciences.

Awarding body: The Franklin Institute, Benjamin Franklin Parkway at 20th St., Philadelphia, Pa. 19103, U.S.A.

Recipients include: Theodosius G. Dobzhansky (U.S.A., genetics and biocultural evolution, 1973); Nikolai Bogolyubov (U.S.S.R., mathematical methods in nonlinear mechanics, 1974); John Bardeen (U.S.A., theory and technology of superconductivity and semiconductor devices, 1975); Mahlon B. Hoagland (U.S.A., protein synthesis and its relations to information coded in DNA and RNA, 1976); Dr. Cyril Manton Harris (U.S.A., contributions to acoustical science and engineering, 1977).

Benjamin Franklin Medal

The medal was established by the Royal Society of Arts in 1956 to commemorate the 250th anniversary of the birth of Benjamin Franklin (1706–90) and the 200th anniversary of his election to membership of the Society of Arts. The medal is awarded annually, alternately to a citizen of the United Kingdom and of the United States of America who has forwarded the cause of Anglo-American understanding, particularly in the fields of arts, manufactures or commerce.

Awarding body: Royal Society of Arts, John Adam St., Adelphi, London WC2N 6EZ, England.

Recipients include: Alistair Cooke (U.S.A., 1973); Dame Margot Fonteyn de Arias (U.K., 1974); Dr. W. S. Lewis (U.S.A., 1975); Sir Harold Macmillan (U.K., 1976); Dr. Ivor Richards (U.S.A., 1977).

Miles Franklin Literary Award

This award was created under the terms of the will of the late Stella Maria Sarah Miles Franklin, an Australian authoress, who died in September 1954. It is given annually for the novel or play of the highest literary merit, written by an Australian, presenting aspects of Australian life, and published during the preceding year. There is no limit on the number of entries submitted by one candidate, and books written by more than one author are also eligible. The winner receives a cash prize of a sum determined by the Trustees, at present $1,750.

Awarding body: Permanent Trustee Company Ltd., 23/25 O'Connell Street, Sydney, Australia.

Recipients include: Dal Stivens (*A Horse of Air*, 1970); David Ireland (*The Unknown Industrial Prisoner*, 1971); Thea Astley (*The Acolyte*, 1972); Ronald McKie (*The Mango Tree*, 1974); Xavier Herbert (*Poor Fellow My Country*, 1975).

Frankuchen Award

The Frankuchen Award was founded in 1971, in memory of Isadore Frankuchen, late Professor of Physics at the Polytechnic Institute of Brooklyn. The award is made every three years to an outstanding crystallographer or X-ray diffractionist of any nationality, who has also made significant contributions to the teaching of the subject (although he need not be a teacher by profession). The recipient will present the Frankuchen Memorial Lecture at the A.C.A. meeting at the time of the award, at the Polytechnic Institute of Brooklyn, and at two additional institutions to be decided. The award consists of a certificate and $1,500, plus an additional sum to cover expenses.

Awarding body: American Crystallographic Association, 335 East 45 St., New York, N.Y. 10017, U.S.A.

Recipients: Martin J. Buerger (U.S.A., 1971); André Guinier (France, 1974); Dorothy C. Hodgkin (U.K., 1977).

Sir John Fraser Memorial Lecture

The lecture was founded in memory of the late Sir John Fraser, Bt., K.C.V.O., M.C., Hon. Surgeon in Scotland to H.M. King George VI, Regius Professor of Clinical Surgery (1925–44) and Principal and Vice-Chancellor of Edinburgh University (1944–47). The lecture is delivered every three years.

Awarding body: Edinburgh University, Edinburgh EH8 9YL, Scotland.

Lecturers include: Sir John Bruce (1972); Prof. Sir Andrew Kay (1977).

Frazer Lectureship in Social Anthropology

The lectureship was founded by subscription at Cambridge University in 1920 in commemoration of the services contributed to learning by Sir James George Frazer, Fellow of Trinity College, Cambridge. The lectures are delivered every four years in rotation at the Universities of Oxford, Cambridge, Glasgow and Liverpool. The lecturer is required to deliver a lecture on some subject connected with social anthropology.

Awarding bodies: Universities of Oxford, Cambridge, Glasgow and Liverpool.

Lecturers include: Cambridge: Prof. Fred Eggan (1971); Glasgow: E. A. Gellner (Dept. of Sociology, L.S.E., 1977).

Charles Lang Freer Medal

This award is made in recognition of distinguished contributions to the knowledge and understanding of Oriental civilizations as reflected in their arts. It was established in 1956 in memory of Charles Lang Freer (1856–1919), a Detroit industrialist who assembled one of the world's most significant collections of Oriental art. Freer gave his collection in trust to the Smithsonian Institution in 1906, providing funds for a building to house it. He also established an endowment, the income of which was to be used for research into the civilization of the East related to the objects in the collection and to make purchases of additional works of Oriental art. The award consists of a bronze medal which is presented irregularly as merited.

Awarding body: Smithsonian Institution, 1000 Jefferson Drive, S.W., Washington, D.C. 20560, U.S.A.

Recipients include: Osvald Siren (Sweden, Chinese art specialist, 1956); Ernst Kuhnel (specialist in Islamic art, 1960); Yukio Yashiro (Japanese scholar, 1965); Tanaka Ichimatsu (specialist in Japanese painting, 1973).

Simon W. Freese Environmental Engineering Lecture

This lectureship was established in 1975 by the Environmental Engineering Division of the ASCE and endowed by the firm of Freese and Nichols in honour of their partner, Simon Wilke Freese, F.A.S.C.E. At about yearly intervals a distinguished person, selected without membership or nationality restrictions, is invited to deliver a lecture at a meeting of the Society; he receives a certificate and an honorarium of $1,000.

Awarding body: American Society of Civil Engineers, 345 East 47th St., New York, N.Y. 10017, U.S.A.

Fresenius-Preis

The prize was established in 1961 by the Society of German Chemists in memory of Professor Dr. C. Remigius Fresenius, analytical chemist, and honorary member of the former German Chemical Society and Association of German Chemists. The prize is awarded to Germans for outstanding contributions to the development of analytical chemistry. It takes the form of a sum of money and a gold medal. It is not awarded regularly.

Awarding body: Gesellschaft Deutscher Chemiker, 6000 Frankfurt (Main) 90, Carl Bosch-Haus, Varrentrappstr. 40–42, Federal Republic of Germany.

Recipients include: Prof. Egon Stahl (1966); Prof. Walter Koch (1970); Prof. Gerhard Hesse (1972); Dr. Erwin Lehrer (1972); Prof. Hermann Kienitz (1975).

Sigmund-Freud-Preis

This prize was founded in 1964 by the German Academy for Language and Poetry to foster a fuller appreciation of German scholarly prose and its further development. It is named after the philosopher and scholar, Sigmund Freud, who criticized the neglect of this genre in Germany as compared with other European countries. The award is made annually and consists of a cash prize of DM6,000.

Awarding body: Deutsche Akademie für Sprache und Dichtung, Alexandraweg 23 (Glückert-Haus), 6100 Darmstadt, Federal Republic of Germany.

Recipients include: Erik Wolf (lawyer, 1972); Karl Rahner (theologian, 1973); Günter Busch (art historian, 1974); Ernst Bloch (philosopher, 1975); Jürgen Habermas (1976).

Alfred M. Freudenthal Medal

This medal was established in 1975 by the Engineering Mechanics Division of ASCE in honour of Alfred M. Freudenthal, F.ASCE. It is normally presented every two years to an individual, regardless of age, nationality or ASCE membership, who has made a distinguished contribution to safety and reliability studies in any branch of civil engineering.

Awarding body: American Society of Civil Engineers, 345 East 47th St., New York, N.Y. 10017, U.S.A.

Recipients include: Emilio Rosenblueth (contributions to probabilistic methods in earthquake engineering, 1976).

E. K. Frey-Preis

This prize was donated by the paint factories of Bayer AG, and is given annually to a physician or scientist from a German-speaking country for studies in the area of enzyme inhibitors. It takes the form of a certificate and cash prize of DM10,000. It is awarded in rotation by the German Surgical Society, the Society of Internal Medicine and the Society for Gynaecology.

Awarding body: Deutsche Gesellschaft für Chirurgie, 1000 Berlin 15, Kurfürstendamm 179, Federal Republic of Germany.

Recipients include: Prof. Paul Matis (Fed. Rep. of Germany, 1969); Prof. F.-K. Mörl (Fed. Rep. of Germany, 1969).

Friedenspreis des Deutschen Buchhandels
(Peace Prize of the German Book Trade)

This award was established in 1950 by a group of German publishers, and is made annually to an individual whose activities, chiefly in such areas as literature, science and art, have contributed substantially to the realization of the ideals of peace and universal understanding. There are no restrictions as to nationality or religion, and nominations are welcomed from anybody. The award takes the form of DM10,000 and a certificate.

Awarding body: Börsenverein des Deutschen Buchhandels e.V., 6 Frankfurt am Main 1, Grosser Hirschgaben 17/21, Federal Republic of Germany.

Recipients include: The Club of Rome (1973); Frère Roger, Prior of Taizé (1974); Alfred Grosser (1975); Max Frisch (1976); Leszek Kolakowski (1977).

Frink Medal for British Zoologists

The medal was established in 1973 by the Zoological Society of London, a society founded for 'the advancement of Zoology and Animal Physiology and the introduction of new and curious subjects of the Animal Kingdom'. A medal is awarded for substantial and original contributions by professional zoologists to the advancement of their science. The medal may be awarded annually; the winner is announced in January or February, and the presentation takes place in April or May of the following year. Recommendations for the award are normally made without the candidate's knowledge. Candidates must be British citizens resident in the United Kingdom and whose work is based there. Serving members of the Council of the Zoological Society are not eligible.

Awarding body: The Zoological Society of London, Regent's Park, London NW1 4RY, England.

Recipients include: Sir Julian Huxley, F.R.S. (1973); Prof. J. Z. Young, F.R.S. (1974); Prof. Alastair Graham (1975).

John Fritz Medal

This award consists of a gold medal and certificate, and is international and unrestricted. It was established in 1902 by the associates and friends of John Fritz, one of America's pioneers in the iron and steel industries, on the occasion of his 80th birthday. The award is made annually by a board appointed in equal number from the membership of the five founder societies of the United Engineering Trustees, Inc. (American Society of Civil Engineers; American Institute of Mining, Metallurgical and Petroleum Engineers, Inc.; American Society of Mechanical Engineers; American Institute of Chemical Engineers; Institute of Electrical and Electronics Engineers). The award is for notable scientific or industrial achievement, maintaining the standards set by John Fritz.

Awarding body: United Engineering Trustees Inc., 345 East 47th St., New York, N.Y. 10017, U.S.A.

Recipients include: Lyman D. Wilbur (1973); H. I. Romnes (1974); Manson Benedict (1975); Thomas O. Paine (1976); George R. Brown (1977).

William Froude Medal

This gold medal is awarded from time to time to a person of any nationality who, in the judgement of the Council of the Royal Institution of Naval Architects, has made some conspicuous contribution to naval architecture and/or shipbuilding, and whose outstanding services and personal achievements in this direction merit special consideration. The medal may be awarded only to a person and not to an organization or other corporate body.

Awarding body: Royal Institution of Naval Architects, 10 Upper Belgrave St., London SW1X 8BQ, England.

Recipients include: J. M. Murray, M.B.E. (1965); Prof. Dr. Ing. G. Weinblum (1971); Prof. Ir. G. Aertssen (1972); Dr. R. S. Guilloton (1974); Prof. E. V. Telfer (1975).

Fuels and Petrochemical Division Annual Award

This award is primarily honorary in nature, and is presented by a Division of the American Institute of Chemical Engineers to individuals who have made substantial contributions to the technology and advancement of the fuels and petrochemical industries. Varying qualities such as technical, managerial and academic skills are taken into account. The recipient should have a long and recognized record of achievement, and should be currently (or recently) the chief executive officer of his company. He should be a chemical engineer, possibly a member of the Institute, and in his selection the fuels and petrochemical industries should be given equal prominence.

Awarding body: Fuels and Petrochemical Division of the American Institute of Chemical Engineers, 345 East 47th St., New York, N.Y. 10017, U.S.A.

Fujihara Prize

The Fujihara Foundation of Science was established in 1959 by the late Ginjiro Fujihara, President of the Oji Paper Company, on the occasion of his 90th birthday. He contributed 100 million yen from his personal fortune, the income from which is used to award the Fujihara Prize. The sum has since been increased with donations from the Oji group and other paper companies. Currently two prizes of 10 million yen each and a gold medal are awarded annually for outstanding contributions to the advancement of science in all its branches: mathematics, physics, engineering, chemistry, biology, medicine or agriculture. Any Japanese scientist is eligible; nominations are made to the Foundation by appropriate institutions – universities, research laboratories, etc.

Awarding body: Fujihara Foundation of Science, Oji Building, Ginza 4-7-5, Chuo-ku, Tokyo 104, Japan.

Recipients include: Prof. Masao Yoshiki (engineering, 1968); Prof. Ryogo Kubo (physics, 1970); Prof. Osamu Hayaishi (medicine, 1975); Dr. Takashi Sugimura (medicine, 1975).

Futura Prize

This award is presented at the international television competition held every two years in West Berlin. It was established by Sender Freies Berlin (Radio Free Berlin) in 1969 with the aim of promoting international co-operation in television broadcasting and encouraging the introduction of new subjects, contents and forms. All broadcasting organizations which are authorized by national and international law are eligible to submit a maximum of two productions. These should be free from advertising, and should be of no more than 90 minutes' duration (120 minutes in the case of a single entry). The official languages are English, French, German, and Russian. The productions must have been televised within the two years prior to the competition, and should not have been awarded prizes by the European Broadcasting Union. Prizes are awarded on the basis of constructive contributions to the future of civilization, considered either in relation to an individual country or to the entire world. There is an international jury, and the awards are given by the sponsoring bodies: Sender Freies Berlin and Zweites Deutsches Fernsehen. The Futura Prize is awarded in gold, silver and bronze, each prize carrying a replica, two scrolls of honour, and a sum of money (DM10,000, DM6,000, DM4,000 respectively). The authors of the winning productions receive a scroll and the cash prize, while the television organizations entering the productions receive the prize replica and the second scroll of honour. The Gold Prize is indivisible.

Awarding body: Sender Freies Berlin, 1000 Berlin 19, Masurenallee 8–14, Federal Republic of Germany.

Recipients include: ARD/WDR, Fed. Rep. of Germany (Gold Prize for *Smog*, 1975); BBC, U.K. (Silver Prize for *The Writing on the Wall*, 1975); ZDF, Fed. Rep. of Germany (Silver Prize for *Künstliche Errinerungen*, 1975); NOS, Netherlands (Silver Prize for *Hakuna Kazi*, 1975); BBC, U.K. (Silver Prize for *Prophecies*, 1977); FR3, France (Silver Prize for *Des Enfants à la Carte*, 1977).

G

Gabriel Awards

These were established in 1964 by the Catholic Broadcasters Association of America and transferred to the Catholic Association for Broadcasting and Allied Professions (UNDA-USA) on its foundation in 1972. The awards are intended to encourage the production of radio and television programmes which reflect Judaeo-Christian principles and aim at improving the human condition. They are presented annually, usually in December, for outstanding programmes produced in the U.S.A. and Canada between 1 July of one year and 30 June the following year. There are six classes and 27 categories of award and also the Gabriel Award for Personal Achievement, which is presented to individuals who have made a notable contribution to broadcasting. The award consists of a nine-inch silver figure mounted on a base of black wood. The awards are open to production agencies and individuals from the U.S.A. and Canada. There is an entry fee of $25 for radio and $50 for television entries, but no fee for the Personal Achievement Award.

Awarding body: UNDA-USA, 1027 Superior Ave., Room 630, Cleveland, Ohio 44114, U.S.A.

Recipients include: Rev. Agnellus Andrew (Pres., UNDA London, 1972); Robert Hyland (Vice-Pres., CBS Radio, 1973); Pamela Ilott (Dir., Cultural Broadcasting, CBS, 1974); Frederick Wiseman (Documentarian, 1975); Scott Craig (Documentarian, 1976).

Yuri Gagarin Gold Medal

This award was established in memory of the Russian cosmonaut Yuri Gagarin, the first man to enter space. It is made annually to an astronaut who, in the previous year, has advanced the conquest of space for peaceful purposes.

Awarding body: Fédération Aéronautique Internationale, 6 rue Galilée, Paris 16, France.

Recipients include: Donald K. Slayton (U.S.A.), Vance D. Brand (U.S.A.), Valeri Nikolaevitch Kubasov (U.S.S.R.) (Apollo-Soyuz Project), 1975.

Gairdner Foundation International Awards

The Gairdner Foundation was incorporated in 1957, and its funds derive from the personal gift of its founder, the late James Arthur Gairdner (1893–1971) of Oakville, Canada. Its awards are presented for significant, tangible achievements in medicine, and are divided into three classes: the Award of Merit, worth $25,000, is awarded from time to time to an individual or group for an outstanding discovery or contribution; the Annual Awards, a series of prizes of $10,000 each, or $5,000 each for a joint award to two persons, are similarly awarded for outstanding discoveries or contributions; the Wightman Award, worth $25,000, is given from time to time to a Canadian who has demonstrated outstanding leadership in medicine and medical science. All the awards include individual scrolls bearing citations and are presented at a formal dinner in Toronto each year. Nominations are made by the Foundation's correspondents. Winners present brief papers covering their prize-winning work; these are known as the Gairdner Foundation Lectures.

Awarding body: The Gairdner Foundation, 255 Yorkland Blvd., Willowdale, Ont., Canada.

Recipients include: Henry G. Friesen (Canada, Wightman Award, 1977); Prof. J.-P. Changeux (France) and Dr. Terenius (Sweden), neurobiology, Dr. S. Freedman and Dr. P. Gold (Canada), cancer research, Annual Awards, 1978.

Gairn EEC Gold Medal

Mr. Stanley Nash Bruce Gairn, F.S.E., President of the Society of Engineers in 1972, established this medal in 1973. It is a biennial award for an outstanding contribution to contemporary engineering or science within the Common Market.

Awarding body: The Society of Engineers, 21/23 Mossop St., London SW3 2LW, England.

Recipients include: Alfred Champagnat (protein feed from oil, 1973); Prof. Ing. Dr. Bruck (PAL television, 1975).

Galathea medaljen

This medal is awarded occasionally by the Royal Danish Geographical Society. It was established in 1916, and named after the expedition with the corvette 'Galathea' when Admiral Steen Andersen Bille circumnavigated the globe during the years 1845 to 1847. The award is given to outstanding scientists for geographical research outside the Arctic area.

Awarding body: Det Kongelige Danske Geografiske Selskab, Haraldsgade 68, DK-2100 Copenhagen Ø, Denmark.

Recipients include: Prof. dr. Johs. Humlum (studies on irrigation and agriculture, especially in China, 1976); Prof. dr. Johs. Nicolaisen (ethnographical studies, especially among the Tuaregs, Sahara, 1976).

Gallie Memorial Lecture

The lecture is normally on a surgical topic, and is delivered at the annual meeting of the Royal College of Physicians and Surgeons of Canada. It was established in memory of Dr. William Edward Gallie, Professor of Surgery at Toronto University. The lecturer is selected jointly by the President of the College and the Chairman of the Department of Surgery at the University of Toronto.

Awarding body: Royal College of Physicians and Surgeons of Canada, 74 Stanley Ave., Ottawa, Ont. K1M 1P4, Canada.

Recipients include: Dr. Frederick G. Kergin (1973); Dr. G. Tom Shires (1974); Dr. E. Harry Botterell (1975); Dr. Frederick P. Dewar (1976); Dr. E. Bruce Tovee (1977).

Gamgee Prize

The prize was established by the World Veterinary Association in 1963 on the occasion of the 100th anniversary of the World Veterinary Congresses. A gold medal is awarded to a veterinarian for outstanding services to veterinary science and the profession. The award is made at world veterinary congresses (held every four years), if a suitable candidate is found. The prize is in memory of Professor John Gamgee (1831–94) who organized the first International Veterinary Congress in 1863.

Awarding body: World Veterinary Association, 70 Route du Pont Butin, 1213 Petit-Lancy/ Geneva, Switzerland.

Recipients include: Sir Thomas Dalling (1963); Prof. Dr. W. I. B. Beveridge (1975).

Gandhi Peace Award

The award was established in 1960 by Promoting Enduring Peace, Inc. in memory of Mohandas Gandhi (1869–1948), leader of the movement for national independence in India, who preached a philosophy of non-violence. A medal and certificate are awarded annually for significant contributions made in the promotion of international peace and goodwill.

Awarding body: Promoting Enduring Peace, Inc., P.O.B. 103, Woodmont, Conn. 06460, U.S.A.

Recipients include: Dr. Jerome Davis (1967); Sen. Wayne Morse (1970); U Thant (1972); Dorothy Day (1975); Daniel Ellsberg (1976).

Manuel Garcia Prize

This award is sponsored by the Swiss pharmaceutical company, Sandoz AG, and presented by the International Association of Logopedics and Phoniatrics every three years at its Congress. It was established jointly by the two organizations in 1968 in memory of Manuel Garcia, who invented the laryngeal mirror. The award consists of a cash prize of 1,000 Swiss francs and a diploma, and is given for the best article published in *Folia Phoniatrica*, the Association's official journal, during the three-year period.

Awarding body: International Association of Logopedics and Phoniatrics, c/o Dr. B. Fritzell, Västanvägen 4, 146 00 Tullinge, Sweden.

Recipients: N. Yanagihara, Y. Koike and H. von Leden (U.S.A., 1968); Harry Hollien (U.S.A., 1971); Jürgen Wendler (German Dem. Rep., 1974).

Garvan Medal

The award was established in 1936 through a donation from Francis P. Garvan, and is supported by a fund set up at that time. It is intended to recognize distinguished service to chemistry by women chemists who are citizens of the U.S.A. It consists of $2,000, a suitably inscribed gold medal and a bronze replica of the medal.

Awarding body: American Chemical Society, 1155 Sixteenth St., N.W., Washington, D.C. 20036, U.S.A.

Recipients include: Mary L. Good (1973); Joyce J. Kaufman (1974); Marjorie C. Caserio (1975); Isabella L. Karle (1976); Marjorie G. Horning (1977).

Gas Turbine Award

This annual award takes the form of a medal accompanied by a certificate. It is open to any resident of Australia, New Zealand or a territory administered by these countries, who has made an outstanding original contribution to gas turbine technology. Nominations are made by individual members of the Society of Automotive Engineers – Australasia or by Division or independent Group Committees to the Society's Council.

Awarding body: Society of Automotive Engineers–Australasia, National Science Centre, 191 Royal Parade, Parkville, Vic. 3052, Australia.

Gas Turbine Power Award

The award was established in 1963, and is given in recognition of an outstanding individual or multiple-author contribution to the literature of combustion gas turbines or gas turbines thermally combined with nuclear or steam power plants. The paper may be devoted to design aspects or overall gas turbines or individual components and/or systems such as compressors, combustion systems, turbines, controls and accessories, bearings, regenerators, inlet air filters, silencers, etc. It may cover topics specifically related to gas turbines, such as high temperature materials or fuel considerations, including erosion and corrosion complications. It can also be devoted to application or operation aspects of gas turbines in such uses as aircraft propulsion and ground power units, automotive, electric utility, gas pipeline pumping, locomotive, marine, oil field pumping, petrochemical, space power, steel, etc. Papers published anywhere in the world are eligible. Authors are not restricted by nationality, age, profession, nor membership in any engineering society or organization. The award is made annually if warranted, at the Annual Conference of the Gas Turbine Division of ASME, and consists of a turbine wheel with a bronze insert in the hub.

Awarding body: American Society of Mechanical Engineers, United Engineering Center, 345 East 47th St., New York, N.Y. 10017, U.S.A.

Recipients include: F. B. Metzger, D. B. Hanson (1973); John Moore (1975); G. L. Commerford, Lynn E. Snyder (1976).

Gdańsk International Ceramics Prizes
These prizes are awarded every three years and are sponsored by the Polish Ministry of Culture and Art, the Union of Polish Artists and the Department of Culture (PWRN) in Gdańsk. There are five prizes of equal cash amounts.
Awarding body: Department of Culture (PWRN), Toruńska 1, 80-822 Gdańsk, Poland.

Portia Geach Memorial Award
This award is made annually for the best portraits from life of a person distinguished in Art, Letters or the Sciences by a female artist resident in Australia. It was established under the terms of the will of the late Florence Kate Geach, who died in 1962, in memory of her sister, Portia, a noted portrait artist, who died in 1957. The amount of the award is regulated by the Trustees of the bequest and at present is $2,500. The competition is open only to Australian and British women whose home is in Australia and who have resided in Australia for the 12 months preceding the competition. The portrait must have been completed within the 12 months preceding 30 June of the year of the competition.
Awarding body: Permanent Trustee Company Ltd., 23/25 O'Connell St., Sydney, Australia.
Recipients include: Elisabeth Cummings (*Jean Appleton*, 1972); Sylvia Tiarks (*Self Portrait*, 1973); Lesley Haselwood Pockley (*Hugh Paget*, 1974); Sister Mary Brady (*Elizabeth Rooney*, 1975); Jocelyn Maughan (*George Bouckley*, 1976).

Murray Geddes Memorial Prize
This award is made for the encouragement of astronomy in New Zealand. It was established in the late 1940s in memory of Murray Geddes, the first Director of the Carter Observatory, Wellington. The prize is awarded at intervals of not more than five years and not more often than once a year, to an individual whose work in the field of astronomy is considered to be of sufficient merit. The prize, which consists of a book or books to the value of $NZ40, chosen by the recipient and affixed with a suitably inscribed book-plate, is presented at the Annual General Meeting of the Royal Astronomical Society of New Zealand. The recipient must be resident in New Zealand.
Awarding body: Royal Astronomical Society of New Zealand, P.O.B. 3181, Wellington, New Zealand.

Reina Prinsen Geerligs Prijs
This cash prize of 350 Dutch guilders is awarded every three years by the Reina Prinsen Geerligs Foundation for plays, prose or poetry in Afrikaans. The award was established by relatives of Reina Prinsen Geerligs (1922–43) who was shot in Germany during the war. She was a Dutch student of literature and was interested in the connection between the Dutch, Flemish and Afrikaans languages. Entrants for the prize must be between 20 and 30 years old.
Awarding body: The Secretary, Algemeen Nederlands Verbond, P.O.B. 4543, Cape Town 8000, South Africa.

General Diagnostics Lectureship in Clinical Chemistry
Established by Warner-Lambert Company, the award is now sponsored by General Diagnostics Corporation, a laboratory reagents firm. The award is intended to honour a distinguished clinical chemist through a scholarly lecture at each annual meeting of the AACC. The lecturer also receives a scroll, an honorarium of $1,500 and travelling expenses.
Awarding body: American Association for Clinical Chemistry (AACC), 1725 K St., N.W., Suite 1402, Washington, D.C. 20006, U.S.A.
Recipients include: Linus Pauling (1973); Russell Eilers (1974); Martin Rubin (1975); Evan and Marjorie Horning (1976).

Geneva International Musical Performance Competition
Founded in 1939 by Henri Gagnebin and Dr. F. Liebstoeckl, this annual competition is for young musicians in various categories of musical disciplines: singing, piano, woodwind, conducting, etc. Cash prizes are given in all categories, the value varying each year.
Awarding body: International Musical Performance Competition, 12 rue de l'Hôtel de Ville, CH-1204 Geneva, Switzerland.
Recipients of first prizes include: Sir Georg Solti (1943); Victoria de los Angeles (1947); Heinz Holliger (1959); Jennifer Vyvyan.

Genootschapsmedaille (*Medal of the Netherlands Association for the Advancement of Natural, Medical and Surgical Sciences*)
Founded by the Association in 1840, the medal is for outstanding contributions to science in general. It is not awarded regularly.
Awarding body: Genootschap ter bevordering van Natuur-, Genees- en Heelkunde, Plantage Muidergracht 12, Amsterdam, Netherlands.
Recipients include: Sir Henry Dale (U.K., 1954); Sir Hans Krebs (U.K., 1958); Prof. J. D. van der Waals, Jr. (Netherlands, 1965); Prof. Britton Chance (U.S.A., 1965).

Thomas P. Gerrity Award
This national award is made annually by the U.S. Air Force Association to an individual or organization for outstanding contributions in the field of systems and logistics. It takes the form of a plaque, and was instituted in 1968 in honour of Gen. Thomas P. Gerrity (1913–68), Commander of the Air Force Logistics Command.
Awarding body: Air Force Association National Awards Committee, 1750 Pennsylvania Ave., N.W., Washington, D.C. 20006, U.S.A.

Recipients include: Col. Owen J. McGonnell (1972); Col. Allen R. Rodgers (1973); Brig. Gen. Jack W. Waters (1974); Lt. Gen. Charles E. Buckingham (1975); Col. James A. MacDougald (1976).

Leo Gershoy Award

Established in 1977, this award is given biennially for the most outstanding work in English on any aspect of the field of 17th- and 18th-century European history. It is a cash prize of $1,000.
Awarding body: American Historical Association, 400 A St., S.E., Washington, D.C. 20003, U.S.A.

J. Paul Getty Wildlife Conservation Prize

The cash prize of $50,000 is awarded annually by an international jury to an individual or organization for an outstanding contribution of direct or indirect international impact in the conservation of wildlife. It is intended that the recognition accorded by the prize will increase public appreciation of the importance of conserving wildlife. The prize was established with a gift from the late Paul Getty to the World Wildlife Fund in 1974.
Awarding body: World Wildlife Fund – U.S., 1319 18th St., N.W., Washington, D.C. 20036, U.S.A.
Recipients include: Felipe Benavides (protection of the Vicuna in Peru, 1974); Dr. S. A. Ali (promoting knowledge and conservation of birds in India, 1975); Major Ian Grimwood (fmr. Chief Game Warden of Kenya, responsible for saving Arabian oryx, 1976).

Guido Gezelleprijs

The prize was established in 1941 by the Belgian Royal Academy of Dutch Language and Literature in memory of Guido Gezelle (1830–99), priest and poet. An award of 10,000 Belgian francs is made every five years for the best volume of Dutch poetry submitted, published or unpublished. Recipients must be Belgian nationals.
Awarding body: Koninklijke Academie voor Nederlandse Taal- en Letterkunde, Koningstraat 18, B-9000 Ghent, Belgium.
Recipients include: M. Brauns (*Zangen van Onmacht*, 1946); J. L. de Belder (*Ballade der Onzekerheden*, 1951); Jos de Haes (*Gedaanten*, 1956); G. Helderenberg (*dichtbundels verschenen in die periode*, 1961); René Verbeeck (*De zomer staat hoog en rijp*, 1966).

Ştefan Gheorghiu Prize

This prize for history was founded in 1948 by the Romanian Academy. It is named after Ştefan Gheorghiu (1879–1914), champion of the working class movement in Romania, and one of the initiators of the struggle for the reorganization of the Social-Democratic Party. The award is given for published contributions to the study of any period of history, including contemporary. It is presented annually at a General Assembly of the Academy, and consists of 10,000 lei and a diploma.
Awarding body: Academy of the S.R. of Romania, 125 Calea Victoriei, Bucharest, Romania.

Giblin Memorial Lectureship

This lectureship was established by the Australian and New Zealand Association for the Advancement of Science (ANZAAS) in memory of Lyndhurst Falkiner Giblin (1872–1951), the economist. The first lecture was given in 1958. The person appointed is chosen for his distinguished contributions in the fields of economics and the art of public administration and government, and for his capacity for lucid exposition. He receives a fee of $50 from the Association's funds. The lecture is given at each ANZAAS Congress and subsequently published in the Association's journal *Search*.
Awarding body: Australian and New Zealand Association for the Advancement of Science, 157 Gloucester St., Sydney, N.S.W. 2000, Australia.
Recipients include: T. W. Swan (1972); M. Parkin (1973); Peter Karmel (1975); Sir Roland Wilson (1976); Hon. Dr. Joseph E. Isaac (1977).

Gibson Literary Award

This award is made annually for the best 'first' English novel by a Canadian. Any Canadian author or landed immigrant with no previously published novel is eligible. The award is a cash prize of $1,000. It was established in 1975 by Canadian Gibson Distillery Ltd.
Awarding body: Canadian Gibson Distillery Ltd., 2085 Union St., Suite 865, Montreal, Que. H3A 1B9, Canada.
Recipients include: Ian McNiel (*Battle for Salt Bucket Beach*, 1976); Betty Wilson (*André-Tom MacGregor*, 1977).

Gibson Literary Merit Award

This award is made annually to an author for a work or a body of works deemed to have made a most significant contribution to Canadian letters. Any Canadian author or landed immigrant is eligible. The award is a cash prize of $1,000. It was established by Canadian Gibson Distillery Ltd. in 1977.
Awarding body: Canadian Gibson Distillery Ltd., 2085 Union St., Suite 865, Montreal, Que. H3A 1B9, Canada.
Recipients include: Bruce Hutchison (1977).

J. M. Gibson Lectureship in Advanced Surgery

In 1963 the University of Oxford accepted a gift of £1,000 from Sir Paul Patrick, K.C.I.E., C.S.I., M.A., Corpus Christi College, to maintain, in accordance with the desire of the donor, a lectureship in Advanced Surgery to be awarded triennially as a commemoration of John Monroe Gibson, B.A., University College, F.C.S.C. The lecturer is appointed by a Board of the Faculty of Medicine on the recommendation of the Nuffield Professor of Surgery.
Awarding body: Faculty of Medicine, University of Oxford, Wellington Square, Oxford OX1 2JD, England.
Lecturers include: Walter Burdette (Yale Univ., 'The Management of neoplastic disease in prospect', 1966).

Karin Gierow Prize for Cultural Information Achievements

This prize is given annually by the Swedish Academy for dedicated work in promoting Swedish culture. It was endowed in 1967 by Dr. Karl Ragnar Gierow, and consists of two cash prizes – at present 10,000 Swedish kronor each. The prize is given to Swedish writers, journalists, teachers and others engaged in communications. It cannot be applied for.

Awarding body: The Swedish Academy, Börshuset, Källargränd 4, S-111 29 Stockholm, Sweden.

Karin Gierow Prize for Promotion of Knowledge

This prize is given annually by the Swedish Academy for the promotion of knowledge through the written word and other means by Swedish publicists. It was endowed in 1967 by Dr. Karl Ragnar Gierow and consists of a cash prize (at present 10,000 Swedish kronor). It cannot be applied for.

Awarding body: The Swedish Academy, Börshuset, Källargränd 4, S-111 29 Stockholm, Sweden.

Gifford Lectureships in Natural Theology

The lectureship, held at the four older Scottish universities, is for promoting, advancing, and diffusing the study of Natural Theology in the widest sense and as a strictly natural science. It was founded in 1887 in terms of a Trust Disposition and Settlement by Adam, Lord Gifford, a Senator of the College of Justice. The lecturer is appointed by the Senatus Academicus of each university, normally for a two-year period during which a course of lectures is given. It is provided that the lectures be open to the public and that the lecturer be not subject to any test, religious or otherwise.

Awarding bodies: Universities of Aberdeen, Edinburgh, Glasgow and St. Andrews, Scotland.

Lecturers include: Prof. B. G. Mitchell (Glasgow, 1974–75); Prof. J. Z. Young (Aberdeen, 1975–76); Dr. J. P. Jossua (Edinburgh, 1976–77); Prof. R. Hooykaas (St. Andrews, 1975–77); Prof. Sir John Eccles (Edinburgh, 1977–79).

Gill Memorial Award

The award was established in 1887 by Miss Gill in memory of her brother, Captain W. J. Gill, R.E. (1843–82), surveyor and explorer in Persia and the Far East. It is a monetary award made annually by the Royal Geographical Society to encourage geographical research, but may be taken in any suitable form such as survey instruments, plate or books. There is no application for the award; it is made by the Society's Council on the recommendation of a special committee, and the criteria are the academic or other achievements of the recipient.

Awarding body: Royal Geographical Society, 1 Kensington Gore, London SW7 2AR, England.

Recipients include: Dr. O. H. K. Spate (1949); Mlle M. Foncin (1962); Prof. T. W. Freeman (1975); Prof. M. J. Kirkby (1976); Prof. A. Wilson (1978).

Gill Memorial Medal

This award is made every three years for outstanding contributions to the ornithology of geographical South Africa. Such contribution shall be a significant published scientific work or works, or other exceptional services to the advancement of ornithology, or both. The award is not restricted to members of the SAOS.

Awarding body: South African Ornithological Society, P.O.B. 87234, Houghton, 2041 Johannesburg, South Africa.

Federico Giolitti Steel Medal

This award was established in 1958 by the Italian Metallurgical Association in honour of Federico Giolitti (1880–1946), metallurgist and engineer. It is presented every three years for outstanding achievements in the field of iron and steel metallurgy.

Awarding body: Associazione Italiana di Metallurgia, Piazzale Rodolfo Morandi 2, 20121 Milan, Italy.

Recipients include: Domenico Taccone (Italy, 1966); Ernesto Manuelli (Italy, 1969); Herbert Trenkler (Austria, 1973); Bruno Falck, Mario Marchesi (Italy, 1976).

Glazebrook Medal and Prize

A silver gilt medal and a prize of £250 are awarded annually for outstanding contributions in the organization, utilization or application of science. The award was established in 1965 by the Council of the Institute of Physics and the Physical Society, and named after Sir Richard Glazebrook, first President of the Institute of Physics and first Director of the National Physical Laboratory. Candidates are considered on the recommendation of members of the Institute and of its Awards Committee.

Awarding body: The Institute of Physics, 47 Belgrave Square, London SW1Z 8QX, England.

Recipients include: Francis Edgar Jones (1971); Gordon Brims Black McIvor Sutherland (1972); Kurt Hoselitz (1973); Basil John Mason (1974); Walter Charles Marshall (1975).

Gmelin-Beilstein-Denkmünze

This silver medal was established in 1954 by the dye manufacturers, Hoechst Aktiengesellschaft, in memory of Leopold Gmelin and Friedrich Beilstein, founders respectively of the handbooks on inorganic and organic chemistry. The medal, together with a certificate, is awarded to Germans or non-Germans who have distinguished themselves as writers on chemistry or as historians of chemistry, and who have thus fulfilled the aims of the Society of German Chemists.

Awarding body: Gesellschaft Deutscher Chemiker, 6000 Frankfurt (Main) 90, Carl Bosch-Haus, Varrentrappstr. 40–42, Federal Republic of Germany.

Recipients include: Prof. Erich Pietsch (Fed. Rep. of Germany, 1962); Prof. Jean Baptiste Gillis (Belgium, 1965); Eduard Kreuzhage (Fed. Rep. of Germany, 1966); Prof. Werner Schultheis (Fed. Rep. of Germany, 1973); Prof. Hans Rudolf Christen (Fed. Rep. of Germany, 1976).

Goddard Astronautics Award

Established by the AIAA in 1975 to honour Robert H. Goddard, the engineer, the award replaces the former Goddard Award and is the highest distinction the Institute can bestow for the most notable achievement in the field of astronautics. A medal and certificate of citation are presented at the Annual Meeting of the Institute.

Awarding body: American Institute of Aeronautics and Astronautics, 1290 Avenue of the Americas, New York, N.Y. 10019, U.S.A.

Recipients include: James S. Martin, Jr. (1977).

Godlove Award

This award is made every two years by the American Inter-Society Color Council for a contribution to any aspect of the field of colour, either directly by encouraging the application of colour, or by dissemination of knowledge by writing or lecturing. The award, which takes the form of a medal, was established in 1956 in memory of Dr. I. H. Godlove, chairman of the Council's first committee on measurement and specification and editor of its Newsletter. The medal is given to a resident of the U.S.A. or Canada with at least five years' experience in his field of colour.

Awarding body: Inter-Society Color Council, c/o Dr. Fred W. Billmeyer, Jr., Dept. of Chemistry, Rensselaer Polytechnic Institute, MRC Rm. 217, Troy, N.Y. 12181, U.S.A.

Recipients include: Edwin I. Stearns (1967); Harry Helson (1969); Norman Macbeth (1971); Dorothea Jameson Hurvich and Leo Hurvich (1973); Vincent C. Vesce (1975).

Goethe-Medaille

This prize was established in 1954 by the Goethe-Institut in Munich in memory of Johann Wolfgang von Goethe (1749–1832). It is awarded for outstanding scientific, literary, educational or organizational achievements which have improved cultural relations between Germany and other countries. It takes the form of a gold medal and is awarded annually.

Awarding body: Goethe-Institut zur Pflege der deutschen Sprache im Ausland und zur Förderung der internationalen kulturellen Zusammenarbeit e.V., 8 Munich 2, Lenbachplatz 3, Federal Republic of Germany.

Recipients include: Prof. L. Zabrocki (Poland, 1974); Prof. V. Zmegac (Yugoslavia, 1974); Prof. A. Grosser (France, 1975); Prof. Ingerid Dal (Norway, 1976); Prof. Paranjpe (India, 1977).

Goethepreis der Stadt Frankfurt am Main
(Frankfurt am Main Goethe Prize)

This award is presented every three years by the town of Frankfurt am Main, the birthplace of the poet and playwright Johann Wolfgang Goethe (1749–1832). It was established by Ernst Sutter and Alfons Paquet in 1927 to distinguish those who have already achieved recognition through their creative works and are considered worthy of an award dedicated to the memory of Goethe. The award consists of a parchment certificate and a cash prize of DM50,000.

Awarding body: Stadt Frankfurt am Main, Amt für Wissenschaft und Kunst, Brückenstr. 3–7, 6000 Frankfurt am Main 70, Federal Republic of Germany.

Recipients include: Benno Reifenberg (author and journalist, 1964); Carlo Schmid (scientist and politician, 1967); Georg Lukács (philosopher and humanist, 1970); Arno Schmidt (author, 1973); Ingmar Bergman (film director, 1976).

Harry Gold Award

The family of the late Harry Gold donated this award for the purpose of honouring excellence in the teaching of pharmacology to undergraduate, graduate, professional or postdoctoral students. The award is given annually, and consists of a certificate and $1,000. Candidates must be nominated by a member of ASPET, and nominees must be actively engaged in teaching.

Awarding body: American Society for Pharmacology and Experimental Therapeutics, Inc., 9650 Rockville Pike, Bethesda, Md. 20014, U.S.A.

Gold Baton Award

This award is made for distinguished service to music and the arts. It was established in 1948 by the American Symphony Orchestra League. It is given annually, and takes the form of a presentation baton.

Awarding body: American Symphony Orchestra League, Box 669, Vienna, Va. 22180, U.S.A.

Recipients include: Leonard Bernstein (young people's concerts); Mrs. Martha Baird Rockefeller (philanthropy); Leopold Stokowski (opportunities for young musicians); American Federation of Musicians (educational programmes); Mrs. Jouett Shouse (founding of America's first national park for the arts).

Maurice Goldblatt Cytology Award

The award was established in 1961 by the International Academy of Cytology to honour Maurice Goldblatt, President of the Cancer Research Foundation in Chicago. The prize is awarded annually for pioneering achievements in the field of clinical cytology and is issued every three years at the International Congress of Cytology. It comprises a gold medal, a certificate and a cheque for $1,500. Researchers and prominent clinicians who have contributed significantly to the development and progress of clinical cytology are eligible.

Awarding body: International Academy of Cytology, 5841 Maryland Ave., HM 449, Chicago, Ill. 60637, U.S.A.

Recipients include: Dr. Arthur I. Spriggs (U.K., 1970); Prof. S. F. Patten, Jr. (U.S.A., 1971);

Prof. T. O. Caspersson (Sweden, 1972); Prof. H.-J. Soost (Fed. Rep. of Germany, 1973); Prof. G. Riotton (Switzerland, 1974).

Golden Berlin Bear

This is the main award given at the Berlin International Film Festival for the best film (long or short). The sculpture of a bear is presented on the last evening of the annual Festival held in June–July. The Festival, established in 1951, has the objective of informing a wide public of the development of international film art, of gathering film personalities from all over the world for an exchange of views, and of encouraging better understanding between nations. The proposed films must not have been completed before May of the preceding year. They may have been shown theatrically only in their countries of origin or in countries where the original language of the film is spoken, but they must not have been shown on television; German-speaking films must not have run in Berlin. Films already shown competitively at other international film events are not eligible. Besides the Golden Bear awards, Silver Bears are also given for the best director, best actor, best actress in long films, and for other outstanding achievements in short films.

Awarding body: Berlin International Film Festival, Bundesallee 1–12, 1000 Berlin 15, Federal Republic of Germany.

Recipients include: Pier Paolo Pasolini (Italy, (*Canterbury Tales*, 1972); Robert Altman (U.S.A., *Buffalo Bill and the Indians or Sitting Bull's History Lesson*, 1976); Larissa Chepitko (U.S.S.R., *Ascension*, 1977); Peter Lilienthal (Fed. Rep. of Germany, *David*, 1978).

Golden Egg International Prize for Zootechnics

This annual prize was established in 1964 by Francesco Vismara, S.p.A., a firm which specializes in the feeds and meat packing industry. It is awarded in March during the international agricultural fair in Verona. It consists of a gold replica of a hen's egg and a certificate, and is awarded for scientific and practical progress in the field of zootechnics.

Awarding body: Associazione Premio Internazionale per la Zootecnia Uovo d'Oro, Via Mameli 10, 22064 Casatenovo, Italy.

Recipients include: Profs. Ivo Peli (Italy) and Carlos Luis de Cuenca (Spain), 1975; Profs. Albert de Vuyst (Belgium) and Alfio Falaschini (Italy), 1976; Profs. Kurt Nehring (German Dem. Rep.) and Marino Gasparini (Italy), 1977.

Golden Globe Award

This award was started in 1943 by a group of Hollywood foreign correspondents. An annual presentation of golden statuettes takes place in January for achievements in motion pictures and television during the previous year. At the first award ceremony three prizes were given: for the best motion picture drama, best actor and best actress; the number of awards has now risen to 28, and includes recognition for foreign films, directing, writing, music, etc.

Awarding body: Hollywood Foreign Press Association, 8732 Sunset Blvd., Suite 210, Los Angeles, Calif. 90069, U.S.A.

Recipients include: Rocky (best motion picture – drama), *A Star is Born* (best motion picture – musical), Peter Finch (best actor – drama), Faye Dunaway (best actress – drama), Sidney Lumet (best director), 1977.

Golden Harp Television Festival

The Golden Harp is the main award made annually at the Golden Harp Television Festival for the best television programme entered. The festival was established by Radio Telefís Éireann under the patronage of the European Broadcasting Union in 1966. It is open to broadcasting organizations which are members or associated members of the International Telecommunications Union. Programmes must not be less than 12 minutes or more than 35 minutes in duration. Second and third prizes of a Silver Harp and a Bronze Harp are also awarded. The Golden Harp trophy is in the form of a gold-plated harp on a marble base, designed by a leading Irish sculptor.

Awarding body: Radio Telefís Éireann, Donnybrook, Dublin 4, Ireland.

Recipients include: Finnish Broadcasting Corporation (*The Last Laments*, 1973); British Broadcasting Corporation (*Look Stranger – The Hobby Horse Man*, 1974); Yugoslav Television (*The Thirst of the Dead*, 1975); London Weekend Television (*Finnan Games*, 1976); Radiotelevisión Española (*Adivina Adivinanza*, 1977).

Golden Pen of Freedom

The International Federation of Newspaper Publishers (FIEJ) established the award in 1948 to pay tribute to an individual, a group or an institution having, by its writings or its actions, rendered outstanding service to the freedom of the press. The annual award consists of a gold pen in a case, with an engraved plaque. Applications for the award may be made personally, or candidates may be nominated by anyone connected with the press.

Awarding body: International Federation of Newspaper Publishers (FIEJ), 6 rue du Faubourg Poissonnière, 75010 Paris, France.

Recipients include: Julio de Mesquita Neto (*O Estado de São Paolo*, Brazil, 1974); Dr. Sang-Man Kim (*Dong-A Ilbo*, Rep. of Korea, 1975); Raul Rêgo (*Republica* and *A Luta*, Portugal, 1976); Robert Lilley (*Belfast Telegraph*, U.K., 1977).

'Golden Prague' International Television Festival

This annual competition was founded in 1964 by Czechoslovak Television, with the aim of furthering international co-operation in the field of television and of providing a platform for the broadest possible examination of the results of creative work. There are two categories: drama, and musical programmes. The Festival is open to any public television organization. Only original programmes created specially for television and produced in the last year are eligible. Maximum screening time is 90 minutes for drama and 60 minutes for musical programmes. The main prize in each category is the 'Golden Prague', which takes the form of a bronze statuette. There are 14 other prizes (for the best script, best direction, best camera work, etc.), as well as special mentions.

Awarding body: 'Golden Prague' International Television Festival, Czechoslovak Television, 29–30 Gorkého nám., Prague 1, Czechoslovakia.

Recipients include: U.S.S.R. (drama, *Strannye Vzroslye*, 1975); NHK, Japan (drama, *Ghuou Ryusa*, 1976); ČST, Czechoslovakia (musical, *Balady Na Slova Moravské Lidové Poezie*, 1975); U.S.S.R. (musical, *Phantasia*, 1976).

Golden Rose of Montreux

Each year in May the Swiss city of Montreux organizes an international contest of television light entertainment programmes, under the patronage of the European Broadcasting Union and with the collaboration of the Swiss Broadcasting Corporation. Variety shows, light entertainment (with scenario), personality shows and programmes of songs, light music, jazz and pop music are all eligible. Dancing, pantomime, folk music, cabaret, circus and informative pieces are admissible only as elements of a programme. Programmes should be 15–60 minutes in length, and should have been screened during the previous 14 months. Those that have already obtained an international award are not eligible. Participation is open to all organizations which operate a national television service, but each organization may enter one programme only. The Golden Rose carries with it a cash prize of 10,000 Swiss francs; four other prizes are awarded: a silver rose; a bronze rose; the special prize of the city of Montreux for the funniest entry; and the Press prize (awarded by a jury of television critics and journalists). The latter two prizes take the form of statuettes. The competition was instituted in 1960 by Marcel Bezençon.

Awarding body: Société Suisse de Radiodiffusion et Télévision, Giacomettistr. 1, 3000 Berne 15, Switzerland.

Recipients include: Sveriges Radio, *The N.S.V.I.P.'s* (Sweden, 1973); Televisión española, *Don Juan* (Spain, 1974); Radiotelevisione Italiana, *Fatti e Fattaci* (Italy, 1975); Norsk Rikskringkasting, *The Nor-Way to Broadcasting* (Norway, 1976); ITV/ATV, *The Muppet Show* (U.K., 1977).

Goldene Medaille der Goethe-Gesellschaft in Weimar (*Gold Medal of the Weimar Goethe Society*)

This prize was first awarded in 1910. It is for special literary services.

Awarding body: Goethe-Gesellschaft in Weimar, 53 Weimar, Burgplatz 4, Schloss, German Democratic Republic.

Recipients include: Prof. Dr. Andreas Bruno Wachsmuth (1970); Prof. Dr. Erich Trunz, Prof. Helmut Holtzhauer, Prof. Dr. Wilhelm Girnus, Prof. Dr. Hans Tümmler (1975).

V. M. Goldschmidt Medal

A gold medal and certificate are awarded annually or at the discretion of the Geochemical Society's Council for a major achievement in geochemistry or cosmochemistry consisting of either a single contribution or series of publications having great influence in the field.

Awarding body: Geochemical Society, c/o Dr. Peter R. Buseck, Chemistry Dept., Arizona State University, Tempe, Ariz. 85281, U.S.A.

Gonin Medal

The gold medal is awarded for the best worldwide achievement in the field of ophthalmology. It is awarded every four years at the International Congress of Ophthalmology, and was established in 1946 by Lausanne University in memory of J. Gonin, professor of ophthalmology at the university and inventor of the surgical techniques for curing detached retina.

Awarding body: International Council of Ophthalmology.

Recipients include: J. François (1962); H. Goldmann (1966); Meyer Schwickerath (1970); D. G. Cogan (1974); Norman H. Ashton (1978).

Goodacre Medal and Gift

This award for outstanding contributions to astronomy made over many years of investigation and endeavour, was established about 1930 at the bequest of Walter Goodacre, the distinguished lunar observer and cartographer. It is made not more than once in two years and consists of a silver-gilt medal and about £20. Recipients must be members of the British Astronomical Association and the terms of the award imply seniority.

Awarding body: British Astronomical Association, Burlington House, Piccadilly, London W.1, England.

Recipients include: B. M. Peek (authority on Jupiter, 1957); F. J. Hargreaves (great planetary observer and outstanding telescope-maker, 1959); Dr. W. H. Steavenson (perhaps the greatest amateur of the century, 1961); Dr. A. F. O'D. Alexander (authority on Saturn, 1962); Dr. G. Merton (authority on comets, 1963).

Harry Goode Memorial Award

Established in 1964, the award is in memory of Harry Goode (1909–60), who was a pioneer in the field of system engineering and Chairman of the National Joint Computer Committee. A medal and certificate are awarded annually to honour and encourage outstanding contributions to the information processing field.

Awarding body: American Federation of Information Processing Societies, Inc.

Recipients include: Allen Newell (1971); Seymour Cray (1972); Edsger Dijkstra (1974); Kenneth Iverson (1975); Lawrence Roberts (1976).

Jeffrey A. Gottlieb Memorial Award

This prize was established in 1976 in honour of the late Jeffrey A. Gottlieb, Chief of the Chemotherapy Service at M. D. Anderson Hospital and Tumor Institute, who died of cancer in 1975 at the age of 35. The award is given to a physician for significant contributions to clinical therapeutic cancer research. It is presented annually at the time the recipient delivers the Gottlieb Award Lecture in Houston, and consists of a certificate and an honorarium.

Awarding body: The University of Texas System Cancer Center, M. D. Anderson Hospital and Tumor Institute, Texas Medical Center, Houston, Tex. 77030, U.S.A.

Recipient: Dr. Vincent T. DeVita, Jr. (1976).

Murray Gottlieb Prize Essay Award

This prize is intended to stimulate the writing of American medical history. It was established by Mrs. Johanna Gottlieb in memory of her husband, and has been awarded annually since 1956. It consists of a cash prize of $100 and publication of the essay in the *Bulletin* of the Medical Library Association.

Awarding body: Medical Library Association, 919 North Michigan Ave., Chicago, Ill. 60611, U.S.A.

Gottschalk Medal

Established in 1977 by the Australian Academy of Science, the medal is in memory of the late Dr. Alfred Gottschalk, Fellow of the Academy. The medal and an honorarium of A$200 are awarded annually for distinguished work in either or both medical and biological sciences to a scientist not over the age of 36, and who is not a member of the Academy. The work should have been carried out mainly in Australia.

Awarding body: Australian Academy of Science, P.O.B. 783, Canberra City, A.C.T. 2601, Australia.

Gouden KNCV-Medaille (*KNCV Gold Medal*)

This medal was established as an annual award in 1963 by the Board of the Royal Netherlands Chemical Society to promote the interest of young Dutch chemists in scientific research and to enable the discovery of new talent in this field.

Awarding body: Koninklijke Nederlandse Chemische Vereniging, Burnierstraat 1, The Hague, The Netherlands.

Gouden Penseel (*Gold Paintbrush*)

This award, established in 1973, is given annually during Children's Book Week in the Netherlands for the best illustrations for a children's book by a Dutch artist. It consists of a gold paintbrush and a cash prize of 2,500 guilders.

Awarding body: Collectieve Propaganda van het Nederlandse Boek, Langestraat 61, Amsterdam, The Netherlands.

Recipients include: Wim Hofman (1974); Paul Hushof (1975); Lidia Postma (1976).

Gouden en Zilveren Griffels (*Gold and Silver Pencils*)

These awards are made annually during Children's Book Week in the Netherlands. They were established in 1971. A maximum of three gold pencils and a cash prize of 2,500 guilders each are given for the best children's books published in Holland in the preceding year. Further awards of silver pencils (maximum eight) are given for the best Dutch or translated children's books.

Awarding body: Collectieve Propaganda van het Nederlandse Boek, Langestraat 61, Amsterdam, The Netherlands.

Recipients include: Simone Schell, Alet Schouten (1975); Guus Kuijer (1976).

Goue Akademiemedalje vir natuurwetenskaplike prestasie (*Gold Academy Medal for Achievement in Natural Sciences*)

In 1955 a committee of the Faculty of Natural Science and Technology of the South African Academy recommended that an honour be awarded for creative work in the field of technology – i.e. work of practical discovery and ingenuity coupled with an element of technical ability. It is intended to reward work which falls outside the scope of the Academy's Havenga Prize (*q.v.*). The medal is donated by the South African Chamber of Mines, and is now awarded every three years.

Awarding body: Suid-Afrikaanse Akademie vir Wetenskap en Kuns, Posbus 538, Pretoria 0001, South Africa.

Recipients include: P. A. L. Steyn (1972); Dr. C. J. G. Niehaus (1973); T. G. la G. Joubert (1974); R. S. Loubser (1977).

Governor General's Literary Awards

These awards were established in 1937 by the Canadian Authors Association and given their title with the agreement of the then Governor General of Canada, Lord Tweedsmuir, widely known as John Buchan, novelist and historian. They are presented annually to the authors of the best books in three categories: fiction; non-fiction; and poetry and drama (one in English, one in French in each category), written and published by Canadians during the preceding calendar year. Each of the six winners receives a cash prize of $5,000 and a specially bound copy of his/her book, presented by the Governor General.

Awarding body: Canada Council, P.O.B. 1047, Ottawa, Ont. K1P 5V8, Canada.

Recipients include: Milton Acorn (*The Island Means Minago*), Marion MacRae and Anthony Adamson (*Hallowed Walls*), Brian Moore (*The Great Victorian Collection*), Louis-Edmond Hamelin (*Nordicité canadienne*), Anne Hébert (*Les enfants du sabbat*), Pierre Perrault (*Chouennes*), 1975.

Sir Frederick Gowland Hopkins Medal

This award was established in 1958 in memory of Sir Frederick Gowland Hopkins, the eminent biochemist, who died in 1947. It is made every two years for distinction in the field of biochemistry. Biochemists of any nationality are eligible. A cash prize of £100 accompanies the medal, which is bestowed after the delivery of a lecture assessing the impact of recent advances in a field, chosen by the lecturer, on progress in biochemistry.

Awarding body: The Biochemical Society, 7 Warwick Court, London WC1R 5DP, England.

Recipients include: H. A. Barker ('Biochemical Functions of Corrinoid Compounds', 1967); F. J. W. Roughton, F.R.S. ('Some Recent Work on the Interactions of Oxygen, Carbon Dioxide and Haemoglobin', 1969); F. Sanger, C.B.E., F.R.S. ('Nucleotide Sequences in Bacteriophage RNA', 1971); M. F. Perutz, C.B.E., F.R.S. ('The Molecular Pathology of Human Haemoglobin', 1973); E. Racker ('Reconstitution, Mechanism of Action and Control of Ion Pumps', 1975).

Reinier de Graafmedaille

Founded in 1952 by the Netherlands Association for the Advancement of Natural, Medical and Surgical Sciences, the medal is awarded every nine years for outstanding scientific contributions to medicine. It is named after Reinier de Graaf, the famous Dutch physician (1641–73).

Awarding body: Genootschap ter bevordering van Natuur-, Genees- en Heelkunde, Plantage Muidergracht 12, Amsterdam, The Netherlands.

Recipients include: Prof. Paul Govaerts (Belgium, 1952); Prof. S. van Crefeld (Netherlands, 1961); Prof. B. G. Ziedses des Plantes (Netherlands, 1970).

Duncan Graham Award

This award is presented by the Royal College of Physicians and Surgeons of Canada to an individual of international renown in the field of medical education.

Awarding body: Royal College of Physicians and Surgeons of Canada, 74 Stanley Ave., Ottawa, Ont. K1M 1P4, Canada.

Recipients include: Dr. Douglas E. Cannell (1972); Dr. Robert C. Dickson (1974); Dr. William Boyd (1975); Dr. Eugène Robillard (1976); Dr. John F. McCreary (1977).

Gran Medalla Nacional General Francisco de Paula Santander *(General Francisco de Paula Santander National Grand Medal)*

The Colombian Ministry of Education established this international award in 1974 to honour the memory of the national hero, General Francisco de Paula Santander. The purpose of the award is to encourage and reward outstanding services to Colombian education and culture, or to the enrichment of the national heritage. The medal is awarded in two classes, Officer and Commander, and can be conferred at any time.

Awarding body: Ministerio de Educación Nacional, Bogotá, Colombia.

Gran Premio Anual 'Pedro Domingo Murillo' *('Pedro Domingo Murillo' Annual Grand Prize)*

These annual monetary prizes were established in 1953 and are awarded by the 'Franz Tamayo' cultural institute of La Paz. They are given in the following disciplines: painting, sculpture, kinetic art or montage, engraving, water colour and drawing. A prize may be withheld if no exhibit reaches the required standard.

Awarding body: Dirección General de Cultura, Casilla 5881, La Paz, Bolivia.

Recipients include: Gonzalo Ribero Morales (painting, *Refugio de los Dioses*, 1975); César Jordán Córdova (kinetic art or montage, *Relieve I*, 1975); Max Condori Vargas (engraving, *Olvido Permanente*, 1976); Octavio Vargas (water colour, *Inicio de Vuelo*, 1976); Edgar Arandia Quiroga (painting, *Niños Jugando con la Muerte*, 1976).

Gran Premio de Honor *(Grand Prize of Honour)*

This annual prize awarded by the Argentine Writers' Society comprises a gold medal and diploma and is given to an Argentinian writer whose complete works are judged to have made a lasting contribution to literature. It is presented on 13 June, the Día del Escritor (Writer's Day).

Awarding body: Sociedad Argentina de Escritores, Uruguay 1371, Buenos Aires, Argentina.

Recipients include: Raúl González Tuñon (1972); Manuel J. Castilla (1973); Ernesto Sabato (1974); Adolfo Bioy Casares (1975); José Isaacson (1976).

Grand Aigle d'Or de la Ville de Nice *(Golden Eagle of the Town of Nice)*

This international literary prize was established in 1970 by the town of Nice to mark the occasion of the International Book Fair held in Nice. It is presented annually in May during the Fair to a writer of any nationality for his/her entire literary work. The winner receives 30,000 French francs.

Awarding body: Secrétariat du Festival International du Livre, 5 rue Stanislas, 75006 Paris, France.

Recipients include: Julio Cortázar (Argentina, 1976); Louis Guilloux (France, 1978).

Grand Prix de l'Association Aéronautique et Astronautique de France *(French Aeronautical and Astronautical Association Grand Prize)*

This prize is awarded annually to a person of any nationality, in recognition of outstanding services or work in the field of aeronautics or astronautics. Nominations should be presented by two members of the above association. The winner receives a diploma and a medal.

Awarding body: Association Aéronautique et Astronautique de France, 80 rue Lauriston, 75116 Paris, France.

Recipients include: Lucien Servanty (1973); Jean Boulet (1974); Henri Deplante (1975).

Grand Prix de la Critique Littéraire *(Literary Critics Grand Prize)*

This annual prize for literary criticism was established in 1948 by Robert Kemp. Works should be submitted about three months before the award, which is made every autumn. The winner receives a cash prize of 2,000 francs.

Awarding body: Syndicat des Critiques Littéraires, Hôtel de Massa, 38 rue du Faubourg Saint Jacques, 75014 Paris, France.

Recipients include: Maurice Bardèche (*Marcel Proust, romancier*, 1971); André Wurmser (*Conseils de révision*, 1972); Pierre Barbéris (*Le Monde de Balzac*, 1973); Jean-Pierre Richard (*Proust et le Monde terrible*, 1974); José Cabanis (*Saint-Simon l'Admirable*, 1975).

Grand Prix International de Poésie (*International Grand Prize for Poetry*)

The prize was founded in 1956 at the 'Biennales Internationales de Poésie' held in Knokke, Belgium, by the International House of Poetry which also created the Biennale. A monetary prize of 100,000 Belgian francs, it is awarded for the published works of a poet of international repute. The jury consists of poets and critics of various nationalities. No applications are accepted.

Awarding body: Maison Internationale de la Poésie, 147 Chaussée de Maecht, 1030 Brussels, Belgium.

Recipients include: Léopold Sédar Senghor (Senegal, 1970); Yannis Ritsos (Greece, 1972); Vladimir Holan (Czechoslovakia, 1974); Miguel Torga (1976).

Grand Prix Littéraire de l'Afrique Noire (*Black Africa Literary Grand Prize*)

Founded in 1960, this annual prize of 2,000 francs is given either for one particular book or for the whole of an author's work. All literary genres are acceptable. Books submitted should have been published during the preceding year, and authors should be citizens of one of the French-speaking Black African countries. Three of the ten-member jury are ambassadors from African countries accredited to France.

Awarding body: Association des Ecrivains de Langue Française (Mer et Outre-Mer), 38 rue du Faubourg-Saint-Jacques, 75014 Paris, France.

Recipients include: Etienne Yanou (Cameroon, *L'homme Dieu de Bisso*, 1975); Mme Aoua Keita (Mali, *Femme d'Afrique*, 1976); Sory Camara (Guinea, *Gens de la Parole, Essai sur la condition et le rôle des Griots dans la Société Malinke*, 1977).

Grand Prix Littéraire de Madagascar (*Madagascar Literary Grand Prize*)

Re-founded in 1961 after a lapse, this prize of 2,000 French francs is given in even-numbered years either for one particular work published during the previous two years, or for an author's total published work. It is given either to a Malagasy author writing in French or to a French author writing on a theme dealing with Madagascar. Authors and publishers are invited to submit books in any literary genre (poetry, novel, drama, reporting, short stories, essay, historical or geographical study).

Awarding body: Association des Ecrivains de Langue Française (Mer et Outre-Mer), 38 rue du Faubourg-Saint-Jacques, 75014 Paris, France.

Recipients include: Pierre Randrianarisoa (Madagascar, *La diplomatie malgache face à la politique des grandes puissances*, 1972); Alain Spacensky (France, Madagascar: *50 ans de vie politique de Ralaimongo à Tsiranana*, 1972); Raymond Delval (France, *Radama II*, 1974); Daniel Coulaud (France, *Les Zafimaniry*, 1974); Pelandrova Dreo (Madagascar, *Pelandrova*, 1976).

Grand Prix Littéraire de la Ville de Montréal (*City of Montreal Grand Prize for Literature*)

The prize was established in 1965 by the Mayor of Montreal, Mr. Jean Drapeau, and the Municipal Council. An award of $3,000 is made annually to the author of a literary work published in Montreal during the previous year. Authors are not limited to one entry.

Awarding body: The Greater Montreal Council of Arts, 700 St. Antoine St. East, Suite 112, Montreal, Que. H2Y 1A6, Canada.

Recipients include: Antonine Maillet (*Mariagélas*, 1974); Hubert Aquin (*Neige noire*, 1975); Guy Robert (*Lemieux*, 1976); Gilles Marcotte (*Le roman à l'imparfait*, 1977).

Grand Prix de Littérature (*Grand Prize for Literature*)

This annual prize of 50,000 francs is one of the major awards of the French Academy. It is given to a prose writer or a poet for either one or several works which show great inspiration and noteworthy style. It may not be shared, and writers may not submit their own work.

Awarding body: Académie Française, 23 Quai de Conti, Paris 6e, France.

Recipients include: Marguerite Yourcenar (for her complete works, 1977); Paul Guth (1978).

Grand Prix de la Mer (*Grand Prize of the Sea*)

Established in 1970, this annual prize of 2,000 French francs is given for one particular book or for the whole of an author's published work which, directly or indirectly, concerns the sea. Authors and publishers are invited to submit works of creative literature written in French and published during the preceding year.

Awarding body: Association des Ecrivains de Langue Française (Mer et Outre-Mer), 38 rue du Faubourg-Saint-Jacques, 75014 Paris, France.

Recipients include: Gérard Janichon (*Damien*, 1974); Bernard Gorsky (*La mer retrouvée* and complete works, 1975); Jean-François Deniau (*La mer est ronde*, 1976); Jean Laine (*Les Naufrageurs*, 1976); Georges Aubin (complete works, 1977).

Grand Prix National de l'Architecture (*National Grand Prize for Architecture*)

First awarded in 1976, this is the most recent of the national prizes established by the French Ministry of Culture. It is awarded annually at the same time (mid-December) as the prizes for literature, art, music, theatre and film. The prize money is currently 20,000 francs.

Awarding body: Secrétariat d'Etat à la Culture, 3 rue de Valois, 75001 Paris, France.

Recipients include: Roger Taillibert (1976).

Grand Prix National des Arts (*National Grand Prize for Art*)
This prize is awarded annually to a French artist for outstanding work in one of the fine arts. It is awarded by the Ministry of Culture in mid-December, at the same time as the other national prizes for literature, architecture, music, theatre and film. The prize money is currently 20,000 francs.
Awarding body: Secrétariat d'Etat à la Culture, 3 rue de Valois, 75001 Paris, France.
Recipients include: Arpad Szenes (painter, 1978).

Grand Prix National du Cinéma (*National Grand Prize for Cinema*)
The prize is awarded annually for achievement in some aspect of the cinema world which has contributed to the cultural life of France. The award is made annually in mid-December at the same time as the other national prizes for literature, art, architecture, music and theatre. The prize money is currently 20,000 francs.
Awarding body: Secrétariat d'Etat à la Culture, 3 rue de Valois, 75001 Paris, France.
Recipients include: Robert Bresson (1978).

Grand Prix National des Lettres (*National Grand Prize for Literature*)
This prize is awarded to a French writer whose entire work, in whatever genre, has contributed to the glory of French language and literature. The prize is awarded annually in mid-December, at the same time as the equivalent national prizes for art, architecture, music, theatre and cinema. Nominations may not be submitted. Founded in 1950, the prize is currently worth 20,000 francs.
Awarding body: Secrétariat d'Etat à la Culture, 3 rue de Valois, 75001 Paris, France.
Recipients include: Jean Cassou (1971); Marguerite Yourcenar (1974); André Dhôtel (1975); Armand Lunel (1976); Roger Caillois (1978).

Grand Prix National de la Musique (*National Grand Prize for Music*)
The prize, founded in 1967, is awarded annually to a French musician for outstanding contributions to national culture in this field. It is awarded annually by the Ministry of Culture at the same time as the other national prizes for literature, art, architecture, theatre and film. The prize money is currently 20,000 francs.
Awarding body: Secrétariat d'Etat à la Culture, 3 rue de Valois, 75001 Paris, France.
Recipients include: Georges Auric (1978).

Grand Prix National du Théâtre (*National Grand Prize for Theatre*)
This prize is awarded annually to an exceptional theatre personality – actor, director, manager, etc. – for the whole of his/her work which has benefited the cultural life of France. It is awarded in mid-December with the other national prizes for literature, art, architecture, music and cinema. The prize money is currently 20,000 francs.

Awarding body: Secrétariat d'Etat à la Culture, 3 rue de Valois, 75001 Paris, France.
Recipients include: Jacques Noël (1978).

Grand Prix de Poésie de la Fondation Roucoules (*Roucoules Foundation Grand Prize for Poetry*).
Under the terms of this Foundation an annual prize of 25,000 francs is awarded to a French poet. This prize is not competitive and authors may not submit entries.
Awarding body: Académie Française, 23 Quai de Conti, Paris 6e, France.
Recipients include: Robert Mallet and Marie-Jeanne Durry (shared, 1977); Charles Le Quintrec (1978).

Grand Prix du Rayonnement de la Langue Française (*Grand Prize for the Dissemination of the French Language*)
This is one of the few prizes awarded by the French Academy which are open to foreigners as well as French nationals. It is an annual monetary prize (20,000 francs in 1978), and may be awarded to more than one person at a time. Authors may not present their work for consideration.
Awarding body: Académie Française, 23 Quai de Conti, Paris 6e, France.
Recipients include: Prof. Joseph Hanse (Belgium, Pres., *Conseil International de la Langue Française*, 1977); Alliance Française (1978).

Grand Prix des Sciences (*Grand Prize for Science*)
This is an annual prize instituted by the National Convention in the 18th century and therefore one of the oldest-established of French prizes. It is paid from the national budget and its value is now 40,000 francs. The prize is awarded by the Academy of Science alternately for work in either mathematics and physics or chemistry and natural sciences.
Awarding body: Académie des Sciences, 23 Quai de Conti, Paris 6e, France.
Recipients include: Mme Hélène Charniaux-Cotton (experimental biology, 1977); Noël Felici (mathematics and physics, 1978).

Grande Médaille d'Or (*Grand Gold Medal*)
This is the highest award of the French Academy of Architecture, given to a French citizen or a foreigner for outstanding achievement or service in this field. It is usually given annually but may be deferred. It was established in 1965. (The Academy also confers silver and silver-gilt medals for achievement in allied fields (e.g. landscaping) and in art history.)
Awarding body: Académie d'Architecture, Hôtel de Chaulnes, 9 place des Vosges, 75004 Paris, France.
Recipients include: Sir Basil Spence (U.K., 1974); Josep Lluis Sert (U.S.A., 1975); Marcel Breuer (U.S.A., 1976); Kevin Roche (U.S.A., 1977); Pedro Ramirez Vasquez (Mexico, 1978).

Dr. Jan Graulsprijs

The prize was established in 1973 by the Belgian Royal Academy of Dutch Language and Literature in memory of Dr. Jan Grauls (1887–1960), philologist and civil servant. An award of 20,000 Belgian francs is made every five years for the best submitted essay, written in Dutch, in the field of Dutch linguistics or folklore. Preferred subjects are semantics, onomastics, dialects, proverbs and purism. Recipients must be Belgian nationals.

Awarding body: Koninklijke Academie voor Nederlandse Taal- en Letterkunde, Koningstraat 18, B-9000 Ghent, Belgium.

Graves Lecture, Prize and Medal

Two awards are made annually under this title. The first was established in 1961 by the Irish Royal Academy of Medicine and the Medical Research Council of Ireland in memory of Robert James Graves, a Dublin physician who first described Graves Disease and first instituted formal clinical teaching. The second award was established in 1975 by the Irish Royal Academy of Medicine and Saint Luke's Hospital, Dublin, which is the Oncology and Radiotherapy Centre for Ireland. The conditions governing both awards are the same. Each one is made following a public lecture on a special subject and the lecturer receives a cash prize of £150 and a silver medal. Candidates for the awards should be preferably under 40 years of age and the lecture should embody clinical research carried out wholly or partly in Ireland. Nominations must be made by two Fellows of the Irish Royal Academy of Medicine.

Awarding bodies: Irish Royal Academy of Medicine, Medical Research Council of Ireland, Saint Luke's Hospital, Dublin, Ireland.

Lecturers include: (Graves Lecture) Prof. E. Bourke, M.R.C.P. (Edin.); Prof. M. I. Drury, F.R.C.P.I.; Prof. P. Elmes, F.R.C.P.; (Saint Luke's Lecture) Dr. J. J. Fennelly, F.R.C.P.I.; Dr. J. Murphy, M.R.C.P.I., M.R.C.O.G.

Gordon Gray Award

Formerly called the Special Award, and established in 1968, the Gordon Gray Award was renamed in honour of the second Chairman of the U.S. National Trust. It is given in recognition of outstanding achievement in special areas in support of historic preservation, though not necessarily in the field of preservation itself. These areas may include: banking, business and industry; communications media; scholarship; restoration architecture; traditional crafts; adaptive use of historic structures; public agencies; legislation. It consists of a trophy or scroll or both, and is awarded annually.

Awarding body: The National Trust for Historic Preservation, 740–748 Jackson Place, N.W., Washington, D.C. 20006, U.S.A.

Recipients include: St. Louis Symphony Orchestra and James Marston Fitch, Columbia Univ. (1974); College of Charleston, S.C. (1975); Childs Bertman Tseckares Associates, Boston, and Sigma Chi Fraternity, Univ. of Wisconsin Chapter (1976).

L. H. Gray Medal

This award was established in 1967 by the International Commission on Radiation Units and Measurements, to honour outstanding contributions in scientific fields of interest to ICRU. It commemorates Louis Harold Gray, physical scientist and former Vice-Chairman of ICRU. The medal is awarded every four years, at the International Congress of Radiology, when the recipient is invited to deliver a lecture.

Awarding body: International Commission on Radiation Units and Measurements, 7910 Woodmont Ave., Suite 1016, Washington, D.C. 20014, U.S.A.

Recipients include: Lewis V. Spencer (1969); John W. Boag (1973); Mortimer M. Elkind (1977).

Samuel Arnold Greeley Award

This award was established in 1968 by the Sanitary (now Environmental) Engineering Division of the ASCE, in honour of Samuel A. Greeley, past Director and Hon. M.ASCE. The award is made to the member whose paper makes the most valuable contribution to the environmental engineering profession; only those engaged in the private practice of environmental engineering are eligible. The award consists of a plaque and certificate.

Awarding body: American Society of Civil Engineers, 345 East 47th St., New York, N.Y. 10017, U.S.A.

Recipients include: Ralph G. Berk ('Disposal Well Problems in Chicago and Bakersfield Areas', 1973); James A. Mueller, Thomas J. Mulligan and Dominic M. di Toro ('Gas Transfer Kinetics of Pure Oxygen System', 1974); R. Stone ('Landfill Disposal of Liquid Sewage Sludge', 1976).

Kate Greenaway Medal

The Library Association established the award in 1955 in honour of Kate Greenaway to recognize the importance of illustrations in children's books. It is awarded annually to the artist who has produced the most distinguished work for a children's book published in the U.K. during the preceding year. Recommendations are made by members of the Library Association.

Awarding body: The Library Association, 7 Ridgmount St., London WC1E 7AE, U.K.

Recipients include: Raymond Briggs (*Father Christmas*, 1973); Pat Hutchins (*The Wind Blew*, 1974); Victor Ambrus (*Horses in Battle* and *Mishka*, 1975); Gail Haley (*The Post Office Cat*, 1976); Shirley Hughes (*Dogger*, 1977).

A. P. Greensfelder Construction Prize

The St. Louis Regional Planning and Construction Foundation Trust founded the ASCE Construction Engineering Prize in 1939, and in 1961 its name was changed to the A. P. Greensfelder Construction Prize. The award is annual, and open to non-members of the ASCE; it consists of a cash prize of $150, a plaque and a certificate. It is given for the best original scientific or educational article on construction published in *Civil*

Engineering. The article should deal primarily with the construction phase of an engineering project.

Awarding body: American Society of Civil Engineers (ASCE), 345 East 47th St., New York, N.Y. 10017, U.S.A.

Recipients include: Edward Peterson and Peter Frobenius ('Soft-Ground Tunneling Technology on the BART Project', 1973); Ernest C. Harris and John A. Talbott ('Longest Concrete-Arch Bridge in North America', 1974); A. P. Bezzone ('Pine Valley Creek Bridge – A First', 1976).

Herbert E. Gregory Medal

This medal is awarded for a distinguished research contribution in the Pacific in anthropology, botany, geology or zoology, plus a distinguished contribution to the development of institutions and organizations sponsoring and supporting Pacific research. The medal is presented every five years at the Congress of the Pacific Science Association. First presented in 1961, the award is bestowed by the Trustees of Bishop Museum, Honolulu, in honour of Herbert E. Gregory, the founder of the Pacific Science Association and Director of the Museum from 1920 to 1936.

Awarding body: The Pacific Science Association, U.S.A.

Recipients include: Prof. A. P. Elkin (Australia, 1961); Prof. G. P. Murdock (U.S.A., 1966); Dr. F. R. Fosberg (U.S.A., 1971); Dr. J. Linsley Gressitt (1976).

John Grierson International Technical Award

Established by the Society of Motion Picture and Television Engineers, the award is in honour of John Grierson (1898–1972), the pioneer British documentary film maker. The award is made annually for outstanding contributions to the science and technology of equipment, processes or techniques related primarily to the production of documentary motion pictures.

Awarding body: Society of Motion Picture and Television Engineers, 862 Scarsdale Ave., Scarsdale, N.Y. 10583, U.S.A.

Grillparzer Prize

The prize was established in 1871 on the occasion of the 80th birthday of the Austrian poet Franz Grillparzer (1791–1872). Although the award of the prize lapsed in 1976, the Austrian Academy of Sciences still retains the right to make the award. The prize, a certificate and a sum of money, is given for a dramatic work in the German language, which in the preceding three years has been performed with success on a well-known stage in a German-speaking area. The work must not have received any other prize.

Awarding body: Österreichische Akademie der Wissenschaften, 1010 Vienna, Dr.-Ignaz-Seipel-Platz 2, Austria.

Recipients include: Gerhart Hauptmann; Arthur Schnitzler; Karl Schönherr, Franz Werfel; Max Mell.

Grillparzer-Ringe

The Grillparzer rings are awarded by the Austrian Ministry of Education and Arts at the recommendation of a special jury, to scholars, theatre directors, managers or actors who have made a special contribution in connection with the works of the Austrian dramatist, Grillparzer. Both Austrians and non-Austrians are eligible.

Awarding body: Bundesministerium für Unterricht und Kunst, 1014 Vienna, Minoritenplatz 5, Austria.

Recipients include: Prof. Dr. Zdenko Skreb, Prof. Piero Rismondo (1975).

Gebrüder-Grimm-Preis (*Brothers Grimm Prize*)

The prize is awarded every two years to theatre groups which have presented a play for children or young people, and is designed to encourage this genre. It consists of a cash prize of DM10,000, and is named after the famous Brothers Grimm, the German children's story writers.

Awarding body: Der Senat von Berlin, Senatskanzlei, 1000 Berlin 62, John-F.-Kennedy-Platz, Federal Republic of Germany.

Recipients include: Grips-Theater.

Adolf-Grimme-Preis

Several awards, made annually since 1963, are given under this title for outstanding work in television. Their number and function have varied over the years. At present they are given for programmes of general interest (gold, silver, bronze and honourable mention); to honour a particular individual or institution; occasionally for the most interesting experimental work; and, since 1974, for educational and cultural series (gold, silver, bronze and honourable mention – replacing an earlier similar award). Special prizes are awarded by the Donors Association for promoting Sciences and Humanities, and by the regional government of North Rhine-Westphalia, and occasionally by other sources.

Awarding body: Deutscher Volkshochschulverband e.V., D-4370 Marl, 'die insel', Eduard-Weitsch-Weg 25, Federal Republic of Germany.

Recipients include: Hans Gottschalk (script) and Rainer Erler (direction, *Der Attentäter*, SDR, 1969); Herbert Ballmann (script), Wolfgang Patzsche (direction) and Herbert Stass (principal role, *Interview mit Herbert K.*, ZDF, 1970); Peter Stripp, Peter Beauvais, Rosemarie Fendel, Johanna Hofer and Wolfgang Kieling (*Im Reservat*, ZDF, 1973); Daniel Christoff and Peter Beauvais (*Sechs Wochen im Leben der Brüder G.*, SFB, 1974); Eberhard Fechner (script and direction, *Unter Denkmalschutz*, HR, 1975).

Grindley Medal

This award is made annually by the Agricultural Institute of Canada to a Canadian who has made a particular contribution to the country's agriculture, the impact of which has been of far-reaching importance, and recognized during the past five years. The award consists of a medal, certificate and citation, and was established in 1968 in memory of Frederick F. Grindley, first Secretary of the Canadian Society of Technical Agriculturists from 1920 to 1930.

Awarding body: Agricultural Institute of Canada, Suite 907, 151 Slater St., Ottawa, Ont. L1P 5H4, Canada.

Recipients include: C. W. Owen (breeding of soy beans, 1968); Fred Dimmock (breeding of corn varieties, 1970); R. K. Downey (breeding of low euric acid rape seed varieties, 1973); V. D. Burrows (breeding of high protein oats, 1975); Ernest Reinbergs and Kenneth J. Kasha (developing a method of obtaining pure lines of barley, 1976).

Grosser Österreichischer Staatspreis (*Grand Austrian State Prize*)

This award is presented by the Austrian Ministry of Education and Arts in recognition of the total creative work of an individual in the field of literature, music, fine arts or cinema. Candidates are proposed by the Arts Senate. The award is a cash prize of 100,000 Schillings.

Awarding body: Bundesministerium für Unterricht und Kunst, 1014 Vienna, Minoritenplatz 5, Austria.

Recipients include: Karl Schwanzer (fine arts, 1975).

Grosser Österreichischer Staatspreis für Filmkunst (*Grand Austrian State Prize for Cinematic Art*)

This award was instituted in 1975 by the Austrian Ministry of Education and Arts in recognition of the cinema as the art form of the 20th century. The prize is 100,000 Schillings.

Awarding body: Bundesministerium für Unterricht und Kunst, 1014 Vienna, Minoritenplatz 5, Austria.

Recipients include: Axel Corti (1975).

Grosser Preis der Stadt Oberhausen (*Grand Prize of the City of Oberhausen*)

This prize, consisting of a cash sum of DM5,000 and a certificate, is awarded for the best film or films screened at the Oberhausen Short Film Festival. This festival was founded by the city of Oberhausen and the Association of Adult Education in West Germany and is held annually. The jury is international and the films must not be more than two years old. The prize is usually awarded to the director of a film rather than to the producer and may be divided among several recipients.

Awarding body: Westdeutsche Kurzfilmtage, Grillostr. 34, 42 Oberhausen, Federal Republic of Germany.

Recipients include: Heynowski and Scheumann (German Dem. Rep., *Mitbürger*, 1974); Paolo Pietrangeli (Italy, *La Nostalgia del Dinosauro*, 1974); Donjo Donev (Bulgaria, *De Facto*, 1974); Hans Stürm, Nina Stürm and Mathias Knaur (Switzerland, *Ein Streik ist keine Sonntagsschule*, 1975); Rolf Orthel (Netherlands, *A Shadow of Doubt*, 1976); Martha Rodriguez and Jorge Silva (Colombia, *Campesinos*, 1976).

Grosvenor Medal

The medal was established in 1949 by the National Geographic Society in honour of Gilbert Grosvenor, editor of the *National Geographic* from 1899 to 1949. The medal is awarded as and when merited for outstanding service to geography.

Awarding body: National Geographic Society, 17th and M Streets, N.W., Washington, D.C. 20036, U.S.A.

Recipients: Gilbert Grosvenor (1949); John Oliver La Gorce (1955).

Otto von Gruber Award

This prize is awarded at the quadrennial Congresses of the International Society for Photogrammetry to the author of an outstanding article on photogrammetry or photo-interpretation written in the four years preceding the Congress. The recipient must have graduated or done postgraduate work in photogrammetry in the previous 12 years. Applications for the award are invited, but it may be given to a non-applicant. It consists of a gold medal and a cash prize of not more than 500 Dutch guilders. It was established in 1964 by the Office of the International Training Centre Foundation in honour of the services rendered to photogrammetry by Otto von Gruber.

Awarding body: International Society for Photogrammetry, U.S. Geological Survey 516, Reston, Va. 22092, U.S.A.

Recipients include: Prof. F. Ackermann (1964); Dr. H. Ebner (1972); Dr. J. Höhle (1972); Dr. F. Leberl (1976).

Andreas Gryphius-Preis

Instituted in 1957, this annual award is made by the Federal German Artists' Guild for literary works (prose, lyric, drama or essays) which have appeared in the last five years and are concerned with Eastern or Middle Germany, or contact between Germans and their neighbours to the east. The principal award is worth DM10,000 and three secondary awards are worth DM4,000 each. The awards are accompanied by diplomas. (The Federal Länder donate DM18,000, and the Ministry of the Interior DM4,000.) People born in the eastern regions of Germany are eligible. The prize commemorates the Silesian poet, Andreas Gryphius (1616–64).

Awarding body: Die Künstlergilde e.V., 7300 Esslingen N., Webergasse 1, Federal Republic of Germany.

Recipients include: Günter Eich (1972); Wolfgang Weyrauch (1973); Peter Huchel (1974); Dr. Frank Thiess (1975); Karin Struck (1976).

Guardian Award for Children's Fiction

Established in 1967, the award is made annually in March by *The Guardian* newspaper. The sum of £105 (100 guineas) is given for an outstanding contribution to imaginative literature for children. The author must be from Britain or the Commonwealth, and the book must have been published in the previous 12 months.

Awarding body: The Guardian, 119 Farringdon Rd., London EC1, England.

Recipients include: Barbara Willard (*The Iron Lily,* 1974); Winifred Cawley (*Gran at Coalgate,* 1975); Nina Bawden (*The Peppermint Pig,* 1976); Peter Dickinson (*The Blue Hawk,* 1977); Diana Wynne Jones (*A Charmed Life,* 1978).

Guardian Fiction Prize

This is a cash award of £210 (200 guineas) given annually by *The Guardian* newspaper in November for a novel of originality and promise. The author must be from Britain or the Commonwealth, and the novel must have been published within the preceding 12 months.

Awarding body: The Guardian, 119 Farringdon Rd., London EC1, England.

Recipients include: Beryl Bainbridge (*The Bottle Factory Outing,* 1974); Sylvia Clayton (*Friends and Romans,* 1975); Robert Nye (*Falstaff,* 1976); Michael Moorcock (*The Condition of Muzak,* 1977); Roy A. K. Heath (*The Murderer,* 1978).

Ernest Guenther Award in the Chemistry of Essential Oils and Related Products

Established in 1948 by Fritzsche Dodge & Olcott Inc., this annual award is intended to recognize and encourage outstanding achievements in analysis, structure elucidation, chemical synthesis of essential oils, isolates, flavours and related substances. Special consideration is given to the independence of thought and originality shown. The award is granted without regard to age, nationality or sex. It consists of $2,000 and a gold medal. An allowance of $300 is provided for travelling expenses to the meeting at which the award will be presented.

Awarding body: American Chemical Society, 1155 Sixteenth St., N.W., Washington, D.C. 20036, U.S.A.

Recipients include: William G. Dauben (1973); Günther Ohloff (1974); S. Morris Kupchan (1975); Alastair I. Scott (1976); Robert E. Ireland (1977).

Daniel Guggenheim Medal Award

Established in 1929, the award is intended to honour those who make notable achievements in the advancement of aeronautics. A medal and certificate are presented annually. The award is sponsored jointly by the American Institute of Aeronautics and Astronautics, the American Society of Mechanical Engineers and the Society of Automotive Engineers.

Awarding body: United Engineering Trustees, 345 East 47th St., New York, N.Y. 10017, U.S.A.

Recipients include: William C. Mentzer (1972); William McPherson Allen (1973); Floyd L. Thompson (1974); Duane Wallace (1975); Marcel Dassault (1976).

Bires Chandra Guha Memorial Lecture

This lecture was established in 1965 by the Indian National Science Academy. The lectureship is awarded for distinguished contributions in the fields of biochemistry and nutrition, food and allied subjects. It is awarded every three years and the lecturer receives an honorarium.

Awarding body: Indian National Science Academy, Bahadur Shah Zafar Marg, New Delhi 110001, India.

Recipients include: V. Subramanyan (1969); A. Sreenivasan (1972); J. Ganguly (1975); M. G. Deo (1978).

Guldbaggen (*Gold Bug*)

This prize consists of a glazed metal sculpture, awarded annually to the best director and actor/actress respectively in a Swedish film released during the previous fiscal year, or to some other person who has made a special achievement in the field of Swedish cinema. The award was instituted by the Svenska Filminstitutet (Swedish Film Institute) in 1964. The award is made by a 12-man jury.

Awarding body: Svenska Filminstitutet, Box 27 126, 102 52 Stockholm 27, Sweden.

Recipients include: Liv Ullmann (best actress) and Bo Widerberg (best director), 1969; Harriet Andersson (best actress) and Sven Nykvist (best photographer), 1973; Vilgot Sjöman (best director), 1974.

Guldberg and Waage's Law of Mass Action Memorial Medal

This medal is given to Norwegian chemists for outstanding scientific and/or technological work carried out in Norway. It was established in 1963 and is awarded irregularly.

Awarding body: Norwegian Chemical Society, P.O.B. 1107, Blindern, Oslo 3, Norway.

Recipients include: Prof. dr. Håkon Flood (1966); Cand. pharm. Per Laland (1966); Prof. dr. Nils Andreas Sørensen (1966); Siv. ing. Erik Samuelsen (1973); Prof. dr. Olav Foss (1973).

Gullstrand Medal

The Swedish Society of Medical Sciences founded this gold medal in 1922 in honour of Dr. Allvar Gullstrand (1862–1930), who received the Nobel Prize for Physiology in 1911. The medal is awarded every ten years to a scientist of any nationality for an outstanding contribution to the development of ophthalmology.

Awarding body: Swedish Society of Medical Sciences, P.O.B. 558, S-101 27 Stockholm, Sweden.

Recipients include: Sir Stewart Duke-Elder (U.K.), 1952); Prof. Hans Goldmann (Switzerland, 1962); Prof. E. Custodis (Fed. Rep. of Germany, 1972).

Gunlogson Countryside Engineering Award

This award is presented annually by the American Society of Agricultural Engineers to encourage and to recognize outstanding engineering contributions which have resulted in significant progress in or towards the development of Countryside U.S.A. Recipients must be ASAE members and have contributed to the technology of countryside development or to plans, programmes or other leadership activities which have promoted development of the countryside. The award consists of an engraved and mounted plaque.

Awarding body: American Society of Agricultural Engineers, 2950 Niles Rd., St. Joseph, Mich. 49085, U.S.A.

Neil Gunn International Fellowship

The award was established in 1972 by the Scottish Arts Council in memory of Neil Gunn (1891–1973), novelist. A £1,000 fellowship is awarded every two years to a novelist of international standing, elected by the Scottish Arts Council. Writers may not themselves submit applications. The recipient visits Scotland for a three-week period as the Council's guest and is expected to give one public lecture.

Awarding body: Scottish Arts Council, 19 Charlotte Square, Edinburgh EH2 4DF, Scotland.

Recipients include: Chinua Achebe (Nigeria, 1975); Saul Bellow (U.S.A., 1977); Ruth Prawer Jhabvala (India, 1979).

Guthrie Medal and Prize

A silver gilt medal and a prize of £250 are awarded annually to a physicist of international reputation for his contributions to physics. The award was instituted in 1965 by the Institute of Physics and the Physical Society in place of the Guthrie Lecture, established in 1914 in memory of Prof. Frederick Guthrie, founder of the Physical Society. Candidates are considered on the recommendation of members of the Institute and of its Awards Committee.

Awarding body: The Institute of Physics, 47 Belgrave Square, London SW1X 8QX, England.

Recipients include: John Ashworth Ratcliffe (1971); Brian David Josephson (1972); Hermann Bondi (1973); Rudolf Ludwig Mössbauer (1974); David Tabor (1975).

Manfred S. Guttmacher Award

This award, established in 1967, is made annually for an outstanding contribution to the literature of forensic psychiatry in the form of a book, monograph, paper, film or other work submitted to a professional meeting during the year. It consists of a plaque and honorarium of $250.

Awarding body: American Psychiatric Association, 1700 18th St., N.W., Washington, D.C. 20009, U.S.A.

Gyulai Zoltán Prize

An annual prize was established in 1968 by the Hungarian Physical Society in honour of Zoltán Gyulai (b. 1887), the physicist. A sum of 5,000 forints is awarded to young research workers for outstanding results in solid-state physics.

Awarding body: 'Eötvös Loránd' Fizikai Társulat, 1061 Budapest VI, Anker-köz 1, Hungary.

H

H.M. the King's Medal of Merit

This medal was instituted by King Haakon VII of Norway in 1908 as a reward for merit in the fields of art, science and commerce or in the discharge of public office. The medal may be awarded in gold or silver, and is accompanied by a warrant. It has been awarded in rare cases to a foreigner.

Awarding body: Norwegian Government, Oslo, Norway.

Hermann-Haack-Medaille

This silver medal is awarded to an individual or a group for outstanding achievements in various areas of geography and cartography. Up to four awards may be made, at intervals of three to four years. The award was instituted by the GDR Geographical Society in 1960 on the occasion of the 175th anniversary of the founding of the Gotha Geographical-Cartographical Institute, and honours Prof. Dr. h.c. Hermann Haack (1872–1966), who carried out eminent work in the field of school cartography.

Awarding body: Geographische Gesellschaft der DDR, 701 Leipzig, Dimitroffplatz 1, German Democratic Republic.

Recipients include: Prof. Dr. G. Jacob (1969); Prof. Dr. H. Kohl (1969); Prof. Dr. G. Mohs (1969); Prof. Dr. H. Richter (1969); Prof. Dr. A. Zimm (1972).

Michael Haberlandt-Medaille

This silver medal is awarded by the Ethnological Society of Vienna to those whose services to the Society and to the Ethnological Museum of Vienna have made a particular contribution to the study of Austrian folklore. The award was established in 1974 on the occasion of the Society's 80th anniversary in memory of Michael Haberlandt, who founded both the Society and the Ethnological Museum.

Awarding body: Verein für Volkskunde in Wien, Laudongasse 15–19, A-1080 Vienna, Austria.

Recipients include: Prof. Dr. Oskar Moser (1976); Dr. Franz Koschier (1976); Helmut Prasch (1976); Prof. Dr. Helene Grünn (1977); Dr. Friederike Prodinger (1977).

Otto-Hahn-Preis für Chemie und Physik
(*Otto Hahn Prize for Chemistry and Physics*)

Established in 1955 by the central committee of the combined German chemical organizations and the Union of German Physics Societies, the prize is in honour of Otto Hahn (1879–1968), who won the 1944 Nobel Prize for Chemistry for his discovery of nuclear fission. It is awarded to Germans for outstanding contributions to the development of chemistry or physics. The award is a particularly high distinction and therefore is generally awarded only at intervals of several years. The prize takes the form of a sum of money and a gold medal.

Awarding body: Gesellschaft Deutscher Chemiker, 6000 Frankfurt (Main) 90, Carl-Bosch-Haus, Varrentrappstr. 40–42, Federal Republic of Germany.

Recipients include: Prof. Hans Meerwein (1959); Dr. Manfred Eigen (1962); Prof. Erich Hückel (1965); Prof. Georg Wittig (1967); Prof. Friedrich Hund (1974).

Haldane Essay Competition

The Haldane Silver Medal and £100 are awarded for significant and original contributions to the study of the practice and the history of public administration. The competition was established in 1924 by the Royal Institute of Public Administration, a non-political body whose objects are to advance the study of public administration and to promote the exchange of information and ideas on all aspects of the subject. The competition is associated with the name of Viscount Haldane of Cloan, K.T., O.M. (1856–1928), first president of the Institute. The award is made annually in January, and additional money awards are made if the judges consider other contributions to be of high merit. The competition is open to all past and present members of the public services throughout the world. Essays of between 7,500 and 12,500 words should be submitted under a *nom de plume*.

Awarding body: Royal Institute of Public Administration, Hamilton House, Mabledon Place, London WC1H 9BD, England.

Haley Space Flight Award

The award was established in 1954 as the Astronautics Award and renamed in honour of Andrew G. Haley, one of the founders of the American Rocket Society. It is given for outstanding contributions by an astronaut or flight test personnel to the advancement of the art, science or technology of astronautics. It comprises a medal and certificate of citation, and is presented biennially, alternating with the Chanute Flight Award (*q.v.*), at the Aerospace Sciences Meeting.

Awarding body: American Institute of Aeronautics and Astronautics, 1290 Avenue of the Americas, New York, N.Y. 10019, U.S.A.

Recipients include: Gerald Carr, William Pogue, Edward Gibson (1975); William H. Dana (1976).

Halley Lectureship

In 1910 the University of Oxford accepted an offer of £600 made by the late Henry Wilde, F.R.S., to found an annual lecture on Astronomy and Terrestrial Magnetism in honour and in memory of Edmond Halley, sometime Savilian Professor of Geometry. The lecturer may be of any nationality, and is appointed by a Board of Electors consisting of various professors of the University.

Awarding body: University of Oxford, Wellington Square, Oxford OX1 2JD, England.

Lecturers include: D. G. King-Hele ('Truth and Heresy over Earth and Sky', 1973–74); W. H. McCrea, F.R.S. ('Solar System as Space Probe', 1974–75).

Alice Berger Hammerschlag Trust Award

This award of £300, for which the Arts Council of Northern Ireland acts as Trustee, is given for achievement in the field of the arts.

Awarding body: Arts Council of Northern Ireland, 181a Stranmillis Rd., Belfast BT9 5DU, Northern Ireland.

Recipients include: John Byrne (sculptor), Stephen G. Allen (designer, 1974); Ken Norris (sculptor, 1975).

Hanbury Memorial Medal

The Council of the Pharmaceutical Society is the trustee of a fund raised to establish a memorial to Daniel Hanbury, who died in 1875. The memorial takes the form of a gold medal given biennially for 'high excellence in the prosecution or promotion of original research in the Natural History and Chemistry of Drugs', the medallist being required to deliver an evening lecture on his work that formed the basis of the award. He receives an honorarium of 40 guineas. The award is made by a committee comprising the Presidents of the Chemical, Linnean and Pharmaceutical Societies, the Chairman of the British Pharmaceutical Conference, and one pharmaceutical chemist.

Awarding body: The Pharmaceutical Society of Great Britain, 1 Lambeth High St., London SE1 7JN, England.

Recipients include: Maurice M. Janot (1968); Robert B. Woodward (1970); Sir Ernst Chain (1972); Arnold H. Beckett (1974); Frederick Sanger (1976).

Hancor Soil and Water Engineering Award

This award (formerly the Hancock Brick and Tile Soil and Water Engineering Award) is made for noteworthy contributions to the advancement of soil and water engineering in teaching, research, planning, design, construction or management, or methods and materials. These contributions shall have been either in the form of published litera-ture, notable performance, or specific actions which have served to advance the science of soil and water engineering. A candidate for the award must be sponsored by members of the American Society of Agricultural Engineers.

Awarding body: American Society of Agricultural Engineers, 2950 Niles Rd., St. Joseph, Mich. 49085, U.S.A.

C. F. Hansen Medal

The award was established in 1830 by the Danish Academy of Fine Arts in honour of C. F. Hansen (1756–1845), the outstanding architect and sometime president of the Academy. A medal is awarded annually for distinguished achievement in architecture. Recipients must be of Danish nationality save in exceptional cases.

Awarding body: Akademiet for de skønne Kunster, Akademiraadet, Kgs. Nytorv 1, 1050 Copenhagen K, Denmark.

Hansischer Goethe-Preis *(Hanseatic Goethe Prize)*

Founded in 1949 by the FVS Foundation of Hamburg, this award of DM25,000 is intended to honour a European who has shown a way of thinking, and humanitarian aspirations and achievements, reflecting the spirit of Johann Wolfgang Goethe (1749–1832), the most famous of German poets and thinkers. Since 1973 the Foundation has also awarded a Goethe Gold Medal.

Awarding body: Stiftung FVS, Georgsplatz 10, 2 Hamburg 1, Federal Republic of Germany.

Recipients include: Dr. Giorgio Strehler (Italy, 1972); Prof. Albin Lesky (Austria, 1973); Manès Sperber (Austria, 1973); Lord Duncan Sandys (U.K., Gold Medal, 1975); National Trust (U.K., Gold Medal, 1977).

Hantken Miksa Memorial Medal

Founded by the Hungarian Geological Society in 1963, the medal is awarded every three years for a scholarly publication in the field of palaeontology or stratigraphy. It is named after Miksa Hantken (1821–93), a noted palaeontologist.

Awarding body: Magyarhoni Földtani Társulat, Budapest 1061, Anker-köz 1, Hungary.

Hal Williams Hardinge Award

This award is made annually by the American Institute of Mining, Metallurgical, and Petroleum Engineers for outstanding achievement which has benefited the field of industrial minerals, by means such as writing, teaching, research or administration. Candidates of all nationalities are eligible, provided they are proposed by a member of the Institute and have not previously received an Institute award. The award takes the form of a bronze plaque, and was established in 1958 by Mrs. Hal Williams Hardinge in memory of her husband, an inventor and President of the Hardinge Co., manufacturers of mining and milling equipment.

Awarding body: American Institute of Mining, Metallurgical, and Petroleum Engineers, Inc., 345 East 47th St., New York, N.Y. 10017, U.S.A.

Recipients include: Kenneth Knight Landes (1973); Elburt Franklin Osborn (1974); R. Gill Montgomery (1975); Haydn H. Murray (1976); Thomas D. Murphy (1977).

Clarence H. Haring Prize

This award is made every five years for the most outstanding book on Latin American history, by a Latin American, published in the preceding five years. The prize consists of a cash award of $500.

Awarding body: American Historical Association, 400 A St., Southeast, Washington, D.C. 20003, U.S.A.

Albert J. Harris Award

This award is presented for outstanding contributions to the diagnosis and treatment of reading disabilities. It is made annually, if the standard of entries is sufficiently high, for a work published in the preceding year. It was established in 1974 in honour of Albert J. Harris, an eminent educator and past President of the International Reading Association. The award consists of a cash prize which varies annually.

Awarding body: International Reading Association, 800 Barksdale Rd., Newark, Dela. 19711, U.S.A.

Recipients include: Dr. Harry Singer (*IQ Is and Is Not Related to Reading Ability*, 1974).

Harrison Memorial Medal

This medal is purchased from the fund raised in memory of the late Colonel Edward Frank Harrison, a distinguished pharmaceutical chemist, who was Director of Chemical Warfare in 1918. Originally the medal was open for competition; in 1927 it was decided to change the terms of reference and institute a lectureship and medal to be called respectively the Harrison Memorial Lectureship and the Harrison Lectureship Medal. The award is made annually; the lecture must be on a subject relating to the science and practice of pharmacy, and the lecturer receives the medal in silver and an honorarium of 30 guineas.

Awarding body: The Pharmaceutical Society of Great Britain, 1 Lambeth High St., London SE1 7JN, England.

Recipients include: Cecil A. Johnson (1972); Thomas D. Whittet (1973); John B. Stenlake (1974); James W. Fairbairn (1975); Peter H. Elworthy (1976).

Harrison Memorial Prize

This prize was created in 1922 to commemorate the devoted services of the late Colonel Edward Frank Harrison, formerly Deputy Controller of the Chemical Warfare Department, for the protection of the British Forces from poison gas in the 1914–18 war. The prize, not exceeding 100 guineas, is awarded normally at intervals of three years to the chemist of either sex, being a British subject by birth and not over 30 years of age, who,

during the previous five years, has conducted the most meritorious and promising investigations in chemistry and has published the results in a scientific periodical. The selection committee consists of the Presidents of the Chemical Society, the Royal Institute of Chemistry, the Society of Chemical Industry and the Pharmaceutical Society. The prize, which is accompanied by a bronze plaque, is presented by the President of the Chemical Society at a meeting of the Society, usually the Annual General Meeting following the announcement of the award.

Awarding body: The Chemical Society, Burlington House, London W1V 0BN, England.

Recipients include: G. Williams (1965); G. R. Luckhurst (1968); G. M. Bancroft (1971); C. Masters (1975).

Harrison Prize

The prize is awarded every three years, if there is a suitable candidate, for the best fundamental work on a bacteriological subject, excluding work done for direct clinical application in human or veterinary medicine, but including work of general scientific importance, published by an investigator domiciled in Canada for at least the preceding five years. The prize consists of C$150 and a scroll. It was established in 1952 by Francis Charles St. Barbe Harrison (1871–1952).

Awarding body: The Royal Society of Canada, 395 Wellington, Ottawa, Ont. K1A 0N4, Canada.

Recipients include: P. C. Fitz-James (1963); J. J. Miller (1966); J. J. R. Campbell (1969); L. C. Vining (1972); H. J. Jennings (1975).

Wilhelm-Hartel-Preis

The prize was established by the Austrian Ministry of Education in 1957 in memory of Wilhelm R. von Hartel (1839–1907), professor of classical philology. It is awarded for outstanding scholarly achievements in the arts. It consists of a certificate and a sum of money, and is awarded generally every year in May or June.

Awarding body: Österreichische Akademie der Wissenschaften, 1010 Vienna, Dr.-Ignaz-Seipel-Platz 2, Austria.

Recipients include: Viktor Kraft; Herbert Koziol; Heinz Kindermann; Hermann Vetters; Otto Pächt.

Sir Harold Hartley Medal

This silver medal is awarded annually by the British Institute of Measurement and Control for a contribution of outstanding merit to the technology of measurement and control. It was instituted in 1969 in honour of the late Sir Harold Hartley, F.R.S. (1878–1972), former President of the Institute.

Awarding body: The Institute of Measurement and Control, 20 Peel St., London W8 7PD, England.

Recipients include: Prof. R. V. Jones (U.K., 1972); Prof. H. E. M. Barlow (U.K., 1973); Prof. J. H. Westcott (U.K., 1974); Prof. T. J. Williams (U.S.A., 1975); R. S. Medlock (U.K., 1976).

Eugen-Hartmann-Preis

This annual prize, consisting of a certificate and cash prize of DM1,000, is awarded by the Society for Measurement and Automatic Control (GMR), attached to the Associations of German Engineers and Electrical Engineers. It is for exceptional work during the preceding year in the field of measurement and automatic control. Eligibility is restricted to those of 35 years or under, and preference is given to GMR members. The award was instituted in 1975 by Eugen W. Hammann-Kloss, in memory of Eugen Hartmann, the distinguished scientist and engineer and founder of the organization.

Awarding body: VDI/VDE Gesellschaft für Mess- und Regelungstechnik (GMR), Federal Republic of Germany.

Recipients include: Prof. Dr.-Ing. D. Franke (1976).

Hartnett Award

This annual award, named after a past president of the Society of Automotive Engineers – Australasia, takes the form of a medal accompanied by a certificate. It is open to any resident of Australia, New Zealand or a territory administered by these countries, who has made an outstanding original contribution to automotive or aeronautical knowledge or practice. Nominations are made by individual members of the Society or by Division or independent Group Committees to the Society's Council.

Awarding body: Society of Automotive Engineers – Australasia, National Science Centre, 191 Royal Parade, Parkville, Vic. 3052, Australia.

Bogdan Petriceicu Hasdeu Prize

This prize for contributions in the field of philology was founded in 1948 by the Romanian Academy. It is named after Bogdan Hasdeu (1836–1907), historian, linguist and writer, who was Professor of Comparative Philology at the University of Bucharest, and founder of Romanian scientific linguistics and lexicography. The award is presented annually at a General Assembly of the Academy, and consists of 10,000 lei and a diploma.

Awarding body: Academy of the S.R. of Romania, 125 Calea Victoriei, Bucharest, Romania.

Clara Haskil Competition

This is a biennial piano competition founded by the Clara Haskil Association and the Lucerne Festival in memory of the famous pianist. The first competition was in 1963; in 1973 it was taken over by the Montreux-Vevey Festival of Music and takes place in September during the Festival. Clara Haskil (1895–1960) was born in Romania and was famous for her interpretation, mainly of Mozart and Schubert works. The competition is open to young pianists (age limit 32) of any nationality. The winner receives a cash prize of 10,000 Swiss francs and various concert engagements.

Awarding body: Montreux-Vevey Music Festival, 27 bis Av. des Alpes, CH-1820 Montreux, Switzerland.

Recipients include: Richard Goode (1973); Michel Dalberto (1975).

Havengapryse

With the foundation in 1942 of a Faculty of Natural Science and Technology within the South African Academy of Science and Arts, the need was felt for a prize in this field as a counterpart to the Hertzog Prize (*q.v.*) for literature. In 1944 an award was established, and in 1947 it was decided to name it after Mr. N. C. Havenga, who had promised to donate £50 a year for the prize. In his will Mr. Havenga bequeathed R4,000 to the Academy; in 1969 a further R14,000 was received from the estate of Mrs. Olive Havenga. From these gifts the Havenga prizes (currently R250 each) are awarded. They are given for outstanding work in the field of natural science or technology in the form of original research and publications. The latter are the most important criteria; the candidate must, *inter alia*, have published quality work in Afrikaans. Two or three prizes are awarded annually in a three-yearly cycle for work in the various disciplines: mathematics, physics, medicine; chemistry, biology, engineering and architecture; geology, agricultural science.

Awarding body: Suid-Afrikaanse Akademie vir Wetenskap en Kuns, Posbus 538, Pretoria 0001, South Africa.

Recipients include: Prof. C. H. W. T. Pistorius (physics), Prof. H. W. Snymon (medicine), Prof. G. J. Hauptfleisch (mathematics), 1976; Prof. M. J. Toerien (biology), Prof. C. F. Garbers (chemistry), Dr. J. J. Wannenburg (engineering), 1977.

Haworth Memorial Lectureship

This award was founded in 1969 to commemorate the name of Sir Norman Haworth, President of the Chemical Society from 1944 to 1946. The terms of the lectureship, which may be varied at the discretion of Council, provide that the lecturer shall deal with advances in any subject of carbohydrate chemistry, including the contributions which studies on carbohydrates can make to a better understanding of other branches of chemical science. The lecturer receives a bronze medal and £100.

Awarding body: The Chemical Society, Burlington House, London W1V 0BN, England.

Recipients include: M. Stacey (1971); H. Isbell (1973); J. K. N. Jones (1975); R. U. Lemieux (1978).

Hawthornden Prize

Established in 1919 by Miss Alice Warrender, the prize is given annually for the best work of imaginative literature by an author under 41. Its value is £100 but it carries considerable prestige. It is designed to encourage young authors, and the word 'imaginative' is used in a broad sense to include most literary genres.

Awarding body: Society of Authors, 84 Drayton Gardens, London SW10 9SD, England.

Recipients include: Oliver Sacks (*Awakenings,* 1975); Robert Nye (*Falstaff,* 1977); Bruce Chatwin (*In Patagonia,* 1978).

John Hay Memorial Lectureship in Medicine

The lectureship was established in 1965 with an endowment of £1,200 raised by private subscription to commemorate the late Emeritus Professor John Hay, Professor of Medicine at Liverpool University from 1924 to 1934. The appointment is made every two years by the University Council. The lecturer delivers a lecture or course of lectures on Medicine. The remuneration is £100.

Awarding body: The University of Liverpool, P.O.B. 147, Liverpool L69 3BX, England.

Hayden-Harris Award

This annual award, instituted in 1967, takes the form of a plaque and is made for outstanding contributions to the history of dentistry. It was established in memory of Horace H. Hayden and Chapin A. Harris, co-founders in 1840 of the first dental school in the world, in Baltimore, U.S.A.

Awarding body: American Academy of the History of Dentistry, c/o Dr. Milton B. Asbell (Secretary), 1001 N. Kings Highway, Cherry Hill, N.J., U.S.A.

Recipients include: Alfred J. Asgis (1972); Neil Macauley (1973); Alfred W. Chandler (1974); Milton B. Asbell (1975); W. Harry Archer (1976).

Heat Transfer Memorial Award

This award was established by the Heat Transfer Division of ASME in 1959 and operated as a divisional award until 1974, when it was converted to a Society award. It is bestowed on individuals who have made outstanding contributions to the field of heat transfer through teaching, research, design or publications. Each award is based on papers in an area of heat transfer or on a paper dealing with the science or art of heat transfer. Three awards may be made annually, one in the science of heat transfer, one in the art of heat transfer, and one in the general subject of heat transfer. Recipients are not restricted by nationality, age or society membership. The award consists of a memorial booklet and a certificate.

Awarding body: American Society of Mechanical Engineers, United Engineering Center, 345 East 47th St., New York, N.Y. 10017, U.S.A.

Recipients include: Peter Griffith, Simon Ostrach (1975); Warren H. Giedt, Raymond Viskanta (1976).

Heath Memorial Award

This prize was established in 1965 by the late William W. Heath, former Chairman of the University of Texas System Board of Regents, in honour and in memory of his three brothers. The prize is given in recognition of an outstanding contribution to the better care of cancer patients through the clinical application of basic research knowledge. It is awarded annually at the Clinical Conference on Cancer held in Houston, and consists of a medallion and an honorarium.

Awarding body: The University of Texas System Cancer Center, M. D. Anderson Hospital and Tumor Institute, Texas Medical Center, Houston, Tex. 77030, U.S.A.

Recipients include: Dr. Leo G. Rigler (1973); Dr. C. Gordon Zubrod (1974); Dr. Elson B. Helwig (1975); Dr. Wataru W. Sutow, Dr. Franz M. Enzinger (1976).

Hegel-Preis

This award was first made in 1970 to commemorate the bicentenary of the birth of Georg Wilhelm Friedrich Hegel (1770–1831), the German philosopher who was born in Stuttgart. It is presented every three years by the city of Stuttgart to an individual who has contributed to the development of the human sciences in the broadest sense. The prize takes the form of DM15,000 and a certificate.

Awarding body: Kultur- und Schulreferat der Stadt Stuttgart, 7000 Stuttgart 1, Rathaus, Postfach 161, Federal Republic of Germany.

Recipients: Prof. Dr. Bruno Snell (philology, 1970); Prof. Dr. phil. Jürgen Habermas (sociology and philosophy, 1973); Prof. Sir Ernst Gombrich (Dir., Warburg Inst., London, 1976).

Heine-Preis der Landeshauptstadt Düsseldorf (*Heine Prize of the Provincial Capital of Düsseldorf*)

This prize was established in 1972 in memory of the German poet, Heinrich Heine (1797–1856), on the 175th anniversary of his birth, by the Council of the city of Düsseldorf, where he was born. The prize is awarded to people who through their work have broadened the social and political awareness and strengthened the basic rights of mankind. It consists of a certificate and a cash sum of DM25,000, and is awarded every three years.

Awarding body: Rathaus, Düsseldorf, Federal Republic of Germany.

Recipients include: Dr. h.c. Dr. phil. h.c. Carl Zuckmayer (1972); Prof. Pierre Bertaux (1975).

Dr. H. P. Heineken Prize

In 1963 the Dutch brewery firm of Heineken established the Heineken Foundation with the aim of promoting science and culture; its first initiative was to establish this prize in honour of Dr. Henri Pierre Heineken (1886–1971), who was the firm's managing director, then president, for many years. The prize is awarded once every three years for work in the fields of biochemistry and biophysics, and is open to scientists of any nationality. It consists of a cash prize of 100,000 guilders and a crystal trophy bearing a replica of the microscope of Antonie van Leeuwenhoek, the Dutch founder of microbiology. The Royal Netherlands Academy of Science acts as adjudicator in the election of the prize-winner.

Awarding body: Heineken Foundation, 21 Tweede Weteringplantsoen, Amsterdam, The Netherlands.

Recipients include: Prof. J. L. A. Brachet (Belgium, 1967); Prof. B. Chance (U.S.A., 1970); Prof. Christian de Duve (Belgium, 1973); Dr. L. L. M. Van Deenen (Netherlands, 1976); Dr. Aaron Klug (U.K., 1979).

Dannie Heineman Prize

This prize is awarded every two years by the Academy of Sciences in Göttingen for outstanding work mainly in the field of natural science. It was established in 1962 by the Minna James Heineman Foundation in Hanover in honour of its founder, the American engineering executive, educator and philanthropist, Dannie N. Heineman (1872–1962). The award is open to scientists of all nationalities and consists of a cash prize of DM30,000.

Awarding body: Akademie der Wissenschaften in Göttingen, 34 Göttingen, Prinzenstr. 1, Federal Republic of Germany.

Recipients include: Prof. Brian Pippard (U.K., for work on the dynamics of electron transport chains in metals, 1969); Prof. Neil Bartlett (U.S.A., for experimental research into electropositive gas compounds, 1971); Prof. Igor R. Schafarevitsch (U.S.S.R., for work on algebra and theory of numbers, 1973); Prof. Philip W. Anderson (U.S.A., for theoretical contributions to condensed matter physics, 1975).

Dannie Heineman Prize for Mathematical Physics

Established in 1959 by the Heineman Foundation for Research, Educational, Charitable and Scientific Purposes, Inc., the prize is administered jointly by the American Physical Society and the American Institute of Physics. It is awarded annually to recognize an outstanding publication in the field of mathematical physics. 'Publication' is defined as a single paper, a series of papers, a book or any other communication which can be considered a publication. The prize may be awarded to more than one person on a shared basis; there are no restrictions on a candidate's citizenship or country of residence. The prize consists of $5,000 and a certificate citing the contributions made by the recipient.

Awarding bodies: American Institute of Physics, American Physical Society, 335 East 45th St., New York, N.Y. 10017, U.S.A.

Recipients include: Kenneth G. Wilson (1973); Subrahmanyan Chandrasekhar (1974); Ludwig Dmitriyevich Faddeev (1975); Stephen Hawking (1976); Steven Weinberg (1977).

W. H. Heinemann Literature Award

Established under the W. H. Heinemann bequest to the Royal Society of Literature, the award is intended to encourage genuine contributions to literature, with preference for publications less likely to command large sales (poetry, biography, criticism, philosophy, history), though novels will not be overlooked. Similar preference will be shown towards younger authors not yet widely recognized, while not excluding well-known authors from consideration. One, two, or three prizes may be given annually, though an award may be withheld if no work is considered to be of sufficient merit. Books submitted must have been published during the current year and must be written in the English language.

Awarding body: Royal Society of Literature, 1 Hyde Park Gardens, London W2 2LT, England.

Recipients include: Malcolm Bradbury (*The History Man*) and William Trevor (*Angels at the Ritz*), 1975; Philip Ziegler (*Melbourne*) and Edward Crankshaw (*The Shadow of the Winter Palace*), 1976; Christopher Hill (*Milton and the English Revolution*), F. S. L. Lyons (*Charles Stewart Parnell*) and N. and J. Mackenzie (*The First Fabians*), 1977.

Helmholtz-Preis

The prize was established by the Helmholtz Fund in 1973 on the occasion of its 60th anniversary. It is named after Hermann von Helmholtz (1821–94), who became the first president of the German Physical-Technical Institute in 1887. The prize, which consists of DM5,000 and a certificate, is awarded every two years for a scientific paper relating to research and development in precision measurement of physical quantities. Physicists and engineers in the Federal Republic of Germany (including West Berlin) whose work is in the field of metrology, may compete for the prize. Papers submitted must be original and unpublished.

Awarding body: Helmholtz-Fonds e.V., c/o Präsident, Physikalisch-Technische Bundesanstalt, Bundesallee 100, 3300 Braunschweig, Federal Republic of Germany.

Recipients: Dr.-Ing. Walter Farr (1974); Dr.-Ing. W. Fuhrmann and Dr. V. Kose (1977).

Gottfried-von-Herder-Preis

This prize was instituted in 1963 by DDr. h.c. Alfred Toepfer in memory of Gottfried von Herder (1744–1803), the German philosopher, writer and folklore specialist. It is awarded through the University of Vienna, and takes the form of a medal, certificate and cash prize of DM20,000. Its intention is to encourage cultural relations with the peoples of eastern and south-eastern Europe. It is awarded annually to seven individuals from these countries who have accomplished outstanding work in the field of literature, music, painting, sculpture, architecture, folklore or the care of historical monuments, and thereby contributed to the European cultural tradition. The prize is one of many administered by the F.V.S. Foundation in Hamburg to promote the cause of European unity.

Awarding body: Kuratorium des Gottfried von Herder-Preises der Stiftung F.V.S. zu Hamburg, D-2 Hamburg 1, Georgsplatz 10, Federal Republic of Germany.

Recipients include: Jagoda Buić (Yugoslavia), Prof. Marin Goleminov (Bulgaria), Prof. Dr. Joannis Th. Kakridis (Greece), Prof. Dr. Dezsö

Keresztury (Hungary), Nichita Stănescu (Romania), Prof. Dr. Rudolf Turek (Czechoslovakia), Prof. Dr. Kazimierz Wejchert (Poland), 1976.

Rudolph Hering Medal

This award was established in 1924 by the Sanitary (now Environmental) Engineering Division of the ASCE, in honour of Rudolph Hering, former Vice-President of the Society. It consists of a bronze medal and a certificate, and is presented annually to a member of the ASCE for the best previously unpublished paper presented to the Society on water works, sewerage works, drainage, refuse handling or any other branch of environmental engineering.

Awarding body: American Society of Civil Engineers, 345 East 47th St., New York, N.Y. 10017, U.S.A.

Recipients include: Kenneth S. Price, Richard A. Conway and Albert H. Cheely ('Surface Aerator Interactions', 1974); W. C. Boyle, P. M. Berthouex and T. C. Rooney ('Pitfalls in Parameter Estimation for Oxygen Transfer Data', 1975); C. F. Guarino, M. D. Nelson and A. B. Edwards ('Philadelphia Pilots – Builds Oxygen Activated Sludge', 1976).

Herman Ottó Medal

The Hungarian Speleological Society founded this medal in 1962 for outstanding work promoting the advancement of speleological activity in Hungary. One or more prizes of 3,000 forints each are awarded annually. The medal is named after Ottó Herman (1835–1914), a world-famous scholar, biologist, palaeo-anthropologist and ethnographer.

Awarding body: Magyar Karzst- és Barlangkutató Társulat, 1055 Budapest, Kossuth Lajos tér 6–8, Hungary.

Mayo D. Hersey Award

This award was established in 1965 to recognize the splendid leadership in lubrication science and engineering of Mayo D. Hersey. It is bestowed on an individual in recognition of distinguished and continued contributions over a substantial period of time to the advancement of lubrication science and engineering. Distinguished contributions may result from significant original research in one or more of the many scientific disciplines related to lubrication, from excellence and creativity in lubrication engineering practice, or from sustained and forthright efforts and dissemination of information on the theory and practice of lubrication. The recipient need not be a member of ASME. The award takes the form of a bronze plaque.

Awarding body: American Society of Mechanical Engineers, United Engineering Center, 345 East 47th St., New York, N.Y. 10017, U.S.A.

Recipients include: Sydney J. Needs (1972); Donald F. Wilcock (1973); David Tabor (1974); Arthur F. Underwood (1975); John Boyd (1976).

Christian A. Herter Memorial Award

Established by the World Affairs Council of Boston in 1973, this has replaced the Council's Annual Award. It is given in memory of the late Christian A. Herter (1895–1967), a former Governor of Massachusetts and Secretary of State in the Eisenhower Administration. The award of a bronze medal is presented annually to individuals whose commitment to better international understanding has been demonstrated in a significant way through their professional work. Anyone is eligible to receive the award.

Awarding body: World Affairs Council of Boston, 70 Hereford St., Boston, Mass. 02115, U.S.A.

Recipients include: Elliot L. Richardson (1974); Edward M. Kennedy (1975); Henry A. Kissinger (1976); Robert S. McNamara (1977).

Gustav-Hertz-Preis

This award was established in 1977 by the GDR Physical Society to recognize outstanding achievements in theoretical and applied physics. It commemorates Prof. Dr. Gustav Hertz (1887–1975), Nobel Prize-winner, whose work provided experimental proof of Max Planck's quantum theory. Two awards may be made each year, to an individual and to a group of not more than four people. The prize takes the form of a diploma and a medal or cash prize, to the value of 2,000 DDR-Marks for individuals and 4,000 DDR-Marks for groups. The achievements for which it is awarded must have been undertaken during the previous two years.

Awarding body: Physikalische Gesellschaft der D.D.R., 108 Berlin, Am Kupfergraben 7, German Democratic Republic.

Heinrich Hertz Prize

The Badenwerk Foundation and the University of Karlsruhe founded this prize jointly in 1975, on the occasion of the 150th anniversary of the University of Karlsruhe. It is a triennial prize of DM50,000 and a medal, and is given for excellent scientific and technological achievements in the field of energy technology. It is named in memory of Heinrich Hertz who discovered electromagnetic waves, and who was a professor at the University of Karlsruhe from 1885 to 1889. The award is open to scientists of any nationality.

Awarding body: Badenwerk Foundation and University of Karlsruhe, 7500 Karlsruhe, Kaiserstr. 12, Federal Republic of Germany.

Recipients include: Alvin M. Weinberg (U.S.A., 1975).

Hertzogprys

This is the most prestigious prize in Afrikaans literature, and is named after one of the greatest champions of Afrikaans: General J. B. M. Hertzog. It was established in 1914 with a donation to the South African Academy of Science and Arts from General Hertzog, and is awarded annually in rotation for published work in three literary categories: prose, poetry and drama. The prize money consists of the interest on the capital of the gift, and is currently about R900.

Awarding body: Suid-Afrikaanse Akademie vir Wetenskap en Kuns, Posbus 538, Pretoria 0001, South Africa.

Recipients include: P. G. du Plessis (drama, *Siener in die suburbs* and *Die nag van Legio*, 1972); Chris Barnard (prose, *Mahala en Duiwel-in-die-bos*, 1973); Uys Krige (poetry, *Uys Krige: 'n keur uit sy gedigte*, 1974); Anna M. Louw (prose, *Kroniek van Perdepoort*, 1976); Wilma Stöckenstrom (poetry, *Van vergetelheid en van glans*, 1977).

Hermann-Hesse-Preis

This prize was established in 1956 by the Association for the Advancement of German Art, in honour of the German writer, Hermann Hesse (1877–1962). In 1968 the city of Karlsruhe became a co-patron of the award. The prize is given for a work of fiction or in the sphere of philosophy, history or sociology, written in German by an author of any nationality. The cash prize of DM10,000 is awarded every three years. The presentation ceremony takes place, if possible, on 2 July, the anniversary of Hesse's birthday. As the award was established to encourage young writers in particular it is not given to an author who has already received a prize. Works submitted need not have been published. No one may submit more than one work.

Awarding body: Förderungsgemeinschaft der deutschen Kunst e.V., 7500 Karlsruhe 1, Kantstr. 6, Federal Republic of Germany.

Recipients include: Ernst Augustin (*Der Kopf*, 1962); Hubert Fichte (*Das Waisenhaus*, 1965); Hans Saner (*Kants Weg vom Krieg zum Frieden*, 1968); Mario Szenessy (*Fälschungen*, 1971); Adolf Muschg (*Albissers Grund*, 1974).

Otto-Heubner-Preis

This gold medal is awarded by the Federal German Society of Paediatrics at intervals of at least three years to one of its members who has made a notable contribution in the area of paediatrics. Names can be put forward by any member of the Society. The prize originated in the years preceding the First World War, but was confirmed in its present form in 1953.

Awarding body: Deutsche Gesellschaft für Kinderheilkunde e.V., D-5000 Cologne 60, Amsterdamer Strasse 59, Federal Republic of Germany.

Recipients include: Prof. Dr. Widukind Lenz (1964); Prof. Dr. K. Kundratitz (1967); Prof. Dr. Hans Kleinschmidt (1970); Prof. Dr. H. Dost (1973); Prof. Dr. Guido Fanconi (1976).

Georg von Hevesy Medal and Memorial Lecture

This award, consisting of a medal and invitation to deliver the memorial lecture to the European Society of Nuclear Medicine, is made for long-standing contributions to the development of nuclear medicine by a scientist of any nationality. Instituted in 1970, it is generally presented annually, and commemorates Georg von Hevesy (1885–1966), Nobel prize-winning pioneer in the field of nuclear medicine.

Awarding body: Georg von Hevesy-Stiftung für Nuklearmedizin, Waserstr. 53, 8053 Zürich, Switzerland.

Recipients include: E. Eric Pochin (U.K., 1970); John H. Lawrence (U.S.A., 1973); H. J. Severing (Fed. Rep. of Germany, 1975); H. Levi (Denmark, 1975); H. N. Wagner (U.S.A., 1976).

Georg von Hevesy Prize for Nuclear Medicine

This award is made annually to a scientist of any nationality, not more than 40 years of age, for a publication in the field of nuclear medicine. It consists of a certificate and cash prize of about 10,000 Swiss francs. First presented in 1969, it commemorates Georg von Hevesy (1885–1966), Nobel prize-winning pioneer in the field of nuclear medicine.

Awarding body: Georg von Hevesy-Stiftung für Nuklearmedizin, Waserstr. 53, 8053 Zürich, Switzerland.

Recipients include: H. S. Winchell (U.S.A., 1969); G. Meuret (Fed. Rep. of Germany, 1972); H. Maseri a.o. (Italy, 1974); D. A. Goodwin a.o. (U.S.A., 1974); H. P. Breuel (Fed. Rep. of Germany, 1975).

Hickman Medal

The medal is awarded every three years by the Royal Society of Medicine for original work of outstanding merit in anaesthesia, or in subjects directly connected therewith, to any person of any nationality not necessarily medically qualified.

Awarding body: Royal Society of Medicine, 1 Wimpole St., London W1M 8AE, England.

David Higham Prize for Fiction

The prize was established in 1975 by David Higham's firm of literary agents, to celebrate his 80th birthday. The prize of £500 is administered by the National Book League and is awarded annually on 17 November, the anniversary of David Higham's birthday (Mr. Higham died in 1978). It is given for a first novel written in English by a citizen of the Commonwealth, Eire or South Africa, which shows promise for the future.

Awarding body: National Book League, 7 Albemarle St., London W1X 4BB, England.

Recipients include: Jane Gardam (*Black Faces, White Faces*) and Matthew Vaughan (*Chalky*), jointly, 1975; Caroline Blackwood (*The Stepdaughter*, 1976); Patricia Finney (*A Shadow of Gulls*, 1977); Leslie Norris (*Sliding*, 1978).

Karl Emil Hilgard Hydraulic Prize

This prize was established in 1939 with funds bequeathed by K. E. Hilgard, M.ASCE, and is given annually for the paper which deals best with a problem of flowing water, either in theory or in practice; preferably the paper should not have received another Society award. The prize consists of a wall plaque and a certificate. When the excellence of more than one paper justifies it, a second paper may be designated as of 'second order of merit'; this may be entered for the next year's award.

107

Awarding body: American Society of Civil Engineers, 345 East 47th St., New York, N.Y. 10017, U.S.A.

Recipients include: George D. Ashton and John F. Kennedy ('Ripples on Underside of River Ice Covers', 1974); Eduard Naudascher and Frederick A. Locher ('Flow-Induced Forces on Protruding Wall', 1975); Task Committee for the Preparation of the Manual on Sedimentation of the Hydraulics Division Sedimentation Committee ('Sedimentation Engineering', 1976).

Hindi Literary Awards

These awards were established by the Union Ministry of Education and Social Welfare to encourage authors whose mother tongue is an Indian language other than Hindi, and who live in a non-Hindi-speaking state, to write in Hindi. Sixteen prizes of 1,500 rupees each are awarded annually in the following categories: literature, fine arts and humanities, sciences, social sciences, technology. Translations of standard works from other Indian languages into Hindi are also eligible. Only books published during the preceding three years are considered for the awards.

Awarding body: Ministry of Education and Social Welfare, Central Hindi Directorate, West Block No. 7, Rama Krishna Puram, New Delhi 110022, India.

Julian Hinds Award

This award was endowed by John R. Kiely, F.ASCE, in memory of the outstanding professional contributions of Julian Hinds, Hon. M.ASCE, and established by the American Society of Civil Engineers in 1974. The award is given for the most meritorious contribution to the field of water resources development, in the form of a published paper. It is an annual award, and restricted to members of ASCE unless a joint paper is submitted, in which case only one author need be a member. The award consists of a wall plaque, a certificate and an honorarium of $1,000.

Awarding body: American Society of Civil Engineers, 345 East 47th St., New York, N.Y. 10017, U.S.A.

Recipients include: Victor A. Koelzer (1975); Harvey O. Banks (role in California Water Project and many contributions to water resource policies, 1976).

Axel Hirsch Prize

The award was endowed by Axel Hirsch in 1967, and is given every two years by the Swedish Academy. A monetary prize (currently 50,000 Swedish kronor) is awarded for biographical or historical work by Swedish writers or scientists, published during the previous two years. It cannot be applied for.

Awarding body: The Swedish Academy, Börshuset, Källargränd 4, S-111 29 Stockholm, Sweden.

History Manuscript Award

This award goes to the winner of an annual competition for the best historical manuscript

dealing with the science, technology and/or impact of aeronautics and astronautics on society. Its purpose is to provide professional recognition for an author making a major and original contribution to the history of aeronautics and astronautics. The award carried a medal and certificate of citation.

Awarding body: American Institute of Aeronautics and Astronautics, 1290 Avenue of the Americas, New York, N.Y. 10019, U.S.A.

Recipients include: Richard C. Lukas (1971); Richard K. Smith (1972); William M. Leary, Jr. (1973); Richard P. Hallion (1975); Thomas Crouch (1977).

Hodgkins Medal and Prize

This award is made to promote and to recognize noteworthy contributions to environmental studies from scientific and social points of view. It was established in 1893 in memory of Thomas George Hodgkins (1803–92) who willed his fortune to the Smithsonian Institution. He designated that a portion of the income from the fund named after him be used to promote atmospheric research. In 1965 the terms of the award were revised and the award is now made for 'important contributions to knowledge of the physical environment bearing upon the welfare of man'. The award consists of a gold medal and a cash prize and is presented annually or biennially by the Secretary of the Institution who may arrange for a lecture at the time of presentation. There are no restrictions on eligibility.

Awarding body: Smithsonian Institution, 1000 Jefferson Drive, S.W., Washington, D.C. 20560, U.S.A.

Recipients include: Jule Gregory Charney (1969); Arie Haagen-Smit (1969); Lewis Mumford (1971); Walter Orr Roberts (1973); E. Cuyler Hammond (1976).

Wilhelm-Hoff-Preis

The prize was established in 1964 by the German Society for Aeronautics, the predecessor of the German Aerospace Research and Experimental Establishment (DFVLR) in Cologne. The prize commemorates the aeronautical scientist Wilhelm Hoff (1883–1945), who was head of the German Experimental Establishment for Aeronautics (DVL) in Berlin-Adlershof from 1920 onwards. The prize consists of a certificate and a sum of money of up to DM5,000, and is awarded every two years for published papers or lectures given about their scientific achievements by persons working with the DFVLR.

Awarding body: Deutsche Forschungs- und Versuchsanstalt für Luft- und Raumfahrt e.V., Postfach 90 60 58, D-5000 Cologne 90, Federal Republic of Germany.

Paul G. Hoffman Awards

These biennial awards were established by the Society for International Development in 1976 in memory of Paul G. Hoffman (1891–1974), administrator of the United Nations Development

Programme. There are two awards: one for significant contribution to international co-operation for development, and another for significant contribution to national economic and social development. Each award is worth $5,000.

Awarding body: Society for International Development, 1346 Connecticut Ave., N.W., Washington, D.C. 20036, U.S.A.

August-Wilhelm-von-Hofmann-Denkmünze

Established in 1902 by the German Chemical Society, this was originally known as the Hofmann prize for outstanding achievements in experimental chemistry. The gold medal commemorates the first President of the Society, August Wilhelm von Hofmann. In 1951 the award was taken over by the new Society of German Chemists, founded in 1946, with the stipulation that the medal should be awarded either to foreign chemists or to German scientists who, without being chemists, have distinguished themselves in chemistry. The award is made irregularly.

Awarding body: Gesellschaft Deutscher Chemiker, 6000 Frankfurt (Main) 90, Carl Bosch-Haus, Varrentrappstr. 40–42, Federal Republic of Germany.

Recipients include: Prof. Viktor N. Kondratiev (U.S.S.R., 1967); Sir Lawrence Bragg, F.R.S. (U.K., 1967); Prof. Vladimir Prelog (Switzerland, 1967); Prof. Costin D. Nenitzescu (Romania, 1970); Prof. Edgar Heilbronner (Switzerland, 1974); Prof. Albert Eschenmoser (Switzerland, 1976).

Holleman Prize

Professor A. F. Holleman initiated this prize in 1952. It is awarded by the Royal Netherlands Academy of Arts and Sciences once every five years, and is for outstanding research work in chemistry. Its value is 2,500 guilders.

Awarding body: Koninklijke Nederlandse Akademie van Wetenschappen, Kloveniersburgwal 29, 1011 JV Amsterdam, The Netherlands.

Recipients include: Prof. Dr. H. J. den Hartog (1964); Prof. Dr. G. J. M. van der Kerk (1969); Prof. Dr. Th. J. de Boer (1975).

Holley Medal

The Holley Medal was established in 1924 to honour Alexander L. Holley, Charter Member of the American Society of Mechanical Engineers. The medal is bestowed only on one who, by some great act of genius of an engineering nature, has accomplished a great and timely public benefit. Attention is concentrated on the brilliance of his art – not on the man. The achievement should be of such public importance as to be worthy of the gratitude of the nation and to call forth admiration of engineers. Following an amendment of 1973, the medal may also be awarded to more than one individual for a single achievement, provided that each individual made an equal or comparable contribution. Gold medals, engrossed certificates and lapel buttons are awarded.

Awarding body: American Society of Mechanical Engineers, United Engineering Center, 345 East 47th St., New York, N.Y. 10017, U.S.A.

Recipients include: Harold E. Edgerton and Kenneth J. Germeshausen (1973); George M. Grover (1975); Emmett N. Leith and Juris Upatnieks (1976).

Gilles Holst Medal

The Royal Netherlands Academy of Arts and Sciences founded this gold medal in 1960 in honour of Dr. Gilles Holst (1886–1968), Director of the N.V. Philips Laboratories. The medal is awarded every four years for research in the fields of applied physics or applied chemistry. Scientists of Dutch nationality only are eligible.

Awarding body: Koninklijke Nederlandse Akademie van Wetenschappen, Kloveniersburgwal 29, 1011 JV Amsterdam, The Netherlands.

Recipients include: Prof. Dr. W. G. Burgers (1963); Dr. M. C. Teves (1967); Prof. Dr. J. D. Fast (1971); Prof. Dr. P. M. de Wolff (1976).

Winifred Holtby Memorial Prize

Miss Vera Brittain has given to the Royal Society of Literature a sum of money to provide an annual prize of £100 in honour of the late Winifred Holtby. The prize is for the best regional novel of the year written in the English language. The writer must be of British or Irish nationality, or a citizen of the Commonwealth. Translations, unless made by the author of his/her own work, are not eligible.

Awarding body: Royal Society of Literature, 1 Hyde Park Gardens, London W2 2LT, England.

Recipients include: John Stewart (*Last Cool Days*, 1971); Graham King (*Pandora Valley*, 1974); Jane Gardam (*Black Faces, White Faces*, 1975); Eugène McCabe (*Victims*, 1976); Anita Desai (*Fire on the Mountain*, 1977).

Holweck Medal and Prize

A gold medal and a prize of £150 are awarded for distinguished work in experimental physics, or in theoretical physics if closely related to experimental work, which should either still be in progress or have been carried out within the preceding ten years. The award was instituted in 1945 jointly by the French and British Physical Societies as a memorial to Fernand Holweck, Director of the Curie Laboratory of the Radium Institute in Paris, who was killed by the Gestapo during the German occupation of France in 1940–44. Since 1974 the award has been made in odd-dated years to a French physicist by the Council of the Institute of Physics, and in even-dated years to a British physicist by the Council of the Société Française de Physique. The selection is made from a list of three nominees submitted by the other Council.

Awarding body: The Institute of Physics, 47 Belgrave Square, London SW1X 8QX, England.

Recipients include: Ionel Solomon (1972); Brian David Josephson (1973); Philippe Nozières and Antony Hewish (1974); Evry Schatzman (1975); Prof. W. F. Vinen (1978).

Honeywell International Medal

This award is made annually by the British Institute of Measurement and Control to chartered measurement and control technologists (or their equivalent) for distinguished work on control in any area. It was established in 1975 by Honeywell International, manufacturers of control equipment, and commemorates the granting of a Royal Charter to the Institute.

Awarding body: The Institute of Measurement and Control, 20 Peel St., London W8 7PD, England.

Recipients include: S. T. Lunt.

Honeywell Prize

This award is made annually by the British Institute of Measurement and Control for the best article in the Journal section of *Measurement and Control*. It takes the form of a cash prize of £20, and was established in 1971 by Honeywell Ltd., manufacturers of control equipment.

Awarding body: The Institute of Measurement and Control, 20 Peel St., London W8 7PD, England.

Hood Medal

This is awarded annually for meritorious performance in some branch of photography, with particular emphasis on any exhibit which represents an outstanding advance in photography for public service.

Awarding body: The Royal Photographic Society of Great Britain, 14 South Audley St., London W1Y 5DP, England.

Recipients include: Stephen Dalton (1971); Pat Whitehouse (1972); John Chittock (1973); R. M. Callender (1974); Heather Angel (1975).

P. C. Hooft-prijs

The Dutch Ministry of Culture, Recreation and Social Work awards an annual prize for outstanding and original literature written in Dutch. The prize amounts to 8,000 guilders, and is the most important of the national literary prizes. It is awarded in rotation for poetry, a novel, and an essay.

Awarding body: Ministerie van Cultuur, Recreatie en Maatschappelijk Werk, Steenvoordelaan 370, Rijswijk (ZH), The Netherlands.

Recipients include: Simon Carmiggelt (1977).

C. P. Hoogenhout Award for Children's Literature in Afrikaans

The award was established in 1960 to be given annually for an outstanding children's book in Afrikaans (age limits 7–12) published in the preceding year. It consists of a gold medal and certificate, and is presented during the South African Library Association Conference.

Awarding body: South African Library Association, c/o Ferdinand Postma Library, Potchefstroom University, Potchefstroom 2520, South Africa.

Recipients include: Pieter W. Grobbelaar (*Die mooiste Afrikaanse sprokies*, 1968); Alba Bouwer (*Katrientjie van Keerweder* and *'n Hennetjie met kuikens*, 1971); Frede Linde (*Snoet-Alleen* and *By die oog van die fontein*, 1974).

Friedrich-Hopfner-Medaille

The award, named after the Professor of Higher Geodesy at the Vienna Technical College, was instituted by the Austrian Commission for International Geodesy to be presented every four years, beginning in 1977. The medal is awarded for outstanding work in any area which comes within the scope of the International Geodetic Association. It is generally awarded to Austrian citizens only. Members of the Austrian Commission, who are not themselves eligible, may propose candidates.

Awarding body: Österreichische Kommission für die Internationale Erdmessung, 1040 Vienna 4, Gusshausstr. 27–29, Austria.

Chandra Kala Hora Medal

This medal was established in 1945 by the Indian National Science Academy. It is awarded every five years for exceptional contributions to the development of fisheries in India during the preceding five years.

Awarding body: Indian National Science Academy, Bahadur Shah Zafar Marg, New Delhi 110001, India.

Recipients include: B. S. Bhimachar (1965); N. K. Panikkar (1970); S. Z. Qasim (1975).

Sunder Lal Hora Medal

Established in 1957 by the Indian National Science Academy, this medal is awarded for outstanding contributions in the field of life sciences. It is awarded every three years.

Awarding body: Indian National Science Academy, Bahadur Shah Zafar Marg, New Delhi 110001, India.

Recipients include: K. Ramiah (1969); Salim Ali (1971); T. S. Sadasivan (1973); L. S. Ramaswami (1975); G. P. Talwar (1978).

Wesley W. Horner Award

This award consists of a plaque and certificate, and is made annually to the author or authors of the best paper dealing with hydrology, urban drainage or sewerage published in the previous year by the ASCE. Preference is given to authors in the private practice of engineering. The award was established in 1968 in honour of W. W. Horner, former President of the ASCE, and is endowed by his office partners and family.

Awarding body: American Society of Civil Engineers, 345 East 47th St., New York, N.Y. 10017, U.S.A.

Recipients include: Charles V. Gibbs, Stuart A. Alexander and Curtis P. Leiser ('System for Regulation of Combined Sewage Flows', 1974); C. G. Gunnerson ('Environmental Design for Istanbul Sewage Disposal', 1975); W. R. Giessner, R. T. Cockburn, F. H. Moss and M. E. Noonan ('Planning and Control of Combined Sewerage Systems', 1976).

Horning Memorial Award
The award was established in 1938 in memory of Henry L. Horning, a former President of the Society of Automotive Engineers. A medal and certificate are presented annually to the author or authors of the best paper or combination of papers relating to the adaptation of fuels and internal combustion engines, which has been presented at a meeting of the Society, or any of its sections, during the previous calendar year. Papers are judged primarily for the originality of their contribution to such knowledge. The award is also open to an individual for distinguished achievements in engine–fuel relationships.
Awarding body: Society of Automotive Engineers, Inc., 400 Commonwealth Drive, Warrendale, Pa. 15096, U.S.A.
Recipients include: Ather A. Quader (General Motors Research Laboratory, 'Lean Combustion and Misfire Limits in Spark Ignition Engines', 1975).

Hospital and Community Psychiatry Institute Achievement Awards
These awards, established in 1949, are made for outstanding treatment programmes for the mentally ill and retarded. They consist of three gold plaques presented annually by the Hospital and Community Psychiatry Institute in conjunction with the American Psychiatric Association.
Awarding body: American Psychiatric Association, 1700 18th St., N.W., Washington, D.C. 20009, U.S.A.

Høst-Madsen-Medal
This medal was founded in 1953 by the Danish Pharmacists' Association, to be given to the winner of a competition for the best scientific paper. Although it was originally intended to encourage research by young pharmaceutical scientists, in practice it has always been awarded to senior members of that discipline. The first award, a gold medal, was made in 1955 to Dr. Erik Høst-Madsen, the Dutch pharmacologist who was President of the International Pharmaceutical Federation from 1935 to 1953. Since then it has been cast in bronze. It is normally awarded to a single recipient every two years at the General Assembly of the Federation.
Awarding body: International Pharmaceutical Federation, Alexanderstraat 11, The Hague, The Netherlands.
Recipients include: Prof. R. Ruyssen (Belgium, 1968); Prof. H. Flück (Switzerland, 1970); Prof. J. Wagner (U.S.A., 1972); Prof. M. Guillot (France, 1974).

Valentin-Hottenroth-Denkmünze
This medal is presented by the West German Association of Pulp and Paper Chemists and Engineers (Zellcheming) for an outstanding work on the subject of cellulose and its processing. Nominations must be made by members of Zellcheming. The award was instituted in 1955 by Zellcheming and the Waldhof cellulose factory to commemorate Zellcheming's golden jubilee, and honours Dr. Valentin Hottenroth and his industrial research into cellulose and synthetic fibres.
Awarding body: Verein der Zellstoff- und Papier-Chemiker und Ingenieure, 6100 Darmstadt, Berliner Allee 56, Federal Republic of Germany.
Recipients include: Dir. Dr. phil. Rudolf Schepp (1955); Dr. phil. Arthur Zart, Dir. Dr.-Ing. Erwin Schmidt (1958); Prof. Dr.-Ing. Georg Jayme (1961); Dir. Dr.-Ing. Waldemar Nippe (1965); Dr. rer. nat. Otmar Töppel (1970).

Bernardo A. Houssay Science Prize
This annual prize was instituted in 1972 by the Inter-American Council for Education, Science and Culture in memory of Dr. Bernardo Houssay (1887–1971), the Argentinian scientist and Nobel prize-winner. The prize is awarded to a research worker who has made notable contributions in a Latin-American country in one of the following fields: biological sciences; exact sciences; agricultural sciences; technological research related to development. The prize consists of U.S.$30,000, a certificate, and paid travel expenses for two people for the presentation ceremony.
Awarding body: Inter-American Council for Education, Science and Culture, Constitution Ave., N.W., Washington, D.C. 20006, U.S.A.
Recipients include: Dr. Alberto Hurtado (Peru, biological sciences, 1972); Dr. Venancio Deulofeu (Argentina, exact sciences, 1973); Dr. Arturo Burkart (Argentina, agricultural sciences, 1974); Dr. José Salvador Gandolfo (Argentina, technical research related to development, 1975); Dr. Roberto Caldeyro-Barcia (Uruguay, biological sciences, 1976).

Ebenezer Howard Memorial Medal
The award was established in 1938 by the Town and Country Planning Association, in memory of Sir Ebenezer Howard (1850–1927), founder of the Garden Cities (now New Towns) Movement and sometime President of the International Federation for Garden Cities and Town Planning (now International Federation for Housing and Planning). The medal is awarded for consistent and distinguished contribution to the advancement of ideas on town and country planning, garden cities and new towns, as originally articulated by Sir Ebenezer Howard. The award is made whenever a suitable candidate is found.
Awarding body: Town and Country Planning Association, 17 Carlton House Terrace, London SW1 5AS, England.
Recipients include: Sir Raymond Unwin (1938); Sir Barry Parker (1938); Sir Patrick Abercrombie (1943); Lewis Mumford (1946); Sir Frederic Osborn (1968).

Ernest E. Howard Award
This award was established in 1954 by Mrs. Howard in honour of her husband, a former President of the American Society of Civil Engineers. It is awarded annually to a member of the Society for a definite contribution to the

advancement of structural engineering, either in research, planning, design or construction, in written form or through notable action or performance. The award consists of a gold medal, a bronze replica, a certificate, a brochure describing the accomplishment and a cash prize of $300. 'Second and third order of merit' papers can be designated, which can be reconsidered for the prize in the two following years.

Awarding body: American Society of Civil Engineers, 345 East 47th St., New York, N.Y. 10017, U.S.A.

Recipients include: George S. Richardson (1972); C. Martin Duke (1973); Bruce G. Johnston (1974); George E. Brandow (1975); Egor P. Popov (long research in mathematics and its application to modern structures, 1976).

C. D. Howe Award

This award is presented annually by the Canadian Aeronautics and Space Institute for achievement in the fields of planning, policy making and overall leadership in Canadian aeronautics and space activities. It was established in 1966, and consists of a silver plaque.

Awarding body: Canadian Aeronautics and Space Institute, Suite 406, 77 Metcalfe St., Ottawa, Ont. K1P 5L6, Canada.

Recipients include: P. C. Garratt (1966); G. R. McGregor (1967); T. E. Stephenson (1968); A. Bandi (1969); D. A. Golden (1970); Dr. G. N. Patterson (1972).

Howe Medal

This medal is awarded annually by the American Ophthalmological Society to an ophthalmologist of any nationality who has distinguished himself through either some notable discovery, conspicuous service as a writer or teacher, or outstanding original investigation. It was established in 1919 by Dr. Lucien Howe.

Awarding body: American Ophthalmological Society (c/o Robert W. Hollenhurst, M.D.), 420 5th Ave., S.W., Rochester, Minn. 55901, U.S.A.

Recipients include: Dr. Algernon B. Reese (1950); Dr. Francis H. Adler (1952); Dr. David G. Cogan (1965); Dr. C. Wilbur Rucker (1971); Dr. Edward W. D. Norton (1976).

Howells Medal

This medal is given in honour of William Dean Howells, President of the American Academy of Arts and Letters from 1908 to 1920. It is given every five years in recognition of the most distinguished work of American fiction published during that period.

Awarding body: American Academy and Institute of Arts and Letters, 633 West 155th St., New York, N.Y. 10032, U.S.A.

Hubbard Medal

The medal was established in 1906 by the National Geographic Society in honour of Gardiner Greene Hubbard, first President of the Society. It is

awarded as and when merited for distinction in exploration, discovery and research.

Awarding body: National Geographic Society, 17th and M Streets, N.W., Washington, D.C. 20036, U.S.A.

Recipients include: American Mount Everest Expedition (1963); Juan T. Trippe (1967); Apollo 8 Astronauts (Col. Frank Borman, Capt. James A. Lovell, Jr., Lt. Col. William A. Anders, 1969); Apollo 11 Astronauts (Neil A. Armstrong, Col. Edwin E. Aldrin, Lt. Col. Michael Collins, 1970); Dr. Alexander Wetmore (1975).

Manley O. Hudson Medal

This award is made occasionally by the American Society of International Law to an individual of any nationality who has contributed to the scholarship and achievement of his time in international law. It takes the form of a gold medal and certificate. Established by Ralph G. Albrecht, the medal was first awarded in 1956 to Manley O. Hudson (1886–1960), a distinguished scholar in international law and member of the International Court of Justice.

Awarding body: American Society of International Law, 2223 Massachusetts Ave., N.W., Washington, D.C. 20008, U.S.A.

Recipients include: Lord McNair (1959); Philip C. Jessup (1964); Charles De Visscher (1966); Paul Guggenheim (1970); Myres S. McDougal (1976).

Hufeland-Preis

The Colonia Life Insurance Company of Cologne established this annual award in 1959 and dedicated it to the memory of Christoph Wilhelm Hufeland (1762–1836), a doctor and founder-member of the University of Berlin and the Charité Medical Centre. The award was founded to promote the knowledge and use of preventive medicine, and is presented annually for scientific work in this field. The work must be based on first-hand medical knowledge which is considered to be essentially scientifically founded, and must not have been published previously. German doctors and dentists are eligible for the award, which consists of a certificate and a cash prize of DM20,000.

Awarding body: Stiftung Hufeland-Preis, Federal Republic of Germany.

Recipients include: Prof. Dr. Georg-Wilhelm Löhr and Doz. Dr. Hans Dierck Waller (1965); Prof. Dr. Dietrich Schmähl and Prof. Dr. Hans Osswald (1970); Privatdoz. Dr. med. habil. Jürgen Krämer (1972); Prof. Dr. Kurt Biener (1976).

Hughes Medal

In 1900 Professor D. E. Hughes bequeathed £4,000 to the Royal Society. With the income from this fund a silver gilt medal, bearing a bust of Professor Hughes, is awarded annually to such person as the President and Council of the Society may consider the most worthy recipient, without restriction of sex or nationality, as the reward of original discovery in the Physical Sciences, par-

112

ticularly electricity and magnetism or their applications, such discovery or applications having been published not less than one year before the award. A gift of £200 accompanies the medal.
Awarding body: Royal Society of London, 6 Carlton House Terrace, London SW1Y 5AG, England.
Recipients include: Prof. P. H. Fowler (1974); Prof. R. H. Dalitz (1975); Dr. S. W. Hawking (1976); Prof. A. Hewish (1977); Prof. W. Cochran (1978).

Hughlings Jackson Medal and Lecture

A lecturer is appointed every three years to lecture on a neurological subject. He receives a medal and an honorarium.
Awarding body: The Royal Society of Medicine, 1 Wimpole St., London W1M 8AE, England.

Alexander von Humboldt Medal

This gold medal is presented for services to nature and landscape conservation. It is named in memory of Alexander von Humboldt (1769–1859), the German naturalist.
Awarding body: Stiftung FVS, Georgsplatz 10, 2 Hamburg 1, Federal Republic of Germany.
Recipients include: Sir Peter Smithers (U.K., 1971).

Humboldt Prize

This award for senior U.S. scientists was established by the Government of the Federal Republic of Germany in 1972. It was announced by the then Chancellor, Willy Brandt, speaking at Harvard University on 5 June 1972, the 25th anniversary of the inauguration of the Marshall Aid Programme. The prize is administered by the Alexander von Humboldt Foundation, from which it takes its name. Its aim is to promote scientific co-operation between institutions in the Federal Republic of Germany and the U.S.A. It is awarded to American scientists who have gained an international reputation by their research and teaching. Winners receive a sum of money ranging from DM25,000 to DM72,000 plus travelling expenses and the opportunity to carry out research at institutes in the Federal Republic of Germany. Professors, and scientists of equal standing outside the universities, whose work is in the fields of mathematics, physics, chemistry, biology, medicine, engineering, computer and earth sciences, are eligible. As many as 80 prizes may be awarded in any year. There is no application; nominations are accepted only from leading German researchers and institutions.
Awarding body: Alexander von Humboldt-Stiftung, Federal Republic of Germany.
Recipients include: Prof. Hans Neurath (biochemistry, 1974); Prof. Klaus Hofmann (biochemistry, 1976); Prof. Ernst Mayr (ornithology, 1976); Prof. David M. Prescott (plant biology, 1977).

Hungarian P.E.N. Club Memorial Medal

This award is made occasionally to writers, poets, translators, editors and others for outstanding literary translations from Hungarian into foreign languages, and dissemination of Hungarian literature abroad. It was established in 1948, and takes the form of a medal and certificate.
Awarding body: Magyar P.E.N. Club, 1051 Budapest, Vörösmarty tér 1, Hungary.
Recipients include: Sava Babić (Yugoslavia, 1971); François Gachot (France, 1972); Edwin Morgan (U.K., 1972); Bernard Vargaftig (France, 1976); David Scheinert (Belgium, 1976).

Hungarian People's Republic State Prize

This annual prize was established by the Presidential Council in 1963 and is awarded by the Council of Ministers. It consists of honorary recognition with the 'Grand Prize' and a medal, in three categories. It is given for outstanding achievement in the furtherance of socialist society in the fields of science and technology, national economy, medicine, education and instruction.
Awarding body: Committee for the State Prize, Council of Ministers, Kossuth Lajos tér 1, Budapest V, Hungary.

John Hunter Medal and Triennial Prize

Founded by the Court of Assistants in 1820, the prize of £50 and a bronze medal is awarded to a Fellow or Member of the Royal College of Surgeons, not on the Council, who has during the preceding ten years done such work in anatomy, physiology, histology, embryology or pathological anatomy as in the opinion of the adjudicating committee deserves special recognition.
Awarding body: The Royal College of Surgeons of England, 35–43 Lincoln's Inn Fields, London WC2A 3PN, England.
Recipients include: Gilbert Washington Causey (outstanding contribution to the study of electron microscopy and his work in connection with re-establishing the Hunterian museum, 1961–63); Joseph Mendel Yoffey (work on the lymphocyte and the lymphatic system, 1964–66); Roderic Alfred Gregory (outstanding contributions in the field of the physiology of the gastro-intestinal tract, 1967–69); William James Hamilton (outstanding contributions to anatomy and embryology, 1970–72); David Ernest Poswillo (contributions to experimental teratology, 1973–75).

Hunterian Oration

This oration is to be delivered biennially in the Royal College of Surgeons on 14 February, John Hunter's birthday, by a member of the Council, 'such oration to be expressive of the merits in comparative anatomy, physiology, and surgery, not only of John Hunter, but also of all persons, as should be from time to time deceased, whose labours have contributed to the improvement or extension of surgical science'. It was founded in 1813 by Dr. Matthew Baillie and Sir Everard Home, executors of John Hunter, who made a gift to the College to provide an annual oration (for which there is an honorarium of £10) and a dinner for Members of the Court of Assistants and others. In 1853 the oration and dinner became biennial.

Awarding body: The Royal College of Surgeons of England, 35–43 Lincoln's Inn Fields, London WC2A 3PN, England.

Orators include: Sir Hedley John Barnard Atkins, K.B.E. (1971); Sir Thomas Holmes Sellors (1973); Sir Rodney Smith, K.B.E. (1975); Richard Harrington Franklin (1977); George Qvist (1979).

Dragomir Hurmuzescu Prize

The Romanian Academy established this prize for physics in 1948. It is presented annually at a General Assembly of the Academy, and consists of 10,000 lei and a diploma. It is named after Dragomir Hurmuzescu (1865–1954), the physicist who made remarkable contributions in the fields of electricity and X-ray physics; he worked with the Curies, and created the electroscope which bears his name.

Awarding body: Academy of the S.R. of Romania, 125 Calea Victoriei, Bucharest, Romania.

Huxley Memorial Medal and Lecture

The highest honour awarded by the Royal Anthropological Institute, the Huxley Memorial Medal and Lecture is awarded annually by ballot of the Council, to a scientist of any nationality distinguished in any field of anthropology. It was established in 1900 in memory of Thomas Henry Huxley (1825–95), the great English student of anatomy and evolution.

Awarding body: Royal Anthropological Institute of Great Britain and Ireland, 36 Craven St., London WC2N 5NG, England.

Lecturers include: Prof. Marcel Mauss (1938); Prof. A. L. Kroeber (1945); Prof. A. R. Radcliffe-Brown (1951); Prof. J. B. S. Haldane (1956); Prof. Claude Lévi-Strauss (1965).

Huy International Film Festival

Inaugurated in 1960 by Georges Warzee, this Festival is held annually in October. It is open to all non-professional film-makers. Two prizes are awarded: Le Cwerneu d'Or, a gold statuette, for the amateur category; Le Coq Hardi, a pewter statuette, for the independent category.

Awarding body: Festival Mondial du Cinéma du Huy, 5 rue Nokin, 5250 Antheit, Belgium.

Samuel Hyde Memorial Lecture in Rheumatology and Rehabilitation

A lecturer is appointed every three years and receives an honorarium.

Awarding body: The Royal Society of Medicine, 1 Wimpole St., London W1M 8AE, England.

I

ICI Prize
This award is made annually by the British Institute of Measurement and Control for the best paper in the *Transactions* of the Institute on the application of the theory of automatic control. It takes the form of a cash award of £50, and was instituted in 1975 by ICI Ltd., the processing company.
Awarding body: The Institute of Measurement and Control, 20 Peel St., London W8 7PD, England.

IVAs Brinellmedalj (*Swedish Academy of Engineering Sciences Brinell Medal*)
The Academy established the medal in 1936 in honour of Johan August Brinell. It is given at irregular intervals for outstanding contributions in the sphere of mining and metallurgy, and is open to scientists and engineers of all nationalities.
Awarding body: Ingenjörsvetenskapsakademien, Box 5073, S-102 42 Stockholm 5, Sweden.
Recipients include: Prof. Gudmar Kihlstedt (Sweden, 1970); Dr. Thaddeus Sendzimir (U.S.A., 1974).

IVAs Guldmedalj (*Swedish Academy of Engineering Sciences Gold Medal*)
The medal was founded in 1921 for meritorious contributions within the Academy's sphere of activity, preferably in engineering and technology. Three medals are awarded annually, and recipients must not be members of the Academy.
Awarding body: Ingenjörsvetenskapsakademien, Box 5073, S-102 42 Stockholm 5, Sweden.
Recipients include: Ing. Henrik Björling, Ing. Fredrik Palmqvist, Ing. Isac Rosén, Dir. Nils Ståhl (1973); Fil. dr. Erik Lundblad, Övering. Sigurd Nordblad (1974).

IVAs Stora Guldmedalj (*Swedish Academy of Engineering Sciences Grand Gold Medal*)
The Academy founded the medal in 1921, and the regulations were revised in 1974. It is given at irregular intervals for distinguished work over many years within the Academy's field of activity, and especially for technological research and development.
Awarding body: Ingenjörsvetenskapsakademien, Box 5073, S-102 42 Stockholm 5, Sweden.
Recipients include: Dr. Håkan Sterky (development of telecommunications, 1969); Gunnar Ljungström (development of SAAB motor cars,

1971); Baltzar von Platen and Carl Munters (many years' successful activity as inventor and innovator of industrial products, 1974).

Ibero-American Bureau of Education Gold Medal
The award was established in 1960 and is given annually to a person or institution for distinguished service to the IABE. This is an intergovernmental organization for educational, scientific and technological co-operation between the Ibero-American countries.
Awarding body: Oficina de Educación Iberoamericana, Ciudad Universitaria s/n, Madrid 3, Spain.
Recipients include: José Luis Villar Palasí (Spain, 1973); Patronato Regional de Iberodidacta (Spain, 1974); Dr. Angel Rosenblat (Venezuela, 1975); Gen. Carlos P. Romulo (Philippines, 1976).

Ignasi Iglesias Prize
An annual prize of 250,000 pesetas, founded in 1977, is awarded for the best dramatic work written in Catalan. It is named after Ignasi Iglesias (1871–1928), the Catalan dramatist, and is awarded on 23 April (National Book Day).
Awarding body: Institut i Museu del Teatre, Diputació Provincial de Barcelona, Conde del Asalto 3, Barcelona, Spain.

Imamura Sho (*Imamura Memorial Prize*)
This annual award was established in 1969 by the Japanese Society for Tuberculosis in memory of Prof. Arao Imamura (1887–1967), a pioneer in studies on BCG vaccination and mass radiography. The award is made to encourage young research workers (under 45 years of age). It is given to members of the Society for papers published in the Society's official journal or presented at the general assembly or regional scientific meetings within the previous three years. The prize takes the form of a certificate and 100,000 yen in cash, and is usually awarded to two researchers per year.
Awarding body: Nihon Kekkakubyo Gakkai, c/o Research Institute of Tuberculosis, Japanese Anti-Tuberculosis Association, 3-1-24 Matsuyama Kiyose-shi, Tokyo 180-04, Japan.
Recipients include: Dr. Tatsuichiro Hashimoto ('Mechanism of tuberculin reaction') and Dr. Shunsaku Ohshima ('Growth inhibiting factors of tubercle bacilli found in the urine of healthy

persons', 1973); Dr. Kotaro Ohizumi ('Acting mechanism of antituberculous drugs', 1974); Dr. Takeshi Yamada and Dr. Kuniji Masuda ('Hereditary-biochemical studies on drug resistance to mycobacteria', 1975).

Immermann-Preis für Literatur
The town of Düsseldorf established this prize in 1964 in memory of Karl Leberecht Immermann as a tribute to his services to German literature and the development of dramatic art. The award, which consists of a cash prize of DM20,000, is conferred every three years either for one piece of literary work or for an author's collected works written during the preceding ten years. Recipients must have been born within the boundaries of the former German Reich of 1937 and have at least one parent of German nationality, or alternatively must have taken German nationality. Prizewinners are chosen by a Board consisting of seven members selected by the town council.
Awarding body: Landeshauptstadt Düsseldorf, Federal Republic of Germany.
Recipients include: Dr. Gerd Gaiser (1959); Dr. Eckart Peterich (1960); Sigismund von Radecki (1961); Ernst Jünger (1964); Wolfgang Koeppen (1967).

Imperial Tobacco Awards for Radio
Imperial Tobacco Ltd. in conjunction with the Society of Authors established the awards in 1976. Trophies are given annually for achievement in various categories: performance by an actor; performance by an actress; radio presenter; specialist programme; music documentary; documentary feature; light entertainment; talks; local radio; dramatized feature; drama – adaptation; drama – original; and a special gold award is given for the most outstanding contribution to radio during the year, in the judges' opinion (no nominations). Nominations for the other awards may be made by members of the Radiowriters Association of the Society of Authors, BBC and IBA departments, and radio critics.
Awarding body: Imperial Tobacco Ltd. and Society of Authors, London, England.
Recipients include: Kenny Everett (light entertainment, *Captain Kremmen*, 1976, 1977); Colin Blakely (outstanding actor in *Judgement*, 1977); Rosemary Leach (outstanding actress in *Moonshine*, 1977); Desmond Briscoe (gold award, *A Wall Walks Slowly*, 1977); Tom Vernon (radio presenter, *News Stand*, 1978).

Imperial Tobacco Cello Festival
Established in 1975 by Imperial Tobacco Ltd. under the Presidency of M. Paul Tortelier, the Festival is held biennially in October. Cellists under 30 years old of any nationality may enter the competition. Awards are made in three categories: gold medal and £1,000 cash prize; silver medal and £500 cash prize; bronze medal and £250 cash prize. The gold medallists perform in a gala concert at the end of the Festival with the Bournemouth Symphony Orchestra.

Awarding body: Imperial Tobacco Ltd., Imperial House, 1 Grosvenor Place, London SW1X 7HB, England. (Festival enquiries to the Director, Imperial Tobacco Cello Festival, Kallaway Arts Sponsorship Management, 2 Portland Rd., London W11 4LA, England.
Recipients include: Reiner Hochmuth (Fed. Rep. of Germany), Mirel Iancovici (Romania), 1975.

Inco Medal
This award, which was established in 1933 by the International Nickel Co. of Canada, is presented annually for a meritorious and practical contribution of outstanding importance to the mining and metallurgical industry of Canada. Nominations must be endorsed by not fewer than five members of the Canadian Institute of Mining and Metallurgy. The Inco Medal is platinum, with a replica in nickel.
Awarding body: The Canadian Institute of Mining and Metallurgy, 400-1130 Sherbrooke St. West, Montreal, Que. H3A 2M8, Canada.
Recipients include: C. C. Huston (1972); John R. Bradfield (1973); Arvid Thunaes (1974); J. D. Simpson (1975); James B. Redpath (1976).

Incorporated Society of Valuers and Auctioneers Property Journalist of the Year Award
This award is made annually to the journalist who has consistently expressed the most balanced, constructive views on property. This applies equally to residential and commercial property and includes such aspects as planning and architecture. A minimum of four articles is taken into account in the selection. The winner receives £250 and a silver-plated salver.
Awarding body: The Incorporated Society of Valuers and Auctioneers, 3 Cadogan Gate, London SW1X 0AS, England.

Indian Institute for Islamic Studies Award
This prize was established in 1967 to stimulate interest in those branches of Islamic studies which call for greater attention and to ensure that adequate light is thrown on the relevance of the teachings of Islam to the social, political and economic conditions of the present-day world. It is given periodically for original work written in English or Arabic and consists of a cash sum of 15,000 rupees.
Awarding body: Indian Institute of Islamic Studies, Panchkuin Rd., New Delhi 110001, India.
Recipients include: Prof. Ghulam Dastgir Rasheed.

Indian Language Prizes
A scheme of awarding prizes for books or manuscripts written in any Indian language other than Hindi, Sanskrit or the author's mother tongue was set up in 1969 by the Union Ministry of Education and Social Welfare to promote national integration through exchange of ideas by writers of different languages, and to encourage Indians to learn the

anguages of other regions than their own. Books and manuscripts in the following categories are eligible for the prizes: literature, fine arts and humanities, sciences, social sciences, technology. The prizes are each worth 2,000 rupees. Translations of standard works of one regional language into another are also eligible for a prize of 1,000 rupees. The prizes are awarded annually.

Awarding body: Ministry of Education and Social Welfare, Central Hindi Directorate, West Block No. 7, Rama Krishna Puram, New Delhi 110022, India.

Recipients include: Madhurima Sarma, Nahendra Padun, Nripendra Mohan Sarma, Mavinakere Ranganathan, Kollegal Simha, Chandrabhushan Umashankar Kulshreshtha, C. Pachiammal, Baduizzaman Khawar, Bawa Krishan Gopal (1974–75).

Indian National Science Academy Silver Jubilee Commemoration Medal

Established in 1962, this medal is awarded for outstanding contributions in the fields of agriculture and applied sciences. It is awarded every three years.

Awarding body: Indian National Science Academy, Bahadur Shah Zafar Marg, New Delhi 110001, India.

Recipients include: S. Rangaswami (1970); M. S. Swaminathan (1973); A. K. Sharma (1976).

Industrial Achievement Award

This award is made annually by the American Institute of Food Technologists in recognition of an outstanding food process or product which represents a significant advance in the application of food technology to food production, and which has been successfully implemented in commercial operation for at least six months, but not more than four years. The award consists of a bronze plaque given to the company, and engraved plaques for individuals. Candidates are nominated by members of the Institute.

Awarding body: Institute of Food Technologists, Suite 2120, 221 North La Salle St., Chicago, Ill. 60601, U.S.A.

Recipients include: Western Regional Res. Lab., ARS, USDA (1972); Armour & Co., Food Research Div. (1973); Kelco Co. and Northern Regional Res. Lab., ARS, USDA (1974); Clinton Corn Processing Co., Div. of Standard Brands, Inc. (1975); Bisphoric Products Co. and Purdue Univ. (1976).

Information Systems Award

Established by the AIAA in 1975, the award is presented for technical and/or management contribution in space and aeronautics computer and sensing aspects of information technology and science. The award comprises a medal and certificate of citation and is presented every two years at an appropriate conference. It alternates with the Aerospace Communications Award (*q.v.*).

Awarding body: American Institute of Aeronautics and Astronautics, 1290 Avenue of the Americas, New York, N.Y. 10019, U.S.A.

Recipients include: Albert Hopkins, Jr. (1977).

Ingold Lectureship

This lectureship was founded in 1973 to commemorate the name of Sir Christopher Ingold, President of the Chemical Society from 1952 to 1954. The lecture should deal with the relation between structure and reactivity in chemistry, or any aspect of this theme that can be associated with the name of Sir Christopher Ingold. Lecturers receive a bronze medal and £100.

Awarding body: The Chemical Society, Burlington House, London W1V 0BN, England.

Recipients include: P. D. Bartlett (1974–75); C. Eaborn (1976–77).

Innis-Gérin Medal

The medal is awarded every two years, if there is a suitable candidate, for a distinguished and sustained contribution to the literature of the social sciences including human geography and social psychology. The award consists of a bronze medal and C$1,000. Canadian citizens or persons who have been Canadian residents for the five years preceding the award are eligible. The medal was established by the Royal Society of Canada in 1966 to honour two of its former presidents: the economic historian H. A. Innis (1894–1952) and the sociologist Léon Gérin (1863–1951).

Awarding body: The Royal Society of Canada, 395 Wellington, Ottawa, Ont. K1A 0N4, Canada.

Recipients include: Esdras Minville (1967); Alexander Brady (1969); Jacques Henripin (1971); Jean-Charles Falardeau (1973); Noël Mailloux (1975).

Institute of Actuaries Gold Medal

A gold medal was established by the Institute in 1919 but rarely awarded until revised regulations were laid down in 1963. It is given in honour of work which is of pre-eminent importance, either in originality, or content, or consequence, in the actuarial field. So far as published work is relevant, it may be considered for the purpose of making an award, even if it has not appeared in the Institute's *Journal*.

Awarding body: Institute of Actuaries, Staple Inn Hall, High Holborn, London WC1V 7QJ England.

Recipients include: Wilfred Perks (1964); William Phillips (1964); Frank M. Reddington (1968); Prof. Bernard Benjamin (1975).

Institute of Foresters of Great Britain Medal

This award was instituted in 1943 by the then Society of Foresters of Great Britain, and is presented when appropriate for eminent services to British forestry. The Institute is the representative of the forestry profession in Great Britain and Northern Ireland.

Awarding body: Institute of Foresters of Great

Britain, 6 Rutland Square, Edinburgh EH1 2AU, Scotland.

Recipients include: J. A. B. Macdonald (1966); Sir Harry Champion, K. N. Rankin, The Duke of Buccleuch and Queensberry (1972); Prof. J. D. Matthews (1976).

Institute of Journalists Gold Medal

Established in 1963, the medal is awarded to persons of any nationality, as occasion merits, for outstanding service to journalism and the fundamental freedom of the press. Nominees may be: non-journalists who have spoken out for the freedom of the press; persons such as politicians, lawyers, journalists, who have laboured to break down barriers or amend constrictive laws; journalists who have been prepared to suffer for the freedom of the written word, and whose courage and devotion have been inspiring.

Awarding body: Institute of Journalists, 1 Whitehall Place, London SW1A 2HE, England.

Recipients include: Laurence Gandar (Editor, *Rand Daily Mail*, 1964); Dr. Ahmed Emin Yalman (President, Turkish Press Institute and Editor, *Vatan*, 1966); Mrs. Helen Vlachos (Greek newspaper owner, 1968); Hubert Beuve-Mery (founder, and for 25 years Editor, of *Le Monde*, 1970); Brian R. Roberts (lately Editor, *Sunday Telegraph*, 1971).

Institute of South African Architects Gold Medal

The Institute founded this award in 1958 in order to recognize an outstanding contribution to architecture by an architect of any nationality. The award is normally made every second year, and consists of the medal and a citation.

Awarding body: Institute of South African Architects, P.O.B. 31750, Braamfontein 2017, South Africa.

Recipients include: Prof. Lord Holford; Prof. N. L. Hanson; Prof. G. E. Pearse; N. M. Eaton; Revel Fox.

Inter-American Agricultural Medal

This is an annual prize established in 1959 by the Technical Advisory Council of the Inter-American Institute of Agricultural Sciences of the OAS. It is open to those professionals in the field of agricultural sciences who have distinguished themselves through their outstanding contributions to the development of agriculture and the improvement of rural life in America. The candidates are nominated by the Council Representative of each country. The prize consists of a gold medal and a diploma.

Awarding body: Consejo Técnico Consultivo del Instituto Interamericano de Ciencias Agrícolas, Apdo. 10281, San José, Costa Rica.

Recipients include: Dr. Alvaro Barcellos Fagundes (Brazil, 1971); Dr. Pierre G. Sylvain (Haiti, 1972); Prof. Carlos Muñoz Pizarro (Chile, 1973); Dr. Oscar Brauer Herrera (Mexico, 1974); Jorge Ortíz Méndez (Colombia, 1975).

Inter-American Association of Writers Prizes

The Association holds two competitions, the Inter-American Literary Competition and the Argentinian Literary Competition, both of which were established in 1950. The Inter-American competition takes place every four years and the national competition every two years. The prizes consist of medals, diplomas or plaques. Candidates must be citizens of an American country.

Awarding body: Inter-American Association of Writers, Humberto 1°, 431, Casilla de Correo 4852, Buenos Aires, Argentina.

Recipients include: Miguel Alvarez Acosta (poetry); Diego A. Del Pino (legend); María Delia Barros (short stories); Carlos Waldemar Acosta (novel); Raúl Marcó del Pont (essay); Natalio Budasoff (play).

Inter-American Council for Education, Science and Culture Award for Historians or Writers of the Americas

Established in 1970, this annual award is made for the best essay on an outstanding historical or literary personality of the Americas. The essay subject is chosen by the judges. Entries must be unpublished and specially written for the competition in Spanish, English, Portuguese or French; entrants must be citizens of an American country. The award comprises US$5,000 and a diploma.

Awarding body: Organization of American States, Washington, D.C. 20006, U.S.A.

Recipients include: Prof. Helena Costábile de Amorín and Prof. María del Rosario Fernández Alonso (Uruguay, 1973); Prof. Ivie A. Cadenhead, Jr. (U.S.A., 1973); Dr. Dionisio Petriela (Argentina, 1974); Dr. Carlos Daniel Valcárcel (Peru, 1975); Dr. Leslie T. Crawford (Uruguay, 1976).

Inter-American Council for Education, Science and Culture Prizes

Since 1970 the Council has held a number of competitions in honour of heroes, representative figures and movements of historic significance in the hemisphere, in order to promote historical and literary research in the American countries. A prize consisting of U.S.$5,000 and a diploma is awarded to the author (North or South American) of the best work submitted on a specific topic; the Council also undertakes to publish this work. Each competition is held in co-operation with a relevant national academic body. The works presented must be unpublished and written specifically for the competition in Spanish, English, Portuguese or French. Recent commemorative events include: the 150th anniversary (in 1975) of the independence of Bolivia; the 100th anniversary (in 1976) of the death of Juan Pablo Duarte, the father of the Dominican Republic; the bicentennial (in 1976) of the independence of the United States of America; the bicentennial (in 1978) of the birth of Bernardo O'Higgins, the Chilean national hero.

Awarding body: Inter-American Council for Education, Science and Culture, General Secretariat of the OAS, 17th St. and Constitution Ave., N.W., Washington, D.C. 20006, U.S.A.

International Aeronautical Federation Gold Air Medal

This award is made for outstanding contributions to the development of aeronautics, through achievement, initiative or devotion to the cause of aviation.

Awarding body: Fédération Aéronautique Internationale, 6 rue Galilée, Paris 16, France.

Recipients include: Curtis H. Pitts (U.S.A., 1975).

International Aeronautical Federation Gold Space Medal

This award is made to astronauts for exceptional achievements in space.

Awarding body: Fédération Aéronautique Internationale, 6 rue Galilée, Paris 16, France.

Recipients include: Thomas P. Stafford (U.S.A.), Alexei Arkhipovich Leonov (U.S.S.R.) (Soyuz-Apollo Project), 1975.

International Award of Merit in Structural Engineering

This annual award was established in 1975 by the executive committee of the International Association for Bridge and Structural Engineering (IABSE), in recognition of outstanding contributions in the field of constructional engineering, with special reference to their usefulness to society. A parchment certificate is presented at the annual conference of IABSE.

Awarding body: International Association for Bridge and Structural Engineering, ETH-Hönggerberg, CH-8093 Zürich, Switzerland.

Recipients include: Prof. Dr. Kiyoshi Muto (the safety of constructions in earthquakes, 1976).

International Book Award

Instituted in 1973 by the International Book Committee of UNESCO, the annual award is given for outstanding services by an individual or an institution to the cause of books in general. It is an honorary distinction consisting of a diploma which is usually presented at one of the international book fairs.

Awarding body: International Book Committee, Place de Fontenoy, 75700 Paris, France.

Recipients include: U.S.S.R. National Cttee. for International Book Year (1975); Ronald Barker (U.K. (posthumously), 1976); Julian Behrstock (U.S.A., 1977).

International Catholic Film Association Awards

The Association presents various awards, in the form of bronze works of art, for films which encourage a perception of spiritual, social and human values. Awards are made at various film festivals, including those at Cannes, Berlin and San Sebastian. A special award is made at the Berlin agricultural film festival for a film which encourages human co-operation in the fight against hunger throughout the world. An African prize has been awarded at the Ouagadougou film festival and an Asian prize at the Pusan festival. The Association began making awards at film festivals in 1948.

Awarding body: International Catholic Film Association, 8 rue de l'Orme, 1040 Brussels, Belgium.

Recipients include: Berlin, *Die Plötzliche Einsamkeit des Konrad Steiner* (K. Gloor, Switzerland, 1976); San Sebastian, *Na Samote u Lesa* (Jiří Menzel, Czechoslovakia, 1976); Ouagadougou, *Muna Moto* (Dikongue-Pipa, Cameroon, 1976); Pusan, *Children of the Snow Country* (Hiromi Higuchi, Japan, 1976).

International Chamber Music Competition

Established in 1968 in Colmar, this annual competition draws entrants from most European countries. Each year the competition is reserved for different branches of chamber music: one year for string trios and quartets with piano, the next for string quartets only, another year for reed instrument trios and wind quintets, etc. The prizes vary but there is a first prize of 6,000 francs (5,000 francs given by the French Ministry of Culture and 1,000 francs by a local organization) and an *objet d'art* given by the Mayor of Colmar. The winning group is also invited to give a concert and make a radio broadcast. The average age of participants must not exceed 35.

Awarding body: Association 'Culture et Loisirs', Office du Tourisme, 4 rue d'Unterlinden, 68000 Colmar, France.

Recipients of first prize include: Quintette à Vent du Val de Loire (France), Trio 'Avenia' (Belgium), 1976.

International Charlemagne Prize of the City of Aachen

Created on Christmas Day 1949 by prominent citizens of Aachen, the award is made annually for the most notable achievement in the service of international understanding and co-operation in Europe. The purpose is to further the creation of a United States of Europe through this annual appeal to public opinion. The recipient may be of any nationality, religion or race and is selected by a committee of 15 known as the jury. The prize consists of an illuminated document and a medallion, and the sum of DM5,000. A presentation ceremony is held in Aachen, normally on Ascension Day.

Awarding body: Stadtverwaltung, 5100 Aachen, Federal Republic of Germany.

Recipients include: François Seydoux de Clausonne (fmr. Ambassador of France to the Fed. Rep. of Germany, 1970); Rt. Hon. Roy Jenkins (U.K., 1972); Don Salvador de Madariaga (Spain, 1973); Léo Tindemans (Prime Minister of Belgium, 1976); Walter Scheel (Pres. of Fed. Rep. of Germany, 1977).

119

International Citation of Merit

This biennial award is made for outstanding contributions to the field of reading on the international level. Entry is open and is generally by nomination.

Awarding body: International Reading Association, 800 Barksdale Rd., Newark, Dela. 19711, U.S.A.

International Competition for Musical Performers

Established in 1939 by Henri Gagnebin, this event takes place annually in Geneva. All branches of music are represented, but each year the competition is restricted to different disciplines, resulting in a variation in the rules and prizes given. In general, competitors must be under 35, and the prizes consist of cash awards, medals and certificates. A traditional prize-winners' concert is broadcast. Various special prizes are available, and winners also receive invitations for concert engagements.

Awarding body: Secretariat, International Competition for Musical Performers, 12 rue de l'Hôtel de Ville, CH-1204 Geneva, Switzerland.

Recipients include: Dusan Bogdanovic (Yugoslavia, guitarist, 1975); Peter Dvorsky (Czechoslovakia, singer, 1975); Katherine Ciesinski (U.S.A., singer, 1976); Tatiana Chebanova (U.S.S.R., pianist, 1976); Magda Sirbu (Romania, violinist, 1976).

International Competition for Young Conductors

Held as part of the Besançon-Franche-Comté international music festival, the competition is an annual event for young musicians under the age of 30. It was founded in 1951 by Emile Vuillermoz, musicologist and music critic, whose name is given to the main prize. This consists of 10,000 francs donated by the French Ministry of Culture and Environment, and a Golden Harp. A further sum of money is donated by the Société des Auteurs, Compositeurs et Editeurs de Musique.

Awarding body: Concours International de Jeunes Chefs d'Orchestre, Parc des Expositions, B.P. 1913, 25020 Besançon, France.

Recipients include: Yoël Levi (Israel, 1978).

International Conductors Award

The award was established in 1974 by the Western Orchestral Society. It is given biennially, and applications are accepted from conductors of any nationality who are under the age of 30 on the first day of the competition. The winner receives a trophy and a £7,000 two-year contract to conduct the Western Orchestral Society's orchestras.

Awarding body: Bournemouth Symphony Orchestra and the Western Orchestral Society, Westover Mansions, Gervis Place, Bournemouth BH1 2AW, England.

Recipients include: Simon Rattle (U.K., 1974); Gerard Oskamp (Netherlands, 1976).

International Confederation of Societies of Authors and Composers Triennial Prize

The prize is awarded as the result of a competition to the author of a work dealing with author copyright and preferably a problem of international author copyright. It should be either unpublished, or published within the preceding three years. The prize consists of a cash award of 10,000 French francs, and was established in 1949 by the Confederation, which is concerned to protect the interests of creative artists.

Awarding body: International Confederation of Societies of Authors and Composers, 11 rue Keppler, 75116 Paris, France.

International Drawing Triennial

This competition is held every three years and has been international since 1977. The awards consist of a first prize (Grand Prix), five major prizes and ten distinctions. The competition is sponsored by the District Union of Polish Artists in Wrocław, the Office of Voivodship in Wrocław, and the Wrocław Museum of Architecture.

Awarding body: Museum of Architecture, Bernardyńska 5, 50-156 Wrocław, Poland.

International Editor of the Year Award

The award was established in 1975 by the editors of the American *Atlas World Press Review.* The International Editor of the Year is selected for 'courage, enterprise, and leadership on an international level in advancing press freedom and responsibility, enhancing world understanding, defending human rights, and fostering journalistic excellence'. Any editor (not an American) of a publication outside the U.S.A. is eligible for the award, which is presented in the spring of each year. The winner receives a plaque. The deadline for nominations is 1 February.

Awarding body: Atlas World Press Review, 230 Park Ave., New York, N.Y. 10017, U.S.A.

Recipients: Harold Evans (*The Sunday Times,* U.K., 1975); André Fontaine (*Le Monde,* France, 1976); Julio Scherer García (*Excelsior,* Mexico, 1977).

International Geigy Rheumatism Prize

In 1967 scientific circles impressed on J. R. Geigy S.A. (now Ciba-Geigy) that inadequate public funds were available for supporting rheumatological research. Geigy responded by establishing a prize to further clinical, therapeutic and experimental research. Entry is open to groups as well as individuals and to non-medical researchers as well as physicians. Work submitted should have been published during the preceding five years. The prize is given every four years at the International Rheumatology Congress, and consists of 50,000 Swiss francs, to be divided into three parts of which the first part (i.e. first prize) must consist of not less than half. The prize is sponsored by the International League Against Rheumatism, which provides the panel of judges, and the prize is administered by the ILAR Secretariat.

Awarding body: International League Against Rheumatism, P.O.B. 145, 4011 Basel, Switzerland.

Recipients include: W. M. Kelly (U.S.A., 1969); Jacob Natvig and team (Norway, 1973); Dr. R. Bluestone and team (U.S.A.) and Dr. D. Brewerton and Dr. D. James (U.K.), jointly, 1977.

International Geological L. A. Spendiarov Prize of the U.S.S.R. Academy of Sciences

This prize was established in memory of L. A. Spendiarov, a young Russian geologist who died in 1897 while participating in the seventh IGC pre-Congress excursion. His father deposited funds in the State Bank, the interest from which would constitute the prize money. The award was not made between 1917 and 1926 because of nationalization of private funds in the State Bank, but in 1926 it was re-established as the U.S.S.R. International Geological Spendiarov Prize (and altered to its present title in 1976). The prize is given to a person who has contributed fresh knowledge to the geological sciences, and is presented at the International Geological Congress held every four years. It consists of a cash sum of 500 roubles and a diploma. Since 1945 the prize has usually been awarded to a geologist from the country hosting the Congress.

Awarding body: U.S.S.R. National Committee of Geologists, U.S.S.R. Academy of Sciences, 101017 Moscow ZH-17, Pyzhevsky 7, U.S.S.R.

Recipients include: M. Alvarez (Mexico, 1956); S. Tarrarinsson (Iceland, 1960); D. K. Ray (India, 1964); H. R. Wynne-Edwards (Canada, 1972); N. H. Fisher (Australia, 1976).

International Industrial Film Festival

This annual festival was established in 1961 by the Council of European Industrial Federations, and is held in a different European city each year. Films entered are judged in eight categories: four for films on various industrial and social topics intended primarily for a general audience, and four for those which envisage more specialized audiences (such as industrial or educational establishments). The number of prizes awarded in each section varies, depending on the number of entries, but there are ten main prizes: one for each of the eight categories and in addition two CEIF Grands Prix, awarded to the best films in the general and specialized groups. The awards take the form of trophies and certificates.

Awarding body: Council of European Industrial Federations.

International Institute for Applied Systems Analysis Honorary Scholar Award

Established in November 1975 by the Council of the Institute, this award is bestowed irregularly in recognition of outstanding contributions to the development of the Institute and to the advancement of its objectives, and for exemplary dedication to IIASA's ideals and distinguished scholarly achievements.

Awarding body: International Institute for Applied Systems Analysis, 2361 Schloss Laxenburg, Austria.

Recipients include: Prof. Harrison Brown (U.S.A.); Prof. Helmut Koziolek (German Dem. Rep.); Prof. Howard Raiffa (U.S.A.).

International Institute of Refrigeration Prize

Founded in 1961 by the executive committee of the International Institute of Refrigeration, the prize is awarded every four years in recognition of original studies in the field of low temperatures presented in the form of papers or reports at a congress or meeting of the Institute. The winners receive a cash prize of between 1,000 and 3,000 French francs, a medal or a certificate. The value of the cash prize varies according to the number of awards made and the scientific and technical level of the study.

Awarding body: International Institute of Refrigeration, 177 Blvd. Malesherbes, 75017 Paris, France.

Recipients include: Mme. Hôte-Baudart (Belgium, 'Etudes sur l'évolution des matières azotées au cours de la conservation en congélation de caillé et fromage du type Camembert', 1967); Mr. Najork (German Dem. Rep., 'Investigations on the closing of self-acting valves in high-speed R-12 compressors', 1967); Mr. Eber (Switzerland, 'A new analysis of rectification in absorption refrigeration', 1967); Mr. van der Ree (Netherlands, 'Views concerning the design of an evaporator for the regasification of cryogenic liquids', 1967); G. Comini and C. Bonacina (Italy, 'Application de l'ordinateur aux problèmes de changement de phase dans les aliments', 1975).

International League Human Rights Award

Established in 1968, International Human Rights Year, the award is made annually in recognition of contributions to and defence of human rights. Anyone active in this field is eligible to receive it. The prize takes the form of a plaque, a certificate and a lithograph.

Awarding body: International League for Human Rights, 777 UN Plaza (6F), New York, N.Y. 10017, U.S.A.

Recipients include: Andrei Sakharov; Roger Baldwin; David Morse; Mstislav Rostropovich; Andrei Amalrik.

International Lenin Peace Prize

The Presidium of the U.S.S.R. Supreme Soviet established this annual prize in 1950 in memory of V. I. Lenin, founder of the U.S.S.R. It is given for outstanding activity in promoting peace among nations through any medium – science, literature, art, etc. Winners receive a diploma, a gold medal, and a cash award of 25,000 roubles (or equivalent in any currency). The international committee awards several prizes annually, and the announcement is made on 1 May.

Awarding body: International Lenin Peace Prize Committee, The Kremlin, Moscow, U.S.S.R.

Recipients include: Janos Kadar (Hungary, 1st Sec. of Hungarian Socialist Workers' Party central cttee.), Antonio Agostinho Neto (Pres. of Angola), Samora Moises Machel (Pres. of Mozambique), Hortensia Bussi de Allende (Chile, Vice-Pres., Women's Int. Democratic Fed.), Sean Macbride (Ireland, UN Supreme Commr. for Namibia), Pierre Poujade (France, leader of the peace movement), Yannis Ritsos (Greece, poet), 1977.

International Meteorological Organization Prize

The World Meteorological Organization (formerly the International Meteorological Organization) established the prize in 1955 to recognize eminent research work in the field of meteorology. Consideration is given equally to the scientific value of the recipient's work and his/her work for the IMO. The prize is awarded annually, and consists of a gold medal, a diploma and U.S.$1,200. Candidates must be proposed by a member of the Organization; members of the Executive Committee, as jury, are ineligible. The WMO is a UN Specialized Agency.

Awarding body: World Meteorological Organization, 41 ave. Giuseppe Motta, C.P. 5, 1211 Geneva 20, Switzerland.

Recipients include: Dr. C. H. B. Priestley (Australia) and J. S. Sawyer (U.K., 1973); Prof. J. Smagorinsky (U.S.A., 1974); Dr. W. L. Godson (Canada, 1975); Acad. E. K. Fedorov (U.S.S.R., 1976).

International Music Competition

The competition, which is held annually, was instituted in 1952 by the Broadcasting Corporations of the Federal Republic of Germany (ARD), and awards are made for outstanding performance in the various categories of instruments (these vary from year to year, including voice). First prizes range from DM5,000 to DM6,000, second prizes from DM3,500 to DM4,000 and third prizes from DM2,000 to DM2,500. In addition, first prize-winners are invited to take part in concerts and make recordings. The competition is open to young musicians of all nationalities. The age limits are 17 to 30 years, with the exception of the voice and chamber music sections.

Awarding body: Internationaler Musikwettbewerb, Bayerischer Rundfunk, 8 Munich 2, Federal Republic of Germany.

First prize-winners include: Jessye Norman (U.S.A., soprano, 1968); Tokyo Quartet (Japan, string quartet, 1970); James Tocco (U.S.A., piano, 1973); Anthony and Joseph Paratore (U.S.A., piano duo, 1974); Yuri Baschmet (U.S.S.R., viola, 1976).

International Music Competition Vienna (Beethoven Competition)

Music competitions are held each year in Vienna under the auspices of the University of Music and Dramatic Art and the Austrian Ministry of Science. Every four years since 1961 the competition has been devoted to the piano works of Beethoven. It is open to pianists of any nationality between the ages of 17 and 32. First, second and third prizes of 60,000 Schillings, 40,000 Schillings and 20,000 Schillings respectively are awarded, and there are also three further prizes of 10,000 Schillings each. The first prize-winner is offered engagements in Vienna and other Austrian cities. The competition is open to the public.

Awarding body: International Music Competition Secretariat, Hochschule für Musik und Darstellende Kunst, Lothringerstr. 18, 1030 Vienna 3, Austria.

Recipients include: John O'Connor (Ireland, 1973); Natalia Pankova (U.S.S.R., 1977).

International Optometric and Optical League Medal

The League established this award in 1963, to be given at irregular intervals in recognition of outstanding contributions by individual optometrists or other persons to the advancement of the science or profession of optometry or ophthalmic optics. Nominations must be made by member organizations of the IOOL. The recipient may be invited to lecture on the subject for which the award is made.

Awarding body: International Optometric and Optical League, 65 Brook St., London W1Y 2DT, England.

Recipients include: Prof. H. W. Hofstetter (1968); Hermann Barry Collin (1969); Peter Abel (1973).

International Organ Competition 'Grand Prix de Chartres'

Founded in 1971 by Pierre Firmin-Didot as an annual event, the competition has been held biennially since 1974. It is open to organists of any nationality under 35. There are two prizes of 15,000 francs each: one for interpretation and one for improvisation. If one or other prize is not awarded a medal of honour is presented. Winners also receive a number of concert engagements. The finals of the competition are held in public in Chartres cathedral.

Awarding body: Association des Grandes Orgues de Chartres, 75 rue de Grenelle, 75007 Paris, France.

Recipients include: Daniel Roth and Yves Devernay (France, both prizes jointly, 1971); Charles Benbow (U.S.A., interpretation, 1972); Wolfgang Rubsam (Fed. Rep. of Germany, interpretation, 1973); Philippe Lefebvre (France, improvisation, 1973); George C. Baker (U.S.A., interpretation, 1974). No awards 1976.

International Poster Prizes

These prizes are awarded every two years for the best posters. The first, second and third prizes consist of gold, silver and bronze medals respectively, and a cash prize accompanies each medal. The prizes are sponsored by the Polish Ministry of Culture and Art and the Union of Polish Artists.

Awarding body: Central Office of Artistic Exhibitions, Plac Małachowskiego 3, 00-063 Warsaw, Poland.

International Prize for Architecture

This prize consists of two annual awards, one for the design of one-family houses and the other for that of apartment blocks. The sum of 250,000 Belgian francs is divided between the two prize-winners, each of whom receives a certificate. Candidates must be professional architects and nationals of member states of the EEC. The building in question must be situated in an EEC country. The prize was founded by the Belgian National Institute of Housing in 1957.

Awarding body: Institut national du logement, 10 Blvd. Saint-Lazare, 1030 Brussels, Belgium.

International Publications Cultural Award

The Japanese Publishers Association for Cultural Exchange founded this prize in 1967 to promote cultural exchange between Japan and other countries and to stimulate the development of Japanese publications in foreign languages. The award of a medal and a certificate is given annually to a Japanese publisher for the best book published in the previous twelve months in a language other than Japanese introducing Japanese culture to foreign readers.

Awarding body: Publishers Association for Cultural Exchange, 1-2-1, Sarugaku-cho, Chiyoda-ku, Tokyo 101, Japan.

Recipients include: Economic Development of Asia Perspective (1970); *Imperial Gardens of Japan* (1972); *An Introduction to Earthquake Engineering* (1974); *Arts of Korea* (1976).

International Reading Association Citation of Merit

This award is made for outstanding contributions to the field of reading. It is presented annually, when merited. Entry for the award is open and is generally by nomination.

Awarding body: International Reading Association, 800 Barksdale Rd., Newark, Dela. 19711, U.S.A.

International Salon of Photography 'Photo Expo 69' Prizes

These prizes are awarded every two years for the best photographs. They consist of a first prize (Grand Prix), three gold medals, four silver medals and six bronze medals. The prizes are sponsored by the Photographers Society of Poznań and the District Union of Polish Artists-Photographers in Poznań.

Awarding body: Photographers Society of Poznań, ul. Paderewskiego 7, 61-770 Poznań, Poland.

International Robert Schumann Competition

This international competition is held every three years in Zwickau, German Democratic Republic. Prizes are awarded in two branches of music: piano and singing. The age limit for pianists is 28 years, and for singers 30 years. There are five prizes for piano, totalling 18,500 D.D.R.-Marks, and four prizes in each category (male and female voice) for singing, totalling 17,500 D.D.R.-Marks. The competition is named after the famous German composer, Robert Schumann (1810–56), who was born in Zwickau.

Awarding body: Organisationsbüro des Robert-Schumann-Wettbewerbs, Münzstr., 95 Zwickau, German Democratic Republic.

Recipients include: Pawel Jegorow (U.S.S.R., piano), Mitsuko Shirai (Japan, female voice), Laszlo Polgàr (Hungary, male voice), 1974.

International Society for Human and Animal Mycology Award

Established in 1971, the award is for merit in medical mycology. It takes the form of a cash prize and a certificate, and is presented at the General Assembly of the International Society for Human and Animal Mycology, which takes place every four years. There are no restrictions as to eligibility, except that preference is given to ISHAM members.

Awarding body: International Society for Human and Animal Mycology, Gelleristr. 11a, CH-4052 Basel, Switzerland.

Recipients include: Prof. G. Segretain (France, 1975).

International Tapestry Design Competition

This competition is held every two years in Gdańsk. It is sponsored by the Cepelia Co-operative Union of Folk Arts and Crafts in Warsaw, the Voivodship Office in Gdańsk, the ARTES Work Co-operative of Artistic Handicrafts in Gdańsk and the regional management of the Union of Polish Artists in Gdańsk. First, second and third prizes are awarded, each consisting of a medal, a diploma and a sum of money, and 14 honourable mentions are made, each accompanied by a diploma and a sum of money.

Awarding body: Union of Polish Artists, ul. Peplińskiego 4, 80-335 Gdańsk, Poland.

International Tchaikovsky Competition

The competition is held every four years in Moscow. Prizes are given for the best performances of Tchaikovsky's music. The rules and prizes vary with each competition; in 1978 it was open to singers of any nationality between the ages of 18 and 30, and to pianists, violinists and cellists between the ages of 16 and 32. Eight monetary prizes and medals are given in the strings section and six in the vocal section. First prize is 2,500 roubles and a gold medal. The first three prize-winners take part in concert tours in the U.S.S.R.

Awarding body: Organizing Committee, International Tchaikovsky Competition, 15 Neglinnaya St., Moscow, U.S.S.R.

International Union of Forestry Research Organizations Scientific Achievement Award

The award was established in 1969 to recognize distinguished individual scientific achievement in forestry research in the fields covered by IUFR. The award takes the form of a gold medal and scroll together with a small honorarium. It is presented formally at each congress (every three to five years). Up to five awards may be made at a

123

time. Those nominated must be under 45 years of age and belong to a member organization of IUFRO. The award is given for a piece of specific research or a major accomplishment over an extended period; it is based on published results demonstrating either originality or their importance for the advancement of forestry, or both.

Awarding body: International Union of Forestry Research Organizations, A-1131 Vienna, Schönbrunn, Austria.

Recipients include: P. Hakkila (Finland), A. S. Isayev (U.S.S.R.), A. Nanson (Belgium), A. Petty (U.K.), D. E. Reichle (U.S.A.), 1976.

International Henryk Wieniawski Competitions

These three competitions were inaugurated in 1935 by Adam Wieniawski, in memory of his uncle Henryk Wieniawski (1835–80), the Polish violinist-virtuoso and composer. The competition for violin-playing is open to violinists of any nationality under the age of 30, and is held every five years. The first prize is 50,000 złotys and a gold medal, and the winner is invited on a concert tour of Poland. The winners of the second and third prizes receive a silver medal and 40,000 złotys, and a bronze medal and 30,000 złotys, respectively. Seven other cash prizes are awarded. The violinmakers' competition is also held every five years, and is open to professional violinmakers of any age or nationality. The first prize is worth 40,000 złotys, and there are six other cash prizes. The Henryk Wieniawski Composers' Competition is open to composers of all nationalities. This is held every five to ten years. The winner receives a prize of 40,000 złotys, and other cash prizes are also awarded.

Awarding body: The Secretariat of the International Henryk Wieniawski Competitions, Wodna Street 27, 61-781 Poznań, Poland.

Recipients include: Tatiana Grindienko (U.S.S.R., violin competition, 1972); Mieczysław Bielański (Poland, violinmakers' competition, 1972); Ivo Petrič (Yugoslavia, composers' competition, 1976).

Ion Ionescu de la Brad Prize

Established in 1948 by the Romanian Academy, the prize is for contributions to agriculture. It is presented annually at a General Assembly of the Academy, and consists of 10,000 lei and a diploma. It is named after Ion Ionescu de la Brad (1818–91), economist, statistician and agronomist, who contributed to the modernization of agriculture by the use of machinery.

Awarding body: Academy of the S.R. of Romania, 125 Calea Victoriei, Bucharest, Romania.

Irish American Cultural Institute Awards

These awards are made annually for achievement by an Irish citizen in literature, art or music. The literature award, established in 1968, consists of a cash prize of $10,000, and the art and music awards, established in 1975, consist respectively of $10,000 and $5,000. Nomination and selection is by a committee.

Awarding body: Irish American Cultural Institute, 683 Osceola Ave., St. Paul, Minn. 55105, U.S.A.

Recipients include: Mairtin Ó Cadhain (literature); Cecil King (painting); James Coleman (painting); Bill Kirk (photography); Sean Ó Riordan (literature); John Montague (literature).

Ralph H. Isbrandt Automotive Safety Engineering Award

Established in 1972, the award is presented annually to the author or authors of the best paper or combination of papers relating to automotive safety engineering, presented at a meeting of the Society, or any of its sections, during the previous calendar year. Papers are judged primarily for the originality of their contribution to this branch of engineering. The award is also open to an individual, in recognition of distinguished active service in the field of automotive safety engineering; he must first agree to present a Ralph H. Isbrandt Memorial Lecture on an appropriate subject at a designated meeting of the Society. The award consists of a bronze medal and certificate, and is presented at the Automobile Engineering and Manufacturing Meeting each October.

Awarding body: Society of Automotive Engineers, Inc., 400 Commonwealth Drive, Warrendale, Pa. 15096, U.S.A.

Recipients include: L. M. Patrick, Nils Bohlin and Ake Andersson ('Three-Point Harness Accident and Laboratory Data Comparison', 1975).

Israel Prize

Established in 1953 on the fifth anniversary of the foundation of Israel, the prize is administered by the Ministry of Education through the Israel Prize Office. It is awarded annually on Israel Independence Day for an outstanding contribution in a given area of the arts or sciences or for life-long achievement or service in a specified field. Any Israeli citizen resident in Israel is eligible.

Awarding body: Office of Israel Prizes, Ministry of Education and Culture, 10 Mordechai Ben-Hilel St., Jerusalem, Israel.

Italia Prize

An international competition was established in 1948 in Capri by the most important radio and television organizations in the world, on the initiative of RAI (Radiotelevisione Italiana). Its aims are to stimulate the continuous improvement, both in substance and form, of the product of radio and TV. The competition is held annually in September, and six Italia prizes, amounting to 15,000 Swiss francs each, are awarded for the best programmes in three categories: music, drama and documentary (three for radio and three for TV). In addition, six RAI prizes are awarded amounting to 1,250,000 lire each.

Awarding body: Secretariat of Italia Prize, RAI Viale Mazzini 14, Rome, Italy.

Recipients include: Imaginary Diary (radio music Italy, RAI), *Lullaby for Grown Ups* (radio drama,

Japan, NHK), *Why Have I Done It?* (radio documentary, Hungary, MR), 1975; *St. Nicolas Cantata* (TV music, U.K., Thames Television), 1977; *The Spongers* (TV drama, U.K., BBC), *Hospital* (TV documentary, U.K., BBC), 1978.

Frederic Ives Medal

This award was endowed in 1929 by Herbert E. Ives in memory of his father who is remembered for his pioneering contribution to colour photography, photo-engraving, three-colour process printing, and other branches of applied optics. The award, a silver medal and a citation, is the highest award of the Optical Society of America for overall distinction in optics.

Awarding body: Optical Society of America, 2000 L St., N.W., Suite 620, Washington, D.C. 20036, U.S.A.

Recipients include: Dr. Rudolf Kingslake (1973); Dr. David L. MacAdam (1974); Dr. Ali Javan (1975); Dr. Arthur L. Schawlow (1976); Dr. Emil Wolf (1977).

J

Jacksonian Prize

The award was established in 1800 by Samuel Jackson, F.R.S., M.R.C.S., as an annual prize of £10 for a dissertation on a practical subject in surgery. The award now consists of £52.50 and a bronze medal. Those eligible are Fellows or Members, or Fellows in Dental Surgery or Fellows in the Faculty of Anaesthetists of the Royal College of Surgeons. The dissertation may be the work of more than one applicant; the subject is open, but must be approved by the Council of the College in advance. Members of the Council are not eligible.

Awarding body: The Royal College of Surgeons of England, 35-43 Lincoln's Inn Fields, London WC2A 3PN, England.

Recipients include: Manickavasagar Balasegaram (1970); John Phillimore Mitchell (1971); Andreas Nicos Nicolaides (1972); Gerald White Milton (1973); Christopher Edward Aldridge Holden (1975).

Jacobson Lecture

The lecture is associated with the Jacobson Visiting Lectureship at the University of Newcastle upon Tyne, which is endowed by a generous gift from the Ruth and Lionel Jacobson Fund. This lecture is on some aspect of medicine, and is delivered annually. It is subsequently published.

Awarding body: University of Newcastle upon Tyne, 6 Kensington Terrace, Newcastle upon Tyne NE1 7RU, England.

Lecturers include: D. G. Cogan (Harvard Medical School, 1973); Dr. W. F. Ballinger (Washington Univ. School of Medicine, 1974); Prof. Dr. Klaus Wolff (Vienna, 1975); Prof. M. Rubin (Georgetown Univ. Hospital, Washington, D.C., 1976); M. A. R. Freeman (Consultant Orthopaedic Surgeon, London Hospital, 1977).

Jaén International Piano Competition

This annual competition was established in 1956 by Pablo Castillo García-Negrete, and is open to pianists of any nationality, with the exception of those who have already obtained the Jaén Prize. The winner of the first prize receives 200,000 pesetas and a gold medal, and several concert engagements. Three other cash prizes are awarded.

Awarding body: Instituto de Estudios Giennenses, Excma. Diputación Provincial, Jaén, Spain.

Recipients include: Marioara Trifán (U.S.A.) and Elza Kolodziei (Poland), 1973; Jean François Helsser (France, 1974); Boris Bloch (U.S.S.R., 1975); Michiko Tsuda (Japan, 1976).

Anders Jahres pris

In 1953 the Norwegian ship owner and barrister, Anders Jahre, gave a sum of money to Oslo University with which to establish a fund for the promotion of science. Two annual prizes were founded for excellent work in the field of medical science. The main prize of 200,000 kroner is awarded to a scientist of any age from one of the Scandinavian countries. The second prize of 100,000 kroner goes to a scientist under the age of 40.

Awarding body: University of Oslo, Blindern, Oslo 3, Norway.

Recipients include: Prof. Med. Dr. Rolf Luft (Sweden, 1973); Prof. Med. Dr. Arvid Carlsson (Sweden, 1974); Prof. dr. med. Erik Strømgren (Denmark, 1975); Prof. dr. med. Lorentz Eldjarn (Norway, 1976); Dr. med. Niels A. Lassen (Denmark, 1977).

Max Jakob Memorial Award

This award was established in 1961 by the ASME Heat Transfer Division; in 1962 the American Institute of Chemical Engineers joined in the award. It is in honour of Max Jakob (1879–1955), pioneer in the science of heat transmission, to commemorate his outstanding contributions as a research worker, educator and author. It is bestowed in recognition of eminent achievement or distinguished service in the area of heat transfer. Given annually, without regard to society affiliation or nationality, the award consists of a bronze plaque, an honorarium and an engrossed certificate.

Awarding body: American Society of Mechanical Engineers, United Engineering Center, 345 East 47th St., New York, N.Y. 10017, U.S.A.

Recipients include: James W. Westwater (U.S.A., 1971); Karl A. Gardner (U.S.A., 1972); Ulrich Grigull (Germany, 1973); Peter Grassmann (Switzerland, 1974); Robert G. Deissler (1975).

Wenzel Jaksch-Preis

This award is given for distinguished services to culture and scholarship in dealing with the problem of refugees from the former German areas, the preservation of the heritage of the labour movement in the German Sudetenland, and the peaceful reorganization of Europe on the basis of recognition of the present-day rights of national groups. It has been presented annually since 1968 by the Seliger Community of Sudeten German Social Democrats, and is financed by the West German Ministry of the Interior. It takes the form of a cash prize of DM5,000 and a certificate, and is named after Wenzel Jaksch, a politician from the Sudetenland.

Awarding body: Seliger-Gemeinde, 7000 Stuttgart 1, Charlottenplatz 17/Eingang 3, Federal Republic of Germany.

Recipients include: Karl Gerberich (F.R.G., 1972); Albert Exler, Artur Schober (F.R.G., 1973); Axel Granath (Sweden, 1974); Henry E. Weisbach (Canada, 1975); Dr. Josef Mühlberger (F.R.G., 1976).

Jancsó Miklós Commemorative Medal

This award, consisting of a medal and 1,000 forints in cash, is presented annually by Szeged University of Medicine to a scientist of any nationality who has made valuable contributions to medical science. Established in 1969, it commemorates Prof. Miklós Jancsó (1903–66), a distinguished pharmacologist.

Awarding body: Szegedi Orvostudományi Egyetem, 6720 Szeged, Dugonics-tér 13, Hungary.

Recipients include: Prof. Dr. Miklós Julesz (1972); Prof. Dr. György Ivánovics (1973); Prof. Dr. Károly Tóth (1974); Prof. Dr. István Huszák (1975); Prof. Dr. János Szentágothai (1976).

R. S. Jane Memorial Lecture Award

The award was established in 1960 by The Chemical Institute of Canada to commemorate Dr. Robert Stephen Jane, in recognition of his contribution to the chemical profession and the chemical industry in Canada. The award is given annually to a person who, while resident in Canada, has made an exceptional achievement in the field of chemical engineering or industrial chemistry. The winner is required to deliver a lecture about his achievements to the Canadian Chemical Engineering Conference of the Canadian Society for Chemical Engineering. The lecture is published in a journal of The Chemical Institute of Canada, preferably *The Canadian Journal of Chemical Engineering*. In addition to the title of 'The R. S. Jane Memorial Lecturer', the winner receives a cash prize of $300. Nominations are made by members of The Chemical Institute of Canada and/or the Canadian Society for Chemical Engineering.

Awarding body: The Chemical Institute of Canada, 151 Slater St., Ottawa, Ont. K1P 5H3, Canada.

Recipients include: N. S. Grace ('Three C's for Accomplishment – Creativity, Communication and Cooperation', 1972); O. C. W. Allenby ('Down with the "Cargo Cults"', 1973); A. Cholette (1974); I. E. Puddington ('Technology and the Good Life', 1975); James Hyne (1977).

Japan Academy Prize

Nine prizes are awarded annually under this title: five for outstanding achievements in the field of pure science and its applications, and four for outstanding achievements in the field of humanities and social sciences (corresponding to the two sections of the Academy). Of these, one from each section is considered the most distinguished, and is named the Imperial Prize. The awards were established in 1911 by the Academy, and any living Japanese researcher is eligible, with the exception of Academy members. The awards consist of a certificate, a medal, and a cash prize of 500,000 yen each; the Imperial Prize consists of a certificate and the Imperial Gift of a silver vase with a chrysanthemum crest on it.

Awarding body: The Japan Academy, Ueno Park, Tokyo 110, Japan.

Recipients include: Dr. Jôkichi Takamine (discovery of adrenalin, 1912); Prof. Kotaro Honda (research on the physical properties of iron, 1916); Profs. Masao Kotani and Shin-ichiro Tomonaga (oscillation mechanism of a magnetron and theoretical study on wave guides and resonators, 1948); Dr. Leo Esaki (research on Esaki Diodes, 1965).

Japan Art Prize

The prize was established with two others (Japan Literature Prize and Shincho Prize) in 1969 by Mr. Ryoichi Sato, President of the Shinchosha Publishing Company. The Art Prize is given annually for the best work in any branch of art, submitted during the year. The award consists of one million yen and a souvenir.

Awarding body: Shincho Foundation, Shinchosha Publishing Company, 71 Yarai-cho, Shinjuku-ku, Tokyo, Japan.

Recipients include: Hiroaki Kondo (1975); Ario Hirayama (1976); Kyubei Kiyomizu (1977).

Japan Literature Prize

The prize was established with two others (Japan Art Prize and Shincho Prize) in 1969 by Mr. Ryoichi Sato, President of the Shinchosha Publishing Company. The Literature Prize is given annually to the author of the best literary work (any genre) published during the year. The award consists of one million yen and a souvenir. The four judges are chosen from among Japan's most distinguished writers.

Awarding body: Shincho Foundation, Shinchosha Publishing Company, 71 Yarai-cho, Shinjuku-ku, Tokyo, Japan.

Recipients include: Kazuo Dan, Odaka Haniya (1976); Yoshie Wada, Boku Hagitani (1977).

Japan Medical Association Supreme Award for Merit

This award was established in 1960 by Dr. Taro Takemi, President of the Association, and is presented annually on 1 November, the anniversary of the founding of the Association. It takes the form of a shield, and is given for distinguished service in medical education, voluntary emergency medical work, or contributions to prophylactic inoculation; or to physicians in private practice who have rendered distinguished service in the academic field, and to local medical associations which have promoted community activities in co-operation with other organizations. It may also be awarded to officers and committee members of the Association who have held office for over ten years and Presidents of prefectural medical associations who have held office for more than ten years.

Awarding body: Japan Medical Association, 5 Kanda Surugadai 2-chome, Chiyoda-ku, Tokyo, Japan.

Recipients include: Dr. Tadasu Shinoda (1974) and Dr. Toshio Kurokawa (1975) for distinguished service in the field of medical education; Dr. Saburo Sugiura (1974), Dr. Yutaka Mizutani (1975) and Dr. Tatsuaki Matsushima (1976) for distinguished service in the academic field.

Japan Prize International Educational Programme Contest

The prize was established by the Japan Broadcasting Corporation (NHK) in 1965. It is an international award for the best radio and TV programmes which are considered to have high educational value and fully demonstrate the important role and great potential of broadcasting in the field of education. The prize is awarded every two years and consists of a trophy and a cash sum of U.S.$2,000. Various other prizes are awarded in different categories: the Minister of Education Prize for a primary or secondary education radio programme; the Governor of Tokyo Metropolis Prize for a secondary or adult education radio programme; the Minister of Posts and Telecommunications Prize for a primary or secondary education TV programme; the Abe Prize for a secondary or adult education TV programme; the Maeda Prize (in honour of a former President of NHK) for a radio or TV programme judged conducive to the promotion of better understanding and closer co-operation among the nations of the world; the Hoso-Bunka Foundation Prize for a pre-school-age radio or TV programme; the UNICEF Prize for a TV programme dealing with the life of children in the developing countries. Contestants must be broadcasting organizations from a country that is a member of the International Telecommunication Union.

Awarding body: Nippon Hoso Kyokai (NHK), Jinnan, Shibuya-ku, Tokyo 150, Japan.

Recipients include: Jumping and Winding (Magyar Rádió, Hungary, radio, 1975); *Heil Caesar* (BBC, U.K., TV, 1975); *Lesson 171* (Proyecto Matemática por Radio, Nicaragua, radio, 1977); *The Silkworm Miracle – Metamorphosis* (NHK, Japan, TV, 1977).

Japan Society of Library Science Prize and Incentive Award

The prize is awarded annually for distinguished achievements in the field of library science, and comprises a certificate and a cash prize of 20,000 yen. The Incentive Award is given for outstanding scientific research in library science and comprises a certificate and a cash prize of 10,000 yen. Both prizes were established in 1972 on the 20th anniversary of the Society's foundation and are open to full members of the Society.

Awarding body: Japan Society of Library Science, c/o National College of Library Science, 1-1 Shimouma 4-chome, Setagaya-ku, Tokyo, Japan.

Recipients include: Masami Kanô (*An annotated bibliography of education*); Tsutomu Kuroki (*An introduction to Japanese government publications*).

Japan Welding Society Prize

The prize was established in 1944 for distinguished achievement in education and technology in the field of welding, or for outstanding contributions to the Society. It consists of a certificate and 100,000 yen in cash. Candidates must be proposed by a member of the Society. The prize is awarded on an irregular basis.

Awarding body: Yosetsu Gakkai, 1-11 Sakuma-cho Kanda, Chiyoda-ku, Tokyo, Japan.

Japanese Minister of State for Science and Technology Prize

The prize was established in 1959 by the Japanese Science and Technology Agency. It is given annually in the form of a certificate to those who have made outstanding contributions to science and technology either by research or by practical work in laboratories and workshops.

Awarding body: Science and Technology Agency, 2-2-1, Kasumigaseki, Chiyoda-ku, Tokyo 100, Japan.

Recipients include: Akio Shindo (invention of the production system of carbon textiles, 1972); Tasuku Date, Tadashi Kume and Shizuo Yagi (development of the Compound Vortex Controlled Combustion System engine, 1973); Ichiro Chibata (fixation of enzyme and micro-organism and development of the utilization system, 1976); Jun Hayashi (development of highly sensitive colour film, 1977).

Japanese Society of Veterinary Science Award

An annual prize established in 1959, it is awarded to a member of the Society for his outstanding work in the field of veterinary science, usually published in the Society's journal. It comprises a medal and certificate.

Awarding body: Japanese Society of Veterinary Science, c/o Faculty of Agriculture, University of Tokyo, Yayoi, 1-1-1, Tokyo 113, Japan.

Jászai Mari Prize for Theatrical Art

Instituted by the Hungarian Council of Ministers in 1953, the prize is awarded annually by the Minister of Culture. It is an honorary distinction, divided into three classes, and given to actors and actresses for outstanding performance. It is named in honour of Mari Jászai (1850–1926), Hungary's great tragedienne.

Awarding body: Committee for the Jászai Mari Prize, Ministry of Culture, Szalay-utca 10, Budapest V, Hungary.
Recipients include: Árpád Csányi (stage designer, National Theatre), István Iglódi (actor-director, 25th Theatre), 1976.

Jatiya Chalachitra Purashkar (*National Film Award*)

The Bangladeshi Ministry of Information and Broadcasting introduced this annual award in 1976 for films released in the preceding year. Awards are given in various categories: best actor, best actress, best screenplay, etc. Winners in all categories receive a certificate, and the producer of the best film and the best director each receive a cash prize of 25,000 taka. Only Bangladeshi nationals are eligible.
Awarding body: Ministry of Information and Broadcasting, Government of Bangladesh, Dacca, Bangladesh.

Jefferson Lecture in the Humanities

The National Endowment for the Humanities, wishing to give leadership in affirming the relationship between thinker, scholar, and citizen, in 1972 established this lecture so that thinkers of international reputation might have a forum for their ideas, that humanistic insights of importance might reach the public, and that living issues might be the test of humane learning. Thomas Jefferson (1743–1826) epitomized the scholar in touch with his own time; President of the American Philosophical Society as well as President of the United States, the thinker and scholar within him informed the citizen and man of action. The lecture is given annually in Washington, D.C. before an invited audience of scholarly, cultural, and public leaders. It carries a stipend of $10,000, and the lecturer is expected to publish the lecture or series.
Awarding body: National Endowment for the Humanities, Washington, D.C. 20506, U.S.A.
Lecturers include: Erik H. Erikson ('Dimensions of a New Identity', 1973); Robert Penn ('Democracy and Poetry', 1974); Paul A. Freund ('Liberty: The Great Disorder of Speech', 1975); John Hope Franklin ('Racial Equality in America', 1976); Saul Bellow ('The Writer and His Country Look Each Other Over', 1977).

Jeffries Medical Research Award

The award was established in 1940 to honour the memory of John Jeffries, the American physician who made the earliest recorded scientific observations from the air. The award is made for outstanding contribution to the advancement of aerospace medical research and consists of a medal and certificate of citation. It is usually presented at the Aerospace Sciences Meeting.
Awarding body: American Institute of Aeronautics and Astronautics, 1290 Avenue of the Americas, New York, N.Y. 10019, U.S.A.
Recipients include: Harald von Beckh (1977).

John Wilfred Jenkinson Memorial Lectureship

The lectureship was established at Oxford University soon after the second world war at the bequest of Constance Hannah Jenkinson in memory of the pioneering work of her nephew in the field of embryology.
Awarding body: University of Oxford, Wellington Square, Oxford OX1 2JD, England.
Lecturers include: Dr. Susumo Ohno (City of Hope Medical Center, Calif., U.S.A., 1972–73); Prof. Ruggero Cappellini (1973–74); Prof. A. K. Tarkowski (Univ. of Warsaw, 1974–75).

Jenner Medal

The medal is awarded by the Royal Society of Medicine for distinguished work in epidemiological research or for pre-eminence in the prevention and control of epidemic disease.
Awarding body: Royal Society of Medicine, 1 Wimpole St., London W1M 8AE, England.

Jephcott Medal and Lecture

A lecturer is appointed every two years to lecture on a subject related to the advancement of the cause of education or on scientific and/or medical subjects generally. He receives a medal and an honorarium.
Awarding body: The Royal Society of Medicine, 1 Wimpole St., London W1M 8AE, England.

Jerusalem Prize

This international biennial prize of $2,000 is offered by the city of Jerusalem and presented at the Jerusalem International Book Fair. It is given to an author whose work expresses 'the freedom of the individual in society'. The prize was instituted in 1963.
Awarding body: Jerusalem International Book Fair, P.O.B. 1508, Jerusalem 91000, Israel.
Recipients include: Simone de Beauvoir (France, 1975); Octavio La Paz (Mexico, 1977); Sir Isaiah Berlin (U.K., 1979).

John Jeyes Medal, Award and Lectureship

This international award was founded in 1877 by an endowment from the Jeyes Group to commemorate the initiative of John Jeyes. The lecture should deal with a general theme, 'Advances in Chemistry Relating to a Better Environment', and the award is given to the individual who has made the most meritorious contributions to this theme. He/she receives a gold medal and £100.
Awarding body: The Chemical Society, Burlington House, London W1V 0BN, England.
Recipients include: R. L. Wain (1976–77).

Jnanpith Literary Award

This award was established in 1963 by the cultural institute Bharatiya Jnanpith, and is given for outstanding creative literary work. This must be written in one of the 15 Indian languages recognized by the Indian Constitution. The award is

129

made annually and consists of a cash sum of 100,000 rupees, a gold and silver citation plaque and a bronze-cast statuette of Vagdevi, the goddess of learning. The recipient must be an Indian citizen.

Awarding body: Bharatiya Jnanpith, B/45–47, Connaught Place, New Delhi 110001, India.

Recipients include: Vishwanath Satyanarayana (1970); Bishnu De (1971); Ramdhari Singh Dinkar (1972); D. R. Bendre and Gopinath Mohanty (1973); V. S. Khandekar (1974).

Mead Johnson Award for Research in Nutrition

This annual award, presented by the American Institute of Nutrition, was established by Mead Johnson & Co., and is made to a nutritional scientist under the age of 40 for outstanding recent research. This may take the form of either a single outstanding work or a series of papers on the same subject. The award consists of $1,000 and an inscribed scroll.

Awarding body: American Institute of Nutrition. (Nominations to Dr. R. L. Wixom, Dept. of Biochemistry, Univ. of Missouri Medical Center, Columbia, Mo. 65201, U.S.A.)

Recipients include: H. H. Sandstead (1972); V. R. Young (1973); J. W. Suttie (1974); H. E. Ganther (1975); L. D. Steglink (1976).

R. M. Johnston Memorial Medal

This award was established in 1920 in memory of Robert Mackenzie Johnston (1844–1918), the statistician and scientist. It is given annually or biennially to a lecturer who is chosen by the Council of the Royal Society of Tasmania, and who delivers the R. M. Johnston Memorial Lecture. There are no restrictions on eligibility.

Awarding body: Royal Society of Tasmania, P.O.B. 1166M, Hobart, Tasmania 7001, Australia.

Recipients include: L. H. Martin (1946); F. Griffiths Taylor (1948); J. T. Wilson (1950); F. Walker (1957); Edmund Hillary (1959).

Hilary Jolly Award

This annual award for contributions to Australian limnology was established in 1973 in honour of Violet Hilary Jolly (1906–75), co-founder and sometime President of the Australian Society for Limnology. The award consists of an inscribed book and the recipient is invited to deliver the Hilary Jolly Memorial Lecture at the Annual Congress of the Society.

Awarding body: Australian Society for Limnology, c/o Zoology Department, University of Adelaide, Adelaide, S.A. 5000, Australia.

Recipients include: Prof. A. H. Weatherley (1973–74); Dr. I. A. E. Bayly (1974–75).

Lady Jones Lectureship in Orthopaedic Surgery

The lectureship was established in 1918 by the gift of £2,500 from John Rankin, LL.D., to Liverpool University. Sir Robert Jones, Bt., K.B.E., C.B., was Honorary Lecturer from 1919 to 1924. The terms of the lectureship were revised in 1924 and a research scholarship in the same subject established. The appointment is made every two years by the University Council. The lecturer delivers a lecture or course of lectures on Orthopaedic Surgery. The remuneration is £100.

Awarding body: The University of Liverpool, P.O.B. 147, Liverpool L69 3BX, England.

Sydney Jones Lectureship in Art

In 1935 Sir Charles Sydney Jones promised to provide £100 a year for the establishment of this lectureship. The appointment is made annually by the Council of Liverpool University. At least two lectures are given in each Session and are open to the public without charge. The subject of the lectures must be approved by the Board of the Faculty of Arts. The fee payable to the lecturer(s) is £150.

Awarding body: The University of Liverpool, P.O.B. 147, Liverpool L69 3BX, England.

Jordan Award

This is a biennial cash award of £100 for the best contribution to the science or technology of surface coatings, accepted for publication in the Journal of the Oil and Colour Chemists' Association. It was instituted in 1967 by the late Mrs. M. R. Jordan in memory of her husband, Dr. L. A. Jordan, President of the Association in the years 1947–49. Any member of the Association of any nationality, working in either the academic or industrial field, is eligible, provided he/she is under the age of 35.

Awarding body: Oil and Colour Chemists' Association, Priory House, 967 Harrow Rd., Wembley, Middlesex HA0 2SF, England.

Recipients: R. J. King and M. J. B. Franklin (1969); J. R. Groom (1971); D. F. Tunstall (1973); J. G. Balfour and M. J. Hird (1975).

József Attila Prize for Literature

Instituted by the Hungarian Council of Ministers in 1953, the prize is awarded by the Minister of Culture. It is given annually for distinction in the field of literature, and is divided into three classes. It is named in honour of the Hungarian poet, Attila József (1905–37).

Awarding body: Committee for the József Attila Prize, Ministry of Culture, Szalay-utca 10, Budapest V, Hungary.

Recipients include: Erzsébet Galgóczi (writer), István Gáll (writer), Gyula Hernádi (writer), Károly Tamkó Sirató (poet), 1976.

Jubiläumspreis (*Jubilee Prize*)

This prize, awarded for the development of clinical surgery, was donated by the company Braun, Melsungen, in 1972 and is administered by a committee selected by the German Surgical Society. It is presented annually, and takes the form of a silver medal, certificate and cash prize of DM10,000. Physicians and scientists from Germany and Austria are eligible.

Awarding body: Deutsche Gesellschaft für Chirurgie, 1000 Berlin 15, Kurfürstendamm 179, Federal Republic of Germany.

Recipients include: Prof. Dr. F. Holle (Fed. Rep. of Germany, 1973); Prof. Hanno Millesi (Austria, 1974); Dr. Hans Reiner Mittelbach (Fed. Rep. of Germany, 1975); Prof. Dr. Werner Maassen and Dr. Dieter Greschuchna (Fed. Rep. of Germany, 1976).

Jubiläumspreis des Böhlau-Verlages/Wien

(*Jubilee Prize of the Böhlau Publishing House, Vienna*) Established in 1975, the prize is awarded for a learned work on a historical topic taken in its widest sense. The prize is intended for scholars of Austrian citizenship who are not older than 35. They may submit works which have been published or which are intended for publication. The prize, which is a certificate and a sum of money, is awarded in general every year, in May or June.

Awarding body: Österreichische Akademie der Wissenschaften, 1010 Vienna, Dr.-Ignaz-Seipel-Platz 2, Austria.

George Julius Medal

In 1977 this bronze medal replaced the Mechanical Engineering Prize of the Institution of Engineers, Australia, established in 1955. It is given in memory of Sir George Julius who practised in Sydney as a consulting engineer in the mechanical/electrical field. One of his best known achievements was the automatic totalizator before the days of electronics. He was Chairman of the Standards Association of Australia, Chairman of CSIRO (1926–45), a Councillor of the Institution of Engineers, Australia, and its President in 1925. The medal is awarded for the best paper on mechanical engineering selected by the Board of the College of Mechanical Engineers (one of the foundation Colleges of the Institution). The award is open to members of the Institution only.

Awarding body: Institution of Engineers, Australia, 11 National Circuit, Barton, A.C.T. 2600, Australia.

Recipients include: A. L. Carpenter (1970); J. A. Macinante (1973); J. V. Deslandes (1974); J. A. Macinante (1975); R. I. Mair (1976).

Hugo-Junkers-Preis

The prize was established in 1964 by the German Society for Aeronautics, the predecessor of the German Aerospace Research and Experimental Establishment (DFVLR) in Cologne. It commemorates the aircraft designer Hugo Junkers (1859–1935), who designed the first wholly metal aeroplane in 1915. It is intended for persons working with the DFVLR, and is given for works they have published or lectures they have given about their scientific achievements. The prize consists of a certificate and a sum of money of up to DM5,000 and is awarded every two years.

Awarding body: Deutsche Forschungs- und Versuchsanstalt für Luft- und Raumfahrt e.V., Postfach 90 60 58, D-5000 Cologne 90, Federal Republic of Germany.

K

George W. Kable Electrification Award
This award was established by the American Society of Agricultural Engineers in tribute to George W. Kable, a pioneer educator, researcher, author and public servant in farm electrification whose leadership and contributions did much to advance farmstead mechanization during its early stages of development. The award is given to honour individual agricultural engineers for their personal and professional contributions to the progress made in the utilization of electrical energy in the production and processing of agricultural products, and to emphasize the unique role of the agricultural engineering profession in the advancement of agriculture.
Awarding body: American Society of Agricultural Engineers, 2950 Niles Road, St. Joseph, Mich. 49085, U.S.A.

Josef Kainz-Medaille
The award was established by the city of Vienna in 1958 on the 100th anniversary of the birth of the Viennese actor, Josef Kainz. Three prizes are awarded annually to an actor, an actress and a producer for an outstanding theatrical production in a Viennese theatre. In the case of a special achievement a prize may also be awarded to a stage or costume designer. An award is not necessarily made in all of these categories each year. Foreign artists are also eligible for the prize, which consists of a certificate and a medal.
Awarding body: Magistratsabteilung 7, Stadtsrat, Vienna, Austria.

Jakob-Kaiser-Preis
The West German Ministry for Intra-German Relations established two annual prizes in 1960: one for the best television play, and the other for the best television documentary, which take some aspect of Germany (East and West) as their theme. The prize is in memory of the politician Jakob Kaiser (1888–1961), who was Minister for All-German Affairs from 1949 to 1957. The awards consist of DM10,000 each, and a certificate, and may be divided.
Awarding body: Bundesministerium für innerdeutsche Beziehungen, Godesberger Allee 140, Postfach 120250, 5300 Bonn 2, Federal Republic of Germany.
Recipients include: Johannes Hendrick (play, *Maria Morzeck*, 1976); Lutz Lehmann and Peter Schultze (documentary, *Ein Sonntag im August*, 1976); Holger Oehrens (documentary, *Mit Hammer und Zirkel*, 1976).

Kalevalapalkinto (*Kalevala Prize*)
This prize is awarded every three years by the Finnish Academy for the best study of the Kalevala, the Finnish national epic. The prize, a cash award of 4,500 markkaa, was founded by the State Council in 1935.
Awarding body: Suomalainen Tiedakatemia, Finland.
Recipients include: Mikko Korhonen (1968); Osmo Ikola (1971); Hannes Sihvo (1974).

Kalinga Prize
Named after the Kalinga empire, ruled by the Indian emperor Asoka in the third century B.C., the prize was established in 1951 by the Kalinga Trust Foundation with a donation by the Indian industrialist Bijoyanand Patnaik. It is awarded annually for the popularization of science and scientific research. The award is open to individuals with a distinguished career of public service in the interpretation of science and scientific research as writer, editor, speaker or radio programme director. The winner receives £1,000 to travel to India.
Awarding body: UNESCO, 9 Place de Fontenoy, 75700 Paris, France.
Recipients include: Dr. José Reis (Brazil) and Dr. Luis Estrada (Mexico), (1974); Sir George Porter (U.K.) and Acad. A. I. Oparin (U.S.S.R.), (1976); Fernand Séguin (Canada, 1977).

Herbert T. Kalmus Gold Medal Award
Established in 1956 by the Society of Motion Picture and Television Engineers, the award is in honour of Herbert T. Kalmus (1881–1963), the American pioneer photographic expert and President of Technicolor. The medal is awarded annually for outstanding contributions in the development of colour films, processing, techniques or equipment useful in making colour motion pictures for cinema or television use.
Awarding body: Society of Motion Picture and Television Engineers, 862 Scarsdale Ave., Scarsdale, N.Y. 10583, U.S.A.

Martin S. Kapp Foundation Engineering Award

This award was founded in 1973 in memory of Martin S. Kapp, F.ASCE, and is funded from gifts by his friends and associates. The award consists of a plaque and certificate, and is made annually to the originator of the most innovative design or construction of foundations, earthworks, retaining structures or underground construction, with emphasis on the overcoming of problems or the achieving of economies; its description should have been published in a form available to the whole engineering community. The award is open to non-members of the Society. No one may receive it more than once.

Awarding body: American Society of Civil Engineers, 345 East 47th St., New York, N.Y. 10017, U.S.A.

Recipients include: Anthony J. Tozzoli (1974); Ben C. Gerwick, Jr. (direction of the development and construction of the SPTC walls in the BARTD Stations, 1975).

Kardinal-Innitzer-Preise

These awards are made annually by the Cardinal Innitzer Study Foundation. They were instituted in 1962 by Cardinal Franz König, patron of the Foundation, in memory of Cardinal Theodor Innitzer, who started the Foundation, and who was Archbishop of Vienna from 1932 to 1955. The awards are intended primarily for Austrian scientists, and the recipients should be carrying out their work at an Austrian scientific institute. The principal award, worth 100,000 Schillings, is presented for outstanding achievement in a field relevant to the social sciences. Another three prizes, worth 50,000 Schillings each, may be awarded to recognize achievements in the human sciences, natural sciences and journalism. (Further prizes, worth 25,000 Schillings each, may be awarded to encourage work by young scholars in the following seven categories: theology; human sciences; social and commercial sciences; law and civic sciences; human and veterinary medicine; mathematics, natural sciences and technology; journalism.)

Awarding body: Kardinal-Innitzer-Studienfonds, 1010 Vienna, Rotenturmstr. 2, Austria.

Recipients include: Prof. Dr. Willibald Plöchl (ecclesiastical law), Prof. Dr. Wilhelm Weber (economics, 1972); Prof. Dr. Anton Burghardt (sociology, 1973); Prof. Dr. Alfred Verdross-Drossberg (international law, 1974); Prof. Dr. Hans Asperger (paediatrics, 1975); Prof. Dr. Karl Rahner (theology, 1976).

Dr. Heinz Karger Memorial Foundation Award

This international award is presented annually for a paper on a particular scientific subject. It was established in 1963 by Dr. h.c. Thomas Karger in honour of his father, Dr. Heinz Karger (1895–1959), former head of the Swiss publishing house S. Karger AG. The prize consists of 7,000 Swiss francs. The winning manuscript is published in one of the Karger journals.

Awarding body: S. Karger AG, Arnold-Böcklin-Str. 25, 4011 Basel, Switzerland.

Recipients include: Dr. D. Burckhardt (Switzerland, 1972); Dr. J. Schuster and Margarita Ihli (Fed. Rep. of Germany, 1972); Philip R. Wyatt and David M. Cox (Canada, 1976); D. J. H. Brock (U.K., 1976).

Karlovy Vary International Film Festival

This biennial competition was established in 1948 with the two aims of furthering friendship among nations, and introducing outstanding films which, by their artistic merit, contribute to the development of cinematography. Each country may submit one full-length feature film, which must have been made during the preceding year. The main prize, the Crystal Globe, is awarded to the most outstanding film, and there are various other prizes for the best actor and actress, etc.

Awarding body: Festival Committee, Central Management of the Czechoslovak Film, Jindřiská 34, 112 06 Prague 1, Czechoslovakia.

Recipients include: J. Menzel (Czechoslovakia, *Capricious Summer*, 1968); K. Loach (U.K., *Kes*, 1970); D. Khrabrovitski (U.S.S.R., *Taming of Fire*, 1972); A. Mikhalkov-Konchalovski (U.S.S.R., *Lovers' Romance*, 1974); H. Solás (Cuba, *Chilean Cantata*, 1976).

Theodore von Karman Award

This national award is made annually by the U.S. Air Force Association to an individual or organization for outstanding contributions in the field of science and engineering. It takes the form of a plaque. Instituted in 1948, it was originally named the Science Trophy, but was renamed in honour of Theodore von Karman (1881–1963), physicist and expert on rockets and aerodynamics.

Awarding body: Air Force Association National Awards Committee, 1750 Pennsylvania Ave., N.W., Washington, D.C. 20006, U.S.A.

Recipients include: Lt. Col. Donald G. Carpenter (1972); Lt. Col. Roy Robinette, Jr. (1973); USAF's Space and Missile Systems Organization (1974); USAF/industry team including Maj. Gen. Kendall Russell, Brig. Gen. Lawrence A. Skantze and Mark K. Miller (1975); NASA/industry team including James S. Martin, Jr. and Thomas G. Pownall (1976).

von Karman Lectureship in Astronautics

Established by the AIAA in 1975 to succeed the von Karman Lecture (1962), this lecture is given in honour of Theodore von Karman, the world-renowned fundamentalist in aerospace sciences. The award is intended to honour an individual who has performed notably and made a significant technical contribution in the field of astronautics. However, it not only honours a particular person but, by means of the lecture, enables the recipient to share his technological gifts with AIAA membership and the public at large. The award consists of a medal and certificate of citation; the lecture is usually presented at the Annual Meeting.

Awarding body: American Institute of Aeronautics and Astronautics, 1290 Avenue of the Americas, New York, N.Y. 10019, U.S.A.

Recipients include: Joseph V. Charyk (1977); Robert Fuhrman (1978).

Theodore von Karman Medal

The award was established in 1960 by the Engineering Mechanics Division of ASCE, which is responsible for the nomination of the winner. It is awarded annually to an individual in recognition of distinguished achievements in engineering mechanics, applicable to any branch of civil engineering.

Awarding body: American Society of Civil Engineers, 345 East 47th St., New York, N.Y. 10017, U.S.A.

Recipients include: Hans H. Bleich (1973); George W. Housner (1974); John H. Argyris (1975); Yuan-Chang B. Fung (research on problems of mechanics of solids, structures and biomechanics, 1976); Prof. Rodney Hill (U.K., 1978).

Theodore von Karman Memorial Lecture

The lecture was established in 1964 by the Israel Society of Aeronautical Sciences in memory of Theodore von Karman, first Honorary President of the Israel Society of Aeronautics and Astronautics. From 1958 to 1962 the lectureship was known as the Biennial International Lectures. The lecturer is chosen for his outstanding contributions to aeronautical science. Anyone who has made such a contribution is eligible although emphasis is placed on academic achievements, particularly in co-operation with Israeli researchers, or industrial work in co-operation with Israeli industry. The lecture is delivered every two years to the Israel Annual Conference on Aviation and Astronautics. All expenses are met by the Society.

Awarding body: Israel Society of Aeronautics and Astronautics, P.O.B. 2956, Tel-Aviv, Israel.

Recipients include: J. Schijve (National Aerospace Laboratory, Netherlands, 1970); I. E. Garrich (NASA Langley Research Centre, U.S.A., 1972); Richard S. Shevell (Stanford Univ., U.S.A., 1974); W. R. Sears (Aerospace and Mechanical Engineering Dept., Univ. of Arizona, U.S.A., 1976).

Theodore von Karman Prize

Established in 1968 by the American Society for Industrial and Applied Mathematics, the prize is awarded for a notable application of mathematics to mechanics or the engineering sciences made within the previous five or ten years. The prize is awarded every five or ten years and consists of a sum of money.

Awarding body: Society for Industrial and Applied Mathematics, U.S.A.

Recipients include: Sir G. Taylor (1971).

Ratanbai Katrak Lectureship

The lectureship was founded in 1922 at Oxford University by Dr. Nanabhai Navrosji Katrak of Bombay, in memory of his wife. The object of the lectureship is to promote the study of the religion of Zoroaster and of its later developments from a theological, philological and historical point of view. A Board of Management appoints the lecturer, of any nationality, at intervals of not more than ten years, to give a course of not less than six lectures.

Awarding body: University of Oxford, Wellington Square, Oxford OX1 2JD, England.

Lecturers include: Mary Boyce (Prof. of Iranian Studies, School of Oriental and African Studies, Univ. of London, 1974–75).

H. P. Kaufmann-Preis

Established in 1971 by the German Society for the Study of Fats, the prize is in memory of Dr. Hans Paul Kaufmann (1889–1971), professor of pharmacy and chemical technology, and founder and president of the society. Shortly before his death Dr. Kaufmann presented the society with 25 complete sets of the journal *Fette. Seifen. Anstrichmittel,* which he had created as the organ of the society. His wish was that these should form the basic stock for an annual scientific award. Thus the prize, which is for outstanding works on the chemistry and technology of fats and related substances, consists of a complete series of the journal from 1950 to the year of the award, together with a certificate and a plaque. The prize may not be awarded to more than two people each year. Works submitted may be unpublished and may be in the form of dissertations. The author must not be over 35 years old. The prize is presented at the annual congress of the Society for the Study of Fats, which takes place in the autumn.

Awarding body: Deutsche Gesellschaft für Fettwissenschaft e.V., 4400 Münster, Soester Strasse 13, Federal Republic of Germany.

Recipients include: Dr. P. B. van Dam (Netherlands, 1974); Dr. Gad Cegla (Israel, 1974); Dr. Hermann-Josef Drexler (Fed. Rep. of Germany, 1976); Dr. Irene Reichwald (Fed. Rep. of Germany, 1976).

Cherry Kearton Medal and Award

The award was established in 1967 as a result of a bequest to the Royal Geographical Society by the late Mrs. Kearton in memory of her husband, Cherry Kearton (1871–1940), naturalist, traveller and photographer. The bronze medal and a monetary award are given to a traveller concerned with the study or practice of natural history, with a preference for those with an interest in nature photography or cinematography. The award may be made annually but only if a suitable candidate is forthcoming. There are no restrictions of age, nationality or sex. Applications may not be submitted; the award is granted by the Society's Council and the criteria are the achievements of the recipient. The award is made at the Society's Annual Meeting in June.

Awarding body: Royal Geographical Society, 1 Kensington Gore, London SW7 2AR, England.

Recipients include: Heinz Sielmann (1973); Des and Jen Bartlett (1974); Eric Ashby (1975); Dr. Pamela Harrison (1976); Anthony Smith (1978).

Keilin Medal

This award was established in 1964 in memory of the distinguished biochemist David Keilin (1887–1963), by a group of his associates. The medal and a cash prize are awarded biennially to a bio-chemist of any nationality, for distinction in a sphere of biochemistry decided by the awards committee. The medal is bestowed after delivery of a lecture on the sphere of biochemistry nominated. Should the lecture be given outside the U.K., it must be repeated in the U.K.

Awarding body: The Biochemical Society, 7 Warwick Court, London WC1R 5DP, England.

Recipients include: M. Eigen ('Molecular Control in Biology', 1969); E. Margoliash ('The Structural Basis of Cytochrome *c* Function as a Product of the Evolution of Species', 1970); R. J. P. Williams, F.R.S. ('Electron Transfer and Oxidative Energy', 1972); E. C. Slater, F.R.S. ('From Cytochrome to Adenosine Triphosphate and Back', 1974); S. M. E. Magnusson ('Restrictive Activation and Limited Proteolysis, Modular Design of Regulatory Zymogen Structures (Prothrombin, Plasminogen, Factors X and IX)', 1976).

Kelvin Medal

The medal was founded in 1914, and first awarded in 1920 in memory of Lord Kelvin. The Institution of Civil Engineers is Trustee of the fund, and the Award Committee consists of the Presidents of the Institutions of Civil, Mechanical, Electrical, and Mining Engineers, the Royal Institution of Naval Architects, the Institution of Mining and Metallurgy, the Institution of Engineers and Shipbuilders in Scotland, and the Metals Society. The award is made every three years.

Awarding body: Institution of Civil Engineers, Great George St., London SW1P 3AA, England.

Recipients include: Rt. Hon. Lord Penney (1971); Dr. Charles Stark Draper (1974); Rt. Hon. Lord Hinton of Bankside (contributions to the British electric power supply industry, including the development of nuclear reactor generating stations, 1977).

Robert F. Kennedy Journalism Awards

These awards were instituted in memory of the politician and social reformer Robert F. Kennedy, and are presented for outstanding coverage of the problems of the disadvantaged. Established in 1968, they are sponsored by the Journalism Awards Committee on the Problems of the Disadvantaged, with the assistance of the Robert F. Kennedy Memorial. They are made annually for work during the previous year in six categories: newspaper, magazine, photo-journalism, television, radio, and student. For the 1977 awards, it was decided that three cash prizes of $1,000 each would be awarded to the entries judged most

outstanding in the print (newspaper and magazine), broadcast (TV and radio), and photo-journalism categories. From among the three winners, the recipient of a grand prize of an additional $2,000 would be selected.

Awarding body: Robert F. Kennedy Journalism Awards Committee on the Problems of the Disadvantaged, 1035 30th St., N.W., Washington, D.C. 20007, U.S.A.

Recipients include: Gene Miller and *The Miami Herald* (newspaper), Michael O'Brien (*The Miami News*, photo-journalism), Tom Pettit (NBC News, television), Bob Cain and Cathleen Gurley (WWVA, West Virginia, radio), *The Cavalier Daily* (Univ. of Virginia, student), 1976.

Mzee Jomo Kenyatta Prize for Literature

Four cash prizes are awarded under this title as follows: K£250 to the author of the best book published in English, K£250 to the author of the best book published in Swahili, K£150 to the author of the best first book published in English, and K£150 to the author of the best first book published in Swahili. The books must have been published between 1 January and 30 June of the year of the award (it is presented on 20 October: Kenyatta Day). Translations are not eligible. Any book entered for the competition shall not qualify unless its publisher agrees to spend not less than K£200 on direct media advertising of the book, to have not less than 1,000 copies of the winning books in stock locally and available to booksellers throughout East Africa. Authors must be citizens of East Africa (Kenya, Tanzania, Uganda or Zanzibar). The prize was established in 1972 in honour of the President of the Republic of Kenya.

Awarding body: The Kenya Publishers' Association, c/o Box 45314, Nairobi, Kenya.

Recipients include: Charles Mangua; Abdilatif Abdalla; Meja Mwangi; Okot P'Bitok; Ahmed Nassir; Salim Kibao.

W. P. Ker Lectureship

Founded in 1938 at Glasgow University by the bequest of John Brown Douglas, M.A., writer in Glasgow, the lectureship is in memory of William Paton Ker, Professor of English Literature, University of London and Professor of Poetry, University of Oxford. The foundation provides for an annual (since 1958 biennial) lecture on some branch of literary or linguistic studies. The lecture is subsequently published.

Awarding body: University of Glasgow, Glasgow G12 8QQ, Scotland.

Lecturers include: Prof. J. F. Kermode (Lord Northcliffe Prof. of Modern English Literature, Univ. Coll., London, 1972); Prof. Denis Donoghue (Prof. of Modern English and American Literature, Univ. Coll., Dublin, 1974); E. Peter M. Dronke (Univ. of Cambridge, 1976).

Donald Q. Kern Award in Heat Transfer or Energy Conversion

This award of the Heat Transfer and Energy Conversion Division of the American Institute of

Chemical Engineers is made to individuals who have demonstrated outstanding expertise in some area of heat transfer or energy conversion. The award, which is not restricted to Institute members, consists of an engraved plaque and $300. The recipient will be asked to provide a written review of his special field for distribution to members of the Division, and will be the invited lecturer at the National Heat Transfer Conference in the year of his award. Nominations are made in the year preceding such a Conference.

Awarding body: Heat Transfer and Energy Conversion Division of the American Institute of Chemical Engineers, 345 East 47th St., New York, N.Y. 10017, U.S.A.

Kinder- und Jugendbuchpreise der Stadt Wien (*City of Vienna Prizes for Children's and Juvenile Books*)

Established in 1954, three prizes are awarded annually for the best newly published books for children and juveniles. The books must be by living Austrian authors and have been published either in the current or the previous year by a Viennese publishing house. The awards are made in the following categories: a book for small children; a book for children up to the age of 14; a book for juveniles up to the age of 18. The prizes consist of a diploma and a sum of money. A separate prize may also be given to the illustrator of a book.

Awarding body: Magistratsabteilung 7, Stadtsrat, Vienna, Austria.

King Faisal's Prize

The King Abdul Aziz Research Centre founded the prize in 1975 for the best treatise compatible with the objectives of the Centre: studies on the history, geography or literature of Saudi Arabia, as well as the Arab Peninsula, Arab countries and the Islamic world in general. Provision is made for annual prizes of 20,000 riyals (first prize), 7,000 riyals (second prize) and 5,000 riyals (third prize).

Awarding body: King Abdul Aziz Research Centre, P.O.B. 2945, Riyadh, Saudi Arabia.

Recipients include: Dr. Abdul Fattah Abu Alya (1976).

Coretta Scott King Award

This annual prize was established in 1969 by a group of librarians and publishers, and the Englewood (N.J.) Library Council. It was founded in memory of Rev. Dr. Martin Luther King, Jr. (1929–68), and is named in honour of Mrs. Coretta Scott King, his widow, for her courage and determination to realize Dr. King's dreams. The prize is given for a book published the preceding year, which can be rated as having made the greatest contribution to promoting world brotherhood, non-violent social change, and world peace, as exemplified by the life and philosophy of the late Dr. King. The award aims to inspire children and young people to dedicate their talents and energies to achieving the above goals, and encourage them to make Dr. King's dream their own. The prize is presented at the annual Convention of the American Library Association. The winner receives an honorarium of $250, a set of *Encyclopaedia Britannica*, a laminated plaque, and is the guest of honour at an award breakfast or luncheon.

Awarding body: The Coretta Scott King Award, 1236 Oakcrest Dr. S.W., Atlanta, Ga. 30311, U.S.A.

Recipients include: Elton C. Fax (*Seventeen Black Artists*, 1972); Alfred Duckett (*I Never Had It Made: The Autobiography of Jackie Robinson*, 1973); Sharon Bell Mathis, author, and George Ford, illustrator (*Ray Charles*, 1974); Dorothy W. Robinson, author, and Herbert Temple, illustrator (*The Legend of Africania*, 1975); Pearl Bailey (*Duey's Tale*, 1976).

Martin Luther King Memorial Prize

This is an annual prize of £100, awarded for a literary work reflecting the ideals to which Dr. King dedicated his life. The work may be a novel, a non-fiction book, a play (for stage, screen or radio) or a poem over 500 lines in length. It must have been published or performed in the U.K. during the calendar year preceding the award. The prize is awarded on 4 April, the anniversary of Dr. King's death.

Awarding body: Martin Luther King Memorial Prize, c/o National Westminster Bank, 7 Fore St., Chard, Somerset TA20 1PJ, England.

Recipients include: Evan Jones (*The Fight Against Slavery*, TV documentary, 1976); James L. Watson (ed. *Between Two Cultures*, 1978).

Mary Kingsley Medal

The medal was established in 1903 by the Liverpool School of Tropical Medicine, in memory of the explorer Miss Mary Kingsley (1862–1900). The medal is awarded from time to time for distinguished achievement in the field of tropical medicine and kindred subjects.

Awarding body: Liverpool School of Tropical Medicine, Pembroke Place, Liverpool L3 5QA, England.

Recipients include: Charles Morley Wenyon (protozoology, 1929); Samuel Rickard Christophers (entomology, 1934); Emile Brumpt (parasitology, 1938); Warrington Yorke (chemotherapy, 1949); Percy Cyril Claude Garnham (malaria, 1973).

Otto Kinkeldy Award

This award is given to a U.S. or Canadian author of the most notable full-length study in any branch of the discipline of musicology published in the preceding year. It was established in 1967 in memory of Otto Kinkeldy (1878–1966), scholar-librarian and first President of the American Musicological Society (1934–36). The award is presented annually and consists of a cash prize of U.S.$400 and a scroll.

Awarding body: American Musicological Society.

Recipients include: Albert Seay (*Jacobus Arcadelt, Opera Omnia*, vol. II, 1972); H. Colin Slim (*A Gift of Madrigals and Motets*, 1973); Robert L. Marshall

(*The Compositional Process of J. S. Bach*, 1974); Vivian Perlis (*Charles Ives Remembered, an Oral History*, 1975); David P. McKay and Richard Crawford (*William Billings of Boston: eighteenth-century composer*, 1976).

Kinma Awards

To encourage film-making in Taiwan, the Government Information Office established in 1958 the Kinma ('Golden Horse') awards for the best films, best film-makers, best performers, and other contributors to the art.

Awarding body: Government Information Office, Taipei 100, Taiwan, Republic of China.

Recipients include: Hsu Feng (best actress), Chang Feng (best actor), Chang Pei-cheng (best director), *Victory* (best motion picture), 1976.

Frederic Stanley Kipping Award in Organosilicon Chemistry

Established in 1960 by the Dow Corning Corporation, the award commemorates the achievements of Professor Frederic Stanley Kipping. It will be presented biennially in even-numbered years from 1978, and is intended to recognize distinguished achievement in research in organosilicon chemistry and, by such example, to stimulate the creativity of others toward further advancement of this field of chemistry. A nominee must have accomplished such research during the ten years preceding the year of the award. The measure of this achievement should focus primarily on the nominee's significant publications in the field of organosilicon chemistry but may include consideration of his contributions to the related field of organometallic chemistry, particularly embracing the elements of Group IV. There are no limits as to age or nationality. The award consists of $2,000 and a certificate. An allowance will be provided to cover travelling expenses incidental to conferment of the award.

Awarding body: American Chemical Society, 1155 Sixteenth St., N.W., Washington, D.C. 20036, U.S.A.

Recipients include: Dietmar Seyferth (1972); Adrian G. Brook (1973); Hubert Schmidbaur (1974); Hans Bock (1975); Michael F. Lappert (1976).

Klinck Lectureship

Established in 1966 by the Agricultural Institute of Canada, the lectureship is in memory of Leonard S. Klinck, first President of the Institute and subsequently Dean of Agriculture, then President of the University of British Columbia. The lectureship is awarded annually to a renowned agriculturist and entails the delivery of a series of lectures throughout Canada for two weeks during the winter months. Expenses are paid, and the lecturer receives a certificate and $1,000 honorarium.

Awarding body: Agricultural Institute of Canada, Suite 907, 151 Slater St., Ottawa, Ont. K1P 5H4, Canada.

Recipients include: M. F. Baumgardner ('Remote Sensing', 1972); D. R. Bergmann ('European Common Market', 1973); R. G. Anderson ('Second Look at the Green Revolution', 1974); M. E. Brunk ('Agriculture and Public Policy', 1975); J. C. Gilson ('Canadian Agriculture and Public Policy', 1976).

Kodansha Prize

Two awards are given annually under this title by the Kodansha publishing company. One, founded in 1970, is awarded to a publisher for a book published in the previous year which is outstanding in one of the following areas: illustrations, non-fiction, photographs, design; the prize consists of a clock and a sum of 300,000 yen. The second prize, founded in 1977, is for the best cartoon book published in the previous year; it consists of a clock and 500,000 yen.

Awarding body: Kodansha Ltd., 2-12-21, Otowa, Bunkyo-ku, Tokyo 112, Japan.

Ilona Kohrtz Prize

The Ilona Kohrtz Prize is given by the Swedish Academy to a Swedish writer of either prose or poetry. The prize consists of an annual pension of about 4,000 Swedish kronor for the rest of the recipient's life. The prize was instituted in 1962 by Ilona Kohrtz.

Awarding body: The Swedish Academy, Börshuset, Källargränd 4, S-111 29 Stockholm, Sweden.

Beatrice J. Kolliner Award for a Young Israeli Artist

A prize of I£9,000 is awarded annually to an Israeli artist at the International Council meetings of the Israel Museum.

Awarding body: The Israel Museum, P.O.B. 1299, Jerusalem 91000, Israel.

Recipients include: Hedi Tarjan; Mordechai Mizrachi.

Käthe-Kollwitz-Preis

This prize was established in 1962 by the Council of Ministers of the German Democratic Republic in memory of the artist Käthe Kollwitz (1867–1945). It is presented annually to an artist whose work or works are executed in the service of socialism. All artists, excluding members of the Academy of Arts, are eligible for the award, which consists of a certificate, a plaque, and a sum of money.

Awarding body: Akademie der Künste der D.D.R., 104 Berlin, Hermann-Matern-Strasse 58/59, German Democratic Republic.

Recipients include: Renè Graetz (sculptor, 1973); Wieland Förster (sculptor, 1974); Verner Stötzer (sculptor, 1975); Harald Metzkes (painter and graphic artist, 1976); Horst Zickelbein (painter and graphic artist, 1977).

Kolthoff Gold Medal Award

Established in 1967 by the American Pharmaceutical Association, the Kolthoff Gold Medal

Award in Analytical Chemistry is presented biennially to a scientist who has contributed significantly to the advancement of pharmaceutical analysis. In addition to a medal the award includes a cash prize of $1,000, which is contributed by the CIBA Pharmaceutical Company.
Awarding body: American Pharmaceutical Association, 2215 Constitution Ave., N.W., Washington, D.C. 20037, U.S.A.
Recipients include: I. M. Kolthoff (1967); A. J. P. Martin (1969); Lyman C. Craig (1971); Egon Stahl (1973); Sidney Siggia (1975).

Kongelige danske Landhusholdningsselskab's medalje (*Royal Danish Agricultural Society Medals*)
Established in 1769, three medals or silver cups are awarded once or twice a year to honour outstanding scientific, practical or organizational activities in agriculture. Recipients must be Danish citizens.
Awarding body: Royal Danish Agricultural Society, Rolighedsvej 26, Copenhagen V, Denmark.
Recipients include: Johannes Jespersen (1964); Johannes Dons Christensen (1969); Flemming Juncker (1971); A. W. Nielsen (1975); Viggo Lund (1977).

Joseph-König-Gedenkmünze
This bronze medal was established in 1934 by the Association of German Food Chemists, in commemoration of the food chemist Joseph König (1843–1930). It lapsed after 1945 and was taken up again in 1951 by the Society of German Chemists, founded in 1946. The medal is awarded, on the recommendation of the Food Chemistry branch of the Society, to Germans or non-Germans who have distinguished themselves by their contribution to the development of food chemistry. A sum of money is awarded with the medal.
Awarding body: Gesellschaft Deutscher Chemiker, 6000 Frankfurt (Main) 90, Carl Bosch-Haus, Varrentrappstr. 40–42, Federal Republic of Germany.
Recipients include: Prof. Josef Schormüller (1963); Prof. Josef Eisenbrand (1966); Prof. Rudolf Heiss (1972); Prof. Friedrich Kiermeier (1974); Prof. Rudi Franck (1976).

Koninklijke/Shell prijs (*Royal Dutch/Shell Prize*)
Founded in 1969 under the auspices of the Dutch Society of Sciences (Hollandsche Maatschappij der Wetenschappen), this prize is awarded annually to Dutch scientists or to scientists working in the Netherlands, for work in the exact sciences, life sciences or social sciences. The prize consists of 25,000 Dutch guilders, and is sponsored by the Royal Dutch Shell Company.
Awarding body: Hollandsche Maatschappij der Wetenschappen, Spaarne 17, Haarlem, The Netherlands.
Recipients include: Dr. P. W. M. Glaudemans (nuclear physics, 1971–72); Prof. D. de Wied

(pharmacology, 1972–73); Dr. L. G. Suttorp (theoretical physics, 1973–74); Dr. M. J. van der Wiel (atomic physics, 1975–76).

Korean Translation Award
This annual award was established in 1957, and has been given regularly since 1961. It is awarded by the Korean P.E.N. Center to any Korean national for the best translation of a literary work into Korean or from Korean into English. The award consists of a cash prize of $600 and a certificate.
Awarding body: The Korean P.E.N. Center of the International P.E.N., 163 Ankuk-dong, Jongno-ku, Seoul, Republic of Korea.
Recipients include: Lee Tong-hyun (Dostoevski, *Brat'ja Karamazovy*, 1970); Chang Sun-yung (Cervantes, *Don Quixote*, 1971); Lee Ka-hyung (A. Malraux, *L'Espoir*, 1972); Son U-sung (Montaigne, *Essais*, 1974); Kwack Bok-nock (Thomas Mann, *Der Zauberberg*, 1976).

Kossuth Prize of the Hungarian People's Republic
Founded by Parliament in 1948, the prize is awarded annually by the Council of Ministers. It consists of a 'Grand Prize' and a medal, in three categories. It is given for outstanding contributions in the field of culture and the arts which have benefited the whole nation. The prize is named in honour of Lajos Kossuth (1802–94), the Hungarian patriot and politician.
Awarding body: Committee for the Kossuth Prize, Council of Ministers, Kossuth Lajos tér 1, Budapest V, Hungary.

Kosutány Tamás Memorial Medal
The Hungarian Society for Food Industry founded this medal in 1956 for members of the Society whose outstanding scientific activities have significantly contributed to the advancement of the Society and the food industry. An annual cash prize of 5,000 forints accompanies the medal. It is named after Tamás Kosutány, a university professor, who worked on the problems of the chemistry of wheat, wine and foodstuffs.
Awarding body: Magyar Élelmezésipari Tudományos Egyesület, 1054 Budapest V, Akadémia u. 1–3, Hungary.

Richard Kovacs Lecture in Rheumatology and Rehabilitation
A lecturer is appointed every three years and receives an honorarium.
Awarding body: The Royal Society of Medicine, 1 Wimpole St., London W1M 8AE, England.

Kranichsteiner Musikpreis (*Kranichstein Music Prize*)
This prize was established in 1952 by the Darmstadt International Music Institute. It is awarded every two years for achievements in the composition and interpretation of new music during the 'International Holiday Course for New Music'. The winner may be of any nationality but

must not be over 30 years of age. The prize consists of a diploma and a sum of DM4,000, which may be shared among two or more people.

Awarding body: Internationales Musikinstitut Darmstadt, 6100 Darmstadt, Nieder-Ramstädter Strasse 190, Federal Republic of Germany.

Recipients include: Jorge Zulueta (piano, 1956); Werner Taube (cello, 1956); Léon Spierer (violin, 1957); Bruno Canino (piano, 1960); Herbert Henck (piano, 1972); Ulrich Stranz (composition, 1976).

Kariamanikam Srinivasa Krishnan Memorial Lecture

This lecture was established in 1965 by the Indian National Science Academy. The lectureship is awarded for distinguished contributions in any branch of natural science. It is awarded every six years and the lecturer receives an honorarium.

Awarding body: Indian National Science Academy, Bahadur Shah Zafar Marg, New Delhi 110001, India.

Recipients include: R. K. Asundi (1969); A. P. Mitra (1975).

August Krogh Lecture

The lecture was established in 1969 on the occasion of the 50th anniversary of the Danish Medical Society. Each year a prominent Danish physician is invited to lecture at the Society, and receives an award of 10,000 kroner. The lecture is named in memory of August Krogh (1874–1949), the Danish physiologist, famous for his studies in capillary physiology, for which he received the Nobel Prize in 1920.

Awarding body: Dansk Medicinsk Selskab, Copenhagen, Denmark.

Recipients include: Dr. med. Johannes Ipsen (1973); Dr. med. Poul Riis (1974); Dr. med. Axel Harrestrup Andersen (1975); Dr. med. Poul Bonnevie (1975); Dr. med. Kaj Kalbak (1976).

Nadezhda K. Krupskaya Prize

This prize was inaugurated by the Government of the U.S.S.R. in 1969. It is awarded annually for meritorious work in literacy, and is worth 5,000 roubles. The award is open to institutions, organizations or individuals displaying outstanding merit and achieving special success in contributing to literacy.

Awarding body: UNESCO, 9 Place de Fontenoy, 75700 Paris, France.

Recipients include: Education Corps (Iran, 1972); Literacy Project in the Western Lake Region (Tanzania, 1973); Cercle pour le Développement de la Commune de Shyorongi – CEDECOS (Rwanda, 1974); Abdirizak Mohamoud Abukar (Somalia, 1975); Literacy Department of the Ministry of Education and Culture (Syria, 1976).

Kshanika Oration Award

This award was established by Dr. M. N. Sen in 1976. It is intended for a woman scientist for research in the field of bio-medical sciences. It is an annual prize of 1,000 rupees. The recipient is expected to deliver an oration on her work, which is also published in the *Indian Journal of Medical Research.*

Awarding body: Indian Council of Medical Research, Ansari Nagar, Post Box 4508, New Delhi 110016, India.

Richard-Kuhn-Medaille

Established in 1968 by the aniline and soda manufacturers, Badische Anilin- & Soda-Fabrik AG, of Ludwigshafen, the award is in memory of Richard Kuhn (1900–67), who won the 1938 Nobel Prize for Chemistry for his work on carotenes and the vitamins A and B_2. The gold medal and a sum of money are awarded to German or non-German scientists in recognition of outstanding achievements in the field of biochemistry. The award is made not more than once every two years. The recipient delivers the Richard Kuhn Memorial Lecture about his work to a meeting of the Society of German Chemists, and the lecture is then published in the Society's journal, *Angewandte Chemie* (Applied Chemistry).

Awarding body: Gesellschaft Deutscher Chemiker, 6000 Frankfurt (Main) 90, Carl Bosch-Haus, Varrentrappstr. 40–42, Federal Republic of Germany.

Recipients include: Prof. Hans Georg Zachau (Fed. Rep. of Germany, 1968); Prof. Kurt Wallenfels (Fed. Rep. of Germany, 1970); Prof. Hermann Schildknecht (Fed. Rep. of Germany, 1974).

Kultur- und Förderungspreise des Landes Niederösterreich *(Province of Lower Austria Cultural Prizes)*

These prizes have been awarded annually by the Province of Lower Austria since 1960. One prize of 40,000 Schillings and two research grants of 15,000 Schillings are given each year. Each of the awards is accompanied by a certificate. The awards are made to individuals who are Austrian citizens and who were either born in Lower Austria, or live there, or whose work emphasizes the importance of Lower Austria as a centre of art and science, or is concerned with Lower Austria. The prizes and awards are given in the fields of literature, music, painting and science.

Awarding body: Niederösterreichische Landesregierung, 1014 Vienna, Herrengasse 11–13, Austria.

Recipients include: Karl Korab (fine arts, 1972); Prof. Dr. Erik Werba (music, 1974); Prof. Heinrich Strecker (music, 1975); Hans Weigel (literature, 1976); Dr. Josef Stummvoll (science, 1976).

Kulturális Kapcsolatok Intézete emlékérme *(Institute of Cultural Relations Commemorative Medal)*

This award is made occasionally by the Hungarian Institute of Cultural Relations (a government body co-ordinating the international activities of all Hungarian organizations engaged in the fields of culture, education, science and technology. It is for contributions to the dissemination of Hungarian culture abroad. The award was instituted in 1969, and consists of a medal and certificate.

Awarding body: Kulturális Kapcsolatok Intézete, 1368 Budapest, Dorottya u.8, Hungary.

Recipients include: Prof. Eugenius Mroczko (Poland, 1973); T. Ikeda (Japan, 1974); Prof. K. Tanimoto (Japan, 1974); Hugo Albornoz (Ecuador, 1974); Bruna Gobbi (Italy, 1975).

Kulturpreis des Landes Oberösterreich
(Province of Upper Austria Prize for Culture)
This prize was established in 1975 by the provincial government of Upper Austria. It is awarded annually in four categories: literature, art, music and science. Persons born in Upper Austria or who are Austrian citizens and have lived in Upper Austria for five years are eligible. The prize-winning work must have been produced in the previous three years. The winner in each category receives a cash prize of 50,000 Schillings.

Awarding body: Oberösterreichische Landesregierung, Landhaus, Promenade, 4020 Linz, Austria.

Recipients include: Prof. Erwin Gimmelsberger (literature), Alois Riedl (art), Richard Kittler (music), Prof. Otfried Kastner (science), 1976.

Felix-Kuschenitz-Preis
Established in 1940 by the factory director, Felix Kuschenitz, the prize is awarded for the furthering of independent research in chemistry or physics. It is primarily for completed work, but may be awarded for projects still in progress. The prize consists of a diploma and a sum of money. It is awarded in general every year, in May or June.

Awarding body: Österreichische Akademie der Wissenschaften, 1010 Vienna, Dr.-Ignaz-Seipel-Platz 2, Austria.

140

L

John Labatt Limited Award

The award was established in 1976 by The Chemical Institute of Canada, and is financed by John Labatt Ltd. First made in 1977, it is given annually in recognition of outstanding achievements in chemical or biological research or development pertinent to the food and beverage sciences, in terms of supply, manufacture, quality or nutritional value. Scientists resident in Canada or who have carried out the major portion of their applicable work in Canada are eligible. The award consists of an honorarium of $1,000 and a commemorative scroll; these are presented at the Annual Conference of The Chemical Institute of Canada. The recipient is required to present a lecture at this conference or at a suitable symposium of the Institute, and is known as 'The Labatt Lecturer'; his travelling expenses to the conference may be provided. Nominations for the award are made by members of The Chemical Institute of Canada.

Awarding body: The Chemical Institute of Canada, 151 Slater St., Ottawa, Ont. K1P 5H3, Canada.

John Oliver La Gorce Medal

The medal was established in 1967 by the National Geographic Society in honour of John Oliver La Gorce. The medal is awarded as and when merited for accomplishment in geographic exploration, or in the sciences, or for public service that advances international understanding.

Awarding body: National Geographic Society, 17th and M Streets N.W., Washington, D.C. 20036, U.S.A.

Recipients: American Antarctic Mountaineering Expedition 1966–67 (1967); Harold E. Edgerton (1968); Philip Van Horn Weems (1968).

Dr. Elizabeth Laird Lecture

The bequest of Dr. Elizabeth Laird, a distinguished Canadian radar research physicist, to the University of Winnipeg, provided the institution with funds to establish an 'occasional public lecture in the field of science or social studies'. One lecture is held every year. The first was in 1975.

Awarding body: University of Winnipeg, 515 Portage Avenue, Winnipeg, Man. R3B 2E9, Canada.

Lecturers include: Dr. Kenneth Hare (Dir., Inst. of Environmental Studies, Univ. of Toronto, 1975); Dr. Louis Siminovitch (Prof. of Biophysics, Univ. of Toronto and Geneticist-in-Chief, Hospital for Sick Children, Toronto, 1976).

Lamme Award

This is an annual award established in memory of Benjamin Garver Lamme (1864–1924), an inventor and developer of electrical machinery. It is bestowed upon a distinguished engineering educator for excellence in teaching and for contributions to the art of teaching, to research and technical literature and to the advancement of the profession, and for engineering college administration. The Lamme Trust Fund provides the funds for the award which consists of a gold medal, a bronze replica and a certificate.

Awarding body: American Society for Engineering Education, Suite 400, One Dupont Circle, Washington, D.C. 20036, U.S.A.

Recipients include: Glenn Murphy (1972); Max S. Peters (1973); George W. Hawkins (1974); John R. Whinnery (1975); John J. McKetta (1976).

Will-Lammert-Preis

This award was established in 1961 with an endowment from the family of the sculptor, Will Lammert (1892–1957). It is presented every three years by the Academy of Arts of the German Democratic Republic for work executed in the style of Will Lammert. The artist must be no more than 35 years of age and must have begun work on his sculptures during the preceding two years. The prize consists of a certificate and cash award.

Awarding body: Akademie der Künste der DDR, 104 Berlin, Hermann-Matern-Strasse 58/59, German Democratic Republic.

Recipients include: Gerhard Rommel (1967); Margret Middell (1969); Friedrich B. Henkel (1971); Bernd Göbel (1973); Christa Sammler (1976).

Lamont Poetry Selection

The Academy of American Poets was founded in 1934 to assist the careers of American poets; the Lamont Poetry Selection award, made annually since 1954, was established by a bequest of the late Mrs. Thomas W. Lamont. It was originally awarded for an American poet's first published book of poems; it now ensures the publication of his second collection. Each year, U.S. publishers are invited to submit manuscripts of once-published poets to the Academy for consideration.

Awarding body: The Academy of American Poets, 1078 Madison Ave., New York, N.Y. 10028, U.S.A.

Recipients include: Stephen Dobyns (*Concurring Beasts*, 1971); Peter Everwine (*Collecting the Animals*, 1972); Marilyn Hacker (*Presentation Piece*, 1973); John Balaban (*After Our War*, 1974); Lisel Mueller (*The Private Life*, 1975).

Lampitt Medal

The medal was instituted by the Society of Chemical Industry in 1958, and given for outstanding service to the Society through its Subject Groups and Local Sections. The medal commemorates Dr. Leslie H. Lampitt who for 37 years played an active and major part in the Society's affairs, holding the offices of President, Hon. Treasurer and Hon. Secretary (Foreign). The medal is normally awarded every two years.

Awarding body: Society of Chemical Industry, 14 Belgrave Square, London SW1X 8PS, England.

Recipients include: F. Gamble (1969); H. Hayhurst (1971); J. J. Hastings (1972); W. E. Cowley and A. Pollard (1975).

Vice Admiral 'Jerry' Land Medal

This award was established in 1952 by the Society of Naval Architects and Marine Engineers in honour of Vice Admiral Emory Scott ('Jerry') Land (1879–1971), a past president and honorary member of the Society. It is awarded annually for outstanding accomplishments in the marine field and takes the form of a medal.

Awarding body: Society of Naval Architects and Marine Engineers, Suite 1369, One World Trade Center, New York, N.Y. 10048, U.S.A.

von Langenbeck-Preis

This prize is awarded annually by the German Surgical Society and consists of a cash prize of DM10,000 and certificate. It was founded in 1953, and is given to members of the Society at the level of senior physician or assistant, for scientific essays and the development of young talent.

Awarding body: Deutsche Gesellschaft für Chirurgie, 1000 Berlin 15, Kurfürstendamm 179, Federal Republic of Germany.

Recipients include: Dr. Gerhard Zimmermann (1973); Dr. Claus-Peter Schrader (1973); Dr. Claus Hammer and Dr. Christian Chaussy (1975); Dr. Hartmut Seidel, A. Eggert, H. Huland, J. Ruhnke (1975); Dr. Arnulf Thiede (1976).

Langley Medal

This gold medal is awarded for specially meritorious investigations in connection with the science of aeronautics and astronautics. It was established in 1908 by the Smithsonian Board of Regents in honour of Samuel P. Langley (1887–1906), third Secretary of the Smithsonian Institution and a famous pioneer in aeronautics. The award is made irregularly.

Awarding body: Smithsonian Institution, 1000 Jefferson Drive, S.W., Washington, D.C. 20560, U.S.A.

Recipients include: Alan B. Shepard, Jr. (1964); Wernher von Braun (1967); Samuel Phillips (1971); James Webb (1976); Grover Loening (1976).

Irving Langmuir Prize in Chemical Physics

Established in 1964 by the General Electric Foundation as a memorial to, and in recognition of the accomplishments of Irving Langmuir, the prize is intended to recognize and encourage outstanding interdisciplinary research in chemistry and physics in the spirit of Irving Langmuir. It is awarded to one person who has made an outstanding contribution in the fields of physical chemistry or chemical physics within the ten years prior to the award. The recipient must be a citizen of the U.S.A. at the time of selection and the prize money must be spent in the U.S.A. or its possessions. In even-numbered years, the American Chemical Society selects the prize-winner and presents the prize. In odd-numbered years, the American Physical Society does so. The prize consists of $5,000 and a certificate citing the contributions made by the recipient; an allowance is provided for travelling expenses incurred in attending the General Meeting of the Society at which the prize is bestowed.

Awarding bodies: American Physical Society, 335 East 45th St., New York, N.Y. 10017; American Chemical Society, 1155 16th St., N.W., Washington, D.C. 20036, U.S.A.

Recipients include: Peter M. Rentzepis (1973); Harry G. Drickamer (1974); Robert H. Cole (1975); John S. Waugh (1976); Aneesur Rahman (1977).

Karl Spencer Lashley Prize

The Lashley Fund was established in 1957 with the gift of $65,000 from Mr. Lashley to the American Philosophical Society. The income is used for an award (currently $2,000) to be made from time to time in recognition of useful and significant work in the field of neurobiology.

Awarding body: American Philosophical Society, 104 South Fifth St., Philadelphia, Pa. 19106, U.S.A.

Recipients include: János Szentágothai (Hungary, 1973); Vernon B. Mountcastle, Jr. (U.S.A., 1974); Paul Weiss (U.S.A., 1975); Roger W. Sperry (U.S.A., 1976); David H. Hubel and Torsten N. Wiesel (U.S.A., 1977).

James Laurie Prize

The prize was established in 1912 by the American Society of Civil Engineers in honour of its first President; from this date until 1965 it was awarded under the rules of the Thomas Fitch Rowland Prize (*q.v.*) for the paper judged to be next in order of merit. From 1966 the prize has been awarded for contributions to transportation engineering. The contribution may be in written form or through notable performance or actions which have served to advance transportation engineering. The prize consists of a plaque and certificate; no one may receive it more than once.

Awarding body: American Society of Civil Engineers, 345 East 47th St., New York, N.Y. 10017, U.S.A.

Recipients include: Donald S. Berry (1972); Robert W. Brannan (1973); William A. Bugge (1974); Thomas M. Sullivan (1975); John Veerling (role in directing the planning, design and construction of airports in New Jersey/New York, 1976).

Lauro D'Oro Tiberino (*Tiberine Golden Laurel*)

This award, consisting of a golden laurel wreath and diploma, is made annually by the Accademia Tiberina in Rome in recognition of some distinguished scientific, literary, artistic or social achievement. It was established in 1960.

Awarding body: Accademia Tiberina – Istituto di Cultura Universitaria e di Studi Superiori, Via del Vantaggio 22, 00186 Rome, Italy.

Recipients include: Gen. Domenico Furbini (economist and jurist, Italy); Prof. ing. dr. Giovanni Colamarino (electrical engineer, Italy); Prof. dott. Karl von Frisch (bacteriologist, Fed. Rep. of Germany); Prof. Marino Moretti (writer and poet, Italy); Giovanni Omiccioli (painter, Italy).

Alphonse Laveran Gold Medal

This award was established in 1927 by the French Society of Exotic Pathology, in memory of its founder, Alphonse Laveran. It is given every two years alternately to a Frenchman and an Englishman for work overseas in the field of exotic pathology.

Awarding body: Société de Pathologie Exotique, Institut Pasteur, 25 rue du Docteur Roux, 75015 Paris, France.

Recipients include: M. Montel (1964); A. Dubois (1966); M. Vaucel (1968); P. C. C. Garnham (1971); F. Blanc (1977).

Ernest Orlando Lawrence Memorial Awards

These awards were established in 1959 in memory of the late Dr. Lawrence, the inventor of the cyclotron, and are given for recent work in any of the following scientific fields related to atomic energy: reactors, chemistry and metallurgy, life sciences, physics, national security. Not more than five awards are made in any one year and each winner receives $5,000 and a citation. Candidates must be American citizens and preference is given to young scientists (not more than 45 years old). Nominations are invited from members of the National Academy of Sciences, officers of scientific and technical societies whose interests are related to fields in which the award is to be granted, and other individuals with special knowledge and competence.

Awarding body: Energy Research and Development Administration, 20 Massachusetts Ave., N.W., Washington, D.C. 20545, U.S.A.

Recipients include: A. Philip Bray (thermal and hydraulic phenomenon associated with boiling water reactors), James W. Cronin (major experimental contributions to particle physics), Kaye D. Lathrop (outstanding contributions to nuclear reactor theory), Adolphus L. Lotts (leadership and innovative contributions to the development of the thorium 233-uranium fuel cycle), Edwin D. McClanahan (significant contributions to nuclear weapons metallurgy and fabrication technology), 1976.

Lázár Deák Memorial Medal

The award was established in 1958 by the Hungarian Geodesy and Cartography Society in memory of Deák Lázár. Two medals are awarded annually for outstanding work in the Society's field of activity.

Awarding body: Geodéziai és Kartográfiai Egyesület, Budapest VI, Anker-köz 1, Hungary.

Gheorghe Lazăr Prize

The Romanian Academy established this prize in 1948 for mathematics or astronomy. It is presented annually at a General Assembly of the Academy, and consists of 10,000 lei and a diploma. It is named after Gheorghe Lazăr (1779–1823), scholar of the Enlightenment, who first taught in the national language in Wallachia, and who contributed to the creation of scientific and technological terminology in the Romanian language.

Awarding body: Academy of the S.R. of Romania, 125 Calea Victoriei, Bucharest, Romania.

Adolf-Ledebur-Denkmünze

This prize, a bronze medal, was established in 1934 by the German Society of Foundry Engineers in memory of Adolf Ledebur for his contributions to the technical development of foundry engineering. It is awarded for outstanding services to the Society and for contributions in the field of foundry engineering.

Awarding body: Verein Deutscher Giessereifachleute, 4 Düsseldorf, Sohnstr. 70, Federal Republic of Germany.

Recipients include: Prof. Dr.-Ing. Karl Roesch (1965); Prof. Dr.-Ing. Rudolf Spolders (1968); Prof. Dr.-Ing. Günther Schwietzke (1969); Otto Paes (1973); Prof. Dr.-Ing. Philipp Schneider (1975).

Leah Lederman Lecture

A lecturer is appointed every two years to lecture on a subject connected with cancer of the breast or female genital tract. He receives an honorarium.

Awarding body: The Royal Society of Medicine, 1 Wimpole St., London W1M 8AE, England.

Leeds International Pianoforte Competition

This triennial competition was established in 1963 by the Leeds International Pianoforte Competition Committee. It is open to professional pianists of all nationalities under the age of 30 on 1 September of the year of the competition. The first prize is the Princess Mary Gold Medal and

£750. Nineteen other cash prizes are awarded, and winners carry out over 50 engagements in eight countries. The last competition was in September 1978.

Awarding body: Leeds International Pianoforte Competition, c/o The Bursar's Dept., University of Leeds, Leeds LS2 9JT, England.

Recipients include: Rafael Orozco (Spain, 1966); Radu Lupu (Romania, 1969); Murray Perahia (U.S.A., 1972); Dmitry Alexeev (U.S.S.R., 1975); Michel Dalberto (France, 1978).

Leeds National Musicians' Platform

This occasion provides an opportunity for young professional singers and instrumentalists to give public recitals before interested parties, and is open to solo singers, instrumentalists and ensembles of not more than four players (solo pianists are not eligible). They should be of British nationality or resident in the U.K., under 30 years of age, and should have studied in this country. Organized by the Leeds International Pianoforte Competition (*q.v.*), the Platform was started in 1974, and is held every three years. After preliminary auditions 24 participants are selected for the Leeds Platform Recitals, for which they receive £40 each, and the finalists take part in the Leeds Platform Final Concert for a further fee of £60 each. Two further awards up to a total of £300 may be given. Many performers are offered professional engagements.

Awarding body: Leeds International Pianoforte Competition, c/o The Bursar's Dept., University of Leeds, Leeds LS2 9JT, England.

Finalists include: Michael Bochman (violin), Robert Bramley (clarinet), Anne-Marie Connors (soprano), Lawrence Foster (cello), Peter Knapp (baritone), Graham Salter (oboe), Graham Titus (baritone), 1974.

Leeuwenhoek Lecture

The George Gabb Fund was established in 1948 by a bequest of £1,000 from Mr. George Gabb to the Royal Society. It is for an annual lecture in the field of microbiology which is named after Antony van Leeuwenhoek, F.R.S. (1632–1723), the Dutch microbiologist. The fee paid to the lecturer is £100.

Awarding body: Royal Society of London, 6 Carlton House Terrace, London SW1Y 5AG, England.

Lecturers include: Dr. Aaron Klug (1973); Dr. Renato Dulbecco (1974); Prof. Joel Mandelstam (1975).

Leeuwenhoek Medal

The Royal Netherlands Academy of Arts and Sciences founded this gold medal in 1875 to commemorate Antonie van Leeuwenhoek (1632–1723), the Dutch microbiologist. The medal is awarded every ten years to a scientist of any nationality for research in the field of microscopic organisms.

Awarding body: Koninklijke Nederlandse Akademie van Wetenschappen, Kloveniersburgwal 29, 1011 JV Amsterdam, The Netherlands.

Recipients include: Selman A. Waksman (U.S.A., 1950); André Lwoff (France, 1960); C. B. van Niel (U.S.A., 1970).

Wilhelm-Lehmbruck-Preis der Stadt Duisburg (*Wilhelm Lehmbruck Prize of the City of Duisburg*)

This prize was established in 1964 by the city of Duisburg in memory of Wilhelm Lehmbruck (1881–1919), the sculptor, who was born in Duisburg-Meiderich. A cash prize of DM20,000 is awarded every five years in recognition of an internationally renowned work by a sculptor of any age or nationality.

Awarding body: Dezernat für Kultur und Bildung der Stadt Duisburg, Rathaus, 4100 Duisburg 1, Federal Republic of Germany.

Recipients: Eduardo Chillida (Spain, 1965); Norbert Kricke (Fed. Rep. of Germany, 1970); Jean Tinguely (1975).

A. E. Leighton Memorial Award

The award was established in 1965 by the Royal Australian Chemical Institute and Miss Anne Leighton in memory of her father, Arthur Edgar Leighton (1873–1961), President of the Institute in 1953. A medal is awarded annually for an outstanding contribution to chemistry. The award is made irrespective of nationality or membership of the Institute.

Awarding body: The Royal Australian Chemical Institute, Clunies Ross House, 191 Royal Parade, Parkville, Vic. 3052, Australia.

Eugen-Lendholt-Denkmünze

This medal is presented by the West German Association of Pulp and Paper Chemists and Engineers (Zellcheming) for outstanding scientific or technical achievements in the sodium and sulphate pulp and paper industry. It was instituted in 1957 by Zellcheming and the Kraft Paper Association in honour of the late Eugen Lendholt's fifty years in the industry. Nominations must be made by members of Zellcheming.

Awarding body: Verein der Zellstoff- und Papier-Chemiker und Ingenieure, 6100 Darmstadt, Berliner Allee 56, Federal Republic of Germany.

Recipients include: Dir. Eugen Lendholt (1957); Dir. Ernst Laubscher (1963); Dr.-Ing. Friedrich Burgstaller (1968); Erich P. Petermann (1973).

Lenin State Prizes

These prizes are awarded every two years to Soviet citizens on the anniversary of Lenin's birth. They are given for outstanding achievements in all branches of science, technology and the arts.

Awarding body: Committee for Lenin State Prizes, Presidium of the Supreme Soviet of the U.S.S.R., Ul. Neglinnaya 15, Moscow, U.S.S.R.

Recipients include: Aleksandr Chakovsky (literature), Maksim Tank (literature), Acad. Nikolai Tsitsin (agriculture), Acad. Vladimir Platonov (mathematics), Acad. Mikhail Krasnov (medicine), 1978.

Peter-Joseph-Lenné-Preis

This award, which consists of a cash prize of DM6,000, was established by Dr. Peter Joseph Lenné, General Director of the Royal Gardens in West Berlin. It is presented annually by the Senate of West Berlin, and is intended to provide a stimulus and opportunity to young planners and scientists to solve problems in the developing of landscape and open spaces, and to promote progressive thought in this area. Both individuals and groups are eligible, provided none of the participants is over 40 years of age.

Awarding body: Der Senat von Berlin, Senatskanzlei, 1000 Berlin 62, John-F.-Kennedy-Platz, Federal Republic of Germany.

Lentz International Peace Research Award

The award was established in 1973 by friends of the late Dr. Theodore F. Lentz (1888–1976), who founded the Peace Research Laboratory, to honour those who have made an outstanding contribution to the field of Peace Research, through either their research work or organizational activities. A sculpture, created specially for the award, and a cheque for $1,000 are presented annually; anyone concerned with peace research anywhere is eligible, but the recipient must be nominated for the award.

Awarding body: Peace Research Laboratory, 438 N. Skinker Blvd., St. Louis, Mo. 63130, U.S.A.; nominations to Arun K. Mitra, LIPRA, 270 Radcliffe Ave., St. Louis, Mo. 63130, U.S.A.

Recipients include: Dr. Bert V. A. Roling (Polemologisch, Netherlands, 1973); Dr. Hanna Newcombe and Dr. Alan Newcombe (Canadian Peace Research Inst., 1974); Dr. Anatol Rapoport (Univ. of Toronto, Canada, 1975).

Aldo Leopold Award

Founded in 1949, the award is in memory of Aldo Leopold (1886–1948), founder of the science and art of wildlife management. The award is given for distinguished service to wildlife conservation to a candidate considered to be entirely worthy; it is the highest honour bestowed by the Wildlife Society. The winner receives a bronze medal and automatic honorary membership of the Society. The award is made annually.

Awarding body: The Wildlife Society, 7101 Wisconsin Ave., Suite 611, Washington, D.C. 20014, U.S.A.

Recipients include: Joseph J. Hickey (1972); Gustav A. Swanson (1973); Lucille F. Stickel (1974); Russell E. Train (1975); John S. Gottschalk (1976).

Ian Murray Leslie Awards

The awards scheme was introduced in 1977 by the Institute of Building to encourage development of the communication skills of its members, and to facilitate the exchange of knowledge, thereby benefiting the industry at large. The scheme is named after Mr. Ian Murray Leslie, Honorary Fellow of the Institute, and editor of *Building* for many years. Entries must be unpublished and have as a theme a subject related to building technology, building economics, building management or education and training for building. Three awards are confined to members of the Institute: a prize of £100 and a silver medal is awarded for the best paper submitted; a prize of £50 and a bronze medal is awarded for the best paper by a member under 30; a prize of £50 and a bronze medal is awarded for the best paper by a non-corporate member. There is also an open award of £50 and a bronze medal for the best paper by a non-member on a given topic.

Awarding body: The Institute of Building, Englemere, Kings Ride, Ascot, Berks. SL5 8BJ, England.

Lesmüller-Medaille

This prize was established in 1949 by the Association of German Chambers of Pharmacists on the occasion of the 75th birthday of Max Lesmüller (1874–1952), then President of the Bavarian Chambers of Pharmacists, in recognition of his services to pharmacy in Germany and particularly in Bavaria. The prize is awarded annually to a pharmacist for services to German pharmacy. It consists of a medal and a certificate.

Awarding body: Arbeitsgemeinschaft der Berufsvertretungen Deutscher Apotheker, 6000 Frankfurt am Main, Beethovenplatz 1, Federal Republic of Germany.

Recipients include: Dr. Helmut Häussermann (1969); Dr. Hans Klingmüller (1970); Hugo Friedrich-Sander (1971); Jakob Kranzfelder and Erwin Schmidt (1972); Jobst Mielck (1973).

Lessing-Preis für Literatur (*Lessing Prize for Literature*)

The prize was established in 1929 by the city council of Hamburg on the occasion of the 200th anniversary of the birth of the German writer and dramatist Gotthold Ephraim Lessing (1729–81). Poets, writers and scholars who belong to the German Cultural Circle may be selected for the award. Exceptionally, however, in recognition of literary achievements which are of particular significance to Hamburg, the prize may be awarded to someone outside the German Cultural Circle. The prize of DM15,000 is awarded every three years, and is presented if possible on 22 January, the anniversary of Lessing's birthday.

Awarding body: Senat der Freien und Hansestadt Hamburg, 2 Hamburg 1, Rathaus, Federal Republic of Germany.

Leverhulme Medal

In 1960 the Trustees of the Leverhulme Trust Fund expressed a desire to mark the occasion of the tercentenary of the Royal Society by the award of a gold medal. It is awarded by the Society every three years to the individual who, in the opinion of its Council, shall have made the most significant contribution in the field of pure or applied chemistry or engineering, including chemical engineering. The medal is accompanied by a monetary award of £500.

Awarding body: Royal Society of London, 6 Carlton House Terrace, London SW1Y 5AG, England.

Recipients include: Hans Kronberger (1969); Dr. J. B. Adams (1972); Dr. F. L. Rose (1975).

Bernard Lewis Medal

Established in 1958 by the Combustion Institute, this biennial award is given for brilliant research in the field of combustion, particularly on kinetics and combustion waves. It is presented at the Institute's International Symposium.

Awarding body: The Combustion Institute, 986 Union Trust Building, Pittsburgh, Pa. 15219, U.S.A.

Recipients include: Dr. Guenther von Elbe (U.S.A., 1976).

John F. Lewis Prize

The prize was established in 1935 by the gift of $10,000 to the American Philosophical Society from Mrs. John F. Lewis in memory of her husband. The income (currently $300) is used annually as an award to the American citizen who shall announce at any general or special meeting of the Society, and publish among its papers some truth which the Council of the Society shall deem worthy of the award.

Awarding body: American Philosophical Society, 104 South Fifth St., Philadelphia, Pa. 19106, U.S.A.

Recipients include: Neal A. Weber ('Gardening Ants, the Attines', 1973); George Kennan ('The Historiography of the Early Political Career of Stalin', 1974); Frederick A. Pottle ('Wordsworth in the Present Day', 1975); Owen Gingerich ('From Copernicus to Kepler', 1976); Choh Hao Li ('Hormones of the Anterior Pituitary', 1977).

Warren K. Lewis Award for Contributions to Chemical Engineering Education

This award is sponsored by Exxon International Company and Exxon Research and Engineering Company, and consists of a certificate and $2,000. It is generally made annually. It is given by the American Institute of Chemical Engineers to an individual, who need not be a member of the Institute, who has made distinguished and continuing contributions to education in that field. Factors to be taken into account include success as a teacher; the compilation of educational aids such as lectures, textbooks and laboratory techniques; creative ability evidenced in literature, inventions, work in industry or government, or consultancy; the administration of a department or equivalent group which has made similar contributions.

Awarding body: American Institute of Chemical Engineers, 345 East 47th St., New York, N.Y. 10017, U.S.A.

Erich Lexer-Preis

This award is sponsored by the company Ethicon GmbH, Norderstedt, and is made annually to a surgeon of any nationality for studies in the area of reconstructive surgery. It takes the form of a silver medal and cash prize of DM10,000. It is awarded alternately by the German Surgical Society and the German Society for Orthopaedics and Traumatology.

Awarding body: Deutsche Gesellschaft für Chirurgie, 1000 Berlin 15, Kurfürstendamm 179, Federal Republic of Germany.

Recipients include: Prof. O. Hilgenfeldt (Fed. Rep. of Germany, 1973); Prof. Max Lange (Fed. Rep. of Germany) and Prof. Peter-Friedrich Matzen (German Dem. Rep.), 1974; Dr. Gerhard Stellbrink (Fed. Rep. of Germany, 1975); Prof. Dr. A. N. Witt (Fed. Rep. of Germany, 1976).

Lichtwark-Preis für bildende Kunst (*Lichtwark Prize for Fine Art*)

Established in 1951 by the city council and parliament of Hamburg, the prize marks the occasion of the 100th anniversary of the birth of Alfred Lichtwark, who was director of the museum of art in Hamburg (Hamburger Kunsthalle) from 1886 to 1914. The prize is awarded to painters, graphic artists or sculptors selected because their work has brought originality to present-day fine arts. Recipients should belong to the German Cultural Circle, but the prize may exceptionally be awarded to a non-member in recognition of artistic achievements which have some particular significance for Hamburg. The prize of DM15,000 is awarded every three years, and is presented if possible on 14 November, anniversary of the birthday of Alfred Lichtwark.

Awarding body: Senat der Freien und Hansestadt Hamburg, 2 Hamburg 1, Rathaus, Federal Republic of Germany.

Liebig-Denkmünze

This medal was established by the Association of German Chemists in 1903, the 100th anniversary of the birth of the great German chemist, Justus von Liebig, and awarded by the Association until 1940 for outstanding achievements by German chemists. In 1950 the Society of German Chemists, founded in 1946, took over the award. The medal is silver, and bears on the obverse the profile of Liebig and commemorative wording. There is a classical scene on the reverse. The medal is presented at the Society's annual general meeting. A sum of money is also part of the award.

Awarding body: Gesellschaft Deutscher Chemiker, 6000 Frankfurt (Main) 90, Carl Bosch-Haus, Varrentrappstr. 40–42, Federal Republic of Germany.

Recipients include: Prof. Erich Thilo (1967); Prof. Oskar Glemser (1970); Prof. Hans Werner Kuhn (1972); Prof. Leopold Horner (1973); Prof. Horst Pommer (1976).

Justus von Liebig Prize

This is one of many awards given by the FVS Foundation in Hamburg for contributions by Europeans to various aspects of cultural and scientific life. The Justus von Liebig Prize is given annually for services to agriculture, either in a practical way, or by scientific and technical work. The prize money amounts to DM20,000. Justus von Liebig (1803–73) was a German chemist, famous for his work in organic chemistry.

Awarding body: Stiftung FVS, Georgsplatz 10, 2 Hamburg 1, Federal Republic of Germany.

Recipients include: Klaus Kleeberg (Fed. Rep. of Germany) and Prof. Dr. Harald Skjervold (Norway), 1972.

Lilienthal Medal

This award is made for a remarkable performance in gliding, or for eminent services over a long period on behalf of gliding.

Awarding body: Fédération Aéronautique Internationale, 6 rue Galilée, Paris 16, France.

Recipients include: Adela Dankowska (Poland, 1975).

Eric Liljencrantz Award

This prize was established by the Aerospace Medical Association in memory of Commander Eric Liljencrantz, whose career in aviation medicine was cut short by his death in an aeroplane accident in 1942. It is given annually in May for basic research into the problems of acceleration and altitude. The prize is sponsored by Smith Kline & French Laboratories, and consists of $500 and a certificate.

Awarding body: Aerospace Medical Association, Washington National Airport, Washington, D.C. 20001, U.S.A.

Recipients include: Capt. Marvin D. Courtney (1972); Dr. Adolf P. Gagge (1973); Commander Donald J. Sass (1974); Wing Commander John Ernsting (1975); Dr. Ulrich C. Luft (1976).

T. Y. Lin Award

This award was established as the ASCE Prestressed Concrete Award in 1968, endowed by T. Y. Lin, F.ASCE, and was changed in 1969 to the T. Y. Lin Award. It consists of a wall plaque, a certificate and a cash prize of $500. It is awarded to the best paper written by a member of the ASCE or one of its Student Chapters which deals with prestressed concrete. Preference is given to younger authors. The American Concrete Institute and the Prestressed Concrete Institute each nominate one paper selected from their respective publications, and the Structural Division of ASCE nominates one paper from any ASCE publication.

Awarding body: American Society for Civil Engineers, 345 East 47th St., New York, N.Y. 10017, U.S.A.

Recipients include: Raouf Sinno and Howard L. Furr ('Computer Program for Predicting Prestress Loss and Camber', 1974); Paul Zia and W. D. McGee ('Torsion Design of Prestressed Concrete', 1975); Maher K. Tadros, Amin Ghali and Walter H. Dilger ('Time-Dependant Prestress Loss and Deflection in Prestressed Concrete Members', 1976).

Linacre Lecture

The lecture was endowed by Thomas Linacre (born 1460), first President of the Royal College of Physicians, and Physician to Henry VIII. It was reconstituted on an annual basis in 1908. A stipend of £150 is awarded, and the lecturer appointed is a scientist distinguished for his work in the life sciences.

Awarding body: St. John's College, Cambridge, CB2 1TP, England.

Lecturers include: Prof. E. F. Gale ('Perspectives in Chemotherapy', 1973); Rt. Hon. Lord Todd ('Science, Medicine and Society', 1974); Prof. R. R. Porter ('Immunity to Infection', 1975); Prof. Sir Richard Doll ('The Prevention of Cancer', 1976); Prof. Sir Frank Young (1977).

Linden-Medaille

This gold medal is awarded occasionally by the Stuttgart Geographical and Ethnological Society for outstanding achievements in the field of geography. It was established in 1907 under the Society's former title, Württembergischer Verein für Handelsgeographie e.V., to commemorate its 25th anniversary. The medal is named in memory of Graf Karl von Linden, former Chairman of the Society.

Awarding body: Gesellschaft für Erd- und Völkerkunde zu Stuttgart e.V., Stuttgart, Federal Republic of Germany.

Recipients: Graf Karl von Linden; Dr. med. Albert Tafel; Friedrich von Eckstein; Theodor G. Wanner.

Max-Lingner-Preis

This prize was established in 1973 with an endowment from the family of the artist, Max Lingner (1888–1959). It is awarded biennially by the Academy of Arts of the German Democratic Republic to individuals or a group whose work makes a significant contribution to the development of socialist art as defined by Max Lingner, either through encouragement, popularization and research, or by means of creative work in the fields of painting, graphics and aesthetics. The award consists of a certificate and a cash prize.

Awarding body: Akademie der Künste der DDR, 104 Berlin, Hermann-Matern-Strasse 58/59, German Democratic Republic.

Recipients include: Nuria Quevedo (1973); Ingo Bach (1976).

Lister Medal

This bronze medal is given triennially, irrespective of nationality, in recognition of distinguished contributions to surgical science. The recipient is required to give an address in London under the auspices of the Royal College of Surgeons; there is an honorarium of £500. The award was established by public subscription as a mark of lasting respect to the memory of the Rt. Hon. Lord Lister, O.M., F.R.S., F.R.C.S., and in grateful appreciation of his eminent services to the science of surgery and the signal benefit thereby conferred on mankind. The fund has been administered by the Royal College of Surgeons since 1920.

Awarding body: The Royal College of Surgeons of England, 35–43 Lincoln's Inn Fields, London WC2A 3PN, England.

Recipients include: Sir Charles Frederic William Illingworth, C.B.E. (1963); The Lord Brock (1966); Sir Michael Francis Addison Woodruff (1969); John Webster Kirklin (1972); John Charnley, C.B.E. (1975).

Liszt Prize

The Liszt Society, which exists to promote knowledge and appreciation of the works and ideals of the composer and pianist Franz Liszt (1811–86), sponsors the British Liszt Piano Competition to give young pianists an opportunity to explore the repertoire of Liszt's works. Competitors must be under 31 years old. Prizes are given in various categories; the first prize (Liszt Prize) consists of a cash sum ($£500$ in 1976) and a diploma; the winner also receives a series of concert and recital engagements. The competition was held first in 1961, and subsequently in 1968 and 1976.

Awarding body: The Liszt Society Ltd., c/o Alan Paul, 59 Leopold Rd., London SW19 7JG, England.

Recipients include: John Ogdon (1961); John Owings (1968); Terence Judd (1976).

Liszt Ferenc Prize for Musical Recital

Instituted by the Hungarian Council of Ministers in 1953, the prize is awarded annually by the Minister of Culture. It is an honorary distinction, divided into three classes, and bestowed on outstanding musical performers. It is named in honour of Liszt (1811–86), the outstanding Hungarian composer and piano virtuoso.

Awarding body: Committee for the Liszt Prize, Ministry of Culture, Szalay-utca 10, Budapest V, Hungary.

Recipients include: Ferenc Béres (singer), Ádám Medveczky (conductor, State Opera House), Sylvia Sass (singer, State Opera House), 1976.

Liversidge Lectureship

The Liversidge Lectureship was founded in 1927 to commemorate the name of Professor Archibald Liversidge (1847–1927), a benefactor of the Chemical Society. In accordance with the terms of the bequest, the lecture should deal as far as practicable with the description of new knowledge, and the lecturer should point out the directions in which further research in general, physical, and inorganic chemistry is desirable. The lecture is delivered in alternate years, and the lecturer receives a silver medal and $£100$.

Awarding body: The Chemical Society, Burlington House, London W1V 0BN, England.

Recipients include: Sir George Porter (1969–70); J. Chatt (1971–72); R. P. Bell (1973–74); C. C. Addison (1975–76); J. S. Rowlinson (1977–78).

Liversidge Research Lectureship

This lectureship, first awarded in 1930, was established by the Australasian Association for the Advancement of Science, forerunner of the Aus-

tralian and New Zealand Association for the Advancement of Science (ANZAAS), in accordance with the will of the late Professor Archibald Liversidge (1847–1927), first holder of a chair of chemistry in Australia, at Sydney University. He had been professor of geology at the same university, and in a wide-ranging career he paid particular attention to metallurgy and the study of minerals. The person appointed as lecturer is chosen for his distinguished contributions to chemistry in accordance with Professor Liversidge's will: 'The lectures shall be upon recent researches and discoveries, and the most important part of the Lecturer's duty shall be to point in which direction further researches are necessary and how he thinks they can best be carried out.' The lecturer receives a fee of $50 from the Lectureship Fund, and the lecture is published in the ANZAAS journal *Search*.

Awarding body: Australian and New Zealand Association for the Advancement of Science, 15 Gloucester St., Sydney, N.S.W. 2000, Australia.

Recipients include: N. S. Bayliss ('Complexes in Solution', 1972); A. J. Parker ('Hydrometallurgy of Copper and Silver in Solvent Mixtures', 1973); R. W. Rickards ('Chemistry and Micro-organisms', 1975); L. E. Lyons ('Some Photoelectric Effects in Organic Solids', 1976); Dr. D. H. Solomon ('Minerals, Macromolecules and Man', 1977).

David Livingstone Centenary Medal

This award was established in 1913 to commemorate the centenary of the birth of David Livingstone, the famous explorer. A gold, silver or bronze medal is given intermittently for scientific achievement in the field of geography of the southern hemisphere.

Awarding body: American Geographical Society, Broadway at 156th St., New York, N.Y. 10032, U.S.A.

Recipients include: William Edward Rudolph (1959); Bassett McGuire (1965); Preston E. James (1966); William H. Phelps, Jr. (1968); Akin L. Mabogunje (1972).

Lloyd Roberts Lecture

A lecturer is chosen yearly, in turn by the Royal College of Physicians, the Medical Society of London and the Royal Society of Medicine. He receives an honorarium.

Awarding body: The Royal Society of Medicine, 1 Wimpole St., London W1M 8AE, England.

Locarno International Film Festival

The festival is held annually in August, and is recognized by the International Federation of Film Producers Associations (IFFPA). It is subsidized by the Swiss Federal Government and the Canton of Ticino. Its purpose is to provide a forum for innovations in stylistic or thematic perspective leading to freer cinematic expression, in particular for the alternatives proposed by new directors and young national film industries. Feature-length fiction films which have been completed and screened within the past twelve months and have no previously been shown in Switzerland or gained an award at a festival recognized by the IFFPA are eligible. The International Jury awards the Golden Leopard Grand Prix for the best film, and the Ernest Artaria Prize, in memory of the Swiss cameraman (1926–71), for outstanding technical achievement contributing to the success of one of the films shown. They may also award a Silver Leopard special prize for an outstanding first or second film or one produced by a young film industry, and a Jury Grand Prix of a Bronze Leopard to an outstanding director or actor. The Ecumenical, Youth and FIPRESCI (International Federation of Film Critics) Juries may also present awards.

Awarding body: Société Suisse des Festivals Internationaux de Cinéma, Case postale 98, 1260 Nyon, Switzerland.

Grand Prix recipients include: Krzysztof Zanussi (Poland, *Iluminacja*, 1973); Istvan Szabo (Hungary, *Tuzolto Utca 25*, 1974); Jean-Jacques Adrien (Belgium, *Le Fils d'Amr est Mort*, 1975); Francis Reusser (Switzerland, *Le Grand Soir*, 1976).

Logie Award

Founded in 1958 by the Australian magazine *TV Week*, the award is named in memory of John Logie Baird, inventor of television. Two gold statuettes are awarded annually for the best Australian male and female personalities. Other awards are given for distinction in various categories: most popular actor and actress, most popular show, etc.; special awards are given in addition for the best script in various categories, best news report, best documentary, etc.

Awarding body: TV Week, 32 Walsh St., West Melbourne, Vic. 3003, Australia.

Recipients include: Jeanne Little (best female personality, 1977); Don Lane (best male personality, 1977).

Russell Loines Award for Poetry

This award is given periodically to an American or British poet in recognition of merit, preferably not widely recognized. It is given by the National Institute of Arts and Letters under the terms of the Russell Loines Memorial Fund which is administered by the Institute. The award consists of a cash prize of $2,500.

Awarding body: American Academy and Institute of Arts and Letters, 633 West 155th St., New York, N.Y. 10032, U.S.A.

Adolph Lomb Medal

Adolph Lomb was the Treasurer of the Optical Society of America from its foundation until his death in 1932. In recognition of his devotion to the interests of the Society and the advancement of optics, the Adolph Lomb Memorial Fund was established, and in 1940 as a result of this the Adolph Lomb Medal was founded. The award consists of a silver medal and a citation, and is presented biennially to a person who has made a noteworthy contribution to optics published before he or she has reached the age of 30, and

who has not reached the age of 32 on 1 January of the award year.

Awarding body: Optical Society of America, 2000 L St., N.W., Suite 620, Washington, D.C. 20036, U.S.A.

Recipients include: Dr. Douglas C. Sinclair (1968); Dr. Marlan O. Scully (1970); Dr. Robert L. Byer (1972); Dr. James Forsyth (1974); Dr. Marc D. Levenson (1976).

Raymond F. Longacre Award

This prize was established by the Aerospace Medical Association to honour the memory of Maj. Raymond F. Longacre, M.C. It is given annually in May for outstanding accomplishment in the psychological and psychiatric aspects of aerospace medicine. It consists of $500 and a trophy.

Awarding body: Aerospace Medical Association, Washington National Airport, Washington, D.C. 20001, U.S.A.

Recipients include: Rosalie K. Ambler (1972); Dr. Claude J. Blanc (1973); Dr. Herbert C. Haynes (1974); Alan J. Benson (1975); Dr. W. Dean Chiles (1976).

Longstaff Medal

The Longstaff Medal, first awarded in 1881, was instituted to commemorate the name of Dr. George Dixon Longstaff, an original Fellow and benefactor of the Chemical Society. In accordance with the terms of the bequest the medal is awarded every three years to the Fellow of the Society who, in the opinion of the Council, has done the most to promote the science of chemistry by research. The bronze medal is accompanied by a monetary prize of £100.

Awarding body: The Chemical Society, Burlington House, London W1V 0BN, England.

Recipients include: J. Monteath Robertson (1966); R. G. W. Norrish (1969); Sir Derek Barton (1972); J. S. Anderson (1975).

Edward Longstreth Medal

This silver medal is awarded for inventions of high order and for particularly meritorious improvements and developments in machines and mechanical processes. It was founded in 1890 by Mr. Edward Longstreth of Philadelphia.

Awarding body: The Franklin Institute, Benjamin Franklin Parkway at 20th St., Philadelphia, Pa. 19103, U.S.A.

Recipients include: Samuel Ruben (mercuric-oxide zinc battery, 1972); Gerhard W. Goetze (secondary electron conduction tube, 1973); Edward S. Bristol (automatic control system to balance boiler inputs against electric power demands, 1975); Walter L. Bond (contributions to crystallography, 1976); Norris Fitz Dow (inventor of extra-strong triaxial fabric, 1977).

Clive Lord Memorial Medal

This award, established in 1930 in honour of Clive Lord (1889–1933), Director of the Tasmanian Museum (1917–33), is made every three years.

The recipient delivers the Clive Lord Memorial Lecture. There are no restrictions on eligibility.

Awarding body: Royal Society of Tasmania, G.P.O. Box 1166M, Hobart, Tasmania 7001, Australia.

Recipients include: J. Burke (1951); P. G. Law (1958); V. V. Hickman (1960); W. M. Curtis (1966); W. Bryden (1976).

Lorentz Medal

The Royal Netherlands Academy of Arts and Sciences founded this gold medal in 1926 in honour of Professor H. A. Lorentz (1853–1928), the physicist and Nobel prize-winner. It is awarded every four years to a scientist of any nationality for achievement in the field of theoretical physics.

Awarding body: Koninklijke Nederlandse Akademie van Wetenschappen, Kloveniersburgwal 29, 1011 JV Amsterdam, The Netherlands.

Recipients include: R. E. Peierls (U.K., 1962); Freeman J. Dyson (U.S.A., 1966); G. E. Uhlenbeck (U.S.A., 1970); J. H. van Vleck (U.S.A., 1974); N. Bloembergen (U.S.A., 1978).

Josef Loschmidt-Medaille

This award is presented by the Austrian Chemical Society in memory of Josef Loschmidt (1821–95) who established the Loschmidt Number. It recognizes distinguished contributions to the field of chemistry. It is given annually, and consists of a medal and certificate.

Awarding body: Verein Österreichischer Chemiker, 1010 Vienna, Eschenbachgasse 9, Austria.

Recipients include: Otto Kratky (1968); Hans Nowotny (1972).

Losey Atmospheric Sciences Award

In 1940 the Robert M. Losey Award was established in memory of Captain Losey, a meteorological officer who was killed while serving as an observer for the U.S. Army, the first officer to die in the service of the U.S.A. in the second world war. The present title of the award was adopted in 1975. It is presented annually in recognition of outstanding contribution to the science of meteorology as applied to aeronautics. The award comprises a medal and certificate of citation and is usually presented at the Aerospace Sciences Meeting.

Awarding body: American Institute of Aeronautics and Astronautics, 1290 Avenue of the Americas, New York, N.Y. 10019, U.S.A.

Recipients include: Robert Knollenberg (1977).

Loudon Lectureship in Engineering Production

Founded in 1926, the lectureship was endowed by Mr. George F. Loudon, engineer and machine tool maker, of Glasgow, and his wife. The lectureship is attached to the Department of Mechanical Engineering of Glasgow University. The lecturer is required to deliver a course of class lectures of not less than 40 hours and five public lectures on 'Machine Tool Types, the Art of Cutting Metals, and the Methods of Production'.

Awarding body: University of Glasgow, Glasgow G12 8QQ, Scotland.

Lecturers include: M. Fores (Senior Economic Adviser, Dept. of Industry, 1976); Franz Koenigsberger (Emer. Prof. of Machine Tool Engineering, Manchester Univ. Inst. of Science and Technology, 1976); G. Robertson (Scottish Organizer, General and Municipal Workers Union, and Board Member, Scottish Development Agency, 1976); G. L. Reid (Manpower Services Comm., 1977); J. A. Kelly (General Motors, Scotland, Ltd., 1977).

Maurice Lubbock Memorial Lecture

In 1963 the University of Oxford accepted an offer from the Trustees of the Maurice Lubbock Memorial Fund of a sum to be paid to a lecturer invited to speak on a topic related to the industrial applications of engineering science.

Awarding body: University of Oxford, Wellington Square, Oxford OX1 2JD, England.

Lecturers include: C. H. Villiers (Chair. Guinness, Mahon & Co. Ltd., 1971); F. J. M. Laver (Nat. Research Development Corpn., 1974); Prof. J. S. Forrest, F.R.S. (1975).

Anthony F. Lucas Gold Medal

This award is made annually by the American Institute of Mining, Metallurgical and Petroleum Engineers for distinguished achievements in improving the technique and practice of finding or producing petroleum. Candidates of all nationalities are eligible, provided they are proposed by a member of the Institute and have not previously received an Institute award. The medal was established in 1936 by admirers of Captain Anthony Francis Lucas, mining engineer and discoverer of the 'Lucas Gusher' oil well on Spindletop, Texas.

Awarding body: American Institute of Mining, Metallurgical and Petroleum Engineers, Inc., 345 East 47th St., New York, N.Y. 10017, U.S.A.

Recipients include: Albert Geyer Loomis (1972); William Ludwig Horner (1974); Michel Thomas Halbouty (1975); J. Clarence Karcher (1976); Marshall B. Standing (1977).

Carl-Lueg-Denkmünze

This prize, a gold medal, was established in 1903 by the Association of German Iron Metallurgists in honour of Carl Lueg (1833–1905), who was President of the Association for twenty-five years. It is awarded irregularly for outstanding contributions to the science of iron metallurgy.

Awarding body: Verein Deutscher Eisenhüttenleute, 4000 Düsseldorf 1, Breite Strasse 27, Federal Republic of Germany.

Recipients include: Dr.-Ing. Kurt Thomas (1967); Dr.-Ing. Hermann Schenck (1968); Karl Kaup, Dr. Iwan N. Stranski (1972); Ulrich Petersen (1975).

Thomas Ranken Lyle Medal

Established in 1931 by the Australian National Research Council, the medal is now administered by the Australian Academy of Science. It is in memory of Sir Thomas Ranken Lyle, F.R.S., who was Professor of Natural Philosophy at the University of Melbourne from 1889 to 1915 and President of the then National Research Council. A bronze medal is awarded no more frequently than every second year at the Annual General Meeting of the Academy to the living author of such researches in mathematics and physics as may appear to the Council to be most deserving of such honour. The research should have been done in the preceding five years. The award is restricted to workers in Australia, and is by invitation only.

Awarding body: Australian Academy of Science, P.O.B. 783, Canberra City, A.C.T. 2601, Australia.

Recipients include: G. Szekeres (1968); R. Hanbury Brown (1970); H. A. Buchdahl (1975); K. Mahler (1977).

Theodore C. Lyster Award
This award was established by the Aerospace Medical Association to honour the memory of Brigadier General Theodore C. Lyster, the first Chief Surgeon of the Aviation Section of the U.S. Army Signal Corps. It is given for outstanding achievement in the general field of aerospace medicine and is sponsored by the Purdue Frederick Company and the Keith Loring Gentilcore Memorial Fund. It is awarded annually in May and consists of $500 and a trophy.

Awarding body: Aerospace Medical Association, Washington National Airport, Washington, D.C. 20001, U.S.A.

Recipients include: Dr. Joseph P. Pollard (1972); Dr. Andre Allard (1973); Col. Stanley C. White (1974); Dr. Merrill H. Goodwin (1975); Maj. Gen. Heinz S. Fuchs (1976).

M

Macbeth Award

This award is made every two years by the American Inter-Society Color Council in recognition of recent important contributions in the field of colour, including accomplishments related to colour in science, art, industry, education or merchandising; preferably these should have been made within the preceding five to ten years. The award, which takes the form of a medal, was established in 1970 by Norman Macbeth, Jr., in memory of Norman Macbeth (1873–1936), founder of the Macbeth Corporation and pioneer in the use and control of illumination for viewing colour.

Awarding body: Inter-Society Color Council, c/o Dr. Fred W. Billmeyer, Jr., Dept. of Chemistry, Rensselaer Polytechnic Institute, MRC Rm. 217, Troy, N.Y. 12181, U.S.A.

Recipients: Peter C. Goldmark (1972); Midge Wilson (1974); Richard S. Hunter (1976).

R. B. McCallum Memorial Lecture

This annual lecture was established in 1975 by subscriptions of old members of Pembroke College, Oxford. It is in memory of Ronald Buchanan McCallum, Master of Pembroke 1955–67, Fellow 1925–55, and Hon. Fellow 1968–73. The lecturer appointed is required to be a scholar of international repute in the field of political history. An honorarium is awarded.

Awarding body: Pembroke College, Oxford, England.

· *Lecturers include:* J. William Fulbright (fmr. U.S. Senator, Hon. Fellow, Pembroke Coll., and pupil and friend of R. B. McCallum, 1975).

McColvin Medal

The Library Association established this annual medal in 1970 in honour of Lionel Roy McColvin, former City Librarian of Westminster. It is given for an oustanding reference book first published in the U.K. during the preceding year.

Awarding body: The Library Association, 7 Ridgmount St., London WC1E 7AE, England.

Recipients include: W. F. Maunder (ed. *Reviews of United Kingdom Statistical Sources*, 1974); Peter Kennedy (*Folksongs of Britain and Ireland*, 1975); C. G. Allen (*A Manual of European Languages for Librarians*, 1976).

Robert Earll McConnell Award

This award is made annually by the American Institute of Mining, Metallurgical and Petroleum

Engineers for beneficial service to mankind b engineers, whose achievements have advanced th nation's standard of living or replenished i natural resources (e.g., the discovery or develoj ment of a major source of minerals supply). Cai didates of all nationalities are eligible, provide they are proposed by a member of the Institu and have not previously received an Institu award. The award consists of a bronze troph representing the Institute symbol, and was inst tuted in 1968 as the Engineering Achieveme Award, with a donation from the Robert Eai McConnell Foundation. It was renamed in 197 following the death of Mr. McConnell, a prom nent mining engineer and financier.

Awarding body: American Institute of Minin; Metallurgical and Petroleum Engineers, Inc., 3 East 47th St., New York, N.Y. 10017, U.S.A.

Recipients include: Maurice Ewing (1973); C. Pa Besse (1974); Norwood B. Melcher (1975); Robe H. McLemore (1976); Geoffrey G. Hunkin (1977

Cyrus Hall McCormick Medal

This gold medal is awarded by the America Society of Agricultural Engineers for exception; and meritorious engineering achievement in agr culture. Recipients may achieve their distinctio through invention, research, education, manag ment, or other areas of engineering endeavou Only ASAE members in good standing ma sponsor candidates for the medal.

Awarding body: American Society of Agricultur; Engineers, 2950 Niles Rd., St. Joseph, Mic] 49085, U.S.A.

McCurdy Award

This is the premier award of the Canadian Aeri nautics and Space Institute and is presente annually for outstanding achievement in ar science and engineering relating to aeronauti and space. It was established in 1954 by th Institute of Aircraft Technicians (a constituei body of the Aeronautics and Space Institute), an honours Air Commodore The Hon. J. A. I McCurdy. It takes the form of a trophy and silve medal.

Awarding body: Canadian Aeronautics an Space Institute, Suite 406, 77 Metcalfe St Ottawa, Ont. K1P 5L6, Canada.

Recipients include: Dr. G. V. Bull (1968); Pro B. Etkin (1969); F. C. Phillips (1970); F. H. Bull (1971); E. L. Smith (1972).

John A. MacDonald Prize for History
The Canadian Historical Association and Manufacturers' Life Insurance Company established this prize in 1977 in the name of the first President of Manufacturers'. The prize of $5,000 is given annually for a work, published in the preceding year, deemed to have made the highest contribution to the better understanding of Canadian history. Submissions are invited in English or in French.
Awarding body: MacDonald Prize Secretariat, 548 Merton St., Toronto, Ont. M4S 1B3, Canada.

Sir William Macewen Memorial Lectureship in Surgery
The lectureship was founded in 1926 and endowed from a fund promoted to commemorate the work of Sir William Macewen, Regius Professor of Surgery in the University of Glasgow. A lecture is delivered biennially on a subject connected with the advancement of surgery. The general public may attend. The lecture is subsequently published.
Awarding body: University of Glasgow, Glasgow G12 8QQ, Scotland.
Lecturers include: John W. Kirklin (Prof. of Surgery, Univ. of Alabama, U.S.A., 1970); Sir Hedley Atkins (fmr. Prof. of Surgery, Guy's Hospital, and Past Pres., Royal Coll. of Surgeons, 1972); Sir Michael Woodruff (Prof. of Surgery, Edinburgh Univ., 1975).

Agnes Purcell McGavin Award
This award was established in 1964 by the estate of the late Dr. Agnes P. McGavin and is made to a psychiatrist for outstanding work in the previous year related to the preventive aspects of the emotional disorders of childhood. Normally made annually, the award is non-competitive and consists of a certificate and honorarium of $500.
Awarding body: American Psychiatric Association, 1700 18th St., N.W., Washington, D.C. 20009, U.S.A.

James H. McGraw Award
This is an annual award established in 1950 by the McGraw-Hill Book Company to recognize outstanding service in engineering technology education. It consists of $1,000 in cash and a certificate, and is presented to a teacher, author, or administrator who is, or has been, affiliated with an institution which provides engineering technology education. Nominations may be made by any person, organization or group other than members of the Award Committee and employees of McGraw-Hill.
Awarding body: American Society for Engineering Education, Suite 400, One Dupont Circle, Washington, D.C. 20036, U.S.A.
Recipients include: Richard J. Ungrodt (1972); G. Ross Henninger (1973); Merritt A. Williamson (1974); Louis J. Dunham, Jr. (1975); Eugene Wood Smith (1976).

Ernst-Mach-Preis
The prize was established in 1964 by the German Society for Aeronautics, the predecessor of the German Aerospace Research and Experimental Establishment (DFVLR) in Cologne. The prize commemorates the physicist and philosopher, Ernst Mach (1838–1916), whose particular achievements were in the field of ballistics and supersonic speeds. The prize consists of a certificate and a sum of money of up to DM5,000, and is awarded every two years to persons working with the DFVLR for works they have published or lectures they have given about their scientific achievements.
Awarding body: Deutsche Forschungs- und Versuchsanstalt für Luft- und Raumfahrt e.V., Postfach 90 60 58, D-5000 Cologne 90, Federal Republic of Germany.

Machine Design Award
This annual award was founded in 1958 by the Machine Design Division of the American Society of Mechanical Engineers. It is given in recognition of eminent achievement or distinguished service in the field of machine design, which is considered to include application, research, development or teaching of machine design. The award consists of a bronze plaque and an engrossed certificate.
Awarding body: American Society of Mechanical Engineers, United Engineering Center, 345 East 47th St., New York, N.Y. 10017, U.S.A.
Recipients include: Walter L. Starkey (1971); Ferdinand Freudenstein (1972); Allen S. Hall, Jr. (1974); George N. Sandor (1975); Charles W. Radcliffe (1976).

McKenzie Travelling Lectureship in Education
This lectureship was established in 1971 by the New Zealand Council for Educational Research from funds made available by the McKenzie Foundation, established by R. A. McKenzie, a well-known philanthropist and businessman (son of the late Sir John McKenzie). A lecturer is chosen annually on the basis of his/her distinctive leadership in scholarly activities related to the improvement of the professional knowledge of teachers (or others associated with education), combined with the ability to convey fresh perspectives in seminars or meetings. The lecturer receives an allowance covering travel and expenses incurred during a lecture tour within the country over a period of 40–50 days. Recipients are chosen generally from English-speaking countries but there are no other restrictions.
Awarding body: New Zealand Council for Educational Research.
Lecturers include: Prof. J. F. Kerr (Univ. of Leicester, U.K., curriculum development); Prof. Brian Sutton-Smith (Teacher's Coll., Columbia, U.S.A., growth of imagination in children); Peter McPhail (Cambridge Univ., U.K., moral development of children); Prof. Betty Watts (Univ. of Queensland, Australia, involving the parents of ethnic minorities in schooling); Prof. Judith

Torney (Univ. of Illinois, Chicago Circle, U.S.A., growth of civic attitudes).

Mackie Medal

Founded in 1961, this medal is in memory of Professor Alexander Mackie (1876–1955) who made many influential and notable contributions to the teaching profession. The medal is presented annually to an individual, group or institution in recognition of work completed within the preceding two years, and judged to be the most significant contribution to the study of education. The recipient must be a citizen of Australia or New Zealand or have been resident in one or other country for the two years prior to the award.

Awarding body: Australian and New Zealand Association for the Advancement of Science, 157 Gloucester St., Sydney, N.S.W. 2000, Australia.

Recipients include: C. E. Beeby, C.M.G. (1971); W. C. Radford, M.B.E. (1972); J. L. Ewing (1973); Peter Karmel (1975); W. F. Connell (1977).

Mackintosh Lecture

The Mackintosh Charity instituted an annual lecture to be given in the University of East Anglia on the subject of the Christian religion, its theology or ethical teaching, or its relations with other faiths, or contemporary issues. The lecturer is appointed by the Chaplaincy Committee.

Awarding body: University of East Anglia, Norwich NR4 7TJ, England.

McMurray Lectureship in Orthopaedic Surgery

The lectureship was established in 1955 from funds, amounting to some £1,300, subscribed by friends, relatives and former pupils of the late Emeritus Professor T. P. McMurray, Professor of Orthopaedic Surgery at Liverpool University from 1939 to 1948. The appointment is made every two years by the University Council. The lecturer delivers a lecture or course of lectures on orthopaedic surgery. The remuneration is £90.

Awarding body: The University of Liverpool, P.O.B. 147, Liverpool L69 3BX, England.

Donald J. McParland Memorial Medal

This award is made annually by the Canadian Institute of Mining and Metallurgy for outstanding performance in the minerals industry in the field of mechanical, electrical or civil engineering design, general plant design, project engineering and mine plant installations and management. It was instituted in 1972, in memory of Donald J. McParland, a Canadian engineer and co-founder of the Institute's Mechanical-Electrical Division. Nominations must be endorsed by not fewer than five members of the Institute, and it is preferred that the recipient should also be a member.

Awarding body: The Canadian Institute of Mining and Metallurgy, 400-1130 Sherbrooke St. West, Montreal H3A 2M8, Canada.

Recipients include: Harold M. Wright (1974); C. M. Barrett (1975); G. L. Tiley (1976).

MacRobert Award

This is considered the major engineering award in Great Britain. It is made annually by the Council of Engineering Institutions on behalf of the MacRobert Trusts, and consists of a gold medal and £25,000. It is presented in recognition of an outstanding contribution by way of innovation in engineering or the physical technologies or in the application of the physical sciences, which has enhanced or will enhance the prestige and prosperity of the United Kingdom. The MacRobert Trusts instituted the award in 1968 with the aim of honouring individuals or small teams of individuals.

Awarding body: The Council of Engineering Institutions, 2 Little Smith St., London SW1P 3DL, England.

Recipients include: Dr. S. Jones, Dr. K. H. Spring, Dr. A. O. Gilchrist, M. Newman, A. Wickens (contributions to British Rail's Advanced Passenger Train) and J. Speechley, B. A. B. Rogers, K. T. McKenzie, D. E. H. Balmford, G. J. Smith-Pert (contributions to Westland Helicopters' Lynx helicopter), jointly, 1975; a five-man team from the Royal Signals and Radar Establishment and Malvern Instruments (work on photon correlation, 1977); Pilkington Bros. (development of Ten-Twenty Laminated Windscreen by their subsidiary, Triplex Safety Glass, 1978).

Otto-Mader-Preis

Established in 1964 by the German Society for Aeronautics, the predecessor of the German Aerospace Research and Experimental Establishment (DFVLR) in Cologne, the prize commemorates the motor expert Otto Mader (1880–1944), who developed the Junkers aircraft diesel engine. The prize, which consists of a certificate and a sum of money of up to DM5,000, is awarded every two years to persons working with the DFVLR for works they have published or lectures they have given about their scientific achievements.

Awarding body: Deutsche Forschungs- und Versuchsanstalt für Luft- und Raumfahrt e.V., Postfach 90 60 58, D-5000 Cologne 90, Federal Republic of Germany.

John Madsen Medal

In 1977 this bronze medal replaced the Electrical Engineering Prize, originally founded in 1927 by the Electrical Association of Australia. The medal is in memory of Sir John Madsen who was foundation Professor of Electrical Engineering at the University of Sydney from 1920 to 1949. He was one of Australia's great electrical engineers and a leader in the development of radar in Australia. The medal is awarded for the best paper in the discipline of electrical engineering, selected by the Board of the College of Electrical Engineers (a foundation College of the Institution of Engineers, Australia). The award is open to members of the Institution only.

Awarding body: Institution of Engineers, Australia, 11 National Circuit, Barton, A.C.T. 2600, Australia.

Recipients include: J. R. Gumley (1973); D. Darveniza (1974); C. J. McRae (1975); P. M. Roberts (1976); H. E. Green (1977).

Magellanic Premium

The Magellanic Fund was established in 1786 by the gift of 200 guineas from John Hyacinth de Magellan, of London, for a gold medal to be awarded from time to time 'to the author of the best discovery or most useful invention relating to navigation, astronomy, or natural philosophy (mere natural history only excepted)'. The award is made on the recommendation of the Committee on the Magellanic Premium of the American Philosophical Society.

Awarding body: American Philosophical Society, 104 South Fifth St., Philadelphia, Pa. 19106, U.D.A.

Recipients include: W. H. Pickering (leadership in the exploration of the Moon and Venus by jet-propelled vehicles, 1966); Paul M. Muller and William L. Sjogren (discovery of the lunar mascons leading to the first detailed gravimetric map of the moon, 1971); Ralph A. Alpher and Robert Herman (prediction of the black-body relict radiation from the early 'explosion' of the universe, 1975).

Kurt-Magnus-Preis

Awarded each year since 1963 on 28 March, the prize marks the birthday of Kurt Magnus, the distinguished broadcaster and founder of German sound broadcasting. The object is to encourage young qualified personnel in sound broadcasting. The specially created Kurt Magnus Foundation provides an annual sum of DM30,000, and the awards consist of cash prizes, grants for further training and commissions for new projects as appropriate. Qualified radio broadcasting staff of any member station of the Federal German Working Group of Public Radio Broadcasting Corporations (ARD) may be nominated for awards, and the jury is a commission of three members appointed by the radio station concerned, the Conference of Programme Directors and the Hessian Radio Corporation.

Awarding body (on behalf of the ARD): Hessischer Rundfunk.

Recipients include: Martin Buchhorn (SR), Barbara Feldmann (HR), Georg Felsberg (SWF), Gabriele Finger-Hoffmann and Christiane Sprenger (SDR), Winfried Göpfert (SFB), Wolfgang Herles (BR), Rüdiger Kremer (RB), Jürgen Krönig (DLF), Caspar Richter (RIAS), Rüdiger Siebert (DW), 1975.

Ramon Magsaysay Awards

These awards were founded in 1957 with a grant from the Rockefeller Brothers Fund and contributions from individuals and organizations from the Philippines and abroad, to honour the late President of the Philippines, killed in a plane crash in 1957, and to recognize those persons in Asia (either Asian or working in Asia) who exemplify his greatness of spirit, integrity and devotion to liberty. Five awards (for government service; public service; community leadership; journalism, literature and creative arts; international understanding) are made annually and carry a cash prize of U.S.$10,000 each, plus a gold medal and a certificate. The awards are presented on 31 August, the anniversary of Ramon Magsaysay's birthday.

Awarding body: Ramon Magsaysay Award Foundation, Ramon Magsaysay Center, Roxas Blvd., P.O.B. 3350, Manila, Philippines.

Recipients include: George Verghese (India, journalism, 1975); Fr. Patrick J. McGlinchey (Ireland, international understanding, 1975); Sombhu Mitra (India, drama, 1976); Henning Holck-Larsen (Denmark, international understanding, 1976).

P. C. Mahalanobis Medal

This medal was established in 1975 by the Indian National Science Academy. It is awarded every three years for outstanding contributions in the field of engineering and technology.

Awarding body: Indian National Science Academy, Bahadur Shah Zafar Marg, New Delhi 110001, India.

D. F. Malan-medalje

In 1961 the South African Academy of Science and Arts decided to establish a gold medal 'as a lasting tribute to the memory of the late Dr. D. F. Malan for the great service he has rendered to the furthering of Afrikaans language and culture'. Dr. Malan (1874–1959) was Prime Minister of South Africa and also a founder member and Council member of the Academy. The award, regarded as a particularly eminent distinction, is given to those who have produced work of the highest standard in the furthering of Afrikaans culture in the areas in which Dr. Malan was prominent. It is financed by an annual donation from Homes Trust Life, and is awarded usually every three years.

Awarding body: Suid-Afrikaanse Akademie vir Wetenskap en Kuns, Posbus 538, Pretoria 0001, South Africa.

Recipients include: C. M. van Niekerk (1962); Prof. G. B. A. Gerdener (1967); H. Recht Malan (1972); Prof. H. B. Thom (1975).

Harold Malkin Prize

Established in 1971 by Mr. Harold Malkin, the prize of £25 is awarded annually to a candidate for, or a holder of, the membership of the Royal College of Obstetricians and Gynaecologists who undertakes the best original work whilst holding a registrar or senior registrar post in a hospital in the U.K. or the Republic of Ireland. The record of the work can be submitted as an original manuscript or as a reprint of a published article.

Awarding body: Royal College of Obstetricians and Gynaecologists, 27 Sussex Place, Regent's Park, London NW1 4RG, England.

Recipients include: B. Spurrett (1972); Dr. Arnold Gillespie (1973); G. H. Randle (1974); B. Alderman (1976); Dr. A. K. Ghosh (1977).

Mallingkrodt Award

This is an annual prize established by the Japanese Society of Nuclear Medicine in 1968 for distinguished original work in the field of nuclear medicine. It is a cash prize of U.S.$1,500 to cover the costs of travelling to the U.S.A. to attend the Annual Meeting of the Society of Nuclear Medicine. The winner must be a scientist of Japanese nationality under 45 years of age and have been a member of the Society for at least four years.

Awarding body: Japanese Society of Nuclear Medicine, c/o Japanese Radioisotope Association, 2-28-45, Honkomagome, Bunkyo-ku, Tokyo 113, Japan.

Recipients include: Minoru Irie, M.D. (1975); Toyoharu Isawa, M.D. (1976); Norihisa Tonami, M.D. (1977).

Man in his Environment Book Award

This annual award has recently been established by the publishers E. P. Dutton & Co. of New York for a work of adult non-fiction dealing with the past, present or future of man in his environment. The prize-winning book must be published during the year of the award, and the author is guaranteed a minimum of $10,000 as an advance against all earnings. Entries will be judged by the editors of E. P. Dutton & Co. Both U.S.A. and overseas authors are eligible, but entries must be submitted in English. Academic dissertations or theses, unless suitably revised, are not acceptable, nor are works which have previously been published in book form in the U.S.A. Only entries of 50,000 words or more will be considered.

Awarding body: E. P. Dutton & Co., Inc., 201 Park Ave. South, New York, N.Y. 10003, U.S.A.

Manly Memorial Medal

The Society of Automotive Engineers established the medal in 1928 to commemorate the late Charles Matthews Manly, the engineer. The scope of the award was broadened in 1960. The medal is awarded annually to the author of the best paper relating to theory or practice in the design or construction of, or research on, aerospace engines, their parts, components, or accessories, which has been presented to the Society, or any of its sections, during the previous calendar year. Papers are judged primarily for their value as new contributions to knowledge. All papers presented to a Society meeting are automatically considered.

Awarding body: Society of Automotive Engineers, Inc., 400 Commonwealth Drive, Warrendale, Pa. 15096, U.S.A.

Recipients include: Frederick B. Metzger and Rose Worobel ('New Low Pressure Ratio Fans for Quiet Business Aircraft Propulsion', 1973); Theodore Katsanis and William D. McNally ('Quasi-Three-Dimensional Flow Solution by Meridional Plane Analysis', 1974); Robert A. Howlett ('Engine Design Considerations for Second Generation Supersonic Transports', 1975).

Heinrich-Mann-Preis

The Government of the German Democratic Republic established this literary prize in 1950 in memory of Heinrich Mann, the novelist and essayist (1871–1950). The prize is awarded annually to no more than two authors at a time, whose works must be written in German and must make a significant contribution to the democratic and socialistic development of the people, as defined by Heinrich Mann. Each winner receives a certificate and a cash prize.

Awarding body: Akademie der Künste der DDR, 104 Berlin, Hermann-Matern-Strasse 58/59, German Democratic Republic.

Recipients include: Annemarie Auer (1976); Joachim Nowotny (1976); Erich Köhler (1977).

Thomas-Mann-Preis

The prize was established by the Hanseatic city of Lübeck in 1975, on the occasion of the 100th anniversary of the birth in Lübeck of the poet and writer, Thomas Mann (1875–1955). He subsequently emigrated to the U.S.A. and was made an honorary citizen of Lübeck in 1955. The prize is awarded for work in the field of literature or the history of literature written in the humanitarian spirit, which was a characteristic of the work of Thomas Mann. The prize is awarded every three years and consists of DM10,000 and a certificate. Submissions for the prize are not accepted; a special jury meets in private to decide on the winner.

Awarding body: Dir Bürgerschaft der Hansestadt Lübeck, Rathaus, 2400 Lübeck, Federal Republic of Germany.

Recipients include: Peter de Mendelssohn (research work on Thomas Mann, 1975).

Mannheim Grand Prize

This award is given annually by the town of Mannheim for a first feature film, which should not have been made more than two years before. Established in 1961, the award takes the form of a certificate and a cash prize of DM10,000. Several other prizes are also given, including the Lord Mayor's special prize for a documentary of social-political commitment (DM6,000), the Josef von Sternberg Prize for the most original film (DM3,500), the Mannheim Film Ducat and a special prize for the best TV film.

Awarding body: Stadt Mannheim, Federal Republic of Germany.

Recipients include: Miguel Bejo (Argentina, 1972); Yoichi Takabayashi (Japan, 1973); Gyula Maár (Hungary, 1974); Krzysztof Kieslowski (Poland) and István Dárday (Hungary, 1975); Gábor Bódy (Hungary, 1976).

Carl-Mannich-Medaille

This award was established in 1959 by the German Pharmaceutical Society in memory of Carl Mannich (1877–1947), its long-standing President and former Director of the Pharmacy Institute of the University of Berlin. The award is given for outstanding achievements in the field of pharmacy, and consists of a silver medal and a certificate. It is awarded irregularly.

Awarding body: Deutsche Pharmazeutische Gesellschaft e.V., 6100 Darmstadt, Frankfurter Strasse 250, Federal Republic of Germany.

Recipients include: Prof. Dr. Friedrich von Bruchhausen (1961); Prof. Dr. Kurt Mothes (1965); Prof. Dr. Karl Winterfeld (1966); Prof. Dr. Eugen Baumann (1969); Prof. Dr. Horst Böhme (1969).

Katherine Mansfield Memorial Award

This award was established in 1959 by the New Zealand Women Writers' Society and the Bank of New Zealand, to commemorate New Zealand's most famous writer and to encourage young New Zealand writers. The award is sponsored by the Bank of New Zealand because Katherine Mansfield's father, Sir Harold Beaucamp, was a Director of the Bank and its Chairman for 15 years. The award is made every two years for an unpublished short story of not more than 7,000 words. In 1975 the winner received N.Z.$300. Only citizens of New Zealand or those who have been resident in New Zealand continuously for five years are eligible, and each entrant may only submit one story. The winner of the previous award is not eligible.

Awarding body: New Zealand Women Writers' Society, c/o Bank of New Zealand, P.O.B. 2392, Wellington 1, New Zealand.

Recipients include: Maurice Shadbolt (1967); Alice Glenday (1969); Wystan Curnow (1971); Margaret Sutherland (1973); Kerry Hulme (1975).

Katherine Mansfield Menton Short Story Prize Awards

These triennial awards were established in 1959 by the city of Menton to commemorate Katherine Mansfield's residence there. The equivalent of £100 is offered for the best English and the best French story, chosen by judges appointed by the English and French centres of International PEN (International Association of Poets, Playwrights, Editors, Essayists and Novelists). Stories must not exceed 10,000 words in length, and must have been published in the previous three years. For the English award, stories must have appeared in the U.K., Eire, the Commonwealth or South Africa; stories by American writers are not eligible. The awards are presented at a special ceremony in Menton.

Awarding bodies: English Centre of International PEN, 62/63 Glebe Place, London SW3 5JB, England; Maison Internationale des PEN Clubs, 6 rue François Miron, Paris 4e, France.

Manson Medal

This bronze medal is the highest mark of distinction of the Royal Society of Tropical Medicine and Hygiene. It is awarded every three years for original work in any branch of tropical medicine or hygiene. Sir Patrick Manson, G.C.M.G., F.R.S., was the most eminent figure in the field of tropical medicine at the beginning of this century, and was the first President of the Society. In 1921 his friends and admirers subscribed to a Portrait Fund as a mark of their esteem for him and his work. On completion of the portrait (which hangs in the London School of Hygiene and Tropical Medicine) it was decided to use the surplus of the Fund to found the Medal. No restrictions are imposed as to the recipient of the award, but nominations must be made by Fellows of the Society.

Awarding body: Royal Society of Tropical Medicine and Hygiene, Manson House, 26 Portland Place, London W1N 4EY, England.

Recipients include: Dr. Edmond Sergent (1962); Prof. P. C. C. Garnham (1965); Brig. Sir John S. K. Boyd (1968); Maj.-Gen. Sir Gordon Covell (1971); Dr. Cecil A. Hoare (1974).

T. W. Manson Memorial Lecture

The T. W. Manson Memorial Lectureship in New Testament Studies was founded in 1960 by a gift of a sum subscribed by colleagues, pupils and friends of the late Professor T. W. Manson at Manchester University.

Awarding body: University of Manchester, Manchester M13 9PL, England.

Lecturers include: Rev. D. E. Nineham ('The Genealogy in St. Matthew and its significance for the study of the Gospels', 1975); Prof. Etienne Trociné ('Why Parables? A study of Mark IV', 1976).

Marconi International Fellowship

The Fellowship was first announced in 1974 to mark the centennial of Marconi's birth. It commemorates his contributions to scientific invention, engineering and technology, and his commitment to their use for the betterment of the human condition. The Fellowship's goal is to recognize and inspire scientific achievements by living men and women whose lives are characterized by a similar dedication. The Fellowship is to be awarded once a year until the end of the 20th century, and is accompanied by a $25,000 grant and a replica of an original sculpture. The Fellowship commissions significant creative works that will add to knowledge and understanding of how communications sciences and technologies can be applied to the improvement of human life. The Fellowship is granted to an individual in recognition of outstanding contributions towards this goal with the clear understanding that the grant is made to commission scholarly work by the recipient or some other designated person. The recipient is asked to deliver a public lecture based on the commission.

Awarding body: Aspen Institute for Humanistic Studies, Program in Science, Technology and Humanism, 1919 Fourteenth St., No. 811, Boulder, Colo. 80302, U.S.A.

Recipients include: Dr. James R. Killian, Jr. (U.S.A., 1975); Prof. Hiroshi Inose (Japan, 1976); Prof. Arthur L. Schawlow (U.S.A., 1977).

Gheorghe Marinescu Prize

The prize was founded in 1948 by the Romanian Academy. It is for achievement in the field of medical science, and is named after Gheorghe Marinescu (1863–1938), the founder of the Romanian school of neurology. The award is presented annually at a General Assembly of the Academy, and consists of 10,000 lei and a diploma.

Awarding body: Academy of the S.R. of Romania, 125 Calea Victoriei, Bucharest, Romania.

Howard R. Marraro Prize

The Marraro Prize of $500 is awarded annually for the best work on any epoch of Italian cultural history or of Italian-American relations.

Awarding body: American Historical Association, 400 A St., S.E., Washington, D.C. 20003, U.S.A.

Marsden Medal for Outstanding Service to Science

The medal is awarded annually for services to the cause or profession or use of sciences in the widest sense in New Zealand. It was established in 1951 in memory of Sir Ernest Marsden, Head of the Department of Scientific and Industrial Research from its foundation in 1926 until after the second world war, and patron of the New Zealand Association of Scientists.

Awarding body: New Zealand Association of Scientists, P.O.B. 1874, Wellington, New Zealand.

Recipients include: Professor J. A. R. Miles, Professor J. F. Duncan, P. C. Alve, Dr. Lucy B. Moore, A. H. Ward.

Alan Marsh Medal

This medal is awarded annually to a British pilot in recognition of outstanding helicopter pilotage achievement. The medal was founded in 1955 by the Helicopter Association of Great Britain (now the Rotorcraft Section of the Royal Aeronautical Society) to commemorate the work of Alan Marsh, the outstanding helicopter test pilot who was killed in an air crash in 1950.

Awarding body: The Royal Aeronautical Society, 4 Hamilton Place, London W1V 0BQ, England.

Recipients include: Commdr. L. G. Locke (1971); Capt. D. H. Eastwood (1972); L. R. Moxam (1973); Capt. A. C. Gordon (1974); Flt. Lt. J. R. A. Whitney (1976).

Paul-Martini-Medaille

This gold medal was first awarded posthumously in 1966 to Prof. Dr. med. Paul Martini (1889–1964), a distinguished scientist in the field of clinico-therapeutic research, and has since been presented occasionally in his honour to individuals with a long and distinguished career in clinical pharmacology.

Awarding body: Paul Martini-Stiftung der Medizinisch Pharmazeutischen Studiengesellschaft e.V., 6000 Frankfurt am Main, Humboldtstr. 94, Federal Republic of Germany.

Recipients: Prof. Dr. med. Paul Martini (1966); Prof. Dr. med. H. H. Bennhold (1973); Prof. Dres. Dr. h.c. Wolfgang Wirth (1973); Prof. Dr. med. F. H. Dost (1975).

Paul-Martini-Preis

This annual award was established by the Paul Martini Foundation of the Society for Medico-Pharmaceutical Studies and the German Society for Medical Documentation, Information and Statistics, in memory of Prof. Dr. med. Paul Martini (1889–1964), a distinguished scientist in the field of clinico-therapeutic research. It is made for recent contributions to the development of scientific methods of evaluation in the clinical, pharmacological and therapeutic fields. There are no restrictions as to age or nationality. The award was first made in 1969, and now amounts to DM20,000.

Awarding body: Paul Martini-Stiftung der Medizinisch Pharmazeutischen Studiengesellschaft e.V., 6000 Frankfurt am Main, Humboldtstr. 94, Federal Republic of Germany.

Recipients include: Dr. Alasdair Muir Breckenridge and Dr. Michael L'Estrange Orme (1974); Prof. Dr. Lucius Dettli, Dr. Alan Richens (1975); Priv.-Doz. Dr. Michel T. Eichelbaum, Priv.-Doz. Dr. Bodo-Eckehard Strauer (1976).

John Masefield Memorial Award

This award was established in 1965 in honour of the English Poet Laureate by Dr. Corliss Lamont, a friend of Masefield's. It is given for a narrative poem in English not exceeding 200 lines. It is usually made annually, and is worth $500.

Awarding body: The Poetry Society of America, 15 Gramercy Park, New York, N.Y. 10003, U.S.A.

Recipients include: Siv Cedering Fox; Alvin Reiss; Sallie Nixon; Donald Justice; Penelope Schott.

Massey Medal

This award is made annually for outstanding personal achievement in the exploration, development or description of the geography of Canada, and takes the form of a silver gilt medal. It was established in 1959 by Sir Vincent Massey, first Canadian-born Governor General of Canada. The award is normally limited to Canadian citizens (if it is to be made to a non-Canadian, the agreement of the Massey Foundation must be obtained).

Awarding body: Royal Canadian Geographical Society, 488 Wilbrod St., Ottawa, Ont. K1N 6M8, Canada.

Recipients include: Dr. F. K. Hare (specialist in Canadian climatology, 1974); William M. Gilchrist (President of Northern Transportation Ltd., 1975); Louis Edmond Hamelin (specialist in the Canadian North, 1976); Thomas H. Manning (responsible for exploring and mapping much of the Canadian North, 1977).

Massey-Ferguson Educational Award

This award was established as a tribute to Daniel Massey, a pioneer-innovator and agricultural machinery manufacturer, and Harry Ferguson, an inventor whose unique educational approaches made a lasting contribution to world-wide agricultural mechanization. The award is given to honour those whose dedication to the spirit of learning and teaching in the field of agricultural engineering has advanced with distinction agricultural knowledge and practice and whose efforts serve as an inspiration to others.

Awarding body: American Society of Agricultural Engineers, 2950 Niles Road, St. Joseph, Mich. 49085, U.S.A.

Massey-Ferguson National Award for Services to U.K. Agriculture

This is an annual award consisting of a prize of £1,000, a medallion and a trophy (held only for one year). It is for a proven practical and outstanding contribution to the advancement of agriculture in the U.K. The award was established in 1964 by Massey-Ferguson (U.K.) Ltd., the farm machinery manufacturers. The award is for farmers, farm managers and those engaged in the supporting services of agriculture, in person. Organizations as such are ineligible, as are those whose contributions to agriculture arise from whole-time commercial employment.

Awarding body: Massey-Ferguson (U.K.) Ltd., Banner Lane, Coventry, Warwickshire, England.

Recipients include: Cadzow Brothers (development of the Wing breed, 1972); Dr. G. D. H. Bell (plant breeding, 1973); The Duke of Northumberland (national services to agriculture, 1974); W. H. Cashmore (services to farm mechanization, 1975); Sir Nigel Strutt (national services to agriculture, 1976).

Masson Memorial Lectureship

The Australian and New Zealand Association for the Advancement of Science (ANZAAS) created this medal, first awarded in 1935, in honour of Sir David Orme Masson, F.R.S. (1858–1954). He held the Melbourne University Chair of Chemistry from 1886 to 1924, and, apart from his valuable contributions to chemistry, he created standards in teaching and research that still have influence through his students, and set an outstanding example by his many public and social services. The Masson Lectureship Fund provides for a fee of $50 to be paid for a lecture to be given every fourth year at the ANZAAS Congress. The person appointed as the Masson Lecturer is chosen on account of his distinguished contributions to astronomy, chemistry, economics and statistics, engineering, mathematics, meteorology, mining and metallurgy, or physics. The lecture is published in *Search*, the ANZAAS journal.

Awarding body: Australian and New Zealand Association for the Advancement of Science, 157 Gloucester St., Sydney, N.S.W. 2000, Australia.

Recipients include: R. J. W. le Fevre ('Chemistry – Proliferation or Progress', 1967); J. P. Wild ('Solar Explosions', 1971); H. K. Worner ('The Modern Vulcans', 1975).

Frank M. Masters Transportation Engineering Award

This award was endowed from a bequest to the American Society of Civil Engineers by Frank M. Masters, Hon. M.ASCE, and established in his memory by the Society in 1975. The award consists of a plaque and certificate, and is awarded annually to the member who has published the best example of noteworthy planning, design or construction of transportation facilities.

Awarding body: American Society of Civil Engineers, 345 East 47th St., New York, N.Y. 10017, U.S.A.

Recipients include: S. Starr Walbridge (creation of the first grade-separated highway interchange, 1976).

Mather Lecture

The Textile Institute established this annual lecture in 1919 in honour of Sir William Mather (1838–1920), its generous benefactor, and President from 1915 to 1918; he was Chairman of Mather & Platt Ltd., manufacturers of textile-finishing and other machinery, and contributed personally to the development of his company's products. The lecture is given in the course of the Institute's Annual Conference.

Awarding body: The Textile Institute, 10 Blackfriars St., Manchester M3 5DR, England.

Recipients include: Hans W. Krause ('New Ways of Producing Textiles – How "New" are "New Ways"?', 1972); Frank Howlett ('The Impact of Modern Technology in Industrial Textiles', 1973); P. W. Smith ('Textile Industries in Developed Countries: Some Criteria for their Existence and Development', 1974); Prof. Malcolm Chaikin ('Success and Failure in Textile Technical Innovation', 1975); David Brunnschweiler ('From Spinneret to Fabric', 1976).

Sir Robert Matthew Award

This award is conferred on an architect who has contributed to the education of architects in developing countries. It was founded in 1978 by the International Union of Architects.

Awarding body: International Union of Architects, 1 rue d'Ulm, 75005 Paris, France.

Somerset Maugham Awards

These annual awards were established in 1947 by the author Somerset Maugham. Published works of poetry, fiction, criticism, biography, history, philosophy, belles-lettres and travel are eligible, but not dramatic works. Entrants must be British subjects by birth, ordinarily resident in the United Kingdom and under the age of 35 on 31 December of the year of the awards. The winners receive a sum of money (£500 each in 1978) which must be used for a period of foreign travel of not less than three months.

Awarding body: The Society of Authors, 84 Drayton Gardens, London SW10 9SD, England.

Recipients include: Martin Amis (*The Rachel Papers*, 1974); Dominic Cooper (*The Dead of Winter*) and Ian McEwan (*First Love, Last Rites*, 1976); Richard Holmes (*Shelley: the Pursuit*, 1977); Tom Paulin (*A State of Justice*, poetry) and Nigel Williams (*My Life Closed Twice*, novel), 1978.

Matthew Fontaine Maury Medal

This gold medal is awarded for distinguished contributions in underwater ocean science. It was established in 1970 in memory of Matthew Fontaine Maury (1806–73), a U.S. naval officer, recognized as the founder of the science of oceanography. The medal is presented irregularly as merited. There are no restrictions as to eligibility.

Awarding body: Smithsonian Institution, 1000 Jefferson Drive, S.W., Washington, D.C. 20560, U.S.A.

Recipients include: Edwin A. Link and J. Seward Johnson (invention and development of the Johnson-Sea-Link, the first of a pioneer class of submersible research vehicles, 1971); Robert M. White (first administrator of the National Oceanic and Atmospheric Administration, fostered research on a national level in the ocean sciences, 1976).

Maxwell Medal and Prize

The prize was established in 1961 by the Institute of Physics and the Physical Society for outstanding contributions to theoretical physics made in the ten years preceding the date of the award. A bronze medal and a prize of £150 are awarded annually. Candidates should normally be not more than 35 years old, and are considered on the recommendation of members of the Institute and of its Awards Committee.

Awarding body: The Institute of Physics, 47 Belgrave Square, London SW1X 8QX, England.

Recipients include: John Bryan Taylor (1971); Volker Heine (1972); David James Thouless (1973); Samuel Frederick Edwards (1974); Anthony James Leggett (1975).

James Clark Maxwell Prize for Plasma Physics

The prize was established in 1975 by Maxwell Laboratories, Inc., of San Diego, California, to recognize outstanding contributions to the field of plasma physics. The prize is awarded annually to U.S. residents for work done primarily in the U.S.A.; the work should contribute to the advancement and diffusion of the knowledge of properties of highly ionized gases of natural or laboratory origin. The prize consists of $3,500 and a certificate citing the contributions made by the recipient.

Awarding body: American Physical Society, 335 East 45th St., New York, N.Y. 10017, U.S.A.

Recipients include: Lyman Spitzer (1975); Marshall N. Rosenbluth (1976).

Mechanics and Control of Flight Award

The award was established by the AIAA in 1967 for an outstanding recent technical or scientific contribution by an individual to the mechanics, guidance or control of flight in space or atmosphere. It comprises a medal and certificate of citation and is presented annually at the AIAA Guidance, Control and Flight Dynamics Conference.

Awarding body: American Institute of Aeronautics and Astronautics, 1290 Avenue of the Americas, New York, N.Y. 10019, U.S.A.

Recipients include: John V. Breakwell (1972);

Henry J. Kelley (1973); Harold Roy Vaughn (1974); Bernard Etkin (1975); Charles Murphy (1976).

Medaille der Mozartstadt Salzburg (*Mozartian City of Salzburg Medal*)

Medals in honour and in memory of Wolfgang Amadeus Mozart (1756–91), who was born in Salzburg, have been awarded by the city since 1950. They are for outstanding musical achievement which is of special significance to Salzburg. Four grades of medal are awarded: the Grand Gold, the Gold, the Grand Silver and the Silver. They bear Mozart's profile on the obverse, and on the reverse the inscription 'Amico Salisburgensis laus et honor', the Salzburg coat of arms and a laurel branch. A certificate is also presented, and a record of the award is entered in the city's Golden Book of Honour. The presentation ceremony takes place when possible on one of Salzburg's commemoration days. The award is not made regularly, and the medals may be held only by a limited number of people at one time. On the death of the holder the medal is returned to the city and preserved in the Carolino-Augusteum Museum. The holder must relinquish the award if he is proved unworthy of it.

Awarding body: Landeshauptstadt Salzburg, A-5024 Salzburg, Austria.

Recipients include: International Mozart Foundation (Grand Gold, 1956); Vienna Philharmonic Orchestra (Grand Gold, 1956); Wilhelm Backhaus, pianist (Gold, 1969); Josef Kaut, Pres. of Salzburg Festival (Gold, 1974).

Médaille Archambault

The medal was created in 1953 in honour of Urgèle Archambault, founder-director of the Ecole Polytechnique in Montreal, with a gift from Monsieur Ignace Brouillet, then President of the Corporation of the Polytechnic and former President of the French-Canadian Association for the Advancement of Science. The medal is awarded for exceptional contributions in the field of applied research and technological development or, more generally, for practical work of a kind that promotes the progress of scientific research. The medal, awarded annually, is accompanied by a cash prize of $2,000 donated by Aluminium du Canada. Candidates must be of French-Canadian nationality.

Awarding body: Association Canadienne-Française pour l'Avancement des Sciences, C.P. 6060, Montreal H3C 3A7, Canada.

Recipients include: Jean-J. Archambault and Lionel Cahill (1974); Hans Selye (1975); Roger Boucher (1976).

Médaille André H. Dumont

This medal is awarded every year for outstanding work carried out during the preceding decade in the fields of geology, petrography, mineralogy, physical geography or palaeontology. It may be an important discovery or the realization of a significant advance in theoretical concepts. The award was established by the Belgian Geological Society in 1949 in memory of the famous Belgian geologist André H. Dumont (1809–57). It is open to scientists of any nationality.

Awarding body: Société Géologique de Belgique, Place du Vingt-Août 7, B-4000 Liège, Belgium.

Recipients include: E. Stensiö (Sweden); L. S. B. and M. Leakey (Kenya); R. F. Legget (Canada); A. L. Washburn (U.S.A.); J. H. Brunn (France).

Médaille d'Or du Centre National de la Recherche Scientifique *(Gold Medal of the National Centre for Scientific Research)*

Established in 1954, the medal is awarded annually to a person who has, in various ways, contributed to the prestige of French scientific research, and rewards a body of work or a scientific career of international renown. Silver and bronze medals are also awarded for the best post-thesis and thesis work in any year.

Awarding body: Centre National de la Recherche Scientifique, 15 quai Anatole-France, 75700 Paris, France.

Recipients include: Prof. Edgard Lederer (biochemist, 1974); Mme. Christiane Desroches-Noblecourt (egyptologist) and Prof. Raymond Castaing (physicist), 1975; Henri Cartan (mathematician, 1976); Prof. Maurice Allais (economist) and Pierre Jacquinot (physicist), 1978.

Médaille Pariseau

Originally named *Médaille de l'ACFAS*, the medal was created in 1944 with a donation from Léo Pariseau, the first President of ACFAS. It is intended to recognize meritorious work by French-Canadians in the field of basic research. It is accompanied by a cash prize of $2,000, given by the Banque Canadienne Nationale. It is awarded annually in rotation for work in one of three areas: humanities and social sciences; physical and mathematical sciences; biological sciences.

Awarding body: Association Canadienne-Française pour l'Avancement des Sciences, C.P. 6060, Montreal H3C 3A7, Canada.

Recipients include: Antoine d'Iorio (1974); Pierre Angers (1975); Paul Marmet (1976).

Médaille Vincent

The medal was established in 1975 with a gift from Marcel Vincent, President of Bell Canada. It is awarded to a young (under 40) French-Canadian for outstanding basic or applied research work, carried out in Canada. The medal is awarded annually and is accompanied by a cash prize of $2,000.

Awarding body: Association Canadienne-Française pour l'Avancement des Sciences, C.P. 6060, Montreal H3C 3A7, Canada.

Recipients include: Pierre Deslongchamps (1975); Fernand Labrie (1976).

Medalha 'Ciência para a Amazônia' *('Science for Amazonia' Medal)*

Instituted in 1976 by Warwick Estêvão Kerr, Director of INPA (National Institute for Research in Amazonia), the medal is awarded annually to scientists or other persons who have made a direct or indirect contribution to the scientific and technological development of the Amazonian region of Brazil.

Awarding body: Instituto Nacional de Pesquisa da Amazônia (INPA), P.O.B. 478, 69000 Manaus, Amazonas, Brazil.

Recipients include: Dr. Djalma Batista; Dr. Felisberto Camargo; Dr. Paulo Vanzolini; Dr. Harald Sioli.

Medalla del Instituto Colombiano Agropecuaria *(Colombian Agricultural Institute Medal)*

The Institute (ICA) established the medal in 1972 to recognize outstanding achievements by scientists – Colombian or foreign – working at the Institute. It is given at irregular intervals, and in three categories: gold, silver, bronze.

Awarding body: Instituto Colombiano Agropecuario, Calle 37 No. 8 – 43 Of. 811, Bogotá, Colombia.

Recipients include: Clímaco Cassalett Dávila (1977).

Medalla al Mérito Ecológico y al Mérito Conservacionista *(Medal of Merit for Ecology and Conservation)*

This biennial prize was established in 1973 by the Colombian National Institute for Natural Resources and the Environment. The award for ecological merit is given to persons or institutions who have made an outstanding contribution to the development of natural resources; the conservationist award is bestowed upon members of the League of Conservation who have made a notable contribution to the conservation of the natural environment.

Awarding body: Instituto Nacional de los Recursos Naturales Renovables y del Ambiente (INDERENA), Bogotá, D.E., Colombia.

Medalla de Oro Antonio Raimondi *(Antonio Raimondi Gold Medal)*

This prize was established in 1935 by the Lima Geographical Society and is awarded every four years to an eminent geographer, explorer, scientist or author who has made a significant contribution to geography and related fields. The Society also awards the Luis Carranza Gold Medal to distinguished authors of geography text books, and the Eulogio Delgado Gold Medal for work on demarcating Peru's national frontiers.

Awarding body: Sociedad Geográfica de Lima, Jirón Punto 456, Casilla 1176, Lima, Peru.

Recipients include: Gen. Bernardino Vallenas; Gen. Guillermo Barriga; Dr. Bolivar Ulloa; Ing. Gustavo Lama; Rear-Admiral Manuel R. Nieto.

Media Club of Canada Memorial Awards/ Club Média du Canada Concours National Annuel

These awards are made to the authors of the best article, news story, and column or editorial submitted to the Media Club. The top prize in each category is a medal and $100. The awards are a tribute to past members of the Club and are intended to foster a high standard of writing among Canadian writers and journalists.

Awarding body: Media Club of Canada, Box 182, Station H, Montreal, Quebec, Canada.

Medical Association of South Africa Gold Medal

This is the highest of a series of medals and awards made by the Association. It was established in about 1928 and is normally awarded annually to a member who, by serving the Medical Association, has also made an outstanding contribution to the medical profession. The Silver and Bronze Medals and the Pro Meritis Award recognize services to the advancement of medical science in South Africa from a wider range of candidates.

Awarding body: The Medical Association of South Africa, P.O.B. 20272, Alkantrant 0005, South Africa.

Recipients of Gold Medal: Prof. C. N. Barnard (achievement in human heart transplantation, 1968); Prof. Dr. S. F. Oosthuizen (distinctive contribution to the art and science of medicine, 1969); Prof. H. Grant-Whyte (services to the profession, 1970); Dr. D. McKenzie (services to the profession, 1974).

C. E. K. Mees Medal

This award was established in 1961 in memory of C. E. K. Mees, who contributed pre-eminently to the development of scientific photography. It was endowed by the family of Dr. Mees, and consists of a silver medal and a citation. It is presented biennially to a recipient who exemplifies the thought that 'optics transcends all boundaries' – interdisciplinary and international alike.

Awarding body: Optical Society of America, 2000 L St., N.W., Washington, D.C. 20036, U.S.A.

Recipients include: Dr. Charles H. Townes (1968); Dr. Giuliano Toraldo di Francia (1971); Prof. Erik P. Inglestam (1973); Dr. William D. Wright (1975); Dr. André Maréchal (1977).

William F. Meggers Award

This award, which was endowed in 1970 by the family of William Meggers, several individuals, and a number of optical manufacturers, honours Dr. Meggers for his notable contributions to the field of spectroscopy and metrology. It is awarded annually for outstanding work in spectroscopy, and consists of a silver medal and a citation.

Awarding body: Optical Society of America, 2000 L St., N.W., Washington, D.C. 20036, U.S.A.

Recipients include: Curtis J. Humphreys (1973); Harry L. Welsh (1974); Jean Blaise (1975); Dr. W. R. S. Garton (1976); Dr. Mark S. Fred and Dr. Frank S. Tomkins (1977).

Meisinger Award

This award is made annually to an individual in recognition of research achievements that are, at least partly, aerological in character. Preference is given to promising atmospheric scientists 35 years of age or younger, who have recently shown outstanding ability.

Awarding body: American Meteorological Society, 45 Beacon St., Boston, Mass. 02108, U.S.A.

Recipients include: Robert E. Dickinson, James R. Holton (1973); Keith A. Browning (1974); John M. Wallace (1975); Thomas W. Flattery (1976).

Meldola Medal and Prize

This bronze medal is the gift of the Society of Maccabaeans and commemorates Raphael Meldola who was President of both the Society and the (then) Institute of Chemistry. It is now accompanied by a prize of £100, and is awarded to the chemist who, being a British subject and under 30 years of age, shows the most promise as indicated by his or her published chemical work. There are no restrictions as to the kind of work or the place where it is conducted. Nominations may be made to the Council of the Royal Institute of Chemistry, or candidates may apply personally.

Awarding body: Royal Institute of Chemistry, 30 Russell Square, London WC1B 5DT, England.

Recipients include: J. N. L. Connor and B. P. Roberts (1973); P. J. Derrick (1974); J. K. M. Sanders (1975); J. K. Burdett and M. Poliakoff (1976).

David Mellor Lecture on Chemical Education

The University of New South Wales established this lecture in 1970 in recognition of the contributions of David P. Mellor, Emeritus Professor of Chemistry at the University, in the field of chemical education. Lectures are given at irregular intervals. Lecturers are chosen for their contributions to chemical education and receive an honorarium to cover expenses. The University is unable to invite lecturers from outside Australia unless they happen to be visiting Australia.

Awarding body: The University of New South Wales, Kensington, N.S.W. 2033, Australia.

Recipients include: Prof. L. E. Strong (U.S.A., 'Developments in Chemical Education', 1972); Prof. J. H. Wotiz (U.S.A., 'Higher Education in Chemistry in the USSR and Other East European Countries', 1974); Dr. D. M. Adams (U.K., 'What Chemistry for 1984?', 1975).

Melville Medal

The Melville Medal was first awarded in 1927, and was established by the bequest in 1914 of Admiral George W. Melville, Honorary Member and eighteenth President of the American Society of Mechanical Engineers. This is the highest ASME honour for the best current original paper presented before ASME during the preceding calendar year, or published or approved for publication by the Society. The paper may have more than one author but one of the authors should be an ASME corporate member. The paper should be specifically recommended for the medal by a review committee or qualified individual. The medal of gold plated bronze is accompanied by an engrossed certificate and an honorarium of $1,000.

Awarding body: American Society of Mechanical Engineers, United Engineering Center, 345 East 47th St., New York, N.Y. 10017, U.S.A.

Recipients include: David M. Sanborn, A. V. Turchina, Ward O. Winer (1975); Bernard J. Hamrock, Duncan Dowson (1976).

Mendel-Medaille

This prize was established by the Leopoldina German Academy of Researchers in Natural Sciences in 1965 on the occasion of the Mendel Jubilee. (Johann Gregor Mendel (1822–84) was a pioneer in the fields of hybridization and heredity.) The medal is awarded for outstanding new achievements in the field of biology.

Awarding body: Deutsche Akademie der Naturforscher Leopoldina, 401 Halle/Saale, August-Bebel-Strasse 50A, German Democratic Republic.

Recipients include: Prof. Dr. Max Delbrück (U.S.A., 1967); Dr. Sydney Brenner (U.K., 1970); Prof. Dr. Nikolai Timofeev-Resovsky (U.S.S.R., 1970); Prof. Dr. Erwin Chargaff (U.S.A., 1973); Prof. Dr. Curt Stern (U.S.A., 1975).

William C. Menninger Memorial Award

This award, which is supported by the Menninger Foundation, was established in 1967 and is bestowed for distinguished contributions to the science of mental health. It is presented annually, and takes the form of a medal.

Awarding body: American College of Physicians, 4200 Pine St., Philadelphia, Pa. 19104, U.S.A.

Recipients include: Dana L. Farnsworth (1970); Ewald W. Busse (1971); Theodore Lidz (1972); John Romano (1973); Ephraim T. Lisansky (1974).

Dr. Kamala Menon Medical Research Award

This award of 5,000 rupees was instituted in 1975 by Shri T. K. N. Menon in memory of his late wife. It is awarded annually, alternately for work in the fields of internal medicine and paediatrics. It is given to an eminent scientist for outstanding and sustained research over several years.

Awarding body: Indian Council of Medical Research, Ansari Nagar, Post Box 4508, New Delhi 110016, India.

Recipients include: Dr. S. Padmavati (1975); Dr. Shanti Ghosh (1976).

Mental Health Association Research Achievement Award

Established in 1972 in memory of William R. McAlpin, the award is presented annually to a researcher whose work makes a significant contribution to the understanding of the causes of mental illness. It consists of a stipend and a medal.

Awarding body: Mental Health Association, 1800 N. Kent St., Arlington, Va. 22190, U.S.A.

Recipients include: Dr. Seymour S. Kety; Dr. Robert Coles; Prof. Erik Erikson; Dr. Alexander Leighton; Dr. William E. Bunney, Jr.

Menuhin Prize for Young Composers

A competition was established in 1973 by the City of Westminster Arts Council. It is named after Yehudi Menuhin, who is Chairman of the Council, and the prize is awarded every three years for a musical composition. Conditions of entry vary with each competition, but entrants must be resident in the U.K., and there is usually an upper age limit of 30. The winner receives a cash prize of £500, plus a first performance in a central London concert hall.

Awarding body: City of Westminster Arts Council, c/o The Honorary Secretary, Menuhin Prize Management Committee, Marylebone Library, Marylebone Rd., London NW1 5PS, England.

Recipients include: Michael Blake Watkins (1973).

Dr. Fritz Merck-Preis

The prize was established in 1960 at the Justus Liebig University of Giessen by the company E. Merck AG of Darmstadt, on the occasion of the 70th birthday of Dr. Fritz Merck, honorary senator of the University. The prize is awarded primarily to young scientists of German citizenship or resident in Germany, in recognition of scientific achievements, whose object has been the explanation or elimination of disturbances in the biosphere. Employees of industrial or commercial companies are not eligible. The prize of DM10,000 is awarded annually on the decision of a board consisting of representatives of the University and the company.

Awarding body: Justus Liebig-Universität Giessen, 6300 Giessen 2, Ludwigstr. 23, Postfach 21440, Federal Republic of Germany.

Johann-Heinrich-Merck-Preis

This prize of DM6,000 was founded in 1964 by the German Academy for Language and Poetry to promote literary criticism and essays. It is dedicated to the memory of Johann Heinrich Merck (1741–91), an early critic and essayist.

Awarding body: Deutsche Akademie für Sprache und Dichtung, Alexandraweg 23 (Glückert-Haus), 6100 Darmstadt, Federal Republic of Germany.

Recipients include: Horst Krüger (1972); H. H. Stuckenschmidt (1973); Joachim Günther (1974); Walter Höllerer (1975); Peter Rühmkorf (1976).

Merck Sharp & Dohme Lecture Award

Established in 1955 by the Chemical Institute of Canada, the award is made to scientists residing in Canada who have made distinguished contributions in the fields of organic chemistry or biochemistry, while working in Canada. It is an annual award. The recipient delivers the lecture at the Institute's Annual Conference. He is known for the year as the 'Merck Sharp & Dohme Lecturer' and receives $500 prize money, which is provided by Merck Sharp & Dohme of Canada, Ltd. Nominations signed by at least three professional members of the Chemical Institute of Canada must be submitted by 1 January of each year and they remain valid for three years. Nominees should be under the age of 40.

Awarding body: The Chemical Institute of Canada, 151 Slater St., Ottawa, Ont. K1P 5H3, Canada.

Recipients include: S. Wolfe ('Sulfur-free Penicillin Derivatives', 1972); J. W. ApSimon ('Terpenoid Meanderings', 1973); S. Hannessian ('New Synthetic Methods: From Carbohydrates to Antibiotics and Beyond', 1974); L. D. Hall ('A Fourth Dimension for NMR Spectroscopy', 1975); B. O. Fraser-Reid (1976).

Arthur Merghelynckprijs

The prize was established in 1946 by the Belgian Royal Academy of Dutch Language and Literature in memory of Arthur Merghelynck (1853–1908), art collector and benefactor of the Academy. Two awards may be made every three years for the best literary works submitted, one for prose and one for poetry. Both awards are of 5,000 Belgian francs. Recipients must be Belgian nationals.

Awarding body: Koninklijke Academie voor Nederlandse Taal- en Letterkunde, Koningstraat 18, B-9000 Ghent, Belgium.

Recipients include: Karel Jonckheere (*De Hondenwacht*, 1951); Hubert Lampo (*Terugkeer naar Atlantis*) and Hubert van Herreweghen (*Gedichten*), 1954; Johan Daisne (*Lago Maggiore*, 1957); Jos Vandeloo (*De Muur*, 1960).

Merlin Medal and Gift

The award was established in 1961 from funds bequeathed by the late Elliot Merlin, a member of the British Astronomical Association. The silver medal and a monetary award of about £20 are given for outstanding discoveries in astronomy. The award is made not more than once in two years (more frequently in earlier years). The recipient must be a member of the British Astronomical Association.

Awarding body: British Astronomical Association, Burlington House, Piccadilly, London W1, England.

Recipients include: B. G. Marsden (calculation of comet orbits, etc., 1965); H. Joy (variable stars, 1966); W. M. Baxter (exceptional solar photography, 1967); A. F. A. L. Jones (comets, 1968); H. Hill (solar observations, 1969).

Messel Medal

This is regarded as the senior award of the Society of Chemical Industry. It was instituted in 1921 to commemorate Dr. Rudolf Messel who bequeathed one-fifth of the residue of his estate to the Society (the Messel Fund), the income from which to be applied in a manner conducive to the furtherance of scientific research and such other scientific objects as the Society may determine. Dr. Messel (1848–1920) was an eminent international chemist and a founder member of the Society; he was its Hon. Secretary (Foreign) and President. The medal carries an honorarium of £250 and is

awarded every two years to a person who has secured meritorious distinction in science, literature, industry or public affairs and who is prominently concerned with the welfare of the Society. Recipients present an address and the award is usually made at the Society's Annual Meeting.

Awarding body: Society of Chemical Industry, 14 Belgrave Square, London SW1X 8PS, England.

Recipients include: Sir Paul Chambers ('The International Problems of the Chemical Industry', 1968); Sir E. Rideal ('Matter in the Boundary State and Technology', 1970); Prof. A. R. Ubbelohde ('From Spark to Blaze in Graphite Research', 1972); Dr. Jean Rey (untitled, 1974); Dr. K. L. Blaxter ('The Art and Science of Agriculture', 1976).

Vicky Metcalf Award

This annual award of $1,000 was established by Mrs. Vicky Metcalf to encourage Canadians to write books for children. Entries may be fiction, non-fiction or even picture-books; authors will be judged by their complete works.

Awarding body: Canadian Authors Association, 22 Yorkville Ave., Toronto, Ont. M4W 1L4, Canada.

Recipients include: William E. Toye (1972); Christie Harris (1973); Jean Little (1974); Lyn Harrington (1975); Suzanne Martel (1976).

Adolf Meyer Lectureship

This lectureship was established in 1957 by a grant from a private sponsor. The lecturer, selected by the American Psychiatric Association, is an outstanding psychiatric investigator from the U.S.A. or abroad. The purpose of the lecture series is to advance psychiatric research by enabling American psychiatrists to exchange ideas and information with their eminent colleagues. The award is made annually, and consists of an honorarium and expenses totalling $1,500.

Awarding body: American Psychiatric Association, 1700 18th St., N.W., Washington, D.C. 20009, U.S.A.

Hans-Meyer-Medaille

This award was created in 1971 to replace an earlier Honorary Presentation, at a joint meeting of the executive bodies of the German Pharmacists' Representative Group (ABDA), the Association of German Chambers of Pharmacists and the German Association of Pharmacists. It consists of a medal in gold or silver with pin and a certificate, and is awarded each year. The three organizations select the winners jointly for distinguished services in the profession of pharmacy in Germany. The medal is in honour of Dr. Hans Meyer, for his services in the organization of the profession of pharmacy as Chief Executive of the ABDA from 1950 to 1964.

Awarding body: Arbeitsgemeinschaft der Berufsvertretungen Deutscher Apotheker (ABDA), 6000 Frankfurt am Main, Beethovenplatz 1, Federal Republic of Germany.

Recipients include: Dr. Hans Meyer (1971); Dr. Wolfgang Stammberger (1971, gold), Enno Ries 1971, silver); Gustav Tauber, Dr. Werner Luckenbach, Willy Etzbach, Hermann Krause, Werner Klie, Dr. Wolfram Scheel (1972, all silver); Dr. Heinrich Danner (1973, gold).

Albert A. Michelson Medal
Dr. George S. Crampton (1874–1962) was a member of the Franklin Institute, and a distinguished physician and optical engineer. In his will he left a donation to the Franklin Institute to establish an award in optics in honour of Dr. Albert A. Michelson. Dr. Michelson (1852–1931) was a professor of physics and winner of the Nobel Prize for Physics in 1907. The award is a gold medal and is given annually, regardless of nationality.
Awarding body: The Franklin Institute, Benjamin Franklin Parkway at 20th St., Philadelphia, Pa. 19103, U.S.A.
Recipients include: Herbert Friedman (solar and X-ray astronomy, 1972); S. Jocelyn Bell Burnell, Antony Hewish (discovery of pulsars, 1973); Peter P. Sorokin (discovery of the organic dye laser, 1974); Irwin I. Shapiro (use of radar astronomy to investigate planets, cosmology and general relativity, 1975); Dr. Albert V. Crewe (inventor of the scanning transmission electron microscope (STEM), 1977).

Constantin Miculescu Prize
The Romanian Academy established this prize for physics in 1948. It is presented annually at a General Assembly of the Academy, and consists of 10,000 lei and a diploma. It is named after Constantin Miculescu (1863–1937), physicist and professor, who did valuable research in optics, acoustics and thermodynamics.
Awarding body: Academy of the S.R. of Romania, 125 Calea Victoriei, Bucharest, Romania.
Recipients include: Deniza Popescu and Jakub Mirza (1974).

Thomas A. Middlebrooks Award
This award consists of a certificate and the income from a fund set up in 1955 in recognition of the outstanding professional accomplishments of T. A. Middlebrooks, A.M.ASCE. It is awarded annually to the author or authors of the paper published by the Society which has made the greatest contribution to geotechnical engineering. Preference is given to papers by young engineers. The winner has the option of taking his prize in books or in cash.
Awarding body: American Society of Civil Engineers, 345 East 47th St., New York, N.Y. 10017, U.S.A.
Recipients include: Aleksandar S. Vesic ('Analysis of Ultimate Loads of Shallow Foundations', 1974); Kenneth L. Lee, Bobby Dean Adams and Jean-Marie J. Vagneron ('Reinforced Earth Retaining Walls', 1975); Kenneth L. Lee and John A. Focht, Jr. ('Liquefaction Potential at Ekofisk Tank in North Sea', 1976).

Midsummer Prize
The Corporation of London established this award in 1968 to be given to the British artist, sculptor, musician, writer, or person of learning in literary or cultural matters who, in the opinion of the Prize Committee, has made an outstanding contribution to the cultural life of the nation, or who, in their opinion, has not been adequately rewarded by appreciation or otherwise, or who needs help at an early stage of his/her career. The prize of £1,500 is awarded annually by the Lord Mayor at the Midsummer Banquet held at the Mansion House.
Awarding body: Corporation of London, Guildhall, London EC2.
Recipients include: Norman Marshall (theatre, 1971); George Daniels (watchmaker, 1974); Jacqueline du Pré (musician, 1975); Kenneth Martin (sculptor, 1976); Prunella Clough (painter, 1977).

Mikola Sándor Prize
Two prizes of 5,000 forints each are awarded annually by the Hungarian Physical Society for work promoting better physics teaching based on modern experimental techniques. The award was established in 1961, in honour of Sándor Mikola.
Awarding body: 'Eötvös Loránd' Fizikai Társulat, 1061 Budapest VI, Anker-köz 1, Hungary.

O. M. Miller Cartographic Medal
This gold medal is awarded for outstanding contributions in the field of cartography or geodesy. The award was founded in 1968, and is made intermittently.
Awarding body: American Geographical Society, Broadway at 156th St., New York, N.Y. 10032, U.S.A.
Recipients include: Richard Edes Harrison (1968).

Willet G. Miller Medal
The medal is awarded every two years, if there is a suitable candidate, for outstanding research in any branch of the earth sciences. The prize consists of a gold medal and C$1,000. Canadian citizens or persons who have been Canadian residents for the five years preceding the award are eligible. The medal was established in 1941 by friends of Willet G. Miller (1867–1925), a distinguished geologist.
Awarding body: The Royal Society of Canada, 395 Wellington, Ottawa, Ont. K1A 0N4, Canada.
Recipients include: R. A. Jeletzky (1969); R. W. Boyle (1971); R. Thorsteinsson (1973); J. R. Mackay (1975); A. M. Goodwin (1977).

Mining and Metallurgical Society of America Gold Medal
The medal is awarded for conspicuous professional or public service for the advancement of the science of Mining and Metallurgy, or of Economic Geology; for the betterment of the conditions under which these industries are carried on, for the protection of mine investors, and especially for

the better protection of the health and safety of workmen in the mines and metallurgical establishments. The medal, first awarded in 1914, is given at irregular intervals, and recipients must be members of the Mining and Metallurgical Society.

Awarding body: Mining and Metallurgical Society of America, 230 Park Ave., New York, N.Y. 10017, U.S.A.

Recipients include: Louis S. Cates (distinguished service in mining and related industrial activities, 1955); Donald M. Liddell (contribution to the art of non-ferrous metallurgy, 1957); John F. Thompson (original research, development of new metal uses, and guidance of a great metallurgical enterprise, 1966); Thayer Lindsley (application of encyclopedic geological knowledge, 1974); Plato Malozemoff (leadership and financial skills in developing mining enterprises, 1976).

Minkowski Prize

This prize, consisting of DM10,000 and a certificate, is awarded annually for distinction manifested by publications which contribute to the advancement of knowledge concerning *diabetes mellitus*. The prize is open to persons under 40 years of age, resident in Europe, whose relevant research has been carried out in Europe. The award was founded in 1966 by the European Association for the Study of Diabetes, sponsored by Farbwerke Hoechst AG. The prize commemorates Oscar Minkowski (1858–1931) who in 1889 operated to remove the pancreas from a dog which developed diabetes.

Awarding body: European Association for the Study of Diabetes, 3/6 Alfred Place, London WC1E 7EE, England.

Recipients include: W. J. Malaisse (Belgium, 1972); L. Orci (Italy, 1973); E. Cerasi (Sweden, 1974); P. Freychet (France, 1975); K. D. Hepp (Fed. Rep. of Germany, 1976).

Sisir Kumar Mitra Lecture

This lecture was established in 1963 by the Indian National Science Academy. The lectureship is awarded for distinguished contributions in any branch of natural science. It is given every six years and the lecturer receives an honorarium.

Awarding body: Indian National Science Academy, Bahadur Shah Zafar Marg, New Delhi 110001, India.

Recipients include: K. R. Ramanathan (1966); R. N. Chakravarty (1972); T. Ramachandra Rao (1978).

Alexander-Mitscherlich-Denkmünze

This medal is presented by the West German Association of Pulp and Paper Chemists and Engineers (Zellcheming) for outstanding scientific and technical achievements which have served to advance the paper and cellulose industry. Nominations must be made by members of Zellcheming. The award was instituted in 1936, and commemorates the centenary of the birth of Alexander Mitscherlich (1836–1918), founder of the German sulphite cellulose industry.

Awarding body: Verein der Zellstoff- und Papier-Chemiker und Ingenieure, 6100 Darmstadt, Berliner Allee 56, Federal Republic of Germany.

Recipients include: Prof. Dr. Erich Schmidt (Fed. Rep. of Germany, 1965); Dr. Herbert F. Rance (U.K., 1970); Prof. Lennart Stockman (Sweden, 1973); Prof. Dr.-Ing. Waldemar Jensen (Finland, 1974); Dr. Theodor N. Kleinert (Canada, 1976).

Mofolo-Plomer Prize

This annual award of R500 was established in 1976 by Nadine Gordimer, the novelist, with the backing of three Johannesburg publishers, to encourage South African literature in English. It is for an unpublished novel or short story by a Southern African citizen or resident who is not yet an established writer. Thomas Mofolo and William Plomer were distinguished novelists during the formative years of South African literature in English.

Awarding body: Mofolo-Plomer Prize Committee, c/o Ravan Press, P.O.B. 31134, Braamfontein 2017, South Africa.

Recipients include: Mbulelo Mzamane (short stories, 'My Cousin Comes to Jo'burg') and Peter Wilhelm (novel, 'An Island Full of Grass'), jointly, 1976.

Moisseiff Award

This award was established in 1947 by friends of Leon S. Moisseiff, M.ASCE, in recognition of his achievements in structural design. The prize consists of a bronze medal and certificate, and is awarded, normally every year, to an important paper published by the Society which deals with the broad field of structural design, including applied mechanics as well as the theoretical analysis, or constructive improvement, of engineering structures. Papers recognized for award of other Society prizes are not eligible.

Awarding body: American Society of Civil Engineers, 345 East 47th St., New York, N.Y. 10017, U.S.A.

Recipients include: Paul Weidlinger ('Shear Field Panel Bracing', 1975); C. S. Lin and A. Scordelis ('Nonlinear Analysis of RC Shells of General Form', 1976).

Molson Prizes

These awards for outstanding contributions to the arts, humanities or social sciences, are made by the Canada Council, an independent agency founded in 1957 to foster and promote work in the above fields. The prizes were instituted in 1963 by the Council, financed initially by a gift of $900,000 from the Molson Foundation, a philanthropic organization, and supplemented by a further $100,000 in 1975. Normally, three prizes of $20,000 each are awarded every year. The recipients must be Canadian citizens.

Awarding body: Canada Council, P.O.B. 1047, Ottawa, Ont. K1P 5V8, Canada.

Recipients include: Alex Colville (painter, 1974); Margaret Laurence (writer, 1974); Pierre Dansereau (ecologist, 1974); Jon Vickers (opera singer, 1975); Denise Pelletier (actress, 1975); Orford String Quartet (1975).

John Monash Medal
This bronze medal was established in 1976 and perpetuates the memory of Sir John Monash who is recognized as Australia's greatest military commander, and who was an engineer of exceptional and diversified talents. The medal is awarded for the paper selected by the Board of the General College of Engineering (one of the foundation Colleges of the Institution of Engineers, Australia) as the best paper on engineering related to General College interests. The award is open to members of the Institution only.
Awarding body: Institution of Engineers, Australia, 11 National Circuit, Barton, A.C.T. 2600, Australia.

Ludwig Mond Lectureship
The lectureship was founded in 1923 under a bequest of £2,000 made by the late Mrs. Frederike Mond for the institution of lectures in the University of Manchester in memory of her husband.
Awarding body: University of Manchester, Manchester M13 9PL, England.
Lecturers include: Prof. Sir Frederick Warner ('Education and the Professions in the European Economic Community', 1972–73); Joseph Needham ('China and the Origins of Medical Chemistry', 1973–74); Lord Ashby ('Politics and the Environment', 1974–75); Prof. Edward Ullendorf ('The Life of the Emperor Haile Selassie of Ethiopia', 1975–76); Prof. Sir Fred Hoyle ('The Case for Nuclear Energy', 1976–77).

Montaigne Prize
This is one of four similar prizes given annually by the FVS Foundation for outstanding achievements in the arts, town and country planning, folklore and human sciences. It consists of DM25,000, and is especially for those who live in the area of Europe where Romance languages are spoken. The prize is named in memory of the French moralist, Montaigne (1533–92), famous for his *Essais.* (*See also* Shakespeare, Steeffens, Vondel prizes.)
Awarding body: Stiftung FVS, Georgsplatz 10, 2 Hamburg 1, Federal Republic of Germany.
Recipients include: Philippe Jaccottet (Switzerland, 1972).

Monte Carlo International Television Festival
Established in 1960, the Festival is held annually in February. Television organizations from countries which are members of the International Union of Telecommunications are invited to submit entries for prizes in all categories of television filming. The main prize goes to the best programme of the entire festival. Other prizes (gold and silver 'Nymphs') go to actors, actresses, writers and directors, and there are categories for documentaries, news reporting, children's programmes, and environmental programmes, as well as a special Critics Prize.
Awarding body: Monte Carlo International Television Festival, c/o Palais des Congrès, Monte Carlo, Monaco.
Recipients include: *The Fire Next Door* (U.S.A., best programme, 1978); *The Prisoner of the Caucasus* (U.S.S.R., Critics Prize, 1978); *Cinéma Romain* (France, best programme, 1979).

Montevideo International Piano Competition
Founded by the pianist Eliane Richepin in 1966, the competition is administered by the 'Asociación Eliane Richepin por el desarrollo de la cultura musical'. It is held every three years in November. Contestants must be between 15 and 32 years old. The cash prizes amount to $5,000; medals and certificates are also awarded, and winners receive concert engagements. The competition is affiliated to the Federation of International Music Competitions.
Awarding body: Secretariat, 'Ciudad de Montevideo' International Piano Competition, Enrique Muñoz 815, Montevideo, Uruguay.
Prize-winners include: Vladimir Bakk, Yuri Slesarien (U.S.S.R., 1972); Julian Martin (U.S.A.), Elsa Perdono (Uruguay), 1975.

Montreal Medal of The Chemical Institute of Canada
Established in 1956, the medal is awarded to persons resident in Canada in recognition of their leadership in or outstanding contributions to the profession of chemistry or chemical engineering in Canada (e.g. administrative work within the Institute and other professional organizations, teaching, or work by staff members of chemical industries). The medal is provided by the Montreal Section of the Institute, and is awarded annually at a National, Regional or Divisional Conference. Nominations are made by members of the Institute.
Awarding body: The Chemical Institute of Canada, 151 Slater St., Ottawa, Ont. K1P 5H3, Canada.
Recipients include: H. S. Sutherland ('It Depends on the Approach', 1972); W. G. Schneider ('Science in Transition', 1973); R. Gaudry ('Chemistry for What?', 1974); B. B. Migicovsky ('Contributions of Chemistry to Food Production', 1975); J. W. T. Spinks (1977).

Professor W. R. A. D. Moore Memorial Lecture
The lecture was established in 1969 in memory of Professor Moore, Professor of Polymer Science at Bradford University. A Memorial Fund was established from contributions from industry and academics, designed to finance an annual lecture given by a person of eminence either in the field of polymer science or in some other field which uses plastics.
Awarding body: University of Bradford, Bradford, West Yorkshire BD7 1DP, England.

Lecturers include: Prof. C. H. Bamford ('Polymers and Catalysts', 1972); Prof. R. J. W. Reynolds ('Polymer Pioneers of the Northern Counties', 1973); Dr. W. F. Watson ('University Research and the Needs of Industry', 1974); Donald Longmore ('Polymers in Organ Replacement', 1975); Sir Misha Black ('The Aesthetics of Plastics', 1977).

Sir Gilbert Morgan Medal

This award commemorates Sir Gilbert Morgan, Chairman of the Birmingham and Midlands Section of the Society of Chemical Industry, 1924–25, and President of the Society, 1931–32. Sir Gilbert exerted a profound influence on both pure and applied chemistry in Great Britain. The award is made for a paper submitted by a candidate under 30 years of age, describing original work in a field of pure and applied chemistry, providing sufficient material for a half-hour lecture. Papers are assessed for originality, experimental content, potential and general presentation.

Awarding body: Society of Chemical Industry, 14 Belgrave Square, London SW1X 8PS, England.

Recipients include: Dr. D. J. Greenwood ('Nitrogen Transformation in the Distribution of Oxygen in Soil', 1962); R. A. Cross ('The Enrichment of Gases of Low Calorific Value with Liquid Petroleum Gases', 1966); A. J. Pearson ('Kinetics and Mechanisms of the Auto Oxidation of Petrahydro Pterins', 1973).

Emil-Mörsch-Denkmünze

This prize was founded in 1938 by the German Concrete Association in honour of Professor Emil Mörsch (1872–1950), a pioneer in construction techniques using concrete. It is awarded for outstanding achievements and advances in the use of concrete and ferro-concrete. The prize is given every two years and consists of a silver medal and a certificate.

Awarding body: Deutscher Beton-Verein e.V., 6200 Wiesbaden 1, Postfach 21 26, Federal Republic of Germany.

Recipients include: Dr.-Ing. Fritz Leonhardt (1967); Nicolas Esquillan (1969); Dr.-Ing. Hans Minetti (1971); Dr.-Ing. habil. Kurt Walz (1973); Ir. Pieter Blokland (1975).

Robert T. Morse Writers Award

This award was established in 1964 in memory of Robert T. Morse, M.D., and is awarded to any writer for the general public who has made a major contribution to the public understanding of psychiatry over a period of time. In 1976 it was extended to cover comparable contributions to the mental health cause in a region, state or metropolitan area. It is made annually, and consists of a plaque and honorarium of $500. Selection is by nomination only.

Awarding body: American Psychiatric Association, 1700 18th St., N.W., Washington, D.C. 20009, U.S.A.

Samuel Finley Breese Morse Medal

This occasional award in the form of a gold medal was established in 1872 for the encouragement of geographical research. It commemorates Samuel Morse (1791–1872), inventor of the Morse code.

Awarding body: American Geographical Society, Broadway at 156th St., New York, N.Y. 10032, U.S.A.

Recipients include: Sir George Hubert Wilkins (1928); Archer M. Huntington (1945); Gilbert Grosvenor (1952); Charles B. Hitchcock (1966); Wilma B. Fairchild (1968).

Moscow International Film Festival

This is an annual event, with an international jury awarding prizes for different kinds of film in various categories. The main prize is a gold medal for the best feature film; silver and bronze medals are awarded for runners-up in this category. Gold, silver and bronze medals are also given for short films, children's films and documentaries. There are also awards for the best actor and actress, and special prizes which vary each year.

Awarding body: Moscow International Film Festival, c/o U.S.S.R. State Committee for Cinema, M. Gnezdnikovsky per. 7, Moscow, U.S.S.R.

Recipients include: *The Fifth Seal* (Zoltan Farbi, Hungary), *The Bridge* (Juan Antonio Barden, Spain), *Mimino* (Georgi Danelia, U.S.S.R.), 1977.

Harry G. Moseley Award

This prize was established by the Aerospace Medical Association in memory of Col. Harry G. Moseley, U.S.A.F., M.C., in recognition of his material contributions to flight safety. It is awarded annually in May for the most outstanding contribution to flight safety, and consists of a certificate. The award is sponsored by the Lockheed Aircraft Corporation.

Awarding body: Aerospace Medical Association, Washington National Airport, Washington, D.C. 20001, U.S.A.

Recipients include: A. Howard Hasbrook (1972); Capt. Frank H. Austin, Jr. (1973); Dr. Stanley R. Mohler (1974); Dr. Richard G. Snyder (1975); Harry W. Orlady (1976).

Mountbatten Lectureship

This lectureship, on some aspect of Defence, is named after Admiral of the Fleet Lord Mountbatten, who delivered the first of the series in 1962.

Awarding body: Edinburgh University, Edinburgh EH8 9TL, Scotland.

Lecturers include: General Farrar-Hockley (1977).

Mozart-Medaille

This award was established in 1950 by the Vienna Mozart Society. It is given annually to artists, scientists, journalists and organizers for outstanding achievements in connection with Mozart's work. Up to four medals may be awarded annually.

Awarding body: Mozartgemeinde Wien, 1030 Vienna III, Metternichgasse 8, Austria.
Recipients include: Fritz Kreisler; Henryk Szeryng; Leopold Wlach; Karl Öhlberger; Amadeus String Quartet.

Samuel Edward Mqhayi-prys vir Bantoeletterkunde *(Samuel Edward Mqhayi Prize for Bantu Literature)*

Samuel Edward Mqhayi was a famous Xhosa writer and poet, particularly known for writing the words of 'N'kosi sikelel'i Afrika'. He is known among the Xhosas as 'the true folk poet'. The Mqhayi Prize is given for original literary work in a South African Bantu language, written by a Bantu living in South Africa, and is intended as an encouragement to a writer who has shown promise in his/her first published work. The prize money of R100 is donated by Shell (S.A.).
Awarding body: Suid-Afrikaanse Akademie vir Wetenskap en Kuns, Posbus 538, Pretoria 0001, South Africa.
Recipients include: M. T. Mazibuko *(Ithongwane)* and I. T. Maditsi *(Monamolomo bolela)*, 1971; Oliver Kgadime Matsepe *(Megokgo ya Bjoko,* 1973).

Mueller Medal

Founded in 1902 by the Australian and New Zealand Association for the Advancement of Science, the medal is in memory of Baron Sir Ferdinand von Mueller, K.C.M.G., M.D., Ph.D., F.R.S. (1825–96), who did pioneering work in botany, geography and explorations, as well as administration and advancement of science generally in Australia. The interest from the Mueller Medal Fund is used annually to provide a bronze medal to be awarded at each ANZAAS Congress to the author of important contributions of anthropological, botanical, geological or zoological science, preference being given to work having special reference to Australasia. The money remaining after purchase of the medal is awarded as an accompanying prize.
Awarding body: Australian and New Zealand Association for the Advancement of Science, 157 Gloucester St., Sydney, N.S.W. 2000, Australia.
Recipients include: D. F. Waterhouse (entomology, 1972); R. J. Moir (agriculture, 1973); A. E. Ringwood (geology, 1975); L. D. Pryor (botany, 1976); A. K. McIntyre (physiology, 1977).

Mullard Medal

The Royal Society Mullard Award, which consists of a gold medal and a prize of £1,000, was provided by a gift to the Society by the Board of Directors of Mullard Ltd. in 1967. It is awarded annually to an individual or individuals who, in the opinion of the Council of the Society, have made an outstanding contribution to the advancement of science or engineering or technology leading directly to national prosperity in the United Kingdom of Great Britain and Northern Ireland.
Awarding body: Royal Society of London, 6 Carlton House Terrace, London SW1Y 5AG, England.
Recipients include: Sir Charles Oatley (1973); F. B. Mercer (1974); J. Bingham (1975); Dr. G. H. Hitchings (1976); Dr. J. W. Black (1978).

Hugo Muller Lectureship

This award was founded in 1918 to commemorate the name of Dr. Hugo Müller, President of the Chemical Society from 1885 to 1887, and one of its benefactors. The subject of the lecture deals with the relation between chemistry and either botany or mineralogy. The lecture is delivered every three years, and lecturers receive a silver medal and £100.
Awarding body: The Chemical Society, Burlington House, London W1V 0BN, England.
Recipients include: D. M. Hodgkin (1968–69); A. R. Battersby (1971–72); G. Eglinton (1974–75); L. Crombie (1977–78).

Munkácsy Mihály Prize for Visual and Applied Arts

Instituted by the Hungarian Council of Ministers in 1953, the prize is awarded annually by the Minister of Culture. It is an honorary distinction, and is divided into three classes. It is named in honour of the Hungarian painter, Mihály Munkácsy (1844–1900).
Awarding body: Committee for the Munkácsy Mihály Prize, Ministry of Culture, Szalay-utca 10, Budapest V, Hungary.
Recipients include: Ernó Tóth (painter), József Németh (painter), István Szabó (sculptor), 1976.

Murchison Award

This award is intended for the advancement of geographical science by supporting travellers in pursuit of knowledge, authors of memoirs, or those actually employed in enquiries bearing on the science of geography. It is an annual monetary award, but can be taken in the form of survey instruments, plate or books. The award was founded in 1882 as a result of a bequest of Sir Roderick Murchison, Bt. (1792–1871), one of the founder members of the Royal Geographical Society, a leading exponent of geography and a promoter and encourager of geographical exploration. There is no application for the award, which is granted by the Council of the Royal Geographical Society on the recommendation of a special committee. The criteria are the academic and other achievements of the recipients.
Awarding body: Royal Geographical Society, 1 Kensington Gore, London SW7 2AR, England.
Recipients include: Prof. Stanley H. Beaver (1962); Prof. A. Austin Miller (1963); Prof. W. B. Fisher (1973); Emeritus Prof. W. G. Hoskins (1976); Prof. Kenneth Walton (1978).

Gheorghe Munteanu-Murgoci Prize

The prize was founded in 1948 by the Romanian Academy. It is given for achievements in the fields of geography or geology, and is named after Gheorghe Murgoci (1872–1925), the founder of pedology in Romania. The prize is presented annually at a General Assembly of the Academy, and consists of 10,000 lei and a diploma.

Awarding body: Academy of the S.R. of Romania, 125 Calea Victoriei, Bucharest, Romania.

E.V. Murphree Award in Industrial and Engineering Chemistry

Established in 1955 by Exxon Research and Engineering Company, the award is intended to stimulate fundamental research in industrial and engineering chemistry, the development of chemical engineering principles and their application to industrial processes. The award is granted annually without regard to age, nationality or sex. A nominee must have accomplished outstanding research of a theoretical or experimental nature in the fields of industrial chemistry or chemical engineering. The award consists of $2,000 and a certificate. An allowance of not more than $350 is provided for travelling expenses to the presentation ceremony.

Awarding body: American Chemical Society, 1155 Sixteenth St., N.W., Washington, D.C. 20036, U.S.A.

Recipients include: Thomas K. Sherwood (1973); Herman S. Bloch (1974); Donald L. Katz (1975); James F. Roth (1976); Alexis Voorhies, Jr. (1977).

Glenn Murphy Award

Established by the Nuclear Engineering Division of ASEE, this annual award is made to a distinguished nuclear engineering educator in recognition of notable professional contributions to the teaching of undergraduate and/or graduate nuclear engineering students. The award, consisting of an honorarium and engraved certificate, is sponsored by former students and friends of Dr. Murphy in recognition of his many contributions in this field. The recipient must be a full-time member of a college faculty and actively engaged in teaching in the United States or Canada at the time of the award selection.

Awarding body: American Society for Engineering Education, Suite 400, One Dupont Circle, Washington, D.C. 20036, U.S.A.

Recipients include: Raymond L. Murray (1976).

David Murray Lectureship

Founded in 1929, the lectureship is in memory of David Murray, M.A., LL.D. One or more lectures are delivered biennially on the history of learning, especially in relation to history, archaeology, law or bibliography. The choice of lecturer and subject of the lectures are made by the Glasgow University Court. The lectures are published at regular intervals.

Awarding body: University of Glasgow, Glasgow G12 8QQ, Scotland.

Lecturers include: C. H. S. Fifoot (Hon. Fellow of Hertford Coll., Oxford, 1970); J. K. S. St. Joseph (Dir. in Aerial Photography, Cambridge Univ., 1973); Prof. William Beattie (Inst. for Advanced Studies in the Humanities, Edinburgh Univ., 1976).

John Courtney Murray Award

This award was originally established in 1947 as the Cardinal Spellman Award by the Catholic Theological Society and Cardinal Spellman. In 1972 it was established under its present title by the Catholic Theological Society of America in honour of John Courtney Murray, S.J., one of the most distinguished North American Catholic theologians of the 20th century. The prize is awarded for distinguished achievement in theology through scholarly research and writing and/or teaching. Any Catholic theologian, usually from the United States or Canada, is eligible. It is awarded annually and consists of a medal, a scroll and a cash sum of $250.

Awarding body: The Catholic Theological Society of America, St. Mary of the Lake Seminary, Mundelein, Ill. 60060, U.S.A.

Recipients include: Charles E. Curran (1972); Bernard J. F. Lonergan, S.J. (1973); George H. Tavard, A.A. (1974); Carl J. Peter (1975); Richard P. McBrien (1976).

Musgrave Medal

Three medals are awarded annually in December. They were established in 1888 to commemorate Sir Anthony Musgrave, Governor of Jamaica from 1877 to 1883 and founder of the Institute of Jamaica in 1879. The gold medal is awarded for eminence in literature, science or art in connection with the West Indies, especially Jamaica. The silver medal is awarded for outstanding merit in the promotion of literature, science or art, and the bronze medal for outstanding individual achievement in the same fields. There are no conditions of age, sex or nationality.

Awarding body: Council of the Institute of Jamaica, 12–16 East St., Kingston, Jamaica, West Indies.

Gold Medal recipients include: Alvin Marriot (sculpture), Amy Jacques Garvey (history), Prof. Michael Smith (anthropology), Albert Huie (painting), Victor Stafford Reid (literature).

Musician of the Year

In 1976 the Incorporated Society of Musicians drew attention to the need for wider recognition of the real achievements of contemporary British musicians. As a positive lead in this direction the Society established its own award. It takes the form of a silver-gilt medal and is awarded annually for the most outstanding contribution to music.

Awarding body: Incorporated Society of Musicians, 10 Stratford Place, London W1N 9AE, England.

Recipients: Alexander Gibson, C.B.E. (1976); Sir William Walton, O.M. (1977); Sir Peter Pears (1978).

Henry Myers Lecture

This lecture, instituted in 1945 in memory of Henry Myers (died 1947), is delivered every two years (it alternates with the Curl Lecture). The lecturer is nominated by the Council of the Royal

Anthropological Institute and delivers a formal lecture on the subject of religion in society.

Awarding body: Royal Anthropological Institute of Great Britain and Ireland, 36 Craven St., London WC2N 5NG, England.

Lecturers include: Prof. Joseph Needham (1964); Prof. Sir Edmund Leach (1966); Prof. Louis Dumont (1970); Prof. Mary Douglas (1972); Prof. C. von Fürer-Haimendorf (1974).

Myres Memorial Lectureship

In 1959 the University of Oxford accepted a sum from certain learned bodies and friends of the late Professor Sir John Myres to provide a memorial lecture to be given from time to time on subjects in which Sir John was chiefly engaged: fields of Ancient History, European and Near Eastern Archaeology, Ancient Geography and Ethnology, with special reference to Mediterranean lands. The lecture is given every other year.

Awarding body: University of Oxford, Wellington Square, Oxford OX1 2JD, England.

Lecturers include: Prof. A. D. Momigliano (University Coll., London, 1973–74); C. F. C. Hawkes (Hon. Fellow, Keble Coll., Oxford, 1974–75).

N

NIN Critics Award

The award was established by *Nedeljne Informativne Novine* (NIN), the weekly periodical, in 1954. A cash prize of 20,000 dinars and a certificate is presented for the best novel to have been published in the preceding year.

Awarding body: NIN, Makedonska 29, Belgrade, Yugoslavia.

Recipients include: Danilo Kiš (1973); Mihailo Lalić (1974); Jure Franičević (1975); Miodrag Bulatović (1976); Alexsander Tišma (1977).

Otto Naegeli-Preis

This prize is given by the Naegeli Foundation and is the most important Swiss prize in the field of medical research. It is currently worth 100,000 Swiss francs which the winner is expected to use to further his research.

Awarding body: Otto Naegeli-Stiftung, c/o Präsident, Dr. W. Staehelin, Bleicherweg 58, 8002 Zürich, Switzerland.

Recipients include: Prof. Hugo Studer (1977).

Theodor Naegeli-Preis

This prize, founded in 1971, is awarded every three years to physicians from German-speaking countries for medical research into thromboembolism, geriatrics and gerontology. It consists of a cash prize and a grant for further research, totalling 20,000 Swiss francs. It is awarded by the Naegeli Foundation through a committee including representatives from the German and Swiss Surgical Societies and the University of Tübingen.

Awarding body: Theodor Naegeli-Stiftung, Basel, Switzerland.

Recipients include: Dr. Ulrich F. Gruber (Switzerland, 1973); Dr. Kristian Lüders (Fed. Rep. of Germany, 1973).

Nagroda imienia Włodzimierza Mozołowskiego (*W. Mozolowski Memorial Prize*)

This prize was established in 1968 by the Polish Biochemical Society; in 1975 its name was changed in honour of Włodzimierz Mozołowski (1895–1975), an outstanding biochemist. It is awarded annually, usually to several people at a time, for outstanding written or oral contributions at annual meetings of the Society by biochemists under the age of 30. The prize consists of a certificate and a cash sum of a varying amount.

Awarding body: Polskie Towarzystwo Biochemiczne, Zarząd Główny, ul. Freta 16, 00-227 Warsaw, Poland.

Nagroda imienia Jakuba Karola Parnasa (*J. K. Parnas Prize*)

This prize was established in 1961 by the Polish Biochemical Society in memory of Jakub Karol Parnas (1884–1949), an outstanding biochemist. It is awarded annually to a biochemist or group of biochemists for the best experimental work accomplished in a laboratory in Poland and published in Poland during the preceding year. The prize consists of a cash sum of 10,000 złotys and a certificate.

Awarding body: Polskie Towarzystwo Biochemiczne, Zarząd Główny, ul. Freta 16, 00-227 Warsaw, Poland.

Nagroda imienia Bolesława Skarżyńskiego (*B. Skarżyński Prize*)

Established in 1960 by the Polish Biochemical Society, this prize was given the name of Bolesław Skarżyński in 1965 in honour of Skarżyński (1901–63), an outstanding Polish biochemist. It is awarded annually for the best review article published during the preceding year in *Postępy Biochemii* (quarterly, 'Advances in Biochemistry'). The prize consists of a certificate and a cash sum of 8,000 złotys, which may be divided among more than one person.

Awarding body: Polskie Towarzystwo Biochemiczne, Zarząd Główny, ul. Freta 16, 00-227 Warsaw, Poland.

Nagroda imienia Henryka Swidzinskiego (*Henryk Swidzinski Prize*)

This prize was founded in 1970 by Mrs. Lucyna Swidzinska in memory of her husband Henryk Swidzinski (1907–69), a former President of the Geological Society of Poland. It is awarded annually for an outstanding paper published in Poland on the geology of the Carpathian Mountains and/or the Holy Cross Mountains. The prize consists of a cash sum of 3,000 złotys. Recipients must be members of the Geological Society of Poland and under 40 years of age.

Awarding body: Polskie Towarzystwo Geologiczne, Oleandry 2a, 30-063 Cracow, Poland.

Recipients include: Dr. S. Weclawik (1970); Dr. W. Sikora (1971); Dr. A. Slaczka (1972); Dr. N. Oszczypko (1974).

Nagroda imienia Ludwika Zejsznera (Ludwik Zejszner Prize)

This prize was established in 1964 by the Geological Society of Poland in memory of Ludwik Zejszner, an eminent geologist of the first half of the 19th century. The prize is awarded annually for the best paper published in the Society's journal *Rocznik Polskiego Towarzystwa Geologicznego*. The winner receives a cash sum of 3,000 złotys. Recipients must be members of the Society, and must not have reached professional status.

Awarding body: Polskie Towarzystwo Geologiczne, Oleandry 2a, 30-063 Cracow, Poland.

Recipients include: Dr. W. Moryc (1972); Dr. H. Niedzielski (1973); Dr. S. Poltowicz and A. Starczewska-Popow (1974); Dr. M. Sass-Gustkiewicz (1975); Dr. Z. Baranowski (1976).

Nagroda Państwowa (National Prize)

This prize was established in 1949 by the Polish Council of Ministers to promote and stimulate the development of pure and social sciences, technology, agriculture, medicine, literature and the arts in Poland. The prize is awarded for creative achievements of national and international importance in any of these fields of activity. It is awarded every two years on Polish National Day (22 July) and is usually for work done in the preceding two years. The prize is divided into two classes: first class (gold medal) and second class (silver medal). The medals are accompanied by a certificate and a sum of money.

Awarding body: Sekretariat Komitetu Nagród Państwowych, Polska Akademia Nauk, Pałac Kultury i Nauki, 00-901 Warsaw, Poland.

Naito Prize

This is an annual prize established in 1969 to commemorate the 88th birthday of Mr. Toyoji Naito, Chairman emeritus of Eisai Co. Ltd. A cash prize of two million yen is awarded for the most outstanding contribution to the life sciences. Only Japanese nationals are eligible.

Awarding body: The Naito Foundation, 4-6-10 Koishikawa, Bunkyo, Tokyo 112, Japan.

Recipients include: Prof. Hidemasa Yamazaki (1972); Prof. Tokindo Okada (1973); Prof. Teruaki Mukaiyama (1974); Prof. Goro Kikuchi (1975); Prof. Yutaka Oomura (1976).

Fridtjof Nansens belønning (Fridtjof Nansen Award)

The Nansen and Affiliated Funds for the Advancement of Science and the Humanities established this prize in 1896 in honour of Fridtjof Nansen (1861-1930), the natural scientist, explorer, diplomat and philanthropist. It is for outstanding achievement in science and/or the humanities, and is awarded to Norwegian citizens only. It consists of 10,000 kroner and a certificate, and is presented annually on 3 May, the annual meeting of the Norwegian Academy of Science and Letters.

Awarding body: Nansenfondet og de dermed forbundne fond, Norway.

Recipients include: Prof. Dr. Georg H. M. Waaler (medicine), Prof. Dr. Per M. Grøtvedt (linguistics), 1976; Prof. Dr. Arnt Eliassen (meteorology), Prof. Dr. Ragnar Fjørtoft (meteorology), Prof. Andreas Holmsen (history), 1977.

Naoki Prize

This well-known Japanese literary prize was established in 1935 by the late Kan Kikuchi, founder of the Bungei-Shunju publishing company which sponsors the Society for the Promotion of Japanese Literature. The prize is in memory of Sanjūgo Naoki (1891-1934) who was a well-known popular novelist. It is awarded twice a year in February and August for the best novel published in the previous six months. The winner receives 300,000 yen and an inscribed watch.

Awarding body: Society for the Promotion of Japanese Literature, Bungei-Shunju Building, 3 Kioi-cho, Chiyoda-ku, Tokyo 102, Japan.

Recipients include: Masuji Ibuse; Akiyuki Nosaka; Ryotaro Shiba; Masaaki Tachihara; Giichi Fujimoto.

Dr. Y. S. Narayana Rao Oration Award in Microbiology

This prize was instituted in 1971 following a donation by Smt. Kamla Narayana Rao in memory of her late husband, Dr. Y. S. Narayana Rao, a former director of King Institute, Guindy, Madras. The prize of 1,000 rupees is given annually to an eminent microbiologist who delivers a lecture on his/her work.

Awarding body: Indian Council of Medical Research, Ansari Nagar, Post Box 4508, New Delhi 110016, India.

Recipients include: Dr. K. Bhaskaran (1972); Dr. T. Ramachandra Rao (1973); Dr. N. Veeraraghavan (1974); Dr. Dharmendra (1975); Dr. L. N. Mohapatra (1976).

Narvesen Pris

Established in 1954 by Narvesen Ltd., the newspaper and magazine distributors, the prize is for excellence in journalism. It is awarded annually, and consists of a certificate and 15,000 kroner in cash. Norwegian journalists and editors working in any of the media are eligible. The prize may be given for a single article or for excellence over many years.

Awarding body: Narvesen Committee, c/o Norsk Presseforbund, Rosenkrantzgt. 3, Oslo 1, Norway.

Recipients include: Gerd Benneche (*Dagbladet*, 1974); Rolf W. Thanem and Geir Tønset (*Adresseavisen*, 1975); Berit Eriksen (freelance, 1976).

National Academy of Engineering Founders Award

The award was established in 1965 for outstanding engineering accomplishments over a long period of time and of benefit to the people of the United States. Any engineer is eligible except a founding member of the Academy. The prize is given annually and consists of a gold-plated medal, a bronze medal, and a certificate. The recipient is generally invited to deliver a lecture.

Awarding body: National Academy of Engineering, 2101 Constitution Ave., N.W., Washington, D.C., U.S.A.

Recipients include: Edwin H. Land (1972); Warren K. Lewis (1973); J. Erik Jonsson (1974); James B. Fisk (1975); Manson Benedict (1976).

National Book Awards

These awards are presented annually for books written by American citizens and published in the United States during the previous calendar year which are the most distinguished works in their respective categories. At present there are seven categories: poetry, biography and autobiography, history, contemporary thought, translation, children's literature, and fiction. The awards amount to $1,000 each. Between 1950 and 1974 they were sponsored by the American Book Publishers Council and the National Book Committee, Inc. Since 1975 they have been given under the auspices of the National Institute of Arts and Letters (amalgamated 1976 with the American Academy of Arts and Letters). The awards are funded from various sources including major companies and the publishing industry.

Awarding body: American Academy and Institute of Arts and Letters, 633 West 155th St., New York, N.Y. 10032, U.S.A.

Recipients include: Walter Jackson Bate (biography, *Samuel Johnson*, 1978).

National Book Development Council of Singapore Book Awards

Established in 1972, the first awards were made in 1976 for books published between 1972 and 1974. They are given for the best books in the following five categories: fiction; non-fiction; poetry; drama; and children's and young people's books, published in Singapore or abroad. For fiction and non-fiction the cash prize ranges from S$500 to S$1,000, and for the other categories from S$250 to S$500. A certificate and trophy are also awarded to each prize-winner. Only Singapore citizens and/or permanent residents of Singapore are eligible. The books must have been published within a specified period of three years and may be written in any one of the four official languages (Malay, English, Chinese and Tamil). The awards may be made every three or four years or every year if there are books of sufficient merit.

Awarding body: National Book Development Council of Singapore, c/o National Library, Stamford Road, Singapore 6, Republic of Singapore.

Recipients for 1976: Goh Poh Seng (*If we dream too long*) and Michael Soh (*A son of a mother*), fiction in English; Arthur Yap (*Only lines*), poetry in English; Lee Sheng Yi (*The monetary and banking development of Malaysia and Singapore*) and Yeo Kim Wah (*Political developments in Singapore, 1945–55*), non-fiction in English; Kwan Shan Mei (illustrations for the Alpha Press Moongate collection of Folk-tales from the Orient), children's book in

English; Hsieh Ching (*The god is sobbing*), poetry in Chinese; Soon Cheong Jin (*Principles, methods, techniques and application of audio-visual education*), non-fiction in Chinese; Chew Kok Chang (*Poems for children*), children's book in Chinese.

National Crafts Competition Prizes

First, second and third prizes are awarded for craftwork of merit in the annual National Crafts Competition of the Royal Dublin Society. The entries are judged on the standard of workmanship, design and competence. Cash prizes of £50, £25 and £15 are awarded and all winners receive a Certificate of Merit of the Royal Dublin Society. The competition, established in 1968, is open to individual craftworkers, students of schools of art or training colleges or technical and vocational schools and apprentices of any nationality. All works submitted must have been executed in Ireland and none may be entered in more than one class. All works must have been executed within the two years prior to the competition.

Awarding body: Royal Dublin Society, Ballsbridge, Dublin 4, Ireland.

Recipients include: Kathleen Flanagan (Carrickmacross lace veil, 1974); Leonora Fowler (woven vestment, 1975); Catriona O'Connor (batik, 1975); Evelyn Lyndsay (woven chasuble, 1976); Cecil Hyde (woodwork, 1976).

National Crop Improvement Committee Award

This prize was established in 1973 by Dr. Dagnatchew Yirgou, then General Manager of the Institute of Agricultural Research of Ethiopia. The award is normally given annually for work which has made a positive contribution to the development of the country. Dedication, initiative and innovation are very important. The winner should also display qualities of leadership, such as the encouragement of young agricultural scientists, and the ability to promote a team effort in solving agricultural problems. A trophy is presented to the winner at the annual National Crop Improvement Committee meeting.

Awarding body: Institute of Agricultural Research, P.O.B. 2003, Addis Ababa, Ethiopia.

Recipients: F. F. Pinto (1973); Guy Rouanet (1974); Dr. Tessfaye Tessema (1975); Dr. Berhane G. Kidan (1977).

National Culture Awards for Arts and Sciences

The El Salvador National Culture Award was established by a legislative decree in 1975. It is awarded annually on 5 November, in recognition of an outstanding cultural achievement. Any person of Salvadorean nationality who, through research or creative work in the arts or sciences, has made a positive contribution to the cultural development of the country, is eligible. Candidates may only be proposed by officially recognized cultural and scientific institutions of El Salvador. Dedication and originality are considered very important. The award is bestowed by the President of El Salvador. The winner receives a diploma of merit, a gold medal and 15,000 colones. National or international publicity may be given to the winning work.

Awarding body: Ministry of Education, San Salvador, El Salvador, Central America.

Recipients include: José Mejía Vides (painter, sculptor and engraver), Jesús Merino Argueta (phytobiologist), 1976.

National Geographic Society Special Gold Medal

Established in 1909, the medal is awarded as and when merited for extraordinary geographic achievement.

Awarding body: National Geographic Society, 17th and M Streets, N.W., Washington, D.C. 20036, U.S.A.

Recipients include: Amelia Earhart (1932); Thomas C. Poulter (1937); Mrs. Robert E. Peary (1955); Prince Philip, Duke of Edinburgh (1957); Capt. Jacques-Yves Cousteau (1961).

National Institute of Arts and Letters Gold Medal

This award is given annually to two artists for their distinguished achievement in two categories of the arts. In all twelve categories are recognized. These are (as paired every sixth year): architecture and poetry; drama and graphic art; belles lettres and criticism, and painting; biography and music; the novel and sculpture; the short story and history. The award is based on the entire work of the recipient, who is not necessarily a member of the Institute or of the Academy of Arts and Letters. (The Institute and Academy were amalgamated in 1976.)

Awarding body: American Academy and Institute of Arts and Letters, 633 West 155th St., New York, N.Y. 10032, U.S.A.

National Medal of Science Award

Established by Congress in 1959, the prize is awarded annually by the President of the U.S.A. to individuals deserving special recognition by reason of their outstanding contributions to knowledge in the physical, biological, mathematical or engineering sciences. The first medal was presented in 1962.

Awarding body: National Medal of Science Committee, c/o National Science Foundation, 1800 G St., N.W., Washington, D.C. 20550, U.S.A.

Recipients include: Nicolaas Bloembergen, Britton Chance, Erwin Chargaff, Paul John Flory, William Alfred Fowler, Kurt Gödel, Rodolf Kompfner, James Van Gundia Neel, Linus Carl Pauling, Ralph Brazelton Peck, Kenneth Sanborn Pitzer, James Augustine Shannon, Abel Wolman (1974).

National Trust President's Award

Founded in 1976, the award recognizes achievement in preservation that is of significance to the local community either in its usefulness as a community service through adaptive use, or because of the local historical importance of the structure or site concerned. It is awarded annually, and consists of a scroll or trophy or both.

Awarding body: The National Trust for Historic Preservation, 704–748 Jackson Place, N.W., Washington, D.C. 20006, U.S.A.

Naumann-Thienemann Memorial Medal

This medal is awarded for outstanding achievements and contributions to all aspects of theoretical and applied limnology. It was established in memory of two eminent limnologists, Einar Naumann (Sweden) and August Thienemann (Germany). Both these men are considered founders of modern theoretical and applied limnology. The medal is awarded annually or, alternatively, a maximum of three medals are awarded at the triennial International Congress of the International Association of Theoretical and Applied Limnology. The award consists of a bronze medal depicting the busts of Naumann and Thienemann. Only members of the International Association of Theoretical and Applied Limnology are eligible.

Awarding body: International Association of Theoretical and Applied Limnology, c/o Gen. Sec., Prof. R. G. Wetzel, W. K. Kellogg Biological Station, Michigan State University, Hickory Corners, Mich 49060, U.S.A.

Recipients include: V. I. Shadin (U.S.S.R., 1965); Tonolli (Italy, 1968); Y. A. Kuznetsov (U.S.S.R., 1971); W. Ohle (Fed. Rep. of Germany, 1971); W. Rodhe (Sweden, 1974).

Naumburg Chamber Music Awards

The Walter W. Naumburg Foundation was established in 1926 by the late Walter Wehle Naumburg 1867–1959), banker and amateur musician, with the purpose of enabling young musicians to give New York recitals. In 1965 an award was first made to chamber groups, and was instituted on an annual basis in 1972. A maximum of two groups is chosen each year, and, in addition to sponsored New York appearances, the winners are enabled to commission a new work from a composer chosen by them in consultation with the Foundation. The National Endowment for the Arts acts as co-sponsor.

Awarding body: Walter W. Naumburg Foundation, 144 West 66th St., New York, N.Y. 10023, U.S.A.

Recipients include: Cambridge Consort, Da Capo Chamber Players (1973); American String Quartet, Francesco Trio (1974); New York Renaissance Band (1975).

Naumburg Competition

The Walter W. Naumburg Foundation was established in 1926 by the late Walter Wehle Naumburg (1867–1959), banker and amateur musician, with the purpose of enabling young musicians to give New York recitals. In 1961 a competition was established with the idea that the winner would receive a substantial cash prize for use in furthering his/her career, a two-year contract with a professional management, a solo recording, and an appearance with the New York Philharmonic on a Naumburg-sponsored concert. Since 1971 the three traditional categories of piano, strings and voice have usually rotated on a triennial basis, and the winners receive not only the cash prize but several recital appearances.

Awarding body: Walter W. Naumburg Foundation, 144 West 66th St., New York, N.Y. 10023, U.S.A.

Recipients include: Dickran Atamian (piano), Elmar Oliveira (violin), Clamma Dale and Joy Simpson (voice) (1975).

Jawaharlal Nehru Award for International Understanding

The award was instituted by the Indian Government in 1964 in memory of Jawaharlal Nehru (1889–1964), former Prime Minister of India, who was the chief architect of modern India and who strove tirelessly for national unity and international peace and understanding. The award is given annually for an outstanding contribution to the promotion of international understanding, goodwill and friendship. It is worth 100,000 rupees. Nominations may be made by former members of the jury, previous recipients, Indian Members of Parliament, Nobel Laureates, the UN Secretary-General and other leaders of international organizations, heads of academic institutions and learned societies, or heads of Indian Missions abroad. The seven-man jury consists of prominent Indian citizens.

Awarding body: Indian Council for Cultural Relations, Azad Bhavan, Indraprastha Estate, New Delhi, India.

Recipients include: President Julius Nyerere (Tanzania, 1973); Raúl Prebisch (Argentina, 1974); Jonas Salk (U.S.A., 1975); Giuseppe Tucci (Italy, 1976).

Mrs. Patrick Ness Award

This award is intended for the encouragement of travellers who have successfully carried out their plans or wish to pursue or follow up investigations which have been partially completed. It is an annual monetary award, but can be taken in the form of survey instruments, plate or books. The award was established in 1954 by Mrs. Patrick Ness (died 1962), an extensive traveller and the first woman to become a member of the Council of the Society. There is no application for the award, which is granted by the Council of the Royal Geographical Society on the recommendation of a special committee. The criteria are the achievements of the recipients.

Awarding body: Royal Geographical Society, 1 Kensington Gore, London SW7 2AR, England.

Recipients include: Dr. D. R. Stoddart (1965); E. C. Evans and J. P. M. Long (1966); Dr. J. D. Thornes (1970); Squadron-Leader T. H. Sheppard (1976); F. Aylene Street (1978).

Neuhausenske Legat's konkurrence (*Neuhausen Foundation Award*)

The award was established in 1838 by the Danish Academy of Fine Arts in memory of Jens Neuhausen (1774–1816), the master painter. A cash prize of 35,000 Danish kroner is awarded every four years for the best submitted work in the field of architecture, sculpture or fine art. The work must have been completed within a given period of two years. The award is open to anyone with a permanent address in Denmark.

Awarding body: Akademiet for de skønne Kunster, Akademiraadet, Kgs. Nytorv 1, 1050 Copenhagen K, Denmark.

Neumann János Memorial Medal

Founded in 1976 by the Neumann János Society for Computer Science, the medal is awarded to members of the Society who have made outstanding contributions to some branch of computer science, and who have given many years of service to the cause of the Society, thus contributing to the promotion of computer technology in Hungary. Prizes of 5,000 forints each are awarded either annually to up to three people, or every two years to between three and six people.

Awarding body: Neumann János Számitógéptudományi Társaság, 1061 Budapest, Anker-köz 1, Hungary.

John von Neumann Lecture

Established in 1960 by the American Society for Industrial and Applied Mathematics, this lecture takes place annually. It surveys and evaluates a significant field of pure mathematics in the light of its contribution to major advances in applied mathematics. The lecturer receives a cash award of $1,000.

Awarding body: Society for Industrial and Applied Mathematics, U.S.A.

Recipients include: J. H. Wilkinson (1970); Paul A. Samuelson (1971); Jule Charney (1974); Sir James Lighthill (1975); Rene Thom (1976).

Senator-Neumann-Preis

Established by the city council of Hamburg in 1973, the prize is awarded for the creation of buildings or installations which in some particular way cater for the needs of the handicapped. The cash prize is awarded every two years; grants are also awarded from the prize foundation. Prizewinners are selected by a seven-member prize jury appointed by the city council of Hamburg.

Awarding body: Senat der Freien und Hansestadt Hamburg, 2 Hamburg 1, Rathaus, Federal Republic of Germany.

Neustadt International Prize for Literature

This prize was originally known as the *Books Abroad* International Prize for Literature, and then as the *Books Abroad*/Neustadt International Prize for Literature. It was established in 1970 by *Books Abroad: An International Literary Quarterly* (now *World Literature Today*), and permanently endowed in 1971 by the Neustadt family of Oklahoma. The award is made every two years for distinguished and continuous artistic achievement in the fields of poetry, drama or fiction. Any living writer whose work is available in a representative selection in French or English is eligible, but candidates must be nominated by a member of the Prize jury. The award consists of a certificate, $10,000 in prize money and a symbolic eagle feather cast in silver. In addition, one issue of *World Literature Today* is dedicated to the prize-winner.

Awarding body: World Literature Today, 630 Parrington Oval, Univ. of Oklahoma, Norman, Okla. 73019, U.S.A.

Recipients include: Giuseppe Ungaretti (Italy, 1970); Gabriel García Márquez (Colombia, 1972); Francis Ponge (France, 1974); Elizabeth Bishop (U.S.A., 1976).

New England Theatre Conference Annual Awards

The following three prizes were established by the NETC in 1957: the major award 'for outstanding creative achievement in the American Theatre'; the Special Awards for outstanding achievements in, or contributions to, the theatre on a national level; and the Regional Citations for outstanding achievements in, or contributions to, regional theatre activity. The NETC also gives a Community Theatre Drama Festival Award (trophy and plaque) for the best one-act plays or scenes or cuttings from full-length plays; certificates are also presented for Best Director, Actor, Actress, etc. The 'John Gassner Memorial Playwriting Award' was established in 1963 in memory of John Gassner (1903–67), a distinguished personality in the professional and academic theatre. It is awarded annually on a national level for the best original, commercially unproduced and unpublished new one-act play; first prize is $150. The 'Moss Hart Memorial Award', in memory of the playwright Moss Hart (1904–61), is given to stimulate the production of plays which demonstrate human courage and affirm human purpose and dignity; the award is a silver trophy and is given to a New England theatre group.

Awarding body: New England Theatre Conference, 50 Exchange St., Waltham, Mass. 02154, U.S.A.

Recipients include: Adrian Hall (outstanding creative achievement in the American Theatre); Alois Nagler, Theater in America; Theatre Communications Group (Special Award); Bread and Puppet Theatre; Michael P. Price/Goodspeed Opera House; Ralf Coleman; Gustave Johnson (Regional Citations); Garrett Players, Lawrence, Mass. ('1776', Community Theatre Drama Festival Award); Theatre Workshop, Ludlowe High School, Fairfield, Conn. ('The Miracle Worker', Moss Hart Memorial Award), 1976.

New York Drama Critics Circle Award

This award, established in 1935, is made annually at the close of the season for the best plays (excluding revivals) presented during the theatrical year in New York City. The categories are: Best Play; Best American or Foreign Play (whichever has not won the principal award); and Best Musical. Scrolls are presented to the winning authors, and $1,000 for the Best Play.

Awarding body: New York Drama Critics Circle, U.S.A.

Recipients include: Jean Giraudoux (*Tiger at the Gates*, 1955); Eugene O'Neill (*Long Day's Journey into Night*, 1956); Tennessee Williams (*The Night of the Iguana*, 1961); Peter Shaffer (*Equus*, 1975); Tom Stoppard (*Travesties*, 1976).

New York Film Critics Circle Awards

These annual awards in the form of plaques were established in 1936 by the critics of New York's daily newspapers and weekly magazines for the best film, director, screenplay, actor, actress, supporting actor and supporting actress in the films released in New York City during the calendar year.

Awarding body: New York Film Critics Circle, U.S.A.

New Zealand Association of Scientists Research Medal

The medal was founded in 1969 and is awarded annually for outstanding work by someone under the age of 40 in the natural, physical or social sciences during the preceding three years.

Awarding body: New Zealand Association of Scientists, P.O.B. 1874, Wellington, New Zealand.

Recipients include: Dr. D. E. Wright, M. P. Hartshorn, A. H. Kirton, Dr. B. Halton, Dr. A. F. M. Barton.

New Zealand Award for Achievement

This award was established in 1956 by the New Zealand Literary Fund Advisory Committee. It is an annual cash prize of N.Z.$500 and is presented in recognition of one person's contribution to New Zealand literature. Only New Zealand residents are eligible.

Awarding body: Minister for the Arts, Department of Internal Affairs, Private Bag, Wellington, New Zealand.

New Zealand Book Awards

The New Zealand Literary Fund established these awards in 1976. Three cash prizes of N.Z.$2,000 each are given annually for the best book published in the preceding year, in three categories: poetry, fiction, non-fiction. Although the awards are restricted to New Zealand citizens, writers need not be resident in New Zealand, nor need the books have been published in New Zealand.

Awarding body: New Zealand Literary Fund Advisory Committee, Dept. of Internal Affairs, Private Bag, Wellington, New Zealand.

New Zealand Society of Dairy Science and Technology Distinguished Service Award

The award is made to recognize distinguished service and outstanding achievements in the dairy industry. Both members of the Society and non-members are eligible. It is made generally on an

annual basis and was established in 1966 by the Society. The winner receives a certificate.
Awarding body: New Zealand Society of Dairy Science and Technology.
Recipients include: Dr. F. H. McDowall; J. D. Sargent; Dr. J. Cox; Dr. H. Whitehead; A. Yarrall.

Newcomen Medal

This gold medal was founded in 1943 by the American Branch of the Newcomen Society, to be given for outstanding achievement in the field of steam, to be bestowed not oftener than once in three years. It is named in honour of Thomas Newcomen (1663–1729), the inventor of one of the first steam engines.
Awarding body: The Franklin Institute, Benjamin Franklin Parkway at 20th St., Philadelphia, Pa. 19103, U.S.A.

Nathan M. Newmark Medal

This medal was instituted in 1975 by the Engineering Mechanics and Structural Divisions of ASCE; it was endowed by the former students of Nathan M. Newmark at the University of Illinois, in memory of his outstanding contributions to structural engineering and mechanics. The award consists of a gold medal and an engraved certificate, presented annually to the member of ASCE whose written work in structural mechanics has most helped to strengthen the scientific base of structural engineering.
Awarding body: American Society of Civil Engineers, 345 East 47th St., New York, N.Y. 10017, U.S.A.
Recipients include: John E. Goldberg (1976).

Nihon-kaiyo-Gakukai-sho (*Japan Oceanographical Society Prize*)

This annual prize was established in 1966 by the Society and is awarded for outstanding achievements in the field of oceanography. The prize consists of a medal, a certificate and 100,000 yen in cash. Members of the Society over the age of 36 years are eligible.
Awarding body: Nihon-kaiyo-Gakukai, c/o Ocean Research Institute, University of Tokyo, 1 Minamidai, Nakano, Tokyo, Japan.
Recipients include: Dr. Shunei Ichimura (biological oceanography, 1971); Dr. Shiberu Motoda (biological oceanography, 1972); Dr. Sanae Unoki (physical oceanography, 1973); Dr. Ken Sugawara (chemical oceanography, 1974); Dr. Kinjiro Kajiura (physical oceanography, 1975).

Nihon Kikai Gakkai Sho (*Japan Society of Mechanical Engineers Award*)

This prize is awarded annually in April and was established in 1958 by the Society to commemorate its 60th anniversary. A medal and certificate are awarded for outstanding theoretical or practical achievements in the field of mechanical engineering. It is open to members of the Society only.

Awarding body: Nihon Kikai Gakkai, Sanshin Hokusei Building, 4-9, Yoyogi 2-chome, Shibuya-ku, Tokyo, Japan.

Martinus Nijhoff Prize

The Prince Bernhard Fund established this annual literary prize in 1953 in memory of the Dutch poet Nijhoff, who was also an important translator of lyric poetry and drama. A cash award of 5,000 guilders is given for translation of a literary work from or into Dutch.
Awarding body: Prins Bernhard Fonds, Leidsegracht 3, Amsterdam C, The Netherlands.
Recipients include: Adrienne Dixon (U.K., 1974); C. A. G. van den Broek (Netherlands, 1974); Barber van de Pol (Netherlands, 1975); H. R. Radian (Romania, 1976).

Nile Gold Medal

This award was established in 1972, and is made to individuals or organizations for distinguished work in the field of aerospace education.
Awarding body: Fédération Aéronautique Internationale, 6 rue Galilée, Paris 16, France.
Recipients include: Maj.-Gen. A. A. Rafat (Iran, 1975).

Nippon Kinzoku Gakkai Shō (*Japan Institute of Metals Gold Medal*)

Established by the Institute in 1937, the award is in memory of the late Dr. Kotaro Honda (1870–1954), the inventor of KS steel and New KS steel. It is awarded annually in April together with a certificate. It is conferred upon a scientist or engineer who has made the most valuable contribution to the development of theories or technology related to metals. It is open to scientists or engineers of all nationalities regardless of age or sex.
Awarding body: Nippon Kinzoku Gakkai, Aoba Aramaki, Sendai 980, Japan.
Recipients include: Edgar C. Bain (U.S.A., high-speed steel); Seiji Kaya (Japan, physical magnetic properties); Morris Cohen (U.S.A., martensite transformation); Werner Köster (Fed. Rep. of Germany, iron and non-ferrous metals); John Chipman (U.S.A., process metallurgy).

Frederick Niven Award

The award was established in 1956 by Mrs. Pauline Niven, widow of the author Frederick Niven, a Scot who emigrated to Canada, best known for his novels which have Scottish or Canadian settings. The prize of £100 for a novel by any Scottish writer is awarded every three years. No writer can receive the award more than once and entries, which must be made by the publisher concerned, must have been published during the preceding three years.
Awarding body: International PEN Scottish Centre, c/o Miss Mary Baxter, Hon. Secretary, 18 Crown Terrace, Glasgow G12 9ES, Scotland.
Recipients include: Allan Campbell McLean (*The Islander*) and Alastair Mair (*The Devil's Minister*),

jointly, 1965; James Allan Ford (*The Brave White Flag*, 1968); Mary Stewart (*The Crystal Cave*, 1971); Maureen O'Donoghue (*Wild Honey Time*, 1974).

Nobel Prizes

These are probably the best-known and certainly the most prestigious prizes in the world. Five of the six prizes were established under the terms of the will of Alfred Bernhard Nobel (born Stockholm 1833, died San Remo 1896), who wished that the invested capital of his estate should constitute a fund, the interest on which should be annually distributed in the form of prizes to those 'who, during the preceding year, shall have conferred the greatest benefit on mankind. The said interest shall be divided into five equal parts, which shall be apportioned as follows: one part to the person who shall have made the most important discovery or invention within the field of physics; one part to the person who shall have made the most important chemical discovery or improvement; one part to the person who shall have made the most important discovery within the domain of physiology or medicine; one part to the person who shall have produced in the field of literature the most outstanding work of an idealistic tendency; and one part to the person who shall have done the most or the best work for fraternity between nations, for the abolition or reduction of standing armies and for the holding and promotion of peace congresses.... It is my express wish that ... no consideration whatsoever shall be given to the nationality of the candidates, but that the most worthy shall receive the prize...'. A sixth prize, the Alfred Nobel Memorial Prize in Economic Sciences, was endowed in 1968 by the Central Bank of Sweden to mark its tercentenary. All the prizes are presented on 10 December each year: the date of Nobel's death and Commemoration Day of the Nobel Foundation. The Peace Prize is presented in Oslo, the rest in Stockholm. The value of the prizes in 1978 was 725,000 Swedish kronor each; recipients are also awarded a gold medal and certificate. None of the prizes may be applied for; selection is made by the Nobel Committee of the relevant awarding body (*see* below).

Awarding bodies: Royal Swedish Academy of Sciences, Frescati, 104 05 Stockholm 50, Sweden (Physics, Chemistry and Economics prizes); Karolinska Institutet, Faculty of Medicine, Solnavägen 1, Fack, 104 01 Stockholm 60, Sweden (Physiology and Medicine prize); Swedish Academy, Börshuset, Källargränd 4, 111 29 Stockholm, Sweden (Literature prize); Norwegian Parliament Nobel Cttee., Drammensveien 19, Oslo 2, Norway (Peace prize).

Recipients include:

Prize for Physics: Burton Richter (U.S.A.) and Samuel Ting (U.S.A.), for pioneering work in the discovery of a heavy elementary particle of a new kind, 1976; Philip W. Anderson (U.S.A.), Sir Nevill Mott (U.K.), and John Van Vleck (U.S.A.), for research on the electronic structure of magnetic and 'disordered' systems, 1977; Dr.

Arno Penzias (U.S.A.) and Dr. Robert Wilson (U.S.A.), for work in cosmic microwave background radiation, and Dr. Piotr Leonidovich Kapitsa (U.S.S.R.), for work in the area of low-temperature physics, 1978.

Prize for Chemistry: William N. Lipscomb (U.S.A., for studies on the structure of boranes illuminating problems of chemical bonding), 1976; Ilya Prigogine (Belgium, for his extension of thermodynamic theory to systems which are far from thermodynamic equilibrium), 1977; Dr. Peter Mitchell (U.K., for his contribution to the understanding of biological energy transfer through the formulation of the chemiosmotic theory), 1978.

Prize for Physiology or Medicine: Baruch S. Blumberg and D. Carleton Gajdusek (U.S.A., for their discoveries concerning new mechanisms for the origin and dissemination of infectious diseases), 1976; Rosalyn Yalow (U.S.A., for the development and radio-immunoassays of peptide hormones), Roger Guillemin and Andrew V. Schally (U.S.A., for analysing and synthesizing the peptide hormones of the brain), 1977; Prof. Daniel Nathans (U.S.A.), Prof. Hamilton O. Smith (U.S.A.) and Prof. Werner Arber (Switzerland), for their discovery of restriction enzymes and their application to problems of molecular genetics, 1978.

Prize for Literature: Saul Bellow (U.S.A., for his human understanding and subtle analysis of contemporary culture), 1976; Vicente Aleixandre (Spain, for creative poetic writing which illuminates man's condition in the cosmos), 1977; Isaac Bashevis Singer (U.S.A., for his impassioned narrative art, 1978.

Peace Prize: Betty Williams and Mairead Corrigan (U.K., Northern Ireland Peace Movement), 1976; Amnesty International, 1977; Anwar Sadat (Egypt) and Menahem Begin (Israel), 1978.

Economics Prize: Milton Friedman (U.S.A.) for achievements in the field of consumption analysis, monetary history and theory and for his demonstration of the complexity of stabilization policy, 1976; James E. Meade (U.K.) and Bertil Ohlin (Sweden) for their contributions to the theory of international trade and international capital movements, 1977; Prof. Herbert Simon (U.S.A.), for his pioneering research into the decision-making process within economic organizations, 1978.

John Noble Craft Awards

These awards were established by the Saltire Society in 1972 in memory of the late John Noble of Ardkinglas, a former President of the Society. They are made every two or three years to Scottish craftsmen/women, or those resident in Scotland, for various categories of crafts. Entries must have been made in Scotland within the previous two years. In 1975 there were four awards of £50 and a scroll each.

Awarding body: The Saltire Society, Saltire House, 13 Atholl Crescent, Edinburgh EH3, Scotland.

Noma Prize

Two awards are given annually under this title by the Kodansha publishing company: one for the best work in the field of polite literature, and one for the best work in the field of juvenile literature. The first prize was established in 1941 and consists of a medal and 1,000,000 yen. The second prize was established in 1962 and consists of a medal and 500,000 yen. They are awarded at the end of the year for books published between October of the preceding year and September of the award year.

Awarding body: Kodansha Ltd., 2-12-21, Otowa, Bunkyo-ku, Tokyo 112, Japan.

Noranda Lecture Award

Established in 1963 by The Chemical Institute of Canada, the annual award is sponsored by Noranda Mines Ltd. Scientists resident in Canada may receive the award for distinguished contributions in physical, inorganic or analytical chemistry. Nominations are made by members of the Institute. The recipient, who takes the title of 'Noranda Lecturer', delivers the lecture at the Annual Conference of the Institute, and is awarded $500 as well as travelling expenses. The award may not be given to a person who has received the Fisher Scientific Lecture Award (*q.v.*) for the same year.

Awarding body: The Chemical Institute of Canada, 151 Slater St., Ottawa, Ont. K1P 5H3, Canada.

Recipients include: J. Trotter ('X-ray Diffraction Studies in Inorganic Structural Chemistry', 1972); T. P. Schaeffer ('Reminiscences of an Old-fashioned NMR Spectroscopist', 1973); W. R. Cullen ('Unnatural Products', 1974); B. R. James ('Rhodium – Expensive, but Rich in Chemistry', 1975); Christopher E. Brion (1977).

Norman Medal

The medal was instituted and endowed by George H. Norman in 1872, and its administration taken over by the American Society of Civil Engineers in 1897. The award consists of a gold medal, bronze duplicate and certificate, and is awarded annually to a member or members of the Society, for a previously unpublished paper which has made a meritorious contribution to engineering science.

Awarding body: American Society of Civil Engineers, 345 East 47th St., New York, N.Y. 10017, U.S.A.

Recipients include: James R. Cofer ('Orange County Water District's Water Factory', 1974); Roy E. Olson, David E. Daniel, Jr., and Thomas K. Liu ('Finite Difference Analyses for Sand Drain Problems', 1975); Charles C. Ladd and Roger Foott ('New Design Procedure for Stability of Soft Clays', 1976).

Normann-Medaille

The medal was established in 1940 by the German Society for the Study of Fats in honour and in memory of Wilhelm Normann (1870–1939), whose many patented discoveries in the field of fats and oils include the discovery of the method of solidifying fats. The medal is awarded every year for research in the science of fats. The Society may award two medals, one for outstanding scientific and technical achievements in the field of fats and fat products, the other for particular contributions to the advancement of fat research. The medal is presented at the Society's Annual Congress.

Awarding body: Deutsche Gesellschaft für Fettwissenschaft e.V., 4400 Münster, Soester Strasse 13, Federal Republic of Germany.

Recipients include: Dr. rer. nat. B. Werdelmann (Fed. Rep. of Germany, 1973); Prof. Dr. P. Desnuelle (France, 1974); Prof. Dr. Dr. G. Schettler (Fed. Rep. of Germany, 1975); Prof. Dr. E. Baer (Canada, 1975); Prof. Dr. L. Acker (Fed. Rep. of Germany, 1976).

James Flack Norris Award in Physical Organic Chemistry

The award was established in 1963 by the Northeastern Section of the American Chemical Society in commemoration of James Flack Norris. It is presented annually to encourage and reward outstanding contributions to physical organic chemistry. It consists of $2,000 and a suitably inscribed certificate. An allowance of not more than $350 is provided for travelling expenses to the meeting at which the award will be presented.

Awarding body: American Chemical Society, 1155 Sixteenth St., N.W., Washington, D.C. 20036, U.S.A.

Recipients include: Kenneth B. Wiberg (1973); Gerhard L. Closs (1974); Kurt M. Mislow (1975); Howard E. Zimmerman (1976); Edward M. Arnett (1977).

Norsk kulturråds ærespris (*Norwegian Cultural Council Prize of Honour*)

The prize was established in 1968 to reward valuable contributions to Norwegian culture. It is an annual award of 25,000 kroner (tax-free) and is open to Norwegian citizens only.

Awarding body: Norsk kulturråd, Rosenkrantzgt. 11, Oslo 1, Norway.

Recipients include: Klaus Egge (music, 1972); Hans Heiberg (theatre, 1973); Hans J. Henriksen (Lapp culture, 1974); Ingeborg Refling Hagen (education, 1975); Sigbjørn Bernhoft Osa (folk music, 1976).

Norsk kulturråds musikpris (*Norwegian Cultural Council Music Prize*)

The prize was established in 1970 for valuable contributions to Norwegian musical life. It is an annual award of 15,000 kroner (tax-free) and is open to Norwegian citizens only.

Awarding body: Norsk kulturråd, Rosenkran tzgt 11, Oslo 1, Norway.

Recipients include: Gunnar Sønstevold (1972); Kjell Bækkelund (1973); Karsten Andersen (1974); Antonio Bibalo (1975); Ludvig Nielsen (1976).

Norsk kulturråds oversetterpris (*Norwegian Cultural Council Translation Prize*)
Founded in 1968, the prize is for translations of fiction, poetry or drama from foreign literature into Norwegian. It is an annual prize of 15,000 kroner (tax-free) and is open to Norwegian citizens only.
Awarding body: Norsk kulturråd, Rosenkrantzgt. 11, Oslo 1, Norway.
Recipients include: Trygve Greiff (1973); Carl Fredrik Engelstad (1974); Olav Rytter (1975); Lotte Holmboe (1976).

Norsk kulturråds pris for lokalhistorisk arbeid (*Norwegian Cultural Council Prize for Local History*)
Established in 1973, the prize is for contributions by study, research, collections, etc., within the field of local history and traditions in Norway. It is an annual prize of 15,000 kroner, and is open to Norwegian citizens only.
Awarding body: Norsk kulturråd, Rosenkrantzgt. 11, Oslo 1, Norway.
Recipients include: Knut Hermundstad (1973); Olav Kolltveit (1974); Halldor O. Opedal (1975); Hans Hyldbak (1976).

Norske Sivilingeniørers Forening's Miljøvernpris (*Norwegian Society of Chartered Engineers Environmental Pollution Control Prize*)
Established by the Society in 1976, the prize is given annually to persons who have shown great interest and initiative in the area of environmental pollution control, and who are actively engaged in work of this sort when nominated for the prize. The cash value of the award varies according to the sum available. Norwegians or foreigners are eligible, whether resident in Norway or not. Nominations are invited by the Society.
Awarding body: Norske Sivilingeniørers Forening, Kronprinsens gate 17, Oslo 2, Norway.

Novobátzky Károly Prize
The prize was established in 1968 by the Hungarian Physical Society in honour of Károly Novobátzky (b. 1884), the physicist. An annual award of 5,000 forints is awarded to young research workers for outstanding results in theoretical physics.
Awarding body: 'Eötvös Loránd' Fizikai Társulat, 1061 Budapest, VI, Anker-köz 1, Hungary.

Novoprisen (*Novo Prize*)
Established in 1963 by the Novo Foundation, the prize rewards an outstanding achievement in the field of medical science. It takes the form of 50,000 kroner and a certificate, and is awarded annually in February. Preference is given to Danish scientists, but those from other Scandinavian countries are eligible.
Awarding body: Novo's Fond, Novo Allé, DK 2880 Bagsvaerd, Denmark.
Recipients include: Prof. K. A. Marcker (research in molecular biology, 1973); Prof. Michael Schwartz (research into pernicious anaemia, 1974); Dr. Georg Mandahl-Barth (research into bilharziasis, 1975); Prof. Niels Tygstrup (research and treatment of liver diseases, 1976); Prof. Erik Amdrup (development of parietal cell vagotomy, 1977).

George C. Nowlan Lectures
The George C. Nowlan Lectures are delivered every two years at Acadia University by persons of note in the field of politics and government. They were established in 1965 through an endowment by the Progressive Conservative Party of Canada, in memory of the late Hon. George C. Nowlan, former Federal Minister of Finance.
Awarding body: Acadia University, Canada.
Lecturers include: Dr. George P. Grant (1969–70); The Hon. Eric Kierns, M.P. (1971–72); The Rt. Hon. John G. Diefenbaker, M.P. (1973–74); The Hon. Robert L. Stanfield, M.P. (1976–77).

Marcia C. Noyes Award
The American Medical Library Association established this award in 1949 to honour outstanding contributions to medical librarianship. It is normally given every two years, and takes the form of an engraved silver tray.
Awarding body: Medical Library Association, 919 North Michigan Ave., Chicago, Ill. 60611, U.S.A.

Nuffield Medal and Lecture
A lecturer is appointed periodically and reads a paper on a subject devoted to the advancement of the science and art of medicine. He receives a medal and an honorarium.
Awarding body: The Royal Society of Medicine, 1 Wimpole St., London W1M 8AE, England.

Numismatic Art Award for Excellence in Medallic Sculpture
This award, popularly known as the 'Sculptor of the Year Award', is presented by the American Numismatic Association for outstanding achievement in the field of medallic sculpture. It was established in 1965, and is made annually in August. It takes the form of a gold medal.
Awarding body: American Numismatic Association, P.O.B. 2366, Colorado Springs, Colo. 80901, U.S.A.
Recipients include: Elizabeth Jones (1972); Gertrude Lathrop (1973); Abram Belskie (1974); Robert Weinman (1975); Adolph Block (1976).

Nyholm Lectureship
This lectureship was founded in 1973 to commemorate the name of Sir Ronald Nyholm, President of the Chemical Society from 1968 to 1970. The lecture, as far as is practicable, should be concerned with subjects of interest to either the Dalton Division or the Education Division of the Society, and have regard to the wide international interests of Sir Ronald Nyholm. The lecturer receives a silver medal and £100.
Awarding body: The Chemical Society, Burlington House, London W1V 0BN, England.

Recipients include: H. F. Halliwell (1973–74); J. Lewis (1974–75); D. J. Millen (1975–76); J. Chatt (1976–77); A. K. Holliday (1977–78).

Nyon International Film Festival

The festival is held annually in October, and is recognized by the International Federation of Film Producers' Associations (IFFPA). It is subsidized by the Swiss Federal Government and the Canton of Vaud. The Festival's aim is to screen documentary films dealing with the social and psychological aspects of human life. Priority is given to those dealing with a current problem, or requiring specialized distribution. Films of any length are eligible, provided they have been completed and screened in the previous twelve months, and have not previously been shown in Switzerland or gained an award at a festival recognized by the IFFPA. The International Jury awards the Golden Sesterce Grand Prix, up to three Silver Sesterces and, at its discretion, other special prizes. Swiss Television and the Youth Jury may also present awards.

Awarding body: Société Suisse des Festivals Internationaux de Cinéma, Case postale 98, 1260 Nyon, Switzerland.

Grand Prix recipients include: Giuseppe Ferrara (Italy, *La Città del Malessere*, 1973); Joel L Freedman (U.S.A., *Broken Treaty at Battle Mountain*, 1974); Per Mannstaedt (Denmark, *Flere Atomkraftwaerker*, 1976).

O

Rufus Oldenburger Medal

This award was established in 1968 by the Automatic Control Division of the American Society of Mechanical Engineers, to honour Rufus Oldenburger for his distinctive achievements in the field of automatic control, and for his service to ASME and the above Division. The medal is awarded in recognition of significant contributions and outstanding achievements in the field of automatic control. Such achievements may be, for example, in the areas of education, research, development, innovation and service to the field and profession. Nominations are not restricted by profession, nationality or Society membership. The award consists of a bronze medal and a certificate.

Awarding body: American Society of Mechanical Engineers, United Engineering Center, 345 East 47th St., New York, N.Y. 10017, U.S.A.

Recipients include: Clesson E. Mason (1973); Herbert W. Ziebolz (1974); Hendrik W. Bode, Harry Nyquist (1975); Rudolf Emil Kalman (1976).

J. Robert Oppenheimer Memorial Prize

Established in 1969 by the University of Miami Center for Theoretical Studies, the prize is in memory of J. Robert Oppenheimer (1904–67), the eminent American theoretical physicist. A cash prize of $1,000, a gold medal and a citation are awarded annually for outstanding contributions to the theoretical natural sciences and to the philosophy of science.

Awarding body: Center for Theoretical Studies, P.O.B. 9055, University of Miami, Coral Gables, Fla. 33124, U.S.A.

Recipients include: Edwin E. Salpeter (1974); Nicholas Kemmer (1975); Yoichiro Nambu (1976); Feza Gursey and Sheldon Glashow (1977).

Orden del Mérito Agrícola (*Order of Merit for Agriculture*)

This prize, designed to reward those who have contributed to the development of Colombian agriculture, was founded by a decree of the Ministry of Agriculture in 1969. The award consists of a cross conferred annually in four classes: Grand Cross, Grand Officer, Commander, and Knight.

Awarding body: Ministerio de Agricultura, Bogotá, Colombia.

Orden Nacional de Miguel Antonio Caro y Rufino José Cuervo (*National Order of Miguel Antonio Caro and Rufino José Cuervo*)

The Caro and Cuervo Institute established this international award in 1970 to distinguish those who have made significant contributions to the enrichment of the national heritage and cultural life in Colombia. The award can be made at any time in any of six classes: Grand Cross with Gold Insignia, Grand Cross, Grand Officer, Knight Commander, Officer and Knight. Title-holders receive a chain of honour.

Awarding body: Instituto Caro y Cuervo, Apdo. Aéreo 51502, Bogotá, Colombia.

Recipients include: Dr. Amadou Mahtar M'Bow (Dir.-Gen. of UNESCO, 1976); Ministers of Education of Bolivia, Chile, Ecuador, Peru and Venezuela (1976).

Orden Pour le Mérite für Wissenschaften und Künste (*Order of Merit for Sciences and Arts*)

This award, originally founded by King Frederick the Great of Prussia and given a Foundation Charter in 1842 by Frederick Wilhelm IV, was continued by the Prussian Ministry of State and then the Federal Republic of Germany. Membership of the Order is bestowed on men and women who have given outstanding services to science or the arts. The number of members forming the Chapter of the Order must not exceed thirty; this number is completed whenever a member leaves the Order. The humanities, natural sciences and the arts are normally represented by ten members each. Apart from its thirty national members, the Chapter may elect foreign members. The Order's decoration is a medal, worn round the neck on a ribbon.

Awarding body: Orden pour le Mérite, Bundesministerium des Innern, 53 Bonn, Rheindorfer Str. 198, Federal Republic of Germany.

Orpheus Statuette

This bronze statuette is awarded annually by the Polish Musicians Association (SPAM) for the best contemporary musical composition performed at the International Festival of Contemporary Music, 'Warsaw Falls'.

Awarding body: Polish Musicians Association (SPAM), ul. Krucza 24/26, 00-525 Warsaw, Poland.

George Orwell Memorial Prize

The prize was established in 1975 by Penguin Books in memory of George Orwell (1903–50), and to mark Penguin's 40th anniversary in July 1975. The annual award of £750 is given for an article, essay or series of articles commenting on current cultural, social or political issues anywhere in the world. The work must have been published in the U.K., either in a newspaper, periodical or pamphlet, in the preceding year.

Awarding body: Penguin Books Ltd., Harmondsworth, Middlesex, England.

Recipients include: Ludvík Vaculík (Czechoslovakia, 'Impermissible Thoughts', 1976); Paul Bailey (U.K., 'The Limitations of Despair', 1978).

Bernhard-Osann-Medaille

This prize was established in 1962 by the German Society of Foundry Engineers on the occasion of the 100th anniversary of the birth of Prof. Dr.-Ing. Bernhard Osann, an honorary member of the Society. The medal, with a certificate, is awarded annually to a member for outstanding contributions to the work of the Society.

Awarding body: Verein Deutscher Giessereifachleute, 4 Düsseldorf, Sohnstrasse 71, Federal Republic of Germany.

Recipients include: Dr.-Ing. Heiko Pacyna (1971); Dr.-Ing. Alois Dahlmann, Dipl.-Ing. Diethard Schock (1972); Anton Alt (1973); Dipl.-Ing. Erhard Weisner (1975).

Osborne and Mendel Award of the Nutrition Foundation

This annual award, presented by the American Institute of Nutrition, was established by The Nutrition Foundation, Inc. for the recognition of outstanding recent achievements in the field of nutrition research. Preference is given to candidates resident in the U.S.A. and Canada. The award takes the form of $1,000 and an inscribed scroll.

Awarding body: American Institute of Nutrition. (Nominations to Dr. D. G. Cornwell, Dept. of Physiological Chemistry, Ohio State Univ., 333 West 10th Ave., Columbus, Ohio 43210, U.S.A.)

Recipients include: E. T. Mertz (1972); H. F. DeLuca (1973); DeWitt S. Goodman (1974); B. Connor Johnson (1975); Myron Winick (1976).

O'Shannessy Award

This annual award, named after a past president of the Society of Automotive Engineers – Australasia, takes the form of A$100 and a certificate. It is open to any person under 30 years of age who has presented an outstanding written paper to any Division or Group of the Society or has had a paper published in the Society's Journal during the previous calendar year. Candidates must also be residents of Australia, New Zealand or territories administered by these countries. Nominations are made by Divisions or independent Group Committees to the Society's Council.

Awarding body: Society of Automotive Engineers – Australasia, National Science Centre, 191 Royal Parade, Parkville, Vic. 3052, Australia.

'Paloma O'Shea' International Piano Competition

Señora O'Shea founded the annual competition in 1974. It takes place in Santander in the summer under the auspices of the Spanish Ministry of Culture and various local organizations. Competitors must be between the ages of 15 and 32. The cash prizes vary in amount and number, as many are donated by individuals, families or organizations. The main prize – the Paloma O'Shea International Prize – consists of 250,000 pesetas, a gold medal, six recitals in Spain, and a recital at the next Santander International Festival.

Awarding body: Concurso Internacional de Piano Paloma O'Shea, Hernán Cortes 3, Santander, Spain.

Recipients include: Ruriko Kikuchi (Japan, 1974); Marioara Trifan (U.S.A., 1975); Huseyin Sermet (Turkey, 1976); Ramzi Yassa (Egypt, 1977).

Osler Lectureship

The Osler Lecture is delivered annually in April at McGill University on a topic dealing with the health and welfare of mankind. The lecturer will have made exceptional contributions in some area of this field, but need not be a physician or scientist. The lecture was established in 1977 by McGill University's Faculty of Medicine and Osler Society, and commemorates Sir William Osler (1849–1919), one of Canada's most eminent physicians.

Awarding body: McGill University Faculty of Medicine, Canada.

Inaugural lecturer: Dr. Jean Mayer (U.S.A., 1977).

Ossian Prize

This award was established in 1973 to recognize the services of creatively active individuals and organizations in the preservation of autonomous linguistic and cultural communities within Europe whose cultural identity is endangered by outside influences or modern developments. It is an annual award of DM20,000, and is named after the legendary Scottish bard, Ossian.

Awarding body: Stiftung FVS, Georgsplatz 10, 2 Hamburg 1, Federal Republic of Germany.

Recipients include: Prof. Derick Thomson (U.K., Scottish Gaelic poet and scholar, 1974); Societ Retorumantscha (Switzerland, preservation of the Romansch language, 1975); Dr. Francesco de B Moll (Spain, preservation of the Catalan language, 1978).

Österreichische Kinder- und Jugendbuchpreise (*Austrian Prizes for Children's and Young People's Literature*)

These prizes are awarded annually by the Ministry of Education and Arts in five principal

categories: three for children's books (age ranges of up to 8 years old, 8 to 11, and 11 to 14); one for a book for young people; one for a work of non-fiction; one for illustration; and one for translation. They take the form of cash prizes and diplomas; the total sum available is 125,000 Schillings. In the case of original work, the book must have been published in Austria during the last twelve months (the last ten years in the case of translations). Both authors and publishers may nominate books.
Awarding body: Bundesministerium für Unterricht und Kunst, Abteilung für ausserschulische Jugenderziehung, Postfach 65, 1014 Vienna, Minoritenplatz 5, Austria.
Recipients include: Karl Bruckner; Auguste Lechner; Vera Ferra-Mikura; Oskar Jan Tauschinski; Mira Lobe.

Österreichischer Staatspreis für Europäische Literatur (*Austrian State Prize for European Literature*)

The award is made annually at the recommendation of a specially constituted jury. It is presented by the Austrian Ministry of Education and Arts, and is worth 100,000 Schillings. European authors, whose work is known beyond their homeland, are eligible.
Awarding body: Bundesministerium für Unterricht und Kunst, 1014 Vienna, Minoritenplatz 5, Austria.
Recipients include: Pavel Kohout (Czechoslovakia, 1977); Simone de Beauvoir (France, 1978).

Österreichischer Staatspreis für Gute Form (*Austrian State Prize for Design*)

Established by the Ministry of Trade on the recommendation of the Austrian Institute of Design, this prize is given to Austrian companies for outstanding design of industrial products as regards quality of material, function and appearance. More than one prize may be given annually and citations are also awarded. Each prize consists of 25,000 Schillings and a certificate (the designer is also given a certificate) and each citation is accompanied by a cash prize of 5,000 Schillings and a certificate. A maximum amount of 85,000 Schillings may be awarded in each year.

Awarding body: Bundesministerium für Handel, Gewerbe und Industrie, Stubenring 1, 1010 Vienna, Austria.
Recipients include: Stubai Werkzeugindustrie and Eumig Elektrizitäts- und Metallwarenindustrie (1976).

Österreichischer Staatspreis für journalistische Leistungen im Interesse der Jugend (*Austrian State Prize for Journalistic Achievements in the Interests of Young People*)

The prize is awarded annually by the Ministry of Education and Arts, and recognizes sustained journalistic achievement in all branches of the media which concerns itself with the extra-curricular problems and activities of young people. Only Austrian citizens are eligible for the prize, which consists of a diploma and a cash sum of 40,000 Schillings. Both authors and publishers may nominate contributions, which must have appeared during the past twelve months.
Awarding body: Bundesministerium für Unterricht und Kunst, Abteilung für ausserschulische Jugenderziehung, Postfach 65, 1014 Vienna, Minoritenplatz 5, Austria.

Karl-Ernst-Osthaus-Preis

The award was founded in 1946 by the town of Hagen; it is made for a special achievement in the plastic arts, generally shown by one or more items in the exhibition of the West German Association of Artists (WKB) in the Karl Ernst Osthaus Museum, Hagen. It is awarded every two years, as an encouragement to artists and to commemorate the arts patron Karl Ernst Osthaus (1874–1921), founder of the Folkwang Museum in Hagen and the German Museum for Art in Commerce and the Trades; he is also well known for his encouragement of modern architecture. The prize is a cash award of DM10,000. Selection is normally based on the most recent period of an artist's work.
Awarding body: Karl-Ernst Osthaus-Museum, 58 Hagen, Hochstr. 73, Federal Republic of Germany.
Recipients include: Kurt Sonderborg (1956); Emil Schumacher (1958); Richard Oelze (1964); F. Dahmen (1966); Voré (1974).

P

PEN Translation Prize

This cash award of $1,000 is given annually by the American Center of PEN for the best book-length translation from any language into English in the United States during the preceding calendar year.

Awarding body: PEN American Center, 156 Fifth Ave., New York, N.Y. 10010, U.S.A.

Recipients include: Gregory Rabassa (*The Autumn of the Patriarch* by Gabriel Marquez, 1976).

'Nicolò Paganini' International Violin Prize

Instituted in 1954 by the municipality of Genoa on the initiative of On. Avv. Vittorio Pertusio, this annual competition takes place in October to celebrate Christopher Columbus Day and Genoa's festival day: 12 October. The competition is named after the famous Italian violinist, Paganini (1782–1840), who was born in Genoa. Violinists of any nationality may compete, but must be under the age of 35. The Paganini Prize of 3 million lire is awarded to the best player, and five other prizes are awarded. The Paganini prize-winner plays Paganini's own violin at a special concert, and is asked to play with the Orchestra del Teatro Comunale dell'Opera during the following season.

Awarding body: Segreteria Generale del Premio 'N. Paganini', Via Garibaldi 9, Genoa, Italy.

Recipients include: Mose Secler (1971); Eugene Fodor (1972); Alessandro Kramarov (1973); Yuri Korcinsky (1975); Lenuta Ciulei (1976).

Pahlavi Environment Prize

The prize was established in 1975 by the Shah of Iran to recognize outstanding contributions in the environmental field. An annual cash award of $50,000 is given by the Iranian Government through the United Nations, and, if possible, presented on World Environment Day.

Awarding body: The Government of Iran, Teheran, Iran.

Recipients include: Maurice Strong (Canada), 1976; Jacques-Yves Cousteau (France) and Sir Peter Scott (U.K.), 1977; Thor Heyerdahl (Norway) and Prof. Mohammed E.-Kassas (Egypt), 1978.

Mohammed Reza Pahlavi Prize

This annual prize for meritorious work in literacy was established in 1967 by H.I.M. the Shahinshah of Iran. The award is open to institutions, organizations or individuals displaying outstanding merit and achieving special success in contributing to literacy, and is worth approximately U.S.$2,000.

Awarding body: UNESCO, 9 Place de Fontenoy, 75700 Paris, France.

Recipients include: Paulo Freire (Brazil, 1975); Pasteur Jacques Kofi Adzomada (Togo, 1976); Mwanza Functional Literacy Project (Tanzania, 1978).

Thomas Paine Lecture

The benefaction given to the University of East Anglia in 1970 by Mr. Jesse Collins, a member of the Thomas Paine Society, constitutes a trust fund, the income from which is used to provide one lecture every two years on some aspect of Thomas Paine's life and times. The lectures are subsequently published.

Awarding body: University of East Anglia, Norwich NR4 7TJ, England.

Panetti Prize

This award is made (usually every two or three years) by the Turin Academy of Sciences for distinguished research during the last ten years in the field of applied mechanics. Nominations for the award are made by members of the Academy and the presidents of other scientific academies both in Italy and abroad. Members of the Academy are not eligible. The award consists of a gold medal and cash prize of between 1 million and 3 million lire. It was instituted in memory of Prof. Modesto Panetti (1875–1957), professor of engineering, who specialized in the field of aerodynamics. The prize has great international prestige, and is considered the equivalent of a Nobel prize for mechanics.

Awarding body: Accademia delle Scienze di Torino, Italy.

Recipients include: Sir James Lighthill (U.K., 1965); Prof. Clifford Truesdell (U.S.A., 1967); Prof. Nicolai Muskelishvili (U.S.S.R., 1969); Prof. W. T. Koiter (Netherlands, 1971); Prof. Ronald S. Rivlin (U.S.A., 1975).

Paper Prize

Established by the Japan Welding Society in 1950, this annual prize is awarded for the most outstanding paper on welding education and technology published within the previous year. It consists of a certificate and a medal.

Awarding body: Yosetsu Gakkai, 1-11 Sakuma-cho Kanda, Chiyoda-ku, Tokyo, Japan.

Paracelsusring der Stadt Villach 1953 (*Paracelsus Ring of the Town of Villach 1953*)
In 1953 the Town Council of Villach dedicated this award to the memory of the Swiss doctor Theophrastus Bombast von Hohenheim (1493–1541), known as Paracelsus, and to his father, Wilhelm Bombast von Hohenheim, who worked as a doctor in Villach for 32 years. The ring is awarded for research into the life of the two Bombasts in their adopted home of Carinthia, or the surrounding area; for other scientific works connected with Paracelsus; for scientific or artistic achievements in the spirit of Paracelsus, or for services as special benefactors to and promoters of the Carinthian Paracelsus tradition. The award is made every three years; a certificate is presented with the ring.
Awarding body: Gemeinderat der Stadt Villach, Rathaus, 9500 Villach, Austria.
Recipients include: Prof. Dr. Lorenz Böhler (Austria, 1963); Prof. Dr. Hans Moritsch (Austria, 1966); Dr. Robert N. Braun (Austria, 1969); Prof. Dr. Konrad Lorenz (Austria, 1973); Prof. Dr. Robert-Henri Blaser (Switzerland, 1976).

Jacques Parisot Foundation Award
To perpetuate the memory of Professor Jacques Parisot, former President of the World Health Assembly, Madame Parisot established a fund in order to arrange a lecture on a scientific subject during a session of the World Health Assembly. Lectures were given annually from 1969 to 1975. Then it was felt that the lecture no longer achieved the founder's purpose, and the Foundation Committee decided to award instead a research fellowship in social medicine or public health, fields which had been of special interest to Professor Parisot. The fellowship is awarded every other year, or as funds allow, and consists of a cash award (currently 5,000 Swiss francs) and a medal.
Awarding body: World Health Organization, Avenue Appia, 1211 Geneva 27, Switzerland.
Recipients include: Prof. Mohamed Hilmy Wahdan (Egypt, 1978).

Vasile Pârvan Prize
This prize for history or archaeology was founded by the Romanian Academy in 1948. It commemorates Vasile Pârvan (1882–1927), historian, archaeologist and professor, who contributed to the creation of the Romanian school of archaeology. The award is presented annually at a General Assembly of the Academy, and consists of 10,000 lei and a diploma.
Awarding body: Academy of the S.R. of Romania, 125 Calea Victoriei, Bucharest, Romania.

Pasteur Medal
The medal was founded in 1892 by the Swedish Society of Medical Sciences in honour of the famous French chemist and biologist, Louis Pasteur (1822–95). It is a pure gold medal, and is awarded every ten years to a scientist of any nationality for valuable contributions to the advance of bacteriology or hygiene. It may not be applied for; nominations are made to the Society by an elected jury.
Awarding body: Swedish Society of Medical Sciences, P.O.B. 558, S-101 27 Stockholm, Sweden.
Recipients include: Prof. Michael Heidelberger (U.S.A., 1960).

Clifford Paterson Lecture
The General Electric Co. Ltd. covenanted in 1975 to provide £2,500 a year over seven years to endow the Clifford Paterson Lecture at the Royal Society. The lecture is on electrical science and technology, inclusive of the science and technology of electronic materials, components and systems. The lecture is annual, and the lecturer's gift is £200.
Awarding body: Royal Society of London, 6 Carlton House Terrace, London SW1Y 5AG, England.

Pattantyús Ábrahám Géza Memorial Medal
The Hungarian Society of Mechanical Engineers founded this medal in 1957 in memory of Pattantyús (1885–1956) who made notable contributions to technology with his work on rolling measurements. The medal is awarded to members of the Society for outstanding technical publications or teaching and research. Three cash prizes of 7,000 forints each are awarded as well as a medal.
Awarding body: Gépipari Tudományos Egyesület, 1372 Budapest V, P.O.B. 451, Hungary.

Dr. V. N. Patwardhan Prize
This annual prize of 1,000 rupees is awarded to a scientist under 40 years old for original contributions in the field of nutrition.
Awarding body: Indian Council of Medical Research, Ansari Nagar, Post Box 4508, New Delhi 110016, India.
Recipients include: Dr. Mehtabs Bamji (1973); Dr. Kamala S. Jaya Rao (1974); Dr. R. K. Chandra (1975); Dr. Leela Rahman (1976).

Pawsey Medal
This silver medal was established by friends and colleagues of the late Dr. J. L. Pawsey, F.A.A., to commemorate his unique contributions to science in Australia. It is awarded for distinguished research in experimental physics carried out mainly in Australia by a scientist not over the age of 35. It is awarded annually at the Academy's AGM.
Awarding body: Australian Academy of Science, P.O.B. 783, Canberra City, A.C.T. 2601, Australia.
Recipients include: D. B. Melrose (1974); R. J. Baxter (1975); W. M. Goss (1976); J. N. Israelachvili (1977); R. N. Manchester (1978).

Pawsey Memorial Lecture
This was instituted in 1964 by the Australian Institute of Physics in memory of J. R. Pawsey

(1908–1962), who was prominent in the field of radio astronomy. Individuals selected for the honour are distinguished in some area of physical science, and receive a small honorarium.

Awarding body: Australian Institute of Physics, Science Centre, 35–43 Clarence St., Sydney, N.S.W. 2000, Australia.

Recipients include: Prof. Hanbury Brown (1972); Prof. W. N. Christiansen (1973); Prof. B. Y. Mills (1974); John Bolton (1975); Prof. R. D. Brown (1976).

Péch Antal Memorial Medal

Founded in 1963 by the Hungarian Mining and Metallurgical Society, the medal is awarded to members of the Society who have shown distinction in the technical development of mining and metallurgy and the practical application of scholarly research, and have given an account of these activities in the Society's journal. Three prizes of 5,000 forints each are awarded annually. The medal is named after Antal Péch (1822–95), a mining engineer who was the first to use machine drilling, and who began a professional journal for mining and metallurgical engineers.

Awarding body: Országos Magyar Bányászati és Kohászati Egyesület, Budapest VI, Anker-köz 1, Hungary.

Pedler Lectureship

The Pedler Lectureship was founded in 1927 to commemorate the name of Sir Alexander Pedler, a benefactor of the Chemical Society. The lecture should deal as far as practicable with the description of new knowledge, and the lecturer should point out in his lecture the directions in which further research is desirable in any branch of organic chemistry. The lecture is delivered in alternate years, and the lecturer receives a silver medal and £100.

Awarding body: The Chemical Society, Burlington House, London W1V 0BN, England.

Recipients include: J. W. Cornforth (1968–69); D. H. Hey (1970–71); R. A. Raphael (1972–73); A. W. Johnson (1974–75); G. W. Kenner (1976–77).

Cuthbert Peek Award

The award was established in 1883 by Cuthbert E. Peek, later Sir Cuthbert Peek (1855–1901), who served on the Council of the Royal Geographical Society for different periods over some twenty years. He was a patron of scientific work, whose main interests were astronomy and meteorology. The award is made to persons who have explored or intend to explore a region, with the object of extending geographical knowledge. They must have complete knowledge of field astronomy, exploratory survey and geology or economic botany. The award is monetary, but can be taken in the form of survey instruments, plate, books, etc. It is usually made annually, but only if a suitable candidate is found. Persons of any age, sex or nationality are eligible. There is no applica-

tion; the award is granted by the Council of the Society on the recommendation of a special committee, and the criteria are the academic and other achievements of the recipients.

Awarding body: Royal Geographical Society, 1 Kensington Gore, London SW7 2AR, England.

Recipients include: T. H. Harrisson (1936); V. E. (later Sir Vivian) Fuchs (1937); Dr. T. E. Armstrong (1954); Prof. J. K. St. Joseph, O.B.E., F.S.A. (1976); Dr. J. C. Doornkamp (1978).

Pendray Aerospace Literature Award

The G. Edward Pendray Award was established in 1950 by Dr. Pendray, a founder and past president of the American Rocket Society. The name of the award was changed in 1975. It is presented annually for an outstanding contribution to aeronautical and astronautical literature written in the recent past, preferably within three years of the date of the award. The emphasis should be on the high quality or major influence of the piece rather than the importance of the underlying technological contributions. The award is intended to be an incentive to aerospace professionals to write eloquently and persuasively about their field, and encompasses editorials as well as papers and books. It comprises a medal and certificate of citation.

Awarding body: American Institute of Aeronautics and Astronautics, 1290 Avenue of the Americas, New York, N.Y. 10019, U.S.A.

Recipients include: George Leitmann (1977).

Penrose Medal

Mr. R. A. F. Penrose donated the sum of $5,000 to the Geological Society of America in 1927. The interest from this is used to award an annual gold medal in recognition of eminent research in pure geology. The award is made for outstanding original contributions or achievements which mark a decided advance in the science of geology. Nominees, selected by the Council of the Society, need not be members of the Society, nor American citizens.

Awarding body: Geological Society of America, Inc., 3300 Penrose Place, Boulder, Colo. 80301, U.S.A.

Recipients include: Wilmot H. Bradley (1972); M. King Hubbert (1973); William M. Ewing (1974); Francis J. Pettijohn (1975); Preston Cloud (1976).

Dr. Thomas Percival Lectureship

The lectureship was founded in 1945 by a gift of £300 from the Manchester Literary and Philosophical Society in memory of Dr. Thomas Percival, one of the founders of the Society. The lecture is given by a member of the staff of Manchester University, and is normally delivered annually.

Awarding body: University of Manchester, Manchester M13 9PL, England.

Lecturers include: Prof. A. J. Morton ('Man, the Earth and the Power Engineer', 1975; Prof.

D. S. L. Cardwell ('Science and the European Tragedies', 1976); Prof. T. J. Chandler ('Pollution, Perception and Public Policy', 1977).

Perkin (America) Medal
The medal was founded by the American Section of the Society of Chemical Industry in 1906, to celebrate the 50th anniversary of the coal tar industry. It is named after Sir William Perkin who discovered the first aniline dye: mauve. It is awarded annually to anyone residing in the U.S.A. who is actively engaged in the chemical profession, for successful applied chemistry resulting in outstanding commercial development.
Awarding body: Society of Chemical Industry (American Section), 50 East 41st St., Suite 92, New York, N.Y. 10017, U.S.A.
Recipients include: Robert Burns MacMullin (1972); Theodore L. Cairns (1973); Edwin H. Land (1974); Carl Djerassi (1975).

Auguste Perret Award
This award consists of a diploma conferred every two years for a particularly remarkable project in the field of architecture and technology applied to architecture. The award was founded in 1974 by the International Union of Architects (UIA). It is not intended for personalities whose world-wide repute is already established. The award is a tribute to the memory of Auguste Perret, one of the first Presidents of the UIA.
Awarding body: International Union of Architects, 1 rue d'Ulm, 75005 Paris, France.

Antoinette Perry Award
This award was established in 1947 by the American Theatre Wing for excellence in the theatre. It takes the form of a silver medallion mounted on a base, and is given annually for distinguished achievement in various categories: best actor, best actress, best play, best director, etc. The awards are named in honour of Antoinette Perry (1888–1946), actress, producer, director, Chairman of the Board and Secretary of the American Theatre Wing. The awards are commonly known as 'Tonys'.
Awarding body: League of New York Theatres and Producers Inc., 226 West 47th St., New York, N.Y. 10036, U.S.A.
Recipients include: John Kani and Winston Ntshona (best actors, *Sizwe Banzi is Dead*), Ellen Burstyn (best actress, *Same Time Next Year*), Peter Shaffer (best play – author, *Equus*), John Dexter (best director), 1976.

Perskorprys (*Perskor Award*)
Established in 1964 by Afrikaanse Pers (now Perskor) Publishers, this award began as an annual prize but since 1977 is awarded every two years. It is a cash prize of R3,000, and is given for the best literary work in Afrikaans published during a given period by Perskor.
Awarding body: Perskor Publishers, P.O.B. 845, Johannesburg, South Africa.

Recipients include: Ingrid Jonker (*Rook en Oker*, 1964); Breyten Breytenbach (*Die Ysterkoei Moet Sweet*, 1965); Abraham H. de Vries (*Briekwa*, 1974); Casper Schmidt (*Terra Incognita*, 1975); Henriette Grové (*Toe Hulle Die Vierkleur Op Rooigrond Gehys Het*, 1976).

Petzval József Memorial Medal
The Hungarian Society for Optics, Acoustics and Cinematography founded the medal in 1962 for outstanding technical or scientific achievements in the field of precision engineering: optics, acoustics, photochemistry, film technology and television. Two prizes of 5,000 forints each are awarded annually. The medal is named after József Petzval (1807–95), professor of optics at Pest and Vienna Universities, who invented the double system of lenses in photography.
Awarding body: Optikai, Akusztikai és Filmtechnikai Egyesület, Budapest VI, Anker-köz 1, Hungary.

Georg Michael Pfaff-Medaille
This award was established in 1971 by the Georg Michael Pfaff Gedächtnisstiftung, a foundation which operates nationally and internationally in the fields of education and health. The medal is awarded every two years for innovations in the field of health. It consists of a certificate, a cash sum of DM10,000 and a medal.
Awarding body: Georg Michael Pfaff Gedächtnisstiftung, 675 Kaiserslautern, Eisenbahnstr. 28–30, Federal Republic of Germany.
Recipients include: Arbeitskreis Gesundheitskunde e.V. (1971); Dieter Menninger and Gottfried Gülicher (1973); Fritz Strempfer, Emma Stoll and Hans-Gunther Schumacher (1976).

Georg Michael Pfaff-Preis
This prize was established in 1969 by the Georg Michael Pfaff Gedächtnisstiftung, a foundation which operates nationally and internationally in the fields of education and health. The prize is awarded every two years for innovations in the field of éducation. It consists of a certificate and a cash sum of DM10,000.
Awarding body: Georg Michael Pfaff Gedächtnisstiftung, 675 Kaiserslautern, Eisenbahnstr. 28–30, Federal Republic of Germany.
Recipients include: Ernst Weissert (1971); Horst Speichert (representative of the magazine *Betrifft: Erziehung*, 1971); Martin Bonhoeffer (1973); Planungskommission Kollegschule des Landes Nordrhein-Westfalen (1973).

Pfeifer Ignác Memorial Medal
The Hungarian Chemical Society founded the medal in 1962 for outstanding long-term contributions to technical and economic work in the chemical industry. An annual cash prize of 5,000 forints accompanies the medal. It is named after Ignác Pfeifer (1868–1941), a professor of chemistry at Budapest University.
Awarding body: Magyar Kémikusok Egyesülete, Budapest VI, Anker-köz 1, Hungary.

Wilhelm Leopold Pfeil Prize
This is one of many awards given by the FVS Foundation for contributions to European co-operation, culture or the environment. The Pfeil prize is for services to forestry, and is worth DM20,000.
Awarding body: Stiftung FVS, Georgsplatz 10, 2 Hamburg 1, Federal Republic of Germany.
Recipients include: Prof. Jean Pardé (France) and Kurt Ruppert (Fed. Rep. of Germany), 1972.

Pfizer Award
Established in 1958, the award of $1,000 and a citation is given annually for the best American or Canadian publication in the field of history of science.
Awarding body: History of Science Society, c/o Secretary, School of Physics and Astronomy, University of Minnesota, Minneapolis, Minn. 55455, U.S.A.
Recipients include: Richard S. Westfall (1972); Joseph S. Fruton (1973); Susan Schlee (1974); Frederic L. Holmes (1975); Otto Neugebauer (1976).

Pharmaceutical Society of Great Britain Charter Gold Medal
In 1963 the Council of the Society instituted gold and silver medals to be awarded annually. The gold medal is in recognition of outstanding services rendered by a member to the Society or, generally, in promoting the interests of pharmacy. (The silver medal is for the same services at a local level.) The award is made by the Council on the recommendation of the President, and presented at the Society's Annual General Meeting.
Awarding body: Pharmaceutical Society of Great Britain, 1 Lambeth High St., London SE1 7JN, England.
Recipients include: Miss M. A. Burr, Harry Steinman (1973); Frank Hartley (1974); Allen Aldington (1975); A. G. Fishburn (1976).

Henry M. Phillips Prize
The Phillips Prize Essay Fund, established in 1888 with the gift of $5,000 from Miss Emily Phillips in memory of her brother, allows for the award of a cash prize (currently $2,000) for the best essay of real merit on the science and philosophy of jurisprudence.
Awarding body: American Philosophical Society, 104 South Fifth St., Philadelphia, Pa. 19106, U.S.A.
Recipients include: Karl N. Llewellyn (*The Common Law Tradition: Deciding Appeals*, 1962); John Rawls (*A Theory of Justice*, 1974); Harry W. Jones and Wolfgang Friedman (for various publications, 1976).

John Phillips Memorial Award
This annual award was established in 1929 and is made for distinguished contributions to internal medicine. It takes the form of a medal.
Awarding body: American College of Physicians, 4200 Pine St., Philadelphia, Pa. 19104, U.S.A.

Recipients include: Carl V. Moore (1970); Maxwell Finland (1971); Victor A. McKusick (1972); Willem J. Kolff, Belding H. Scribner (1973); Oscar D. Ratnoff (1974).

Donazione 'Massimo Piccinini'
This award is made annually by the University of Milan to encourage Italian achievement in the field of hydrology. The recipient should have made some practical or theoretical contribution to hydrology (scientific studies in a related field such as medicine, climatology or thalassology are also considered). Applications are envisaged primarily from physicians, but any Italian citizen is eligible. The award is worth 5,000 lire.
Awarding body: Università degli Studi di Milano, Via Festa del Perdono 7, 20122 Milan, Italy.

Picture Book of the Year Award
This award, with the Children's Book of the Year Award (*q.v.*), was established in 1946 by a group of interested librarians, authors and publishers concerned at the lack of good literature for children after the second world war. A medal is presented annually in July (during Children's Book Week in Australia) for the best picture book for children published in the current year. A grant from the Visual Arts Board of the Australia Council (A$1,700 in 1976) is also awarded. Winners must be Australian nationals or resident in Australia for at least five years.
Awarding body: Children's Book Council of Australia.
Recipients include: Ron Brooks (*The Bunyid of Berkeleys Creek*, 1974); Quentin Hole (*The Man from Ironbark*, 1975); Dick Roughsey (*The Rainbow Serpent*, 1976); (no award 1977).

Lorne Pierce Medal
The medal is awarded every two years, if there is a suitable candidate, for an achievement of special significance and conspicuous merit in imaginative or critical literature written in either English or French. Critical literature dealing with Canadian subjects shall have priority. The award consists of a gold medal and C$1,000. Canadian citizens or persons who have been Canadian residents for the preceding five years are eligible. The medal was established in 1926 by Lorne Pierce (1890–1961) who, as Editor of Ryerson Press for forty years, contributed greatly to the development and appreciation of Canadian literature.
Awarding body: The Royal Society of Canada, 395 Wellington, Ottawa, Ont. K1A 0N4, Canada.
Recipients include: Roy Daniells (1970); Desmond Pacey (1972); Rina Lasnier (1974); Douglas LePan (1976); Carl Klinck (1978).

Włodzimierz Pietrzak Award (PAX Award)
This award was established in 1948 by the associates and workers of the socio-cultural Catholic weekly, *Dziś i jutro*, in memory of Włodzimierz Pietrzak (1913–44), a Christian poet, journalist and writer. The award is given annually on the anniversary of the founding of the PAX

Association, for scholarly, literary or artistic achievements by authors who represent or accept the Christian point of view. It consists of a certificate and a cash sum of 25,000 złotys. Further awards are given for writers under the age of 30 and for foreign writers.

Awarding body: Association PAX, Mokotowska 43, Warsaw, Poland.

Recipients include: Rev. Prof. Mieczysław Żywczyński; Rev. Prof. Kazimierz Kłósak; Prof. Alfons Klafkowski; Prof. Józef Chałasiński; Prof. Stefan Skwarczyński.

Pinkerton Award

Mr. J. B. Pinkerton, one of the founders of the Institution of Nuclear Engineers, established this award in 1961. Originally the result of an annual competition, it is now given for outstanding papers which have appeared in the Institution's *Journal*. A cash prize of £100 is available annually, but only awarded when papers of particular merit are presented.

Awarding body: The Institution of Nuclear Engineers, 1 Penerley Rd., London SE6 2LQ, England.

Recipients include: Dr. J. W. Gardner, Dr. J. Lewins (1964); Dr. J. W. Gardner (1972).

Pioneers of Underwater Acoustics Medal

The medal is presented by the Acoustical Society of America to an individual of any nationality who has made an outstanding contribution to the science of underwater acoustics, through publication of research results in professional journals, or by other achievements. The award honours five pioneers in the field: H. J. W. Fay, R. A. Fessenden, H. C. Hayes, G. W. Pierce and P. Langevin.

Awarding body: Acoustical Society of America, 335 East 45th St., New York, N.Y. 10017, U.S.A.

Recipients include: Albert B. Wood (1961); J. Warren Horton (1963); Frederick V. Hunt (1965); Harold L. Saxton (1970); Carl Eckart (1973).

Luigi Pirandello Prizes

Two biennial prizes are awarded – one (the Theatre Award) for the composition of a theatrical work in Italian (this award has the patronage of the President of the Republic); the other (International Award) in recognition of international merit in the theatre. The theatre award is a cash prize of 4 million lire; the international award is a gold plate bearing a bust of Pirandello. The prizes were established (the theatre award in 1966 and the international award in 1970) by the Savings Bank of Sicily in memory of Luigi Pirandello, writer and dramatist (1867–1936). Those eligible for the theatre award are Italian or foreign authors already known in the theatrical field; those eligible for the international award are Italian or foreign personalities of renown in any branch of the theatre. Works must be written in Italian and must be theatrical performances of normal length; they must not have been published

or presented in other competitions, nor performed or transmitted by radio or TV.

Awarding body: Cassa Centrale di Risparmio V.E. per le Province Siciliane, Piazza Cassa di Risparmio, 90133 Palermo, Italy.

Recipients include: Ingmar Bergman (international award, 1971); Girolamo Blunda (theatre award, for *L'inglese ha visto la bifora*, 1973); Giorgio Strehler (international award, 1973); Giorgio Celli (theatre award, for *Le tentazioni del Prof. Faust*, 1975); Eduardo De Filippo (international award, 1975).

Clemens von Pirquet-Preis

This prize was established in 1968 by the Austrian Society for Paediatrics in memory of Clemens von Pirquet (1874–1929), a paediatrician who contributed much in the field of allergy and tuberculin reaction. The prize, awarded to members of the Society only, is for special achievements in the field of paediatrics. Originally it was awarded annually; from 1977 it will be awarded every two years. It consists of a cash prize of 10,000 Schillings.

Awarding body: Österreichische Gesellschaft für Kinderheilkunde, Auenbruggerplatz 30, Universitäts-Kinderklinik, 8036 Graz, Austria.

Recipients include: H. Gleispach (1969); L. Hohenauer, H. Kaloud (1970); L. Reinken (1972); A. Windorfer (1974).

Eugen-Piwowarsky-Preis

This prize was established in 1955 by the German Society of Foundry Engineers in honour of Professor Dr.-Ing. Eugen Piwowarsky (1891–1953), a pioneer in the field of research in foundry engineering. The prize is awarded annually to a member of the Society (upper age limit 35) for a work published during the previous year in either of the Society's journals. The prize consists of a certificate, a medallion and a sum of money, which must be used on a study tour of foundries in other countries.

Awarding body: Verein Deutscher Giessereifachleute, 4 Düsseldorf, Sohnstr. 71, Federal Republic of Germany.

Recipients include: Dr.-Ing. Wolf-Dieter Schneider (1972); Dr.-Ing. Helmut Mücke (1973); Dr.-Ing. Manfred Dette (1974); Dr.-Ing. Rainer Ellerbrok (1975); Dipl.-Ing. Herbert Löblich (1976).

Max-Planck-Medaille

This annual award was instituted in 1929 by the German Physical Society and is given for achievements in the field of theoretical physics, particularly those connected with the work of Max Planck (1858–1947), the famous Nobel prizewinner and originator of the quantum theory. Recipients are selected by the Society on the recommendation of a committee composed of previous winners, who put forward two names. The award takes the form of a medal and certificate, and may be given to scientists of any nationality.

Awarding body: Deutsche Physikalische Gesellschaft, Federal Republic of Germany.

Recipients include: Nikolai N. Bogolubov (1973); Léon C. P. Van Hove (1974); Gregor Wentzel (1975); Ernst C. G. Stueckelberg (1976); Walter E. Thirring (1977).

Platinum Medal
The medal was established in 1938 by the Council of the Institute of Metals (merged with the Iron and Steel Institute to form the Metals Society in 1974). It is awarded annually in recognition of outstanding services to the non-ferrous metals industry, whether on the industrial or the scientific side. It is presented at the Society's Annual General Meeting in May. Anyone who is associated with the science or technology of non-ferrous metals is eligible.
Awarding body: The Metals Society, 1 Carlton House Terrace, London SW1Y 5DB, England.
Recipients include: The Earl of Verulam (U.K., 1972); Dr. K. Van Horn (U.S.A., 1973); Dr. N. P. Inglis (U.K., 1974); Dr. C. Crussard (France, 1975); Prof. Sir Peter Hirsch, F.R.S. (U.K., 1976).

Earle K. Plyler Prize
The prize was established in 1976 by the George E. Crouch Foundation to recognize and encourage notable contributions to molecular spectroscopy. It is awarded annually, and consists of $1,000 and a certificate citing the contributions made by the recipient. Nominations are open to scientists in North America. The prize may be given for experimental or theoretical achievements, for a single dramatic innovation, or for a series of research contributions which, when integrated, amounts to a major contribution to the field of molecular spectroscopy.
Awarding body: American Physical Society, 355 East 45th St., New York, N.Y. 10017, U.S.A.
Recipients include: Charles H. Townes (1977).

Edgar Allan Poe Award
The Academy of American Poets was founded in 1934 to assist the careers of American poets; since 1974 it has presented a group of annual awards, sponsored by the Copernicus Society of America, spanning the full range of American poetic accomplishment. The Edgar Allan Poe Award of $5,000 is made in recognition of the continuing development of a poet 45 years of age or less who has recently published a book of poems.
Awarding body: The Academy of American Poets, 1078 Madison Ave., New York, N.Y. 10028, U.S.A.
Recipients include: Mark Strand (1974); Charles Simic (1975).

Poetry Society of America Awards
Established in 1916, two annual awards of $300 and $200 are made for the two poems voted best of the year in the monthly selections by ballot of the entire Society membership. Only Society members are eligible. The $200 award is known as the John W. Gassner Memorial Award.
Awarding body: The Poetry Society of America, 15 Gramercy Park, New York, N.Y. 10003, U.S.A.

Recipients include: Edgar Lee Masters; Maxine Kumin; Mary Oliver; Daniel Henderson; Constance Carrier.

Polar Medal
This medal is a royal award, conferred on those who have personally made notable contributions to the exploration and/or knowledge of the polar regions and who, in so doing, have undergone the hazards and rigours of the polar environment whether by land, sea or air. Only those who have participated in an expedition which has been the responsibility of one or more governments of Commonwealth countries are eligible. The award may be conferred in recognition of individual service of outstanding quality in the fields of exploration, scientific research or general service on polar expeditions. The medal is silver, octagonal in shape, and bears on the obverse the effigy of the Sovereign, and on the reverse a representation of the ship *Discovery*. The award originated in 1857 when Queen Victoria instituted a medal for Arctic discoveries; Polar medals were instituted by King Edward VII in 1909. They were originally awarded to team-members of specific expeditions, but in 1968 the Royal Warrant was amended to make the medal an award for individual merit. Winners of the medal in the U.K. receive it from the Sovereign at an Investiture ceremony.
Awarding body: Office of the Naval Secretary, Ministry of Defence, Old Admiralty Building, London SW1, England.

Polish Architects Association Honorary Prize
This prize was established in 1966 and is awarded annually to a member of the Polish Architects Association for outstanding achievements in architecture. The prize consists of a medal and a certificate.
Awarding body: Polish Architects Association, Foksal 2, 00-950 Warsaw, Poland.
Recipients include: Prof. Julian Duchowicz and Prof. Zygmunt Majerski (1973); Jadwiga Grabowska-Hawrylak (1974); Henryk Buszko and Aleksander Franta (1975); Prof. Jan Bogusławski (1976).

Polish Composers Union Music Award
The award was founded in 1949 and is given for outstanding achievements in the composition, study and performance of contemporary Polish music. It is given annually and consists of a sum of money and a certificate.
Awarding body: Związek Kompozytorow Polskich, Zarząd Główny, Rynek Starego Miasta 27, 00-272 Warsaw, Poland.
Recipients include: Krzysztof Penderecki (1962); Tadeusz Baird (1965); Jan Krenz (1968); Henryk Mikolaj Górecki (1970); Witold Lutoslawski, (1959, 1973).

Polish Culture Award
This cash award is made annually by the Polish Division of the European Cultural Association for

contributions to the propagation of Polish culture abroad.

Awarding body: Polish Division of the European Cultural Association (SEC), Krakowskie Przedmieście 87/89, 00-322 Warsaw, Poland.

Polish Cultural Merit Badge
This badge is awarded occasionally by the Polish Ministry of Culture and Art to a foreigner for contributions to the propagation of Polish culture abroad.

Awarding body: Department of International Co-operation in the Field of Culture, Ministry of Culture and Art, Krakowskie Przedmieście 15/17, 00-071 Warsaw, Poland.

Polish Ministry of Foreign Affairs Diploma
This diploma is awarded annually to a Polish citizen for outstanding merit in the propagation and dissemination of Polish culture abroad.

Awarding body: Ministry of Foreign Affairs, Aleja 1 Armii WP, Warsaw, Poland.

Polish PEN-Club Prize
This award is given annually for the best translation of Polish literature into a foreign language.

Awarding body: Polish PEN-Club, Pałac Kultury i Nauki, Warsaw, Poland.

Polish Translation Prize
This prize was established in 1966 by the Polish Society of Authors (ZAIKS), which deals with authors' rights. The prize is awarded annually for outstanding literary attainments in translating from and into Polish. It consists of a cash sum of 15,000 złotys and a certificate.

Awarding body: Stowarzyszenie Autorów ZAIKS, 2 ul. Hipoteczna, 00-092 Warsaw, Poland.

Recipients include: Anton M. Raffo (Italy), Jutta Janke (German Dem. Rep.), Anna Maria Linke (Poland), 1975.

Pollák-Virág Award
This award is made annually by the Hungarian Scientific Society for Telecommunication for distinguished contributions to its journal *Magyar Hiradástechnika*. It consists of a certificate and 1,500 forints. The award, which was established in 1960, commemorates Illés Pollák (1852–1930) and József Virág (1870–1901), pioneers of telecommunication techniques in Hungary.

Awarding body: Hiradástechnikai Tudományos Egyesület, 1372 Budapest, P.O.B. 451, Hungary.

George Polya Prize
Established in 1969 by the American Society for Industrial and Applied Mathematics, this prize is awarded every five or ten years for a notable application of combinatorial theory made within the previous five or ten years. It consists of a sum of money.

Awarding body: Society for Industrial and Applied Mathematics, U.S.A.

Recipients include: R. P. Stanley, E. Szemeredi, R. M. Wilson (1975).

Leonard P. Pool Award
This award was established in 1971 by Air Products & Chemicals, Inc., in honour of their founder, and is presented to a member of the American Institute of Internal Auditors in recognition of an outstanding published paper presented before a group of business, professional, governmental or educational leaders. It is generally made annually, and takes the form of a plaque and $500.

Awarding body: The Institute of Internal Auditors, Inc., 249 Maitland Ave., Altamonte Springs, Fla. 32701, U.S.A.

Recipients include: Robert E. Seiler (1972); Aaron Schneider (1974).

Ciprian Porumbescu Prize
This is one of the prizes awarded by the Romanian Academy for achievement in every field of arts and science. This prize is for musicology, and is named after Ciprian Porumbescu (1853–83), the famous composer. It was established in 1956, and is awarded retroactively every other year. It consists of 10,000 lei and a diploma. The award-winning work should have been published in the year for which the prize is given. The Composers' Union, Ministry of Education, Academies of Music, Universities and other relevant institutions make nominations to the Academy for the award.

Awarding body: Romanian Academy, Calea Victoriei 125, Bucharest, Romania.

Howard N. Potts Medal
This gold medal is awarded, without regard to nationality, for distinguished work in science or the arts, particularly for the important development of previous basic discoveries, inventions or products of superior excellence, or for utilizing important principles. The medal was established according to the will of Howard N. Potts (1819–1906) of Philadelphia, who contributed largely to educational, scientific and literary institutions.

Awarding body: The Franklin Institute, Benjamin Franklin Parkway at 20th St., Philadelphia, Pa. 19103, U.S.A.

Recipients include: Howard Vollum (oscilloscope development, 1973); Jay W. Forrester (system dynamics, 1974); Legrand G. van Uitert (new materials for electronic and optical devices, 1975); Stephanie L. Kwolek and Paul W. Morgan (polymer technology, 1976); Godfrey N. Hounsfield (U.K., inventor of the computerized axial tomography (CAT) diagnostic system in radiology, 1977).

Valdemar Poulsen Guldmedaillen (*Valdemar Poulsen Gold Medal*)
The medal was established in 1939 to honour Dr. Valdemar Poulsen (1869–1942). It is awarded irregularly for outstanding achievements in radio and magnetic recording, fields to which Dr. Poulsen made significant contributions.

Awarding body: Valdemar Poulsen Gold Medal Fund, Denmark.

193

Recipients include: Charles P. Ginsburg (1960); John R. Pierce (1963); J. W. Forrester (1969); John B. Gunn (1972); Andrew H. Bobeck (1976).

Ludwig-Prandtl-Ring

This prize was founded in 1956 in honour of Ludwig Prandtl, an expert in aerodynamics, by the German Society for Aeronautics. It is awarded annually for outstanding scientific achievements in research and teaching in the field of aerodynamics.

Awarding body: Deutsche Gesellschaft für Luft- und Raumfahrt e.V., Federal Republic of Germany.

Recipients include: Dipl.-Ing. Ludwig Bölkow (Fed. Rep. of Germany, 1972); Prof. Dr. phil. habil. Klaus Oswatitsch (Austria, 1973); Prof. William Rees Sears (U.S.A., 1974); Prof. Dr.-Ing. August Wilhelm Quick (Fed. Rep. of Germany, 1975); Prof. Alec David Young (U.K., 1976).

Fritz Pregl Prize for Microchemistry

The prize was established in 1930 by Fritz Pregl (1869–1930), professor of microchemistry and a corresponding member of the Austrian Academy of Sciences (which awards the prize). It is given for a learned work in the field of microchemistry, published in the preceding three years, which has not hitherto received an award. It may also be given for a work on chemistry, where it is felt that only the author's skilful mastery of the methods of microchemistry have enabled him to complete his work. The prize is a certificate and a sum of money, and is generally awarded only to an Austrian; it is usually awarded annually in May or June. Full and corresponding members of the Austrian Academy of Sciences, who belong to the Prizes Commission, are not eligible.

Awarding body: Österreichische Akademie der Wissenschaften, 1010 Vienna, Dr.-Ignaz-Seipel-Platz 2, Austria.

Preis der Bayerischen Akademie der Wissenschaften *(Bavarian Academy of Sciences Prize)*

This award is made every two years for a piece of work in German on a set scientific theme, completed during the past two years. It consists of a cash prize of DM8,000, donated by the Donors Association for promoting Sciences and Humanities.

Awarding body: Bayerische Akademie der Wissenschaften, 8000 Munich 22, Marstallplatz 8, Federal Republic of Germany.

Recipients include: Dr.-Ing. Gerd Holtorff, Dipl.-Ing. Dr. Walter Graf, Dipl.-Ing. K. Bormann and Dr.-Ing. E. Häusler (1963); Gerhard Schlichting (1969); Dr. Manfred Sumper, Peter Decker (1971).

Preis der Deutschen Physikalischen Gesellschaft *(German Physical Society Prize)*

This award is made annually by the German Physical Society to one or more young physicists for outstanding published work. Wherever possible, one prize for experimental physics and one for theoretical physics are given each year. The prize, first awarded in 1942, consists of a cash award and certificate.

Awarding body: Deutsche Physikalische Gesellschaft, Federal Republic of Germany.

Recipients include: Albert H. Walenta (1973); Dirk Offermann, Albert Steyerl (1974); Dieter Haidt (1975); Werner Lauterborn (1976); Detlev Buchholz and Gert-Rüdiger Strobl (1977).

Preis der Energietechnischen Gesellschaft im VDE *(Prize of the Power Engineering Society of the German Electrical Engineers Association)*

This annual prize is awarded by the ETG for exceptional publications in the field of electrical power engineering. It was established in 1975, and consists of a certificate and cash prize of DM1,000. Applicants must be VDE members and under 40 years of age, and no one may receive an award more than once. Contributions must have been published during the previous year.

Awarding body: Energietechnische Gesellschaft im VDE (Verband Deutscher Elektrotechniker), D-6000 Frankfurt/Main 70, Stresemannallee 21, Federal Republic of Germany.

Recipients include: Dipl.-Ing. Gerd Balzer and Dr.-Ing. Ralf Gretsch, Dr.-Ing. Hans-Jürgen Haubrich, Dr.-Ing. Joachim Körber, Dr.-Ing. Paul-Gerhard Sperling (1975); Ing. (Grad.) Helmut Schöffel (1976).

Preis für Film- und Fernsehforschung *(Award for research into motion pictures and television)*

This award is made every three years by the Austrian Society for Film Sciences, Communications and Media Research. It was established in 1958 in memory of Joseph Gregor (1888–1960), the Society's first president. It is presented for a written consideration of some aspect of the development of the Austrian cinema or television. (If the author is an Austrian citizen, the subject-matter need not be confined to Austria.) Works submitted should be produced within the previous five years, unpublished, and written in German. The prize-winner receives a diploma and cash prize of 35,000 Schillings; additional prizes of 12,000 Schillings and 10,000 Schillings may also be awarded.

Awarding body: Österreichische Gesellschaft für Filmwissenschaft, Kommunikations- und Medienforschung, 1010 Vienna 1, Rauhensteingasse 5, Austria.

Recipients include: Dr. techn. Siegfried Hermann and Ing. Wilhelm Guha (jointly, 1975).

Preis für Germanistik im Ausland *(Prize for German Philology Abroad)*

This prize was established in 1964 by the German Academy for Language and Poetry, to emphasize the international activities of the Academy. It is awarded annually to a foreigner for outstanding works in German philology, and is a cash prize of DM6,000.

Awarding body: Deutsche Akademie für Sprache und Dichtung, Alexandraweg 23 (Glückert-Haus), 6100 Darmstadt, Federal Republic of Germany.
Recipients include: Ladislao Mittner (Italy, 1972); Gustav Korlén (Sweden, 1973); Herman Meyer (Netherlands, 1974); Elizabeth M. Wilkinson (U.K., 1975); Marian Szyrocki (1976).

Preis der Gesellschaft für Gerontologie der DDR *(East German Gerontology Society Award)*

This award is given annually in three categories: social gerontology and gerohygiene; geriatrics; and basic research in gerontology. The prize in each category consists of 1,000 DDR-Marks and a certificate. It was established in 1974.
Awarding body: Gesellschaft für Gerontologie der DDR, c/o Doz. Dr. sc. med. Udo Jürgen Schmidt, Medizinische Poliklinik, Hermann-Matern-Str. 13a, 104 Berlin, German Democratic Republic.
Recipients include: Prof. Dr. S. Eitner, Doz. Dr. U. J. Schmidt (1975); Dr. Gulbin, Dr. A. Eitner (1976).

Preis der Nachrichtentechnischen Gesellschaft im VDE *(Prize of the Telecommunications Society of the Association of German Electrical Engineers)*

This annual award is made by the NTG for excellent scientific publications in the field of telecommunications. It was established in 1956, and the maximum number of recipients per year is ten. It consists of a certificate and cash prize of DM1,000. Applicants must be NTG members of 40 years of age or under, and no one may receive an award more than once. Contributions must have been published during the previous year.
Awarding body: Nachrichtentechnische Gesellschaft im VDE, D-6000 Frankfurt/Main 70, Stresemannallee 21, Federal Republic of Germany.
Recipients include: Prof. Dr.-Ing. Kurt Antreich, Dr.-Ing. Roland Briechle; Dr.-Ing. Karlheinrich Horninger, Dr.-Ing. Günter Müller, Dr.-Ing. Rüdiger Müller, Prof. Dr.-Ing. Peter Noll, Dipl.-Ing. Gerhard Pfitzenmaier (1976).

Preis für Pharma-Technik *(Prize for Pharmaceutical Technology)*

This award was established in 1963 as the Heinemann Gedächtnispreis, and its present name was adopted in 1977. It is given for articles which have appeared in the publication *Die Pharmazeutische Industrie*. Studies on all aspects of pharmacy – e.g. the development, production and packaging of medicines, good manufacturing practice, and microbiological sterility of medicaments, etc. – are eligible. The first prize, donated by the Pharmaceutical Industry Association in Frankfurt, is worth DM4,000; the second prize, donated by the publishers, Editio Cantor, is worth DM2,000; and the third prize, donated by Frau A. Heinemann of Stuttgart, is worth DM1,000.
Awarding body: Editio Cantor, KG, 7960 Aulendorf, Postfach 1310, Federal Republic of Germany.
Recipients include: Dr. D. Krüger and J. Herschel (first prize, 1977).

Preise der Karl Renner-Stiftung *(Karl Renner Foundation Prizes)*

The Karl Renner Foundation was established in 1951 by the City of Vienna on the occasion of the 80th birthday of the Federal President, Dr. Karl Renner. The prizes are awarded to individuals or groups whose work has contributed to the reputation of Austria and its capital city as focal points of cultural, social and economic activity. Up to six prizes of not less than 100,000 Schillings may be awarded each year.
Awarding body: Magistratsabteilung 7, Stadtsrat, Vienna, Austria.

Preise des Kulturfonds der Stadt Salzburg *(City of Salzburg Cultural Fund Prizes)*

Five prizes, for music, art, literature, science and journalism, were established in 1967 by the Salzburg Cultural Fund for the Advancement of Art, Science and Literature. The first four take the form of a certificate and a cash award of 50,000 Schillings each. They are awarded on an irregular basis in recognition of distinguished work which has some connection with Salzburg. The prize for journalism, the *Kritikpreis*, is an annual award of 15,000 Schillings for the review of an opera, play, ballet or concert forming part of the Salzburg Festival.
Awarding body: Fonds der Landeshauptstadt Salzburg zur Förderung von Kunst, Wissenschaft und Literatur, Kulturverwaltung der Stadt Salzburg, A-5024 Salzburg, Auerspergstr. 7, Austria.
Recipients include: Prof. Dr. h.c. Carl Orff (music, 1970); Prof. Oskar Kokoschka (art, 1971); Dr. h.c. Carl Zuckmayer (literature, 1974); Hans Stuckenschmidt (review, 1975).

Preise der Stadt Wien für Kunst, Wissenschaft und Volksbildung *(City of Vienna Prizes for Art, Science and Popular Education)*

Established in 1947, these prizes are given by the city of Vienna for outstanding achievements in the fields of poetry, journalism, musical composition, painting, popular education, the arts and natural sciences, and technology. The prizes are given for work which draws attention to the importance of Vienna and Austria as cultural centres. Each prize consists of a cash sum of 40,000 Schillings.
Awarding body: Magistratsabteilung 7, Stadtsrat, Vienna, Austria.

Premi Catalònia

This prize of $1,250 was donated by Joan B. Cendrós i Carbonell and is given to foreign researchers studying any aspect of Catalan culture. It is administered by the Institute for Catalan Studies. Candidates must be nominated by a member of a scientific or literary academy or of a learned society, or by a university professor.
Awarding body: Institut d'Estudis Catalans, Apartat 1146, Barcelona, Spain.
Recipients include: Kenneth M. Setton (historical study of the eastern Mediterranean with special reference to the Catalan influence in Greece, 1976); Prof. Friedrich Stegmüller (work on

medieval theology and philosophy at the Rai-mundus Lullus Institute, University of Freiburg, and the critical edition of Ramon Llull's first six works in Latin, 1977).

Premi 'Antonio Feltrinelli' (*Antonio Feltrinelli Prizes*)

Various international and national prizes are awarded by the Italian Academy of Sciences in accordance with the will of Dr. Antonio Feltrinelli (died 1942). They are for outstanding achievement in the sciences and the arts. International prizes may be awarded to Italians as well as foreigners. Awards of varying monetary value are made annually (the first in 1950) in the following order: (1) moral and historical sciences; (2) physical, mathematical and natural sciences; (3) letters; (4) arts; (5) medicine. From time to time a prize may be awarded for an exceptional accomplishment of high moral and humanitarian value. Applications are not submitted; nominations are made by Academy members (who are themselves ineligible) and the presidents of the other major Italian academies (in the case of the international prizes, also the presidents of the major foreign academies).
Awarding body: Accademia Nazionale dei Lincei, Palazzo Corsini, Via della Lungara 10, Rome, Italy.
Recipients include: Alfred Verdross (Austria, international prize for law, 1975); Dinu Adamesteanu (archaeology), Fabrizio Sergio Donadoni (archaeology), Rolando Quadri (law), Giulio Capodaglio (social and political sciences), Giuseppe di Nardi (social and political sciences), national prizes, 1975.

Premi Istituto del Dramma Italiano – Saint Vincent

These annual awards were established in 1949 by the Italian Institute of Drama, and are made to the author and producer of a new Italian play which has been produced during the past theatrical year (with particular emphasis on originality). The prizes take the form of gold medals. Since 1957 actors have also been eligible, and their prizes take the form of masks with gold laurel wreaths. The awards are assigned by a special jury of the Institute and are not open to competition.
Awarding body: Istituto del Dramma Italiano, Via Monte della Farina 42, 00186 Rome, Italy.
Recipients include: Franco Brusati (author); Massimo Castri (producer, 1974–75); Roberto Lerici (author); Orazio Costa (producer, 1975–76).

Premi Enric de Larratea

This prize of 5,000 pesetas was donated by the Enric de Larratea Foundation, and is administered by the Institute for Catalan Studies. It is given for a piece of research on the language, literature, history, art or archaeology of Catalonia or on a scientific subject. The papers submitted must be unpublished and written in any Romance language, English or German.
Awarding body: Institut d'Estudis Catalans, Apartat 1146, Barcelona, Spain.

Premi del Ministro per i Beni Culturali e Ambientali (*Prizes of the Minister for Culture and the Environment*)

Two annual prizes of 4 million lire each were established in 1960 by the Italian Minister of Education; the present title was adopted in 1976. They are for outstanding contributions to science, and are awarded alternately by the two sections of the Academy of Sciences (moral, historical and philological sciences, and physical, mathematical and natural sciences) for work in the various branches of science. Candidates may be nominated by Academy members (who are themselves ineligible) or individual applications may be submitted. The prizes are presented in June at the end of the academic year.
Awarding body: Accademia Nazionale dei Lincei, Palazzo Corsini, Via della Lungara 10, Rome, Italy.
Recipients include: Giovanni Felice Azzone (physiology and pathology, 1974); Bruno Paradisi (law, 1974); Iacopo Barsotti (mathematics and mechanics, 1975); Giulio Bruni Roccia (social and political sciences, 1975).

Premi Nicolau d'Olwer

This prize of $1,000 was founded by the Palma Guillén de Nicolau Foundation, Mexico, and is administered by the Institute for Catalan Studies. It is given for the best work on Catalan history or philology. The papers submitted must be unpublished and may be written in Catalan, Spanish, Portuguese, French, Italian, German or English.
Awarding body: Institut d'Estudis Catalans, Apartat 1146, Barcelona, Spain.
Recipients include: Jaume Riera i Sans ('Noms i cognoms dels conversos jueus als països de la Corona de Catalunya-Aragó fins a l'any 1412', 1976); Albert G. Hauf ('La "Vita Christi" de Fr. Francesc Eiximenis, O.F.M. (1340?–1409?) y la tradición de las "Vitae Christi" medievales. (Aportación al estudio de las principales fuentes e influencias).', 1977).

Premi Josep Ma. de Sagarra

The prize was established in 1977 in honour of the Catalan dramatist, Josep Ma. de Sagarra (1894–1961), for the best play produced or written in Catalan each year. The award of 250,000 pesetas is made on 23 April, National Book Day.
Awarding body: Institut i Museu del Teatre de la Diputació Provincial de Barcelona, Conde del Asalto 3, Barcelona, Spain.

Premio AEI 'Pubblicazioni' (*AEI Publications Prize*)

The prize is awarded by the Italian Electrotechnical and Electronics Association (AEI) in memory of E. Jona, A. Bianchi, and A. Panzarasa. Awarded for the first time in 1919, it consists of a gold medal and certificate, and is given annually in recognition of the entire scientific and technical achievement of a member of the Association over the previous ten years, with particular regard to works published in the AEI's journals and previously given as papers at its meetings.

Awarding body: Associazione Elettrotecnica ed Elettronica Italiana, Viale Monza 259, 20126 Milan, Italy.

Recipients include: Ezio Biglieri (1971–73); Giancarlo Corazza (1974); Marino Valtorta (1975).

Premio AEI 'Ricerche' (*AEI Research Prize*)

The Italian Electrotechnical and Electronics Association (AEI) established the prize in memory of A. Righi, F. Lori and L. Ferraris. First awarded in 1932, it consists of a gold medal and certificate, and is given annually to an AEI member for the best research work published in the previous two years in the field of electrical engineering and electronics, with particular regard to experimental research.

Awarding body: Associazione Elettrotecnica ed Elettronica Italiana, Viale Monza 259, 20126 Milan, Italy.

Recipients include: Giovanni Mamola and Mario Sannino (1971–73); Vincenzo Pozzolo and Dante Del Corso (1974); Mario Soldi (1975).

Premio IEL

The prize was instituted by the Italian firm Industrie Elettriche di Legnano S.p.A. (IEL) for the best memoirs containing original research presented at the previous Annual Reunion of the Italian Electrotechnical and Electronics Association (AEI). It consists of 1 million lire and a diploma, and may be divided if necessary.

Awarding body: Associazione Elettrotecnica ed Elettronica Italiana, Viale Monza 259, 20126 Milan, Italy.

Recipients include: Paolo Antognetti, Sergio Cova and Antonio Longoni; Alessandro Gandoli, C. Nobili, M. Dondi, P. Giuliani, S. Scaglioni, S. Concari and G. N. Guidelli (jointly, 1975).

Premio Academia Nacional de la Historia (*National Academy of History Prize*)

This prize has been awarded every two years since 1966 for the best works on Argentine history. It is given alternately for published works (published in the previous four years) and unpublished works, which must be written in Spanish. The first prize is $4,000, the second prize $1,500 and the third prize $1,000.

Awarding body: Academia Nacional de la Historia, Balcarce 139, Buenos Aires, Argentina.

Recipients include: Edberto Oscar Acevedo (*La Intendencia de Salta del Tucumán en el Virreinato del Río de la Plata*, 1966); Cristina V. Minutolo ('El sitio de Buenos Aires por el coronel Hilario Lagos, 1° de Setiembre de 1852', 1968); Hialmar Edmundo Gammalsson (*Juan Martín de Pueyrredon*, 1970); Horacio Juan Cuccorese ('Historia crítica de la historiografía socioeconómica argentina del

siglo XX', 1972); Horacio Zorraquín Becú (*Tiempo y vida de José Hernández (1834–1886)*, 1974).

Premio Agrícola Aedos (*Aedos Agricultural Prize*)

This award of 100,000 pesetas was established by José Maria Cruzet Sanfeliu in 1960, and is awarded by the Spanish publishing firm, Aedos. It is usually awarded annually on the occasion of an agricultural event. It is for the best original work on an agricultural subject and is designed to promote research in agriculture.

Awarding body: Editorial Aedos, Consejo de Ciento 391, Barcelona 9, Spain.

Recipients include: M. Carbonell (*Tratado de Vinicultura*, 1969); J. L. Leirado (*Manual del Proyectista Agronómico*, 1970); J. Miranda (*Cultivos ornamentales*, 1974); S. Durán (*Replantación de frutales*, 1976).

Premio Acad. Dr. José Aguilar Álvarez (*Acad. Dr. José Aguilar Álvarez Prize*)

This annual prize is sponsored by the Ethicon Division of Johnson & Johnson. It is open to surgeons of Mexican nationality, resident in Mexico and registered with the Ministry of Health and Social Welfare. It is given for the best submitted paper on surgical research which must be unpublished, original and written in Spanish. The prize of 10,000 pesos may be awarded to an individual or a group. If the prize is not awarded the money goes to the Mexican Academy of Surgery to promote its scientific activities.

Awarding body: Academia Mexicana de Cirugía, Centro Médico Nacional del IMSS, Bloque B, 2° piso, Avda. Cuauhtémoc 330, México 7, D.F., Mexico.

Premio Alberdi y Sarmiento

This is an annual prize established in 1950 by the Director of the daily newspaper *La Prensa*, Dr. Alberto Gainza Paz, to commemorate two illustrious Argentinians, Juan Bautista Alberdi and Domingo Faustino Sarmiento, who used both the press and literature to spread and strengthen the ideals of liberty and democracy in Latin America. The prize is awarded for the best contributions to the strengthening of friendship between American nations. The prize consists of a silver plaque, an unspecified sum of money and travelling expenses for the presentation ceremony. The competition is open to distinguished journalists and writers from any American country.

Awarding body: Diario *La Prensa*, Avda. de Mayo 567-75, Buenos Aires, Argentina.

Recipients include: Victoria Ocampo (Argentina, 1967); Guillermo Martínez Márquez (Cuba, 1968); Eduardo Jiménez de Aréchaga (Uruguay, 1971); Donald Marquand Dozer (U.S.A., 1972); Arturo Uslar Pietri (Venezuela, 1973).

Premio Álvarez Quintero

This prize was established by María Jesús Álvarez Quintero in 1949 in memory of her brothers Serafín and Joaquín. It is a monetary prize of

5,000 pesetas and is awarded every two years in turn for the best play, and the best novel or collection of short stories, in a competition held by the Spanish Academy.

Awarding body: Real Academia Española, Calle de Felipe IV 4, Madrid, Spain.

Premio Florentino Ameghino

This award was established in 1974 by the Argentine Palaeontology Association for research work on palaeontology and biostratigraphy published in the Association's quarterly journal, *Ameghiniana.* It is an annual award in the form of a certificate, and is restricted to young authors of under 35 years of age.

Awarding body: Asociación Paleontológica Argentina, Maipú 645, 1° piso, Buenos Aires 1006, Argentina.

Recipients include: Alicia Marta Baldoni (1974).

Premio Anual de Comercio Exterior *(Annual Prize for Foreign Trade)*

Established by the Mexican Institute for Foreign Trade to promote scientific research in this field, the prize is open to Mexican nationals only. Entries may be submitted in the form of essays, special research projects, academic theses or monographs on any theoretical or practical aspect of Mexico's external trade. Papers must be unpublished and written in Spanish. The first prize consists of 100,000 pesos and a special diploma, the second prize is 75,000 pesos and a special diploma and the third prize is 50,000 pesos. A special diploma is also given to any paper considered worthy of mention.

Awarding body: Instituto Mexicano de Comercio Exterior, Dirección de Planeación y Estudios, Asturias No. 50, 3er piso, México 19, D.F., Mexico.

Premio 'José María Arguedas'

This biennial prize was instituted by Goodyear del Perú, S.A. in 1972 to honour the memory of José María Arguedas, the distinguished Peruvian author (1911–69). It is designed to encourage and promote Peruvian literature and to improve standards of writing. It is open to writers of Peruvian nationality only. The prize consists of 100,000 soles, publication of the book and payment of 10 per cent royalties.

Awarding body: Goodyear del Perú, S.A., Paseo de la República 959, La Victoria, Apdo. 1690, Lima, Peru.

Recipients include: Luis Urteaga Cabrera (*Los Hijos del Orden,* 1972); Gregorio Martínez (*Canto de Sirena,* 1976).

Premio Ariel *(Ariel Prize)*

This is an annual prize established in 1946 for the best Mexican film. The award comprises a small gold statue and a special distribution franchise. It is open to any Mexican film produced and shown commercially in Mexico in the year of the competition.

Awarding body: Academia Mexicana de Ciencias y Artes Cinematográficas, A.C., División del Norte 2462, 2°, México 13, D.F., Mexico.

Recipients include: Emilio Fernández; Arturo Ripstein; Jaime Humberto Hermosillo; Felipe Cazals.

Premio 'Doctor Francisco Javier Balmis'

An annual prize consisting of 20,000 pesos, a diploma and medal, is awarded to the researcher of Mexican nationality and resident in the country who has completed the best project on public health to have been published in the three years before the competition.

Awarding body: Academia Nacional de Medicina, Avda. Cuauhtémoc 330 y 350, Bloque B, Unidad de Congresos, Centro Médico Nacional, México 7, D.F., Mexico.

Premio Banamex de Ciencia y Tecnología *(Banamex Science and Technology Prize)*

Established by the Banco Nacional de México, this is an annual prize for the best contributions to science and technology in the fields of industry or agriculture which may be submitted in the form of essays, books or research projects. Practical contributions to the improvement of efficiency and production in these fields may also be submitted. Entries must be of a scientific nature and be considered of practical application in Mexico. The works must have been written or published during the year of the award and if the entry is of a practical nature, the author must submit a written summary of his project. All entries must be in Spanish. The competition is open to Mexican nationals only. The first and second prizes are 100,000 pesos each.

Awarding body: Secretaría del Premio Banamex de Ciencia y Tecnología, 5 de Mayo No. 6 – Mezzanine, México 1, D.F., Mexico.

Recipients include: Lic. Alejandro Nadal Egea ('Instrumento de Política Científica y Tecnología de México', 1977).

Premio Banamex de Economía *(Banamex Prize in Economics)*

This prize was established by the Banco Nacional de México, S.A. and is open to Mexican nationals who have worked individually or collectively in the field of economic development in Mexico. Entries are invited in the form of essays, research projects, lectures, articles, books or theses which have been written or published during the year the prize is awarded. The first prize is 100,000 pesos, the second prize 50,000 pesos, and the sum of 25,000 pesos may be awarded to the author of the best professional thesis submitted. A special diploma may be awarded to any work deemed worthy of special mention.

Awarding body: Banco Nacional de México, S.A., Madero 17, 2° piso, Palacio de Iturbide, México, D.F., Mexico.

Recipients include: Lic. Jesús F. Reyes Heroles González Garza ('Política Fiscal y Redistribución del Ingreso', 1977).

Premio Barbagelata

The prize was established according to the will of Prof. Angelo Barbagelata, former Secretary-General of the Italian Electrotechnical and Electronics Association (AEI). It is given for articles published in the AEI's journals which best summarize and illustrate for the general reader the recent developments in any branch of electrical engineering or electronics. It is an annual prize and consists of 500,000 lire and a diploma. It is restricted to members of the AEI.

Awarding body: Associazione Elettrotecnica ed Elettronica Italiana, Viale Monza 259, 20126 Milan, Italy.

Recipients include: Carlo Alberto Sacchi (1974); Franco Filippazzi (1975); Andrea Abete and Edoardo Barbisio (1976).

Premio Biennale di Letteratura per Ragazzi 'Olga Visentini' (*Olga Visentini Biennial Award for Literature for Young People*)

This award was established in 1966 by the municipality of Cerea in the province of Verona, in memory of the writer Olga Visentini (1893–1961), who for some time lived in Cerea. Previously unpublished prose works for young people by Italian writers are eligible. In selecting the recipients, the emphasis is on the moral content and idealism of the works. The first prize, offered by the municipality of Cerea, consists of 1 million lire; three further prizes, of 500,000 lire, 300,000 lire and 200,000 lire respectively, are given by various local banks.

Awarding body: Comune di Cerea, Provincia di Verona, Italy.

Premio de Biografía Castellana Aedos/Premio de Biografía Catalana Aedos (*Aedos Prizes for Castilian and Catalan Biographies*)

These annual prizes of 100,000 pesetas each were established in 1951 and 1952 respectively by José María Cruzet Sanfeliu and are awarded by the publishing house Aedos. The prizes are for the biography of an important person, and must be written in Castilian (Spanish) and Catalan respectively. The winning books are published by Aedos.

Awarding body: Editorial Aedos, Consejo de Ciento 391, Barcelona 9, Spain.

Recipients include: A. Oliver (Castilian, *Este otro Ruben Darío*, 1959); R. Brown (Castilian, *Becquer*, 1962); R. Grabolosa (Catalan, *Carlins i liberals*, 1971); I. Pujadas (Catalan, *Joan Alsina: Xile al cor*, 1975).

Premio Bonazzi

The prize was established on the basis of a fund instituted by Ottavio Bonazzi, a former emeritus member of the Italian Electrotechnical and Electronics Association (AEI). It is awarded annually for the best work in the field of electronics, preferably experimental, published in one of the AEI's journals in the preceding two years. The prize consists of 500,000 lire and a diploma; it is

indivisible, and is awarded preferably to a member of the AEI who is under 40 years of age.

Awarding body: Associazione Elettrotecnica ed Elettronica Italiana, Viale Monza 259, 20126 Milan, Italy.

Recipients include: Giovanni Soncini (1974); Silvano Donati (1975); Gianfranco Cariolaro (1976).

Premio Bressa

This award is made occasionally by the Turin Academy of Sciences for discoveries or publications during the previous four years in the fields of physical and experimental sciences, natural history, pure and applied mathematics, chemistry, physiology and pathology (occasionally also geology, history, geography or statistics). It was instituted in 1835 by Dr. Cesare Bressa, and takes the form of a gold medal and diploma. The award is made alternately at national and international level. Nominations must be made by Italian members of the Academy (who are not themselves eligible).

Awarding body: Accademia delle Scienze di Torino, Italy.

Recipients include: Giuseppe Pitré (1898); Ernst Haeckel (1899); Sir Ernest Rutherford (1908); Ernesto Schiaparelli (1910); Carlo Ferrari (1936).

Premio Caldas de Ciencias

This prize was established in 1970 by the Colombian Scientific Research Foundation, named after Francisco José de Caldas. It is a national award designed to promote scientific research and awarded annually for work in this field. The prize consists of a gold medal, a certificate and $100,000 in cash.

Awarding body: Fondo Colombiano de Investigaciones Científicas 'Francisco José de Caldas', Apdo. Aéreo 29828, Bogotá, Colombia.

Premio 'Dottor Amilcare Capello'

This award is made for the best work on oto-rhino-laryngology in the field of tuberculosis published during the previous two years. Italian specialists who have graduated from an Italian university not more than six years previously are eligible. The award consists of 120,000 lire.

Awarding body: Università degli Studi di Milano, Via Festa del Perdono 7, 20122 Milan, Italy.

Premio Inocencio Carreño

A competition was established in 1977 by the six signatories of the Andrés Bello Pact: Colombia, Bolivia, Chile, Ecuador, Peru and Venezuela. The object is to stimulate musical composition in the Andean sub-region, and to encourage cultural interchange between the countries concerned. The competition is named after the Venezuelan composer, Inocencio Carreño, and is held every two years, the location being determined on a rotating basis. Executive authority lies with the Venezuelan National Council for Culture in co-operation with the Executive Secretariat of the Andrés Bello Agreement. The prize consists of a cash award, equivalent to U.S.$10,000.

Awarding body: Consejo Nacional de Cultura, Avda. Principal de Chuao, Edificio Los Roques, Apdo. 50, 995, Caracas, Venezuela.

Premio Casa de las Américas

The Casa de las Américas, a cultural institution devoted to the promotion of understanding between the Latin American countries, established this prize in 1960 in order to promote the literary works of Latin American authors. Annual awards of $1,000 each are given for works in all branches of literature. The rules and the number of prizes vary slightly each year; 16 prizes were awarded in 1977. Categories are as follows: fiction (novel, short story, poetry, drama); essay (research, interpretation of criticism); children's book. Those eligible are Caribbean and Latin American writers including those from non-Spanish speaking countries, writers who are not Latin American but who have resided in Latin America for at least five years, and authors from socialist countries in the essay section only. Works presented must be unpublished and in Spanish (except for Brazilian authors and English-speaking Caribbean and Guyanese authors).

Awarding body: Casa de las Américas, Tercera y Calle G, El Vedado, Havana, Cuba.

Recipients include: Carlos José Reyes (Colombia, children's book, 1975); Edward Kamau Braithwaite (Barbados, Anglo-West Indian literature, 1976); Manuel Maldonado Denis (Puerto Rico, essay, 1976); Miguel Acosta Saignes (Venezuela, Simón Bolívar special award, 1977).

Premio Acad. Dr. Gonzalo Castañeda (*Acad. Dr. Gonzalo Castañeda Prize*)

This annual prize is open only to members of the Mexican Academy of Surgery and consists of a first prize of a gold medal and diploma, a second prize of a silver medal and diploma and a third prize of a bronze medal and diploma. It is awarded for the best work presented to the Academy during the year. The work may be submitted by an individual or a group; in the latter case, the principal author must be a member of the Academy.

Awarding body: Academia Mexicana de Cirugía, Centro Médico Nacional, Bloque B, 2° piso, Avda. Cuauhtémoc 330, México 7, D.F., Mexico.

Premio Castellani

The prize was established by Signor Castellani's family according to his will. It provides for the award of ten prizes in even-numbered years (1964–82) for the best contributions to the development of electrical energy. Only members of the Italian Electrotechnical and Electronics Association (AEI) are eligible.

Awarding body: Associazione Elettrotecnica ed Elettronica Italiana, Viale Monza 259, 20126 Milan, Italy.

Recipients include: Arnaldo Maria Angelini (1970); Dante Finzi (1972); Ercole Bottani (1974); Noverino Faletti (1976).

Premio Castillo de Chirel

This prize of 4,000 pesetas was established in 1916 by María del Patrocinio de Muguiro y Finat, Baroness of the Castle of Chirel, in memory of her husband, Carlos de Frígola. It is awarded every four years for a piece of journalistic work published in a newspaper or magazine during the previous four years, the specific subject being chosen by the Spanish Academy.

Awarding body: Real Academia Española, Calle de Felipe IV 4, Madrid, Spain.

Premio Miguel de Cervantes

This is one of the most prestigious literary prizes in Spain. It is given annually for the best novel published during the year, and its value is now five million pesetas. It is named after the famous author, Cervantes (1547–1616), who wrote *Don Quixote de la Mancha*.

Awarding body: Ministerio de Información y Turismo, Av. Generalisimo 39, Madrid 16, Spain.

Recipients include: Jorge Guillén (1977).

Premio Giuseppe Ciardi

The prize is named after Professor Giuseppe Ciardi who established the Ciardi Foundation in 1970 under the auspices of the Italian section of the International Society of Penal Military Law and Law of War. Professor Ciardi, who died in 1974, was a past President of the Society. The prize is given for an original study on military law or subjects associated with it, and may refer to a specific country or deal with the international situation. It is awarded every three years at the Society's International Congress, and is a cash prize of 300,000 lire.

Awarding body: Fondazione Giuseppe Ciardi, Gruppo Italiano della Società Internazionale del Diritto Penale Militare e del Diritto di Guerra, Viale delle Milizie 5/c, Rome, Italy.

Recipients include: Prof. Fritz Kalshoven (Holland, 1973); Dr. Michael Bothe (Fed. Rep. of Germany, 1976); Gen. Pietro Verri (Italy, 1976).

Premio de Ciencias Alejandro Angel Escobar (*Alejandro Angel Escobar Science Prize*)

This prize was established according to the will of Alejandro Angel Escobar (1903–53), and has been awarded by the Alejandro Angel Escobar Foundation annually since 1955. The award, which is intended to promote the applied sciences, is made to two Colombian-born scientists for work accomplished during the preceding year. The prize consists of a medal, a certificate, and a cash sum, which varies according to the interest from the Foundation.

Awarding body: Fundación Alejandro Angel Escobar, Calle 19 6-68, Oficina 603, Bogotá, Colombia.

Recipients include: Alex Enrique Bustillo Pardey and Eduardo Gaitán Marulanda (1976); Alex Enrique Bustillo Pardey and Guillermo Sánchez (1977).

Premio de Ciencias 'Federico Lleras' (*Federico Lleras Prize for Science*)

This award is made annually to encourage the development of the medical sciences among young Colombians. It consists of a cash prize of $20,000, and was established in 1968.

Awarding body: Laboratorios Hormona Colombia S.A., Colombia.

Premio en Ciencias Sociales (*Social Sciences Prize*)

Awarded annually, this prize of 25,000 pesos is designed to encourage young scientists in the field of social sciences, i.e. anthropology, sociology, political science, law, philosophy, philology, history, ethnohistory, economics, psychology and administrative sciences. Any scientist under the age of 40 and resident in Mexico is eligible.

Awarding body: Academia de la Investigación Científica, A.C., Avda. Revolución 1909, 8° piso, México, D.F., Mexico.

Premio Científico Luis Elizondo (*Luis Elizondo Scientific Prize*)

The prize was established in 1967 by Don Luis Elizondo Lozano, industrialist and philanthropist. It is designed to stimulate scientific research and is given to one person (or a group of up to three if the work has been carried out jointly) who has made a significant contribution to cultural or scientific research. Any Mexican citizen is eligible. The prize consists of 400,000 Mexican pesos, a gold medal and a diploma. It is given annually in turn for work in one of the following five fields: medicine and/or biological sciences; agriculture, zootechnics and food production sciences; physics, chemistry and/or mathematics; education; engineering.

Awarding body: Patronato Premio Luis Elizondo, Instituto Tecnológico y de Estudios Superiores de Monterrey, Sucursal de Correos 'J', Monterrey, Nuevo León, Mexico.

Recipients include: Dr. Emilio Rosenblueth Deutsch (engineering, 1973); Dr. Guillermo Soberón Acevedo, Dr. Maximiliano Ruiz Castañeda and Dr. Rafael Méndez Martínez (medicine and biological sciences, 1974); Dr. Celio Barriga Solorio (food production science, 1975); Dr. Xorge Alejandro Domínguez (chemistry, 1976).

Premio Lorenzo Codazzi

The Colombian Society of Engineers awards an annual prize to the author of the best work published in the preceding year which shows knowledge of the territory of Colombia. The prize usually consists of a medal, a diploma and a sum of money.

Awarding body: Sociedad Colombiana de Ingenieros, Carrera 4a, No. 10-41, Apdo. Aéreo 340, Bogotá, Colombia.

Recipients include: Luis Laverde Goubert ('Bibliografía sobre Fronteras – Amazonia y Orinoquia', 1975).

Premio del Colegio de Arquitectos de Venezuela (*Venezuelan Architectural Association Prize*)

This is a biennial prize established in 1963 for outstanding contributions to architectural research and dissemination.

Awarding body: Colegio de Arquitectos de Venezuela, Centro Comercial Chacaito, Locales 9 y 10 sótano, Apdo. 5262, Caracas, Venezuela.

Recipients include: Tomás José Sanabria (1965); Julián Ferris (1967); Guido Bermudez (1971); Ernesto Fuenmayor and Carlos Celis Cepero (1973); Heriberto Gonzáles Méndez (1976).

Premio 'Silvio D'Amico'

This award was established in 1950 by the Italian Institute of Drama, in honour of the distinguished Italian drama critic who lived during the first half of this century. The award is made to the Italian critic whose recent published works have contributed most to the knowledge and appreciation of Italian drama from the year 800 to the present day. The award of 500,000 lire is made every two years, and is assigned by a special jury of the Institute and is not open to competition.

Awarding body: Istituto del Dramma Italiano, Via Monte della Farina 42, 00186 Rome, Italy.

Recipients include: Vittorio Viviani (*Storia del teatro Napoletano*, 1970); Ruggero Jacobbi (*Teatro italiano da ieri a domani*, 1972); Anna Borsotti (*Verga drammaturgo* and *Giuseppe Giacosa*, 1974); Giovanni Antorucci (*Lo spettacolo futurista in Italia*, 1975); Edo Bellingeri (*Dall' intellettuale al politico – Le cronache teatrali di Gramsci*, 1975).

Premio Duque de Alba

This prize was established in 1905 by Jacobo Fitz-James Stuart y Falcó, Duke of Berwick and Alba, in memory of the Duchess, Doña Rosario Falcó y Ossorio, to commemorate the 300th anniversary of the publication of *Don Quijote*. The prize of 12,000 pesetas is given every nine years for original unpublished works written in Spanish by a Spaniard. The subject is chosen by the Spanish Academy.

Awarding body: Real Academia Española, Calle de Felipe IV 4, Madrid, Spain.

Premio per Esperienze di Fisica a carattere didattico della Società Italiana di Fisica (*Italian Physics Society Award for Physics Experiments of an Educational Nature*)

This award is made annually to an individual or group of people for an outstanding contribution to the teaching of physics at any level (in the form of a book, article, experiment, apparatus or similar) as described in a written report. The award is worth 250,000 lire.

Awarding body: Società Italiana di Fisica, Via L. degli Andalò 2, 40124 Bologna, Italy.

Premio Manuel Espinosa y Cortina

This prize of 4,000 pesetas was established in 1891 by the Marquis and Marchioness of Cortina in memory of their son, Manuel Espinosa y Cortina. It is awarded every five years for the best dramatic work performed in Spain, and written by a Spaniard in Spanish, within the previous five years.

Awarding body: Real Academia Española, Calle de Felipe IV 4, Madrid, Spain.

Premio para el Estímulo de Docencia e Investigación en Ingeniería Química (*Prize to Promote Teaching and Research in Chemical Engineering*)
Established by the Mexican Institute of Chemical Engineers (IMIQ), this competition is designed to stimulate original research and practical work in the field of chemical engineering. It is given for the best original paper, either unpublished or published in the preceding year, in the form of an essay, special research project or outstanding achievement which makes an important contribution to development analysis and planning in Mexico and to the promotion of chemical engineering. It is open to members of the IMIQ resident anywhere in the world with the exception of student-members and those under 30 years of age. A diploma and special mention are given to the author of the best paper.

Awarding body: Instituto Mexicano de Ingenieros Químicos, A.C., Londres 188-302, México 6, D.F., Mexico.

Premio Fastenrath
This annual prize was established in 1909 by King Alfonso XIII following a donation to the Spanish Academy from Doña Luisa Goldmann, widow of the famous publisher Juan Fastenrath. It is a monetary prize of 6,000 pesetas and is given in turn for poetry, literary criticism or essays, novels or collections of short stories, historical criticism, biography, general history or the history of politics, literature, art, costume, etc., and dramatic works in prose or verse whether destined for theatrical production or not. No author can receive the prize more than once every ten years for work in the same field. All entries must be written in Spanish by Spaniards.

Awarding body: Real Academia Española, Calle de Felipe IV 4, Madrid, Spain.

Premio Feijoo
The prize was established in 1961 by the Spanish Association for the Advancement of Science in honour of Fray Benito Jerónimo Feijoo (1676–1764), the celebrated Spanish writer. Until 1967 it was awarded annually but is now awarded every two years. The prize is 50,000 pesetas, awarded to the author of the best collection (not less than six) of published articles on recent scientific developments and the importance of scientific research for the industrial and economic progress of the nation. The articles must have been published in non-specialist magazines or newspapers during the previous year.

Awarding body: Asociación Española para el Progreso de las Ciencias, Valverde 24, Madrid 13, Spain.

Recipients include: Miguel Masriera (1966); Octavio Roncero (1967); Pedro Crespo (1969);

Aldemaro Romero (1973); José M. de Pablos (1975).

Premio de Filologia 'Felix Restrepo' (*Felix Restrepo Philology Prize*)
This international prize was founded in 1972 in honour of R. P. Felix Restrepo, S.J. It is awarded annually by the Colombian Academy of Language for the best work in the field of philology, and consists of a cash prize of 50,000 pesos.

Awarding body: Academia Colombiana de la Lengua, Apdo. Aéreo 13922, Bogotá, Colombia.

Premio della Fondazione 'Dott. Giuseppe Borgia' (*'Dr. Giuseppe Borgia' Foundation Prize*)
The foundation was established in 1955 and is administered by the Italian Academy of Sciences. The prize of 1 million lire is awarded annually to Italians under 35 for scientific or literary work. The awards are made in rotation on a five-yearly basis in the following order: in the first four years alternately for a scientific and a literary work; in the fifth year for research or scientific inventions which the Academy deems worthy of a prize. Applications may be submitted (except for the quinquennial prize); Academy members are ineligible.

Awarding body: Accademia Nazionale dei Lincei, Palazzo Corsini, Via della Lungara 10, Rome, Italy.

Recipients include: Prof. Franco Pacini (astrophysics, 1972); Dott. Paola Rigo (literature, 1973); Prof. Andrea Bennici (1974); Dott. Silvia Rizzo (philology and linguistics, 1975); Prof. Piero Sensi (quinquennial prize, 1976).

Premio 'Fondo Hoechst' (*'Hoechst Foundation' Prize*)
This is an annual prize awarded jointly by the Mexican National Academy of Medicine and Química Hoechst de México, S.A. It is designed to promote the development of specific research projects in the field of medical sciences and consists of 40,000 pesos. The prize is open to researchers working in hospital, teaching or research institutes in Mexico who are involved in the field of experimental or clinical medicine.

Awarding body: Academia Nacional de Medicina, A.C., Bloque B, Unidad de Congresos, Centro Médico Nacional, Avda. Cuauhtémoc 330, México 7, D.F., Mexico.

Premio 'Fondo Eli Lilly' (*Eli Lilly Foundation Prize*)
This is an annual prize awarded jointly by the Mexican National Academy of Medicine and the Eli Lilly Laboratories. It consists of 75,000 pesos, and is designed to promote the development of specific research projects in the field of clinical medicine. It is open to researchers involved in experimental or clinical medicine in hospitals, teaching institutes and research institutes in the Mexican Republic.

Awarding body: Academia Nacional de Medicina, Bloque B, Unidad de Congresos, Centro Médico Nacional, Avda. Cuauhtémoc 330, México 7, D.F., Mexico.

Premio del Fondo 'Maria Teresa Roncaglia Eugenio Mari' (*Maria Teresa Roncaglia and Eugenio Mari Fund Prize*)

This award of 3 million lire was instituted under the will of Ing. Eugenio Mari who died in Florence in 1969. It was his wish to establish an annual prize to be awarded alternately for work in the sciences and arts. Nominations are made by members of the Academy of Sciences who are themselves ineligible for the award.

Awarding body: Accademia Nazionale dei Lincei, Palazzo Corsini, Via della Lungara 10, Rome, Italy.

Recipients include: Prof. Talamanca (moral, historical and philological sciences, 1976).

Premio Manuel Forero

This award is given from time to time by the Colombian National Academy of Medicine to Colombians who have performed outstanding services to the Republic in the field of medicine or the related sciences, particularly in experimental research. It was established in 1960, and consists of a medal, diploma and cash prize of $500.

Awarding body: Academia Nacional de Medicina, Carrera 9, No. 20-13, Apdo. Aéreo 23224, Bogotá, Colombia.

Recipients include: Dr. Alfonso Bonilla Naar (1970); Dr. Alfredo Correa Henao (1973); Dr. Augusto Gast Galvis (1976).

Premio Rómulo Gallegos

This literary prize is awarded by the Venezuelan Government in memory of the Venezuelan author and former President, Rómulo Gallegos. A cash prize of 100,000 bolívares ($22,000) is awarded every four years to a writer from Latin America, Spain or the Philippines for a novel written in Spanish.

Awarding body: Comisión por el Premio Gallegos, Consejo Nacional de la Cultura, Caracas, Venezuela.

Recipients include: Carlos Fuentes (Mexico, *Terra Nostra*, 1977).

Premio Francisco Luis Gallejo

The National University of Colombia established this science prize in 1972 to promote scientific research in Colombia. Four awards may be made at a time, each consisting of a diploma and a cash prize of $15,000.

Awarding body: Universidad Nacional de Colombia, Medellín, Colombia.

Premio Prof. D. Ganassini per le Ricerche Mediche (*Prof. D. Ganassini Award for Medical Research*)

This award is made annually by the University of Milan on behalf of the Ganassini Foundation, established in honour of Domenico Ganassini, for an unpublished monograph in the area of biology, biochemistry or pathology. Italian or foreign doctors attached to Italian university or hospital institutes and clinics are eligible. The award is made at the end of the academic year, and consists of a cash prize and the publication, at the Foundation's expense, of the winning manuscript; the second-prize winner also receives a cash prize. The award is also made at international level, to citizens of EEC countries. Both awards are under the patronage of the Ministry of Health.

Awarding body: Università degli Studi di Milano, Via Festa del Perdono 7, 20122 Milan, Italy.

Premio Gastroenterología Nacional (*National Gastroenterology Prize*)

This award was established in 1954 and is given every two years. Its purpose is to stimulate the development and progress of gastroenterology as a specialty in Venezuela. A paper may be entered for the award by any member of the Venezuelan Society of Gastroenterology. The winner receives a gold medal and a certificate.

Awarding body: Sociedad Venezolana de Gastro-enterología, Torre del Collegio, Of. F-1, piso 15, Av. J. M. Vargas, Urb. Santa Fé, Caracas, Venezuela.

Recipients include: Dr. Marcos Matos Villalobos (1976).

Premio Rodrigo Gómez

This annual prize was established in 1971 by the Governors of Latin American banks in honour and memory of Rodrigo Gómez, Director-General of the Banco de México from 1952 until his death in 1970. It is designed to stimulate the preparation of research studies in fields of interest to the central banks. The 30,000-word papers should be original, including doctoral theses, written in Spanish, French, English or Portuguese. Citizens of all Latin American and Caribbean countries are eligible. The prize consists of U.S.$5,000 and the winning paper is published by the Centro de Estudios Monetarios Latinoamericanos.

Awarding body: Centro de Estudios Monetarios Latinoamericanos, Durango 54, México 7, D.F., Mexico.

Recipients include: Aldo Arnaudo (Argentina, Economía Monetaria', 1972); L. R. Seyffert (Mexico, 'Análisis del Mercado de Eurodólares', 1974); Mario I. Blejer (Argentina, 'Money Prices and the Balance of Payments: the case of Mexico', 1976).

Premio Cleto González Víquez

This prize was established in honour of Cleto González Víquez, one of Costa Rica's most distinguished historians, and former President of the Republic (1906–10 and 1928–32). The prize acknowledges the best book on history or geography published in the preceding year. It is awarded annually and consists of a gold medal and certificate.

Awarding body: Academia de Geografía e Historia de Costa Rica, Apdo. Postal 4499, San José, Costa Rica.

Recipients include: Carlos Meléndez (1967); Luz Alba Chacón de Umaña (1969); Marco Antonio Fallas (1973); Samuel Stone (1976); Carolyn Hall (1977).

Premio Historia de Madrid (*Madrid History Prize*)

This annual prize of 300,000 pesetas is donated by the Círculo de la Unión Mercantil e Industrial de Madrid (Madrid Industrial and Mercantile Union Cultural Circle) and is one of the 'Villa de Madrid' prizes awarded in conjunction with the Madrid City Council. It is designed to encourage cultural and artistic activities and is awarded for the best submitted monograph on the origins, organization, operation and recent developments of guilds in Madrid.

Awarding body: Ayuntamiento de Madrid, Plaza de la Villa 5, Madrid, Spain.

Premio Innovazione Elettronica (*Award for Innovation in Electronics*)

This award was established in 1976 by the SELENIA Association of Electronic Industries, to commemorate the 25th anniversary of its foundation. It is awarded every three years for innovative ability as demonstrated in the recent application of scientific discoveries to industrial problems in the field of electronic systems and apparatus. Italian citizens working in Italian electronic companies are eligible. The first prize consists of 4 million lire, and four runners-up each receive 1 million lire.

Awarding body: Istituto Elettrotecnico Nazionale Galileo Ferraris, Corso Massimo D'Azeglio 42, 10125 Turin, Italy.

Premio Integración para América Latina (*Integration for Latin America Award*)

This annual competition was established in 1975 by the Institute for Latin American Integration. It is intended to promote and encourage unpublished papers on the process of Latin American integration and co-operation, and to strengthen current regional trends. A specific subject is chosen each year and the papers may be submitted in Spanish, Portuguese, English or French, by citizens of any Latin American country. The first prize is U.S.$3,000 and publication of the paper; the second prize is U.S.$1,500.

Awarding body: Instituto para la Integración de América Latina (INTAL), Casilla de Correo 39, Sucursal 1, 1401 Buenos Aires, Argentina.

Recipients include: H. Alvez Catalán (Chile, 1975).

Premio Internazionale della Fondazione 'Guido Lenghi' (*Guido Lenghi Foundation International Prize*)

This prize of 2 million lire was established in 1965 by Signora Clara Magrassi Lenghi in memory of her father, Signor Guido Lenghi. It is administered

for the Foundation by the Italian Academy of Sciences, and is awarded every two years for work in the field of biological or clinical virology. The prize may not be awarded to members of the Academy, nor more than once to the same person.

Awarding body: Accademia Nazionale dei Lincei, Palazzo Corsini, Via della Lungara 10, Rome, Italy.

Recipients include: Prof. Robert J. Huebner (1971); Prof. Ferdinando Dianzani (1973); Dr. Giancarlo Vecchio and Dr. Salvatore Venuta (1975).

Premio Internazionale della Fondazione 'Eugenio Morelli' (*Eugenio Morelli Foundation International Prize*)

This prize of 2 million lire was established in 1964 by Signore Giuseppina Savarino Morelli and Emilia Morelli to honour the memory of their father, Senator Professor Eugenio Morelli. It is administered for the Foundation by the Italian Academy of Sciences, and is awarded every two years for outstanding work in the field of pneumology. The prize may not be awarded to members of the Academy, nor more than once to the same person.

Awarding body: Accademia Nazionale dei Lincei, Palazzo Corsini, Via della Lungara 10, Rome, Italy.

Recipients include: Prof. Ramon Viswanathan (1969); Prof. Emilio Agostoni (1971); Prof. Emile M. Scarpelli (1973); Prof. Jean Mathey (1975).

Premio Internazionale della Fondazione 'Francesco Saverio Nitti' (*Francesco Saverio Nitti Foundation International Prize*)

Established in 1956, this prize of 1 million lire is administered for the Foundation by the Italian Academy of Sciences. It is awarded every two years for distinguished work in the fields of finance, economics or statistics.

Awarding body: Accademia Nazionale dei Lincei, Palazzo Corsini, Via della Lungara 10, Rome, Italy.

Recipients include: Prof. Paolo Baffi (1970); Prof. Ernesto D'Albergo (1972); Prof. Manlio Rossi Doria (1974); Prof. Gunner Myrdal (1976).

Premio Internazionale dell'Istituto Nazionale delle Assicurazioni (INA) (*National Insurance Institute International Prize*)

In 1962 the Administrative Council of the INA on the occasion of the 50th anniversary of its foundation, instituted an annual prize of 2 million lire to be awarded for outstanding work in the field of insurance. The prize is intended to draw attention to the growing importance of insurance in all countries, for the better safeguarding of life and property, and is awarded on the recommendation of members of the Italian Academy of Sciences to a living Italian or foreigner for distinguished work in one of the disciplines relating to private insurance. The award is made annually in rotation in the following four

ategories: (i) law; (ii) economics, finance and
statistics of private insurance; (iii) mathematics
and techniques of insurance; in the fourth year it
is awarded for work in a different category, or,
failing that, for work in one of the above three
categories.
Awarding body: Accademia Nazionale dei Lincei,
Palazzo Corsini, Via della Lungara 10, Rome,
Italy.
Recipients include: Prof. André Besson (law,
1974); Prof. Pacifico Mazzoni (quadrennial prize
deferred from 1973), 1974); Prof. Karl Henrick
Borch (economics, finance and statistics of private
insurance, 1975); Prof. Dario Fürst (mathematics
and techniques of insurance, 1976).

Premio de Investigación Científica (*Scientific
Research Prize*)
Two prizes are given annually for research in any
scientific field by young Mexican scientists under
the age of 40. The awards, each of 25,000 pesos,
are made on the basis of published and un-
published works.
Awarding body: Academia de la Investigación
Científica, A.C., Avda. Revolución 1909, 8° piso,
México, D.F., Mexico.

Premio 'Körner'
This award is made by the University of Milan for
the best work on organic chemistry applied to
agriculture produced during the past five years by
an Italian citizen. The prize is worth 10,500 lire.
Awarding body: Università degli Studi di Milano,
Via Festa del Perdono 7, 20122 Milan, Italy.

Premio Letterario Prato (*Prato Literary Prize*)
This prize is for a book on the subject of the
Resistance or those ideals of civilization and
democracy which it inspired. It was established in
1948, and has been awarded since 1955 by the
town council of Prato. It is awarded annually in
September in two categories: 200,000 lire for a
work of fiction; 200,000 lire for a work of non-
fiction. The entries must be by living Italian
authors, published in Italian after 1 August of the
preceding year, and must not have won any other
award.
Awarding body: Secretariat of the Prato Literary
Prize, Palazzo Municipale, Prato, Italy.
Recipients include: Mario Spinella (*Memoria della
Resistenza*), Sergio Solmi (*Poesie complete*), 1974;
Ambrogio Donini (*Storia del Cristianesimo*), Primo
Levi (*Il sistema periodico*), 1975; Giorgio Amendola
(*Una scelta di vita*), Giovanni Macchia (*Il silenzio
di Moliere*), 1976.

Premio Letterario Viareggio (*Viareggio Prize
for Literature*)
This annual award was established in 1929 by the
Italian writer Leonida Repaci and is given by the
city of Viareggio. It is presented in the summer of
each year for the best literary works published
during the previous 12 months. All living Italian
writers are eligible. The prize is currently worth
2,500,000 lire.

Awarding body: Premio Letterario Viareggio,
Via Lima 28, Rome, Italy.
Recipients include: Giorgio Bassani (1962);
Giuseppe Berto (1964); Goffredo Parise (1965);
Mario Praz (1973); Giorgio Strehler (1975).

Premio 'Doctor Eduardo Liceaga' (*'Doctor
Eduardo Liceaga' Prize*)
This is an annual prize of 20,000 pesos and a
diploma awarded jointly by the Mexican National
Academy of Medicine and Productos Científicos
Laboratorios Carnot. It is presented to the
Mexican researcher, resident in the country, who
has completed the best piece of biomedical
research to have been published within the
previous three years.
Awarding body: Academia Nacional de Medicina,
Bloque B, Unidad de Congresos, Centro Médico
Nacional, Avda. Cuauhtémoc 330, México 7,
D.F., Mexico.

Premio Linceo
This prize of 4 million lire is awarded by the
Italian Academy of Sciences. Established in 1971,
it is given annually, each year for work in a
different branch of the sciences. Applications are
not submitted; nominations are made by Academy
members who are themselves ineligible. Awards
are made in June at the end of the academic year.
Awarding body: Accademia Nazionale dei Lincei,
Palazzo Corsini, Via della Lungara 10, Rome, Italy.
Recipients include: Prof. Angelo Mangini (chemistry, 1972); Prof. Giuseppe Grioli (mathematics,
1973); Prof. Ernesto Sestan (history, 1974); Prof.
Giorgio Careri (physics, 1975); Prof. Onofrio
Carruba (linguistics, 1976).

Premio Lope de Vega
This is an annual prize given by the Madrid City
Council as one of the series 'Premios Villa de
Madrid', in memory of the famous Spanish
dramatist, Lope Félix de Vega Carpio (1562–
1635). A first prize of 300,000 pesetas and a
second prize of 75,000 pesetas are awarded to the
authors of the best submitted dramatic works.
Entries must be original, unpublished, not entered
for any previous competition nor performed in
public. They must be in Spanish, and authors
must be Spanish or Latin-American. The play
awarded first prize is performed at the Teatro
Español or at any other suitable national theatre
in Madrid.
Awarding body: Ayuntamiento de Madrid, Plaza
de la Villa 5, Madrid, Spain.

Premio Marqués de Cerralbo
Established under the terms of the will (made in
1922) of the 17th Marquis of Cerralbo, Enrique
Aguilera y Gamboa, this prize is awarded every
four years for the best original and unpublished
work in the field of Spanish language and literature. The Marquis of Cerralbo expressed the wish
that the subject should 'concern either comparative
philology and the study of archaic influences on
the Spanish language and on the various regional

205

languages; or the way these regional languages have adapted to the national language; or the benefits that archaeology has brought to hispanic literature, archaeology in our literature, etc.'.

Awarding body: Real Academia Española, Calle de Felipe IV 4, Madrid, Spain.

Premio Antonio Maura

This is an annual prize of 200,000 pesetas established by the Madrid City Council in the series 'Premios Villa de Madrid'. It is awarded to the author of the best scientific study on environmental problems facing the city of Madrid in the fields of urban development, finance, sanitation, transport, traffic, education, culture, housing, etc. Applicants must have a degree or belong to a research centre. The works become the property of the City Council and royalties will be paid to the instigators of any practical solutions used by the Council.

Awarding body: Ayuntamiento de Madrid, Plaza de la Villa 5, Madrid, Spain.

Premio Ramón Menéndez Pidal

This prize was established in 1958 by Ramón Menéndez Pidal, Director of the Royal Spanish Academy. It consists of 30,000 pesetas and is awarded every two years for a piece of literary or philological research.

Awarding body: Real Academia Española, Calle de Felipe IV 4, Madrid, Spain.

Premio 'Mesonero Romanos'

This annual prize of 100,000 pesetas was established by the Madrid City Council in the 'Villa de Madrid' series of prizes. It is given for the best collection of features, articles, or reports on Madrid which were published, broadcast or televised in the year preceding the competition.

Awarding body: Ayuntamiento de Madrid, Plaza de la Villa 5, Madrid, Spain.

Premio Gustavo Montejo Pinto

The Colombian savings bank, Caja Nacional de Previsión, founded the prize in 1974 to encourage research in the field of medicine. It is an annual prize of 25,000 pesos.

Awarding body: Caja Nacional de Previsión, Colombia.

Premio Enrique Morales

The Colombian Society of Engineers awards an annual prize for the best practical or theoretical work undertaken in the preceding year in the field of electronics or electrical engineering. The prize usually consists of a medal, a diploma and a sum of money.

Awarding body: Sociedad Colombiana de Ingenieros, Carrera 4a, No. 10-41, Apdo. Aéreo 340, Bogotá, Colombia.

Premio 'Perito F. P. Moreno' (*F. P. Moreno Prize*)

This prize for merit in the field of geography was established in 1952 by the Argentine Society for Geographical Studies. It is named after the distinguished scientist, Francisco P. Moreno. It awarded irregularly, and takes the form of a med and diploma.

Awarding body: Sociedad Argentina de Estudi Geográficos, Avda. Santa Fe 1145, Buenos Air 1059, Argentina.

Recipients include: Dr. Federico A. Daus (1957 Prof. Romualdo Ardissone (1961); Col. José Leal (1966); Dr. Ricardo G. Capitanelli (1971 Arq. Patricio H. Randle (1972).

Premio Nacional de Arquitectura (*Nation Architecture Prize*)

This is a biennial prize established in 1963 by t Architectural Association of Venezuela ar awarded for the most outstanding architectur work completed in the preceding two years.

Awarding body: Colegio de Arquitectos (Venezuela, Centro Comercial Chacaito, Local 9 y 10 sótano, Apdo. 5262, Caracas, Venezuela.

Recipients include: Julián Ferris (Aduana (Puerto Cabello, 1965); Tomás Sanabria (Ban Central, 1967); Bernardo Borges and Francis Pimentel (Edificio El Universal, 1971); Jo Miguel Galia (Edificio Seguros Orinoco, 1973 Carlos Gómez de La Llerena and Manuel Fuent (Edificio Torre Europa, 1976).

Premio Nacional de Arte (*National Prize for Ar*

This is one of six prizes given every two years the Chilean Ministry of Education. It is awarde for distinguished work, in Chile or abroad, in ar one of the arts: painting, sculpture, music, dram dance, choreography, etc. The winner receives certificate and a cash prize equal to 50 times t current minimum monthly wage, as well as pension equal to eight times the current month wage.

Awarding body: Ministerio de Educación, Sa tiago, Chile.

Recipients include: Marta Colvin (sculptur 1970); Gustavo Becerra (music, 1971); Agustí Siré (theatre, 1972); Ana Cortés Julian (1974 Jorge Urrutia Blondel (music, 1976).

Premio Nacional de Artes (*National Prize for Ar*

The Colombian Ministry of Education establishe this national prize in 1964 to encourage ar reward artistic activity. It is awarded annually an consists of a certificate and a cash prize ($100,000.

Awarding body: Ministerio de Educacic Nacional, Bogotá, Colombia.

Premio Nacional de Ciencias (*National Pri for Science*)

The Chilean Ministry of Education awards a pri every two years to an individual or a team scientists for achievement in the field of pure (applied sciences. The award takes the form of certificate and a cash prize equal to 50 times t current minimum monthly wage, as well as pension equal to eight times the current month wage.

Awarding body: Ministerio de Educación, Sanago, Chile.
Recipients include: Herbert Appel (organic emistry, 1970); Ricardo Donoso Novoa (human iences, 1971); Joaquín Luco V. (1975).

remio Nacional de Ciencias (*National Prize r Science*)
he Colombian Ministry of Education established is national prize in 1964 to promote and reward ientific activity. It is awarded annually and nsists of a certificate and a cash prize of 100,000.
Awarding body: Ministerio de Educación acional, Bogotá, Colombia.

remio Nacional de Cirugía 'Dr. Francisco lontes de Oca' (*'Dr. Francisco Montes de Oca' ational Surgery Prize*)
his annual prize is awarded by the Ministry of ealth and Social Welfare and the Mexican cademy of Surgery for the best submitted paper surgery which must be unpublished, original id written in Spanish. It is open to surgeons of lexican nationality, resident in Mexico and gistered with the Ministry of Health and Social elfare. The prize consists of 50,000 pesos divided tween first, second and third prize-winners who ceive a gold medal, silver medal and diploma spectively. If the prize is not awarded the money used to promote surgical research.
Awarding body: Academia Mexicana de Cirugía, entro Médico Nacional, Edificio de Academias, loque B, 2° piso, Avda. Cuauhtémoc 330, México D.F., Mexico.

remio Nacional de Cuento (*National Short ory Prize*)
his prize is awarded annually by the Mexican ational Fine Arts Institute and the municipality ' San Luis Potosí, and administered through the stitute's promotional department and the Casa Cultura de San Luis Potosí. It is awarded for e best unpublished book of short stories on any bject and consists of 40,000 pesos and a diploma. is open to any Spanish-speaking writers resident Mexico.
Awarding body: Instituto Nacional de Bellas rtes, Dolores 2, 3°, México 1, D.F., Mexico.

remio Nacional de Cuento Infantil 'Juan : la Cabada' (*'Juan de la Cabada' National ildren's Story Prize*)
nis prize is awarded annually by the Mexican ational Fine Arts Institute and the government the state of Campeche, and is administered by e Casa de la Cultura de Campeche. It consists 30,000 pesos and a diploma, and is awarded for e best unpublished book of children's stories on y theme. It is open to any Spanish-speaking riters resident in Mexico.
Awarding body: Instituto Nacional de Bellas rtes, Dolores 2, 3°, México 1, D.F., exico.

Premio Nacional de Cultura (*National Cultural Prize*)
This is an annual prize, instituted by the Peruvian Ministry of Education in 1950. It is awarded for work in the following fields: literature; art; humanities; natural sciences and mathematics; applied sciences and technology. A prize consisting of a diploma and 200,000 soles is awarded to the winner in each section. Only Peruvian nationals are eligible.
Awarding body: Instituto Nacional de Cultura, Jirón Ancash 390, Lima, Peru.
Recipients include: Emilio Adolfo Vestphalen (literature), Julia Codesido (art), Luis E. Valcarcel (humanities), Ronald Woodman Pollitt (natural sciences and mathematics), Pedro Weiss (applied sciences and technology), 1976.

Premio Nacional de Ensayo Histórico (*National Historical Essay Prize*)
This prize is awarded annually by the Mexican National Fine Arts Institute, the government of the state of Coahuila de Zaragoza and the municipality of Torreón, and is administered by the Institute's promotional department and the Casa de Cultura de Torreón. It consists of 50,000 pesos and a diploma, and is awarded for the best historical essay on a specific subject. In 1977 the subject was the Mexican Revolution in Northern Mexico. Any Spanish-speaking historians or essayists, resident in Mexico, are eligible.
Awarding body: Instituto Nacional de Bellas Artes, Dolores 2, 3°, México 1, D.F., Mexico.

Premio Nacional de Historia (*National History Prize*)
This is a biennial prize given by the Chilean Government for excellence in the field of history. The winner receives a certificate and a cash award equal to 50 times the current minimum monthly wage, as well as a pension equal to eight times the current monthly wage.
Awarding body: Ministerio de Educación, Santiago, Chile.
Recipients include: Prof. Eugenio Pereira Salas (1974); Mario Góngora del Campo (1976).

Premio Nacional de Historia (*National Prize for History*)
The Colombian Ministry of Education established this national prize in 1964 to promote and reward activities in the field of history. It is awarded annually and consists of a certificate and a cash prize of $100,000.
Awarding body: Ministerio de Educación Nacional, Bogotá, Colombia.

Premio Nacional de Ingeniería (*National Engineering Prize*)
The National Engineering Prize of Colombia was inaugurated in 1937 by governmental decree. It is awarded annually for work of outstanding scientific and technical merit, completed in the previous year. Candidates must be of Colombian

207

nationality, and be resident in Colombia. Only professionally qualified engineers are eligible. The winner receives a cash prize.

Awarding body: Sociedad Colombiana de Ingenieros, Carrera 4a, No. 10-41, Bogotá, D.E., Colombia.

Premio Nacional de Letras, Ciencias y Artes (*National Prize for Literature, Science and Arts*)

Awarded by the Mexican Ministry of Public Education, this prize is for outstanding achievements in each of the following fields: research into natural, exact or social sciences; letters (literature, philology, philosophy, history, criticism, essay, film-script); arts (plastic arts, music, dance, drama, film). It is open to all Mexicans (by birth, or naturalized for at least 20 years) and may never be awarded to the same person twice. The prize money is decided each year by the Ministry of Education but is not less than 100,000 pesos for each of the three awards.

Awarding body: Secretaría de Educación Pública, Argentina y González Obregón, 2° piso, Puerta 387, México 1, D.F., Mexico.

Premio Nacional de Literatura (*National Prize for Literature*)

Established in 1964 by the Chilean Ministry of Education, the prize is given every two years to a Chilean writer for work in one of the literary genres: poetry, novel, drama, essay, or criticism. It takes the form of a certificate and a cash award equal to 50 times the current minimum monthly wage, as well as a pension equal to eight times the current monthly wage.

Awarding body: Ministerio de Educación, Santiago, Chile.

Recipients include: Carlos Droguett (1970); Humberto Díaz C. (1971); Edgardo Garrido M. (1972); Sady Zañartu B. (1974); Arturo Aldunate P. (1976).

Premio Nacional de Literatura (*National Prize for Literature*)

The Colombian Ministry of Education established this prize in 1964 to promote and reward literary activity. It is awarded annually and consists of a certificate and a cash prize of $100,000.

Awarding body: Ministerio de Educación Nacional, Bogotá, Colombia.

Premio Nacional de Periodismo (*National Prize for Journalism*)

The Chilean Ministry of Education awards a prize every two years for distinguished work in any field of journalism: editing, reporting, photography, etc. The winner receives a certificate and a cash award equal to 50 times the current minimum monthly wage, as well as a pension equal to eight times the current monthly wage.

Awarding body: Ministerio de Educación, Santiago, Chile.

Recipients include: Arturo Fontaine (1975); Andrés Aburto Sotomayor (1977).

Premio Nacional de Química 'Andrés Manuel del Río' (*'Andrés Manuel del Río' National Chemistry Prize*)

Two medals are awarded annually by the Mexican Chemical Society to individuals who have either contributed through their work to the national and international prestige of the Mexican chemical profession or who have made significant contributions to the teaching of chemistry in Mexico.

Awarding body: Sociedad Química de México, Ciprés 176, México 4, D.F., Mexico.

Premio Nacional 'José Revueltas' de Ensayo Literario (*'José Revueltas' National Literary Essay Prize*)

This prize is awarded annually by the Mexican Fine Arts Institute and the government of the state of Durango, and is administered by the Institute's promotional department and the Casa de la Cultura de Gómez Palacio, Durango. It consists of 40,000 pesos and a diploma, and is awarded for the best essay on the literary work of any distinguished contemporary Mexican writer. It is open to any writers resident in Mexico.

Awarding body: Instituto Nacional de Bellas Artes, Dolores 2, 3°, México 1, D.F., Mexico.

Premio Nazionale del Presidente della Repubblica (*National President of the Republic's Prize*)

This important Italian prize of 5 million lire is awarded annually by the Academy of Sciences. It is given alternately for research or publications in the field of one of the two sections of the Academy: moral, historical and philological sciences, or physical, mathematical and natural sciences. It was established in 1949 and is presented in June by the President of the Republic. Nominations are made by Academy members who are themselves ineligible for the award.

Awarding body: Accademia Nazionale dei Lincei, Palazzo Corsini, Via della Lungara 10, Rome, Italy.

Recipients include: Ennio de Giorgi (1973); Giovanni Paccagnini (1974); Raffaele Raoul Gatto (1975).

Premio Nieto López

This prize was established under the terms of the will of Lorenzo Nieto López and was awarded for the first time in 1973. It consists of 150,000 pesetas and is awarded to an individual or organization for distinguished work benefiting the Spanish language. It is given in turn to a Spanish individual or organization, a Latin American individual or organization, and to an individual or organization outside Spain and Latin America.

Awarding body: Real Academia Española, Calle de Felipe IV 4, Madrid, Spain.

Premio 'Dr. Fernando Ocaranza' (*'Dr. Fernando Ocaranza' Prize*)

An annual prize of 20,000 pesos, a diploma and a medal is given by the Mexican National Academy of Medicine and Laboratorios Lepetit de México

It is presented to the researcher of Mexican nationality and resident in the country who has completed the best piece of research on experimental surgery to have been published within the previous three years.

Awarding body: Academia Nacional de Medicina, Bloque B, Unidad de Congresos, Centro Médico Nacional, Avda. Cuauhtémoc 330, México 7, D.F., Mexico.

Premio Ortega y Gasset

This is an annual prize established by the Madrid City Council in the series 'Premios Villa de Madrid', in honour of the celebrated essayist José Ortega y Gasset (1883–1955). The prize of 200,000 pesetas is awarded to the author of the best original and unpublished essay submitted. Special attention will be given to an essay on Madrid from the sociological, economic, cultural or artistic points of view.

Awarding body: Ayuntamiento de Madrid, Plaza de la Villa 5, Madrid, Spain.

Premio Joel Valencia Paparcén

This award was established in 1965 to acknowledge the contribution made by Dr. Joel Valencia Paparcén to the development of gastroenterology as a medical specialty in Venezuela. It is given for the best paper delivered to the annual meeting of the Venezuelan Society of Gastroenterology, and consists of a gold medal and a certificate.

Awarding body: Sociedad Venezolana de Gastroenterología, Torre del Colegio, Of. F-1, piso 15, Av. J. M. Vargas, Urb. Santa Fé, Caracas, Venezuela.

Recipients include: Dr. Emilio Candia C., Dr. Guillermo Seijas C., Dr. Alberto García Urosa, Dr. Francisco J. Martínez M., Dr. Enrique Dejman, Dr. María de los Angeles Gómez (1972); Dr. Alí Rivas Gómez, Manuel S. Mijares (1975).

Premio Rubén Peréz Ortiz

This is an international prize awarded by the Colombian Association of Librarians (ASCOLBI) to promote librarianship and honour those who have distinguished themselves through their services to the Association, or who have accomplished work worthy of merit. The prize is awarded annually and consists of a parchment certificate and two honourable mentions.

Awarding body: Asociación Colombiana de Bibliotecarios, Calle 10, No. 3-16, Apdo. Aéreo 30883, Bogotá, Colombia.

Premio Planeta

This prize was established by the publishing firm, Planeta, in 1952. It is one of the most valuable literary awards; the prize money is currently 4 million pesetas. It is awarded annually for the best unpublished novel, and is open to writers from all Spanish-speaking countries.

Awarding body: Editorial Planeta, Córcega 273-77, Barcelona 8, Spain.

Recipients include: Jesús Torbado (*En el dia de hoy,* 1977).

Premio di Poesia 'Lerici-Pea' (*Lerici-Pea Award for Poetry*)

This award is made annually by the Italian publishing house Carpena for an unpublished poem in Italian. The prize has been awarded since 1954, and consists of 1 million lire. The prize is indivisible, but smaller awards may also be made at the jury's discretion. Carpena undertakes to publish the prize-winning entries.

Awarding body: Casa editrice Carpena, Sarzana, Italy.

Premio Francisco de Quevedo

This is an annual prize established by the Madrid City Council in the series 'Premios Villa de Madrid', in memory of the celebrated poet and satirist Francisco Gómez de Quevedo y Villegas (1580–1645). The prize of 150,000 pesetas is awarded to the best submitted poem of 600 to 1,000 lines. The poem must be original, unpublished and written in Spanish by any Spanish or Latin American poet. It may be on any subject but special attention is given to those poems which make some reference to Madrid.

Awarding body: Ayuntamiento de Madrid, Plaza de la Villa 5, Madrid, Spain.

Premio Ravani-Pellati

This award, which is made every five years by the Turin Academy of Sciences and takes the form of a gold medal and diploma, is made for publications, inventions or discoveries in the physical and chemical sciences which have appeared during the past five years. Scientists of any nationality are eligible. Nominations must be made by Italian members of the Academy (who are themselves ineligible). The award was established in 1938 in accordance with the will of Luigi Ravani and his wife Maria Pellati; it was first awarded in 1944 and then suspended until 1972.

Awarding body: Accademia delle Scienze di Torino, Italy.

Recipients include: Gian Carlo Wick (theoretical and experimental physics, 1944); Giovanni Battista Bonino (biological chemistry, 1972).

Premio Diódoro Sánchez

The Colombian Society of Engineers awards an annual prize for the best piece of work (either practical or in published form) undertaken during the preceding year, and dealing with some aspect of engineering in Colombia – technical, economic, or historical. The award usually consists of a medal, a diploma and a sum of money.

Awarding body: Sociedad Colombiana de Ingenieros, Carrera 4a No. 10-41, Apdo. Aéreo 340, Bogotá, Colombia.

Recipients include: Ing. Gabriel García Moreno ('La teoría de la elasticidad y sus aplicaciones en la Ingeniería', 1976).

Premio Sociedad Venezolana de Ingeniería Vial (*Venezuelan Society of Road Engineering Prize*)

This is an annual prize established in 1975 to stimulate the study and investigation of problems related to road engineering. It consists of a plaque and is awarded to a civil engineer who specializes in road engineering, for work on road engineering problems and transport, with special reference to Venezuela.

Awarding body: Sociedad Venezolana de Ingeniería Vial, Edificio del Colegio de Ingenieros de Venezuela, Bosque Los Caobos, Apdo. 13024, Caracas 101, Venezuela.

Recipients include: Angel Graterol Tellería and Antonio J. Vincentelli (1976).

Premio 'Elías Sourasky' en Artes, Ciencias y Letras (*'Elías Sourasky' Prize in the Arts, Sciences and Literature*)

A prize of 75,000 pesos is awarded each year by the Fondo de Fomento Educativo (Educational Development Fund) for outstanding achievements in the arts, sciences and literature.

Awarding body: Sr. Ricardo J. Zevada, Secretario del Fondo de Fomento Educativo, Banco General de Cédulas Hipotecarias, Reforma No. 364, piso 18, México, D.F., Mexico.

Premio de Tecnología Química (*Chemical Technology Prize*)

The prize is awarded to promote interest in the teaching of and research into chemical technology with the aim of improving technology, equipment design, etc. The competition is open to Mexican nationals working individually or collectively. The paper submitted must be written in Spanish and have been written or published within the year of the competition. The subject chosen may be from any field of chemistry but in particular inorganic and organic chemistry, physico-chemistry, electrochemistry and chemical engineering. The first prize is 50,000 pesos, the second 10,000 pesos and the third 5,000 pesos.

Awarding body: Celanese Mexicana, S.A., Dirección de Relaciones Públicas, Avda. Revolución 1425, México, D.F., Mexico.

Premio de Tecnología Textil (*Textile Technology Prize*)

The prize is awarded to promote interest in the teaching of and research into textile technology with the aim of improving techniques, equipment design, etc. The competition is open to Mexican nationals working individually or collectively. The paper submitted must be written in Spanish and have been written or published within the year of the competition. The subject may be chosen from any aspect of textile technology and in particular from the following fields: fibrology, textile machinery, equipment and processes. The first prize is 50,000 pesos, the second 10,000 pesos and the third 5,000 pesos.

Awarding body: Celanese Mexicana, S.A., Dirección de Relaciones Públicas, Avda. Revolución 1425, México, D.F., Mexico.

Premio Tonatiuh International

This prize was established by Dr. Octavio I. Romano-V., President of Tonatiuh International Inc., publishers of Chicano literature. It was firs awarded in 1976. Cash prizes of $1,000 each ar given for the best literary work in three categories by a Chicano author resident in the U.S.A.; by ; Mexican author resident in Mexico; and by ; Spanish author resident in Spain. The winnin works are published by Tonatiuh International.

Awarding body: Tonatiuh International Inc. 2150 Shattuck Ave., Berkeley, Calif. 94704, U.S.A

Premio Guillermo Valencio

This prize was founded by the Colombian Ministr of Foreign Affairs in 1973 for outstanding service to Hispanic culture. Recipients can be individual or groups of any nationality and can be nominated at any time. The award is made in three classes Gold Medal with Emerald, Gold Medal, anc Silver Medal.

Awarding body: Ministerio de Relaciones Ex teriores, Bogotá, Colombia.

Premio Vallauri

This prize was established with a bequest of th brothers Riccardo and Giancarlo Vallauri to th Italian Electrotechnical and Electronics Associa tion (AEI). It is a monetary prize of 500,000 lire accompanied by a gold medal and a certificate and is given in even-numbered years for the bes work published in the AEI's journals in th preceding two years, preferably in the field o electromechanical constructions. Candidates mus be members of the AEI and under 40 years of age

Awarding body: Associazione Elettrotecnica e Elettronica Italiana, Viale Monza 259, 2012(Milan, Italy.

Recipients include: Giorgio Molinari (1971–73) Mario Pent (1974–75).

Premio Vallauri

This award, consisting of a gold medal and dip loma, is made every four years by the Turi Academy of Sciences for publications in th alternate fields of physical science and Lati literature. (The last award, made in 1974, was fo physics.) Scholars from all countries are eligible provided the works have been published durin the previous eight years. Nominations must b made by members of the Academy (who ar themselves ineligible). The award was establishe in 1894 by Tommaso Vallauri (1805–97), a dis tinguished Latin scholar.

Awarding body: Accademia delle Scienze d Torino, Italy.

Recipients include: Remigio Sabbadini (Latin 1916); Eduard Norden (Latin, 1926); Wallace M Lindsay (Latin, 1926); Giorgio Pasquali (Latin 1940); Eduard Fraenkel (Latin, 1969).

Premio Maestro Villa

This is an annual prize of 200,000 pesetas in th series 'Premios Villa de Madrid', established b the Madrid City Council in memory of th founding director of the Municipal Orchestra o Madrid, Maestro Ricardo Villa. It is awarded fo the best unperformed symphonic score of 15 t

5 minutes' duration composed especially for the Municipal Orchestra. The winning composition is subsequently performed by the Orchestra at a concert in Madrid.

Awarding body: Ayuntamiento de Madrid, Plaza de la Villa 5, Madrid, Spain.

Premio 3M Italia

The prize was instituted by the Italian firm 3M Italia S.p.A. for the best memoirs containing original research presented at the previous Annual Reunion of the Italian Electrotechnical and Electronics Association (AEI). It is a monetary prize of 1 million lire which may be divided.

Awarding body: Associazione Elettrotecnica ed Elettronica Italiana, Viale Monza 259, 20126 Milan, Italy.

Recipients include: A. Buffa, S. Costa, G. Favarin, Lorenzo Fellin, Gaetano Malesani, A. Maschio, P. L. Mondino, G. F. Nalesso, S. Ortolani, Giorgio Rostagni, A. Stella (1975).

Premios del Conde de Cartagena

These prizes were established in 1929 under the terms of the will of Aníbal Morillo y Pérez, Count of Cartagena and Marquis of La Puerta. The Spanish Academy holds an annual literary competition at which two prizes are awarded, each of 50,000 pesetas. The subjects are chosen by the Academy, and the entries should be unpublished and written in Spanish by Spanish or Latin-American citizens.

Awarding body: Real Academia Española, Calle de Felipe IV 4, Madrid, Spain.

Recipients include: Luis de Miguel González Miranda ('Glosario de Geomagnetismo y Aeronomia'), José Muñoz Garrigós ('Contribución al estudio del léxico de La Celestina'), 1974; Adhemar B. Ferreira Lima and Avenir Rosell Figueras ('Vocabulario de términos estenológicos', 1976).

Premios para la Investigación en Contaduría (*Prizes for Research in Accountancy*)

These biennial prizes were established by the Mexican Institute of Public Accountants. Papers submitted must be unpublished, original and written in Spanish on any aspect of public accountancy. Entries must be accompanied by a letter from the author explaining why he wishes to enter the competition. The first prize is 60,000 pesos, the second 25,000 pesos and the third 15,000 pesos. The prize-winners are also awarded special diplomas.

Awarding body: Instituto Mexicano de Contadores Públicos, A.C., Organismo Nacional, Danubio No. 80 – 5° piso, México 5, D.F., Mexico.

Premios 'Lazarillo'

Established by the Instituto Nacional del Libro Español (Spanish National Book Institute), two prizes of 100,000 pesetas each are awarded annually. One is for the best original book for children under 15, and the other for the best collection of illustrations for children. Although the prizes are independent of each other, they may be awarded to one work if it fulfils both categories. The book must not be longer than 5,000 words, unpublished and written in Spanish. The illustrations must either be unpublished or published in the previous two years.

Awarding body: Instituto Nacional del Libro Español, Santiago Rusiñol 8, Madrid, Spain.

Recipients include: Consuelo Armijo Navarro-Reverter (author, *Los batautos*, 1974); Miguel Calatayud (illustrator, *Cuentos del ano 2100*, 1974); Hilda Perera (author, *Cuentas para Grandes y Chicos*, 1975); Margarita Vazquez de Parga (illustrator, *La Ventana de María*, 1975).

Premios Rivadeneira

These awards were established in 1940 by Manuela Rivadeneira Sánchez in memory of her father, Manuel Rivadeneira. Two prizes, one of 30,000 pesetas and one of 20,000 pesetas, are awarded annually for the best works on the theme 'A study on some aspect of Spanish linguistics or literature'.

Awarding body: Real Academia Española, Calle de Felipe IV 4, Madrid, Spain.

Premios de las Salas Nacionales de Exposición (*National Art Galleries Prizes*)

Annual prizes are awarded for painting, sculpture, engraving, drawing and ceramics by the Argentine National Galleries, sponsored by the Ministry of Culture and Education. There are four prizes for each discipline: Grand Prize, first, second and third prizes. The Grand Prize consists of a silver medal and 150,000 pesos; the first prize is a silver medal and 100,000 pesos; the second prize is a silver medal and 50,000 pesos; and the third prize is a silver medal and 40,000 pesos. The works submitted must be signed originals which have never been previously exhibited in public. The competition is open to all artists who are not pupils of any public or private institution and who have resided in Argentina for at least two years. Other donated prizes are awarded under the auspices of the National Art Galleries.

Awarding body: Salas Nacionales de Exposición, Avda. del Libertador 1248, Buenos Aires, Argentina.

Recipients include: Ary Brizzi (painting), Enrique Romano (sculpture), Alfredo de Vincenzo (engraving), Osvaldo Ernesto Attila (drawing), Leo Tavella (ceramics), 1976.

Prémio Alvarenga do Piauí

The Lisbon Academy of Sciences founded this prize in 1898 in memory of the Portuguese doctor Pedro Francisco da Costa Alvarenga who was born in Piauí (Brazil), and who made notable contributions to the study of heart disease. The prize of 2,500 escudos is given annually for the best original unpublished work on some aspect of medical science, including the history of medicine in Portugal. Applicants should be of Portuguese nationality.

Awarding body: Academia das Ciências de Lisboa, Rua da Academia das Ciências 19, Lisbon 2, Portugal.
Recipients include: José Luis Pulido Valente (1962); J. Cortez Pimentel (1969).

Prémio Rocha Cabral

The Portuguese Academy of Fine Arts established this prize in 1926 in memory of Rocha Cabral. It is given to a painter or sculptor of any nationality whose work is considered to be the best in the annual National Society of Fine Arts exhibition or in an official exhibition. The prize is of nominal value.
Awarding body: Academia Nacional de Belas Artes, Largo da Biblioteca, Lisbon, Portugal.

Prémio Augusto Botelho da Costa Veiga

The Portuguese Academy of History established this prize in 1967 for the best original work on the history of Portugal. It is a triennial prize, worth 36,240 escudos, and is open to Portuguese members of the Academy only.
Awarding body: Academia Portuguesa da História, Palácio da Rosa, Largo da Rosa 5, Lisbon, Portugal.
Recipients include: Prof. Torcato Brochado de Sousa Soares and António Machado de Faria de Pina Cabral (1970–72); Prof. Dr. Humberto Baquero Moreno (1973–75).

Prémio José de Figueiredo

The Portuguese Academy of Fine Arts established this prize in 1940 as a result of the benefaction of Dr. José de Figueiredo (1872–1937), the noted art critic and sometime Director of the National Museum of Ancient Art. It is an annual prize of 3,975 escudos, and is given for the best literary work on the subject of fine art, showing evidence of historical research as well as analytical and critical qualities. Foreign writers are eligible, provided that the subject is art in Portugal.
Awarding body: Academia Nacional de Belas Artes, Largo da Biblioteca, Lisbon, Portugal.
Recipients include: Paulino Montez and Eugénio Corrêa (*Valores de Portugal (Concelho de Viseu – Estradas Romanas,* 1973); Luis Cristino da Silva (*A Sede da Academia Nacional de Belas-Artes,* 1973); José Augusto França (*A Arte em Portugal no Século XX (1911–1961),* 1974).

Prémio Luciano Freire

The Portuguese Academy of Fine Arts established this prize in 1934 in memory of Professor Luciano Martins Freire (1864–1934), the famous painter. The prize is given to an artist of any nationality whose work has appeared in an exhibition in Portugal, and which is judged to be the most exceptional in concept and technique. The award is honorary, with a nominal cash prize of 400 escudos.
Awarding body: Academia Nacional de Belas Artes, Largo da Biblioteca, Lisbon, Portugal.

Prémio Calouste Gulbenkian

The Gulbenkian Foundation established this prize in 1976 to be awarded to the competitor who wins first prize in the Rio de Janeiro International Voice Competition, held every two years. The prize is worth 41,250 escudos.
Awarding body: Fundação Calouste Gulbenkian, Parque Calouste Gulbenkian, Avda. de Berna, Lisbon, Portugal.

Prémio Gulbenkian de Ciência e Tecnologia (*Gulbenkian Prize for Science and Technology*)

The Gulbenkian Foundation established this prize in 1976 to be awarded annually alternately for outstanding work in science and technology. The Foundation was set up under the terms of Calouste Gulbenkian's will, and is a non-profit organization which awards various grants and prizes in all fields of sciences and humanities. This prize worth 100,000 escudos, and is open to Portuguese citizens only.
Awarding body: Fundação Calouste Gulbenkian, Parque Calouste Gulbenkian, Avda. de Berna, Lisbon, Portugal.
Recipients include: Dr. José Avelino Pais de Lima Faria and Eng.ᵃ. Maria Ondina Gonçalves Dionísio Vidigal de Figueiredo (1976).

Prémio Calouste Gulbenkian de História

The Gulbenkian Foundation established this prize in 1975 for the best original work on the history of the Portuguese presence in the world. The prize is worth 20,000 escudos, and is awarded annually. Only members of the Portuguese Academy of History, whether Portuguese or foreign, are eligible.
Awarding body: Academia Portuguesa da História, Palácio da Rosa, Largo da Rosa 5, Lisbon, Portugal.
Recipients include: António Machado de Faria de Pina Cabral (1975); Dr. Joaquim Alberto Iria Júnior and Pl. Manuel Peixeira (1976).

Prémio António Larragoiti

A biennial prize was established in 1945 by the Portuguese Academy of Sciences and the Brazilian Academy of Letters. It is awarded by each Academy alternately for the best original work on a Luso-Brazilian theme in the fields of literature, philology, history, law, politics or social science. Writers must be Portuguese or Brazilian, and the winner receives 12,000 escudos.
Awarding bodies: Academia das Ciências de Lisboa, Rua da Academia das Ciências 19, Lisbon 2, Portugal; Academia Brasileira de Letras, Av. Presidente Wilson 203, Rio de Janeiro, Brazil.
Recipients include: Luis Silveira (*Ensaio de Iconografia das Cidades Portuguesas do Ultramar,* 1956); Alfredo Diogo Júnior (*Angola perante a Escravatura,* 1968).

Prémio Literário Cidade de Lisboa (*Lisbon Literary Prize*)

The Lisbon municipal government established this prize in 1977 to be awarded annually for the best work of fiction by a Portuguese writer published between 1 August of the preceding year and 30 September of the year of the award. It is worth 50,000 escudos.

Awarding body: Câmara Municipal de Lisboa, Portugal.

Prémio Abílio Lopes do Rego

The Lisbon Academy of Sciences established this prize in 1950 for the best original work in Portuguese on some aspect of the history of Portuguese colonization. The work should either be unpublished, or published during the year of the award. Two prizes are given: a first prize of 50,000 escudos, and a second prize of 30,000 escudos.

Awarding body: Academia das Ciências de Lisboa, Rua da Academia das Ciências 19, Lisbon 2, Portugal.

Recipients include: António Jorge Dias and Margot S. Dias (*Os Macondes de Moçambique – Vida Social e Ritual*, Vol. 3, 1970); Manuel de Seabra and Vimala Devi (*A Literatura Indo-Portuguesa*, 1972); Alfredo Pereira de Lima (*História dos Caminhos de Ferro de Moçambique*, 1973).

Prémio Artur Malheiros

The Lisbon Academy of Sciences founded this prize in 1937. It is given annually for unpublished and original work in some branch of science (the discipline is determined in rotation corresponding to the sections of the Academy). The prize is worth 5,000 escudos, and the winner must be a Portuguese citizen.

Awarding body: Academia das Ciências de Lisboa, Rua da Academia das Ciências 19, Lisbon 2, Portugal.

Recipients include: Luis Nandim de Carvalho (juridical, political and social sciences, 1970); Sebastião Formosinho Simões (physical and chemical sciences, 1972); João P. de Carvalho Dias and Hugo J. Beirão da Veiga (mathematics, 1972); António Augusto Pereira (natural sciences, 1973).

Prémio Ricardo Malheiros

The Lisbon Academy of Sciences established this prize in 1933 in memory of Ricardo Malheiros. It is an annual award of 5,000 escudos for the best original work in Portuguese in the form of a novel, novella or short story, published during the year of the award. It is restricted to Portuguese writers.

Awarding body: Academia das Ciências de Lisboa, Rua da Academia das Ciências 19, Lisbon 2, Portugal.

Recipients include: Luis Cajão (*Um Castelo na Escócia*, 1971); Luisa Martinez (*Movimento Pendular*, 1972); Fausto Lopo de Carvalho (*Ouviam-se Vozes ao Longe*, 1974); Romeu Correia (*Um Passo em Frente*, 1976).

Prémio Aboim Sande Lemos

The Lisbon Academy of Sciences founded this biennial prize for the best work, either unpublished or published during the preceding two years, on some aspect of nutrition, especially concerning the third world, and dealing with the professional ethics of hygiene. The prize is worth 20,000 escudos, and the recipient must be Portuguese.

Awarding body: Academia das Ciências de Lisboa, Rua da Academia das Ciências 19, Lisbon 2, Portugal.

Prémio de Tradução Calouste Gulbenkian
(*Calouste Gulbenkian Translation Prize*)

The Gulbenkian Foundation established two prizes in 1975, each worth 20,000 escudos. One is for a translation in prose of foreign literature into Portuguese, and the other is for a translation of poetry. Both should be either unpublished, or published during the year of the award. Portuguese writers only are eligible.

Awarding body: Academia das Ciências de Lisboa, Rua da Academia das Ciências 19, Lisbon 2, Portugal.

Prêmio Frederico de Menezes Veiga

This annual prize of 50,000 cruzeiros was founded in 1975 by the Brazilian company EMBRAPA (Empresa Brasileira de Pesquisa Agropecuária), in memory of Frederico de Menezes Veiga (1911–74), an expert in the study of sugar cane, of which he discovered a new variety. The prize is intended to promote creativity in research and is bestowed on a scientist who has made a distinguished contribution to agronomic research in Brazil. The prize is accompanied by a medal and diploma.

Awarding body: Empresa Brasileira de Pesquisa Agropecuária, S.C.S. Edificio Venancio 2000, 9° andar, 70.000 Brasilia, D.F., Brazil.

Recipients include: Armando Conagin (agricultural statistics), João Murça Pires (tropical agriculture), Johanna Döbereiner (fertilizers), José Mendes Barcelos (research administrator), Leonidas Machado Magalhães (teaching agricultural sciences), 1976.

Premiu Uniunii Scriitorilor din Republica Socialistă România (*Romanian Writers Union Prize*)

This award consists of cash prizes and diplomas awarded to the best literary works published during the preceding year by Romanian citizens. The prizes were established by the Writers Union in 1964.

Awarding body: Writers Union of the Socialist Republic of Romania, Soseaua Kiseleff 10, Bucharest, Romania.

Recipients include: Meliusz Iozsef (poetry, 1973); Marin Sorescu (play, 1974); Eugen Barbu (novel, 1975); Romul Munteanu (criticism, 1975); St. Augustin Doinaș (poetry, 1968, 1975).

President's Award

This award was established in 1975 by the Government of Sri Lanka and is made on the recommendation of the Ministry of Cultural Affairs and the Department of Cultural Affairs. It may be made to any citizen of Sri Lanka who renders outstanding service to the country in the fields of literature and the arts. The award is annual and consists of 5,000 rupees and a certificate.

Awarding body: Government of Sri Lanka.

Recipients include: Martin Wickremasinghe (services to Sinhala literature); Tittawela Gunaya (services to Kandyan dancing).

President's Medal

Instituted in 1962, this award is made from time to time by the President of the Society of Chemical Industry, as a mark of distinction to persons whom he selects as worthy of honour.

Awarding body: Society of Chemical Industry, 14 Belgrave Square, London SW1X 8PS, England.

Recipients include: E. J. Solvay (1962); J. Rogers (1963); Sir Sydney Barratt and Dr. J. S. Gourlay (1966); Sir Ronald Holroyd (1969).

President's Medals

These awards were established in 1941 in recognition of excellence in contemporary Canadian literature. Three prizes of a medal and $1,000 each are given annually for work in the following categories (revised in 1976): literary; scholarly article; general magazine. The work must have appeared in a Canadian publication during the preceding calendar year. Only Canadian citizens or persons residing in Canada are eligible.

Awarding body: The University of Western Ontario, London, Ont., Canada.

Recipients include: Don Gutteridge (single poem, *Death at Quebec*, 1972); Jack Hodgins (short story, *After the Season*, 1973); Grazia Merler (scholarly article, *La réalité dans la prose d'Anne Hébert*, 1972); Peter C. Newman (general article, *Reflections on a Fall from Grace*, 1973).

Priestley Medal

Established in 1922 by the American Chemical Society, this gold medal is intended to commemorate the work of Joseph Priestley and to recognize distinguished services to chemistry. It is presented annually. The only restrictions are that members of the ACS Board of Directors are ineligible, and the medal may not be awarded more than once to the same individual. Travelling expenses incidental to the conferring of the medal are paid. The recipient may be invited to deliver an address at the ACS spring meeting.

Awarding body: American Chemical Society, 1155 Sixteenth St., N.W., Washington, D.C. 20036, U.S.A.

Recipients include: Harold C. Urey (1973); Paul J. Flory (1974); Henry Eyring (1975); George S. Hammond (1976); Henry Gilman (1977).

Prijs Doctor A. De Leeuw-Damry-Bourlart

This quinquennial prize is awarded for outstanding work in mathematics, physics and chemistry. It consists of a cash award of 750,000 Belgian francs. Candidates for the prize must be proposed by three scientists, at least two of whom must be Belgian. The prize is restricted to Dutch

speakers; a companion prize, the *Prix Docteur A. de Leeuw-Damry-Bourlart*, is awarded to a French-speaking scientist.

Awarding body: Fonds National de la Recherche Scientifique, 5 rue d'Egmont, B-1050 Brussels, Belgium.

Recipients include: Prof. Walter Fiers (for his significant contribution to molecular biology, 1975).

Prijs der Nederlandse Letteren (*Netherlands Literature Prize*)

This prize is awarded every three years jointly by the Dutch and Belgian Ministries of Culture for outstanding and original literary work in the Dutch language by a Dutch or Belgian writer. It may be given for one particular book or for an author's complete works. The prize money amounts to 12,000 guilders.

Awarding body: Ministerie van Cultuur, Recreatie en Maatschappelijk Werk, Steenvoordelaan 370, Rijswijk (ZH), The Netherlands.

Prime Movers Committee Award

The Prime Movers Committee of the Edison Electric Institute established this award in 1954. It is given in recognition of outstanding contributions to the literature of thermal electric station practice or equipment which are available through public presentation and publication. Those papers approved by the appropriate Papers Review Committee as meeting ASME standards and available in printed form may be considered for the award. Papers, while usually current, need not necessarily be so, and may be by more than one author. Authors are not restricted by nationality, age, profession, nor membership in any engineering society or other organization. The award is made annually if warranted, and consists of an engrossed certificate.

Awarding body: American Society of Mechanical Engineers, United Engineering Center, 345 East 47th St., New York, N.Y. 10017, U.S.A.

Recipients include: Hans-Gunter Haddenhorst, Wolfgang Mattick, Z. Stanley Stys, Otto Weber (1976).

Prince Philip Award

This gold medal was instituted to commemorate the presentation by the Plastics Institute of its first Honorary Fellowship to the Duke of Edinburgh in 1973. In 1975 the Plastics Institute amalgamated with the Institution of the Rubber Industry to form the Plastics and Rubber Institute. The theme for the award is 'Plastics in the service of man', and the medal is given to applicants, whether members or not, and wherever resident, whose achievements are considered to be beneficial to mankind in improving the quality of life, in easing pain and distress, in conserving or extending the availability of natural resources, material and food. The award is made not more than once in every two years and not less than once in every five years.

Awarding body: The Plastics and Rubber Institute, 11 Hobart Place, London SW1W 0HL, England.
Recipients include: Prof. John Charnley (work with plastics in the development of an artificial hip joint, 1976).

Prince Pierre of Monaco Prize for Musical Composition

Established in 1960 by H.S.H. Prince Pierre of Monaco (1895–1964), patron of arts and letters, the prize is now continued in his memory. Composers of any age and nationality may enter for the award, which is given annually for a symphonic work and for ballet music, alternately. Applicants may submit only one work, which should not have been published or performed in public. The jury decides from a reading and not from a performance of the work. The prize of 30,000 francs is presented in Monte Carlo in the spring. The winning work may be performed in Monaco during the following year, in which case the choice of conductor and performers remains with the administrative board of the National Orchestra of the Monte Carlo Opera and the Prince Pierre Foundation.
Awarding body: Fondation Prince Pierre de Monaco, Ministère d'Etat, Monaco-Ville, Monaco.
Recipients include: Luciuk Juliusz (chamber music, 1974); Giampaolo Coral (sacred music, 1975); Christopher Brown (symphony, 1976); Christian Berte (ballet music, 1977 – first commendation, no prize awarded); Daniele Zannettovich (symphony for baritone and orchestra, 1978).

Pringle Award

This literary award was established in 1962 by the English Academy of Southern Africa, and since 1972 has been awarded annually for work published in South African newspapers and periodicals in each of three categories: book and play reviews; literary articles; creative writing. Any writer is eligible. Winners receive R100 and a certificate. The award is named after a 19th-century Scot, Thomas Pringle, who spent some years in South Africa and was noted for his defence of the freedom of the press.
Awarding body: English Academy of Southern Africa, Ballater House, 35 Melle St., Braamfontein, Johannesburg, South Africa.
Recipients include: Nadine Gordimer (short story, *Inkalamu's Place*, 1969); Alan Paton (review of an Afrikaans book, 1972); Anthony Delius (poem, *Meditation on Main Street*, 1976).

Print Media Award

This award is made for outstanding reportage on reading or related fields by a professional journalist working in the print media. It is made annually, when merited, for work during a given calendar year. It takes the form of a citation.
Awarding body: International Reading Association, 800 Barksdale Rd., Newark, Dela. 19711, U.S.A.

Prix Antoine d'Abbadie

This is a biennial prize of 10,000 francs awarded for work in the field of astronomy. It was awarded for the first time in 1976.
Awarding body: Académie des Sciences, 23 Quai de Conti, Paris 6e, France.
Recipients include: Mme Suzanne Collin-Souffrin and Mme Françoise Praderie (jointly, 1976).

Prix de l'Académie de Dijon

This award, first presented in 1741, was re-established in 1971. It consists of 10,000 francs and a gold medal and is presented annually for the best dissertation submitted on a theme chosen by the Academy. Dissertations must be sent in anonymously before 1 October of the current year. The scope of the prize covers the development and study of the sciences, literature and the arts.
Awarding body: Académie des Sciences, Arts et Belles-Lettres de Dijon, Bibliothèque Municipale, 5 rue de l'Ecole de Droit, F-21000 Dijon, France.
Recipients include: Jean-Jacques Rousseau (1750); Lazare Carnot (1784); Philippe Saint Marc (1971).

Prix de l'Académie Mallarmé

The Mallarmé Academy Prize is awarded annually to a poet whose mother-tongue is French. It is given for the whole of the author's poetic work or for a recently published volume of poems. The prize is a cash award (currently 12,000 francs). No applications are required. The Mallarmé Academy, itself re-established in 1975, founded the prize in 1976 to perpetuate the memory of the great poet, Stéphane Mallarmé (1842–98).
Awarding body: Académie Mallarmé, Société des Gens de Lettres de France, Hôtel de Massa, 38 rue du Faubourg Saint Jacques, 75014 Paris, France.
Recipients include: Andrée Chedid (1976); Marc Guyon (1977); Jean Joubert (1978).

Prix d'Aéronautique de l'Association Aéronautique et Astronautique de France (*Aeronautics Prize of the French Aeronautics and Astronautics Association*)

This annual prize for outstanding work in the field of aeronautics is awarded to a person of French nationality. Nominations should be presented by two members of the above association. A diploma and a medal are awarded.
Awarding body: Association Aéronautique et Astronautique de France, 80 rue Lauriston, 75116 Paris, France.
Recipients include: Alexandre Boudigues (1974); Bernard Gambet (1975).

Prix de l'Afrique Méditerranéenne (*North Africa Prize*)

This annual literary prize of 2,000 francs was founded in 1971 and is given either for one particular book or for the total published work of a French-speaking author from North Africa. All literary genres are acceptable, and the books submitted should have been published in the preceding year. Authors themselves or publishers may submit entries.

Awarding body: Association des Écrivains de Langue Française (Mer at Outre-Mer), 38 rue du Faubourg-Saint-Jacques, 75014 Paris, France.

Recipients include: Andrée Chedid (Egypt, *Néfertiti et le rêve d'Akhnaton*, 1975); Claude Benady (Tunisia, *Marguerite à la source* and complete works, 1976); Albert Bensoussan (Algeria, *Frimaldjezar*, 1977).

Prix Albert 1er de Monaco (*Albert 1st of Monaco Prize*)

This is one of the prizes awarded by the French Academy of Sciences which are open to foreigners. It is a five-yearly prize (next award 1979) of 25,000 francs for work on a subject decided by the Academy. It is not divisible, but may be given to more than one person working jointly on the same project.

Awarding body: Académie des Sciences, 23 Quai de Conti, Paris 6e, France.

Prix Alvarenga de Piauhy (*Brésil*)

This annual prize of 25,000 Belgian francs is for an unpublished memoir or other work in French or Dutch on any subject within any branch of medicine. Members of the Belgian Academy of Medicine are excluded. The prize is named after the Portuguese doctor Pedro Francisco da Costa Alvarenga, who was born in Piauí in Brazil. He was famous for his work on heart disease.

Awarding body: Académie Royale de Médecine de Belgique, Palais des Académies, 1000 Brussels, Belgium.

Prix Ampère

An annual prize of 200,000 francs was founded in 1975 by the company Electricité de France to honour the bicentenary of the birth of the physicist André-Marie Ampère (1775–1836). The prize is awarded by the Academy of Sciences to one or more French scientists for outstanding research in the field of pure or applied mathematics or physics.

Awarding body: Académie des Sciences, 23 Quai de Conti, Paris 6e, France.

Recipients include: Jacques Dixmier (for his work on the algebraic theories of von Neumann and Gelfand, and the theory of representation of groups, 1976); Pierre-Gilles de Gennes (for his work in the field of magnetism of solids, superconductivity and physical chemistry of 'disordered' systems, 1977); Pierre Cartier (1978). ·

Prix Louis Ancel

Monsieur Louis-Etienne-Nicolas Ancelle (died 1920) bequeathed 10,000 francs to the French Society of Physics for a prize for the best work on radiation (electric, light, heat) and especially on the action of light or heat on the electrical conductivity of selenium group materials. The prize is awarded annually and consists of a medal and 1,800 francs.

Awarding body: Société Française de Physique, 33 rue Croulebarbe, 75013 Paris, France.

Recipients include: J. Joffrin (application of hypersonic techniques on different types of crystals and research into phonon echoes, 1973); P. Berge (photon diffusion, and velocity in liquids, 1974); Mme Ch. Caroli (work on superconductivity and study of N-type solids, 1975); G. Jannink (1976); Ph. Monod (atomic and molecular physics, 1977).

Prix Anonyme (*Anonymous Prize*)

This prize is awarded to the author of the best unpublished work in the French or Dutch language which elucidates the pathogenesis and therapy of nervous diseases, particularly epilepsy. The prize of 20,000 Belgian francs is awarded every three years. Members of the Belgian Academy of Medicine are ineligible.

Awarding body: Académie Royale de Médecine de Belgique, Palais des Académies, 1000 Brussels, Belgium.

Prix Guillaume Apollinaire

This prize was established in 1941 by the French poet, Henri de Lescoët, in memory of the distinguished poet, Guillaume Apollinaire (1880–1918). It is awarded annually to a promising French or French-speaking poet under 50 years of age, and is worth 50 francs.

Awarding body: Société des Amis d'Apollinaire, 86 blvd. de Cessole, 06100 Nice, France.

Recipients include: Luc Estang (1968); Gaston Bonheur (1971); Léopold Sédar Senghor (1974); Charles Le Quintrec (1975); Jean-Claude Renard (1978).

Prix Arc-en-Ciel (*Rainbow Prize*)

This annual prize is awarded to a poet who has not yet had a collection of poems published. The works submitted may be on any subject and should comprise a maximum of 100 lines (classical or free verse), either as one poem or several grouped under one title. The value of the prize is 250 francs.

Awarding body: Union Littéraire & Artistique de France, 35 rue Gayet, 42000 Saint-Etienne, France.

Prix Antonin Artaud

This prize was founded in 1952 by the 'Groupe d'Ecrivains de Rouergue' in memory of the three years (1943–46) spent in that province by the poet Artaud (1896–1948). The prize of 2,000 francs is given for a collection of poems published in the preceding two years; the book must not have won a prize before, and should be written in French. The prize is awarded annually in May, during the 'Journées de Poésie de Rodez', an international gathering organized by the Association des Ecrivains du Rouergue.

Awarding body: Association des Ecrivains du Rouergue, 7 rue de Saunhac, 12000 Rodez, France.

Recipients include: André Miguel (*Boule androgyne*, 1973); Simon Brest (*La Ville engloutie*, 1974);

Christian Hubin (*La Parole sans lieu*, 1975); Robert Delahaye (*Saisons*, 1976); Gérard Bayo (*Un printemps difficile*, 1977).

Prix d'Astronautique de l'Association Aéronautique et Astronautique de France (*Astronautics Prize of the French Aeronautics and Astronautics Association*)

This prize is awarded annually to a person of French nationality, in recognition of outstanding work in the field of astronautics. Nominations for the award should be presented by two members of the above association. The prize takes the form of a diploma and a medal.

Awarding body: Association Aéronautique et Astronautique de France, 80 rue Lauriston, 75116 Paris, France.

Recipients include: Claude Poher (1974); Pierre Madon (1975).

Prix Aujourd'hui

This prize is awarded annually to draw the public's attention to a contemporary historical or political work. The award consists of a cash prize of 5,000 francs. Entries must be written in French and have been published in France in the preceding year. The prize was founded in 1962 by a group of journalists, who also constitute the jury.

Awarding body: Association du Prix Aujourd'hui, 12 rue du Quatre-Septembre, 75002 Paris, France.

Recipients include: Michel Jobert (*Mémoires d'avenir*, 1974); Pierre Jakez-Hélias (*Le Cheval d'orgueil*, 1975); Marek Halter (*Le Fou et les Rois*, 1976); Franz-Olivier Giesbert (*François Mitterand ou la Tentation de l'Histoire*, 1977); Hélène Carrère d'Encausse (*L'Empire Eclaté*, 1978).

Prix Professeur Louis Baes

This is a biennial prize of 20,000 francs instituted in 1962 and awarded by the Belgian Royal Academy. It is for the most important discovery or the most significant work in the fields of elasticity, plasticity, resistance of materials, stability of constructions, and machine parts design. The prize is restricted to candidates from Common Market countries, and entries must be in French. If the work is published, it must have appeared in the preceding five years. The prize may not be divided but it may be awarded for the collective work of several people. The Academy may make the award for work which has not been submitted for the prize.

Awarding body: Académie Royale de Belgique, Palais des Académies, rue Ducale 1, 1000 Brussels, Belgium.

Recipients include: J. Kestens and R. Van Geen (1971); R. Maquoi (1973).

Prix Barotte

This prize, established in 1878, is the oldest of the awards given by the French Academy of Agriculture, and by tradition the most important. It is also the only prize which the Academy may award

to one of its own members. It was established with a bequest of 10,000 francs and is awarded for the discovery or invention which is considered the most outstanding and the most profitable to agriculture. The prize is awarded annually in the form of a medal and a diploma.

Awarding body: Académie d'Agriculture de France, 18 rue de Bellechasse, 75007 Paris, France.

Prix André Barre

This is a biennial monetary prize administered by the French Academy for the work which shows the most original thought and the clearest style. The author must be French, and not a member of the clergy of any religion.

Awarding body: Académie Française, 23 Quai de Conti, Paris 6e, France.

Recipients include: Fernand Cathala (1978).

Prix Louis Barthou

This is an annual monetary prize administered by the French Academy. It is awarded to a French writer whose work or life has contributed to the renown and the best interests of France. Submissions may not be made for this prize.

Awarding body: Académie Française, 23 Quai de Conti, Paris 6e, France.

Recipients include: Jean Fayard (1978).

Prix de Behague

Monsieur de Behague, a member and benefactor of the French Academy of Agriculture, donated 12,000 francs to the Academy in 1889 for the establishment of a prize to the author of the best work on the breeding and fattening of livestock, or to the agriculturist who has rendered considerable service by a discovery or by introducing a new breed or new processes in this field.

Awarding body: Académie d'Agriculture de France, 18 rue de Bellechasse, 75007 Paris, France.

Prix Belgique-Canada (*Canada-Belgium Prize*)

This award was established in 1970 through a cultural agreement between the governments of Canada and Belgium, who co-sponsor the prize. It is presented annually, alternately, to a French-Canadian or Belgian writer, on the basis of his/her total work. The prize amounts to C$2,500.

Awarding body: Canada Council, P.O.B. 1047, Ottawa, Ont. K1P 5V8, Canada.

Recipients include: Suzanne Lilar (Belgium, 1973); Réjean Ducharme (Canada, 1974); Pierre Mertens (Belgium, 1975); Marie-Claire Blais (Canada, 1976); Jacques Godbout (Canada, 1978).

Prix Jean-Béraud-Molson

This annual literary prize of $3,000 is given for an unpublished novel or a work of romantic literature by a French-Canadian. Manuscripts should be submitted by 1 June so that the winning novel may be published by the Cercle du Livre de France in time for the Frankfurt Book Fair in the autumn; it is then offered to foreign publishers at the Fair.

Awarding body: Cercle du Livre de France, 8955 blvd. Saint-Laurent, Montreal, Que. H2N 1M6, Canada.

Recipients include: Guy-Marc Fournier (*L'aube*, 1974); Nelson Dumais (*L'embarquement pour Anticosti*, 1975).

Prix Anton Bergmann

A prize of 30,000 francs is awarded at five-yearly intervals by the Belgian Royal Academy. It is for a history or monograph, written in Dutch, on a Flemish town or community in Belgium. Published work must have appeared in the preceding five years, but unpublished work is also eligible. Foreign entrants are not excluded, but their work must be in Dutch and published in Belgium or the Netherlands.

Awarding body: Académie Royale de Belgique, Palais des Académies, rue Ducale 1, 1000 Brussels, Belgium.

Recipients include: Robert Van Passen (1965); Guy Vande Putte (1975).

Prix Madame Claude Berthault

The income from the Madame Claude Berthault Foundation is used to provide various prizes awarded by the Academies of the French Institute. The *Académie des Beaux-Arts* awards one or more annual or bi-annual prizes to one or more painters, sculptors or architects who have executed a beautiful work of art or decoration which is wholly French in concept and shows no foreign influence. The *Académie des Sciences* awards an annual prize of 3,000 francs for a scientific achievement which contributes to the good name of France. The *Académie des Sciences Morales et Politiques* awards prizes for either the encouragement of agricultural workers' or sailors' families from the Channel coast or the Atlantic coast, or to reward artistic or scientific work which has contributed to the good name of the French nation. All these prizes may be awarded only to French nationals, born in France, of wholly French parentage.

Awarding body: Institut de France, 23 Quai de Conti, Paris 6e, France.

Recipients include: Mme Danièle Marty (science, 1977); Marcel Mailloux (science, 1978).

Prix Bertillon

The Bertillon Prize was founded in 1885 by the Bertillon brothers in memory of their father, Adolphe Bertillon (1821–83), the distinguished anthropologist and founder member of the Anthropological Society of Paris. The prize is awarded every three years to a person of any age, sex or nationality, for the best dissertation on an anthropological subject, particularly demography. The award was originally a monetary prize of 500 francs, but the winner of the competition now receives a medal.

Awarding body: Société d'Anthropologie de Paris, 1 rue René Panhard, 75013 Paris, France.

Prix Bianchetti

The Bianchetti Prize was established in 1937 by the Association des Auteurs de Films in memory of the French actress, Suzanne Bianchetti (1889–1936). The award is normally made annually to a promising young film actress. The recipient is presented with a medal, and one or two rare or old editions of books on theatre.

Awarding body: Association des Auteurs de Films, 5 rue Ballu, 75009 Paris, France.

Recipients include: Marie Dubois (1963); Geneviève Bujold (1966); Caroline Cellier (1967); Bulle Ogier (1972); Isabelle Adjani (1974).

Prix Lucien Boisseau

The prize was established in 1947 with a bequest of 25,000 francs to the French Academy of Agriculture from Monsieur Boisseau, a member of the Academy. It is given to a French sheep-breeder or to any other person who by his actions, writings or research has aided and encouraged the breeding, development and amelioration of the ovine species in France. The prize is awarded annually in the form of a medal, on the recommendation of the Stock-breeding section of the Academy.

Awarding body: Académie d'Agriculture de France, 18 rue de Bellechasse, 75007 Paris, France.

Prix Paul Bonduelle

This prize of 700,000 Belgian francs, awarded by the Belgian Royal Academy, is given every three years for a large-scale architectural composition. The award goes to the winner(s) of a competition run by the Fine Arts section of the Academy. Entrants must be of Belgian nationality, and Academy members are excluded. The prize money may be shared if the winning composition is the work of more than one person.

Awarding body: Académie Royale de Belgique, Palais des Académies, rue Ducale 1, 1000 Brussels, Belgium.

Recipients include: J. C. de Brauwer and D. de Surgères (1974).

Prix Bordin

Various monetary prizes of about 4,000 francs each are given under this title by all the Academies of the *Institut de France*. The *Académie Française* gives an annual prize to encourage superior literature. The *Académie des Inscriptions et Belles-Lettres* awards an annual prize in rotation for the best work in the field of each of its three sections: one year the Orient; the second year Classical Antiquity; the third year the Middle Ages and the Renaissance. The *Académie des Sciences* awards a biennial prize for work which promotes the public interest, the good of mankind, scientific progress and national honour. The prize is awarded alternately for work in the fields of the two branches of the Academy: either mathematics and physics or chemistry and natural sciences. The *Académie des Beaux-Arts* awards an annual prize in rotation for the best work produced in the preceding five years in each of its five sections: painting, sculpture, architecture, engraving and music. The *Académie des ciences Morales et Politiques* awards a biennial prize o writers of unpublished memoirs on subjects oncerning the public interest, the good of mankind, scientific progress and national honour. The *rizes* are awarded in rotation on the recommendation of each of the six divisions of the Academy: legislation; political economy; history; philosophy; moral sciences; general section.

Awarding body: Institut de France, 23 Quai de Conti, Paris 6e, France.

*rix Paul-Emile-Borduas

Created in 1977, this is one of five 'Prix du Quebec' awarded annually by the Quebec Ministry of Culture. It is awarded to an artist or a craftsman for the whole of his work in the field of visual arts (architecture, sculpture, photography, painting, etc.). The award consists of $15,000, a certificate and a medal. It is named after the famous Quebecois painter, Paul-Emile Borduas.

Awarding body: Ministère des Affaires Culturelles, Hôtel du Gouvernement, Quebec, Canada.

*rix Albert Brachet

This is a three-yearly prize of 40,000 francs awarded by the Belgian Royal Academy to the best work on embryology (especially 'causal' embryology) published in the preceding three years. The work may be in French, Dutch, German, English or Italian.

Awarding body: Académie Royale de Belgique, Palais des Académies, rue Ducale 1, 1000 Brussels, Belgium.

Recipients include: M. and Mme Julien Fautrez (1970); Alberto Monroy (1973).

*rix Broca

This annual award was inaugurated in 1881 by the widow of the distinguished anthropologist Paul Broca (1824–80), founder of the Anthropological Society of Paris. The prize is awarded for the best dissertation on a subject related to anthropology, particularly human anatomy, comparative anatomy or physiology. The Broca prize was originally worth 1,500 francs, but the Anthropological Society now awards a medal to the winner.

Awarding body: Société d'Anthropologie de Paris, 1 rue René Panhard, 75013 Paris, France.

*rix Broquette-Gonin

Various annual monetary prizes are administered by the French Academy under this title. They are awarded for historical works, and (*Grand Prix*) for philosophical, political or literary works which inspire the love of truth, beauty and virtue.

Awarding body: Académie Française, 23 Quai de Conti, Paris 6e, France.

Recipients include: François Gibault, Henriette Levillain, Isabelle Rouffiance-Darotchetche, Maurice Toesca, Gilbert Gadoffre, Geneviève Viollet-le-Duc, Raymonde-Anna Rey, Denise Basdevant, Stoyan Tzonev, Bernard Pierre 1978).

Prix Georges Bruel

This cash prize of 200 francs is awarded to the author of a work on the geography, history, meteorology, ethnography, or economics of central Africa. Originally awarded triennially, it is now annual.

Awarding body: Académie des Sciences d'Outre-Mer, 15 rue La Pérouse, 75116 Paris, France.

Recipients include: Charles Le Coeur (*Mission au Tibesti*, 1971); Martial Sinda (*Le Messianisme congolais*, 1974).

Prix Henri Buttgenbach

A prize of 20,000 francs awarded every three years by the Belgian Royal Academy for work in the fields of mineralogy, petrography and palaeontology, based on material gathered in Belgium. Preference is given to Belgian nationals, but the prize may be awarded to a Dutch, French or English scientist.

Awarding body: Académie Royale de Belgique, Palais des Académies, rue Ducale 1, 1000 Brussels, Belgium.

Recipients include: J. Moreau (1966); Jan De Coninck (1969).

Prix Carrière

The Dr. Carrière Foundation was established according to the will of Dr. Carrière who left his fortune to the Academies of the French Institute so that the revenue might be used 'to the profit of Science, Letters and the Arts'. The value and frequency of the prizes vary; they are awarded annually in rotation for work in all disciplines of the five Academies.

Awarding body: Institut de France, 23 Quai de Conti, Paris 6e, France.

Recipients include: Haïm Brezis (mathematics, 1976); Christian Willaime (mineralogy, 1976); Roger Temam (mathematics, 1977).

Prix Pierre Carsoel

This is a prize of 50,000 francs awarded every five years by the Belgian Royal Academy to Belgian architects. It is for the most successful work, from the artistic and technical point of view, produced in the preceding five years.

Awarding body: Académie Royale de Belgique, Palais des Académies, rue Ducale 1, 1000 Brussels, Belgium.

Recipients include: Jacques Dolphyn (1973).

Prix Louis Castex

An annual monetary prize of about 5,000 francs was established in 1969 by Béatrice Bretty and is awarded by the French Academy. It is given for a literary work on one of two subjects: either an account of travels or an expedition of considerable note (excluding aviation, and excluding any romantic theme); or an account of archaeological or ethnological discoveries.

Awarding body: Académie Française, 23 Quai de Conti, Paris 6e, France.

Recipients include: J.-M. Barrault, André Turcat (1978).

Prix Eugène Catalan

An award of 32,000 francs is made every five years by the Belgian Royal Academy to a French or Belgian scientist who has made an important advance in the field of pure mathematics. Published works entered for the prize must have appeared within the preceding five years, and must be in French. The prize may not be divided.

Awarding body: Académie Royale de Belgique, Palais des Académies, rue Ducale 1, 1000 Brussels, Belgium.

Recipients include: G. Crombez (1969); Mme J. Goffar-Lombet (1974).

Prix Hercule Catenacci

Under the terms of a Foundation administered by the French Institute, various monetary prizes are awarded annually in rotation by the relevant Academies of the Institute. They are to encourage the publication of luxury illustrated books on poetry, literature, history, archaeology or music. There is also an annual prize for the ornamentation of a building, a square or a public garden.

Awarding body: Institut de France, 23 Quai de Conti, Paris 6e, France.

Recipients include: Jean Ferron, Yves Devaux (1978).

Prix Cazes

The prize was founded in 1935 by Marcellin Cazes, proprietor of the 'Brasserie Lipp', frequented by writers and publishers. The annual prize of 5,000 francs is awarded in the spring for a work of originality and quality to an author whose book was published in the preceding year, and who has not before received a prize.

Awarding body: Secretariat of the Cazes Prize, c/o Henri Philippon, 151 Blvd. Saint-Germain, Paris 6e, France.

Recipients include: José-Luis de Villalonga (*Fiesta*, 1971); Suzanne Prou (*Méchamment les oiseaux*, 1972); François de Closets (*Le bonheur en plus*, 1974); Jean Chalon (*Portrait d'une séductrice*, 1975).

Prix du Centenaire du Maréchal Lyautey

This annual prize of 250 francs goes to an author or a work on the subject of French accomplishments in overseas territories, or contributing to the development of mutual understanding between East and West. The prize is in honour of Marshal Lyautey (*see Prix Maréchal Lyautey*).

Awarding body: Académie des Sciences d'Outre-Mer, 15 rue La Pérouse, 75116 Paris, France.

Recipients include: R. P. Hubert deLeusse (*Afrique-Occident: heurs et malheurs d'une rencontre*, 1973); Raymon Delval (*Radama II*, 1974); Jean-Jacques Luthi (*Introduction à la littérature d'expression française en Egypte 1798–1945*, 1975).

Prix du Cercle du Livre de France (*French Book Circle Prize*)

This prize was established in 1949 and is given for an unpublished French-Canadian novel of outstanding merit. It is sponsored by the Compagnie pétrolière Impériale Ltée-Esso, which offers $5,00 annually. Entries are invited by 1 June, and th prize is awarded in the autumn before th Frankfurt Book Fair, so that the book can b published by the Cercle du Livre, and offered foreign publishers at the Fair.

Awarding body: Cercle du Livre de France, 895 blvd. Saint-Laurent, Montreal, Que. H2N 1M Canada.

Recipients include: Jean-Pierre Guay (*Mise liberté*, 1974); Pierre Stewart (*L'amour d'une autr* 1975); Simone Piuze (*Les cercles concentriques*, 1977

Prix Champlain

Established in 1957, the prize is for a literary wor on any subject by a French-Canadian autho resident outside Quebec, or a Franco-America. The work should have been published in th previous five years. The winner receives $500 an a certificate.

Awarding body: Conseil de la Vie française Amérique, 75 rue d'Auteuil, Quebec, Que. G1 4C3, Canada.

Recipients include: R. P. Germain Lemieu (1973); R. P. Camille-Antonio Doucet (1974 Arthur Godbout (1975).

Prix de Compositeur de l'Association d Musiciens Suisses (*Association of Swiss Musician Award for Composers*)

This award, consisting of a certificate and ca prize of 10,000 Swiss francs, is presented annua (in May or June) to a composer of Swiss natio ality. It was established in 1944 by a legacy memory of Adolphe Hug.

Awarding body: Association des Musicie Suisses, 11 bis av. du Grammont, 1000 Lausan 13, Switzerland.

Recipients include: Othmar Schoeck (1945 Arthur Honegger (1946); Frank Martin (1947 Willy Burkhard (1950).

Prix Cornélis-Lebègue

This prize of 25,000 Belgian francs is intended encourage work on a cure for cancer. It is award every three years for published or unpublishe work in French, Dutch, German, English Italian. Members of the Belgian Academy Medicine are ineligible.

Awarding body: Académie Royale de Médeci de Belgique, Palais des Académies, 1000 Brussel Belgium.

Prix Aimé Cotton

Founded by the Council of the French Society Physics in 1953 in memory of Monsieur Ai. Cotton, the prize is awarded annually to a your physicist working in the field of optics, and pa ticularly in atomic and molecular physics. Th value of the prize is currently 1,800 francs.

Awarding body: Société Française de Physiqu 33 rue Croulebarbe, 75013 Paris, France.

Recipients include: C. Borde (1973); Ph. Cahuz (1974); J. Romestain (1975); M. Gaillard (1976 G. Grynberg (1977).

Prix Franz Cumont

This is a three-yearly prize of 60,000 francs awarded by the Belgian Royal Academy. It is for work on the history of religion or the history of science, both confined to antiquity – i.e. dealing with the peoples of the Mediterranean basin before Mohammed. The prize may be awarded to a Belgian or a foreigner. No application is required, and the prize cannot be shared, unless it is awarded to several authors of one work.
Awarding body: Académie Royale de Belgique, Palais des Académies, rue Ducale 1, 1000 Brussels, Belgium.
Recipients include: Rev. Jean Festugière (1972).

Prix Gaspard-Adolphe Dailly

This prize was established in 1889 with a bequest of 10,000 francs from Monsieur Dailly, a member of the French Academy of Agriculture. There are no special conditions for its award. It is given annually in the form of a medal, on the recommendation of the Cultivation section of the Academy.
Awarding body: Académie d'Agriculture de France, 18 rue de Bellechasse, 75007 Paris, France.

Prix David

The Minister of Culture for Quebec, in the name of the Government, awards five annual prizes – 'Prix du Québec'. This award, established in 1967, is the highest literary distinction in the province, and is given to an author for the whole of his work. All genres of creative literature are eligible (short stories, novel, poetry, essay, drama, children's literature). The award consists of $15,000, a certificate and a medal.
Awarding body: Ministère des Affaires Culturelles, Hôtel du Gouvernement, Quebec, Canada.
Recipients include: Rina Lasnier (1974); Fernand Dumont (1975); Pierre Vadeboncoeur (1976).

Prix De Boelpaepe

This biennial prize of 50,000 Belgian francs is awarded by the Belgian Royal Academy to a Belgian who has made an important discovery which will advance the science of photography. This might be work on the properties of photographic emulsions, or the physical-chemical techniques used in photographic processes, or a new development which contributes to scientific progress.
Awarding body: Académie Royale de Belgique, Palais des Académies, rue Ducale 1, 1000 Brussels, Belgium.

Prix Eve Delacroix

Established in 1956 by Mme. Eve Delacroix, a prize of 10,000 francs is awarded annually for an essay or novel which combines literary merit with a sense of the dignity of man and the responsibility of a writer.
Awarding body: Prix Eve Delacroix, 56 ave. Foch, 016 Paris, France.

Recipients include: Jean Guitton (*Profils parallèles*, 1970); Edouard Bonnefous (*L'homme ou la Nature*, 1971); Jean Bernard (*Grandeurs et Tentations de la Médecine*, 1974); Georges Elgozy (*Le Bluff du Futur*, 1975); Jean Lods (*La Part de l'Eau*, 1978).

Prix Emile De Laveleye

A prize of 32,000 francs awarded at six-yearly intervals by the Belgian Royal Academy. It is awarded to the Belgian or foreign scientist whose work as a whole is considered to have brought about significant progress in political economy and social science, including finance, international and public law, and general or national politics.
Awarding body: Académie Royale de Belgique, Palais des Académies, rue Ducale 1, 1000 Brussels, Belgium.
Recipients include: Robert Triffin (1968); Jean Fourastié (1974).

Prix Docteur A. De Leeuw-Damry-Bourlart

This quinquennial prize is awarded for outstanding work in mathematics, physics and chemistry. It consists of a cash award of 750,000 Belgian francs. Candidates for the prize must be proposed by three scientists, at least two of whom must be Belgian. The prize is restricted to French speakers; a companion prize, the *Prijs Doctor A. de Leeuw-Damry-Bourlart*, is awarded to a Dutch-speaking scientist.
Awarding body: Fonds National de la Recherche Scientifique, 5 rue d'Egmont, B-1050 Brussels, Belgium.
Recipients include: Prof. Pierre Deligne (for his outstanding work on algebraic geometry and the resolution of the A. Weil hypothesis, 1975).

Prix Polydore de Paepe

This prize of 25,000 Belgian francs, awarded by the Belgian Royal Academy, is given every five years to a Belgian or French author for the best paper on spiritualist philosophy based on pure reason or on experience. Other things being equal, preference is given to a work which develops the principles set out by Paul Le Moyne (Polydore de Paepe) in his treatise 'De l'Idée de Dieu, sa transformation, ses conséquences morales et sociales' (1894).
Awarding body: Académie Royale de Belgique, Palais des Académies, rue Ducale 1, 1000 Brussels, Belgium.
Recipients include: André Léonard (1974).

Prix Agathon De Potter

Various scientific prizes are given under this title by the Agathon De Potter Foundation under the auspices of the Belgian Royal Academy. They are restricted to Belgian nationals. Seven prizes of 20,000 Belgian francs each are awarded every three years for original work in astronomy; physics; mathematics; chemistry; mineralogy; animal biology; plant biology.
Awarding body: Académie Royale de Belgique, Palais des Académies, rue Ducale 1, 1000 Brussels, Belgium.

Prix Deslandres

This is one of the prizes awarded by the French Academy of Sciences which are open to foreigners. It is a biennial prize of 25,000 francs awarded in even-dated years to the French or foreign scientist who has produced the best work on spectrum analysis and its application.

Awarding body: Académie des Sciences, 23 Quai de Conti, Paris 6e, France.

Recipients include: Michel Petit and Philippe Waldeufel (1976); François Roddier (1978).

Prix de Stassart

Two prizes are awarded under this title, both by the Belgian Royal Academy, and both at six-yearly intervals. The first, an award of 40,000 francs, is given to a distinguished Belgian, chosen in turn from among historians, writers, scientists and artists. The second, an award of 50,000 francs, is for an outstanding contribution to Belgian national history.

Awarding body: Académie Royale de Belgique, Palais des Académies, rue Ducale 1, 1000 Brussels, Belgium.

Recipients include: Carlo Bronne (1967); Herman Van der Wee (national history, 1967); Michel Nuttinck (1973); Claude Gaier (national history, 1973).

Prix des Deux Magots

This annual prize was established in 1933 by a 13-member jury of writers and painters, each artist having made a contribution of 100 francs. In 1934 the owner of the famous Deux Magots café took responsibility for the award, which today is worth 5,000 francs. The prize is awarded to a young writer for a novel, essay or poetry. It is the only literary prize of which the proceedings are held in public – in fact, at the café in the presence of the customers.

Awarding body: Les Deux Magots, 170 Blvd. Saint-Germain, 75006 Paris, France.

Recipients include: André Hardellet (*Les Chasseurs Deux*, 1973); Geneviève Dormann (*Le Bateau du Courrier*, 1974); François Coupry (*Mille Pattes sans Têtes*, 1975); Catherine Rihoit (*Le Bal des débutantes*, 1978).

Prix Ernest Discailles

An award of 25,000 francs is given at five-yearly intervals by the Belgian Royal Academy. It is awarded alternately for the best work on the history of French literature or on contemporary history. The award is open only to Belgians or foreigners who are studying or have studied at the University of Ghent.

Awarding body: Académie Royale de Belgique, Palais des Académies, rue Ducale 1, 1000 Brussels, Belgium.

Recipients include: Robert Devleeshouwer (contemporary history, 1966); Léon Somville (literature, 1971).

Prix Jules Duculot

This award of 50,000 francs is made every five years for a manuscript or published work, in French, on the history of philosophy. The prize restricted to Belgians or foreigners who ha received a degree at a Belgian university. Pu lished work must have appeared in the precedi five years. The award may be given to someo who did not enter for the prize.

Awarding body: Académie Royale de Belgiqu Palais des Académies, rue Ducale 1, 1000 Brusse Belgium.

Recipients include: Mlle. Simone Van Riet (197

Prix Dumas-Millier

Under the bequest of Monsieur Pierre-Alexand Dumas and Madame Dumas (née Millier) tw annual monetary prizes are administered by t French Institute. One, awarded by the *Acadé Française*, goes to a writer whose work as a wh honours the French language and contributes the dissemination of French thought. The oth awarded by the *Académie des Beaux-Arts*, is p sented alternately to a painter or a sculptor wh work as a whole is inspired by the traditions of t French school. Winners of both prizes must be French nationality and aged over 45.

Awarding body: Institut de France, 23 Quai Conti, Paris 6e, France.

Recipients include: Lucien Gachon (Acadén Française, 1977); Henri Mitterand (Acadén Française, 1978).

Prix Albert-Pierre-Jean Dustin

This prize of 40,000 Belgian francs is award every five years to the French- or Dutch-speaki author of experimental research in the field cellular pathology. It is restricted to Belgi nationals or those whose research was done Belgium, and who are under 40 years of a Members of the Belgian Academy of Medicine a excluded.

Awarding body: Académie Royale de Médeci de Belgique, Palais des Académies, 1000 Brusse Belgium.

Prix Duvernay

Established in 1944, this is an annual prize $1,000. It is given to a French-Canadian wh competence and renown in the intellectual a literary field serve the best interests of the Frenc Canadian community.

Awarding body: Société Saint-Jean-Baptiste Montréal, 82 rue Sherbrooke ouest, Montre Que. H2X 1X3, Canada.

Recipients include: Marcel Rioux (1974); Robe Lionel Séguin (1975); Jacques Brossard (1976).

Prix Léo Errera

This is a three-yearly prize of 40,000 fran awarded by the Belgian Royal Academy to Belgian or foreign author(s) of the best origir work in the field of general biology.

Awarding body: Académie Royale de Belgiq Palais des Académies, rue Ducale 1, 1000 Brusse Belgium.

Recipients include: Thomas Gaspar (197 Thérèse Vanden Driessche-Oedenkoven (1973).

rix Eugène Etienne

his award of 200 francs is made for work in any
ld of science or social science on the subject of
alth, especially in Africa. It may be given for
llective or individual work. Originally triennial,
is now awarded annually.
Awarding body: Académie des Sciences d'Outre-
er, 15 rue La Pérouse, 75116 Paris, France.
Recipients include: Yvonne Turin (*Affrontements
lturels dans l'Algérie coloniale*, 1971); R. P. Jean-
[arie Goarnisson (for his outstanding work in
pper Volta, 1974).

rix Etudes françaises

stablished in 1967 by the literary magazine
tudes françaises, the award is to encourage the
riting of literature in French by members of the
ancophone community outside France. Manu-
ripts of a creative work (novel, poetry, essay)
ay be submitted. Entrants must have spent half
eir lives, or at least seven consecutive years, in a
untry other than France; inhabitants of French
verseas territories are not excluded. The prize of
2,000 is awarded annually. The winning entry is
blished by the University of Montreal Press.
Awarding body: Revue *Etudes françaises*, P.O.B.
128, University of Montreal, Montreal 101,
anada.
Recipients include: Gaston Miron ('L'homme
paillé', poetry, 1970); Juan Garcia ('Corps de
loire', poetry, 1971); Michel Beaulieu ('Varia-
les', poetry, 1973); Fernand Oüellette ('Journal
énoué', essay, 1975); Jean-Claude Soucy ('Un
eu chasseur', novel, 1976).

rix Henri Fauconnier

his prize of 25,000 Belgian francs is awarded
very three years for research work in French or
utch on the subject of a cure for cancer or
berculosis or any other social scourge. The
search must be unpublished. Members of the
elgian Academy of Medicine are ineligible.
Awarding body: Académie Royale de Médecine
e Belgique, Palais des Académies, 1000 Brussels,
elgium.

rix de la Fédération métallurgique fran-
aise (*French Metallurgical Federation Prize*)

donation of 2,000 francs was made to the French
cademy of Agriculture by the Federation in 1924
establish a prize for a French engineer who
erfects an appliance for an agricultural machine.
he prize is given annually in the form of a medal,
n the recommendation of the Academy's Agri-
ultural Engineering section.
Awarding body: Académie d'Agriculture de
rance, 18 rue de Bellechasse, 75007 Paris, France.

rix Fémina

ounded in 1904 by the review *Fémina* in con-
unction with *Vie heureuse*, the prize is intended to
ncourage good literature and to draw women of
tters closer together. An all-female jury meets in
)ecember each year, and the prize of 5,000 francs
awarded for the best literary work of the year,
hether prose or poetry.

Awarding ,body: Comité Fémina, c/o Secrétaire-
Général, 79 blvd. Saint-Germain, 75006 Paris,
France.
Recipients include: Claude Faraggi (*Le Maître
d'Heure*, 1975); Marie-Louise Haumont (*Le Trajet*,
1976); Régis Debray (*La Neige Brûle*, 1977);
François Sonkin (*Un amour de père*, 1978).

Prix de la Fondation Xavier Bernard

This Foundation, a recognized charity, instituted
two prizes to be administered by the French
Academy of Agriculture. One is intended for the
best applied research in the field of plant and
animal production which contributes in some way
to the advancement of agriculture, to better yields,
and to the fight against insects and disease. The
second prize is for the best practical or written
work in the field of agricultural economics which
contributes to better farm management and the
economics of distribution of farm produce. The
prizes are awarded annually on the recommendation of representatives of the Foundation
and the Academy. Their monetary value varies
each year.
Awarding body: Académie d'Agriculture de
France, 18 rue de Bellechasse, 75007 Paris, France.

Prix de la 'Fondation Professeur Lucien Dautrebande'

This triennial prize is intended to reward the
author (or authors) of a work on human or
animal physiopathology, preferably with therapeutic implications. It should permit the recipient
to continue with research which is already at an
advanced stage. The prize consists of a certificate
and a variable sum of money (700,000 Belgian
francs in 1976). Candidates may be of any
nationality. The prize was founded in 1970 in
memory of Professeur Lucien Dautrebande, a
leading researcher in the physiopathology of
respiration.
Awarding body: Fondation Professeur Lucien
Dautrebande, 35 Chaussée de Liège, 5200 Huy,
Belgium.
Recipients include: Prof. Durrer (Netherlands,
cardiology, 1973); Prof. Gajdusek (U.S.A., discovery of slow viruses, 1976).

Prix de la Fondation Maurice Lenglen

The prize was established in 1951 with a donation
of 133,500 francs to the French Academy of
Agriculture. It is to reward or encourage the
judicious and rational use of chemical fertilizers.
It is awarded annually in the form of a medal, on
the recommendation of the Academy's Physical
and Chemical Sciences section.
Awarding body: Académie d'Agriculture de
France, 18 rue de Bellechasse, 75007 Paris, France.

Prix de la Fondation Servant (*Servant Foundation Prize*)

Annual prizes of 10,000 francs are awarded on
behalf of this Foundation by the French Academy
of Sciences. They are given in alternate years on
the recommendation of the Commission for

mathematics prizes and the Commission for physics prizes.

Awarding body: Académie des Sciences, 23 Quai de Conti, Paris 6e, France.

Recipients include: Marc Lefort (physics, 1977); Michel-Robert Herman (mathematics, 1978).

Prix de la Fondation Thorlet

The income from this Foundation is used by all the Academies of the French Institute to provide annual monetary prizes of about 4,000 francs. They are awarded in rotation for work in all disciplines represented by the Academies.

Awarding body: Institut de France, 23 Quai de Conti, Paris 6e, France.

Recipients include: Mme. Anny-Chantal Levasseur-Regourd (sciences, 1976).

Prix Foucault

The prize was established by the Council of the French Society of Physics in 1971 in memory of the physicist Léon Foucault (1919–68). It is for work in the field of applied physics, and is currently worth 1,800 francs.

Awarding body: Société Française de Physique, 33 rue Croulebarbe, 75013 Paris, France.

Recipients include: E. Auzel (1973); Ph. Marchal (1974); M. Borghini (1975); J. P. Taran (1976); J. Trotel (1977).

Prix Foulon

Three separate awards are given under this title by the French Academy of Sciences. Two annual prizes of 5,000 francs each are given for botany and rural economics, and a biennial prize of 6,000 francs is given for zoology.

Awarding body: Académie des Sciences, 23 Quai de Conti, Paris 6e, France.

Recipients include: Gérald Perbal (botany), Huguette de Barjac (rural economics), 1977; Pierre Pecaut (rural economics), Jacques Margara (botany), Robert Meiniel (zoology), 1978.

Prix Paul Fourmarier

A gold medal is awarded every three years to a Belgian or foreign scientist who, in the preceding ten years, has completed work of significance in the field of geology (applied geology, petrography, physical geography, palaeontology). The work should have made an important contribution to knowledge of the general evolution of the world.

Awarding body: Académie Royale de Belgique, Palais des Académies, rue Ducale 1, 1000 Brussels, Belgium.

Recipients include: A. Watznauer (1971); E. Raguin (1974).

Prix France-Canada

The prize was established in 1961 jointly by the Association France-Canada, the Délégation générale du Québec in Paris, and the Quebec Ministry of Culture. It is awarded annually to an author who is French-Canadian or from Quebec, for a book published in France or Canada since the announcement of the previous prize. The award consists of 1,000 French francs.

Awarding body: Délégation générale du Québec, 66 rue Pergolèse, 75116 Paris, France.

Recipients include: Jacques Folch-Ribas (*Un aurore boréale*, 1974); Antonine Maillet (*Mariagéla*, 1975); Réjean Ducharme (*Les enfantômes*, 1976) Louis Caron (*L'emmitouflé*, 1977).

Prix France-Iran

Founded in 1976, this annual literary prize c 2,000 French francs is intended to honour a boo published in French in the previous two years. I even-numbered years it is given to an Irania writer for a book on any subject; in odd-numbere years it goes to a writer of any nationality for book on Iran. Exceptionally, the award may b given for a writer's total published work. Author are invited to submit works of any literary genr (novel, collection of short stories, essay, poetry history, or journalistic report).

Awarding body: Association des Ecrivains Langue Française (Mer et Outre-Mer), 38 rue d Faubourg-Saint-Jacques, 75014 Paris, France.

Recipients include: Djaval Hadidi (*Voltaire l'Islam*, 1976).

Prix France-Luxembourg

Founded in 1976, this annual literary prize c 2,000 francs is given to a French-speaking autho either for a particular book or for his complet published works. It is presented in even-numbere years in Luxembourg to a French author, and i odd-numbered years in France to a Luxembour author. Works of all literary genres are eligibl provided that they were published during the tw previous years.

Awarding body: Association des Ecrivains d Langue Française (Mer et Outre-Mer), 38 rue d Faubourg-Saint-Jacques, 75014 Paris, France.

Recipients include: Joseph-Emile Muller (Luxem bourg, complete works, 1977).

Prix Francqui

The Francqui Prize is awarded annually to distinguished Belgian who has made an importan contribution to science and thus enhanced th reputation of his country. The prize is awarded i the following categories in rotation: (a) mathe matics, physics, chemistry; (b) natural and medica sciences; (c) human sciences. Candidates must b under 50 years of age. The prize of 1 millio Belgian francs was founded in 1932.

Awarding body: Fondation Francqui, Etablisse ment d'Utilité Publique, 11 rue d'Egmont, B-105 Brussels, Belgium.

Recipients include: Jules Horrent (philology 1968); Isidoor Leusen (medicine, 1969); Rad Balescu (biophysics, 1970); Georges Thin (psychology, 1971); Jean-Edouard Desmed (physiology, 1972).

Prix Gérard

Baron Gérard, a member of the French Academ of Agriculture, donated a sum of 20,000 francs t the Academy in 1921. The prize thus establishe

to encourage cattle-breeders in the selection of
ure French dairy and beef cattle. The award is
made annually in the form of a medal, on the
recommendation of the Stock-breeding section of
he Academy.
Awarding body: Académie d'Agriculture de
rance, 18 rue de Bellechasse, 75007 Paris, France.

rix Léon-Gérin

reated in 1977, this is one of five 'Prix du Quebec'
warded annually by the Quebec Ministry of
ulture. It is given in recognition of an exceptional
ontribution to the development of human sciences
aw, philosophy, theology, education, psychology,
eography, history, etc.). The prize consists of
15,000, a certificate and a medal. It is named in
memory of Léon Gérin (1863–1951), the first
Quebecois sociologist.
Awarding body: Ministère des Affaires Cultur-
lles, Hôtel du Gouvernement, Quebec, Canada.
Recipients include: Léon Dion (political science,
977).

rix Henry Gervais

This prize was established in 1920 with a donation
f 400 francs to the French Academy of Agricul-
ure by Monsieur Prosper Gervais in memory of
is son. It is awarded either to the author of the
est study on the problems of viticulture, or to the
ractising viticulturist deemed most worthy of
ecognition. It is awarded annually in the form of a
medal on the recommendation of the Cultivation
ection of the Academy.
Awarding body: Académie d'Agriculture de
rance, 18 rue de Bellechasse, 75007 Paris, France.

rix Théophile Gluge

warded by the Belgian Royal Academy, this
iennial prize of 30,000 francs is for work in the
eld of physiology. It may be awarded to a Belgian
r a foreigner.
Awarding body: Académie Royale de Belgique,
alais des Académies, rue Ducale 1, 1000 Brussels,
elgium.
Recipients include: Karl Hainaut (1974).

rix Gobert

These prizes were established by Baron Gobert
nd are awarded annually by two of the French
cademies. A first prize (currently 30,000 francs)
s given by the *Académie Française* for the most
loquent work on the history of France. A second
rize (10,000 francs) is awarded to the runner-up.
imilar first and second prizes are awarded by the
cadémie des Inscriptions et Belles-Lettres for the most
earned and most profound work on the history of
rance and the research involved.
Awarding bodies: Académie Française and
cadémie des Inscriptions et Belles-Lettres, 23
Quai de Conti, Paris 6e, France.
Recipients include (Académie Française): Yves-
Marie Berce (first prize, *Histoire des Croquants*,
976); Armand Lunel (second prize, *Juifs du
anguedoc, de la Provence et des Etats français du pape*,
976); Georges Duby (first prize, *Le Temps des
Cathédrales*, 1977); Jacques Bariety (second prize,
*Relations Franco-Allemandes après la Première Guerre
Mondiale*, 1977).

Prix Goncourt

The Goncourt Prize has become one of the most
well-known French literary prizes, not least
because of the controversy which has surrounded
it from time to time. It was established in 1901 in
accordance with the will of Edmond de Goncourt
(1822–96), the author, and commemorates both
him and his brother Jules (1830–70). The prize is
awarded annually, preferably to a young writer,
for the best prose work of the year published in
French. The winner receives a symbolic cheque
for 50 francs, and is assured best-seller status. The
announcement is made traditionally at the
Drouant restaurant where the ten Goncourt
Academy members meet to decide the winner.
The prize cannot be applied for.
Awarding body: Académie Goncourt, Restaurant
Drouant, Place Gaillon, 75002 Paris, France.
Recipients include: Pascal Lainé (*La Dentellière*,
1974); Emile Ajar (*La Vie devant Soi*, 1975
(refused)); Patrick Grainville (*Les Flamboyants*,
1976); Didier Decoin (*John l'Enfer*, 1977); Patrick
Modiano (*Rue des boutiques obscures*, 1978).

Prix Grimaud

The grandson of Monsieur Grimaud bequeathed
4,900 francs to the French Academy of Agriculture
in 1905 for the establishment of a prize to be
awarded alternately for the best work on viticulture and on oenology in the south of France.
The prize is awarded annually in the form of a
medal on the recommendation of the Cultivation
section of the Academy.
Awarding body: Académie d'Agriculture de
France, 18 rue de Bellechasse, 75007 Paris, France.

Prix Hamoir

This prize of 20,000 Belgian francs is awarded to
a doctor of veterinary medicine for a published or
unpublished work in French or Dutch on some
aspect of veterinary science. The prize is awarded
every five years, and the work should have been
done in the five years preceding the award. Only
Belgian nationals are eligible, and members of the
Belgian Academy of Medicine are excluded.
Awarding body: Académie Royale de Médecine
de Belgique, Palais des Académies, 1000 Brussels,
Belgium.

Prix Hassan II des documents et manuscrits
(Hassan II Prize for Documents and Manuscripts)
This annual prize was established in 1969 by the
Ministry for Cultural Affairs for work on the study
of documents and manuscripts. More than one
prize may be given at one time, and each consists
of 30,000 dirhams.
Awarding body: Ministry of State for Cultural
Affairs, Ave. Gandi, Rabat, Morocco.
Recipients include: Mohamed Fatmi (documents,
1975); Mohamed Darkaoui (documents, 1975);

Mohamed Bargach (documents, 1976); Larbi Bensai'd (documents, 1976); Mohamed Garbi (manuscripts, 1976).

Prix Hérédia

This is one of the few prizes awarded by the French Academy which are open to foreigners as well as French nationals. It is an annual monetary prize and is awarded in alternate years to (1) a Latin-American writer for a work of prose or poetry written in French; (2) the author of either a published collection of sonnets or a typed volume containing at least one sonnet and at most 14 sonnets. The prize is not divisible.

Awarding body: Académie Française, 23 Quai de Conti, Paris 6e, France.

Prix Gustave Heuzé

This prize was established in 1903 with a donation of 125 francs from Monsieur Heuzé to the French Academy of Agriculture. It provides for an award for the best published work dealing with crops, market-gardening, fruit trees (except vines), silviculture, or exotic plants. The prize is awarded annually in the form of a medal, on the recommendation of the Cultivation and Silviculture sections of the Academy.

Awarding body: Académie d'Agriculture de France, 18 rue de Bellechasse, 75007 Paris, France.

Prix baron Horta

This prize, first awarded in 1971 by the Belgian Royal Academy, is awarded every five years for a work of architecture, either already finished or in the planning stage. The prize money of 250,000 Belgian francs may be shared if more than one person worked on the winning project. This should have been built in, or planned for, one of the EEC countries. Architects of any nationality are eligible, and are invited to send in their work in the December of the relevant five-year period (next 1977–81).

Awarding body: Académie Royale de Belgique, Palais des Académies, rue Ducale 1, 1000 Brussels, Belgium.

Prix de l'Institut Belge des Sciences Administratives (*Belgian Institute of Administration Prize*)

An annual prize of 25,000 Belgian francs was instituted in 1936 for a work in the field of public administration. This may take the form of a doctorate thesis, research report, scientific study, or a book, written in one of the official languages of Belgium. Works by foreigners are not accepted unless they deal with Belgium either exclusively or in comparison with one or more EEC countries. Candidates must be under the age of 50. Works presented should not have won any other prize, and should not have been published before 1 January of the year preceding the award.

Awarding body: Institut Belge des Sciences Administratives, Cité administrative de l'Etat, Quartier Esplanade 3, 8e étage, 1010 Brussels, Belgium.

Prix Inter de la Presse (*International Press Prize*)

This is one of several annual prizes presented during the Nice International Book Festival in May. The award is given for a book on a historical theme, a news item, or a report in any language, published during the preceding year (proof copies are acceptable). The winner receives a diploma and an official Festival medal, and a cash prize of 10,000 French francs donated by well-known newspapers from several different countries, which also provide the jury.

Awarding body: Secrétariat du Prix Inter de la Presse, 5 rue Stanislas, 75006 Paris, France.

Recipients include: Ian Gibson (U.K., *The Death of Lorca*, 1972); Anthony Sampson (U.K., *The Seven Sisters: The Great Oil Companies and the World They Made*, 1976); Michael Herr (U.S.A., *Dispatches*, 1978).

Prix René Janssens

A prize of 30,000 francs is awarded every three years by the Belgian Royal Academy. It is restricted to Belgian artists and is given alternately for excellence in one of two genres of painting either portraiture or interiors. The award takes into consideration the whole of an artist's work.

Awarding body: Académie Royale de Belgique, Palais des Académies, rue Ducale 1, 1000 Brussels, Belgium.

Recipients include: Erik Boone (interior, 1968) Pierre Dulieu (portrait, 1971); Marie Howe (interior, 1974).

Prix Jules et Louis Jeanbernat Barthélemy de Ferrari Doria

This annual prize of about 4,000 francs was founded by Emmanuel Jeanbernat in memory of his two sons killed in the war. It is awarded in turn by each of the five Academies of the French Institute for a work of literature, science or art, by a young French author or artist. It may not be shared.

Awarding body: Institut de France, 23 Quai de Conti, Paris 6e, France.

Prix Jeunesse International

The Prix Jeunesse Foundation was established in 1964 by the Free State of Bavaria, the City of Munich and the Bavarian Broadcasting Service, who were joined in 1971 by the ZDF TV channel. Its aims are the development and utilization of television for the benefit of the young, with particular emphasis on international relations. To this end a contest is held every two years to which broadcasting authorities worldwide are invited to submit entries (no more than two recent programmes). There are two categories: programmes for children; programmes for young people. Three prizes, in the form of a trophy and certificate, may be presented in each category. Judging is carried out by invited experts known as 'accredited participants'. Programmes intended exclusively for use in schools are not eligible.

Awarding body: Stiftung Prix Jeunesse im Bayerischen Rundfunk, D-8000 Munich 2, Rundfunkplatz 1, Federal Republic of Germany.

Recipients include: British Broadcasting Corporation (U.K.), ITA – Thames Television Ltd. (U.K.), Sveriges Radio TV (Sweden), Danmarks Radio TV (Denmark), Norsk Rikskringkasting (Norway), 1976.

Prix Alexandre Joannidès

An annual prize of 40,000 francs is awarded by the French Academy of Sciences. It is for scientific, medical or other research which the Academy deems beneficial to the public good and worthy of encouragement. It is awarded one year for work in the field of mathematical and physical sciences, and the next year for work in the field of chemical and natural sciences.

Awarding body: Académie des Sciences, 23 Quai de Conti, Paris 6e, France.

Recipients include: Jean-Pierre Changeux (medicine, 1977); Bernard Cagnac (1978).

Prix Joliot-Curie

The prize was established in 1956 by the Council of the French Society of Physics in memory of Irène Joliot-Curie (1897–1956), daughter of Pierre and Marie Curie, who, with her husband, Frédéric, is famous for research in nuclear physics. The prize is awarded annually for work in the field of nuclear or corpuscular physics. Its value is currently 1,800 francs.

Awarding body: Société Française de Physique, 33 rue Croulebarbe, 75013 Paris, France.

Recipients include: P. Darriulat (1973); Cl. Detraz (1974); J. P. Vialle (1975); J. Galin (1976); M. Della Negra (1977).

Prix du Docteur Frans Jonckheere

This triennial prize of 12,000 Belgian francs is given for work in Dutch or French contributing to the advancement of the history of medicine. The work may be published or unpublished; the award is restricted to Belgian nationals.

Awarding body: Académie Royale de Médecine de Belgique, Palais des Académies, 1000 Brussels, Belgium.

Prix L. La Caze

This prize is awarded annually by the French Academy of Sciences in rotation for the most outstanding work in the fields of physics, chemistry, and physiology. It is worth 5,000 francs and is indivisible. Foreigners are also eligible.

Awarding body: Académie des Sciences, 23 Quai de Conti, Paris 6e, France.

Recipients include: Alain Veillard (chemistry, 1977); Jacques Roffi (physiology, 1978).

Prix Charles Lagrange

A four-yearly prize of 30,000 francs is awarded by the Belgian Royal Academy to a Belgian or a foreigner for the best mathematical or experimental work constituting an important advance in the mathematical knowledge of the earth.

Awarding body: Académie Royale de Belgique, Palais des Académies, rue Ducale 1, 1000 Brussels, Belgium.

Recipients include: R. O. Vicente (1968); Desmond King-Hele (1972).

Prix Paul Langevin

The prize was established in 1956 in memory of Paul Langevin (1872–1946) by decision of the Council of the French Society of Physics. It is awarded annually for work in the field of theoretical physics. Its value is currently 1,800 francs.

Awarding body: Société Française de Physique, 33 rue Croulebarbe, 75013 Paris, France.

Recipients include: A. Neveu (1973); E. Brezin (1974); D. Vautherin (1975); G. Toulouse (1976); J. Zinn-Justin (1977).

Prix Langlois

An annual monetary prize is awarded by the French Academy for the best translation in verse or prose of a Greek, Latin or other foreign work into the French language.

Awarding body: Académie Française, 23 Quai de Conti, Paris 6e, France.

Recipients include: Madeleine Horst (1978).

Prix de la Langue Française (*French Language Prize*)

Established in 1914, this is one of the few prizes that the French Academy awards to foreigners. An annual prize, it may be awarded to one person, or divided into one prize of 50 francs, two prizes of 20 francs, or take the form of medals (gold, silver or bronze). It is awarded in recognition of services to the French language.

Awarding body: Académie Française, 23 Quai de Conti, Paris 6e, France.

Recipients include: André Chouraqui (gold medal, 1977).

Prix Henri Lavachery

A five-yearly prize of 25,000 francs is awarded for work in the field of ethnology, in its widest sense. Entries may be in the form of written work or a film. The prize is restricted to Belgian nationals, and the work must be in French. The jury may award the prize to work not entered for it. The prize may not be divided (but may be given to more than one person collaborating on the same work).

Awarding body: Académie Royale de Belgique, Palais des Académies, rue Ducale 1, 1000 Brussels, Belgium.

Recipients include: Luc de Heusch (1967); Eric Pollet and Mme. Grace Pollet-Winter (1972).

Prix Le Conte

This is one of the prizes of the French Academy of Sciences which are open to foreigners. It is a three-yearly prize of 22,000 francs for new and significant discoveries in mathematics, physics, chemistry, natural history or medicine; or for new applications of these sciences which must give results far superior to those already obtained.

Awarding body: Académie des Sciences, 23 Quai de Conti, Paris 6e, France.

Prix Yves Le Kervadec

This prize, founded in 1946, is awarded to the author of the best unpublished work in prose or verse on a philosophical, moral or patriotic theme. Submitted entries should not exceed 20 pages of typescript or 100 lines of verse. The prize amounts to 30 francs.

Awarding body: Union Littéraire & Artistique de France, 35 rue Gayet, 42000 Saint-Etienne, France.

Prix Charles Lemaire

A biennial prize of 30,000 francs is awarded by the Belgian Royal Academy to the author of the best memoir on questions relating to public works. This includes: (a) primarily, experiments and practical work connected directly with the art and science of engineering; (b) secondly, theoretical research on the resistance of materials, stability of constructions and hydraulics.

Awarding body: Académie Royale de Belgique, Palais des Académies, rue Ducale 1, 1000 Brussels, Belgium.

Recipients include: A. Blondé and L. Beyers (1970); Eugène Dehan (1972); Henri Hondermarcq (1974).

Prix Joseph Lepoix

This four-yearly prize of 25,000 Belgian francs is for the best work in Dutch or French on the subject of poisons – treatment, symptoms, diagnosis, etc. The work should be of an instructional nature and of interest to the general public, especially parents, doctors, nurses, etc. It may be published or unpublished. Members of the Belgian Academy of Medicine are excluded.

Awarding body: Académie Royale de Médecine de Belgique, Palais des Académies, 1000 Brussels, Belgium.

Prix des Libraires

This annual prize, founded in 1955, is given for a literary work within the romantic genre published during the preceding year. Members of the French Booksellers Federation vote by post from a short-list, and the result is made known to the media at the Federation's General Assembly. There is no award in kind: the prize consists of the title alone.

Awarding body: Fédération Française des Syndicats de Libraires, 117 blvd. Saint-Germain, Paris 75006, France.

Recipients include: Herbert Le Porrier (*Le Médecin de Cordoue*, 1975); Patrick Modiano (*Villa Triste*, 1976); Pierre Moustiers (*Un Crime de Notre Temps*, 1977); Jean Noli (*La Grâce de Dieu*, 1978); Christiane Singer (*La Mort Viennoise*, 1978).

Prix du Professeur Joseph Lignières

Professor Lignières, a member of the French Academy of Agriculture, donated 20,000 francs to the Academy in 1937. The prize is intended to reward the best research work on the subject of the fight against contagious diseases in animals. It is awarded annually in the form of a medal on the recommendation of the Stock-breeding section of the Academy.

Awarding body: Académie d'Agriculture de France, 18 rue de Bellechasse, 75007 Paris, France.

Prix Littéraire de l'Asie (*Asia Literary Prize*)

Founded in 1971, this annual prize of 2,000 French francs is intended for a French-speaking author either originating from Asia or writing about Asia. The award is given for one particular book or for an author's total literary output. Books submitted should have been published in the preceding year, and may be of any literary genre – creative literature, historical (history or biography), or journalistic reports.

Awarding body: Association des Ecrivains de Langue Française (Mer et Outre-Mer), 38 rue du Faubourg-Saint-Jacques, 75014 Paris, France.

Recipients include: Pierre Darcourt (France, *Viet-Nam, qu'as-tu fait de tes fils?*, 1976); Jean-Marc Pottiez (France, *Les vainqueurs de la défaite*, 1976); Tsien Tche Hao (China, *La Chine*, 1977); Pierre-Antoine Perrod (France, *L'affaire Lally-Tollendal*, 1977).

Prix Littéraire des Caraïbes (*Caribbean Literary Prize*)

Founded in 1964, this award of 2,000 francs is intended for French-speaking writers from the Caribbean – i.e. from Haiti, the French Antilles and French Guiana. The prize is awarded every two years either for a particular book or for the whole of a writer's published work. Authors are invited to submit works of creative literature (novel, collection of short stories, essay, history or poetry) published during the previous two years.

Awarding body: Association des Ecrivains de Langue Française (Mer et Outre-Mer), 38 rue du Faubourg-Saint-Jacques, 75014 Paris, France.

Recipients include: Jean Fouchard (Haiti, *Les marrons de la liberté*, 1973); Jean-Louis Baghio'o (Martinique, *Le Flamboyant à fleurs bleues*, 1975); Ghislain Gouriage (Haiti, *La Diaspora d'Haiti et l'Afrique*, 1975).

Prix Littéraire France–Québec Jean-Hamelin (*France–Quebec Jean Hamelin Literary Prize*)

This annual prize of 2,000 francs, founded in 1964, is financed jointly by the Association of Writers in the French Language in Paris and the Quebec Ministry of Cultural Affairs. The prize is given to a French-speaking writer from Canada or the United States for a work of any literary genre published during the preceding year.

Awarding body: Association des Ecrivains de Langue Française (Mer et Outre-Mer), 38 rue du Faubourg-Saint-Jacques, 75014 Paris, France.

Recipients include: Louise Dechêne (*Habitants et marchands de Montréal au 17e siècle*, 1975); Yves Beauchemin (*L'Enfirouapé*, 1975); Jovette Marchessault (*Comme une enfant de la terre*, 1976); Diane Giguère (*Dans les ailes du vent*, 1977).

Prix Littéraire Gibson

This annual prize is awarded for the best 'first' French novel by a Canadian published in the preceding year. Any Canadian author or landed immigrant with no previously published novel is eligible. The prize consists of a cash award of $1,000. It was established in 1976 by Canadian Gibson Distillery Ltd. (*See also* Gibson Literary Award.)

Awarding body: Canadian Gibson Distillery Ltd., 2085 Union Street, Suite 865, Montreal, Que. H3A 1B9, Canada.

Recipient: Nelson Dumais (*L'Embarquement Pour Anticosti*, 1977).

Prix littéraire de La Presse (La Presse *Literary Prize*)

The prize was created in 1974 on the initiative of Roger Lemelin, President of the newspaper *La Presse*, and Canadian member of the Académie Goncourt. The prize is given annually for a work of literature: poetry, novel, history, literary criticism, essay of a philosophical or artistic nature. The author must be French-Canadian, and must have already published at least one book in Canada. The award is intended to stimulate the development of literature in the French language in Canada. It amounts to $7,500 and was originally divided between two authors; from 1977 a single prize is awarded. It cannot be applied for.

Awarding body: La Presse, 7 rue Saint-Jacques ouest, Montreal, Que. H2Y 1K9, Canada.

Recipients include: André Langevin, Michèle Mailhot (1975); Antonine Maillet, Viola Léger (1976).

Prix Littéraire des Mascareignes, des Seychelles et des Comores (*Mascarene Islands, Seychelles and Comoro Islands Literary Prize*)

The Association of Writers in the French Language, continuing its policy of creating a literary prize for every region where French is spoken, established this prize in 1964. It is given every even-numbered year for a particular book or for the whole of a writer's published work. The prize is worth 2,000 francs and is given to a French-speaking writer from the Mascarene Islands in the Indian Ocean, the Seychelles or the Comoro Islands. Any work of creative literature published in the preceding two years is eligible.

Awarding body: Association des Ecrivains de Langue Française (Mer et Outre-Mer), 38 rue du Faubourg-Saint-Jacques, 75014 Paris, France.

Recipients include: Jean Fanchette (Mauritius, *Psychodrame et Théâtre Moderne*, 1972); Marcelle Lagesse (Mauritius, *Sont amis que vent emporte*, 1974); Pierre Renaud (Mauritius, *Les balises de la nuit*, 1976); Alain Lorraine (Reunion, *Tienbo le Rein*, 1976).

Prix Littéraire de la Pensée Wallonne (*Walloon Literary Prize*)

In 1977 the Commission Culturelle de Wallonie Libre established this annual prize of 5,000 Belgian francs. The award is made in rotation for literature in four categories: French prose; prose in a Walloon dialect; French poetry; poetry in a Walloon dialect. Candidates must either originate from Wallonia or be resident in the region. Entries should not have been printed, nor published, nor read in public.

Awarding body: Commission Culturelle de Wallonie Libre, Route d'Obourg 63, 7000 Mons, Belgium.

Prix Littéraire Prince Pierre de Monaco (*Prince Pierre of Monaco Prize for Literature*)

The prize was established in 1951 by H.S.H. Prince Pierre of Monaco (1895–1964), patron of arts and letters, and father of H.S.H. Prince Rainier III. The award is continued in perpetuation of his memory. The prize of 30,000 francs is awarded annually to an author who is either of French nationality, or who writes in French, in recognition of his/her entire work. Applications for the prize are not accepted. The presentation takes place in Monte Carlo in the spring.

Awarding body: Fondation Prince Pierre de Monaco, Ministère d'Etat, Monaco-Ville, Monaco.

Recipients include: Antoine Blondin (1971); Marguerite Yourcenar (1972); Paul Guth (1973); Félicien Marceau (1974); Pierre Gascar (1978).

Prix Littéraire de la Résistance (*Resistance Literary Prize*)

This annual prize was established by the French Resistance Action Committee in 1965. It is awarded for the best literary work which deals with the French Resistance, and is worth 10,000 francs. The book must be published in French.

Awarding body: Comité d'Action de la Résistance, 10 rue de Charenton, 75012 Paris, France.

Recipients include: Catherine Claude and Jeannette L'Herminier (*Le Triangle Rouge*, 1971); François Broche (*Le Bataillon Des Guitaristes*, 1972); Henri Frenay (*La Nuit Finira*, 1973–74); Jean Michel (*Dora*, 1975); Gilberte Brossolette (*Il S'appelait Pierre Brossolette*, 1976).

Prix de Littérature des Alpes et du Jura (*Alps and Jura Literary Prize*)

Founded in 1971, this annual prize of 2,000 francs is intended for French-speaking authors from the Alps-Jura geographical region. This includes writers from Switzerland, from the French-speaking regions of Italy: Val d'Aosta and the Vaudois Valleys of Piemonte, and from the French Alps and Jura region. The prize is given for one particular book or for the whole of an author's published work. Books submitted may be of any literary genre – creative literature, historical (history or biography), or journalistic reports; they should have been published in the preceding year.

Awarding body: Association des Ecrivains de Langue Française (Mer et Outre-Mer), 38 rue du Faubourg-Saint-Jacques, 75014 Paris, France.

Recipients include: Jean-Christian Spahni (Switzerland, *Les Indiens des Andes*, 1975); Jean-Claude Fontanet (Switzerland, *L'effritement*, 1976); Lin Colliard (Val d'Aosta – Italy, *La Culture valdotaine au cours des siècles*, 1977).

Prix de Littérature Franco-Belge (*Franco-Belgian Literature Prize*)

Re-founded in 1964 after a lapse of several years, this prize of 2,000 francs is given annually to a French-speaking writer by the Association of Writers in the French Language. One year it is presented in France to a Belgian writer; the next year it is presented in Belgium to a French writer. Books submitted should have been published during the preceding two years and should be devoted to a maritime or overseas theme (reflecting the origin of the Association, which began as a society for French colonial writers).

Awarding body: Association des Ecrivains de la Langue Française (Mer et Outre-Mer), 38 rue du Faubourg-Saint-Jacques, 75014 Paris, France.

Recipients include: Claude de Groulart (Belgium, *L'Aigle et le dragon*, 1974); Fernand Dumont (France, *L'Anti Sultan, Al Hajj Omar Tal du Fouta, combattant de la Foi*, 1975); Henry Vincenot (France, *Le sang de l'Atlas*, 1975); Sophie Deroisin (Belgium, *L'Auberge des sept mers*, 1976).

Prix Albert-Londres

The prize was founded in 1933 by Florise Martinet-Londres in memory of her father, a famous journalist, lost when the ship 'Georges Philippar' sank in the Red Sea in 1932. The cash prize of 3,000 francs is presented annually on 16 May, the anniversary of Albert Londres' death. The prize is given to the best reporter of the year; candidates should be under 40 years old, and French-speaking, and are invited to submit published articles or books. The jury is composed of 15 eminent journalists and writers.

Awarding body: Association du Prix Albert-Londres, 53 rue Cardinet, 75017 Paris, France.

Recipients include: François Missen (1974); Thierry Desjardins (1975); Pierre Veilletet (1976); François Debré (1977).

Prix Edouard Mailly

A prize of 30,000 francs is awarded every four years by the Belgian Royal Academy to the Belgian (national or naturalized) scientist who has brought about the most progress in the science of astronomy, or who has contributed to the increase in interest and knowledge of the subject throughout the country.

Awarding body: Académie Royale de Belgique, Palais des Académies, rue Ducale 1, 1000 Brussels, Belgium.

Recipients include: Cercle astronomique de Bruxelles (1967); P. Melchior (1971).

Prix Monsieur et Madame Louis Marain

This annual prize of 1,000 francs is awarded to the author of a work on the subject of the human sciences in general, especially ethnography, anthropology, and the relations between the different peoples of the world.

Awarding body: Académie des Sciences d'Outre-Mer, 15 rue La Pérouse, 75116 Paris, France.

Recipients include: Dr. Anne Retel-Laurentin (*Sorcellerie et ordalie, l'épreuve du poison en Afrique Noire, essai sur le concept de la négritude*, 1976).

Prix Joseph-Edmond Marchal

An award of 25,000 francs given at five-yearly intervals by the Belgian Royal Academy to the Belgian author(s) of the best work on national antiquities or archaeology.

Awarding body: Académie Royale de Belgique, Palais des Académies, rue Ducale 1, 1000 Brussels, Belgium.

Recipients include: André Van Doorselaer, André Dasnoy (1967); Villy Scaff (1972).

Prix Maréchal Lyautey

This prize, awarded every five years, is intended to reward the author of a work on Africa which is of an intellectual, scientific, social or moral nature. It is a cash prize of 150 francs, and is named in honour of Marshal Lyautey (1854–1934) who served with distinction in colonial France. (*See also Prix du Centenaire du Maréchal Lyautey.*)

Awarding body: Académie des Sciences d'Outre-Mer, 15 rue La Pérouse, 75116 Paris, France.

Recipients include: Régine Nguyen Van-Chi Bonnardel (*Développement maritime et rural du Kayar*, 1967); Ferdinand N'Songan Agblemagnon (*Sociologie des Sociétés arabes en Afrique Noire*, 1973).

Prix Marie-Victorin

This prize was created in 1967 and originally known as the 'Prix Scientifique'. It is one of five 'Prix du Québec' given annually by the Quebec Ministry of Culture. The award consists of $15,000, a certificate and a medal, and is intended to crown a distinguished career in any of the pure sciences.

Awarding body: Ministère des Affaires Culturelles, Hôtel du Gouvernement, Quebec, Canada.

Recipients include: Dr. Gilles-G. Cloutier (physics, 1976); Dr. Louis-Edmond Hamelin (geography, 1976); Dr. Jacques Genest (1977).

Prix du Maroc (*Morocco Prize*)

This prize is awarded for published or unpublished work in each of three categories: social and human sciences; exact sciences; arts and literature. It was established in 1968 by the Ministry of State for Cultural Affairs, and each prize is worth 13,000 dirhams. Applications, to be considered annually by a jury, are invited from Moroccan nationals or from those who have lived in Morocco for a period of at least two years.

Awarding body: Ministry of State for Cultural Affairs, Av. Gandi, Rabat, Morocco.

Recipients include: Mohamed ben Chakroun (1970); Mohamed Sabagh (*Point d'objection*, 1970); Khnata Banouna (*Le feu et le choix*, 1971); Mohamed Ibrahim L'katani (*Souvenir d'un prisonnier militant*, 1972); Abd Loihab Etazi (*Jamia Karaouine*, 1973).

Prix Charles-Léopold-Mayer

The Charles-Léopold-Mayer Foundation aims to assist scientific progress and encourage research, particularly in the fields of biology, biochemistry and biophysics. This annual prize of 220,000 francs is awarded by the French Academy of Sciences and is one of the largest French monetary awards. Applications are not submitted; nominations are made by the Academy after consultation with various institutions and individuals. The prize may be awarded to anyone of any nationality, but may not be given two years running to nationals of the same foreign country. The winner is expected to use the prize money to further his/her research; for this reason there is an upper age limit of 65.

Awarding body: Académie des Sciences, 23 Quai de Conti, Paris 6e, France.

Recipients include: Walter Gilbert and Mark Ptashne (U.S.A., for work on biological and molecular properties of repressors and operators), Evelyn Witkin (U.S.A., for work on D.N.A.), 1977); Roger Monier (France, for his work on molecular biology) and Prof. Piotr Slonimski (France, for his work on the genetics of the mitochondria of yeast, as well as his work on the respiratory enzymes), 1978).

Prix de Médecine 'Fondation Pfizer' (*Pfizer Foundation Prize for Medicine*)

This biennial prize, established to reward and encourage medical research, is awarded to a Belgian under 50 years of age who has made the best contribution to human medicine. Recipients of another national or international prize may not apply. A commission consisting of three members each of the Dutch- and French-speaking Academies of Medicine, and the Past President of Pfizers, judge the entries and make nominations to the Academy of Medicine. The prize is 200,000 Belgian francs. Members of the Academy of Medicine are excluded.

Awarding body: Académie Royale de Médecine de Belgique, Palais des Académies, 1000 Brussels, Belgium.

Prix Medicis

The prize was established in 1958 by a group of notable literary figures at the suggestion of Jean-Pierre Giraudoux. A cash prize of 4,500 francs is awarded annually for a novel, story or collection of short stories, published in the previous 12 months, which has introduced a new note to French writing. Applications and nominations are not accepted.

Awarding body: Le Jury Medicis, 25 rue Dombasle, Paris 75015, France.

Recipients include: Marc Cholodenko (*Les Etats du Désert*), 1976; Georges Perec (*La Vie Mode d'Emploi*), 1978.

Prix Medicis Etranger (*Medicis Foreign Prize*)

This prize was established in 1970 by the members of the jury for the Medicis Prize (*q.v.*). A cash prize of 4,500 francs is awarded annually for a novel, story or collection of short stories translated into French and published in the previous 12 months. Applications and nominations are not accepted.

Awarding body: Prix Medicis Etranger, 25 rue Dombasle, Paris 75015, France.

Recipients include: Alexander Zinoviev (*L'Avenir radieux*, 1978).

Prix Melsens

This prize of 20,000 Belgian francs is awarded every four years to the Belgian author (writing in French or Dutch) of an outstanding work on professional hygiene. The work may be published or unpublished. Members of the Belgian Academy of Medicine are excluded.

Awarding body: Académie Royale de Médecine de Belgique, Palais des Académies, 1000 Brussels, Belgium.

Prix Jean Mermoz

The Mermoz Prize was established in 1976 by the French Language Cultural and Technical Union, in honour of the aviator Jean Mermoz. It is a biennial award, given to a person of French nationality who is resident abroad, and who has made a significant contribution to the dissemination of French culture and expertise. The winner receives a medal and a prize of 3,000 francs.

Awarding body: L'Union Culturelle et Technique de Langue Française, 47 Blvd. Lannes, 75116 Paris, France.

Prix Narcisse Michaut

A monetary prize is awarded biennially in odd-dated years to the author of the best work of French literature.

Awarding body: Académie Française, 23 Quai de Conti, Paris 6e, France.

Prix Friedrich Miescher

The Swiss Biochemical Society founded the prize in 1970 to commemorate the centenary of the discovery by Friedrich Miescher of nucleic acid. The award is given annually to a young research worker (under 40) for one or more important contributions to biochemistry. The research should have been undertaken in Switzerland, or by Swiss researchers abroad. The prize consists of 5,000 Swiss francs and a medal.

Awarding body: Friedrich Miescher-Institut, Ciba-Geigy AG, Postfach 273, CH-4002 Basel, Switzerland.

Recipients include: Dr. Kaspar Winterhalter (1973); Dr. Kurt Wuthrich (1974); Dr. Jörg Rosenbusch (1975); Dr. Heidi Diggelmann (1976); Dr. Bernard Fulpius (1977).

Prix Mondial Cino del Duca (*Cino del Duca International Prize*)

Founded in 1969 by Madame Simone del Duca according to the wishes of her late husband, the prize is awarded annually for work in the fields of arts or sciences. It is intended to reward and to bring to public attention an author whose work constitutes a message of modern humanism. With a value of 150,000 francs this is one of the largest monetary awards in Europe. The jury consists of members of the French Academy, the Academy of Sciences and the Goncourt Academy.

Awarding body: Fondation Simone et Cino del Duca, 10 rue Alfred-de-Vigny, 75008 Paris, France.

Recipients include: Andrei Sakharov (U.S.S.R., physician, 1974); Alejo Carpentier (Cuba, writer, 1975); Lewis Mumford (U.S.A., social historian, 1976); Germaine Tillion (France, ethnologist and writer, 1977).

Prix Montyon

Various monetary prizes of 6,000 francs each are administered by the French Institute and awarded by the relevant Academy of the Institute. Two annual prizes are given: one literary, for a published work by a French author which is commendable for its high moral character; the other is awarded for work in the fields of medicine and surgery. Four biennial prizes are awarded in even-dated years: one for the invention or perfection of implements useful to the agricultural, mechanical, theoretical or practical sciences; the second in the field of chemistry for the discovery of a method which will make some mechanical process less distasteful; the third is for work in experimental physiology; the fourth is for statistical research of any kind.

Awarding body: Institut de France, 23 Quai de Conti, Paris 6e, France.

Recipients include: René Labbens (mechanical engineering), Georges Le Moan (chemistry), Gaston Heripret (medicine and surgery), Mme. Suzanne Maroux (experimental physiology), Georges Bonnet (statistics), 1976; Guy Deysson (medicine and surgery), 1977.

Prix Laura Mounier de Saridakis

This is a biennial prize of 4,000 francs for a work of pure science, the application of which would promote the progress of medicine, biology, physics and biological or medical chemistry.

Awarding body: Academy of Sciences, 23 Quai de Conti, Paris 6e, France.

Recipients include: Mme. Claude Giessner-Prettre (1976).

Prix Claude-Adolphe Nativelle de Médecine
(*Claude-Adolphe Nativelle Prize for Medicine*)

This international prize is intended to draw attention to the value of basic clinical or therapeutic research into cardiovascular diseases, and also to the diffusion of the French language and of French scientific knowledge. It is awarded every three years and is a cash prize of 500,000 francs. It was established in 1971 but not awarded until 1976. The Claude-Adolphe Nativelle Foundation for Art and Medicine was created in 1971 to commemorate the centenary of the discovery of crystallized digitalis by Nativelle (1812–89). The Foundation's triple purpose is the defence of the

French language; scientific research having a direct or indirect bearing on the health of mankind; the development of European artistic expression. The Nativelle prize is one of several awards and donations contributed by the Foundation in the fields of medicine and art.

Awarding body: Fondation Claude-Adolphe Nativelle pour l'Art et la Médecine, 75015 Paris, France.

Recipients include: Prof. Paul Puech and Dr. Paul Laurens (work on intracardiac conduction and its anomalies, and for their contribution to the spread of scientific knowledge in the French language by their numerous publications, 1976).

Prix Auguste-Napoléon Parandier

A bequest of 63,520 francs made in 1905 to the French Academy of Agriculture established this prize to reward scientific work on the subject of the cultivation of vines and wine-making. It is awarded annually in the form of a medal on the recommendation of the Cultivation section of the Academy.

Awarding body: Académie d'Agriculture de France, 18 rue de Bellechasse, 75007 Paris, France.

Prix Henri Pellet

The prize was established in 1922 with a donation of 2,500 francs to the French Academy of Agriculture. It is awarded to the author of a work or a collection of works on the subjects of agricultural industry, agricultural chemistry, or the cultivation of sugar-producing plants. The prize is awarded annually in the form of a medal, on the recommendation of the Physical and Chemical Sciences section of the Academy.

Awarding body: Académie d'Agriculture de France, 18 rue de Bellechasse, 75007 Paris, France.

Prix Denise Pelletier

Created in 1977, this is one of five 'Prix de Québec' awarded annually by the Quebec Ministry of Culture. It consists of $15,000, a certificate and a medal, and is awarded in recognition of an outstanding career in the field of music, theatre or dance. It is named in memory of the great comedienne who died in 1976.

Awarding body: Ministère des Affaires Culturelles, Hôtel du Gouvernement, Quebec, Canada.

Prix Jean Perrin

In 1972 the Council of the French Society of Physics created a prize in memory of Jean Perrin (1870–1942), the eminent physicist. It is intended to reward a particularly successful attempt to popularize science. All means of expression – written and audio-visual – are admissible. The prize is awarded by the Council of the Society following nominations by a jury of nine people, four of whom are not physicists. The value of the prize is currently 1,800 francs.

Awarding body: Société Française de Physique, 33 rue Croulebarbe, 75013 Paris, France.

Recipients include: Prof. J. Cl. Pecker (books on astronomy and astrophysics, 1974); H. Tazieff

Dir. of Volcanology Laboratory, C.N.R.S., 1975); M. Rouze (producer on radio programme *France-Culture*, 1976); R. Clarke and N. Skrotzky (*Télévision-Française-1* and *France-Culture* respectively, 1977); Charles Penel (Deputy Dir., Palais de la Découverte, 1978).

Prix Petit d'Ormoy

According to the terms of the prize foundation its income must be used by the French Academy of Sciences to provide prizes, half for theoretical scientific work, and half for applied sciences, medical, mechanical or industrial practice. The Academy awards an annual prize of 8,000 francs alternately for mathematics and physics and for chemistry and natural sciences.

Awarding body: Académie des Sciences, 23 Quai de Conti, Paris 6e, France.

Recipients include: Jacques Forest (1976); Hervé Jacquet (1977).

Prix Plumey

An annual prize of 5,000 francs is awarded to a scientist for the improvement of steam engines or for any other invention which has contributed most to navigation.

Awarding body: Académie des Sciences, 23 Quai de Conti, Paris 6e, France.

Recipients include: Michel Delattre (1976); Jean Deveaux (1977).

Prix de Poésie Max d'Arthez

This prize of 30 francs is awarded for an unpublished poetic work on any subject, not exceeding 100 lines.

Awarding body: Union Littéraire & Artistique de France, 35 rue Gayet, 42000 Saint-Etienne, France.

Prix Poétique Français (*French Poetry Prize*)

This prize is awarded for the best manuscript submitted consisting of 12 unpublished poems (maximum 24 lines each), on any subject. The winning work is subsequently published, and the author receives 100 complimentary copies.

Awarding body: Union Littéraire & Artistique de France, 35 rue Gayet, 42000 Saint-Etienne, France.

Prix André Policard-Lacassagne

A triennial prize (last award 1978) of 4,000 francs is awarded to a young scientist (age limit 40) who is not a member of the French Academy of Sciences. It is for distinction in the fields of biochemistry, biophysics or biophysical chemistry. One prize in four may be awarded to a foreigner who has been working in France.

Awarding body: Académie des Sciences, 23 Quai de Conti, Paris 6e, France.

Prix Quinquennal des Sciences Médicales (*Quinquennial Prize for Medical Sciences*)

This prize was instituted by the Belgian Government in 1964. Two awards of 150,000 Belgian francs each are made every five years under this title, one for research in basic medical science, the other for clinical or applied research. Any work, written in French, Dutch, English or German, is eligible provided that the author is Belgian by birth or naturalization. The prize is given for a specific piece of work or for all an author's work completed in the five years preceding the award.

Awarding body: Académie Royale de Médecine de Belgique, Palais des Académies, 1000 Brussels, Belgium.

Prix Quinquennal des Sciences Pharmaceutiques et Thérapeutiques (*Quinquennial Prize for Pharmaceutical and Therapeutic Sciences*)

This prize of 50,000 Belgian francs was founded by the Belgian 'Section centrale des secours médicaux et pharmaceutiques', organized in the 1914–18 war by the 'Comité National de Secours et d'Alimentation'. It is awarded every five years alternately for work in the fields of pharmaceutical and therapeutic sciences. The work may be in French or Dutch, published or unpublished. Authors must be of Belgian nationality, but members of the Belgian Academy of Medicine are ineligible.

Awarding body: Académie Royale de Médecine de Belgique, Palais des Académies, 1000 Brussels, Belgium.

Prix pour la Recherche économique et financière (*Award for Economic and Financial Research*)

This award is intended to encourage research in the fields of savings, the functioning of financial markets and the investment of savings in the modern economy, and all questions relating to investment. It consists of a cash prize of 250,000 Belgian francs awarded every two years to the author of a book or dissertation in a relevant field. The award may be shared. Candidates must be Belgian university graduates. The work submitted may be in French, Dutch, English or German. The award was founded by the Coopération Ouvrière Belge (C.O.B.) in 1968.

Awarding body: C.O.B. Caisse Centrale de Dépôts, Société Coopérative, rue de la Loi 135, 1040 Brussels, Belgium.

Recipients include: Frans Spinnewyn (*Dynamic portfolio selection: A class of models with application to financial institutions*), Willem Moesen (*Het beheer van de staatsschuld en de termijnstructuur van de interestvoeten met een toepassing voor Belgie*), Myriam Deterck-Spilleboudt (*Analyse théorique et empirique de l'évolution des cours à la Bourse de Bruxelles*), 1976.

Prix Renaudot

This prize, sometimes called the 'minor Goncourt' because it is awarded each year in November at the same time as the Goncourt prize, was established in 1925 and named after Théophraste Renaudot (1586–1653) who was a doctor, official historian to the king, and who founded the *Gazette de France*. The prize is given for a work of fiction showing talent and originality. It has no monetary value, and it cannot be applied for.

Awarding body: Secrétariat du Prix Renaudot, Restaurant Drouant, Place Gaillon, 75002 Paris, France.

Recipients include: Michel Henry (*L'amour aux yeux fermés*, 1976); Alphonse Boudard (*Les Combattants du Petit Bonheur*, 1977); Conrad Detrez (*L'Herbe à brûler*, 1978).

Prix Jean Reynaud

Annual prizes of about 4,000 francs each are awarded under this title. The five Academies of the French Institute give a prize each at five-yearly intervals. The awards are for the most deserving work produced in the preceding five years; it must be original, elevated in style, and of an inventive nature. Members of the French Institute themselves are eligible, and the prize may not be shared.

Awarding body: Institut de France, 23 Quai de Conti, Paris 6e, France.

Recipients include: Christian Aimar (mathematics and physics, 1976).

Prix Jean Ricard

Monsieur Jean Ricard, a member of the French Society of Physics, donated a sum of money to the Society in 1970 for the establishment of a prize. It is intended to reward and encourage the author of outstanding and original research work in the field of physical sciences, either theoretical or experimental. The winner must be a French national, and the prize may not be divided. Its value is currently about 50,000 francs.

Awarding body: Société Française de Physique, 33 rue Croulebarbe, 75013 Paris, France.

Recipients include: J. Winter (1974); P. Musset (1975); G. Slodzian (1976); R. Balian (1977); M. Hénon (1978).

Prix Félix Robin

Monsieur Félix Robin, who was killed in 1914 in the first world war, bequeathed the sum of 50,000 francs to the French Society of Physics, with the stipulation that the money be used to reward outstanding scientific work carried out in France by a French national. The annual prize is currently worth 2,000 francs.

Awarding body: Société Française de Physique, 33 rue Croulebarbe, 75013 Paris, France.

Recipients include: P. Aigrain (1974); L. Michel (1975); Jacques Prentki (1976); B. Cagnac (1977); Henri Benoit (1978).

Prix du Roman (*Prize for a Novel*)

An annual monetary prize of 20,000 francs is awarded to a young French prose-writer for a work of imagination and inspiration. Authors may not submit their own work for consideration.

Awarding body: Académie Française, 23 Quai de Conti, Paris 6e, France.

Prix Victor Rossel

This prize of 125,000 Belgian francs is awarded annually for a novel or collection of short stories by a French-speaking Belgian author. The prize was founded in 1938 by Rossel & Cie., publishers of the newspaper *Le Soir*, in memory of the son of the paper's founder.

Awarding body: Société Anonyme Rossel & Cie. Journal *Le Soir*, 112 rue Royale, 1000 Brussels, Belgium.

Recipients include: Victor Misrahi (*Les routes du nord*, 1960); Maud Frère (*Les jumeaux millénaires*, 1962); Mme. Louis Dubrau (*A la poursuite de Sandra*, 1964); Georges Thines (*Le tramway des officiers*, 1973); Sophie Deroisin (*Les Dames*, 1975).

Prix Auguste Sacré

A prize of 50,000 francs is awarded every six years by the Belgian Royal Academy to a Belgian for the invention which has brought about a significant advance in the field of mechanics relating to any industry. The prize may also be awarded to the Belgian author of a publication on mechanics containing new theories which are of real value to this science.

Awarding body: Académie Royale de Belgique, Palais des Académies, rue Ducale 1, 1000 Brussels, Belgium.

Recipients include: Félix Buckens (1964); Jean Ginoux (1970).

Prix Emile Sacré

A prize of 50,000 francs is awarded every six years by the Belgian Royal Academy. It is for the most significant painting to have been executed and publicly exhibited in the preceding six years. The prize is restricted to Belgian painters.

Awarding body: Académie Royale de Belgique, Palais des Académies, rue Ducale 1, 1000 Brussels, Belgium.

Recipients include: Marie-Claire Wodon (1968); Luc Perot (1974).

Prix Georges-Sadoul

This prize was established in 1968 by Ruta Sadoul in memory of her husband, Georges (1904–67), cinema critic and historian. Medals are awarded every year for the best French film and the best foreign film or films. Entries must be the first or second feature-length films made by a director.

Awarding body: Prix Georges-Sadoul, 3 rue Bretonvilliers, 75004 Paris, France.

Recipients include: Bernard Bouthier (France, *Touche pas à mon copain*), Haïlé Jerima (Ethiopia, *La récolte, an 3000*), Kevin Brownlow and Andrew Mollo (U.K., *Winstanley*), Anthony Leach and Gary Kildea (Papua New Guinea, *Trobriand Cricket*), 1976.

Prix Saintour

Various monetary prizes of about 4,000 francs each are awarded under this title by all the Academies of the French Institute. The *Académie Française* gives an annual prize for various types of work in the field of linguistics: lexicons, grammars, critiques, commentaries, etc., on the subject of the French language, particularly from the 16th century onwards. The annual prize awarded by the *Académie des Inscriptions et Belles-Lettres* is given in rotation according to the classification of its three sections: classical antiquity; the Orient; and the Medieval and Renaissance period. The

Académie des Sciences awards a triennial prize alternately for work in the fields of its two sections: either mathematics and physics or chemistry and natural sciences. The *Académie des Sciences Morales et Politiques* awards a biennial prize in rotation on the recommendation of each of its sections: philosophy; moral sciences; legislation; political economy; history.

Awarding body: Institut de France, 23 Quai de Conti, Paris 6e, France.

Recipients include: Pierre Demerseman (science, 1976); Emile Genouvrier, Claude Désirat, Tristan Horde (linguistics, 1978).

Prix Joseph Schepkens

A prize of 15,000 francs is awarded by the Belgian Royal Academy to a Belgian scientist for the best experimental work in one of three branches of science: plant genetics (especially cultivated plants); phytopathology and applied entomology; agronomic research. The prize is awarded once every three years in rotation for work in each category.

Awarding body: Académie Royale de Belgique, Palais des Académies, rue Ducale 1, 1000 Brussels, Belgium.

Recipients include: R. Maréchal (genetics, 1972); G. Pierrard (phytopathology and applied entomology, 1973); P. Dagnelie (agronomic research, 1974).

Prix Scientifique Joseph Maisin (*Joseph Maisin Prize for Science*)

This quinquennial prize is awarded for outstanding work in the natural sciences and medical science. It consists of a cash award of 750,000 Belgian francs. Candidates for the prize must be proposed by three scientists, at least two of whom must be Belgian. The prize is restricted to French speakers; a companion prize, the *Wetenschappelijke Prijs Joseph Maisin*, is awarded to a Dutch-speaking scientist.

Awarding body: Fonds de la Recherche Scientifique Médicale, 5 rue d'Egmont, B-1050 Brussels, Belgium.

Recipients include: Prof. Henri-Géry Hers (for his work on the metabolism of glucides in relation to the pathology of lysosomes, 1975).

Prix Scientifique Ernest-John Solvay (*Ernest-John Solvay Prize for Science*)

This quinquennial prize is awarded for outstanding work in the human sciences. It consists of a cash award of 750,000 Belgian francs. Candidates for the prize must be proposed by three scientists, at least two of whom must be Belgian. The prize is restricted to French speakers; a companion prize, the *Wetenschappelijke Prijs Ernest-John Solvay*, is awarded to a Dutch speaker.

Awarding body: Fonds National de la Recherche Scientifique, 5 rue d'Egmont, B-1050 Brussels, Belgium.

Recipients include: Prof. Jean Ladrière (for his outstanding work on logico-formal systems and their relationship to human discourse and experience, 1975).

Prix Léopold Sédar Senghor

The Senghor Prize was founded in 1969 by the French Language Cultural and Technical Union, in honour of the Senegalese head of state and honorary president of the above union. The award is given to a person of any nationality other than French, in recognition of an outstanding literary work written in French, or in recognition of an outstanding contribution to the dissemination of the French language and culture. The prize is awarded every two years, and the winner receives a medal and 5,000 francs.

Awarding body: L'Union Culturelle et Technique de Langue Française, 47 Blvd. Lannes, 75116 Paris, France.

Prix Claude Sernet

This prize of 1,000 francs is awarded annually to the author of a collection of French poetry published in the two years preceding the award. Since 1976 it has been restricted to foreign French-speaking poets. No applications or nominations are required. The prize was founded in 1969 by the members of the jury of the Antonin Artaud and Ilarie Voronca prizes (*q.v.*), in memory of Claude Sernet (1902–67), a Romanian-born French poet.

Awarding body: Association des Ecrivains du Rouergue, 7 rue de Saunhac, 12000 Rodez, France.

Recipients include: Robert Momeux (*L'envers de l'ombre*, 1973); Serge Wellens (*Santé des Ruines*, 1974); Raoul Becousse (*La Grande Porte*, 1975); Pierre Morency (*Lieu de naissance*, 1976); Marianne Van Hirtum (*La nuit mathématique*, 1977).

Prix Henriette Simont

This prize of 15,000 Belgian francs is awarded every five years for the best work – published or unpublished – in French or Dutch on the treatment of asthma. Members of the Belgian Academy of Medicine are ineligible.

Awarding body: Académie Royale de Médecine de Belgique, Palais des Académies, 1000 Brussels, Belgium.

Prix de la Société Française d'Hydrologie et Climatologie Médicale (*Prize of the French Society for Medical Hydrology and Climatology*)

This award was established in 1965 and is made every two years for original work in clinical or biological climatology or hydrology, which has been submitted to the Society the previous year. It takes the form of a monetary prize of 3,000 francs.

Awarding body: Société Française d'Hydrologie et Climatologie Médicale, 1 rue Monticelli, 75014 Paris, France.

Prix de la Société Royale de Numismatique de Belgique (*Prize of the Royal Numismatic Society of Belgium*)

This prize is awarded every three years to the author of the best original and unpublished scientific dissertation on numismatics or sigillography submitted to the Society before 1 January

235

of the year of the award. The dissertations, which must be submitted anonymously, may be in French, Dutch, English or German. The prize consists of about 20,000 Belgian francs and a certificate. It was founded in 1976 by an anonymous donor and will be awarded for the first time in 1979.

Awarding body: Société Royale de Numismatique de Belgique, President: Em. Brouette, rue Jennay 28, B-5852 Isnes, Belgium.

Prix de Soliste de l'Association des Musiciens Suisses (*Association of Swiss Musicians' Award for Soloists*)

This award, consisting of a diploma and cash prize of 6,000 Swiss francs, is presented to a soloist of Swiss nationality not more than 30 years of age. The winner is selected by means of a competition. The award (presented annually at the end of August) was established in 1961.

Awarding body: Association des Musiciens Suisses, 11 bis av. du Grammont, 1000 Lausanne 13, Switzerland.

Prix Alexandre Straetmans

This triennial prize of 30,000 Belgian francs is awarded to doctors who have contributed to the advance of a cure for cancer. It is given for research work in French or Dutch, either published or deposited with the Belgian Academy of Medicine during the three-year period preceding the award. Academy members are excluded.

Awarding body: Académie Royale de Médecine de Belgique, Palais des Académies, 1000 Brussels, Belgium.

Prix Victor Tourneur

This prize of 25,000 francs is given every five years by the Belgian Royal Academy. It is awarded alternately by the Literature section of the Academy (for studies in numismatics and sigillography) and the Fine Arts section (to encourage the art of designing medals). In the latter category candidates must design a medal with a portrait on the obverse, while the reverse symbolizes the personality of the model; the artist must prove his powers of imagination, invention and culture.

Awarding body: Académie Royale de Belgique, Palais des Académies, rue Ducale 1, 1000 Brussels, Belgium.

Recipients include: Mlle. J. Lallemand (numismatics, 1968); René Harvent (medal design, 1973).

Prix Triennal de la Société Chimique de Belgique (*Belgian Chemical Society Triennial Prize*)

This prize is awarded every three years to a member of the Society for his work in the field of chemistry. It is intended to honour a researcher under 40 years of age who is at the peak of scientific activity and enjoys an international reputation. Candidates must either be working in Belgium or Belgian nationals working abroad. The prize consists of a cash award of 75,000 Belgian francs.

Awarding body: Société Chimique de Belgique, Square Marie-Louise 49, B-1040 Brussels, Belgium.

Prix Auguste Truelle

Monsieur Truelle, a member of the French Academy of Agriculture, donated 6,000 francs to the Academy in 1928 for the establishment of a prize for the best memoir on the subject of pomology. The award is made annually in the form of a medal, on the recommendation of the Cultivation section of the Academy.

Awarding body: Académie d'Agriculture de France, 18 rue de Bellechasse, 75007 Paris, France.

Prix P.-J. et Édouard Van Beneden

Founded by P. Nolf and administered by the Belgian Royal Academy, this prize is awarded every three years to the Belgian or foreign author(s) of the best original work on embryology or cytology. It may be in the form of a manuscript or published during the preceding three years. Its value is 50,000 Belgian francs.

Awarding body: Académie Royale de Belgique, rue Ducale 1, 1000 Brussels, Belgium.

Recipients include: J. Milaire (1974).

Prix Georges Vanderlinden

A prize of 30,000 francs is awarded every two years by the Belgian Royal Academy for the most important discovery or the most significant work in the field of physics, particularly radioelectricity. The prize is alternately national and international. Work entered for the national competition must be written in Dutch or French. Work entered for the international competition may be written in English, German or Italian.

Awarding body: Académie Royale de Belgique, Palais des Académies, rue Ducale 1, 1000 Brussels, Belgium.

Recipients include: René Freymann (international, 1970); Guy Steenbeckeliers (Belgian, 1972); Ralph A. Alpher and Robert Herman (international, 1974).

Prix Victor Van Straelen

This is a biennial prize of 25,000 francs awarded by the Belgian Royal Academy. It is restricted to Belgian nationals only, and is given in rotation for work in one of the following fields: geology and pedology; zoology (animal ecology and zoo-palaeontology); botany (plant ecology and phyto-palaeontology). The Academy may, regardless of work submitted, award the prize for work which it deems most worthy.

Awarding body: Académie Royale de Belgique, Palais des Académies, rue Ducale 1, 1000 Brussels, Belgium.

Recipients include: J. Uytterhoeven (zoology, 1970); J. de Heinzelin de Braucourt, J. Léonard and X. Misonne (botany, 1972); A. Noirfalise (geology and pedology, 1974).

Prix Victor Vermorel

This prize was established in 1918 with a donation of 400 francs to the French Academy of Agriculture from Monsieur Vermorel, a member of the

Academy. It is awarded alternately for research or practical work which has contributed most to the development of viticulture, and for research which has contributed most to the protection of cultivated plants against insects or disease.

Awarding body: Académie d'Agriculture de France, 18 rue de Bellechasse, 75007 Paris, France.

Prix Armand Viellard

Monsieur Viellard, a member of the French Academy of Agriculture, bequeathed 100,000 francs to the Academy in 1905 to establish a prize for the best work on agriculture and silviculture. It is awarded annually in the form of a medal, on the recommendation of the Cultivation and Silviculture sections of the Academy.

Awarding body: Académie d'Agriculture de France, 18 rue de Bellechasse, 75007 Paris, France.

Prix Ilarie Voronca

The Ilarie Voronca prize is awarded annually to a French or French-speaking poet for an unpublished collection of poems. The prize takes the form of publication of the manuscript by the publisher Jean Subervie. The award was founded in 1952 by a group of writers from the province of Rouergue in memory of Ilarie Voronca (1903–46), a French poet of Romanian origin.

Awarding body: Association des Ecrivains du Rouergue, 7 rue de Saunhac, 12000 Rodez, France.

Recipients include: Anne-Marie Bernad (*Entre Sable et Argile*, 1973); Robert Prade (*Marques du Temps*, 1974); André Laude (*Le bleu de la nuit crie au secours*, 1975); Sandra Thomas (*Les Croiselées*, 1976); Marc Vaution (*L'Absence habitée*, 1977).

Prix J. J. Weiss

This is a biennial monetary prize awarded in even-dated years to a French prose-writer. The work must be in the purest classical style, and have as its theme one of the following: travel, literature, literary or drama criticism, or politics. The prize may not be divided.

Awarding body: Académie Française, 23 Quai de Conti, Paris 6e, France.

Prix Adolphe Wetrems

Two prizes of 30,000 francs each are awarded annually by the Belgian Royal Academy for the most useful inventions or discoveries made in the preceding year, one in the field of mathematics and physics, the other in natural sciences. The prize-winners must be Belgian.

Awarding body: Académie Royale de Belgique, Palais des Académies, rue Ducale 1, 1000 Brussels, Belgium.

Recipients include: V. Belevitch (mathematics and physics, 1974); G. Brasseur, S. Cieslik, C. Muller and E. Derouane (mathematics and physics, 1975); J. E. Desmedt (natural sciences, 1975).

Prix Henry Wilde

This is one of the prizes of the French Academy of Sciences which are open to foreigners. It is a triennial prize of 4,000 francs, and is for a discovery or research work in astronomy, physics, chemistry, mineralogy, geology or experimental mechanics.

Awarding body: Académie des Sciences, 23 Quai de Conti, Paris 6e, France.

Recipients include: Henri Mondin (engineering, 1977).

Prix Valentine de Wolmar

This is one of the annual prizes of the French Academy. It is given for the most beautiful novel published during the year or for the most beautiful collection of poetry. The prize may not be divided. It consists of a cash award and also a selection of the jewellery of the foundress.

Awarding body: Académie Française, 23 Quai de Conti, Paris 6e, France.

Pro Musica-Plakette (*Pro Musica Medal*)

This medal is awarded by the President of the Federal Republic of Germany to groups of amateur musicians who have cultivated orchestral music and made valuable contributions to the country's cultural life. The award was established in 1968. Applications are made through a committee to the regional Minister of Culture, and his recommendation is made to the President by the Minister of the Interior. Foreign societies are recommended by the German Foreign Office.

Awarding body: Der Bundespräsident, c/o Bundesministerium des Innern, 5300 Bonn 7, Federal Republic of Germany.

Professional Progress Award for Outstanding Progress in Chemical Engineering

This award is sponsored by the Celanese Corporation of America, and is generally presented annually. It consists of a certificate and $1,000. It is made by the American Institute of Chemical Engineers to an individual of no more than 44 years of age, who need not be a member of the Institute, for significant contributions to chemical engineering. These may consist of the discovery or development of a new principle in this field; the development of a new process or product; the invention or development of equipment; or services to the profession. The recipient is invited to deliver an address to the Institute.

Awarding body: American Institute of Chemical Engineers, 345 East 47th St., New York, N.Y. 10017, U.S.A.

Progress Medal

This award was instituted in 1878 and consists of a silver medal awarded annually in recognition of any invention, research, publication or exhibition which has resulted in an important advance in the development of photography. It carries with it an Honorary Fellowship of the Society.

Awarding body: The Royal Photographic Society of Great Britain, 14 South Audley St., London, W1Y 5DP, England.

Recipients include: K. V. Chibisov (1968); L. E. Hallett (1969); T. Howard James (1973); Man Ray (1974); Beaumont Newhall (1975).

Progress Medal

Established in 1935, the medal is given annually for outstanding technical contributions to the progress of engineering phases of the motion-picture and/or television industries. It is presented at the Annual Conference of the SMPTE.

Awarding body: Society of Motion Picture and Television Engineers, 862 Scarsdale Ave., Scarsdale, N.Y. 10583, U.S.A.

Progress Medal Award

The award was established in 1948 by the Photographic Society of America (PSA). A large PSA medal and embossed scroll are awarded annually to a person who has made an outstanding contribution to photography or an allied subject. Nominations may be made by any PSA member to the Society's Chairman.

Awarding body: Photographic Society of America, Inc., 2005 Walnut St., Philadelphia, Pa. 19103, U.S.A.

Recipients include: Dr. Victor Hasselblad (1971); Dr. Katharine Burr Blodget (1972); H. Lou Gibson (1973); Harris B. Tuttle (1974); Dr. John Nash Ott (1975).

Progressive Architecture Awards

Established in 1954 by the monthly magazine *Progressive Architecture*, the awards are for designs of buildings not yet completed. Eligible also are projects in architectural research, urban design and planning which are scheduled to be adopted in the following calendar year. Projects must have been commissioned by a specific client (i.e. academic studies do not qualify). Awards in the form of a certificate are presented annually in January. Three awards may be given in any or all of three categories: research; urban design and planning; architectural design. American and Canadian architects, designers, urban planners and their clients are eligible.

Awarding body: Progressive Architecture, 600 Summer St., Stamford, Conn. 06904, U.S.A.

Recipients include: Daniel Mann Johnson Mendenhall (Comsat Laboratories, 1968); Gwathmey Siegel Associates (Whig Hall, 1973); Benjamin Thompson (Faneuil Hall Market Restoration, 1975); Bernard Maquet (The Arama Fellowship, 1977).

Giacomo Puccini International Singing Competition

The competition was founded in 1974 by the Puccini Foundation in memory of the famous Italian composer (1858–1924), born in Lucca. The competition is held annually in May, and is open to singers of any nationality under the age of 32. Three cash prizes of 800,000 lire each are awarded for the best male and female singers of various roles from Puccini's operas.

Awarding body: Fondazione G. Puccini, Palazzo Orsetti, Via S. Giustina, Lucca, Italy.

Prize-winners include: Takaghi Nihoko ('Madam Butterfly'), Ramiro Yordi ('Pinkerton'), Maura Aliboni ('Suzuki'), Alessandro Corbelli ('Sharpless'), 1975; Laura Eoli ('Mimi'), Raffanti Dano ('Marcello'), 1976.

J. E. Purkyně University Memorial Medal

The scientific board of the university established the medal in 1965 as a means of recognizing outstanding creative activity and also contributions to the development of the university. The medal is awarded irregularly on significant occasions, and comes in gold, silver or bronze.

Awarding body: J. E. Purkyně University, 601 37 Brno, A. Nováka 1, Czechoslovakia.

Recipients include: Prof. N. P. Dubinin (U.S.S.R., honorary doctor of J. E. Purkyně Univ., outstanding results in the field of genetics, 1965); Prof. John Chadwick (U.K., outstanding research into ancient culture, 1966); Prof. Dr. Roman Heck (Poland, Wroclaw Univ., co-operation with the history dept. of J. E. Purkyně Univ. and author of a history of the Czechoslovak S.R., 1970); Charles University (Czechoslovakia, on the occasion of its 625th anniversary, 1973).

Puskás Tivadar Commemorative Medal

This award is made annually by the Hungarian Scientific Society for Telecommunication for scientific, technological and industrial services in the field of Hungarian telecommunications. It may also be awarded for educational or administrative activities. It takes the form of a medal and cash prize of 5,000 forints. It was instituted in 1957, in honour of Tivadar Puskás (1844–93), who carried out distinguished work in the field of telecommunications and established Hungary's first telephone exchange.

Awarding body: Hiradástechnikai Tudományos Egyesület, 1372 Budapest, P.O.B. 451, Hungary.

Recipients include: I. Littvai (1972); Prof. Dr. I. Barta (1974); B. Dienes (1974); Dr. G. Bognár (1974); Dr. Gy. Tófalvi (1976).

Q

Quaid-i-Azam Academic and Literary Prizes
These are annual prizes, given for works of academic and literary merit based on research on the Quaid-i-Azam or on any aspect of the Pakistan Movement by a Pakistani or a foreign scholar. There are seven prizes of 10,000 rupees each, one to be given for works in each of the following languages: national language, Sindhi, Pushto, Punjabi, Baluchi, Kashmiri, and a foreign language. The prize was established in 1976, the centenary of the birth of Quaid-i-Azam Mohammad Ali Jinnah (1876–1948), the founder of Pakistan. The prizes are open to all persons regardless of nationality, race, creed or sex.
Awarding body: Quaid-i-Azam Academy, Block 52, Pakistan Secretariat, P.O.B. 894, Karachi 1, Pakistan.

Quaid-i-Azam Human Rights International Prize
Established in 1975 in memory of the founder of Pakistan, Quaid-i-Azam Mohammad Ali Jinnah (1876–1948), the prize was awarded for the first time on 25 December 1976, the centenary of his birth. The prize of 500,000 rupees in cash and a citation is awarded for outstanding contributions to the protection and promotion of human rights. It is open to anyone who is recommended in writing by an individual or body considered competent to do so. If the contribution is written, it must be in published form. Only contributions made during the preceding ten years shall be considered.
Awarding body: Quaid-i-Azam Academy, Block 52, Pakistan Secretariat, P.O.B. 894, Karachi 1, Pakistan.
Recipients include: Dr. Kenneth Kaunda (for his contribution to the eradication of colonialism and racism in Africa, 1976).

Queen Elisabeth International Music Competition
Founded in 1951 by Marcel Cuvelier (Comte de Launoit) and Queen Elisabeth of Belgium, the competition is arranged in three sessions which take place in three successive years. The order of sessions is: violin, composition, piano; there is one year in which there is no competition, after which the three-year cycle begins again. The organization of the concerts and musical events at the competition is handled by the Brussels Philharmonic Society. The competition is held under the patronage of Her Majesty Queen Fabiola. Twelve monetary prizes are awarded at each session, as well as medals.
Awarding body: Queen Elisabeth International Music Competition, rue Baron Horta 11, B-1000 Brussels, Belgium.

Queen Elizabeth II Arts Council Fellowship
This is the highest distinction bestowed by the New Zealand Arts Council, and the major arts award in the country. It is given from time to time in recognition of outstanding achievement and service to the arts, and its current monetary value is N.Z.$6,000.
Awarding body: Queen Elizabeth II Arts Council of New Zealand, 110–116 Courtenay Place 1, P.O.B. 6040, Te Aro, Wellington, New Zealand.
Recipients include: Rangimarie Hetet (Maori crafts, 1974); Juan Matteucci (music, 1974); Bruce Mason (drama, 1977); Jon Trimmer (dance, 1977).

'Queen Marie-José' Prize for Musical Composition
In order to encourage gifted musicians Queen Marie-José established a prize for a musical composition; the biennial contest is open to composers of all nationalities without age limit. The subject of the composition is decided by a committee and varies with each contest (e.g. piano concerto in 1976, chamber music 1978). The monetary prize is 10,000 Swiss francs. Works submitted must be unpublished. The award-winning composition is performed as part of the Merlinge concerts in co-operation with Radio-Télévision Suisse Romande.
Awarding body: 'Queen Marie-José' Musical Composition Contest, Merlinge, 1249 GY/Geneva, Switzerland.
Recipients include: Vaclav Kucera (Czechoslovakia, 'Images' for orchestra and piano, 1970); Daniel Kessner (U.S.A., 'Interactions' for flute, cello, piano and tape, 1972); Miro Bazlik (Czechoslovakia, 'Canticum 43' for chamber orchestra, choir and soprano, 1974); (no prize awarded 1976).

Queen's Award for Export Achievement
Queen's Award for Technological Achievement
These two awards were instituted to recognize and encourage outstanding achievements in exporting goods or services from the U.K. (in the case of the

former), and outstanding innovative achievements advancing process or product technology in the U.K. (in the case of the latter). The awards are made annually on 21 April (the Queen's birthday). A winning company receives a Grant of Appointment, with a facsimile signature of H.M. the Queen and the Prime Minister; and an Emblem, consisting of a stainless steel insert encapsulated in an acrylic block, bearing the title and year of the award. This is held for five years, after which the right to display the Emblem lapses. The award scheme was established in 1965 as the Queen's Award to Industry, by a committee chaired by H.R.H. the Duke of Edinburgh; the present titles were instituted in 1975. Any U.K. 'industrial unit' producing goods or services is eligible for the awards provided that it meets the criteria laid down by the administering office.

Awarding body: The Queen's Awards Office, Williams National House, 11–13 Holborn Viaduct, London EC1A 1EL, England.

Queen's Gold Medal for Poetry

The award was established in 1933 by King George V at the suggestion of the Poet Laureate, John Masefield. It is given at no fixed interval, but usually annually, for a book of verse written in English by a British poet. Recommendations are made by a committee of eminent men and women of letters, including the Poet Laureate.

Recipients include: Ted Hughes (1974); Norman Nicholson (1977).

R

Emil Racoviţă Prize
The prize was established in 1948 by the Romanian Academy. It is for contributions in the field of biology, and is presented annually at a General Assembly of the Academy. It consists of 10,000 lei and a diploma. It is named after Emil Racoviţă (1868–1947), founder of bio-speleology, and sometime President of the Romanian Academy. He participated with Amundsen in the 1897–99 expedition to Antarctica.

Awarding body: Academy of the S.R. of Romania, 125 Calea Victoriei, Bucharest, Romania.

Recipients include: M. Şerban, I. Viedman, D. Coman.

Stamford Raffles Award
The award was established by the Zoological Society of London in 1961 in commemoration of Sir Thomas Stamford Raffles (1781–1826), one of the founders of the Society and its first President. It takes the form of a work of art and is given for distinguished contributions to zoology by an amateur zoologist; however, it may exceptionally be given to a professional in recognition of contributions outside the scope of his professional activities and principal specialization. Serving members of the Society's Council are not eligible. The winner's contributions to zoology should normally have been made over a long period and not consist of only one specific piece of work.

Awarding body: The Zoological Society of London, Regent's Park, London NW1 4RY, England.

Recipients include: Dr. Maxwell Savage (for work on amphibians, 1967); Mrs. B. P. Hall (for work on the taxonomy and zoogeography of birds, particularly those of Africa, 1971); L. G. Higgins (for outstanding contributions to knowledge of the Lepidoptera, 1972); G. H. Locket (for contributions to arachnology, 1973); A. E. Ellis (for contributions to the study of molluscs, 1974).

Dr. P. N. Raju Oration Award
This award was established in 1972 with a donation by Dr. Narasimha Raju, a medical practitioner of Visakhapatnam. It is awarded annually to an eminent scientist to give a lecture on his or her work in the field of medicine or public health. The award consists of a cash sum of 1,000 rupees.

Awarding body: Indian Council of Medical Research, Ansari Nagar, Post Box 4508, New Delhi 110016, India.

Recipients include: Prof. G. P. Talwar (1972); Dr. B. K. Aikat (1973); Dr. S. C. Gungal (1974); Dr. Nandini Ani Shoth (1975); Dr. T. R. Bhaskaran (1976).

Srinivasa Ramanujan Medal
Established in 1961 by the Indian National Science Academy, this medal is awarded for outstanding contributions in the fields of physics, chemistry and mathematics. It is awarded every three years.

Awarding body: Indian National Science Academy, Bahadur Shah Zafar Marg, New Delhi 110001, India.

Recipients include: Dr. B. P. Pal (1964); Dr. K. Chandrasekharan (1966); P. C. Mahalanobis (1968); G. N. Ramachandran (1972); Harish Chandra (1974).

Erskine Ramsay Medal
This award is made annually by the American Institute of Mining, Metallurgical, and Petroleum Engineers for distinguished achievement in coalmining (including both bituminous coal and anthracite). Candidates of all nationalities are eligible, provided they are proposed by a member of the Institute and have not previously received an Institute award. The award consists of a gold plated medal and certificate, and was established in 1948 by Erskine Ramsay, industrialist and inventor.

Awarding body: American Institute of Mining, Metallurgy, and Petroleum Engineers, Inc., 345 East 47th St., New York, N.Y. 10017, U.S.A.

Recipients include: Dennis Lee McElroy (1973); John Thomas Ryan, Jr. (1974); Charles Jackson Potter (1975); David A. Zegeer (1976); James D. Reilly (1977).

Charles F. Rand Memorial Gold Medal
This award is made annually by the American Institute of Mining, Metallurgical, and Petroleum Engineers, for distinguished achievement in mining administration (including metallurgy and petroleum). Candidates of all nationalities are eligible, provided they are proposed by a member of the Institute and have not previously received an Institute award. This award, a gold plaquette and certificate, was established in 1932 by

admirers of Charles Frederic Rand, President of the Spanish-American Iron Company and discoverer of the lateritic iron ore deposits of North Cuba.

Awarding body: American Institute of Mining, Metallurgical, and Petroleum Engineers, Inc., 345 East 47th St., New York, N.Y. 10017, U.S.A.

Recipients include: Arthur F. Peterson (1971); Plato Malozemoff (1972); Robert O. Anderson (1975); Theodore W. Nelson (1976); Albert P. Gagnebin (1977).

Ranganathan Award

The award was established in 1976 in memory of the late Dr. R. S. Ranganathan, by the International Federation for Documentation. A Certificate of Merit is awarded biennially to persons recognized for their outstanding contributions to classification research in recent years.

Awarding body: Fédération Internationale de Documentation, 7 Hofweg, The Hague 2001, The Netherlands.

Recipients include: Derek Austin (British Library, 1976).

John Rankin Lectureship in Electrical Engineering

Established in 1928 by John Rankin, LL.D., the appointment is made annually by the Faculty of Engineering at Liverpool University. Remuneration is dependent on the funds available.

Awarding body: The University of Liverpool, P.O.B. 147, Liverpool L69 3BX, England.

Isaac Ray Award in Memory of Margaret Sutermeister

In 1951 the American Psychiatric Association established the Isaac Ray Award, originally financed through the Aquinas Fund, in memory of a co-founder of the Association. In 1973 a bequest of $20,000 in memory of Margaret Sutermeister from her mother, Bertha B. Sutermeister, continued the award for a further ten years. An honorarium of $2,000 is presented annually to a person (not necessarily a psychiatrist) who has made outstanding contributions to forensic psychiatry or the psychiatric aspects of jurisprudence. The recipient undertakes to offer the manuscript for publication, and present one or more lectures. The purpose of the award is to further co-operation between the practitioners of law and psychiatry.

Awarding body: American Psychiatric Association, 1700 18th St., N.W., Washington 9, D.C., U.S.A.

Recipients include: Bruno Cormier (1977).

Rechter Award

The award was established by the Society of Architects in Israel, the Ministry of Housing, and the Rechter family in honour of Zeev Rechter, a distinguished Israeli architect who contributed to the advancement and development of planning in Israel. The monetary award of I£5,000 is given every two years for a completed building in Israel outstanding for its architecture and its contribution to the advancement of architecture in the country. The building should have been completed within the previous ten years.

Awarding body: Association of Engineers and Architects in Israel, 200 Dizengoff St., Tel Aviv, Israel.

Recipients include: Arch. Abraham Yaski and Arch. Yaacov Gil (Hospital for Chronic Diseases, Gedera); Arch. Yitshak Yashar and Arch. Dan Eitan with Moshe Ashkenazi (Tel Aviv Museum); Arch. Daniel and Akhsa Havkin (Student dormitories in Technion City, Haifa); Arch. Ram Karmi (Bedouin market, Beersheva).

Franz-Redeker-Preis

This prize is awarded annually by the German Central Committee to Combat Tuberculosis, and is made for the best work (as yet unpublished) on the combating of tuberculosis from the standpoint of social hygiene. Anyone resident in Germany and professionally active in this field is eligible. The award was established in 1957 in honour of Franz Redeker (1891–1962), General Secretary of the Committee, and consists of a certificate and DM4,000.

Awarding body: Deutsches Zentralkomitee zur Bekämpfung der Tuberkulose, 2000 Hamburg 60, Poppenhusenstr. 14c, Federal Republic of Germany.

Recipients include: W. Lukas (1966); G. Forschbach (1967); R. Hoppe, E. Jensen (1968); R. Grohmann (1976).

Redi Award

The award was established in 1966 by the International Society on Toxinology in honour of Franciscus Redi, the 17th-century Italian anatomist who showed that it was venom, not spirits, which was transferred from snake to victim. An illuminated manuscript and framed award are given every two or three years in recognition of an outstanding career in the field of toxinology.

Awarding body: International Society on Toxinology, c/o Dr. Philip Rosenberg, Section of Pharmacology and Toxicology, University of Connecticut, School of Pharmacy, Storrs, Conn. 06268, U.S.A.

Recipients include: Findlay E. Russell (U.S.A., 1967); Paul Boquet (France, 1970); Andre De Vries (Israel, 1974); Chen-Yuan Lee (Taiwan, 1976).

Reed Aeronautics Award

The AIAA established this award in 1975 to broaden the scope of the former Sylvanus Albert Reed Award to cover the entire field of aeronautical endeavour. The late Dr. Reed, aeronautical engineer and designer, was a founder member of the former Institute of Aeronautical Science. This is the highest aeronautical award of the AIAA and is presented at the annual meeting; it consists of a medal and a certificate of citation.

Awarding body: American Institute of Aeronautics and Astronautics, 1290 Avenue of the Americas, New York, N.Y. 10019, U.S.A.

Recipients include: William C. Dietz (1977).

Raymond C. Reese Research Prize

This prize was endowed by R. C. Reese, Hon. M.ASCE, to recognize outstanding contributions to the application of structural engineering research, and established by the ASCE in 1970. The prize consists of a plaque and certificate. It cannot be won by the same person twice. It is awarded to the author or authors of a paper published by the Society in the previous year which best describes a notable achievement in research in structural engineering and recommends how the research can be applied to design.

Awarding body: American Society of Civil Engineers, 345 East 47th St., New York, N.Y. 10017, U.S.A.

Recipients include: Peter W. Chen and Leslie E. Robertson ('Human Perception Thresholds for Horizontal Motion', 1974); R. J. Hansen, J. W. Reed and E. H. Vanmarcke ('Human Response to Wind-Induced Motion of Buildings', 1975); Joint ASCE-ACI Task Committee 426 on Shear and Diagonal Tension of the Committee on Masonry and Reinforced Concrete of the Structural Division ('The Shear Strength of Reinforced Concrete Members-Slabs', 1976).

Erich-Regener-Preis

The prize was established in 1964 by the German Society for Aeronautics, the predecessor of the German Aerospace Research and Experimental Establishment (DFVLR) in Cologne. It commemorates the physicist Erich Regener (1881–1955), who worked particularly on the physics of the stratosphere. The prize consists of a certificate and a sum of money of up to DM5,000, and is awarded every two years. It is restricted to persons working with the DFVLR, and is given for works they have published or lectures they have given about their scientific achievements.

Awarding body: Deutsche Forschungs- und Versuchsanstalt für Luft- und Raumfahrt e.V., Postfach 90 60 58, D-5000 Cologne 90, Federal Republic of Germany.

Regina Medal

The medal was established in 1959 by Miss Sherrill McMillan and is administered by the Catholic Library Association. A silver medal is awarded annually to a living person for a distinguished and sustained contribution to children's literature. The works under consideration must have been originally written in the English language but the contribution may take any form (author, editor, publisher, illustrator, etc.).

Awarding body: Catholic Library Association, 461 W. Lancaster Ave., Haverford, Pa. 19041, U.S.A.

Recipients include: Frances Clarke Sayers (1973); Robert McCloskey (1974); May McNeer and Lynd Ward (1975); Virginia Haviland (1976); Marcia Brown (1977).

Regnell Prize

The Swedish Society of Medical Sciences founded this prize in 1866 for work in the field of medical research. It is a monetary prize (currently about 20,000 kronor) and is awarded every four years to a Swedish citizen for an unpublished paper. Applications are invited by the Society.

Awarding body: Swedish Society of Medical Sciences, P.O.B. 558, S-101 27 Stockholm, Sweden.

Recipients include: Prof. Börje Uvnäs ('Storage and release of histamine in mast cells', 1970).

Harvey T. Reid Lectures

These lectures are delivered every two years at Acadia University on some topic of public affairs, by individuals of outstanding reputation in this area. They were established in 1958 by Dr. Harvey T. Reid, graduate of Acadia University and Rhodes Scholar.

Awarding body: Acadia University, Canada.

Lecturers include: Dr. Gerald Graham (U.K., 1969); Dr. Hugh R. Trevor-Roper (U.K., 1970); Prof. Dennis Austin (U.K., 1973); The Rt. Hon. Eric Williams (Trinidad and Tobago, 1975); Dr. William H. McNeill (U.S.A., 1977).

Hans Reinhart-Ring

This award consists of a certificate and gold ring, and is presented annually by the Swiss Association for Theatre Research, for outstanding theatrical performance. Both Swiss artistes and foreigners who have been working for some time in Switzerland are eligible. The award was instituted in 1956 in honour of Hans Reinhart (1880–1963), poet, translator and patron of the arts.

Awarding body: Schweizerische Gesellschaft für Theaterkultur, Richard-Wagner-Str. 19, 8002 Zürich, Switzerland.

Recipients include: Carlo Castelli (1972); Inge Borkh (1973); Annemarie Düringer (1974); Charles Joris (1975); Dimitri (1976).

Phillip Reis Medal

The Federal German Ministry of Posts and Telecommunications founded the medal in 1952 for outstanding achievements in this field. It is usually awarded once a year in the autumn, and is open to anyone of any nationality. It is named in memory of Phillip Reis (1834–74), inventor of the telephone.

Awarding body: Bundesministerium für das Post- und Fernmeldewesen, Postfach 80 01, 5300 Bonn 1, Federal Republic of Germany.

Remington Honor Medal

Initiated by the New York Chapter of the American Pharmaceutical Association in 1918, this medal is awarded each year to the individual who has done the most for American pharmacy during the year or whose contributions to the advancement of pharmacy over a period of years have been judged to be the most outstanding.

Awarding body: American Pharmaceutical Association, 2215 Constitution Ave., N.W., Washington, D.C. 20037, U.S.A.

Recipients include: Linwood F. Tice (1971); Glenn Sonnedecker (1972); Grover C. Bowles (1973); Lloyd M. Parks (1974); Albert Doerr (1975).

Hari Om Ashram Prerit Shree Chunilal Vajeram Reshamwala Trust Research Award

This award was established in 1974 by the Hari Om Ashram Foundation in Surat as a memorial to Shree C. V. Reshamwala. It is given to encourage outstanding original research work in one of the following subjects: archaeology, chemistry of man-made and silk fibres, oceanology, social sciences in Gujarat. The award of 3,500 rupees is given each year in rotation for one of the four subjects. Research papers published by applicants in the preceding five years are assessed by a jury appointed by the University.
Awarding body: South Gujarat University, Udhna Magdalla Rd., Surat 395007, India.
Recipients include: Dr. H. D. Sankalia (archaeology, 1974–75); Dr. Bhupendra Patel (oceanology, 1976–77).

Retzius Medal

This gold medal was founded by the Swedish Society of Medical Sciences in 1896, in honour of Anders Retzius. It is awarded every ten years alternately for outstanding work in anatomy and physiology. Scientists of all nationalities are eligible.
Awarding body: Swedish Society of Medical Sciences, P.O.B. 558, S-101 27 Stockholm, Sweden.
Recipients include: Prof. Ragnar Granit (Sweden, physiology, 1957); Prof. Fritiof S. Sjöstrand (U.S.A., anatomy, 1967).

Reuchlinpreis der Stadt Pforzheim

This prize was established by the town of Pforzheim for the promotion of knowledge as defined by Reuchlin (1455–1522), who was born in Pforzheim. The award is given every three years for an outstanding work in German, within the domain of the arts. Nominees are proposed by the Heidelberg Academy of Sciences, and the Lord Mayor and Council of Pforzheim; the final decision rests with the Council. The award consists of a cash prize of DM10,000.
Awarding body: Stadt Pforzheim, 7530 Pforzheim, Postfach 7, Federal Republic of Germany.
Recipients include: Prof. Dr. Karl Rahner, S.J. (theologian, 1965); Prof. Dr. Erich Preiser (sociologist, 1967); Prof. Dr. Gershom Scholem (theologian, 1969); Prof. Dr. Hans-Georg Gadamer (philosopher, 1971); Prof. Dr. Reinhart Koselleck (historian, 1974).

Ernst-Reuter-Preis

In 1960 the West German Ministry for Intra-German Relations established two annual prizes for radio: one for the best play, and one for the best documentary, taking as their theme some aspect of the two Germanies. The prize is in memory of Ernst Reuter (1889–1953), who was Mayor of Berlin from 1951 to 1953. The awards consist of DM10,000 each and a certificate, and may be divided.

Awarding body: Bundesministerium für inner deutsche Beziehungen, Godesberger Allee 140 Postfach 12025, 5300 Bonn 2, Federal Republic o Germany.
Recipients include: Olaf Leitner (play, *Rock-Szen DDR*, 1977); Horst Karasek (play, *Frankfurt-Bebra, hin-und zurück*, 1977); Werner Hill (docu mentary, report on the Weinhold trial, 1977) Wolfgang Meisenkothen (documentary, *Berlin eine geteilte Stadt*, 1977).

Rhind Lectureship

The lectureship consists of an annual award o £400 and a series of six lectures to be delivered i Edinburgh. It was established in 1876 under a endowment of Alexander Henry Rhind (1833–63) a pioneer prehistorian in Scotland who had a wid interest in European and Egyptian archaeology The subject of the lectures is research in archaeo logy, history or historical architecture.
Awarding body: Society of Antiquaries of Scot land, National Museum of Antiquities of Scotland Queen St., Edinburgh EH2 1JD, Scotland.
Lecturers include: D. Winfield ('Byzantine Mosai and Wall Paintings in Cyprus', 1972–73); D. B Stronach ('Aspects of the Archaeology of Iran' 1973–74); S. Maxwell ('Scottish Silversmiths an their Silver', 1974–75); G. Beard ('Interio Decoration in Great Britain 1660–1830', 1975–76) Dr. I. Henderson ('Pictish Art and Society' 1976–77).

Rhodesia Literature Bureau Literary Com petition

Established in 1956, the competition is for the bes manuscripts of a novel, play or translation i Shona or Ndebele. The novel-writing competitio is biennial, and in the alternate years a play writing, translation or short story-writing com petition is held. In each language group the firs prize is R$50, the second prize is R$25, and th third prize is R$15. Only Africans born o domiciled in Rhodesia are eligible.
Awarding body: Rhodesia Literature Bureau Box 8137, Causeway, Salisbury, Rhodesia.
Recipients include: A. C. Moyo (Shona, 1976) G. M. P. Khiyaza (Ndebele, 1976); Julian Chireshe (Shona, play, 1976); Barbara Makhalis (Ndebele, play, 1976).

Rhodesia Scientific Association Gold Medal

Established in 1975 on the Association's 75t anniversary, this annual prize is awarded fo outstanding contributions to scientific knowledg in Rhodesia by any scientist working in Rhodesi The work must have been completed in th previous two years.
Awarding body: Rhodesia Scientific Associatio P.O.B. 978, Salisbury, Rhodesia.
Recipients: Dr. R. Barnes (breeding of Pinu Patula, 1975); Dr. M. Coulton (biology of Tilapi 1976).

John Llewellyn Rhys Memorial Prize

This annual prize was established in 1942 by th widow of John Llewellyn Rhys, a writer-airma killed in action who was posthumously awarded the Hawthornden Prize (*q.v.*). The value of the award is currently £300 and it is given to a writer under 30 from the British Commonwealth for the most promising literary work published in the previous year.

Awarding body: National Book League, 7 Albemarle St., London W1X 4BB, England.

Recipients include: Richard Cork (*Vorticism*, 1977); Andrew Wilson (*The Sweets of Pimlico*, 1978).

Robert H. Richards Award

This award is made annually by the American Institute of Mining, Metallurgical, and Petroleum Engineers for achievement in furthering the art of mineral beneficiation in any of its branches. Candidates of all nationalities are eligible, provided they are proposed by a member of the Institute and have not previously received an Institute award. This award, a silver plaque, was established by the Institute in 1948 in memory of Robert Hallowell Richards, Professor of Mining and Metallurgy at the Massachusetts Institute of Technology.

Awarding body: American Institute of Mining, Metallurgical, and Petroleum Engineers, Inc., 345 East 47th St., New York, N.Y. 10017, U.S.A.

Recipients include: John Dixon Vincent (1973); Robert S. Shoemaker (1974); Douglas W. Fuerstenau (1975); Donald A. Dahlstrom (1976); Denis F. Kelsall (1977).

David Richardson Medal

In setting up the Richardson Medal the Directors of the Optical Society sought to recognize the unique contribution to applied optics and spectroscopy made by David Richardson. The award, which was endowed by Howard Cary, is presented for a distinguished contribution primarily to technical optics, but not necessarily in a manner manifested by an extensive published record or traditional academic reputation. David Richardson received the first award in 1966 for his distinctive contributions to the ruling and replicating of gratings.

Awarding body: Optical Society of America, 2000 L St., N.W., Washington, D.C. 20036, U.S.A.

Recipients include: William G. Fastie (1972); Roderic M. Scott (1974); Karl Lambrecht (1975); John H. McLeod (1976); Walter P. Siegmund (1977).

Rickey Medal

This prize was established in 1947 by Mrs. Rickey in honour of her husband, James W. Rickey, M.ASCE, a leader in hydroelectric engineering. The medal is normally given annually for a paper in hydroelectric engineering which has been published by the Society during the preceding year. Non-members of the Society are eligible, and the prize is usually given to papers not selected for other Society prizes during that year. The prize consists of a gold medal, bronze duplicate and certificate.

Awarding body: American Society of Civil Engineers, 345 East 47th St., New York, N.Y. 10017, U.S.A.

Recipients include: Committee on Hydro Power Project Planning and Design of the Power Division ('Pumped Storage: State-of-the-Art', 1972); Wallace L. Chadwick (1974); Edward Loane and Franklyn Rogers (1976).

Riddell Memorial Lectures

Founded in 1928 at the University of Newcastle upon Tyne, these lectures are in memory of Sir John Walter Buchanan-Riddell, Bart., and are given in alternate years on a subject concerning the relation between religion and contemporary development of thought. The lectures are published.

Awarding body: University of Newcastle upon Tyne, 6 Kensington Terrace, Newcastle upon Tyne NE1 7RU, England.

Lecturers include: Prof. D. M. MacKinnon (Prof. of Divinity, Cambridge Univ., 1970); Prof. Desmond Pond (Prof. of Psychiatry, London Hospital Medical Coll., 1971); Prof. Kathleen Coburn (Prof. of English, Univ. of Toronto, 1973); B. R. Wilson (Reader in Sociology, Oxford Univ., 1974); Prof. D. M. Mackay (Prof. of Communication, Keele Univ., 1977).

Riddet Award

This award is presented to authors of an article or paper published in the previous year's volume of the *New Zealand Journal of Dairy Science and Technology*, judged to be the most significant contribution to dairy science and technology. It was established in 1970 by the Dairy Science Section of the New Zealand Society of Dairy Science and Technology in memory of Professor William Riddet, Logan Campbell Professor of Agriculture and Professor of Dairying, Massey Agricultural College from 1927 to 1956. The award is made annually and consists of a certificate and a cash prize. Only authors under 35 years of age are eligible.

Awarding body: Dairy Science Section, New Zealand Society of Dairy Science and Technology.

Recipients include: M. Parkin; Dr. K. Marshall; Dr. D. Newstead; Dr. T. Thomas; Dr. W. B. Sanderson.

Rink-medalje

This silver medal is presented occasionally by the Greenland Society of Denmark to persons who have made eminent contributions to the exploration of Greenland or to the service of its people. It was established in 1961, in honour of Hinrich J. Rink (1819–93), geologist, cartographer and ethnologist.

Awarding body: Det grønlandske Selskab, 'Kraemerhus', L. E. Bruunsvej 10, 2920 Charlottenlund, Denmark.

Recipients: Dr. Lauge Koch (geological research, 1961); Frederik Nielsen (literary and public service, 1972).

Rivers Memorial Medal

This award was established in 1923 in memory of William Halse Rivers (1864–1922), the physician and anthropologist who took part in the Cambridge University Torres Strait Expedition to New Guinea and Australia in 1898. It is made annually (sometimes two awards are made in one year) for a body of published work on social, physical or cultural anthropology or archaeology. The work must be recent and must have been published over a period of about five years.

Awarding body: Royal Anthropological Institute of Great Britain and Ireland, 36 Craven St., London WC2N 5NG, England.

Recipients include: Prof. Isaac Schapera (1939); Prof. Sir Raymond Firth (1940); Prof. Sir Eric Thompson (1945); Prof. Max Gluckman (1954); Prof. Sir Edmund Leach (1958).

Alexander Robertson Lectureship

The lectureship was founded in 1901 by the Rev. Alexander Robertson for the defence of the Christian religion. The lecturer is appointed not oftener than once every two years by the Glasgow University Court on the nomination of a committee. He must give not fewer than five lectures. These are open to the public.

Awarding body: University of Glasgow, Glasgow G12 8QQ, Scotland.

Lecturers include: Friedrich Gogarten (Prof. of Theology, Göttingen Univ., 1956); Helmut R. Niebuhr (Sterling Prof. of Theology and Christian Ethics, Yale Univ. Divinity School, 1958); Rev. A. R. Vidler (Fellow and Dean, King's Coll., Cambridge, 1964); Prof. Günther Bornkamm (Heidelberg Univ., 1967).

James Alexander Robertson Memorial Prize

The prize was established in 1953 by the Conference on Latin American History, and the terms of reference were amended in 1957. It is awarded annually for an article appearing during the preceding year in one of the four consecutive issues (beginning with the August issue) of the *Hispanic American Historical Review*. The winning article should make an outstanding contribution to Latin American historical literature. The prize carries a $100 award.

Awarding body: Conference on Latin American History, University of Wisconsin-Milwaukee, College of Letters and Science, Center for Latin America, P.O.B. 413, Milwaukee, Wis. 53201, U.S.A.

Recipients include: Friedrich Katz ('Labor Conditions on Haciendas in Porfirian Mexico: Some Trends and Tendencies', 1974); William B. Taylor ('Landed Society in New Spain: A View from the South', 1975); Charles W. Bergquist ('The Political Economy of the Colombian Presidential Election of 1897', 1976).

Robinson Medal

The Library Association established this biennial award in 1968 in honour of Frederick Robinson, former Deputy Borough Librarian of Colchester. It rewards the originality and inventive ability of librarians and other interested persons or organizations in devising new and improved methods in library technology and any aspect of library administration. Devices submitted must have been shown to be effective during the preceding five years, and of wide application or national significance.

Awarding body: The Library Association, Ridgmount St., London WC1E 7AE, England.

Recipients include: Frank Gurney (computer book-changing, 1970); University of Lancaster Library Research Unit (development of simulation games in education for library management 1972).

Robert Robinson Lectureship

The lectureship was founded in 1962 as a result of an endowment received by the Chemical Society from the Sir Robert Robinson Foundation Inc. which was created to receive the royalties donated by the authors of *Perspectives in Organic Chemistry* published in commemoration of Sir Robert Robinson's 70th birthday, and supplemented by contributions from other sources. The lecture which should review progress in any branch of chemistry, is given once every two years, on the occasion of the Society's Annual Congress. The lecturer receives a silver medal and £100.

Awarding body: The Chemical Society, Burlington House, London W1V 0BN, England.

Recipients include: Sir Derek Barton (1970); J. W. Cornforth (1972); M. J. S. Dewar (1974); A. Eschenmoser (1976); Sir Ewart Jones (1978).

Rodda Award

This annual award, named after a past president of the Society of Automotive Engineers – Australasia, takes the form of a medal and a cash prize of A$500. It is made to a member of the Society of any grade who has submitted an outstanding written paper to the Society (in any of its regional divisions) during the previous calendar year. The paper should be concerned with original work and ideas in the fields of design, development, research or management relevant to the automotive industry. Nominations are made by Divisions or independent Group Committees to the Society's Council.

Awarding body: Society of Automotive Engineers – Australasia, National Science Centre, 191 Royal Parade, Parkville, Vic. 3052, Australia.

Rodman Medal

This is awarded for outstanding work in the field of photography, preferably in relation to photomicrography or radiography.

Awarding body: The Royal Photographic Society of Great Britain, 14 South Audley St., London W1Y 5DP, England.

Recipients include: Dr. G. W. W. Stevens (1973); Godfrey Hounsfield (1975).

Ralph Coats Roe Award

The $1,000 annual award is funded by Kenneth A. Roe of Burns and Roe, Inc. in honour of his distinguished father, the co-founder of the comany, and is sponsored by the Mechanical ngineering Division of the ASEE. The award ecognizes a mechanical engineering educator who an outstanding teacher and who has made a otable professional contribution. Nominations re made by any member of the Division although ne nominee need not be a member of the Division r of the ASEE. The recipient must be a full-time nember of a college faculty and actively engaged n teaching in the United States or Canada at the ime of the award.

Awarding body: American Society of Engineering Iducators, Suite 400, One Dupont Circle, Washington, D.C. 20036, U.S.A.

Recipients include: John R. Dixon (1976).

Ralph Coats Roe Medal

This medal was established in 1972 in memory of Ralph Coats Roe, the pioneer and innovator in he design and construction of highly efficient ower plants and advanced desalting processes. The medal is presented annually, if warranted, to he individual selected by the American Society of Mechanical Engineers, for a significant contribuion to a better public understanding and appreiation of the engineer's worth to contemporary ociety. Candidates are not restricted by profession or by membership in any engineering society or rganization. The successful candidate is expected o have the attributes that qualify him as an uthoritative lecturer on his contribution at a reneral session during the winter annual meeting. The award includes a bronze medal, a certificate, n honorarium of $1,000 plus travel expenses.

Awarding body: American Society of Mechanical Engineers, United Engineering Center, 345 East 17th St., New York, N.Y. 10017, U.S.A.

Recipients include: Emilio Q. Daddario (1974); Walter Sullivan (1975).

David Röell-prijs

In 1963 the Prince Bernhard Fund established a orize in memory of Dr. David Röell who had been Director of the Rijksmuseum in Amsterdam, and a nember of the Fund committee. A sum of 15,000 guilders is awarded every two years in recognition of a Dutch artist's contribution to the nation's cultural life. The prize is given for the artist's complete works, and includes the applied and plastic arts and architecture.

Awarding body: Prins Bernhard Fonds, Leidsegracht 3, Amsterdam C, The Netherlands.

Recipients include: Otto Treumann (1970); Lies Cosijn (1972); Constant (1974); Lucassen (1976).

Romanes Lectureship

In 1891 the University of Oxford accepted the offer of the late George John Romanes, LL.D., F.R.S., of a sum for an annual lecture on some subject relating to science, art or literature.

Awarding body: University of Oxford, Wellington Square, Oxford OX1 2JD, England.

Lecturers include: Sir Karl Popper ('On the Problem of Body and Mind', 1972); Sir Ernst Gombrich ('Art History and the Social Sciences', 1973); Rt. Hon. Lord Zuckerman ('Advice and Responsibility', 1974); Iris Murdoch ('Why Plato Banished the Artists', 1976).

Romanian Architects' Union Annual Award

This award consists of a certificate and cash prize and was established in 1953. It is awarded for work of outstanding quality in architecture or planning, completed in the previous year. The award is open to any member of the Union of Architects.

Awarding body: Union of Architects of the Romanian Socialist Republic, 18–20 Academiei St., 70109 Bucharest, Romania.

Recipients include: Prof. Dr. Arch. Octav Doicescu (long-term achievement in architecture, 1972); Prof. Arch. Alexandru Iotzu (National Theatre in Craiova, 1973); Arch. Bujor Gheorghiu, Arch. Nicolae Vladescu and team (National Physics Centre, Bucharest-Măgurele, 1974); Arch. Mircea Dima, Arch. Traian Stănescu, Arch. Constantin Jugurică, Eng. Ioan Ciobotaru and team (Bucharest town planning scheme, 1975).

Romanian Artists' Union Grand Prize

The prize was founded in 1968 and is given annually for exceptional achievement in the field of fine arts (for the execution of a particular piece of work, for a one-man exhibition, for participation in international exhibitions, etc.). The prize is a cash award of 25,000 lei, and is open only to Romanian artists who are members of the Union.

Awarding body: Romanian Artists' Union, Calea Victoriei 155, Sec. 1, Bucharest, Romania.

Recipients include: Milița Petrașcu (sculptor, 1972); Ovidiu Maitec (sculptor, 1973); Dan Haulica (art critic, 1974); Paul Vasilescu (sculptor, 1975).

Romanian Cinema Workers' Association Prizes

In 1971 the Association inaugurated a competition for cinema and television films. It awards 22 annual prizes in different categories for the best short and full-length films, and for documentaries, scientific and animated cartoon films. The films should have first appeared during the preceding calendar year. The prizes consist of a diploma or plaque, and a sum of money which varies according to the prize. The main prize is the Grand Prize which usually goes to the director of the best film, and other prizes are given for best actor, actress, music, screenplay, etc.

Awarding body: Cinema Workers' Association of the S.R. of Romania, 65 Gheorghe Gheorghiu-Dej blvd., Sector 6, Bucharest, Romania.

Recipients include: Malvina Urşianu (Grand Prize, *The Transient Loves,* 1974); Dan Pişa and Mircea Verciu (best direction, *The Spirit of Gold,* 1974); Andrei Blaier (best direction, *Illustrated Postcards with Wild Flowers,* 1975).

Romanian Composers' Union Prize

The prize was established in 1968 and is awarded annually in principle, but often less frequently, for work in the fields of musical composition (all kinds) and musicology. The prize money varies according to the work concerned (opera, symphony, monograph, critical edition, etc.), but is between 3,000 and 10,000 lei. More than one prize is given each year. Prize-winners must be members of the Union. The presentation ceremony takes place at a meeting with all members present, and is followed by a concert at which the winning pieces are performed.

Awarding body: Composers' Union of Romania, Str. Constantin Esarcu 2, Bucharest, Romania.

Romanian Socialist Republic State Prize

The prize was established in 1949 and is given every two years to those who, individually or collectively, create works of great value which contribute to the development of arts and science and to the achievement of the socialist ideal. Winners are given the title 'State Prize Laureate', a sum of money (20,000 to 50,000 lei) and a special badge. Prizes are awarded in all branches of arts, science and technology.

Awarding body: State Prize Committee, Government of the S.R. of Romania, Bucharest, Romania.

Romantic Novelists' Association Major Award

Established in 1960, this annual award is for the best romantic novel of the year. It is open to both members and non-members of the RNA. Entries may be modern or historical (pre-1910), and are eligible only if published in the U.K. in the previous calendar year. A trophy is presented at an annual dinner in May.

Awarding body: Romantic Novelists' Association, Bells Farm House, Spurriers Lane, Melling, nr. Liverpool, Merseyside L31 1BA, England.

Recipients include: Frances Murray (*The Burning Lamp*, 1974); Jay Allerton (*Vote for a Silk Gown*, 1975); Anna Gilbert (*The Look of Innocence*, 1976); Madeleine Brent (*Merlin's Keep*, 1978).

Röntgen-Plakette

This bronze medal has been given annually since 1951 by the West German city of Remscheid, in commemoration of Wilhelm Conrad Röntgen (1845–1923), discoverer of X-rays and founder of medical radiology, who was born in Lennep (now Remscheid-Lennep), a small town near Remscheid in North Rhine-Westphalia. It honours outstanding developments in the field of the X-ray sciences.

Awarding body: Oberbürgermeister der Stadt Remscheid, Federal Republic of Germany.

Recipients include: Prof. Dr. Werner Teschendorf (Canary Islands, 1972); Drs. Liane B. and William L. Russell (U.S.A., 1973); Dr. Frans W. Saris (Netherlands, 1974); Prof. Dr. Wilhelm Hanle (Fed. Rep. of Germany, 1975); Prof. Dr. Josef Becker (Fed. Rep. of Germany, 1976).

Röntgen-Preis

The prize was established in 1974 by the two companies Arthur Pfeiffer GmbH of Wetzlar, and Schunk & Ebe GmbH of Heuchelheim-Giessen,

in commemoration of W. C. Röntgen, who was professor of physics at the University of Giessen from 1879 to 1888. The award is initially guaranteed for six years until 1980. It is awarded primarily to younger scientists in recognition of outstanding written or other contributions to basic research in radio-physics and radio-biology. The prize is DM5,000 and is awarded annually, provided that a suitable recipient is found. A board, consisting of representatives of the two founder companies and the University of Giessen, decides the winner from nominations put forward by a prize committee. In special cases the prize money may be split between several winners.

Awarding body: Justus Liebig-Universität Giessen, 6300 Giessen 2, Ludwigstr. 23, Postfach 21440, Federal Republic of Germany.

Richard and Hinda Rosenthal Foundation Awards

These two awards were established in 1957 by the Richard and Hinda Rosenthal Foundation. A literary award is granted annually for an American novel published during the preceding 12 months which, though not a commercial success, is a considerable literary achievement. A second annual award is given to a young American painter of distinction who has not yet been accorded due recognition. Each award consists of a cash sum of $2,000.

Awarding body: American Academy and Institute of Arts and Letters, 633 West 155th St., New York, N.Y. 10032, U.S.A.

Carl-Gustaf Rossby Research Medal

This annual award, comprising a gold medal and certificate, is presented for outstanding contributions to Man's understanding of the structure or behaviour of the atmosphere. It is the highest award bestowed by the American Meteorological Society.

Awarding body: American Meteorological Society, 45 Beacon St., Boston, Mass. 02108, U.S.A.

Recipients include: Joseph Smagorinsky (1972); Christian E. Junge (1973); Heinz H. Lettau (1974); Charles H. B. Priestley (1975); Hans A. Panofsky (1976).

Thomas Fitch Rowland Prize

The prize was originally instituted by the American Society of Civil Engineers at their Annual Meeting in 1882. It was endowed in 1884 by Thomas Fitch Rowland, past Vice President and Hon. M.ASCE. The award is given to papers describing in detail accomplished works of construction, their cost, and errors in design and execution. The prize consists of a wall plaque and certificate. It is not restricted to members of the Society.

Awarding body: American Society of Civil Engineers, 345 East 47th St., New York, N.Y. 10017, U.S.A.

Recipients include: Russell C. Borden and Carl E. Selander ('Application of Epoxy Resins in Tunnel

ining Concrete Repair', 1974); Daniel J. Smith, . ('Repair of Earthquake Damaged Underound Reservoir', 1976).

oyal Aeronautical Society Bronze Medal

his medal is awarded annually for work leading an advance in aeronautics. It was founded by e Society in 1908.
Awarding body: The Royal Aeronautical Society, Hamilton Place, London W1V 0BQ, England.
Recipients include: Prof. C. G. van Niekerk 972); R. W. Howard (1973); A. B. Haines 974); R. L. Bickerdike (1975); I. C. Taig 976).

oyal Aeronautical Society Gold Medal

his medal is awarded annually for work of an itstanding nature in aeronautics. It was founded 1909 and is the Society's highest honour.
Awarding body: The Royal Aeronautical Society, Hamilton Place, London W1V 0BQ, England.
Recipients include: Prof. A. D. Young (1972); andel Davies (1973); F. W. Page (1974); Prof. . Keith-Lucas (1975); Dr. W. J. Strang (1976).

oyal Aeronautical Society Silver Medal

his medal is awarded annually for work of an itstanding nature in aeronautics. It was founded y the Society in 1909.
Awarding body: The Royal Aeronautical Society, Hamilton Place, London W1V 0BQ, England.
Recipients include: Dr. J. Seddon (1972); W. J. harnley (1973); H. Zeffert (1974); Prof. W. A. lair (1975); L. F. Nicholson (1976).

oyal Architectural Institute of Canada llied Arts Medal

his award is made in recognition of outstanding chievement in the arts connected with archicture, such as mural paintings, sculpture, ecorations, stained glass and industrial design. he award, a silver medal, is presented at least very three years but not more often than once a ear. It was established in 1953 and is open to rtists of any nationality.
Awarding body: The Royal Architectural Insti- te of Canada.
Recipients include: Vancouver Art Kiosk Com- ittee and Art City Group (environmental design, 972); Charles Daudelin (sculptor, 1973); Ed rahanchuk (potter-designer, 1974); Thomas orrestall (artist, 1975); Micheline Beauchemin ainter, 1976).

oyal Architectural Institute of Canada Gold ledal

he medal was established in 1930. It is awarded recognition of outstanding achievements in the eld of architecture and contributions to the pro- ssion by a person of science or letters. The award ay be made annually to a candidate nominated y the Scholarships and Awards Committee of the istitute.
Awarding body: The Royal Architectural Insti- te of Canada.

Recipients include: Jean Drapeau (Mayor of Montreal, 1967); The Rt. Hon. Vincent Massey (fmr. Governor-General of Canada, 1968); Dr. Eric Arthur (Canadian architect, 1970); Prof. Serge Chermayeff (U.S. architect, 1973); Dr. Constantinos Doxiadis (Greece, 1976).

Royal College of Physicians of Canada Medal

This award is made annually to a graduate in medicine either of Canadian nationality, or whose nomination is based on work done in Canada, and who is less than 45 years of age. If the candidate is not himself a Fellow of the College, his application must be sponsored by a Fellow. The award is made for original work in the field of clinical investiga- tion, or in the basic sciences relating to medicine. The prize-winner receives a bronze medal and cash prize of $500.
Awarding body: Royal College of Physicians and Surgeons of Canada, 74 Stanley Ave., Ottawa, Ont. K1M 1P4, Canada.

Royal College of Physicians and Surgeons of Canada Lectures

At the College's annual meeting three lectures are incorporated into the scientific portion of the proceedings. They concentrate primarily on current and controversial practices in the medical and surgical sciences. They were instituted during the presidency of Dr. Wilder Graves Penfield (1939–41). The lecturers are selected by the incumbent President.
Awarding body: Royal College of Physicians and Surgeons of Canada, 74 Stanley Ave., Ottawa, Ont. K1M 1P4, Canada.
Recipients include: Dr. Pierre Grondin, Dr. Robert Laing Noble, Dr. W. B. Spaulding (1976); Dr. Jacques Genest, Dr. Lloyd D. MacLean, Dr. Hector F. DeLuca (1977).

Royal College of Surgeons of Canada Medal

This award is made annually to a graduate in medicine either of Canadian nationality, or whose nomination is based on work done in Canada, and who is less than 45 years of age. If the candidate is not himself a Fellow of the College, his application must be sponsored by a Fellow. The award is made for original work in the field of clinical investiga- tion, or in the basic sciences relating to surgery. The prize-winner receives a bronze medal and cash prize of $500.
Awarding body: Royal College of Physicians and Surgeons of Canada, 74 Stanley Ave., Ottawa, Ont. K1M 1P4, Canada.

Royal College of Surgeons of England Honorary Medal

Established in 1802, a gold medal is awarded for liberal acts or distinguished labours, researches and discoveries eminently conducive to the im- provement of natural knowledge and of the healing art. The medal is accompanied by a document declaratory of the award. Members of the Council of the Royal College of Surgeons are not eligible.

Awarding body: The Royal College of Surgeons of England, 35–43 Lincoln's Inn Fields, London WC2A 3PN, England.

Recipients include: Bruce Wilfred Goodman (1973); Norman Leslie Capener, C.B.E. (1974); Lord Kindersley, C.B.E., M.S. (1974); Lord Brock of Wimbledon (1975); Leslie Norman Pyrah, C.B.E. (1975).

Royal Danish Academy of Sciences and Letters Medals

The Academy awards two medals: the gold for a highly distinguished scholarly achievement; and the silver for one outstanding book or paper, or for scholarly achievement over five years. The gold medal was established by the Academy in 1769, and is awarded irregularly to anyone except Academy members. The silver medal was established in 1781 and has recently been combined with several 18th-century cash awards amounting to Dkr.5,000; it is awarded one year with one of these stipends, and the next year with three combined stipends. It is awarded to young Danish scholars for work in the fields of agriculture or industry.

Awarding body: Det Kongelige Danske Videnskabernes Selskab, 5 Dantes Plads, DK-1556 Copenhagen V, Denmark.

Recipients include: Dr.agro. Hans Laurits Jensen (gold, for lifelong studies of soil microbiology, 1971); Lic.agro. Gunnar Gissel Nielsen (silver, 1973); Fil.dr. Georg Galster (gold, for lifelong studies in numismatics, 1974); Dr.med.vet. Folke Rasmussen and Cand.mag. Claus Bjørn (silver, 1976); Dr.phil. Jørgen Hæstrup (gold, for works on Danish history during World War II, 1977); Dr. med. vet. Erik Brummerstedt (silver, 1977).

Royal Gold Medal for the Promotion of Architecture

This award was instituted in 1848 by Queen Victoria, and is conferred annually by the Sovereign on a distinguished architect or group of architects for work of high merit, or on some other distinguished person whose work has promoted the advancement of architecture. The Royal Institute of British Architects submits nominations and administers the scheme. The medal cannot be awarded posthumously; there are no other restrictions as to eligibility.

Awarding body: Royal Institute of British Architects, London, England.

Recipients include: Sir Leslie Martin (1973); Powell & Moya (1974); Michael Scott (1975); Sir John Summerson, C.B.E. (1976); Sir Denys Lasdun (1977); Jörn Utzon (1978).

Royal Institute of British Architects Architecture Awards

These awards are made annually for buildings which are considered to be outstanding examples of current architecture and excellent of their kind. The awards were established in 1966, superseding the RIBA Bronze Medal which dates back to 1922. The awards are organized on a regional basis; there are 13 regions covering the U.K. and Northern Ireland. A plaque is awarded for each winning building, and diplomas presented to the architects, building owner and building contractor. Buildings should have been completed within a two-year period ending 31 October of the year preceding the award. The architect responsible or, in the case of a firm, at least one of the partners, should be a member of the Institute. Nominations are submitted by Institute members.

Awarding body: Royal Institute of British Architects, London, England.

Recipients include: Bristol Roman Catholic Cathedral (Percy Thomas Partnership, 1974); Herman Miller Factory, Bath (Farrell Grimshaw Partnership), National Theatre, London (Sir Denys Lasdun), Sainsbury Centre, East Anglia Univ., Norwich (Foster Associates), 1978.

Royal Institution of Chartered Surveyors and The Times Conservation Awards Scheme

The scheme, administered by the Institution and run in conjunction with *The Times*, was launched in 1971 as part of the Institution's contribution to European Conservation Year. Various awards are made for outstanding work in the conservation field; they are intended to encourage local authorities, commercial enterprises, private property owners, architects and others to contribute to the preservation and improvement of the physical environment. Special attention is given to the economic aspects of projects. Each year a different theme such as that of industrial projects, coast and countryside or architectural heritage is chosen. Entries are divided into two categories and the winners in each group receive a silver plate and bronze plaques for erection on the winning schemes. Plaques are also presented to the second and third prize-winners in each group. Prize-winners and commendations also receive certificates.

Awarding body: The Royal Institution of Chartered Surveyors, 29 Lincoln's Inn Fields, London WC2A 3DG, England.

Recipients include: Leicestershire County Council (The Battlefield of Bosworth, 1975); James M Kerr, Esq. (Easton Farm Park, Suffolk, 1975); Borough of Berwick-upon-Tweed (conservation and redevelopment of West End, Tweedmouth, 1976); Northamptonshire County Council (Duddington Area Conservation Scheme, 1976).

Royal Medals

Three Royal Medals, known also as The Queen's Gold Medals, are awarded annually by the Sovereign upon the recommendation of the Council of the Royal Society, two for the most important contributions to the advancement of Natural Knowledge (one to each of the two great divisions) and the other for distinguished contributions in the applied sciences, published originally in Her Majesty's Dominions within a period of not more than ten years, and of not less than one year of the date of the award.

Awarding body: Royal Society of London, 6 Carlton House Terrace, London SW1Y 5AG, England.

Recipients include: Prof. J. W. Cornforth, Prof. J. L. Gowans, Dr. A. Walsh (1976); Sir Peter Hirsch (1977); Prof. A. Salam, Prof. R. A. Gregory, Prof. T. Kilburn (1978).

Royal Medals (Founder's and Patron's)

These are awarded by the reigning monarch (the Patron), on the recommendation of the Council of the Royal Geographical Society. They originated from a gift made in 1831 by King William IV (the Founder), 'to contribute a premium for the encouragement and promotion of geographical science and discovery'. King William established the Founder's Medal in 1836. The Patron's Medal was established in 1839 on the recommendation of the Society's Council. The two medals are equal in value and distinction and they are awarded annually to persons of any nationality, age or sex. There is no application; the medals are granted by the Society's Council on the recommendation of a special committee, the criteria being the academic and other achievements of the recipients. The presentation is made at the Society's Annual Meeting in June.

Awarding body: Royal Geographical Society, 1 Kensington Gore, London SW7 2AR, England.

Recipients include: Christian Bonington (1974); Dr. B. B. Roberts (Founder's, 1976); Rear-Admiral Sir Edmund Irving (Patron's, 1976); Prof. Michael Wise (Founder's, 1977); Major-Gen. R. Ll. Brown (Founder's, 1978); Dr. Miezyslaw Klimaszewski (Patron's, 1978).

Royal Over-Seas League Music Festival

The Festival was established in 1952 and is held annually in the spring and early summer. It is intended to encourage young musicians from the United Kingdom and Commonwealth countries. Various prizes are awarded in different categories. Two prizes of £500 each are given for the best performers from the U.K. and from overseas (including former Commonwealth countries). Other prizes are: the Stella Murray Memorial Prize of £150 for the best New Zealand musician; the Miller Prize of £150 for ensembles; the Eric Rice Memorial Prize of £50 for accompanists; the Australian Musicians Overseas Scholarship Society Prize of £500 for Australian pianists (biennial); the Society of Women Musicians Prize of £200 awarded alternately to a female composer and a female performer. Age limits are under 25 for instrumentalists and under 30 for singers.

Awarding body: Royal Over-Seas League, Over-Seas House, Park Place, St. James's St., London SW1A 1LR, England.

Royal Prize

This award was instituted in 1835 by King Karl XIV Johan of Sweden and is administered by the Swedish Academy. It consists of a variable monetary prize, and is presented annually to a Swedish citizen for cultural, literary or artistic work. It cannot be applied for.

Awarding body: The Swedish Academy, Börshuset, Källargränd 4, S-111 29 Stockholm, Sweden.

Royal Scottish Geographical Society Gold Medal

The Society established the medal in 1890 for work of conspicuous merit within the science of geography itself, e.g. by research, whether in the field or otherwise, or by any other contribution or cumulative service to the advancement of geography. It is awarded irregularly, and there are no restrictions as to eligibility.

Awarding body: Royal Scottish Geographical Society, 10 Randolph Crescent, Edinburgh EH3 7TU, Scotland.

Recipients include: Prof. J. A. Steers (contributions to geography, 1969); W. W. Herbert (journey from Canada to Spitsbergen via the North Pole, 1969); Neil Armstrong (first man on the moon, 1972); Lt.-Col. John Blashford Snell (organization and leadership of three expeditions, 1974); 1975 British Everest Expedition (successful ascent of Mt. Everest by the South West Face, 1975).

Royal Society of Arts Bicentenary Medal

The medal was established in 1954 by the Royal Society of Arts to celebrate the Society's bicentenary. It is awarded annually to persons who 'in a manner other than as industrial designers have exerted an exceptional influence in promoting art and design in British industry'.

Awarding body: Royal Society of Arts, John Adam St., Adelphi, London WC2N 6EZ, England.

Recipients include: Leslie and Rosamund Julius (1972); James S. Cousins (1973); Geoffrey E. Dunn (1974); Viscount Eccles (1975); Jack Pritchard (1976).

Royal Society of Medicine Gold Medal

This is awarded every three years to a scientist who has made valuable contributions to the science and art of medicine.

Awarding body: Royal Society of Medicine, 1 Wimpole St., London W1M 8AE, England.

Royal Society for the Protection of Birds Gold Medal

The medal was designed by Aubrey Hayward Jones in 1906 and was initially instituted as first prize in an essay competition. It has subsequently become an award for consistent and exceptional services to bird protection. The medal is awarded at the discretion of the Society's Council, usually annually, and any fully paid-up member of the Society is eligible.

Awarding body: Royal Society for the Protection of Birds, England.

Recipients include: Sir Kenneth Swan (1962); Lord Hurcomb (1967); Eric Hosking (1974); Charles Tunnicliffe (1975); Peter Conder (1976).

Royal Society of Tasmania Medal

Awarded for prolonged research of high merit, this medal is conferred irregularly by the General Meeting of the Society on the recommendation of the Society's Council. Only members of the Royal Society of Tasmania may receive the award, which was established in 1927.

Awarding body: Royal Society of Tasmania, G.P.O. Box 1166M, Hobart, Tasmania 7001, Australia.

Recipients include: A. N. Lewis (1935); V. V. Hickman and W. E. L. Crowther (1940); O. L. Serventy (1970); Donald Martin (1976).

Royal Society of Victoria Medal

This award of a silver medal was instituted in 1959 by the Royal Society of Victoria, the oldest scientific society in the State, to commemorate its centenary year. It is made for distinguished scientific work which must have been carried out in Australia or on Australia, with preference being given to work done in or on Victoria. The award is made on the basis of material published in the preceding six calendar years. In 1974 it was decided that the medal would be presented for work in the fields of natural, physical and social sciences in turn. Nominations must take the form of a written statement by a sponsor, testifying to the merit of the candidate, submitted to the Council of the Society. The award is generally made annually.

Awarding body: Royal Society of Victoria, Royal Society's Hall, 9 Victoria St., Melbourne, Vic. 3000, Australia.

Recipients include: Dr. D. Metcalf (*Studies on myeloid leukaemia,* 1973) and Dr. J. H. Willis (*Taxonomy of Victorian flora,* 1973); Dr. A. W. Snyder (*Physics of vision, optical physics,* 1974); Prof. R. Taft (*Adjustment of immigrants to life in Australia,* 1975); Prof. R. L. Specht (*Ecology of plant communities in Australia and Papua New Guinea,* 1976).

Royal Society of Western Australia Medal

This award is made every four years (more frequently if the Council so decides), for distinguished scientific work connected with Western Australia. It was instituted in 1924 to mark the centenary of the birth of Lord Kelvin (1824–1907), the eminent British physicist.

Awarding body: The Royal Society of Western Australia Inc., c/o Western Australia Museum, Francis St., Perth, Western Australia 6000.

Recipients include: Prof. E. de C. Clarke (geology, 1941); L. Glauert (zoology, 1945); C. A. Gardner (botany, 1949); Dr. H. W. Bennetts (veterinary pathology, 1955); Prof. E. J. Underwood (animal nutrition, 1959).

Royal Town Planning Institute Gold Medal

This award was established in 1953, and is made occasionally for outstanding achievement in the theory, practice or profession of town and country planning. It is open to people of all nationalities.

Awarding body: Royal Town Planning Institute, 26 Portland Place, London W1N 4BE, England.

Recipients include: Prof. Lord Holford (1961); Sir Frederick James Osborn (1963); Prof. Colin Douglas Buchanan, C.B.E. (1971); The Rt. Hon. Lord Silkin of Dulwich, C.H. (1971); Prof. Sir Robert Grieve (1974).

Rózsa Ferenc Prize for Journalism

Instituted by the Hungarian Council of Ministers in 1959, the prize is awarded annually by the Minister of Culture. It is an honorary distinction, divided into three classes, and given for outstanding journalistic activities in the furtherance of socialist society. It is awarded on Hungarian Press Day, 7 December, and is named after Ferenc Rózsa, who was killed in 1944 because of his activities as editor of *Szabad Nép* (Free People), an illegal newspaper.

Awarding body: Committee for the Rózsa Ferenc Prize, Ministry of Culture, Szalay-utca 10, Budapest V, Hungary.

Arthur Rubinstein Prize

The triennial Arthur Rubinstein International Piano Master Competition was established in 1973 by the Israel Festival Committee, on the initiative of its director, J. Bistritzky. It is sponsored by the Ministries of Education and Culture and of Tourism. The competition was founded in honour of the Polish pianist, Arthur Rubinstein (born 1887), who is its Honorary President. Pianists of all nationalities between the ages of 18 and 32 may compete for the prize, which is given for outstanding musicianship and a talent for persuasive, versatile rendering and creative interpretation of musical works, ranging from the pre-classical to the contemporary. The prize consists of a gold medal, $5,000, a diploma, and concert engagements and recording contracts. Additional gold, silver and bronze medals are awarded, as well as further cash prizes. Distinguished musicians form an international jury, which assesses the contestants' performances on a points system. All stages of the competition are held in public.

Awarding body: Arthur Rubinstein International Piano Master Competition, P.O.B. 29404, Shalom Tower, Tel-Aviv, Israel.

Recipients include: Emanuel Ax (U.S.A., 1974); Gerhard Oppitz (Fed. Rep. of Germany, 1977).

Friedrich-Rückert-Preis

This prize was established by the city of Schweinfurt in 1963 on the 175th anniversary of the birth of Friedrich Rückert (1788–1866), the poet. The prize is awarded to a person whose outstanding cultural and scientific achievements reflect the spirit of Rückert's work. It is awarded every three years and consists of a medal (the Friedrich-Rückert-Plakette), a certificate and a cash sum of DM5,000.

Awarding body: Oberbürgermeister der Stadt Schweinfurt, Stadtrat, Schweinfurt, Federal Republic of Germany.

Recipients include: Dr. Annemarie Schimmel (Fed. Rep. of Germany, 1965); Dr. Helmut Prang (Fed. Rep. of Germany, 1968); Prof. Albert Theile (Switzerland, 1971); Jean Mistler (France, 1974).

Rumford Medal

In 1800 Count Rumford, F.R.S., gave £1,000 to the Royal Society. The income from this fund provides a silver gilt medal and a gift of £200 which is awarded every two years 'to the author of the most important discovery or useful improvement which shall be made and published by printing or in any way made known to the public in any part of Europe during the preceding two years on Heat or on Light, the preference always being given to such discoveries as, in the opinion of the President and Council of the Royal Society, tend most to promote the good of mankind'.

Awarding body: Royal Society of London, 6 Carlton House Terrace, London SW1Y 5AG, England.

Recipients include: Dr. B. J. Mason (U.K., 1972); Sir Alan Cottrell (U.K., 1974); Prof. I. Prigogine (Belgium, 1976).

Benjamin Rush Lectureship on Psychiatric History

This lectureship was established by the American Psychiatric Association in 1967, with the support of Roche Laboratories. It is given annually on a broad theme related to the history of psychiatry, by a person who has been acclaimed for his contributions to this subject; he may belong to a discipline other than psychiatry, such as medical history, anthropology or sociology. The lecturer receives a $500 honorarium and expenses.

Awarding body: American Psychiatric Association, 1700 18th St., N.W., Washington, D.C. 20009, U.S.A.

George Russell (A.E. Memorial) Award

This award is made for, or in connection with, work of a literary character. It was established in 1939 from public subscriptions to the A.E. Memorial Fund, in memory of the late George Russell. The award consists of a cash prize of £100 and is made approximately every five years. The Trustee of the Fund gives notice of at least one month before the award is made so that candidates may submit their work for consideration. The award can be made for work already published, for unpublished work or for a plan of work, if it is of sufficient merit and interest. Only those of Irish birth and ordinarily resident in any part of Ireland, under the age of 35, are eligible.

Awarding body: The Governor and Company of the Bank of Ireland, Trustee Department, Head Office, Lower Baggot St., Dublin 2, Ireland.

Recipients include: Richard Murphy (collection of poems, 1951); Patrick O' Connor (excerpts from six works, 1957); Mr. McGahein (*A Novel*, 1961); Brendan Kinnealy *Collection One, Getting up Early,*

Good Souls to Survive, 1967); Seamus Deane (*Gradual Awards,* 1973).

Peter Nicol Russell Memorial Medal

This is the most prestigious award made by the Institution of Engineers, Australia. It is presented at the Annual General Meeting of the Institution for notable contributions to engineering in Australia. The winner, who must be a Fellow of the Institution and over 45 years of age, receives a bronze medal. The award was established in 1923 in memory of Sir Peter Nicol Russell (1816–1905), an industrialist, who played a major role in the development of the Engineering Association of New South Wales, the oldest engineering society in Australia at the time of the foundation of the Institution in 1919.

Awarding body: The Institution of Engineers, Australia.

Recipients include: Dr. W. H. R. Nimmo (1950); R. J. (Sir Russell) Dumas (1952); Dr. L. F. Loder (1954); L. R. (Sir Ronald) East (1957); Sir Albert Axon (1960).

Rutherford Medal and Prize

A bronze medal and a prize of £150 are awarded in even-dated years for contributions to nuclear physics, elementary particle physics or nuclear technology. The award was established in 1965 to replace the Rutherford Memorial Lecture, instituted by the Council of the Physical Society in 1939 in memory of Lord Rutherford of Nelson. Candidates are considered on the recommendation of members of the Institute of Physics and of its Awards Committee.

Awarding body: The Institute of Physics, 47 Belgrave Square, London SW1X 8QX, England.

Recipients include: Brian Hilton Flowers (1968); Samuel Devons (1970); Aage Bohr (1972); James MacDonald Cassels (1973); Albert Edward Litherland (1974).

Rutherford Memorial Lecture

The lecture was established in 1952 as part of the Rutherford Memorial Scheme of the Royal Society. It is delivered at selected university centres in the British Commonwealth overseas, at least one in three to be given in New Zealand.

Awarding body: Royal Society of London, 6 Carlton House Terrace, London SW1Y 5AG, England.

Lecturers include: Prof. S. K. Runcorn (1970); Prof. P. H. Fowler (1971); Prof. P. B. Moon (Monash University, Australia, 1975).

S

SANDOZ Award for Research in Cancer

This award was established in 1970 and is awarded annually to an eminent scientist for an outstanding contribution to cancer research which has been recognized nationally and internationally and has helped towards the control, prevention and cure of cancer. The award consists of 1,000 rupees and a gold medal.

Awarding body: Indian Council of Medical Research, Ansari Nagar, Post Box 4508, New Delhi 110016, India.

Recipients include: Dr. L. D. Sanghvi (1972); Dr. M. B. Sahasrabudho (1973); Dr. B. M. Braganca (1974); Dr. C. R. R. M. Reddy (1975); Dr. Kamal J. Ranadive (1976).

SANDOZ-Preis

This prize was established by the SANDOZ Research Institute on its foundation in 1970. The Institute is concerned with biological research and was founded by the Swiss chemical-pharmaceutical company, SANDOZ AG. The prize is awarded in five categories: biology, chemistry, medicine, human sciences and the arts. Each winner receives a cash prize of 40,000 Schillings and a certificate. The candidates are put forward by various Austrian universities and the winners are selected by a board made up of experts in the subjects concerned. Candidates must not be over 40 years of age.

Awarding body: SANDOZ Forschungsinstitut Gesellschaft m.b.H., 1235 Vienna, Brunner Strasse 59, Austria.

Recipients include: Alban Berg-Quartett (music, 1973); Prof. Dr. Friedrich Höfler (chemistry, 1973); Dr. Johannes Koder (Byzantine studies, 1974); Karl Korab (painting and drawing, 1975), Dr. Werner K. Waldhäusl (medicine, 1975); Dr. Elmar Bamberg (biochemistry, 1976).

S.A.U.K.-pryse (*S.A.B.C. Prizes*)

Since 1961 the Board of Management of the South African Broadcasting Corporation has made available a sum of money for awards for outstanding original radio drama and radio features (and from 1977 for television as well), in Afrikaans and English. The prize money currently amounts to R500 per award. Prizes are given alternately, one year for drama, one year for features, written and broadcast in the two preceding calendar years.

Awarding body: Suid-Afrikaanse Akademie vir Wetenskap en Kuns, Posbus 538, Pretoria 0001, South Africa.

Recipients include: Cobus Robinson (feature, *Die huis waar ek woon,* 1976); Geoff Sims (feature, *The eighteen-hour siege,* 1976); Ampie von Straten (drama, *Pendoring Edms Beperk,* 1977); Norman Partington (drama, *Demigod and Macvelli,* 1977); Annie Basson (TV, *Duskant die Groot See,* 1977).

Wallace Clement Sabine Medal

The medal is presented by the Acoustical Society of America to an individual of any nationality who has furthered the knowledge of architectural acoustics, through contributions to professional publications, or by other achievements.

Awarding body: Acoustical Society of America, 335 East 45th St., New York, N.Y. 10017, U.S.A.

Recipients include: Vern O. Knudsen (1957); Floyd R. Watson (1959); Leo L. Beranek (1961); Erwin Meyer (1964); Hale J. Sabine (1968); Lothar Cremer (1973).

Meghnad Saha Medal

This medal was established in 1957 by the Indian National Science Academy. It is awarded every three years for outstanding contributions in any branch of science falling within the scope of the Academy.

Awarding body: Indian National Science Academy, Bahadur Shah Zafar Marg, New Delhi 110001, India.

Recipients include: D. N. Wadia (1963); D. M. Bose (1965); C. R. Rao (1969); T. R. Seshadri (1971); T. R. Govindachari (1975).

Sahitya Akademi Awards (*National Academy of Letters Awards*)

Established in 1954 by the Indian Government, an annual award of a copper casket and a cash prize of Rs.5,000 is presented to an Indian national judged to have made an outstanding contribution to literature during the three preceding years. The Academy has recognized 22 languages and dialects, and awards may be made for work in each of these in any one year.

Awarding body: Sahitya Akademi, Rabindra Bhavan, 35 Ferozeshah Rd., New Delhi 110 001, India.

St. Olav's Medal

This award was instituted by King Haakon VII of Norway in 1939 in recognition of contributions to the promotion of knowledge about Norway in other countries and the promotion of close ties between expatriate Norwegians and the mother country. The medal is in silver.

Awarding body: Norwegian Government, Oslo, Norway.

Saltire Society Award for the Embellishment of Buildings in Scotland

Established by the Saltire Society in 1971, the award was given originally for sculpture and murals on public buildings in Scotland. It is now given for any embellishment which has been conceived as an integral part of a building at the planning stage. Artists and craftsmen who have designed and/or executed such an embellishment may enter their work for the award; the work must have been completed during the previous two years. The award is made approximately every three years, and takes the form of a scroll. The Society also names commended and highly commended artists and designers.

Awarding body: The Saltire Society, Saltire House, 13 Atholl Crescent, Edinburgh EH3, Scotland.

Recipients include: Alan Davie (designer) and George Garson (executor) (mosaic mural, York Square, Grangemouth, 1976).

Saltire Society Housing Design Award

Established in 1937 by the Saltire Society, the award was begun by Robert Hurd (1905–64), Edinburgh architect and Honorary Secretary of the Society. The award is given for good design in Scottish housing, and takes the form of a plaque for attachment to the winning building, and two scrolls, one for the commissioning authority and one for the architect; the builder receives a scroll or certificate. Owners, builders, public or semi-public bodies who have commissioned works in Scotland, and the architects employed by them, are all eligible. Awards are made annually in three categories: (i) new housing; (ii) restored or reconstructed Scottish housing; (iii) Scottish housing area improvements; (awards for categories (ii) and (iii) in alternate years). In all three categories the work must have been completed within the calendar year prior to the award.

Awarding body: The Saltire Society, Saltire House, 13 Atholl Crescent, Edinburgh EH3, Scotland.

Recipients include: Robert Hurd and Partners (Chessels' Court, Edinburgh (restoration), 1965); Ian G. Lindsay and Partners (Mylne's Court, Univ. of Edinburgh (restoration), 1970); Wheeler and Sproson (Ladyburn, nr. Kirkaldy (restoration), 1971); Michael Spens (Cleish Castle (restoration), 1973); Scottish Special Housing Association (Tweedbank, 1975).

Salzburger TV-Opernpreis (*Salzburg TV Opera Prize*)

This prize was established in 1956 by the city of Salzburg in collaboration with the Austrian Broadcasting Company, the International Music Council and the Vienna International Music Centre. The prize is awarded by a jury for a work which has not yet been produced but is outstanding musically and dramatically. It is awarded every three years and consists of a certificate and a cash sum of 125,000 Schillings. A second prize of 12,500 Schillings is awarded at the same time in recognition of merit. Works may be presented by any broadcasting station and must not be more than three years old.

Awarding body: Magistrat Salzburg, Abteilung II, Kulturamt, Salzburg, Austria.

Recipients include: Japanese Television (1962); Zweites Deutsches Fernsehen (1965); Swedish Television (1968); Danish Radio (1971); Japanese Television NHK (1974).

Samfundet de Nio's Stora Pris (*Nine Swedish Authors' Grand Prize*)

This award was established in 1916, with a legacy from the Swedish poet and author, Lotten von Kraemer, who devoted her life to literature. The prize is presented annually and is open to any author writing in Swedish. It is a cash award of 20,000 kronor.

Awarding body: Samfundet De Nio, Adolf Öhmans Advokatbyrå, Box 1703, 111 87 Stockholm, Sweden.

Recipients include: Frans G. Bengtson (1945); Karl Vennberg (1957); Evert Taube (1959); Erik Lindegren (1961); John Landquist (1971).

San Remo Film Festival

This exhibition of 'author films' – films written and directed by the same person – was founded in 1958 by Nino Zucchelli, who is still its Director. Its specific aim is to contribute to the promotion and development of quality film production and to favour the wider distribution of such films. The main award, the 'Gran Premio', totals 5 million lire and is divided equally between the director and the producer of the best film; gold medals are awarded for the best actor, best actress and the best musical score. The festival is held annually in March at San Remo.

Awarding body: Mostra Internazionale del Film d'Autore, Rotonda dei Mille 1, 24100 Bergamo, Italy.

Recipients (Grand Prize) include: Erkko Kivikoski (Finland, *Laukaus Tehtaalla*, 1973); Tenghis Abuladse (U.S.S.R., *Molba*) and Peter Bacso (Hungary, *Harmadik Nekifutas*), jointly, 1974; Tadashi Imai (Japan, *Takiji Kobayashi*, 1975); Ruszard Czekala (Poland, *Zofia*, 1977).

Sandberg Prize for Israel Art

Established in honour of Dr. Willem Sandberg, the prize of I£20,000 is awarded annually to an

Israeli artist at the International Council meetings of the Israel Museum.

Awarding body: The Israel Museum, P.O.B. 1299, Jerusalem 91000, Israel.

Recipients include: Avital Geva; Michael Druks; Joshua Neustein; Yehezkel Streichman; Anna Ticho.

Eugen-Sänger-Medaille

This prize was established in 1966 in honour of Eugen Sänger, a space scientist, by the German Society for Rocket Technology and Astronautics. The medal is awarded every two years for outstanding contributions to rocket technology and space science.

Awarding body: Deutsche Gesellschaft für Luft- und Raumfahrt e.V., Federal Republic of Germany.

Recipients include: Dr. Walter Dornberger (U.S.A., 1966); John V. Becker (U.S.A., 1968); Dr. George E. Mueller (U.S.A., 1970); Prof. Wernher von Braun (U.S.A., 1973); Dipl.-Ing. Hans Schneider (Fed. Rep. of Germany, 1975).

Shri Hari Om Ashram Prerit Dr. Vikram Sarabhai Award

This award was established in 1974 with an endowment to the Physical Research Laboratory by the Shri Hari Om Ashram (Foundation) in Nadiad, in the name of Dr. Sarabhai. Several awards are given annually for outstanding research in the following fields: electronics and telecommunications; planetary and space sciences; atmospheric physics and hydrology; systems analysis and management science. The winners (who must be under 45 years old) receive a gold medal and a cash sum of 4,000 rupees.

Awarding body: Physical Research Laboratory, Navrangpura, Ahmedabad 380009, India.

Recipients include: Dr. P. P. Kale, Dr. U. R. Rao, Dr. B. M. Reddy, Dr. N. Pant (1976).

David Sarnoff Gold Medal

Established in 1951, the medal is given annually for outstanding contributions to the development of new techniques or equipment which have contributed to the improvement of the engineering phases of television, including theatre television.

Awarding body: Society of Motion Picture and Television Engineers, 862 Scarsdale Ave., Scarsdale, N.Y. 10583, U.S.A.

Sarrazin Lecturer

The Canadian Physiological Society established this lecture in 1977. It is named after Michel Sarrazin (1659–1735), the physician and naturalist. A distinguished Canadian physiologist is invited to give an annual lecture at the Society's Winter Meeting; he receives a commemorative plaque.

Awarding body: Canadian Physiological Society.

Lecturers include: Dr. D. H. Copp (Univ. of British Columbia, 1977); Dr. L. B. Jaques (Univ. of Saskatchewan, 1978).

Sarton Medal

Established in 1955 by the History of Science Society, a medal and citation are awarded annually for distinguished service in the cause of the history of science.

Awarding body: History of Science Society, c/o The Secretary, School of Physics and Astronomy, University of Minnesota, Minneapolis, Minn. 55455, U.S.A.

Recipients include: Kiyosi Yabuuti (1972); Henry Guerlac (1973); I. Bernard Cohen (1974); René Taton (1975); Bern Dibner (1976).

Sarum Lectureship

By an Order of the High Court of Justice, Chancery Division, in 1952, in those years in which the Bampton Lecture (*q.v.*) is not delivered at the University of Oxford, the Sarum Lecture should be given. The stipend payable should not be more than that paid to the Bampton Lecturer of the previous year. The lecture should be 'in support of the Christian Faith'. The only qualification is that the lecturer should be a person of high scholarship who professes the Christian faith.

Awarding body: University of Oxford, Wellington Square, Oxford OX1 2JD, England.

Lecturers include: Rev. A. R. Vidler ('Catholic Modernists', 1968–69); H. H. Price ('Psychical Research and the Philosophy of Religions', 1970–71); Rev. E. J. Yarnold ('Nature and Grace', 1972–73); R. P. Ramsey (1974–75); Prof. J. S. Dunne (1976–77).

Sasaki Memorial Prize

This is an annual prize established in 1954 by the Japan Welding Society in memory of Dr. Shintaro Sasaki, Vice-President of the Society in 1938. It is awarded for distinguished achievement in the development and application of welding technology, or for contributions to education in the field of welding. It comprises a certificate and medal.

Awarding body: Yosetsu Gakkai, 1-11 Sakuma- cho Kanda, Chiyoda-ku, Tokyo, Japan.

William Lawrence Saunders Gold Medal

This award is made annually by the American Institute of Mining, Metallurgical, and Petroleum Engineers for distinguished achievement in the field of mining, other than coal. Candidates of all nationalities are eligible, provided they are proposed by a member of the Institute and have not previously received an Institute award. This award consists of a gold plaquette and certificate, and was established in 1927 as the Mining Medal with a donation from William Lawrence Saunders, President of the Institute in 1915. It was later renamed in his honour.

Awarding body: American Institute of Mining, Metallurgical, and Petroleum Engineers, 345 East 47th St., New York, N.Y. 10017, U.S.A.

Recipients include: Elmer Alonzo Jones (1970); Stanley M. Jarrett (1972); H. Myles Jacob (1974); Charles Dixon Clarke (1975); Frank Coolbaugh (1977).

Traian Săvulescu Prize

The prize was founded by the Romanian Academy in 1948 and is awarded for contributions to agriculture. It is presented annually at a General Assembly of the Academy, and consists of 10,000 lei and a diploma. It is named after Traian Săvulescu (1889–1963), university professor and sometime President of the Romanian Academy. He founded the Romanian school of phytopathology.

Awarding body: Academy of the S.R. of Romania, 125 Calea Victoriei, Bucharest, Romania.

R. Tom Sawyer Award

This award was established in 1972 to honour R. Tom Sawyer, who for over four decades toiled zealously to advance gas turbine technology in all of its aspects. The award is bestowed on an individual who has made important contributions to advance the purpose of the gas turbine industry and to the Gas Turbine Division of the American Society of Mechanical Engineers. The contribution may be in any area of Division activity but must be marked by sustained forthright efforts. The award consists of a bronze plaque bearing the Division emblem, the miniature turbine wheel.

Awarding body: American Society of Mechanical Engineers, United Engineering Center, 345 East 47th St., New York, N.Y. 10017, U.S.A.

Recipients include: R. Tom Sawyer (1972); John W. Sawyer (1973); Waheeb Rizk (1974); Bruce O. Buckland (1975); Curt Keller (1976).

Hugo H. Schaefer Award

The award was established in 1964 by the American Pharmaceutical Association to honour Dr. Schaefer for a lifetime of contributions to the profession of pharmacy, and in particular for his service to the Association. The prize is given in recognition of outstanding voluntary contributions to society as well as to the profession of pharmacy.

Awarding body: American Pharmaceutical Association, 2215 Constitution Ave., N.W., Washington, D.C. 20037, U.S.A.

Recipients include: E. Claiborne Robins (1969); Harry C. Shirkey (1971); Willard B. Simmons (1973); Gaylord A. Nelson (1974); Philip R. Lee (1976).

Schafarzik Medal

The Hungarian Hydrological Society founded the medal in 1943 to be awarded to those members of the Society who have achieved outstanding theoretical or practical results, and also contributed significantly to the development of the Society. Three medals are awarded annually. They are named after Ferenc Schafarzik (1854–1927), a professor at Budapest Technical University who carried out oil and gas prospecting in Transylvania.

Awarding body: Magyar Hidrológiai Társaság, 372 Budapest V, Kossuth Lajos tér 6–8, Hungary.

Scheele-Plakette

This award was created in 1942 to mark the 200th anniversary of the birth of the pharmacist and discoverer Carl Wilhelm Scheele (1742–86). In 1958 the German Pharmacists' Representative Group (ABDA) reactivated the award under a new statute. It consists of a rectangular plate bearing a profile of Scheele, and is awarded at no fixed interval. The recipient may be of any nationality.

Awarding body: Arbeitsgemeinschaft der Berufsvertretungen Deutscher Apotheker, 6000 Frankfurt Am Main, Beethovensplatz 1, Federal Republic of Germany.

Recipients include: Stellan Gullström (Sweden, 1942); Prof. Roland Schmiedel (Fed. Rep. of Germany, 1958); Stephan Dewald (Fed. Rep. of Germany, 1960); Prof. Hans Kaiser (Fed. Rep. of Germany, 1966); Prof. Ferdinand Schlemmer (Fed. Rep. of Germany, 1968).

Scheepersprys vir jeuglektuur (*Scheepers Prize for Children's Literature*)

The prize was made possible by a donation from the late Mr. and Mrs. Fred L. Scheepers who in 1956 donated money to the South African Academy for Science and Arts to be used for the furthering of good quality Afrikaans literature for the older child. After the couple's death their children, Mrs. Seba Cuyler and Mr. J. A. Scheepers, made a further donation to the Scheepers Fund. The prize is currently worth about R250. The deed of gift stipulates that the winning work must show good literary and/or educational quality, and must demonstrate real Afrikaner character and national pride (although this is not a binding requirement). Since 1974 the prize has been awarded every three years.

Awarding body: Suid-Afrikaanse Akademie vir Wetenskap en Kuns, Posbus 538, Pretoria 0001, South Africa.

Recipients include: Karl Kielblock (*Rebel*, 1970); Rykie van Reenen (*Heldin uit die vreemde*, 1971); Anna Rothmann (*Klaasneus-hulle*, 1972); Freda Linde (*Die singende gras*, 1974); Jan Rabie (*Seeboek van die Sonder kossers*, 1977).

Schelenz-Plakette

This award was established in 1929 by the Society for the History of Pharmacy (in Germany); it consists of a bronze plaque bearing a portrait of Hermann Schelenz (1848–1922), pharmacist, entrepreneur in the pharmaceutical industry and author of *The History of Pharmacy* (1904). It was donated by his widow, to commemorate Hermann Schelenz and to encourage and reward writers of papers in the history of pharmacy. Originally for German authors only, it became an international award when reactivated after the war in 1948, with the International Society for the History of Pharmacy as the awarding body.

Awarding body: International Society for the History of Pharmacy, Graf-Moltke-Strasse 46, 2800 Bremen, Federal Republic of Germany.

Recipients include: Umberto Tergolina (Italy, 1968); Armin Wankmüller (Fed. Rep. of Germany, 1970); Glenn Sonnedecker (U.S.A., 1971); Eugene Humbert Guitard (France, 1972); Dr. L. J. Vandewiele (Belgium, 1973).

Melland Schill Lectureship on International Law

The lectureship was founded in 1958 at Manchester University from a bequest of £10,000 received under the will of Miss Olive B. Schill in memory of her brother who died in the 1914–18 war. A series of five public lectures is given in the University in each session and each set of lectures deals with some aspect of international law. They are published by the University Press.

Awarding body: University of Manchester, Manchester M13 9PL, England.

Lecturers include: I. M. Sinclair ('Vienna Convention on the Law of Treaties', 1972–73); Prof. D. P. O'Connell ('The Influence of Law on Sea Power', 1973–74); Prof. Bin Cheng ('The Nature of International Customary Law', 1974–75).

Schillerpreis der Stadt Mannheim (*Schiller Prize of the City of Mannheim*)

This award was established in 1954 by the West German town of Mannheim in memory of Friedrich Schiller (1759–1805), the poet and dramatist, who for two years lived and worked in Mannheim. The award, which is non-competitive, is made to an individual who, through either his entire creative career or one outstanding work, has contributed significantly to cultural development, or whose career shows promise in this area. It is at present made every four years, and takes the form of a certificate and DM25,000.

Awarding body: Gemeinderat der Stadt Mannheim, Rathaus E 5, 6800 Mannheim 1, Federal Republic of Germany.

Recipients include: Prof. Dr. Carl Wurster (1968); Prof. Dr. Hartmut von Hentig (1968); Ida Ehre (1970); Peter Handke (1972); Horst Janssen (1974).

David C. Schilling Award

This national award is made annually by the U.S. Air Force Association to an individual or organization for outstanding contributions in the field of flight. It takes the form of a plaque. Instituted in 1948, it was originally named the Flight Trophy, but was renamed in 1957 in honour of Col. David C. Schilling (1918–56), U.S. Air Force ace.

Awarding body: Air Force Association National Awards Committee, 1750 Pennsylvania Ave., N.W., Washington, D.C. 20006, U.S.A.

Recipients include: 1st Strategic Reconnaissance Squadron, SAC (1972); 17th Air Division, 8th AF (SAC) (1973); Military Airlift Command (1974); Maj. George B. Stokes (1975); Capt. Donald R. Backlund and Capt. Roland W. Purser (1976).

Schlegel-Tieck Prize

This cash award (£900 in 1977) is made annually at the end of the year by the Translators Association for the best translation of a 20th-century German literary work published in the U.K. by a British publisher during the previous year. Entries are submitted by publishers. The award was established in 1964 by G. D. Astley, Secretary of the Association, under the auspices of the Society of Authors with financial support from the Government of the Federal Republic of Germany, the German Publishers' Association, the Arts Council and British publishers.

Awarding body: The Translators Association, 84 Drayton Gardens, London SW10 9SD, England.

Recipients include: Richard Barry (*The Brutal Takeover* by Kurt von Schuschnigg, 1972); Charles Kessler (*Wallenstein – His Life Narrated by Golo Mann*) and Ralph Manheim (*The Resistible Rise of Arturo Ui* by Bertholt Brecht), 1977.

Schleiden-Medaille

This prize was founded in 1955 by the Leopoldina German Academy of Researchers in Natural Sciences in honour of Matthias Jacob Schleiden (1804–81). It is generally awarded every three years to a scholar who has furthered scientific knowledge of the cell. The prize is awarded alternately to a botanist and a zoologist. It consists of a medal on which is engraved Schleiden's profile.

Awarding body: Deutsche Akademie der Naturforscher Leopoldina, 401 Halle/Saale, August-Bebel-Strasse 50A, German Democratic Republic.

Recipients include: Prof. Dr. Wolfgang Bargmann (Fed. Rep. of Germany, 1966); Prof. Dr. Wolfgang Beermann (Fed. Rep. of Germany, 1969); Prof. Dr. Torbjörn Caspersson (Sweden, 1973); Prof. Dr. Irene Manton (U.K., 1973); Prof. Dr. Wilhelm Bernhard (France, 1975).

Erich Schmid-Preis

The prize was established in 1976 by the Austrian Ministry of Science and Research on the occasion of the 80th birthday of the then Vice-President of the Austrian Academy of Sciences, Dr. Erich Schmid (born 1896), emeritus professor of physics, and long-time President of the Academy. The prize is awarded to physicists of Austrian citizenship who are not more than 40 years old, for a valuable achievement in the field of experimental or theoretical physics. The prize is a certificate and a sum of money and is awarded every two years, in May or June.

Awarding body: Österreichische Akademie der Wissenschaften, 1010 Vienna, Dr.-Ignaz-Seipel-Platz 2, Austria.

Schmid Rezsö Prize

The prize was established in 1950 in memory of Rezsö Schmid (1904–43), the physicist. It is awarded by the Hungarian Physical Society to young research workers for outstanding results in theoretical physics. It is an annual prize of 5,000 forints.

Awarding body: 'Eötvös Loránd' Fizikai Társulat, 1061 Budapest VI, Anker-köz 1, Hungary.

eorg-Schmorl-Preis

his award was established in 1963 by the German
ociety for Research into the Spinal Column, in
emory of the German professor (1861–1932)
ho first established a systematic pathological
natomy of that area. The award is made for
utstanding works on the subject of the spine;
ese may either be unpublished, or have appeared
uring the previous two years (provided they have
ceived no other prize). The award is made every
vo years, and takes the form of a certificate and
M3,000.

Awarding body: Gesellschaft fur Wirbelsäulen-
rschung, c/o Dr. med. F.-W. Meinecke, 6000
rankfurt am Main 60, Friedberger Landstr. 430,
ederal Republic of Germany.

Recipients include: Priv. Doz. Dr. H. Scheier
witzerland, 1967); Priv. Doz. Dr. K. Maier
ed. Rep. of Germany, 1967); Priv. Doz. Dr. W.
ihlmann (Fed. Rep. of Germany, 1969); Priv.
oz. Dr. H. Erdmann (Fed. Rep. of Germany,
173); Dr. L. E. Kazarian (U.S.A., 1973).

choeller-Junkmann-Preis

his prize has been donated by Schering AG
erlin and Bergkamen to be awarded annually to
oung scientists for outstanding papers in the field
endocrinology. It is worth DM15,000, of which
e first prize-winner generally receives DM7,000,
e second DM5,000 and the third DM3,000.
pplicants must be no more than 40 years of age,
nd permanently resident in Europe. Works on
e subject of *diabetes mellitus* are not eligible, nor
ose previously published elsewhere.

Awarding body: Deutsche Gesellschaft für Endo-
inolcgie, c/o President, Prof. Dr. G. Bettendorf,
niversitäts-Frauenklinik und -Poliklinik, Ab-
ilung für klinische und experimentelle Endo-
inologie, D-2000 Hamburg 20, Martinistr. 52,
ederal Republic of Germany.

irger Schöldström Prize

his prize was endowed by Birger Schöldström in
160, and is presented once every four years by the
vedish Academy for a work on the history of
terature or a biography. The prize consists of
000 Swedish kronor. It cannot be applied for.

Awarding body: The Swedish Academy, Börs-
set, Källargränd 4, S-111 29 Stockholm,
veden.

tto-Schott-Denkmünze der Deutschen Glas-chnischen Gesellschaft (*Otto Schott Com-morative Medal of the German Society of Glass echnology*)

tablished in 1927 by the Carl Zeiss Foundation
memory of Otto Schott, the medal is awarded
r distinction through scholarly or practical
hievements in glass technology and research. It
awarded every two or three years. It bears on
e obverse the profile of Otto Schott and on the
verse a laurel wreath, a dedication, the date of
e award and the name of the recipient. A
rtificate is also awarded, and the winner's name
added to the list of members of the Society. The

medal is presented to the winner in person who
then gives a speech of technical or scientific
content to the Society.

Awarding body: Deutsche Glastechnische Gesellschaft e.V., 6 Frankfurt am Main, Bockenheimer
Landstrasse 126, Federal Republic of Germany.

Recipients include: Prof. William Turner, F.R.S.
(1955); Ehrensenator Prof. Dr. Erich Schott
(1956); Prof. Dr.-Ing. Hermann Salmang (1960);
Prof. Dr.-Ing. Adolf Dietzel (1964); Prof. Dr.
Hans Jebsen-Marwedel (1972).

Walter-Schottky-Preis für Festkörperfor-schung (*Walter Schottky Prize for Solid State Physics*)

This annual award, established in 1973, is given
by the German Physical Society and financed by
the electrical engineering company, Siemens AG.
It takes the form of a cash prize and diploma, and
is intended to honour recent contributions by
young scientists to research into solid state physics.
The prize is awarded principally to German
researchers, but other Europeans are also eligible.

Awarding body: Deutsche Physikalische Gesellschaft, Federal Republic of Germany.

Recipients include: Peter Ehrhart (1973); Andreas
Otto (1974); Karl-Heinz Zschauer (1975); Franz
Wegner (1976); Siegfried Hunklinger (1977).

Isaac Schour Memorial Award

As a means of honouring Isaac Schour this award
is supported by the College of Dentistry, University of Illinois, Isaac Schour Memorial Fund. The
award, which is considered international in scope,
consists of $300 and a plaque. It is presented
annually to an individual who has made outstanding contributions in research or teaching or
both in the field of anatomical sciences.

Awarding body: International Association for
Dental Research, 211 East Chicago Ave., Chicago,
Ill. 60611, U.S.A.

Olive Schreiner Prize

This literary award was founded in 1961 by Shell
Southern Africa (Pty.) Ltd., and is administered
by the English Academy of Southern Africa. It is
for published work by a new writer of promise.
The award consists of R250 and a certificate, and
is given annually in one of three categories in
rotation: prose; poetry; drama. It is named after
Olive Schreiner (1855–1920), one of the most
important women that South Africa has produced
in the literary and political field; she won fame
with her book *The Story of an African Farm*.

Awarding body: English Academy of Southern
Africa, Ballater House, 35 Melle St., Braamfontein, Johannesburg, South Africa.

Recipients include: Sheila Fugard (novel, *The
Castaways*, 1974); Oswald Mtshali (poems, *Sounds
of a Cowhide Drum*, 1975); Douglas Livingstone
(radio play, *A Rhino for the Boardroom*, 1976).

Erwin Schrödinger Prize

The prize was established by the Austrian Ministry
of Education in 1956 in honour of Erwin Schrö-
dinger (1887–1961), professor of theoretical

physics and joint winner, with P. A. M. Dirac, of the 1933 Nobel Prize for Physics, for their discovery of new and productive aspects of the atomic theory. The prize is awarded for outstanding scholarly achievements in the field of natural sciences, in particular in physics and chemistry. It consists of a certificate and a sum of money. It is awarded generally every year in May or June. Scholars who are working in Austria are eligible.

Awarding body: Österreichische Akademie der Wissenschaften, 1010 Vienna, Dr.-Ignaz-Seipel-Platz 2, Austria.

Recipients include: Peter Weinzierl; Richard Kieffer; Erwin Plöckinger; Ferdinand Stenhauser; Herbert W. König.

Henrik Schück Prize

This prize for the history of literature is awarded annually by the Swedish Academy. It was instituted in 1946 by Henrik Schück, and consists of a cash prize of 7,000 Swedish kronor.

Awarding body: The Swedish Academy, Börshuset, Källargränd 4, S-111 29, Stockholm, Sweden.

Fritz Schumacher Prize

This is one of many prizes awarded annually by the FVS Foundation in Hamburg. It consists of DM20,000, and is given for outstanding achievements by Europeans in the field of architecture, urban and country planning, and engineering. Fritz Schumacher (1869–1947) was an eminent architect and chief director of architecture for Hamburg.

Awarding body: Stiftung FVS, Georgsplatz 10, 2 Hamburg 1, Federal Republic of Germany.

Recipients include: Sir Hubert Bennett (U.K., 1970); Sir Colin Buchanan (U.K., 1971); Prof. Elisabeth Pfeil (Fed. Rep. of Germany, 1972); F. Cordes (Fed. Rep. of Germany) and R. Vassas (France), 1973; F. van Klingeren and H. Hertzberger (Netherlands), 1974.

Fritz-Schumacher-Preis für Architektur

(*Fritz Schumacher Prize for Architecture*)

Established in 1961 by the city council and parliament of Hamburg, the prize is in memory of the architect and town planner, Fritz Schumacher. The prize is awarded to architects or engineers selected for their achievements in town or regional planning or in the theory or practice of architecture. Recipients of the prize must in general be members of the German Cultural Circle, but the prize may be awarded exceptionally to a non-member for planning or architectural achievements of particular significance to Hamburg. The prize of DM15,000 is awarded every three years, and is presented if possible on 3 May, this being the date on which Fritz Schumacher was appointed chief director of architecture in Hamburg.

Awarding body: Senat der Freien und Hansestadt Hamburg, 2 Hamburg 1, Rathaus, Federal Republic of Germany.

Robert Schuman Prize

Established in 1962, this is one of many prize established by the FVS Foundation in Hamburg which annually donates about DM10 millio through a variety of prizes for achievements i international co-operation, culture, or the enviror ment. The title of the Foundation stands for bot Friedrich von Schiller (1759–1805), the Germa poet and symbol of individual freedom, and fc Freiherr vom Stein, champion of social reforn The Schuman Prize is given in honour and i memory of Robert Schuman (1886–1963), th French politician and one of the originators of th European Economic Community. It is wort DM30,000, and is given annually to a person wh has particularly contributed to the unification ‹ Europe. In 1966, in collaboration with the Frienc of Robert Schuman (a French association), th Foundation created a Schuman Gold Medal, als to be awarded annually.

Awarding body: Stiftung FVS, Georgsplatz 1‹ 2 Hamburg 1, Federal Republic of Germany.

Recipients include: Sir Christopher Soam‹ (U.K., 1976); Gaston Thorn (Luxembourg 1977); Prof. Louis Leprince-Ringuet (Franc 1978).

Ludwig-Schunk-Preis

Established in 1961 by Schunk & Ebe GmbH ‹ Heuchelheim-Giessen, the prize is in memory ‹ Ludwig Schunk. It was awarded originally for ou standing · scholarly achievements in veterinar medicine, but since 1969, when new regulatior were introduced, it has been given for achiev‹ ments in any field of medicine. The prize ‹ DM5,000 is awarded annually, going one year t a member of the medical faculty of the Universit of Giessen or its attached institutes and clinics, an the next year to a scientist of any nationality fror outside the University. If in one year no memb‹ of the University is thought worthy of the prize, may be given two years running to a scientist fror outside. A board consisting of a director of th firm Schunk & Ebe, the dean of the faculty ‹ medicine and other representatives of the Unive: sity of Giessen decides on the prize-winner. Th prize is presented during an academic ceremon either at the faculty of medicine or at the Un versity.

Awarding body: Medizinische Fakultät de Justus Liebig-Universität Giessen, 6300 Giessen ‹ Ludwigstr. 23, Postfach 21440, Federal Republi of Germany.

Paul-Schürmann-Preis

This prize was founded in 1966 by the Society fc Military Medicine and Pharmacy, Association ‹ German Sanitary Officers. It consists of a cash su‹ of DM5,000 and is awarded every two year together with the Paul-Schürmann-Erinnerung medaille (memorial medal) for outstandin scientific work in military aspects of medicine an pharmacy, and in military hygiene. It may b awarded to medical officers of the armed force and members of the Society. Paul Schürman (1895–1941) was a professor at the University ‹

Berlin; he founded the Institute for General and Military Pathology; and he died at the front in the Russian campaign in 1941.

Awarding body: Gesellschaft für Wehrmedizin und Wehrpharmazie, Vereinigung deutscher Sanitätsoffiziere, 5300 Bonn, Kölnerstr. 251, Federal Republic of Germany.

Recipients include: Dr. T. Huber (1970); Dr. M. Bierther and Dr. G. Schlüter (1972); Prof. F. Klose and Dr. C. Emmerich (1973).

Robert Livingston Schuyler Prize

This award is presented every five years by the Taraknath Das Foundation for the best work in the field of modern British, British Imperial, and British Commonwealth history, by an American citizen. The prize is a cash award of $500 and will next be awarded in 1981.

Awarding body: American Historical Association, 400 A St., S.E., Washington, D.C. 20003, U.S.A.

Scientific Medal

Originally established by the Zoological Society of London in 1939, the award lapsed until 1961. Up to three medals may be awarded annually for distinguished work in zoology. Candidates must be under 40 years of age. Serving members of the Society's Council are not eligible. Recommendations must be submitted to the Society by 1 October, and the winners are announced in the following January or February; presentation of medals takes place in April or May.

Awarding body: Zoological Society of London, Regent's Park, London NW1 4RY, England.

Recipients include: Dr. Anne MacLaren (the physiology of reproduction in mammals, 1966); Dr. J. B. Gurdon (nuclear transplantation, 1967); Dr. G. A. Horridge (anatomy and physiology of nervous systems of invertebrates, 1968); Dr. R. V. Short (physiology of reproduction, particularly chemical assay of sex hormones, 1969); Dr. P. F. Baker (ionic transport across cell membranes, 1974).

Scott-Moncrieff Prize

This cash award (£700 in 1977) is made annually in the autumn by the Translators Association for the best translation of a 20th-century French literary work published in the U.K. by a British publisher during the previous year. Entries are submitted by publishers. The award was established in 1964 by G. D. Astley, Secretary of the Association, under the auspices of the Society of Authors, with financial support from the French Government, the Arts Council, and British publishers.

Awarding body: The Translators Association, 84 Drayton Gardens, London SW10 9SD, England.

Recipients include: Barbara Bray (*The Erl King* by Michel Tournier, 1973); John and Doreen Weightman (*From Honey to Ashes* and *Tristes Tropiques*, 1975); Peter Wait (*French Society 1789–1970* by Georges Dupeux, 1976); Janet Lloyd (*Gardens of Adonis* by Marcel Detienne) and

David Hapgood (*Totalitarian Temptation* by Jean-François Revel), jointly, 1977.

Second Half Century Award

This is the second highest award of the American Meteorological Society, and is given to members who have made excellent contributions to the geofluid sciences. It was given for the first time in 1970, at the celebration of the Society's 50th anniversary. It is in the form of a medallion, accompanied by a stipend. Not more than three awards are presented annually, and recipients should be about 50 years of age or less.

Awarding body: American Meteorological Society, 45 Beacon St., Boston, Mass. 02108, U.S.A.

Recipients include: Douglas K. Lilly (1973); James W. Deardorff and Tiruvalam N. Krishnamurti (1974); Louis J. Battan (1975); Roger M. Lhermitte (1976).

Selényi Pál Prize

Established in 1964 by the Hungarian Physical Society in honour of Pál Selényi (1884–1954), the prize is awarded to young physicists who achieve results directly utilizable in industry. It is awarded annually and is worth 5,000 forints.

Awarding body: 'Eötvös Loránd' Fizikai Társulat, 1061 Budapest VI, Anker-köz 1, Hungary.

Seligman Crystal

This award was established by the International Glaciological Society in 1962 at a meeting in Austria. It is given from time to time for a unique contribution to glaciology so that the subject is significantly enriched as a result. The award is a glass hexagon engraved with an ice crystal design and the profile of the recipient.

Awarding body: International Glaciological Society, England.

Recipients include: Lyle Hansen (deep drilling, 1972); John Glen (flow of ice; editor of journal, 1972); Stanley Evans (radio echo sounding of ice, 1974); Willi Dansgaard (isotope glaciology, 1976); Barclay Kamb (physics of ice research, 1977).

Sellin-Glueck Award

This is one of four awards established by the American Society of Criminology in the names of individuals who have made major contributions to criminology. The award was established in 1974 and takes the form of a medal. It is given to persons outside the U.S.A. who have gained international recognition for their contributions in criminology.

Awarding body: American Society of Criminology, 1314 Kinnear Rd., Columbus, Ohio 43212, U.S.A.

Recipients include: Franco Ferracuti (Italy, 1975); Sir Leon Radzinowicz (U.K., 1976).

B. R. Sen Award

The award was established at the 14th session of the Food and Agriculture Organization (FAO) Conference in November 1967, as a permanent feature of FAO activity associated with the ex-Director-General, Mr. B. R. Sen, with a view to furthering the goals he served, namely the economic and social progress of the developing world and the fight against hunger and poverty. The award is made for outstanding contribution to the advancement of the country or countries to which any FAO and World Food Program (WFP) field officer has been assigned. The contribution must be clearly identifiable and may take the form of technical innovations in agriculture, fisheries or forestry, institutional or administrative improvements, discoveries of new resources as a result of research, surveys or other investigations, establishment of training and research institutions, or be connected with any of the many tasks assigned to FAO and WFP personnel. One prize is awarded for each calendar year. The awards for the biennium are conferred in a special ceremony during the FAO Conference of Member States, meeting once every two years. A medal bearing the name of the recipient is presented; the winner also receives a scroll describing his/her achievements, a cash prize of $2,000 and a round trip to Rome for the winner and spouse. The award is open to any FAO and WFP officer who has served in the year for which the award is made; a minimum of two years' continuous service in the field is necessary.

Awarding body: Food and Agriculture Organization of the United Nations, Via delle Terme di Caracalla, 00100 Rome, Italy.

Recipients include: A. Aime (Haiti, rural youth work in Dahomey, 1972) and P. Daniel (Switzerland, information work on rural development training in Dahomey, 1972); A. Hafiz (Pakistan, wheat and barley improvement in the Near East, 1973); K. Sargent (U.K., planning and utilization of forest resources in Malaysia, 1974); J. Carvalho Santiago (Portugal, increase and development of wheat production in Brazil, 1975).

M. N. Sen Oration Award

Dr. Sen donated a sum of 68,000 rupees for the establishment of this award and the Kshanika Oration Award (*q.v.*). A prize of 1,000 rupees is awarded for work in the field of biochemical sciences. The recipient delivers a lecture which is also published in the *Indian Journal of Medical Research*. The first award was made in 1977.

Awarding body: Indian Council of Medical Research, Ansari Nagar, Post Box 4508, New Delhi 110016, India.

Senior Captain Scott Memorial Medal

This award was established in 1916 by the South African Biological Society in memory of Sir Robert Falcon Scott (1868–1912), the Antarctic explorer. It is presented annually for outstanding services to biology. The winner may be any biologist in southern Africa who has performed outstanding work in his or her field.

Awarding body: South African Biological Society, P.O.B. 820, Pretoria 0001, Republic of South Africa.

Recipients include: Dr. J. L. Smith (ichthyology); Miss I. C. Verdoom (botany, 1952); Prof. R. A. Dart (palaeontology); Dr. R. C. H. Bigalke (zoology, 1966); Prof. P. V. Tobias (palaeontology, 1973).

Sergelpriset

The prize was established in 1945 by the Swedish Royal Academy of Fine Arts to honour an outstanding Swedish sculptor. A medal and a cash prize are awarded every five years. The medal is named in memory of Johan Tobias Sergel (1740–1814), the famous Swedish sculptor. The award is made on 26 February, the anniversary of Sergel's death.

Awarding body: Kungl. Akademien för de fria Konsterna, Box 16 317, 103 26 Stockholm, Sweden.

Recipients include: Bror Marklund (1965); Arne Jones (1970); Gustaf Nordahl (1975).

Sertürner-Medaille

This silver medal was established in 1929 by the German Pharmaceutical Society. It is awarded for scientific papers of value to the profession of pharmacy published by a German pharmacist. The award is made annually and may not be given more than once to the same recipient. It commemorates Friedrich Wilhelm Adam Sertürner (1783–1841), who discovered the narcotic element in opium and thus opened the way for the development of alkaloid chemistry.

Awarding body: Deutsche Pharmazeutische Gesellschaft e.V., 6100 Darmstadt, Frankfurter Strasse 250, Federal Republic of Germany.

Recipients include: Kurt Liesche (1968); Dr. Joseph Breinlich (1969); Dr. Gerhard Steink (1970); Dr. Günther Gleiche (1971); Peter Franl (1973).

Dr. M. K. Seshadri Prize and Medal

This prize was established with a donation by Mrs. M. K. Seshadri in memory of her late husband. It is awarded to an eminent scientist whose original work has contributed significantly to the practice of community medicine. The medal is accompanied by a cash sum of 5,000 rupees.

Awarding body: Indian Council of Medical Research, Ansari Nagar, Post Box 4508, New Delhi 110016, India.

Professor T. R. Seshadri Seventieth Birthday Commemoration Medal

This medal was established in 1971 by the Indian National Science Academy. It is awarded every three years to an eminent Indian chemist for outstanding work in any branch of chemistry or chemical technology.

Awarding body: Indian National Science Academy, Bahadur Shah Zafar Marg, New Delhi 110001, India.

Recipients include: K. Venkataraman (1973); R. C. Mehrotra (1976).

Shakespeare Prize

This prize is one of four similar awards given by the FVS Foundation for outstanding achievements in the arts, town and country planning, folklore and human sciences. This prize of DM25,000 is especially for British citizens. (*See also* Steffens, Montaigne and Vondel prizes.)

Awarding body: Stiftung FVS, Georgsplatz 10, 2 Hamburg 1, Federal Republic of Germany.

Recipients include: John Pritchard (conductor, 1975); Philip Larkin (poet, 1976); Dame Margot Fonteyn (dancer, 1977); John Dexter (theatre and opera producer, 1978); Tom Stoppard (playwright, 1979).

Shakuntala Amir Chand Prizes

A number of prizes are given annually under this title. They are for the best published research work in any subject in the field of medical sciences, including clinical research. Applicants should be under 40 years old. The prizes of 500 rupees each are awarded to Indian nationals for work undertaken in any Indian institution. Papers published in the previous two years in Indian or foreign journals are eligible.

Awarding body: Indian Council of Medical Research, Ansari Nagar, Post Box 4508, New Delhi 110016, India.

Recipients include: Dr. Gurmohan Singh, Dr. Vijayalaxmi, Dr. Radharaman Jiban Dash, Miss A. V. Lakshmi (1976).

Dr. Mary Share Jones Memorial Lectureship in Law

The lectureship was established in 1956 by a bequest of £1,000 from the late Emeritus Professor J. Share Jones in memory of his wife. The appointment is made every two years by Liverpool University Council. The lecturer delivers a lecture or course of lectures on a subject related to the study or practice of Law. The remuneration is the income from the endowment for the two previous years.

Awarding body: The University of Liverpool, P.O.B. 147, Liverpool L69 3BX, England.

Sharpey Schafer Memorial Lectureship

The lectureship was established in 1933 at Edinburgh University in recognition of the distinguished work, and to perpetuate the memory of Professor Sir Edward Sharpey Schafer who occupied the Chair of Physiology in the University from 1899 to 1933. Lectures are delivered biennially.

Awarding body: Edinburgh University, Edinburgh EH8 9YL, Scotland.

Lecturers include: Prof. G. V. R. Born (1973).

John Gilmary Shea Prize

Established in 1944, the prize is in memory of John Gilmary Shea (1824–92), historian of the Roman Catholic Church in the United States. It is awarded annually for a published book judged to have made the most original and distinguished contribution to knowledge of the history of the Roman Catholic Church. The award of $300 in cash is presented in December, and the book must have been published between 1 October of the preceding year and 30 September of the award year. The author must be a citizen or permanent resident of the United States or Canada.

Awarding body: American Catholic Historical Association, The Catholic University of America, Mullen Library/305, Washington, D.C. 20064, U.S.A.

Recipients include: Robert Ignatius Burns, S.J. (*The Crusader Kingdom of Valencia, Reconstruction on a Thirteenth-Century Frontier*, 1967); Robert Brentano (*Two Churches: England and Italy in the Thirteenth Century*, 1969); Jaroslav Pelikan (*The Emergence of the Catholic Tradition. A History of the Development of Doctrine. Vol. 1. 100–600*, 1971); Emmet Larkin (*The Roman Catholic Church and the Creation of the Modern Irish State, 1878–86*, 1976).

Shelley Memorial Award

This annual award of $1,750 is made by the Poetry Society of America (founded in 1910) for a poet's entire work. The award is not competitive; the recipient is selected on the basis of his previous publications. The award was endowed by the late Mary P. Sears of Massachusetts.

Awarding body: The Poetry Society of America, 15 Gramercy Park, New York, N.Y. 10003, U.S.A.

Recipients include: Galway Kinnell; May Swenson; David Ignatow; William Stafford; Delmore Schwartz.

Sherrington Lectureship

The lectureship was established in 1948 in honour of Sir Charles Scott Sherrington, O.M., G.B.E., M.D., F.R.S., George Holt Professor of Physiology at Liverpool University from 1895 to 1913. The appointment is made every two years by the University Council. The lecturer, who is paid £200 plus expenses, delivers a lecture or course of lectures on Physiology. These are published by the Liverpool University Press.

Awarding body: The University of Liverpool, P.O.B. 147, Liverpool L69 3BX, England.

Sherrington Memorial Medal and Lecture

A neurologist or physiologist is appointed every five years and receives a medal and an honorarium.

Awarding body: The Royal Society of Medicine, 1 Wimpole St., London W1M 8AE, England.

Shincho Prize

The prize was established with two others (Japan Art Prize and Japan Literature Prize) in 1969 by Mr. Ryoichi Sato, President of the Shinchosha Publishing Company. The Shincho Prize is given annually to the most promising new writer of the year, whose works have appeared in the monthly magazine *Shincho*. The award consists of 300,000 yen and a souvenir.

Awarding body: Shincho Foundation, Shinchosha Publishing Company, 71 Yarai-cho, Shinjuku-ku, Tokyo, Japan.

Recipients include: Tokuzo Miyamoto (1975); Jun Kasahara (1976); Taki Shiyuzo (1977).

Shinkishi Hatai Medal

This medal is awarded for a remarkable contribution to marine biology in the Pacific. It is presented every five years at the Congress of the Parific Science Association. Established by the Japan Society for the Promotion of Science in 1966, the award honours the marine biologist Shinkishi Hatai.

Awarding body: Pacific Science Association, U.S.A.

Recipients include: Dr. Deogracias V. Villadolid (Philippines, 1966); Dr. Carl L. Hubbs (U.S.A., 1971); Dr. Lauren R. Donaldson (U.S.A., 1976).

Dr. A. T. Shousha Foundation Prize

The prize is awarded annually to a person having made the most significant contribution to any health problem in the geographical area in which Dr. Shousha served the World Health Organization. The prize consists of a bronze medal and a cash sum awarded from the accumulated interest on the Foundation's capital. Anyone is eligible, and any national health administration in the stipulated geographical area or former recipient of the prize may nominate a candidate. The Foundation was established in 1966 following a proposal to commemorate Dr. Shousha by the WHO Regional Committee for the Eastern Mediterranean.

Awarding body: World Health Organization, Avenue Appia, 1211 Geneva 27, Switzerland.

Recipients include: Dr. Ahmed Abdallah (Egypt, 1977).

Sibelius Medal

The medal was established in 1965 to mark the 100th anniversary of the birth of Jean Sibelius (1865–1957), the Finnish composer. It is awarded annually to a Finnish or a foreign musician who has contributed to making known the works of Sibelius. The medal is designed by Eila Hiltunen, the sculptor, whose Sibelius Monument was unveiled in 1965 in Helsinki.

Awarding body: Sibelius Society, c/o Secretary, Mrs. Liisa Aroheimo, c/o Musiikki Fazer, P.O.B. 260, 00101 Helsinki 10, Finland.

Recipients include: Colin Davis (U.K., 1977).

Jean Sibelius International Violin Competition

This competition for young violinists was founded by the Sibelius Society of Finland in 1965, in memory of the composer Jean Sibelius (1865–1957). It is held every five years, and is open to violinists of all nationalities between the ages of 15 and 33. Eight cash prizes are awarded, ranging in value from U.S.$4,000 for the first prize to U.S.$200 for the eighth prize (in 1975). Certificates are also given.

Awarding body: Jean Sibelius International Violin Competition, The Secretariat, P. Rautatiekatu 9, 00100 Helsinki 10, Finland.

Recipients include: Oleg Kagan (U.S.S.R., 1965); Liana Isakadze (U.S.S.R., 1970) and Pavel Kogan (U.S.S.R., 1970); Yuval Yaron (Israel, 1975).

Joseph A. Siegel Memorial Award

The award was established in 1955 by the Society of Manufacturing Engineers in honour of Joseph A. Siegel, its first President. The gold medal and engraved citation are conferred only on members of the Society. Recipients are those who have made contributions through leadership, voluntary support or other timely acts which benefit the Society.

Awarding body: Society of Manufacturing Engineers, 20501 Ford Rd., Dearborn, Mich. 48128, U.S.A.

Recipients include: Dr. Harry B. Osborn, Jr. (Park-Ohio Industries, 1972); Andrew W. Williams (North Carolina A & T State Univ., 1973); Joseph L. Petz (J. L. Petz Co., 1974); Francis J. Sehn (1975); Clyde A. Sluhan (Master Chemical Corpn., 1976).

Sigma Delta Chi Awards

These awards have been given annually since 1932 for outstanding achievements in journalism. They consist of bronze medallions and accompanying plaques, and are given in various categories for work in all aspects of press, radio and television journalism undertaken during the preceding year. Nominations may be made by the author or any other party.

Awarding body: Society of Professional Journalists, 35 East Wacker Drive, Suite 3108, Chicago, Ill. 60601, U.S.A.

Recipients include: team of Detroit Free Press reporters (general reporting), Sydney H. Schanberg (foreign correspondence), WHBF AM-FM Radio News team (radio reporting), WHAS-TV News (television reporting), 1975.

Sigmond Elek Memorial Medal

The Hungarian Society for Food Industry founded this medal in 1956 in memory of Elek Sigmond (1873–1939), the chemist noted for his work on the problems of soil science, and considered to have founded agrochemistry in Hungary. The award is given to members of the Society with outstanding achievements in research and teaching, or in the organization of research and production. A cash prize of 5,000 forints accompanies the medal.

Awarding body: Magyar Élelmezésipari Tudományos Egyesület, 1054 Budapest V, Akadémia u. 1–3, Hungary.

Silver Combustion Medal

Established in 1958 by the Combustion Institute, this prize is given at each biennial symposium of the Institute for an outstanding paper presented at the preceding symposium.

Awarding body: The Combustion Institute, 986 Union Trust Building, Pittsburgh, Pa. 15219, U.S.A.

Recipients include: Dr. George H. Markstein, Dr. Lawrence Orloff and Dr. John de Ris (U.S.A., 1976).

Silvicultural Prize of the Institute of Foresters of Great Britain

This award is made annually for a paper published in *Forestry*, preferably on the results of the theory and practice of silviculture. It was established in 1966 by a donation from a member of the Institute, and consists of a cash prize of £40.

Awarding body: Institute of Foresters of Great Britain, 6 Rutland Square, Edinburgh EH1 2AU, Scotland.

Recipients include: S. N. Adams, D. A. Dickson and I. S. Cornforth (1975); J. D. Low and B. J. W. Greig (1976).

Thomas Simm Littler Lectureship and Prize

As a result of a gift of £1,000 to the British Society of Audiology by the IXth International Congress of Audiology a Lectureship and Prize Fund were set up, named in honour of the late Dr. Thomas Simm Littler, a pioneer of British audiology. The lecture is delivered every four years during the Society's Conference. The lectureship carries an honorarium of £100 and a memorial scroll. The prize is awarded annually to the best paper given at a meeting of the Society or published in the *British Journal of Audiology*, with preference given to authors below 35 years of age. The prize has a value of £25 with a memorial scroll.

Awarding body: British Society of Audiology, 1 Birdcage Walk, London SW1H 9JJ, England.

Recipients include: (Lecture) Sir Alexander Ewing (1971); Prof. W. Burns (1975); (Prize) Dr. S. D. G. Stephens (1971); A. Markides (1972); Dr. E. F. Evans (1973).

Simon Memorial Prize

A prize of £300, accompanied by a parchment certificate, is awarded approximately every three years for distinguished work in experimental or theoretical low temperature physics. The award was established in 1958 by the Low Temperature Group of the Physical Society (now amalgamated with the Institute of Physics) in memory of Sir Francis Simon.

Awarding body: The Institute of Physics, 47 Belgrave Square, London SW1X 8QX, England.

Recipients include: Henry Edgar Hall and William Frank Vinen (1963); John Charles Wheatley (1965); Kurt Alfred Georg Mendelssohn (1968); Walther Meissner (1970); Peter Kapitza (1973).

Simonsen Lectureship

The Simonsen Lectureship was endowed in 1957 by Lady Simonsen, to commemorate the name of her husband, Sir John Simonsen, who had served the Chemical Society as Vice-President and as Honorary Secretary. It is intended that the lecture should deal with the chemistry of natural products and that the lecturer should be chosen from amongst the young workers in this field. The appointment of the lecturer is not restricted to British chemists. The lecture is given once every three years, and the lecturer receives a silver medal and £100.

Awarding body: The Chemical Society, Burlington House, London W1V 0BN, England.

Recipients include: D. Arigoni (1969–70); G. W. Kenner (1972–73); L. Crombie (1975–76).

Simulation and Ground Testing Award

Established by the AIAA in 1975, the award is made for outstanding achievement in the development or effective utilization of technology, procedures, facilities or modelling techniques for flight simulation, space simulation, propulsion testing, aerodynamic testing or other ground testing associated with aeronautics and astronautics. It comprises a medal and certificate of citation and is presented at either the Aerodynamic Testing Conference, the Visual and Motion Simulation Conference, the Aircraft Systems and Technology Conference, the Propulsion Conference, or the Space Simulation Conference, depending on the recipient's speciality.

Awarding body: American Institute of Aeronautics and Astronautics, 1290 Avenue of the Americas, New York, N.Y. 10019, U.S.A.

Recipients include: Bernhard H. Goethert (1976).

Raja Ravi Sher Singh of Kalsia Memorial Award

This award of 900 rupees was donated in 1967 by Maharani Ranbir Kaur of Kalsia in memory of her son. It is awarded annually to a graduate under 40 years old for outstanding work in the field of cancer research.

Awarding body: Indian Council of Medical Research, Ansari Nagar, Post Box 4508, New Delhi 110016, India.

Recipients include: Dr. Jayasree Roychowdhary (1972); Dr. V. Shanta (1973); Dr. S. C. Gangal (1974); Dr. Nandini Anil Sheth (1975); Dr. Savita Gautam (1976).

Smeaton Medal

This gold medal was established in 1974 by the Council of Engineering Institutions in conjunction with the Smeatonian Society of Civil Engineers to mark the 250th anniversary of the birth of the eminent engineer John Smeaton (1724–92). He was a founder member in 1771 of the Society of Civil Engineers, renamed after his death the Smeatonian Society of Civil Engineers. He is best known for his lighthouse on Eddystone Rock. The medal is given for an outstanding achievement in engineering in the widest sense and not restricted as to discipline.

Awarding body: The Council of Engineering Institutions, 2 Little Smith St., London SW1P 3DL, England.

Recipients include: G. M. Binnie (1974); Sir Leonard Redshaw (1977).

Daniel B. Smith Award

This award was established in 1965 by the American Pharmaceutical Association to honour the first President of the Association, who was a community pharmacist and President of the Philadelphia College of Pharmacy and Science. The award is given to recognize the achievements of a community pharmacy practitioner who has distinguished himself or herself and the profession of pharmacy by outstanding professional performance, both in the recipient's practice setting and in the community in which the practice is located. It consists of a mounted bronze medallion.

Awarding body: American Pharmaceutical Association, 2215 Constitution Ave., N.W., Washington, D.C. 20037, U.S.A.

Recipients include: Paul W. Lofholm (1972); Martin Rein (1973); Kenneth E. Tiemann (1974); Morris Boynoff (1975); Donald J. Wernik (1976).

H. G. Smith Memorial Medal

This award was established in 1929 in memory of Henry George Smith (1852–1924), Assistant Curator and Economic Chemist at the Sydney Technological Museum from 1899 to 1921. He was President of the Royal Society of New South Wales in 1913 and of the New South Wales branch of the Royal Australian Chemical Institute in 1922–23. The medal is awarded annually to a member of the Institute for outstanding contributions to the development of some branch of chemical science. The contribution is judged on the basis of research work published or accepted for publication during the ten years immediately preceding the award. Most of the work should have been carried out in Australia, while the candidate was a member of the Institute. Only those who have been a member of the Institute for at least five years are eligible. The winner receives A$100 and a medal.

Awarding body: The Royal Australian Chemical Institute, Clunies Ross House, 191 Royal Parade, Parkville, Vic. 3052, Australia.

James Arthur Smith Lectureship

The lectureship was established in 1936 with a bequest of £1,000 from the late Emeritus Professor William Blair-Bell, Professor of Obstetrics and Gynaecology at Liverpool University from 1921 to 1931. The appointment is made every three years by the University Council. The lecturer is someone unconnected with the University or the hospitals of Liverpool, who delivers a lecture on some aspect of cancer. The remuneration is the income from the endowment.

Awarding body: The University of Liverpool, P.O.B. 147, Liverpool L69 3BX, England.

Jane M. Smith Award

The award was established in 1911 by a bequest of Jane McGrew Smith, life member of the National Geographic Society. A medal and life membership of the Society are awarded as and when merited in recognition of contributions to geography.

Awarding body: National Geographic Society, 17th and M Sts., N.W., Washington, D.C. 20036, U.S.A.

Recipients include: Edwin A. Link (1959); Sir Bruce Ingram (1959); Arleigh A. Burke (1960); Lyndon B. Johnson (1962); Dr. Calvin H. Plimpton (1964).

S. G. Smith Memorial Medal

The Shirley Institute (Cotton, Silk and Man-made Fibres Research Association) established the medal in 1964 in memory of Stuart Grayson Smith (1906–63), who was Head of the Fibre Structure Department of the Institute. It is given to those recognized as having devoted themselves to the furtherance of scientific knowledge concerned with the structure, properties and processing of fibres, whether such work has been published or not.

Awarding body: The Textile Institute, 10 Blackfriars St., Manchester M3 5DR, England.

Recipients include: J. Sikorski (contributions to instrumental technique and its use in determination of fibre structure and fibre damage, 1971); M. W. H. Townsend (leader of a team of researchers in the field of woollen and worsted processing, 1972); C. R. Jones (work on heat-transfer phenomena, 1973); J. O. Warwicker (contributions to the physical chemistry of dyeing and the structural chemistry of fibres, 1975); Prof. J. W. Lünenschloss (contributions to textile technology, textile physics, and instrument technology, 1976).

W. H. Smith & Son Literary Award

This annual award of £1,000 is one of the biggest literary prizes in the U.K. It was established in 1959 by W. H. Smith & Son, the retail booksellers and newsagents. It is awarded to the book which, in the opinion of the judges, constitutes the most outstanding contribution to English literature during the year under review (i.e. the previous calendar year). The presentation is made in March. The author must reside in the U.K. or a Commonwealth state. The book must have been written originally in English and published in the U.K. No book may be submitted; the procedure for making the award is a matter for the judges' discretion.

Awarding body: W. H. Smith & Son Ltd., Strand House, 10 New Fetter Lane, London EC4A 1AD, England.

Recipients include: Jon Stallworthy (*Wilfred Owen*, 1975); Seamus Heaney (*North*, 1976); Ronald Lewin (*Slim: The Standard-bearer*, 1977); Patrick Leigh Fermor (*A Time of Gifts*, 1978); Mark Girouard (*Life in the English Country House*, 1979).

Smithson Medal

The medal was established in 1965 by the Smithsonian Institution in honour of James Smithson (1765–1829), founder of the Institution. This is the Smithsonian's highest award consisting of a gold medal and an honorarium (where appropriate), and is awarded not on a regular basis but only when merited. It is given in recognition of exceptional contributions to art, science, history, education and technology.

Awarding body: Smithsonian Institution, 1000 Jefferson Drive, S.W., Washington, D.C. 20560, U.S.A.

Recipients include: Royal Society of London (1965); Edgar P. Richardson (1968); Ralph E. Becker (1976); Nancy Hanks (1976).

Smoluchowskiego Medal

This award was established in 1967 by the Polish Physical Society in memory of Marian Smolu-chowski (1872–1917), the famous Polish physicist. The medal is awarded annually to eminent scientists, Polish or foreign, for important contributions to the development of physics.

Awarding body: Polish Physical Society, Hoża 69, 00-681 Warsaw, Poland.

Recipients include: Dr. Leonard Sosnowski (Poland, 1972); Dr. S. Chandrasekhar (U.S.A., 1973); Dr. Georgi N. Florov (U.S.S.R., 1974); Dr. Gerald Pearson (U.S.A., 1975); Dr. Arkadiusz Piekara (Poland, 1976).

Snelliusmedaille

Founded in 1955 by the Netherlands Association for the Advancement of Natural, Medical and Surgical Sciences, the medal is awarded every nine years for outstanding contributions to physics. It is named after the Dutch scientist, Snellius (1580–1626), one of the first physicists.

Awarding body: Genootschap ter bevordering van Natuur-, Genees- en Heelkunde, Plantage Muidergracht 12, Amsterdam, Netherlands.

Recipients include: Prof. F. Zernike (1955); Ir. H. Rinia (1967); Prof. J. H. van der Waals (1976).

Socialist Countries Natural Photography Biennial Prizes

These prizes are awarded for nature photographs. They are sponsored by the Photographic Society of Poznań and the Federation of Polish Amateur Associations of Photographic Art. There are four prizes: a Grand Prix and three medals (gold, silver, bronze).

Awarding body: Photographic Society of Poznań, Paderewskiego 7, 61-770 Poznań, Poland.

Society of Chemical Industry Canada Medal

Founded in 1939, this medal is awarded every two years for outstanding services to the Canadian chemical industry on the nomination of the Canadian Section of the Society for Chemical Industry. An address is given by the recipient on the occasion of the award.

Awarding body: Society of Chemical Industry (Canadian Section), c/o The Hon. Secretary, Cynamid of Canada Ltd., 635 Dorchester Blvd. West, Montreal, Que. H3B 1R6, Canada.

Recipients include: A. A. Cumming ('Are we Legislating Private Enterprise out of Business?', 1968); W. N. Hall ('Some Thoughts on the Canadian Chemical Industry', 1970); Hon.

Maurice Lamontagne ('The Doom Debate and Beyond', 1972); L. Hynes ('Objectives, National Corporate, Personal', 1974).

Society of Chemical Industry International Medal

The medal was instituted in 1947 for award to a person who has furthered international co-operation in the sphere of the Society's interest. The recipient gives an address on the occasion of the award.

Awarding body: Society of Chemical Industry, 14 Belgrave Square, London SW1X 8PS, England.

Recipients: L. H. Lampitt ('Towards International Collaboration in Science', 1950); H. R. Kruyt ('International Co-operation in Chemistry', 1955); F. J. Griffin ('The Contribution of the Society of Chemical Industry in the International Field', 1970).

Society of Chemical Industry's Medal

Since its institution in 1896 this medal has been awarded every two years for conspicuous services to applied chemistry by research, discovery, invention or for improvements to the Society in the furtherance of its objectives. The recipient need not be a member of the Society and may be of any nationality. He gives an address on the occasion of the award.

Awarding body: Society of Chemical Industry, 14 Belgrave Square, London SW1X 8PS, England.

Recipients include: L. Hynes ('The Impact of Technology on Man and His World', 1967); Prof. F. Morton ('University Research and the Chemical Industry: An Academic Viewpoint', 1969); Dr. D. W. Kent Jones ('Modern Food and Food Additives', 1971); G. H. Beeby ('Robens – Catalyst for Change', 1973); Dr. F. L. Rose ('The Drug Revolution', 1975).

Society of Industrial Artists and Designers Design Medal

Established in 1956, the medal is awarded to a professional designer for outstanding achievement in industrial design. It may be given for a single design, a group of related designs, or as recognition of work of exemplary standard over a number of years. The award is made annually, not later than the end of September.

Awarding body: Society of Industrial Artists and Designers, 12 Carlton House Terrace, London SW1Y 5AH, England.

Recipients include: Mary Quant (U.K.); Charles Eames (U.S.A.); Bill Brandt (U.K.); F. H. K. Henrion (U.K.); Dieter Rams (Fed. Rep. of Germany, 1978).

Society of Manufacturing Engineers Education Award

A gold medal and an engraved citation are awarded annually for development of dynamic curricula, fostering sound training methods or inspiring students to enter the profession of tool and manufacturing engineering. The award, established in 1957, is international and nominations are not confined to members of the Society.

Awarding body: Society of Manufacturing Engineers, 20501 Ford Rd., Dearborn, Mich. 48128, U.S.A.

Recipients include: Dr. Arthur E. Keating (Bridgeport Engineering Inst., 1970); Prof. Roger L. Geer (Cornell Univ., 1971); Dr. Shien-Ming Wu (Univ. of Wisconsin-Madison, 1974); Dr. Dell K. Allen (Brigham Young Univ., 1975); Oyvind Bjorke (Univ. of Trondheim, Norway, 1976).

Society of Manufacturing Engineers Engineering Citation

A gold medal and an engraved citation are awarded annually for unusual skill in the development of tool and manufacturing engineering principles, design or practices. The award, founded in 1955, is international and nominations are not confined to members of the Society.

Awarding body: Society of Manufacturing Engineers, 20501 Ford Rd., Dearborn, Mich. 48128, U.S.A.

Recipients include: George Lorenz (Nat. Standards Laboratory, Australia, 1971); Amber N. Brunson (Brunson Instrument Co., 1972); Horace S. Beattie (IBM Corpn., 1973); Dr. Tsunehisa Nagase (Ikegai Iron Works Ltd., Japan, 1974); John T. Parsons (John T. Parsons Co., 1975).

Society of Manufacturing Engineers Gold Medal

The medal and an engraved citation are awarded annually for outstanding service through published literature, technical writings, or papers dealing with tool and manufacturing engineering subjects. Established in 1955, the award is international, and nominations are not confined to members of the Society.

Awarding body: Society of Manufacturing Engineers, 20501 Ford Rd., Dearborn, Mich. 48128, U.S.A.

Recipients include: Clyde A. Sluhan (Master Chemical Corpn., 1972); Roy L. Williams (Union Carbide Corpn., 1973); Dr. John A. Schey (Univ. of Illinois, 1974); Harry Conn (W. A. Whitney Corpn., 1975); Lester V. Colwell (Univ. of Michigan, 1976).

Society of Manufacturing Engineers Interprofessional Cooperation Award

A gold medal and an engraved citation are awarded annually for scientific achievement contributing to or originating in the field of manufacturing engineering, which acknowledges the professional interdependence of men for the enhancement of progress in that field. The award was established in 1965; it is international and nominations are not confined to members of the Society.

Awarding body: Society of Manufacturing Engineers, 20501 Ford Rd., Dearborn, Mich. 48128, U.S.A.

Recipients include: Norman B. Mears (Buckbee-Mears Co., 1972); Carl L. Sadler, Jr. (Sundstrand Corpn., 1973); Dr. Norman A. Copeland (E. I. DuPont de Nemours & Co., 1974); Roy P. Trowbridge (General Motors Corpn., 1975); Hugh E. McCallick (Univ. of Houston, Texas, 1976).

Society of Manufacturing Engineers Progress Award

Established in 1955, a gold medal and an engraved citation are awarded annually for accomplishments in the field of manufacturing processes, methods or management. The award is international and nominations are not confined to members of the Society.

Awarding body: Society of Manufacturing Engineers, 20501 Ford Rd., Dearborn, Mich. 48128, U.S.A.

Recipients include: John R. Conrad (S & C Electric Co., 1972); William L. Naumann (Caterpillar Tractor Co., 1973); William E. Brandt (Park City Chemical Co., 1974); Albert F. Welch (General Motors Corpn., 1975); Robert C. Wilson (Memorex Corpn., 1976).

Society of Manufacturing Engineers Research Medal

A gold medal and an engraved citation are awarded annually for significant published research leading to a better understanding of materials, facilities, principles and operations, and their application to improve manufacturing processes. The award was established in 1957; it is international and nominations are not confined to members of the Society.

Awarding body: Society of Manufacturing Engineers, 20501 Ford Rd., Dearborn, Mich. 48128, U.S.A.

Recipients include: Richard E. Reason (Rank Precision Industries, U.K., 1969); Dr. Kenjiro Okamura (Kyoto Univ., Japan, 1971); Dr. John F. Kahles (Metcut Research Associates, Inc., 1973); Fr. Jacques Peters (Instituut voor Werktuigkunde, Belgium, 1975); Branimir F. von Turkovich (Univ. of Vermont, 1976).

Society of Plastics Engineers International Award in Plastics Science and Engineering

Established in 1961, this award is sponsored by the Society's New York Section in memory of the late Herbert Preiss, President of Plastic Materials and Polymers, Inc., Hicksville, New York. It is awarded annually to stimulate fundamental contributions in plastics science and engineering throughout the world, to acknowledge outstanding achievements by honouring distinguished scientists and engineers, and to disseminate the technical information of Award Lectures among plastics scientists and engineers. The award consists of a gold medal, a certificate, a medal replica and a cash sum of $1,000. The recipient delivers an Award Lecture at the SPE's Annual Technical Conference.

Awarding body: Society of Plastics Engineers, U.S.A.

Recipients include: J. Harry DuBois (1966); Dr. Raymond F. Boyer (1968); Dr. Albert G. H. Dietz (1971); Dr. Michael Szwarc (1972); Dr. Allan S. Hay (1975).

Torald Sollmann Award in Pharmacology

This award was established by Wyeth Laboratories of Philadelphia to commemorate the pioneer work in America of Dr. Torald Sollmann in the fields of pharmacological research and education. A prize of $2,500 and an appropriate medal are presented for life-long significant contributions to the advancement and extension of knowledge in the field of pharmacology. Candidates must be nominated by a member of ASPET. The award is made on the basis of originality and uniqueness of approach, as well as development of new concepts, theories, and techniques which constitute a definite, mature, and sustained significant contribution to the extension and advancement of pharmacology over a period of years. It is a triennial award.

Awarding body: American Society for Pharmacology and Experimental Therapeutics, Inc., 9650 Rockville Pike, Bethesda, Md. 20014, U.S.A.

Sonning Prize

This cash prize is awarded to internationally recognized composers, instrumentalists, conductors or singers. It is given annually by the Danish Sonning Foundation. The sum of money is variable (100,000 kroner in 1978 and 1979). The award cannot be applied for. The Foundation also awards bursaries for further training abroad to musicians from Scandinavia.

Awarding body: Léonie Sonnings Musikfond, Denmark.

Recipients include: Andrés Segovia (Spain, 1974); Dietrich Fischer-Dieskau (Fed. Rep. of Germany, 1975); Mogens Wöldike (Denmark, 1976); Olivier Messiaen (France, 1977).

Sonning Prize

The prize was established under the terms of the Charter of the Sonning Foundation to honour the late C. J. Sonning, Danish writer and editor. A prize of 200,000 Danish kroner is awarded to a man or woman who has signally contributed to the advancement of European civilization. Candidates are recommended by European universities and the recipient is selected by a Committee set up by the Senate of the University of Copenhagen.

Awarding body: Senate of the University of Copenhagen, Frue Plads, 1168 Copenhagen K, Denmark.

Recipients include: Danilo Dolci (1971); Karl Popper (1973); Hannah Arendt (1975); Arne Næss (1977); Hermann Gmeiner (1978).

Sopot International Song Festival

This festival takes place every year in Sopot, Poland. Various prizes are given for the best songs, collections of songs and the best performers of Polish songs. They are sponsored by organizations such as the Polish Artistic Agency, PAGART, the Department of Culture of the Gdansk Voivodship, and the resort of Sopot.

Awarding body: PAA 'PAGART', Plac Zwycięztwa 9, 00-078 Warsaw, Poland.

Wilmer Souder Award

Wilmer Souder is regarded as the father of modern dental materials research. In his honour the Dental Materials Group of the IADR annually presents a plaque in recognition of outstanding achievements in the advancement of the science of dental materials.

Awarding body: International Association for Dental Research, 211 East Chicago Ave., Chicago, Ill. 60611, U.S.A.

South African Geographical Society Medal

The Society awards a medal in recognition of meritorious contribution to geography in Southern Africa. The award is open to members only.

Awarding body: The South African Geographical Society, P.O.B. 31201, Braamfontein 2017, South Africa.

South African Institute of Physics Gold Medal

This medal is awarded every two years for outstanding achievement in physics in South Africa, either in research, technological or industrial development or education. It was established in 1977.

Awarding body: South African Institute of Physics, c/o Southern Universities Nuclear Institute, P.O.B. 17, Faure 7131, South Africa.

South African Library Association Award for Children's Book Illustration

The award was established in 1973 for outstanding illustrations in children's books in Afrikaans or English by a South African illustrator. It takes the form of a gold medal and certificate, and is presented annually at the SALA Conference. Only books published during the preceding year are considered.

Awarding body: South African Library Association, c/o Ferdinand Postma Library, Potchefstroom University, Potchefstroom 2520, South Africa.

Recipients include: Katrine Harries (1974).

Space Science Award

Established in 1961 by the AIAA, this annual award is presented to an investigator distinguished by his scholarly achievement in the study of the physics of atmospheres of celestial bodies, or of the matter, fields and dynamic and energy transfer processes occurring in space, or experienced by space vehicles. It comprises a medal and certificate of citation and is usually presented at the Aerospace Sciences Meeting.

Awarding body: American Institute of Aeronautics and Astronautics, 1290 Ave. of the Americas, New York, N.Y. 10019, U.S.A.

Recipients include: Paul W. Gast (1973); John H. Wolfe (1974); Murray Dryer (1975); Riccardo Giacconi (1976); Bruce Murray (1977).

Space Systems Award
Established in 1968 by the AIAA as the Spacecraft Design Award, this annual award was renamed in 1976. It is intended to recognize outstanding achievement in the field of systems analysis, design and implementation as applied to spacecraft and launch vehicle technology. It comprises a medal and certificate of citation and is usually presented at the Aerospace Sciences Meeting.
Awarding body: American Institute of Aeronautics and Astronautics, 1290 Ave. of the Americas, New York, N.Y. 10019, U.S.A.
Recipients include: Walter O. Lowrie (1977).

Gheorghe Spacu Prize
The Romanian Academy established this prize in 1948. It is for outstanding achievement in chemistry, and is presented annually at a General Assembly of the Academy. It consists of 10,000 lei and a diploma. It is named after Gheorghe Spacu (1883–1955), research chemist, university professor and Academician, and initiator of a series of research in the chemistry of complex combinations.
Awarding body: Academy of the S.R. of Romania, 125 Calea Victoriei, Bucharest, Romania.

Ernst Späth Prize for Organic Chemistry
The prize was established by a general meeting of the Austrian Academy of Sciences in 1961, in memory of Ernst Späth (1886–1946), professor of chemistry. The prize, which is a certificate and a sum of money, is awarded for outstanding works in the field of organic chemistry. It is given every two years, in May or June.
Awarding body: Österreichische Akademie der Wissenschaften, 1010 Vienna, Dr.-Ignaz-Seipel-Platz 2, Austria.

Special Libraries Association Professional Award
This is an annual award established in 1949 to recognize a specific major achievement in, or a special significant contribution to, the field of librarianship or information science, which advances the stated objectives of the Association. The award comprises a certificate and an appropriate inscribed gift.
Awarding body: Special Libraries Association, 235 Park Ave. South, New York, N.Y. 10003, U.S.A.
Recipients include: Beatrice V. Simon (1969); James B. Adler (1972); Marjorie R. Hyslop (1973); Loretta J. Kiersky (1974); Jacqueline D. Sisson (1976).

Elmer A. Sperry Award
The Sperry Award commemorates the life and achievements of Dr. Elmer A. Sperry (1860–1930) by seeking to encourage progress in the engineering of transportation. It was established in 1955 by Dr. Sperry's daughter and son, and is given

annually in recognition of a distinguished engineering contribution which, through application proved in service, has advanced the art of transportation whether by land, sea or air. The award consists of a bronze medal and a certificate, and is sponsored by five American engineering societies (AIAA, IEEE, ASME, SAE and SNAME).
Awarding body: American Society of Mechanical Engineers (ASME), United Engineering Center, 345 East 47th St., New York, N.Y. 10017, U.S.A.
Recipients include: Leonard S. Hobbs and Perry W. Pratt (1972); Jerome L. Goldman, Frank A. Nemec, James J. Henry (1975).

Spiers Memorial Lecture
This lecture commemorates Mr. F. S. Spiers, first Secretary of the Faraday Society from 1903 to 1926. It is given annually on some aspect of chemistry by a lecturer from the U.K. or overseas. The lecturer receives a silver medal and an honorarium of £100.
Awarding body: The Chemical Society, Burlington House, London W1V 0BN, England.
Recipients include: Prof. G. S. Rushbrooke (U.K., 1967); Prof. P. J. Flory (U.S.A., 1970); Prof. G. G. Hall (U.K., 1972); Prof. R. B. Bell (U.K., 1975); Prof. D. R. Herschbach (U.S.A., 1976).

Spirit of St. Louis Medal
This award was founded in 1929 by Philip D. Ball, ASME members and citizens of St. Louis, Mo. A gold medal and an engrossed certificate are awarded for meritorious service in the advancement of aeronautics and astronautics.
Awarding body: American Society of Mechanical Engineers, United Engineering Center, 345 East 47th St., New York, N.Y. 10017, U.S.A.
Recipients include: Clarence L. Johnson (1970); Ralph L. Creel (1971); Neil A. Armstrong (1972); John F. Yardley (1973); Abe Silverstein (1974).

John Campbell Sproule Memorial Plaque
This award, first presented in 1974, is made annually by the Canadian Institute of Mining and Metallurgy for distinguished contributions to the exploration and development of Canada's mineral resources in the northern regions, in such areas as research, innovation, project management or education. It was established on the recommendation of the Institute's Petroleum Society in honour of a former President of the Institute. Nominations must be endorsed by not fewer than five members of the Institute.
Awarding body: The Canadian Institute of Mining and Metallurgy, 400-1130 Sherbrooke St. West, Montreal H3A 2M8, Canada.
Recipients include: T. A. Link (1974); R. A. Hemstock (1975); H. J. Strain (1976).

Staatspreis fur das Kunsthandwerk im Lande Nordrhein-Westfalen (*Prize for Handicrafts in North Rhine-Westphalia*)
This award was instituted in 1974 by the government of North Rhine-Westphalia to encourage the practice of handicrafts in the region. It is given

every two years in the following categories: jewellery; metalwork; woodwork; textiles; ceramics; stonework; glass and paints; leather, paper and photography. An additional prize may be awarded in one of the last two categories. Each recipient is presented with a cash prize of DM7,000, a bronze medal and a diploma. Craftsmen over 25 years of age and permanently resident in North Rhine-Westphalia are eligible.

Awarding body: Der Kultusminister des Landes Nordrhein-Westfalen, 4000 Düsseldorf, Völklinger Strasse 49, Federal Republic of Germany.

Staatsprijs voor Kinder- en Jeugd Literatuur
(State Prize for Children's Literature)
The Dutch Ministry of Culture, Recreation and Social Work offers a prize of 6,000 guilders every three years for a book for children or young people.

Awarding body: Ministerie van Cultuur, Recreatie en Maatschappelijk Werk, Steenvoordelaan 370, Rijswijk (ZH), The Netherlands.

Stalspryse
In 1947 the South African Academy for Science and Arts founded a prize for humanities. In 1955 its title was changed to Stalspryse, in memory of the late Dr. A. J. Stals, Minister of Health and Education in the first Malan cabinet. The prize money (currently R250 for each award) is donated by the Rembrandt Tobacco Corporation. The prize is given for publications of high quality in Afrikaans, and awards are made annually in a three-yearly cycle for work in the various disciplines: music and theatre, cultural history, theology, history of art; political science, economics, history, philosophy; geography, African studies, sociology and criminology, education and psychology.

Awarding body: Suid-Afrikaanse Akademie vir Wetenskap en Kuns, Posbus 538, Pretoria 0001, South Africa.

Recipients include: Prof. J. G. Garbers (education, 1975); Prof. A. van Selms (theology, 1976); Prof. Martin Versveld (philosophy), Prof. C. F. J. Muller (history), Prof. J. A. Lombard (economics), 1977.

Johann Wenzel-Stamitz-Preis
This award, established by the West German Ministry of the Interior, was first made in 1960. It is presented annually by the Artists' Guild either for the total output or for an outstanding single work of a German musician born in East Germany. The main prize consists of DM5,000 and a diploma, and there are two secondary prizes of DM2,000 each, accompanied by diplomas. The prize is named after the Bohemian composer, Johann Wenzel Stamitz (1717-57), founder of the Mannheim School.

Awarding body: Die Künstlergilde e.V., 7300 Esslingen/N., Webergasse 1, Federal Republic of Germany.

Recipients include: Hans Otte (1972); Dr. Karl Thieme (1973); Wolfgang Hildemann (1974);

Prof. Heinrich Konietzny (1975); Prof. Gerhard Schwarz (1976).

Hermann-Staudinger-Preis
Established in 1970 by the aniline and soda manufacturers, Badische Anilin- & Soda-Fabrik AG, of Ludwigshafen, the prize is in commemoration of Hermann Staudinger (1881-1965), who won the Nobel Prize for Chemistry in 1953 for his achievements in the field of macromolecular chemistry. A gold medal and a sum of money are awarded to German or non-German scientists, who have distinguished themselves in the field of macromolecular chemistry. The award is made not more than once every two years.

Awarding body: Gesellschaft Deutscher Chemiker, 6000 Frankfurt (Main) 90, Carl Bosch-Haus, Varrentrappstr. 40-42, Federal Republic of Germany.

Recipients include: Prof. Werner Kern (Fed. Rep. of Germany, 1971); Prof. Günter Viktor Schulz (Fed. Rep. of Germany, 1971); Prof. Otto Bayer (Fed. Rep. of Germany, 1973); Dr. Hans Fikentscher (Fed. Rep. of Germany, 1976).

Steavenson Award
The award was established in 1976 in memory of the amateur astronomer, Dr. W. H. Steavenson. It consists of about £20 and a citation. It is for distinction in astronomical observation, and is awarded not more than once in two years. The terms of the award imply that the recipient should have some seniority, and must be a member of the British Astronomical Association.

Awarding body: British Astronomical Association, Burlington House, Piccadilly, London W1, England.

Recipients include: O. J. Knox (assiduous observer, 1976).

Henrik Steffens Prize
This is one of four similar prizes given annually by the FVS Foundation for outstanding achievements in the arts, town 'and country planning, folklore and human sciences. It consists of DM25,000 and is especially for Scandinavian citizens. (*See also* Shakespeare, Montaigne and Vondel prizes.)

Awarding body: Stiftung FVS, Georgsplatz 10, 2 Hamburg 1, Federal Republic of Germany.

Recipients include: Dr. h.c. Harry Martinson (Sweden, 1972).

Steiner Lajos Memorial Medal
The Hungarian Meteorological Society founded the medal in 1951. It is awarded for outstanding research in meteorology, or for any other work which has advanced the development of meteorology or the Society. Members of the Society and foreign scientists are eligible. Medals are awarded at irregular intervals, at the discretion of the Society's Presidential Council.

Awarding body: Magyar Meteorológiai Társaság, Budapest VI, Anker-köz 1, Hungary.

Stenton Lectures

These lectures were started in 1967 by Professor Holt, Head of the History Department at Reading University, as a memorial to Sir Frank Stenton. Sir Frank Merry Stenton (1880–1967) was Professor of Modern History at Reading University from 1912 to 1946. From 1934 he was Deputy Vice-Chancellor, and from 1946 Vice-Chancellor until his retirement in 1950. He was outstanding among his generation of historians, and in 1948 was knighted for his services to history. These annual lectures are given by eminent historians in November each year and published in booklet form the following autumn.

Awarding body: University of Reading, Whiteknights, Reading RG6 2AA, England.

Lecturers include: Denis Mack-Smith (*Mussolini as a Military Leader*, 1973); J. M. Wallace-Hadrill (*The Vikings in Francia*, 1974); Keith Thomas (*Rule and Misrule in the Schools of Early Modern England*, 1975); Peter Brown (1976).

Heinrich von Stephan Medal

The Federal German Ministry of Posts and Telecommunications founded the medal in 1952 for outstanding achievements in this field. The medal and a certificate are awarded usually once a year in the autumn; anyone of any nationality is eligible. The medal is named after the first German Postmaster General, Heinrich von Stephan (1831–97), who was a co-founder of the Universal Postal Union.

Awarding body: Bundesministerium für das Post- und Fernmeldewesen, Postfach 80 01, 5300 Bonn 1, Federal Republic of Germany.

Edwin Stevens Lecture for the Laity

A lecturer is appointed annually to deliver an address on a matter of current concern both to the medical profession and to the general public. The lecturer receives a gold medal and an honorarium, and the lecture is published and presented to those who attend. The lecture was established in 1970 by Mr. Stevens (the founder of Amplivox) and his wife, with a gift of £50,000 as a means of bringing the public and the medical profession together on matters of common concern.

Awarding body: Royal Society of Medicine, 1 Wimpole St., London W1M 8AE, England.

Recipients include: Most Rev. and Rt. Hon. Donald Coggan ('Dying with Dignity', 1976).

J. C. Stevens Award

This prize consists of books, normally to the value of $50, awarded annually for a discussion paper on hydraulics published by the ASCE. The author must hold some grade of membership in the ASCE. The prize cannot be awarded to the same person twice, but a paper designated 'second order of merit' may compete again the next year. The prize was established in 1943 by John C. Stevens, former President of the Society.

Awarding body: American Society of Civil Engineers, 345 East 47th St., New York, N.Y. 10017, U.S.A.

Recipients include: Charles R. Neill ('Erosion of Sand Beds Around Spur Dikes', 1974); A. R. Thomas ('Sedimentation in Mangla Reservoir', 1975); D. L. Fread ('Comparison of Four Numerical Methods for Flood Routing', 1976).

M. T. Steyn-prys vir natuurwetenskaplike en tegniese prestasie (*M. T. Steyn Prize for Natural Scientific and Technological Achievement*)

The South African Academy established this prize in 1964. It is named after President M. T. Steyn, the great statesman and first Academy Chairman. The prize takes the form of a gold medal; the costs are met by an annual donation from Sasol. This is one of the most important honours bestowed by the Academy, for leadership at the highest level in the field of natural sciences and technology. No one may receive it more than once. A candidate is chosen for his creative contribution to the development of natural sciences and technology, and the successful application thereof in the national interest.

Awarding body: Suid-Afrikaanse Akademie vir Wetenskap en Kuns, Posbus 538, Pretoria 0001, South Africa.

Recipients include: Dr. S. M. Naudé (1970); Dr. H. O. Mönnig (1971); Dr. P. Etienne Rousseau (1973); Dr. S. J. du Plessis (1976); Dr. A. J. A. Roux (1977).

Alfred-Stock-Gedächtnispreis (*Alfred Stock Memorial Prize*)

In 1950 friends and pupils of Alfred Stock (died 1946) set up the Alfred Stock Memorial Foundation, to be administered by the Society of German Chemists. The Alfred Stock Memorial Prize is awarded by the Society on the recommendation of the trustees of the Foundation, for an outstanding independent piece of practical work in the field of inorganic chemistry. The gold medal, together with a sum of money, is usually awarded annually, and is presented at the general meeting of the Society.

Awarding body: Gesellschaft Deutscher Chemiker, 6000 Frankfurt (Main) 90, Carl Bosch-Haus, Varrentrappstr. 40–42, Federal Republic of Germany.

Recipients include: Prof. Harald Schäfer (1967); Prof. Gerhard Fritz (1970); Prof. Max Schmidt (1972); Prof. Rudolf Hoppe (1974); Prof. Heinrich Nöth (1976).

Ernest Stockdale Lecture

The lecture was established in 1975 in memory of Ernest Stockdale, treasurer of the Quaker Peace Studies Trust which was responsible for raising the funds with which the University of Bradford Chair of Peace Studies was established. The lecture is financed from contributions made by his friends. It is given annually by someone involved in the field of peace studies. The first lecture was given in 1976.

Awarding body: University of Bradford, Bradford, West Yorks. BD7 1DP, England.

Lecturers include: Dr. Vithal Rajan (1976).

Simion Stoilov Prize

This prize for mathematics was founded by the Romanian Academy in 1948. It is presented annually at a General Assembly of the Academy, and consists of 10,000 lei and a diploma. It is named after Simion Stoilov (1887–1961), university professor and creator of the Romanian contemporary school of the theory of functions.

Awarding body: Academy of the S.R. of Romania, 125 Calea Victoriei, Bucharest, Romania.
Recipients include: Viorel Barbu (1970).

Sidney L. Strauss Memorial Award

This award was established in 1949 by the New York Society of Architects in honour of a former President of the Society, and is awarded annually to an architect or other person who has rendered outstanding service to the architectural profession within the previous five years. It takes the form of a bronze medal and certificate.

Awarding body: Sidney L. Strauss Memorial Award Committee, New York Society of Architects, 101 Park Ave., Room 831 N.W., New York, N.Y. 10017, U.S.A.
Recipients include: Daniel Schwartzman, F.A.I.A. (1971); Senator Jack Brooks (1972); Fred L. Liebmann (1973); Isadore M. Cohen (1974); Charles J. Urstadt (1975).

Erwin-Stresemann-Preis

This prize was established by the German Society of Ornithologists in 1969 on the occasion of the 80th birthday of Erwin Stresemann (1889–1972), the famous ornithologist. It is awarded for a significant scientific publication dealing with an ornithological topic. The author must not be more than 40 years of age at the time of publication of the work. The prize may not be awarded more frequently than every two years. It consists of a medal, a certificate and a cash sum of DM3,000.

Awarding body: Deutsche Ornithologen-Gesellschaft e.V., Hardenbergplatz 8, Zoologischer Garten, 1 Berlin 30, Germany.
Recipients include: Erwin Stresemann (1969); Eberhard Gwinner (1973).

Structures, Structural Dynamics and Materials Award

Established by the AIAA in 1967, the award of a medal and certificate of citation is presented annually to an individual responsible for outstanding recent technical or scientific contribution in aerospace structures, structural dynamics or materials. It is presented at the Structures, Structural Dynamics and Materials Conference.

Awarding body: American Institute of Aeronautics and Astronautics, 1290 Ave. of the Americas, New York, N.Y. 10019, U.S.A.
Recipients include: Robert T. Schwartz and George P. Peterson (1973); William D. Cowie (1974); Theodore H. H. Pian (1975); Charles Tiffany (1976); Walter J. Mykytow (1977).

Suomalainen Tiedeakatemia – Kunniapalkinto (*Finnish Academy of Science and Letters Prize*)

This prize is awarded annually to a Finnish member of the Academy for distinguished work. It is given alternately to members in the science section and the humanities section. It consists of 7,500 markkaa and a diploma, and was founded by the Academy in 1945.

Awarding body: Suomalainen Tiedeakatemia, Finland.
Recipients include: Prof. Kustaa Inkeri (mathematics, 1972); Prof. Lauri Posti (Baltic-Finnish languages, 1973); Prof. Esko Suomalainen (genetics, 1974); Veikko Väänänen (Latin, romance philology, 1975); Prof. Th. G. Sahama (geochemistry, 1976).

Suomen Kulttuurirahaston Palkinnot (*Finnish Cultural Foundation Prizes*)

These awards were established by the Finnish Cultural Foundation in 1939, and are presented in recognition of valuable and significant contributions to the scientific and cultural life of Finland. There is usually one main prize of 20,000 markkaa, and five additional prizes of 10,000 markkaa; certificates are also given. All Finnish persons are eligible for the prizes, which are awarded once a year on the Eve of Kalevala Day, 27 February.

Awarding body: Suomen Kulttuurirahasto, Bulevardi 5 A 13, PL 203, 00121 Helsinki 12, Finland.
Recipients include: A. E. Martola (international peace and security, 1975); Matti Koskenniemi (education, 1976); Eero A. Kalaja (industrial engineering, 1977).

Support Systems Award

Established by the AIAA in 1975, the award is for significant contributions to the overall effectiveness of aeronautical or aerospace systems through the development of improved support systems technology. It comprises a medal and certificate of citation, and is usually presented at the Aircraft Systems and Technology Conference.

Awarding body: American Institute of Aeronautics and Astronautics, 1290 Ave. of the Americas, New York, N.Y. 10019, U.S.A.
Recipients include: Gene A. Petry (1976).

Surveying and Mapping Award

Individual engineers and engineering firms contributed towards the endowment of this award, which was established in 1969 by ASCE. It consists of a plaque and certificate, and is awarded annually to a member of the Society who has made the most notable contribution to surveying and mapping either in written form, or in some instances through notable performance, long years of service or specific practical advances.

Awarding body: American Society of Civil Engineers, 345 East 47th St., New York, N.Y. 10017, U.S.A.
Recipients include: Curtis M. Brown (1971); William A. Radlinski (1972); Philip Kissam (1973); George D. Whitmore (1974); Kenneth S. Curtis (1976).

Edwin Sutherland Award

This is one of four awards established by the American Society of Criminology in the names of individuals who have made major contributions to criminology. The award takes the form of a medal, and was established in 1960. It is for a major contribution to criminological theory.

Awarding body: American Society of Criminology, 1314 Kinnear Rd., Columbus, Ohio 43212, U.S.A.

Recipients include: Leslie Wilkins (1972); Edwin Lemert (1973); Simon Dinitz (1974); C. Ray Jeffery (1975); Daniel Glaster (1976).

Sverdrup Gold Medal

This award is presented occasionally to researchers of all nationalities who have made outstanding contributions to the scientific knowledge of interactions between the oceans and the atmosphere. The Sverdrup Memorial Fund was established by friends of the late Professor Harald Ulrik Sverdrup. The medal is awarded on the advice of an international committee.

Awarding body: American Meteorological Society, 45 Beacon St., Boston, Mass. 02108, U.S.A.

Recipients include: Kirk Bryan (1970); Klaus Hasselmann (1971); Vladimir Kamenkovich (1972); Owen M. Phillips (1975); Robert W. Stewart (1976).

Swammerdammedaille

Founded by the Netherlands Association for the Advancement of Natural, Medical and Surgical Sciences in 1880, the medal is for outstanding scientific contributions to biology. It is named after the famous Dutch biologist, Jan Swammerdam (1637–80). It is awarded every nine years, and biologists of every nationality are eligible.

Awarding body: Genootschap ter bevordering van Natuur-, Genees- en Heelkunde, Plantage Muidergracht 12, Amsterdam, The Netherlands.

Recipients include: Hugo de Vries (Netherlands, 1910); Max Weber (Germany, 1920); Sir Vincent Wigglesworth (U.K., 1966); Prof. N. Tinbergen (U.K., 1973).

Swedish Academy Grand Prize

This prize in the form of a medal is awarded only occasionally, in recognition of important cultural achievement. The award was established in 1786 by King Gustavus III, and has been given only 16 times during this century. It cannot be applied for.

Awarding body: The Swedish Academy, Börshuset, Källargränd 4, S-111 29 Stockholm, Sweden.

Swedish Academy Prize for Swedish Culture in Finland

This prize was instituted and endowed by the Swedish Academy in 1966 to recognize important achievements in Finland's Swedish cultural life. The prize is given annually to a Finnish citizen, and consists of 30,000 Swedish kronor. It cannot be applied for.

Awarding body: The Swedish Academy, Börshuset, Källargränd 4, S-111 29 Stockholm, Sweden.

Swedish Academy Prize for Swedish Linguistics

This prize consists of a sum of money, currently 5,000 Swedish kronor, awarded annually for the study and promotion of the Swedish language and linguistics. The prize was instituted in 1953. It cannot be applied for.

Awarding body: The Swedish Academy, Börshuset, Källargränd 4, S-111 29 Stockholm, Sweden.

Swedish Academy Prize for Translation into Other Languages

This award was instituted in 1965 by the Swedish Academy to encourage the translation of Swedish literature into other languages. The award is a cash prize, currently 6,000 Swedish kronor, and is given annually. It cannot be applied for.

Awarding body: The Swedish Academy, Börshuset, Källargränd 4, S-111 29 Stockholm, Sweden.

Swedish Academy Prize for Translation into Swedish

This prize was instituted in 1953, and is endowed jointly by the Swedish Academy and two Swedish publishing houses (Albert Bonniers Förlag and P. A. Norstedt & Söners Förlag). A cash prize currently 5,000 Swedish kronor, is awarded annually to the best translation of literature or the humanities into the Swedish language. The prize cannot be applied for.

Awarding body: The Swedish Academy, Börshuset, Källargränd 4, S-111 29 Stockholm, Sweden.

Swedish Academy Theatre Prize

This prize was founded in 1963 to mark the 175th anniversary of the Royal Dramatic Theatre in Sweden. It is an annual award open to Swedish actors and actresses, producers and dramatists; it is a cash prize of 10,000 Swedish kronor. It cannot be applied for.

Awarding body: The Swedish Academy, Börshuset, Källargränd 4, S-111 29 Stockholm, Sweden.

Swedish Society of Medical Sciences Jubilee Prize

The Society founded this prize in 1858 to celebrate its 50th anniversary. A monetary prize (currently about 3,500 kronor) is awarded every year in rotation for published work within the field of one of the Society's five sections. Prize-winners must be Swedish citizens.

Awarding body: Swedish Society of Medical Sciences, P.O.B. 558, S-101 27 Stockholm, Sweden.

Recipients include: Prof. Torbjörn Caspersson M.D. (for work on identification of chromosome with fluorescent techniques, 1973).

Swellengrebel Memorial Lecture

This is an occasional award, established in 1975 in memory of Professor N. H. Swellengrebel (1885–1970), a Dutch parasitologist who was President of the Netherlands Society of Tropical Medicine. The award consists of a visit to Holland, delivery of a paper and its publication in *Tropical and Geographical Medicine*, and a certificate. The award is open to anyone who has achieved outstanding results in parasitology, malariology, tropical medicine or tropical health.

Awarding body: Nederlandse vereniging voor Tropische Geneeskunde, c/o the Secretary, Institute of Tropical Medicine, 33 Rapenburg, Leyde, The Netherlands.

Recipients include: Prof. Bruce-Chwatt (1975).

Swinburne Award

The award was established by the Plastics Institute (amalgamated in 1975 with the Institution of the Rubber Industry to become the Plastics and Rubber Institute). It consists of a gold medal and a sum of money, and is intended to promote the advancement and fusion of (a) the science and technology of plastics and of plastics engineering, and (b) science and technology in any field relating to plastics or to plastics engineering. It is open to members and non-members of the Institute, and is awarded usually every two years.

Awarding body: The Plastics and Rubber Institute, 11 Hobart Place, London SW1W 0HL, England.

Recipients include: L. R. G. Treloar (molecular orientation in polymers, 1970); R. F. Boyer (multiple transitions in semi-crystalline polymers, 1972); A. Keller (the many faces of order in solid polymers, 1974); H. Schnell (the preparation, structure, properties and uses of aromatic polycarbonates, 1976).

Swiss Children's Book Prize

This award was established in 1942 by the Swiss Teachers Association and Swiss Female Teachers Association, and is made annually for one or more works by a writer or illustrator of Swiss nationality. It consists of a cash prize of 3,000 Swiss francs.

Awarding body: Swiss Teachers Association and Swiss Female Teachers Association, Ringstr. 54, 8057 Zürich, Switzerland.

Recipients include: Ernst Kappeler; Cécile Lauber; Olga Meyer; Traugott Vogel; Josef Reinhart.

Sylvester Medal

The medal was established in 1901 in memory of Professor J. J. Sylvester, F.R.S. A bronze medal is awarded triennially for the encouragement of mathematical research, irrespective of nationality. A gift of £200 accompanies the medal.

Awarding body: Royal Society of London, 6 Carlton House Terrace, London SW1Y 5AG, England.

Recipients include: G. F. J. Temple (1970); Prof. J. W. S. Cassells (1973); Prof. D. G. Kendall (1976).

David Syme Research Prize

This award is made for the best original research work in biology, physics, chemistry or geology published in Australia during the preceding two years. Preference is given to work of value to the industrial and commercial interests of the country. The award was established in 1904 by David Syme. It is made annually and consists of a cash prize of A$250 and a medallion. Only those who have spent not less than five out of the seven years prior to the award in Australia are eligible. University professors are not eligible.

Awarding body: University of Melbourne, Grattan St., Parkville, Melbourne, Vic. 3052, Australia.

Recipients include: Dr. David H. Solomon (1976).

Symons Award

The award was established in 1973 by Professor T. H. B. Symons, then Chairman of the Association of Commonwealth Universities and President of Trent University, Ontario. An award of a small gift of silver is made annually to honour individuals who have made outstanding contributions to the A.C.U. and to Commonwealth universities.

Awarding body: Association of Commonwealth Universities, England.

Recipients include: Sir Charles Wilson and Sir Douglas Logan (1973); Prof. James Auchmuty (1974); Dr. John Foster (1975); Dr. Stephen Stackpole (1976).

Synthetic Organic Chemical Manufacturers Association Environmental Chemistry Award

This annual award was established in 1972 in order to recognize outstanding accomplishments in the application of environmental organic chemistry which contribute in a significant way to improving the nation's environment and the general welfare of its citizens. The award consists of a gold medal and a $1,000 honorarium, and is open to any person or team employed by a company in the United States or affiliated with a U.S. government agency or educational institution. First consideration is given to research completed within the last five years.

Awarding body: Synthetic Organic Chemical Manufacturers Association, 1075 Central Park Ave., Scarsdale, N.Y. 10583, U.S.A.

Recipients include: Prof. J. M. Wood (mercury pollution hazards, 1972); Dr. M. Beroza (chemistry of insect control, 1973); Prof. W. W. Eckenfelder (water treatment control, 1974); Prof. H. A. Laitinen (services to environmental studies and automobile pollution studies, 1975); Dr. R. D. Swisher (research on biodegradaiton of organic molecules, 1976).

Syöväntorjuntatyön Ansiomitali (*Cancer Campaign Medal of Merit*)

This award was established in 1956 by the Council of the Cancer Society of Finland, to commemorate the 20th anniversary of the Society. Gold, silver and bronze medals are given at the end of every year in recognition of particular work for the cancer campaign (e.g. voluntary work, significant scientific achievement, an exceptionally large donation).

Awarding body: The Cancer Society of Finland, Liisankatu 21 B, 00170 Helsinki 17, Finland.

Recipients include: Sylvi Siltanen (Governor, 1970); P. J. Myrberg (Chancellor of Univ. of Helsinki, 1964); Eino Palovesi (Governor, 1964); Artturi Ranta (Governor, 1964); Lions International (Multiple District 107, Finland, 1972).

System Effectiveness and Safety Award

Established by the AIAA in 1975, this award is presented annually for outstanding contribution to the field of system effectiveness and safety or its related disciplines. It comprises a medal and certificate of citation, and is usually presented at the Annual Reliability and Maintainability Conference.

Awarding body: American Institute of Aeronautics and Astronautics, 1290 Ave. of the Americas, New York, N.Y. 10019, U.S.A.

Recipients include: Thomas D. Matteson and F. Stanley Nowlan (1977).

Szele Tibor Memorial Medal

The Hungarian 'Bolyai János' Mathematical Society established this award in 1969 to reward those mathematicians who in the course of their research have contributed outstandingly to the introduction of young people to scientific activity.

A medal and cash prize of 7,000 forints is awarded annually.

Awarding body: 'Bolyai János' Matematikai Társulat, Budapest VI, Anker-köz 1, Hungary.

Szentmiklósi Szabó József Memorial Medal

Founded by the Hungarian Geological Society in 1897, the medal is awarded every three years for outstanding work in the field of mineralogy or geology. It is named in memory of József Szabó (1822–94), professor of petrology at Pest University, who was internationally known for setting forth the trachyte system.

Awarding body: Magyarhoni Földtani Társulat, Budapest 1061, Anker-köz 1, Hungary.

Szikla Géza Prize

The Hungarian Energy Economics Society established this prize in 1964 in honour of Géza Szikla. It is for achievements which promote the development of a socialist people's economy in the field of energy economics in its widest sense. In particular, it may be given for outstanding activity in the technical or economic field in organization, work-safety, technical education, planning, or innovation; or for the popularization of work or organizational activity of a high standard within the Society. The prize is given annually in the form of medals, either gold or silver, accompanied by a cash award of 8,000 or 5,000 forints respectively.

Awarding body: Energiagazdálkodási Tudományos Egyesület, Budapest V, Kossuth Lajos tér 6–8, Hungary.

T

Taiwan Ministry of Education Literature and Art Awards

The Kuomintang (National Party) and the Ministry of Education set up a national foundation in 1976 for the promotion of literature, fine arts and music. Ten awards of N.T.$100,000 are made annually for outstanding works of literary theory, poetry, essays, journalism, novels, fine arts, instrumental or vocal compositions, drama.

Awarding body: Ministry of Education, Chung Shan S. Rd., Taipei, Taiwan.

John A. Tamisea Award

This prize was established by the Civil Aviation Medical Association in memory of John A. Tamisea, M.D. It is awarded annually to an outstanding Aviation Medical Examiner for contributions to the art and science of aviation medicine in its application to the general aviation field. The prize consists of $200 and a certificate.

Awarding body: Aerospace Medical Association, Washington National Airport, Washington, D.C. 20001, U.S.A.

Recipients include: Dr. James Y. Bradfield (1972); Dr. Harold N. Brown (1973); Dr. Luis A. Amezcua G. (1974); Dr. Robert L. Wick, Jr. (1975); Dr. Harry L. Gibbons (1976).

Tanaka Memorial Prize

This annual prize was established in 1967 by the Japan Welding Society with a donation from the late Kikundo Tanaka, founder of Tanaka Engineering Works Ltd. It is awarded for distinguished achievements in research into welding technology and its applications. It comprises a certificate and a cash prize of 50,000 yen.

Awarding body: Yosetsu Gakkai, 1-11 Sakuma-cho Kanda, Chiyoda-ku, Tokyo, Japan.

John Torrence Tate International Medal

Established in 1961 by the American Institute of Physics, this medal is given in recognition of distinguished service to physics on an international level. Services that further international understanding and exchange are considered to be of primary importance. The prize is given at infrequent intervals of three to five years and consists of a gold medal and a cash sum of $1,000.

Awarding body: American Institute of Physics, 335 East 45th St., New York, N.Y. 10017, U.S.A.

Recipients include: H. W. Thompson (U.K., 1966); Gilberto Bernardini (Italy, 1972).

Marius-Tausk-Förderpreis

This award is intended to encourage advance in the field of endocrinology, and is given to young scientists for previously unpublished clinical and experimental work in this area (excluding the subject of *diabetes mellitus*). It was first given in 1971, and was donated by the company Organon GmbH München, provisionally for ten years. Scientists resident in Europe, preferably no more than 33 years of age, are eligible. The total value of the award is DM15,000, of which the winner receives DM3,000 in cash (the balance is used to the benefit of his work and further training).

Awarding body: Deutsche Gesellschaft für Endokrinologie, Med. Hochschule, Dept. Innere Medizin, Abt. für klinische Endokrinologie, D-3000 Hannover-Kleefeld, Roderbruchstr., Federal Republic of Germany.

David W. Taylor Award

This award was established in 1935 by the Society of Naval Architects and Marine Engineers in honour of Rear Admiral David Watson Taylor (1864–1940), a distinguished naval constructor. The award is given annually for notable achievement in naval architecture and marine engineering, and takes the form of a medal.

Awarding body: The Society of Naval Architects and Marine Engineers, Suite 1369, One World Trade Center, New York, N.Y. 10048, U.S.A.

J. Hall Taylor Medal

The Taylor Forge and Pipe Works established this award in 1965, to commemorate the pioneering work of J. Hall Taylor in the field of standardization of industrial products and safety codes for their usage. The medal is presented for distinguished service or eminent achievement in the field of codes and standards pertaining to the broad fields of piping and pressure vessels which are sponsored or undertaken by ASME. The scope includes contributions to technical advancement and administration. Candidates should preferably be members of ASME, but this is not an essential criterion. A bronze medal and a certificate are awarded.

Awarding body: American Society of Mechanical Engineers, United Engineering Center, 345 East 47th St., New York, N.Y. 10017, U.S.A.

Recipients include: Walter H. Davidson, Frederic A. Hough, Joe J. King, Burton T. Mast, Andrew J. Shoup (1975).

Taylorian Annual Lectureship

In 1917 the University of Oxford accepted offers from Professor C. H. Firth and Professor J. Wright to endow a Taylorian Special Lectures Fund, the income of which should be applied by the Curators of the Taylor Institution in providing special lectures on subjects connected with modern European literature. One lecturer is appointed annually.

Awarding body: University of Oxford, Wellington Square, Oxford OX1 2JD, England.

Lecturers include: C. Dionisotti ('Europe in 16th-century Italian Literature', 1971); Harry Levin ('Ezra Pound, T. S. Eliot and the European Horizon', 1974); Prof. Yvon Belaval '(Voltaire et Leibniz', 1975).

Nicolae Teclu Prize

The Romanian Academy established this prize for chemistry in 1948. It is presented annually at a General Assembly of the Academy, and consists of 10,000 lei and a diploma. It is named after Nicolae Teclu (1839–1916), Academician and researcher, who invented the 'Teclu lamp' with automatic air and gas current regulation.

Awarding body: Academy of the S.R. of Romania, 125 Calea Victoriei, Bucharest, Romania.

Teheran International Festival of Films for Children and Young Adults

The festival is held annually. Various prizes were established in 1966 by the Institute for the Intellectual Development of Children and Young Adults. The main prize – the Grand Prix of the Golden Statue – is awarded for the best film of the entire festival. Golden Statues are awarded to the best films in each of six categories: live feature film; animated feature film; medium-length live film; medium-length animated film; live short film; animated short film. A Golden Plaque is awarded to a child or young adult for the best performance in a film shown at the festival.

Awarding body: Institute for the Intellectual Development of Children and Young Adults, 31 Jam St., Takhte-Tavous Ave., Teheran, Iran.

Recipients include: Yuri Norstein (U.S.S.R., Grand Prix, *A Hedgehog in the Fog*), Torgny Anderberg (Sweden, live feature film, *Jungle Adventure Campa, Campa*), Arsalan Sassani (Iran, medium-length live film, *The Bamboo Fence*), Otto Foky (Hungary, short animated film, *Scenes with Beans*), Robert Bloomberg (U.S.A., live short film, *Animation Pie*), 1976).

Teknillisten Tieteiden Akatemian ansio-mitali (*Finnish Academy of Technical Sciences Medal of Merit*)

The silver medal was designed in 1976 by the sculptor Terho Sakki, and replaces the Academy's gold medal which was established in 1962. It is granted to an individual or an organization in recognition of outstanding achievements in the fields of techno-scientific research, creative technical work or the general development of technology, or for meritorious support of the activities and goals of the Academy. Except during the Academy's anniversary years, only one medal a year is awarded.

Awarding body: Teknillisten Tieteiden Akatemia, Lönnrotinkatu 37, SF-00180 Helsinki 18, Finland.

Recipients include: President Urho Kekkonen (Patron of the Academy, 1977); Prof. Otto-I. Meurman (teaching, research and application in the field of urban planning, 1977); Dr. Jaakko Pöyry (export of technical knowledge in forest-based industries, 1977); Prof. Pekka Jauho (research and development of techno-scientific research, and activities as President of the Academy and Editor of its magazine, 1977).

Teknillisten Tieteiden Akatemian taitajan-palkinto (*Finnish Academy of Technical Sciences Craftsman's Award*)

The Academy established this award in 1972. It is given in recognition of meritorious achievement connected with technical research and development in which manual dexterity is required. In addition to recognition of the work itself, the award is intended to attract the attention of the general public to the valuable role in research and development played by mechanics and other technical assistants. Inventors or developers with more advanced training, who have themselves built a model or prototype, can receive the award in special circumstances. The competition for the award is announced in January each year. The prize consists of a diploma and a sum of money decided by the Academy (4,000 Fmk. in 1977).

Awarding body: Teknillisten Tieteiden Akatemia, Lönnrotinkatu 37, SF-00180 Helsinki 18, Finland.

Telford Medal

This is the highest award of the Institution of Civil Engineers, and was instituted in 1835 following a bequest by Thomas Telford (1757–1834), first President of the Institution. The income from the endowment fund is used to provide medals and premiums which are awarded annually in connection with papers presented to the Institution.

Awarding body: The Institution of Civil Engineers, Great George St., London SW1P 3AA, England.

Recipients include: A. M. Muir Wood ('Tunnel Hazards: U.K. experience', 1976); D. G. Jobling and A. C. Lyons ('Extension of the Piccadilly Line from Hounslow West to Heathrow Central', 1977); Dr. D. I. Blockley (1978).

Emanoil Teodorescu Prize

The prize was established by the Romanian Academy in 1948. It is for achievement in some branch of biology, and is presented annually at the General Assembly of the Academy. It consists of 10,000 lei and a diploma. It is named after Emanoil Teodorescu (1866–1949), Academician and professor of botany, who made a comprehensive study of Romanian algae.

Awarding body: Academy of the S.R. of Romania, 125 Calea Victoriei, Bucharest, Romania.

Recipients include: Mihail Şerban and Dita Cotariu (1970).

Karl Terzaghi Award

This award was established by the Soil Mechanics and Foundations (now the Geotechnical Engineering) Division of the ASCE in 1960, in honour of Karl Terzaghi, Hon. M.ASCE. The award consists of a plaque and an honorarium of $1,000, and is awarded at intervals of about two years to the author of a paper (generally published by the Society) which has made an outstanding contribution to knowledge in soil mechanics, subsurface and earthwork engineering and construction.

Awarding body: American Society of Civil Engineers, 345 East 47th St., New York, N.Y. 10017, U.S.A.

Recipients include: Ralph B. Peck (1969); Laurits Bjerrum (1971); H. Bolton Seed (1973); T. William Lambe (1975).

Karl Terzaghi Lecture

This lectureship was established by the Soil Mechanics and Foundations (now the Geotechnical Engineering) Division of the ASCE in 1960 in honour of Karl Terzaghi, Hon. M.ASCE. At about yearly intervals a distinguished engineer is invited to deliver a 'Terzaghi Lecture' at a meeting of the Society; he receives a certificate and an honorarium of $300.

Awarding body: American Society of Civil Engineers, 345 East 47th St., New York, N.Y. 10017, U.S.A.

Recipients include: F. E. Richart, Jr. ('Some Effects of Dynamic Soil Properties on Soil-Structure Interaction', 1974); G. G. Meyerhof 'Bearing Capacity of Foundations', 1975); Lymon C. Reese ('The Design and Construction of Drilled Shafts', 1976).

Nikola Tesla Awards

The 'Nikola Tesla' Society for the Promotion of Scientific Knowledge organizes a biennial international film festival with the aim of popularizing science and technology by means of films. It is named after Nikola Tesla (1856–1943), the famous scientist and inventor who was born in Yugoslavia. Gold, silver and bronze plaques are awarded in five categories: scientific research; popular science; science fiction; science information; television science. Various special awards are also given.

Awarding body: 'Nikola Tesla' Society for Promoting Scientific Knowledge, 10 Kneza Miloša, 1000 Belgrade, Yugoslavia.

Recipients include: A Million Years Ahead (Fed. Rep. of Germany, scientific research), *Hamster* (Yugoslavia, popular science), *Memory of Metals* (U.S.S.R., science fiction), *Eclipse 73* (France, science information), *Nature Builds Waterfalls* (Yugoslavia, television science), 1976.

Tessedik Sámuel Memorial Medal

The Hungarian Society of Agricultural Sciences founded the medal in 1960 for outstanding work, in accordance with the Society's aims, which has promoted the development of agricultural sciences and increased yields, and also for outstanding theoretical or practical work in specialist fields. Two or three prizes of 7,000 forints each are awarded on the occasion of the Society's General Meetings. The medal is named after Sámuel Tessedik (1742–1820), educationalist and agriculturalist, who founded one of the first agricultural training colleges.

Awarding body: Magyar Agrártudományi Egyesület, Budapest V, Kossuth Lajos tér 6–8, Hungary.

Textile Institute Jubilee Award

The award, a framed certificate, was established by the Institute in 1960 to commemorate its 50th anniversary. The award is given annually for successful research and invention by teams or groups of research workers, working within any appropriate organization.

Awarding body: The Textile Institute, 10 Blackfriars St., Manchester M3 5DR, England.

Recipients include: Brintons Ltd. (invention of gripper carpet loom, and progress made in the carpet industry in general, 1971); FNF Ltd. and Courtaulds Ltd. (invention of FNF high-speed warp-knitting machine, 1972); Scapa Group Ltd. (contributions to design, development and manufacture of industrial fabrics for special purposes, 1974); Karl Mayer Textilmaschinenfabrik GmbH (development of warp knitting and associated machinery, 1976).

Textile Institute Medal

Founded in 1921, the medal is given for distinguished services to the textile industry in general and to the Textile Institute in particular. It is awarded annually in November.

Awarding body: The Textile Institute, 10 Blackfriars St., Manchester M3 5DR, England.

Recipients include: G. McLeavy (work on product development in several fields, and active participation in Institute activities, 1974); J. G. Martindale (work in processing on the worsted system, development of testing equipment, and education and active participation in Institute activities, 1974); E. R. Trotman (contributions to the wet-finishing industry including authorship of several books, and active participation in Institute activities, 1975); D. C. Snowden (work in fabric structure and weaving mechanisms, and active participation in Institute activities, 1976); Mario Nava (development of stabilized bulked polyester-filament nylon, 1976).

Textile Institute Medal for Design

Established in 1971, the medal is awarded annually in recognition of professional textile designers who have devoted themselves to, and made substantial contributions in, the field of textile design. Designs must be an integral part of the structure of the fabric; success in printed design only will not be recognized.

Awarding body: The Textile Institute, 10 Blackfriars St., Manchester M3 5DR, England.

Recipients include: Marianne Straub (woven fabrics for furnishing, 1972); Tibor Reich (fabrics for interior decoration, 1973); J. C. Doughty (knitwear, 1974); Stanley Kinder (worsted and woollen cloths, 1975).

Thai Prizes for the Compilation of Books on Buddhism

These prizes were instituted by H.M. King Prachathipok of Thailand in 1928 in order to promote education in Buddhism. There is a first prize of 1,000 baht and two second prizes of 500 baht each. Candidates are required to write a book within a period of eight months on a given Buddhist topic, intended for children over the age of 10. Style and doctrinal orthodoxy form the basis of selection. The prizes are awarded annually by the King or his representative in the Royal Ceremony of Visakha Puja Day (the 15th day of the sixth lunar month).

Awarding body: Selection Committee and H.M. the King of Thailand.

Recipients include: Mr. Kasem Bunsi (1941, 1944, 1947, 1957, 1959, 1961, 1962, 1964, 1965, 1968); Mr. Adisak Thongboon (1970, 1971, 1972, 1974); Lieut.-Col. Watchara Khong-adisak (1955, 1956, 1960, 1963, 1973, 1975).

Irving G. Thalberg Memorial Award

The Academy of Motion Picture Arts and Sciences established this prize in 1937 in memory of Irving G. Thalberg (1899–1936), the American film producer. The award is a bronze head of Thalberg, and is given to a creative producer whose body of work reflects a consistently high quality of motion picture production. It may be given annually, but only if voted by the Academy's Governors. No one may receive it more than once.

Awarding body: Academy of Motion Picture Arts and Sciences, 8949 Wilshire Blvd., Beverly Hills, Calif. 90211, U.S.A.

Recipients include: Alfred Hitchcock (1967); Ingmar Bergman (1970); Lawrence Weingarten (1973); Mervyn LeRoy (1975); Pandro S. Berman (1976).

Thermal Conductivity Award

Established in 1970 by the International Thermal Conductivity Conferences, this prize is awarded for outstanding achievements and contributions to the field of thermal conductivity. The award is made at each conference; these were originally held annually but are now held every other year. The award consists of a mounted specimen of Round Robin Armco iron (a material of historical significance in the field) and a certificate.

Awarding body: International Thermal Conductivity Conferences, c/o Thermophysical Properties Research Center, Purdue University, Lafayette, Ind. 47907, U.S.A.

Recipients include: Dr. R. W. Powell (1970); Dr. D. L. McElroy (1971); Dr. P. G. Klemens (1972); Dr. C. F. Lucks (1973); Dr. M. J. Laubitz (1975).

Thermophysics Award

Established by the AIAA in 1975, the award is presented annually for an outstanding recent technical or scientific contribution in thermophysics, specifically as related to the study and application of the properties and mechanisms involved in thermal energy transfer within and between solids, and between an object and its environment, particularly by radiation, and the study of environmental effects on such properties and mechanisms. It comprises a medal and certificate of citation, and is usually presented at the Thermophysics Conference.

Awarding body: American Institute of Aeronautics and Astronautics, 1290 Avenue of the Americas, New York, N.Y. 10019, U.S.A.

Recipients include: Donald K. Edwards (1976); Chang-Lin Tien (1977).

Dr.-Edmund-Thiele-Denkmünze

This medal, instituted in 1937 by the company J. B. Bemberg AG, Wuppertal-Barmen, is presented annually by the West German Association of Pulp and Paper Chemists and Engineers (Zellcheming) for outstanding achievement in the field of viscose and staple rayon, and other artificial silks, preferably on the basis of a work published during the preceding year. It commemorates Dr. Edmund Thiele (1867–1927), inventor and founder of the German cuprammonium rayon industry. Nominations must be made by members of Zellcheming.

Awarding body: Verein der Zellstoff- und Papier-Chemiker und Ingenieure, 6100 Darmstadt, Berliner Allee 56, Federal Republic of Germany.

Recipients include: Gen.-Dir. Dipl.-Ing. Julius C. Funcke (1961); Dr. August Brötz (1967); Dr.-Ing. Walter Frey (1968); Dr. Kurt Götze (1969); Doz. Dr. Erich Treiber (1971).

Hermann-Thoms-Medaille

This medal was established in 1961 by the German Pharmaceutical Society. It may be awarded at any suitable occasion to persons who have given special service in the whole field of pharmacy. It is accompanied by a certificate. The award is governed otherwise by the same rules that apply to the Carl Mannich Medaille (*q.v.*). It commemorates Prof. Hermann Friedrich Maria Thoms (1859–1931), founding President of the German Pharmaceutical Society.

Awarding body: Deutsche Pharmazeutische Gesellschaft e.V., 6100 Darmstadt, Frankfurter Strasse 250, Federal Republic of Germany.

Recipients include: Prof. Ferdinand Schlemmer (1968); Prof. Georg Edmund Dann (1968); Prof. Günther Krebs (1969); Dr. Dr. Werner Luckenbach (1970); Prof. Gerhard Schenk (1973).

Sir George Thomson Gold Medal

This medal is awarded every five years by the British Institute of Measurement and Control for a contribution to measurement science which has resulted in fundamental improvements in the understanding of the physical world. It was instituted in 1975 in honour of the late Sir George Thomson, F.R.S. (1892–1975), first President of the Institute and 1937 Nobel prizewinner for Physics.

Awarding body: The Institute of Measurement and Control, 20 Peel St., London W8 7PD, England.

J. J. Thomson Medal

The medal was established in 1976 and is awarded for outstanding work in electronics theory, practice, development or manufacture over any period of time. It may be awarded to an individual or a group without restriction as to nationality, country of residence or membership of the Institution of Electrical Engineers.

Awarding body: Institution of Electrical Engineers, Savoy Place, London WC2R 0BL, England.

Recipients include: C. W. Earp (lifetime's work on navigational aids, 1976); W. J. Bray (contributions to telecommunications research, 1977).

Thorvaldsen Medal

The award was established in 1838 by the Danish Academy of Fine Arts in honour of Bertel Thorvaldsen (1770–1844), the sculptor. A medal is awarded annually for distinguished achievement in the free arts. Recipients must be of Danish nationality save in exceptional cases.

Awarding body: Akademiet for de skønne Kunster, Akademiraadet, Kgs. Nytorv 1, 1050 Copenhagen K, Denmark.

Thulin Medal

This award was established by the Swedish Society of Aeronautics and Astronautics in 1944 in memory of Enoch Thulin (1881–1919), a Swedish aviation pioneer. It is for outstanding achievement in the field of aeronautics. There are three awards: the gold medal for aeronautical achievement of the highest merit; the silver medal for contributions to aeronautical development; and the bronze medal for contributions to the Society.

Awarding body: Swedish Society of Aeronautics and Astronautics, FFA, Box 11021, S16111 Bromma, Sweden.

Recipients (Gold Medal) include: Tore Edlén (1970); Erik Bratt (1972); Georg Drougge (1974); Thorvald Andersson (1975); Henrik Lindgren (1976).

Tilden Lectureship

The Tilden Lectureship was founded in 1939 to commemorate the name of Sir William Augustus Tilden, President of the Chemical Society from 1903 to 1905. Two Tilden Lecturers are appointed each year, usually from the younger Fellows of the Society. In accordance with the terms of the bequest, each lecturer should deal with the progress in some branch of chemistry. Lecturers receive a silver medal and £100.

Awarding body: The Chemical Society, Burlington House, London W1V 0BN, England.

Recipients include: A. R. Katritzky, J. W. White (1975–76); R. O. C. Norman, M. W. Roberts (1976–77); N. B. H. Jonathan, K. H. Overton (1977–78).

Edgar D. Tillyer Award

At a meeting of the Optical Society of America in 1953, the President accepted from the President of the American Optical Company the dies of a new medal to be known as the Edgar D. Tillyer Medal, together with an endowment sufficient to permit the striking of the medal biennially. The award is presented to a person who has performed distinguished work in the field of vision, including (but not limited to) the optics, physiology, anatomy, or psychology of the visual system. The award honours Dr. Tillyer for his work in vision.

Awarding body: Optical Society of America, 2000 L St., N.W., Washington, D.C. 20036, U.S.A.

Recipients include: Lorrin A. Riggs (1969); Louise L. Sloan (1971); Robert M. Boynton (1972); Yves Le Grand (1974); Floyd Ratliff (1976).

Timoshenko Medal

The Timoshenko Medal is bestowed annually in recognition of distinguished contributions to applied mechanics, without restrictions to nationality or profession. The award was established in 1957 in honour of Stephen P. Timoshenko, to commemorate his contribution to applied mechanics, as author and teacher. The medal is of bronze and accompanied by an engrossed certificate.

Awarding body: American Society of Mechanical Engineers, United Engineering Center, 345 East 47th St., New York, N.Y. 10017, U.S.A.

Recipients include: Jacob Pieter Den Hartog (1972); Eric Reissner (1973); Albert E. Green (1974); Chia-Chiao Lin (1975); Erastus Henry Lee (1976).

Royce J. Tipton Award

R. J. Tipton, Past Vice-President of the ASCE, established this prize in 1964 to recognize contributions by members to the advancement of irrigation and drainage engineering, either in teaching, research, planning, design, construction or management; these contributions may be practical or in the form of written papers. The award consists of a plaque and certificate, and is made annually.

Awarding body: American Society of Civil Engineers, 345 East 47th St., New York, N.Y. 10017, U.S.A.

Recipients include: George D. Clyde (1972); William R. Gianelli (1973); Arthur D. Soderberg (1974); Charles R. Maierhofer (1975); Jerald E. Christiansen (1976).

Gheorghe Tiţeica Prize

The Romanian Academy founded this prize for mathematics in 1948. It is awarded annually at a general meeting of the Academy, and consists of

10,000 lei and a diploma. It is named after Gheorghe Tiţeica (1873–1939), university professor and Academician, and well known internationally for his work on differential geometry.

Awarding body: Academy of the S.R. of Romania, 125 Calea Victoriei, Bucharest, Romania.

Toronto Book Awards

The awards, totalling $3,000 in value, are made annually by Toronto City Council for the best books about Toronto published during the previous year. They are presented at a civic reception in March. The awards were established in 1973.

Awarding body: Toronto City Council, City Hall, Toronto, Ont., Canada.

Recipients include: Robert Harney and Harold Troper (*Immigrants*, 1976); Hugh Hood (*The Swing in the Garden*, 1976); Margaret Atwood (*Lady Oracle*, 1977); Margaret Gibson Gilbrood (*The Butterfly Ward*, 1977).

Henry Marshall Tory Medal

The medal is awarded every two years, if there is a suitable candidate, for outstanding research in a branch of astronomy, chemistry, mathematics, physics or an allied science carried out mainly in the eight years preceding the date of the award, but all the research of the candidate shall be taken into account. The prize consists of a gold medal and C$1,000. Canadian citizens or persons who have been Canadian residents for the preceding five years are eligible. The prize was established in 1941 by Henry Marshall Tory, founder of the Universities of British Columbia and Alberta, the National Research Council Laboratories and Carleton University.

Awarding body: The Royal Society of Canada, 395 Wellington, Ottawa, Ont. K1A 0N4, Canada.

Recipients include: I. Halperin (1967); W. G. Schneider (1969); H. E. Johns (1971); B. N. Brockhouse (1973); W. T. Tutte (1975).

Toulouse International Voice Competition

The competition was established in 1953 by the then Mayor of Toulouse, Monsieur Raymond Badiou. It takes place annually in the first week of October. The administrative expenses are met by the municipality of Toulouse, but the main prizes are donated by the State, and other prizes by various local organizations and the Société des Auteurs, Compositeurs et Editeurs de Musique. The two first prizes, one for male voice and one for female voice, consist of a Sèvres vase presented by the President of the French Republic and 10,000 francs each presented by the city of Toulouse. Candidates must be between 18 and 33 years of age, and may be of any nationality. The competition is held in public.

Awarding body: Concours International de Chant de la Ville de Toulouse, Théâtre du Capitole, 31000 Toulouse, France.

Recipients include: Bozena Porzynska (Poland, 1974); Pietr Gluboky (U.S.S.R., 1974); Betty Lane (U.S.A., 1976).

Joseph Toynbee Memorial Lectureship

A lecturer, qualified to contribute to the advancement of the science and practice of otology, is appointed by a Selection Committee to deliver a lecture every two years at the Royal College of Surgeons of England.

Awarding body: Royal Society of Medicine, 1 Wimpole St., London W1M 8AE, England.

Trans-Canada (McKee) Trophy

The Trans-Canada Trophy, generally known as the McKee Trophy, is presented annually by the Canadian Aeronautics and Space Institute for outstanding achievement in the field of air operations. Established by Dalzell McKee in 1927, it is the oldest aviation award in Canada, and until 1971 was administered by the Department of Defence.

Awarding body: Canadian Aeronautics and Space Institute, Suite 406, 77 Metcalfe St., Ottawa, Ont. K1P 5L6, Canada.

Recipients include: W/Cdr. W. G. Leach (1960); W. W. Phipps (1961); F. A. MacDougall (1963); P. C. Garratt (1966); Lt.-Col. R. A. White (1967).

Erich-Trefftz-Preis

The prize was established in 1964 by the German Society for Aeronautics, the predecessor of the German Aerospace Research and Experimental Establishment (DFVLR) in Cologne. The prize commemorates the applied mathematician Erich Trefftz (1888–1937), who worked with the DFVLR on Prandtl's theory of lifting surfaces and on theories of oscillation and elasticity. The award is restricted to employees of the DFVLR, and is given for published works or lectures they have given about their scientific achievements. The prize consists of a certificate and a sum of money of up to DM5,000, and is awarded every two years.

Awarding body: Deutsche Forschungs- und Versuchsanstalt für Luft- und Raumfahrt e.V., Postfach 90 60 58, D-5000 Cologne 90, Federal Republic of Germany.

Trent-Crede Medal

The medal is presented by the Acoustical Society of America to an individual of any nationality who has made an outstanding contribution to the science of mechanical vibration and shock through publication of research results in professional journals, or by other achievements.

Awarding body: Acoustical Society of America, 335 East 45th St., New York, N.Y. 10017, U.S.A.

Recipients include: Carl Irwin Vigness (posthum. 1969); Raymond D. Mindlin (1971); Elias Klein (1973); J. P. Den Hartog (1975).

Trident Television Award for Communication in Science

In 1975 the British Association for the Advancement of Science collaborated with the Trident Television Group to found this prize. Its purpose is to broaden public knowledge of important ideas current in any area of science. The winner i selected partly for his/her contribution to scientific thought and partly for his/her ability to communicate such ideas. Originality is desirable; equally important is the ability to expound broad scientific concepts. The award is open to all British scientists who have published original work. It consists of a medal, £1,000 in cash and participation in a nationally networked TV programme originated by Yorkshire Television (a member of the Trident Television group).

Awarding body: British Association for the Advancement of Science, Fortress House, 23 Savile Row, London W1X 2AA, England.

Recipients include: Mrs. Cherrie Bramwell and Dr. G. Whitfield (1975); Sir Bernard Lovell (1976); Prof. G. D. Blair (1978).

Trieste City Music Prize

An international competition, established in 1949, is held annually in October and sponsored by the city of Trieste with the G. Tartini State Conservatoire of Music and the G. Verdi Municipal Theatre. The prize of 3 million lire is for an unpublished and unperformed symphonic composition. The award includes the subsequent public performance of the winning work.

Awarding body: Committee for the 'Città di Trieste' Prize, Palazzo Municipale, Piazza dell'-Unità d'Italia 4, Trieste, Italy.

Recipients include: Carlo Pinelli (1950); Martin Wendel (1967); Joseph Gaher (1970); Thomas Schudel (1972); Daniel Zanettovich (1973).

Tschermak-Seysenegg-Preis

The prize commemorates three members of the same family: Gustav von Tschermak-Seysenegg (1836–1927), professor of mineralogy, Armin von Tschermak-Seysenegg (1870–1952), professor of physiology, and Erich von Tschermak-Seysenegg (1871–1962), professor of botany, and founder of the prize in 1961. The prize is awarded to full and corresponding members of the Austrian Academy of Sciences for outstanding learned works, in turn on mineralogy and petrology (the Gustav von Tschermak-Seysenegg Prize), on medical physiology (the Armin von Tschermak-Seysenegg Prize), and on applied botany (the Erich von Tschermak-Seysenegg Prize). The award, a certificate and a sum of money, is made annually, so that each separate branch of the prize is in effect awarded every three years.

Awarding body: Österreichische Akademie der Wissenschaften, 1010 Vienna, Dr.-Ignaz-Seipel-Platz 2, Austria.

Recipients include: Haymo Heritsch; Sir Henry Dale; Josef Kisser; Josef Zemann.

Jean Tschumi Award

This award consists of a diploma conferred every two years for particularly interesting work or activity in the fields of architectural criticism, the education of young architects, or international collaboration on the professional plane. The award was founded in 1974 by the International Union

of Architects (UIA). It is not intended for personalities whose world-wide repute is already established. The award is a tribute to Jean Tschumi, one of the first Presidents of the UIA.

Awarding body: International Union of Architects, 1 rue d'Ulm, 75005 Paris, France.

Türk Dil Kurumu Ödülü (*Turkish Linguistic Society Prize*)

The Society established the prize in 1955 in memory of Kemal Atatürk, the founder of the Turkish Republic and of the Turkish Linguistic Society (1932). Four annual prizes of 10,000 liras each, and a medal, are awarded for achievement in four categories: literature (various sections for all genres); social sciences and humanities; language used in the press; language used on radio and television. The awards are made to Turkish citizens for works published in the preceding year which conform to the principles of the Society, and make the most effective use of the Turkish language.

Awarding body: Türk Dil Kurumu, 217 Atatürk Bulvarı, Ankara, Turkey.

Recipients include: Aziz Nesin (play, 1970); Oktay Rifat (poetry, 1970); Fakir Baykurt (novel, 1971); Salâh Birsel (essay, 1976).

W. Rupert Turnbull Lecture

The lecture is delivered annually at a major meeting of the Canadian Aeronautics and Space Institute. The lecturer, who receives a certificate and honorarium, is elected for his association with some significant achievement in the scientific or engineering fields of aeronautics or space research, and for his qualifications to present a paper on the subject. The lecture was established in 1955 to commemorate Dr. Turnbull's pioneering work in aeronautical engineering.

Awarding body: Canadian Aeronautics and Space Institute, Suite 406, 77 Metcalfe St., Ottawa, Ont. K1P 5L6, Canada.

Recipients include: Prof. H. S. Ribner ('Jets and Noise', 1968); Dr. B. G. Newman ('The Prediction of Turbulent Jets and Wall Jets', 1969); R. J. Templin ('Aerodynamics Low and Slow', 1970); J. P. Beauregard ('The Development of Small Gas Turbine Engines at UACL', 1971); Dr. J. H. de Leeuw ('An Aerodynamicist's View of the Upper Atmosphere', 1972).

Frederick Jackson Turner Award

This award was first established in 1958 as the Prize Studies Award of the Mississippi Valley Historical Association, and redefined as from 1977. It is awarded annually, to the author of a book-length manuscript on some significant phase of American history, who has not previously published such a study. Applications are submitted by university presses who have undertaken to publish the works. The author receives a medal, certificate and $500, and the university press is given a subsidy of $3,000 to be used for the publication of another book on American history by a new author.

Awarding body: Organization of American Historians, 112 North Bryan St., Bloomington, Ind. 47401, U.S.A.

Arnold B. Tuttle Award

This prize was established by the Aerospace Medical Association in memory of Col. Arnold B. Tuttle, U.S.A.F., M.C. It is awarded annually for original research that has made the most significant contribution of the year towards the solution of a challenging problem in aerospace medicine and published in *Aviation, Space, and Environmental Medicine*. It is sponsored by United Air Lines and consists of $500 and a certificate.

Awarding body: Aerospace Medical Association, Washington National Airport, Washington, D.C. 20001, U.S.A.

Recipients include: Dr. Harald J. von Beckh (1972); Surg./Capt. John S. P. Rawlins (1973); Dr. Henning E. von Gierke (1974); Col. Malcolm C. Lancaster (1975); Dr. Russell R. Burton (1976).

Tweejaarlijkse Poëzieprijs De Vlaamse Gids
(De Vlaamse Gids *Biennial Prize for Poetry*)

This prize is awarded for a volume of verse in Dutch by a poet under 40 years of age. It was founded in 1970 by Editors Hoste, publishers of the cultural magazine *De Vlaamse Gids*, and consists of a cash prize of 25,000 Belgian francs.

Awarding body: De Vlaamse Gids, 28 Korte Nieuwstraat, 2000 Antwerp, Belgium.

Recipients include: Mark Insingel (1970); Patrick Conrad (1972); Lucienne Stassaert (1974); Roland Yooris (1976).

Tylecote Lecture

The lecture was founded in 1966 under a bequest to Manchester University of £500 from the estate of Professor Tylecote, Professor of Medicine in the University from 1929 to 1939 and Professor Emeritus until his death in 1965.

Awarding body: University of Manchester, Manchester M13 9PL, England.

Lecturers include: Prof. John Charnley ('Total Hip Replacement and Basic Surgical Sciences', 1976).

John and Alice Tyler Ecology Award

Established in 1973 by Mr. and Mrs. Tyler, the $150,000 award is made annually to the individual or team working on a common project whose accomplishment has been recognized as conferring the greatest benefit on mankind in the fields of ecology and environment. Recipients are expected to give a paper suitable for lecture and/or publication at an annual symposium held in conjunction with Pepperdine University.

Awarding body: Pepperdine University, Malibu, Calif. 90265, U.S.A.

Recipients include: Dr. Charles Elton (Oxford Univ., animal ecology), Dr. Rene Dubos (Rockefeller Univ., microbiology), Dr. Abel Wolman (Johns Hopkins Univ., sanitation and water engineering), 1975.

Tyrrell Medal

The medal is awarded from time to time, with a minimum interval of two years between awards, for outstanding work in the history of Canada. The prize consists of a gold medal and C$1,000. Preference will be given to Canadian citizens or persons who have been Canadian residents for the five years preceding the award. The medal was endowed in 1927 by Joseph Burr Tyrrell (1858–1957), geologist, geographer, explorer, engineer and amateur historian.

Awarding body: The Royal Society of Canada, 395 Wellington, Ottawa, Ont. K1A 0N4, Canada.

Recipients include: Edgar McInnis (1966); G. W. L. Nicholson (1968); Fernand Ouellet (1970); Jean Hamelin (1972); Ramsay Cook (1975).

U

UNESCO Prize for Architecture

This triennial prize was established by UNESCO's General Conference in 1968 to stimulate architectural efforts towards improving the standard of dwellings or town planning. Architectural students from schools throughout the world are eligible for the award, which is worth U.S.$3,000. A competition is organized by the International Union of Architects.

Awarding body: UNESCO, 9 Place de Fontenoy, 75700 Paris, France.

Recipients include: Mitsuo Morozumi (Japan, 1969); Vladimir Kirpitchev (U.S.S.R., 1972); Vidyadhar Chavda and Alka Shah (India, 1975).

UNESCO Science Prize

The prize was established in 1968 by UNESCO's General Conference. It is awarded in recognition of outstanding contribution to the development of a member state or region of UNESCO, especially in the fields of scientific and technological research and education, or in the fields of engineering and industrial development. Any person or group working privately, or as members of the staff of a private or governmental organization, may receive the award, which is made every two years. A cash prize of U.S.$3,000 and an appropriate plaque are presented.

Awarding body: UNESCO, 9 Place de Fontenoy, 75700 Paris, France.

Recipients include: International Maize and Wheat Improvement Centre (Mexico) and International Rice Research Institute (Philippines), 1970; Prof. Victor A. Kovda (U.S.S.R.) and a group of nine Austrian research workers, 1972; Alfred Champagnat (France, 1976); Rothamsted Experimental Station group (U.K., 1978).

Ubersetzerpreis (*Translator's Prize*)

The German Academy for Language and Poetry founded this prize in 1958 for outstanding achievements in the field of literary translation. The prize is awarded annually and consists of a cash prize of DM6,000.

Awarding body: Deutsche Akademie für Sprache und Dichtung, Alexandraweg 23 (Glückert-Haus), 6100 Darmstadt, Federal Republic of Germany.

Recipients include: Peter Gan (Richard Moering) (1973); Herman Meyer (1974); Curt Meyer-Clason (1975); Hanns Grössel (1976).

Union Carbide Award for Chemical Education

The award was established in 1961 as the Chemical Education Award by The Chemical Institute of Canada. It is sponsored by Union Carbide Canada Ltd. It is given primarily in recognition of outstanding contributions to the teaching in Canada, at any level, of chemistry or chemical engineering. Secondary consideration is given to those whose contribution to chemical education has been administrative or otherwise indirect. The award is made annually and takes the form of a commemorative scroll and an honorarium to the amount of $750. A travel grant of up to $400 may also be given to enable the recipient to attend the award ceremony at the Institute's Annual Conference where he/she gives an award address.

Awarding body: The Chemical Institute of Canada, 151 Slater St., Ottawa, Ont. K1P 5H3, Canada.

Recipients include: J. M. Holmes ('Whither Chemical Education?', 1973); K. J. Laidler ('Too Much to Know', 1974); W. E. Harris ('Analysing Teaching', 1975); Brian T. Newbold (1977); Roger Thibert (1978).

Upjohn Award in Pharmacology

The award was donated by the Upjohn Company of Canada to the Pharmacological Society of Canada in 1977. It consists of $1,000 plus travel expenses of up to $500 to the Annual Meeting of the Society, and a plaque. It is given annually for significant contributions to the advancement and extension of knowledge in the field of pharmacology. It is based on originality and uniqueness of approach to laboratory or clinical research that has led to new significant pharmacological knowledge or concepts, or to the development of new therapeutic agents for the treatment of disease. The award is given for work done primarily in Canada by Canadian scientists. The recipient is invited to give an Upjohn Prize Oration on the occasion of the presentation of the award.

Awarding body: Pharmacological Society of Canada, c/o Secretary, Dr. G. D. Bellward, Division of Pharmacology and Toxicology, Faculty of Pharmaceutical Sciences, University of British Columbia, Vancouver, B.C. V6T 1W5, Canada.

George Urdang Medal

This international award was established in 1952 by the American Institute of the History of

Pharmacy at the University of Wisconsin, to mark the 65th birthday of Georg Urdang, German-born co-founder and Director of the Institute and also co-founder and President of the International Society of the History of Pharmacy. The medal is awarded irregularly for scientific papers, chiefly on historical or socio-historical aspects of pharmacy, published anywhere in the world. The recipient is selected by the International Academy for the History of Pharmacy by special request of the American Institute.

Awarding body: American Institute of the History of Pharmacy, University of Wisconsin, Madison, Wis. 53706, U.S.A.

Recipients include: Georg Edmund Dann (Fed. Rep. of Germany, 1962); Antonio E. Vitolo (Italy, 1964); Leslie G. Matthews (U.K., 1968); Wolfgang Schneider (Fed. Rep. of Germany, 1973).

Abbott Payson Usher Prize

This award of $100 and a certificate was established by the Society for the History of Technology to honour the late Dr. Abbott Payson Usher for his many contributions to the history of technology. Its purpose is to encourage the publication of original research of the highest standard in the history of technology. It is given to the author of the best work published by the Society within the preceding three years, either in the Society's international quarterly, *Technology and Culture,* or in book form in the Society's Monograph Series.

Awarding body: Society for the History of Technology, c/o Dr. Carroll Pursell, Jr., Secretary, Dept. of History, University of California, Santa Barbara, Calif. 93106, U.S.A.

Recipients include: Cyril Stanley Smith (1972); R. L. Hills and H. A. Pacey (1973); Carl Mitcham and Robert Mackey (1974); Paul Uselding (1975); Russell I. Fries (1976).

V

Jean Vacher Prize
This prize is awarded for the best paper submitted to the International Congress of Agricultural Medicine, which is held every three years. The prize, consisting of 1,000 Swiss francs, is restricted to members of the International Association of Agricultural Medicine and Rural Health who are under 35 years of age. The prize was founded by the Association in 1973, in memory of Professor Jean Vacher (1924–72), its founder and secretary-general.
Awarding body: International Association of Agricultural Medicine and Rural Health.
Recipients include: Kimio Fujita (Japan, 1975).

Romeo Vachon Award
This award is presented annually by the Canadian Aeronautics and Space Institute for an outstanding contribution of a practical nature to the art, science and engineering of aeronautics and space in Canada. It was established in 1969, and consists of a bronze plaque.
Awarding body: Canadian Aeronautics and Space Institute, Suite 406, 77 Metcalfe St., Ottawa, Ont. K1P 5L6, Canada.
Recipients include: S. N. Green (1969); H. E. Rasmussen (1970); J. F. Fairchild (1971); E. J. McLaren (1972).

Van Cleef Memorial Medal
This gold medal was established in 1970, and is given intermittently for outstanding contributions in the field of applied urban geography.
Awarding body: American Geographical Society, Broadway at 156th St., New York, N.Y. 10032, U.S.A.
Recipients include: John R. Borchert (1970); Harold Rose (1974).

Hoyt S. Vandenberg Award
This national award is made annually by the U.S. Air Force Association to an individual or organization for outstanding contributions in the field of aerospace education. It takes the form of a plaque, and was instituted in 1948, in honour of Gen. Hoyt S. Vandenberg (1899–1954), Second Chief of Staff, U.S. Air Force.
Awarding body: Air Force Association National Awards Committee, 1750 Pennsylvania Ave., N.W., Washington, D.C. 20006, U.S.A.
Recipients include: Maj. Richard L. Craft (1972); Community College of the Air Force (1973);

Lt.-Col. Gregory J. Butler (1974); Aerospace Audiovisual Service, Norton AFB, Calif. (1975); Hon. David P. Taylor (1976).

Toon van den Heever-prys vir regswetenskap
(*Toon van den Heever Prize for Jurisprudence*)
This prize is named after François Petrus (Toon) van den Heever (1894–1956) who, besides being a poet and essayist, was also the most eminent Afrikaans-speaking lawyer of his time. In 1966 the South African Academy decided to remove law from the categories covered by its Stals Prize (*q.v.*) and to introduce a separate prize for this subject. The prize money, R250, is donated by Butterworth's, the publishing firm. The prize is awarded every three years for original legal works in Afrikaans.
Awarding body: Suid-Afrikaanse Akademie vir Wetenskap en Kuns, Posbus 538, Pretoria 0001, South Africa.
Recipients include: Prof. H. S. Cilliers and Prof. M. L. Benade (*Maatskappyereg*, 1969); Prof. S. A. Strauss and Adv. M. J. Strydom (*Die Suid-Afrikaanse geneeskundige reg*, 1972); Prof. C. W. H. Schmidt (*Die Bewysreg*, 1975).

Joost van den Vondel Prize
This is one of four similar prizes given annually by the FVS Foundation for outstanding achievement in the arts, town and country planning, folklore and human sciences. It consists of DM25,000, and is intended for those who live in the Dutch, Flemish and Low German area of cultural influence. It is named in memory of Joost van den Vondel (1587–1679), the Dutch tragic poet, born in Cologne. (*See also* Shakespeare, Steffens, and Montaigne prizes.)
Awarding body: Stiftung FVS, Georgsplatz 10, 2 Hamburg 1, Federal Republic of Germany.
Recipients include: Prof. Fernand Colin (Belgium, 1971); Prof. Horst Gerson, 1972).

Balthasar van der Pol Gold Medal
This award was established in 1963 by the widow of Prof. Balthasar van der Pol, the Dutch radio scientist (1889–1961). The medal is awarded triennially for achievements of particular value in any of the branches of science covered by the Commissions of the International Union of Radio Science (URSI). Candidates must be proposed by one of the 36 National Member Committees of

URSI, and the work must have been carried out mainly during the six-year period preceding the award.

Awarding body: International Union of Radio Science (URSI), Rue de Nieuwenhove 81, B-1180 Brussels, Belgium.

Recipients: Sir Martin Ryle (U.K., application of the phase-switching and aperture-synthesis techniques to antennas for radio astronomy, 1963); Prof. W. E. Gordon (U.S.A., development of the incoherent scatter technique for ionospheric studies, 1966); Dr. J. P. Wild (Australia, radio astronomy, including completion of a notable high-resolution radio-heliograph, 1969); Dr. B. D. Josephson (U.K., electronic effects in superconductors, 1972); Prof. L. B. Felsen (U.S.A., application of ray-optical methods to studies of the propagation and diffraction of electromagnetic waves, 1975).

Simon Van der Stel Foundation Award

This is a medal of honour in gold, silver or bronze, awarded by the Foundation (the South African National Trust) at irregular intervals to mark significant contributions to conservation, preservation and restoration of historic buildings, structures and townscapes. It was established in 1969.

Awarding body: Simon Van der Stel Foundation, P.O.B. 1743, Pretoria 0001, South Africa.

Recipients include: Hon. B. J. Vorster (gold); Caltex Oil Co. of S.A. Ltd (gold); Dr. W. H. J. Punt, Sr. (gold), for initiation of private conservation movement in S.A.; The Hon. B. J. van der Walt (silver), for contribution to conservation in Namibia (S.W.A.); Dr. J. Ploeger (silver) for historical contributions to preservation; Mr. E. Vertue (silver), conservation services and photographic recording of Cape Dutch architecture.

Jan van Riebeeck Medal of Honour

This award was established in 1977 for significant contributions in the field of South African history, especially on the subject of the founding and founder of South Africa, Jan van Riebeeck. The award is made annually on 6 April (Founder's Day). It consists of a medal in silver gilt, silver, or bronze.

Awarding body: Jan van Riebeeck Foundation, P.O.B. 3457, Pretoria 0001, South Africa.

Recipients include: City Council of Cape Town (consistent honouring of Founder's Day); Dr. H. B. Thom (research on Jan van Riebeeck and his times at the Cape); Dr. G. D. Scholz (promoting good relations with the Netherlands); Dr. W. H. J. Punt (initiatives leading to the restoration of van Riebeeck's birthplace in Holland).

Tibor Varga International Violin Competition

This is an annual competition begun in 1964 and named after Tibor Varga, the Hungarian violinist and teacher. Various cash prizes are awarded,

given by different Swiss organizations and municipal bodies (first prize 5,000 Swiss francs). The upper age limit for entrants is 35.

Awarding body: Festival Tibor Varga, B.P. 3374, CH1950 Sion, Switzerland.

Recipients include: Valeriy Gradow (U.S.S.R., 1973); Nam-yun Kim (Korea, 1974) and Helen Armstrong (U.S.A., 1974); Shimizu Takashi (Japan, 1975); Tomoko Okada (Japan, 1976).

Oskar-Vas-Förderungspreis (*Oskar Vas Promotional Award*)

This award was established in 1976 by the Board of Directors of the Austrian Standards Institute on the occasion of the 80th birthday of the President of the Institute, Prof. Dr. Oskar Vas. It is given for outstanding achievements in the field of standardization or for efforts to promote understanding of the principles of standardization. The award consists of a minimum cash prize of 10,000 Schillings and a certificate, and is made annually. The recipient may be a private individual or an organization.

Awarding body: Österreichisches Normungsinstitut, Leopoldsgasse 4, Postfach 130, 1021 Vienna, Austria.

Recipients include: 'Working-Group Standardization and School' (co-ordinating standardization activities with teaching and lecturing, 1976).

Vásárhelyi Pál Prize

The Hungarian Hydrological Society founded the prize in 1970 for outstanding work in some field of water supply management: scientific research, teaching, planning, management, and hydraulic engineering. Annual prizes are awarded in three grades: gold, 8,000 forints; silver, 6,000 forints; bronze, 4,000 forints. The prize is named after Pál Vásárhelyi (1795–1846) who was responsible for first regulating the course of the Lower Danube at the Iron Gate (a canyon through the Carpathians).

Awarding body: Magyar Hidrológiai Társaság, 1372 Budapest V, Kossuth Lajos tér 6–8, Hungary.

Vendl Mária Memorial Prize

The Hungarian Geological Society founded the award in 1964 for a published work of national or international significance in any one of the following fields: crystallography, mineralogy, geochemistry, metallurgy. A cash prize of 3,000 forints is awarded every three years.

Awarding body: Magyarhoni Földtani Társulat, Budapest 1061, Anker-köz 1, Hungary.

Verband Deutscher Elektrotechniker-Ehrenring

This is a gold ring and certificate which is given by the Association of German Electrical Engineers in recognition of exceptional scientific or technical achievements in this field. It was first instituted in 1958 to mark the Association's 65th anniversary, and since then has normally been presented every two years.

Awarding body: Verband Deutscher Elektrotechniker (VDE) e.V., D-6000 Frankfurt/Main 70, Stresemannallee 21, Federal Republic of Germany.

Recipients include: Prof. Dr.-Ing. habil. Wilhelm Bader, Prof. Dr.-Ing. Herbert Döring, Prof. Dr. phil. Herbert W. König (1972); Prof. Dr.-Ing. Alfred Lotze, Dr.-Ing. Erich Uhlmann (1974).

Verco Medal

This bronze medal is awarded for distinguished scientific work. It was established in 1928 in memory of Sir Joseph Verco (1851–1933), former President of the Royal Society of South Australia. He was a notable physician, Dean of the Faculty of Medicine of the University of Adelaide, and an amateur malacologist. The award, usually annual, is open only to Fellows of the Royal Society of South Australia.

Awarding body: Royal Society of South Australia Inc., State Library Building, Adelaide, South Australia 5000.

Recipients include: L. W. Parkin (1972); Prof. H. Wopfner (1973); Mrs. Patricia Thomas (1974); B. P. Thomson (1975); J. T. Hutton (1976).

Frederick H. Verhoeff Lecture

Every two years the American Ophthalmological Society invites an individual outstanding in any branch of medicine to deliver a lecture; on this occasion he receives a plaque and honorarium. He may be of any nationality. The lecture was established in 1959 by Dr. Arthur Bedell in honour of Dr. Frederick H. Verhoeff (1874–1968), ophthalmologist and pathologist.

Awarding body: American Ophthalmological Society (c/o Robert W. Hollenhorst, M.D.), 420 5th Ave., S.W., Rochester, Minn. 55901, U.S.A.

Recipients include: Dr. David Cogan (1969); Dr. Lorenz Zimmerman (1971); Dr. Irving Leopold (1973); Dr. Arthur Gerald Devoe (1975); Dr. Jules Francois (1977).

Vestermark Award

This award was established in 1969 in memory of Seymour Vestermark, Chief of the National Institute of Mental Health, Training Branch. It is given annually by the American Psychiatric Association to an educator who has made an outstanding contribution to the training and development of psychiatrists in either graduate or postgraduate education. The award is made annually, and consists of a plaque and honorarium of $500, given jointly by the Institute and the Association's Vestermark Award Fund.

Awarding body: American Psychiatric Association, 1700 18th St., N.W., Washington, D.C. 20009, U.S.A.

Victoria Medal

The medal was established in 1902 by the Royal Geographical Society in memory of Queen Victoria, who was the Society's Patron during her reign. The medal is for conspicuous merit in scientific research in geography; it may be awarded annually but only if a suitable candidate is forthcoming. There are no restrictions as to nationality, age or sex. Applications may not be submitted; the award is made by the Society's Council on the recommendation of a special committee. The medal is presented at the Society's Annual Meeting in June.

Awarding body: Royal Geographical Society, 1 Kensington Gore, London SW7 2AR, England.

Recipients include: Prof. H. C. Darby (1963); Prof. Henri Marcel Gaussen (1965); Prof. Emer. Carl O. Sauer (1975); Prof. J. N. Jennings (1976); Dr. Terence E. Armstrong (1978).

Viking Fund Medal

This prize was established in 1946 by the Wenner-Gren Foundation, then called the Viking Fund, whose sphere of interest is the support of research in all branches of anthropology and in related disciplines pertaining to the sciences of man. The prize is given to reward and draw attention to individuals of merit for achievement and excellence in the field of anthropology. Prior to 1960 three awards were made annually; since then the medal has been awarded every five years to one recipient, to coincide with the International Congress of Anthropological and Ethnological Sciences. The prize consists of a gilded bronze medal and a sum of money.

Awarding body: Wenner-Gren Foundation for Anthropological Research, Inc., 14 East 71st St., New York, N.Y. 10021, U.S.A.

Recipients include: Dr. E. E. Evans-Pritchard (U.K.), Dr. Louis S. B. Leakey (Kenya), Dr. Robert von Heine-Geldern (Austria), Dr. Sol Tax (U.S.A.), 1961; Dr. Claude Lévi-Strauss (France, 1966); Dr. John Grahame Douglas Clark (U.K., 1972).

Leonardo da Vinci Medal

The purpose of the award is to honour individuals who have made outstanding contributions to the history of technology by research, teaching, publication, or otherwise. It was established in 1962 by Professor Robert S. Woodbury of the Massachusetts Institute of Technology. A bronze medal and a certificate are presented annually at a banquet given by the Society for the History of Technology.

Awarding body: Society for the History of Technology, c/o Secretary, Dr. Carroll Pursell, Jr., Dept. of History, University of California, Santa Barbara, Calif. 93106, U.S.A.

Recipients include: Ladislao Reti (1972); Carl W. Condit (1973); Bern Dibner (1974); Friedrich Klemm (1975); Derek J. de Solla Price (1976).

Aurel Vlaicu Prize

The Romanian Academy established this prize for technology in 1948. It is presented annually at a General Assembly of the Academy, and consists of 10,000 lei and a diploma. It is named after Aurel Vlaicu (1882–1913), aero engineer and pilot, who was a pioneer in world aviation.

Awarding body: Academy of the S.R. of Romania, 125 Calea Victoriei, Bucharest, Romania.

Irene Vogeler-Preis

This prize was established in 1970 by a bequest of Irene Vogeler, a member of the Max-Planck-Gesellschaft, who specified that it should be given to a young scientist for outstanding work in the field of cancer research. The prize is awarded irregularly. It consists of DM10,000 and is awarded either as one prize or as three prizes of differing amounts.

Awarding body: Max-Planck-Gesellschaft zur Fördering der Wissenschaften e.V., Generalverwaltung, 8 Munich 1, Postfach 647, Federal Republic of Germany.

Recipient: Prof. Peter Vogt (U.S.A., 1976).

August Vollmer Award

This is one of four awards established by the American Society of Criminology in the names of individuals who have made major contributions to criminology. The award, established in 1959, is for an outstanding research report in this field, and is presented at the Society's Annual Meeting. It takes the form of a medal.

Awarding body: American Society of Criminology, 1314 Kinnear Rd., Columbus, Ohio 43212, U.S.A.

Recipients include: Jerome Skolnick (1972); E. Preston Sharpe (1973); Patrick Murphy and Sol Rubin (1974); Patricia M. Wald (1976).

Traian Vuia Prize

The Romanian Academy established this prize in 1948. It is given for achievement in the field of technology, and is presented annually at a General Assembly of the Academy. It consists of 10,000 lei and a diploma. It is named after Traian Vuia (1872–1950), the aero engineer and inventor, who in 1906 was the first man to fly an aeroplane taking off under its own power.

Awarding body: Academy of the S.R. of Romania, 125 Calea Victoriei, Bucharest, Romania.

Recipients include: Traian Sălăgean (1962).

W

D. N. Wadia Medal

This medal was established in 1975 by the Indian National Science Academy. It is awarded every three years for contributions in the field of earth sciences.

Awarding body: Indian National Science Academy, Bahadur Shah Zafar Marg, New Delhi 110001, India.

Recipients include: A. G. Jhingran (1977).

Celia B. Wagner Memorial Award

This annual award of $250 is made by the Poetry Society of America (founded 1910) for the best poem worthy of the tradition of the art, in any length or style. It was established in memory of the late wife of the Society's Executive Secretary.

Awarding body: The Poetry Society of America, 15 Gramercy Park, New York, N.Y. 10003, U.S.A.

Wahlner Memorial Medal

Founded in 1926 by the Hungarian Mining and Metallurgical Society, the medal is given to members of the Society for quite exceptional contributions to its field of activity, either by means of invention or innovation of great significance, or through outstanding contributions to the specialist literature. An annual monetary prize of 5,000 forints is awarded with the medal.

Awarding body: Országos Magyar Bányászati és Kohászati Egyesület, Budapest VI, Anker-köz 1, Hungary.

Marjorie Peabody Waite Award

This award was made possible by a gift from Mrs. Elizabeth Ames in memory of her sister. It is conferred on an older artist, writer, or composer, in rotation, for continuing achievement and integrity in his art. The award consists of $1,500.

Awarding body: American Academy and Institute of Arts and Letters, 633 West 155th St., New York, N.Y. 10032, U.S.A.

Wakefield Gold Medal

This medal is awarded by the Royal Aeronautical Society for contributions towards safety in aviation. It was presented in 1926 by Castrol Limited in memory of the company's founder, the late Viscount Wakefield of Hythe.

Awarding body: The Royal Aeronautical Society, 4 Hamilton Place, London W1V 0BQ, England.

Recipients include: J. W. Wilson (1972); J. Keri Williams (1973); G. W. Stallibrass (1974); Lt.-Cdr. J. S. Sproule (1975); R. D. Starkey (1976).

Walker Prize

The prize is awarded quinquennially, irrespective of nationality, to the person who shall be deemed to have done the best work during the preceding five years in advancing the knowledge of the pathology and therapeutics of cancer. The prize of not less than £100 and a document declaratory of the award was established under a trust set up by Charles Clement Walker in 1894. Members of the Council of the Royal College of Surgeons are not eligible.

Awarding body: The Royal College of Surgeons of England, 35–43 Lincoln's Inn Fields, London WC2A 3PN, England.

Recipients include: Cornelius Packard Rhoads (1951–55); Charles Brenton Huggins and Ludwik Gross (1956–60); Sir Stanford Cade (1961–65); Denis Parsons Burkitt (1966–70); Kenneth Dawson Bagshawe (1971–75).

Francis A. Walker Medal

Established in 1947 by the American Economic Association, this silver medal is named after the first President of the Association. It is given every five years to a living American economist who is a member of the Association for the greatest contribution to economics made during his career.

Awarding body: American Economic Association, 1313 21st Ave. South, Nashville, Tenn. 37212, U.S.A.

Recipients include: John Maurice Clark (1952); Frank Hyneman Knight (1957); Jacob Viner (1962); Alvin H. Hansen (1967); Theodore W. Schultz (1972).

William H. Walker Award for Excellence in Contributions to the Chemical Engineering Literature

This award is generally presented annually by the American Institute of Chemical Engineers to a member who is the author or co-author of an outstanding work in chemical engineering published in the preceding three years. His contribution may consist of one or more books, articles or other professional publications. The subject matter need not be original work, but may be a review, research report, theoretical contribution, history of the development of a process,

291

or other material of significance to the profession. The award consists of a certificate, plaque and $1,000.

Awarding body: American Institute of Chemical Engineers, 345 East 47th St., New York, N.Y. 10017, U.S.A.

Otto-Wallach-Plakette

In 1964 the firm DRAGOCO, Gerberding and Co., GmbH, of Holzminden, set up the Otto Wallach Fund, administered by the Society of German Chemists. The fund was established on the occasion of the 70th birthday of the firm's founder, C. W. Gerberding, and in commemoration of Otto Wallach (1847–1931), professor of chemistry, creator of the modern chemistry of the terpenes and winner of the Nobel Prize for Chemistry in 1910. A cash prize is awarded at irregular intervals to young European researchers, in recognition of achievements in the field of volatile oils, the terpenes and polycyclic terpenes or in the field of biochemical coolants. In special cases a gold Otto Wallach Medal may also be awarded.

Awarding body: Gesellschaft Deutscher Chemiker, 6000 Frankfurt (Main) 90, Carl Bosch-Haus, Varrentrappstr. 40–42, Federal Republic of Germany.

Recipients of medal: Prof. Walter Hückel (Fed. Rep. of Germany, 1966); Prof. Guy-Henri Ourisson (France, 1969); Prof. Ferdinand Bohlmann (Fed. Rep. of Germany, 1974).

C. E. Wallis Lecture in the History of Dentistry

A lecturer is appointed every five years and receives an honorarium.

Awarding body: The Royal Society of Medicine, 1 Wimpole St., London W1M 8AE, England.

Albert Wander Lecture

A lecturer is appointed not more than once a year to promote the art and science of the general practice of medicine. He receives an honorarium.

Awarding body: The Royal Society of Medicine, 1 Wimpole St., London W1M 8AE, England.

Warburton Lectureship

The lecture and the Warburton Scholarship in Local Government are provided from the income of a bequest of £1,000 made by the late Thomas Warburton of Manchester, to the Owens College (since incorporated in Manchester University) to be applied in such a way as the Governors might deem best for promoting and encouraging the study of the best methods of Local Government and the Law, for the time being, relating to Local Government.

Awarding body: University of Manchester, Manchester M13 9PL, England.

Lecturers include: A. Hopkinson (Principal of Owens College) ('On the Contracts of Local Authorities', 1899); Sidney Webb ('The Government of Manchester', 1907–08); Prof. Sir Paul Vinogradoff ('The Russian Unions and the Revolution', 1916–17); Sir John Maude ('Relations between Central and Local Government', 1949); P. D. Smithson ('Making the Connection', 1974).

Warburton and Wiseman Memorial Lectures

In 1973 a fund was established at Manchester University by colleagues of the late Professor F. W. Warburton, Professor of Experimental Education, and the late Professor Stephen Wiseman, Professor of Education and Director of the School of Education, to commemorate their services to scholarship.

Awarding body: University of Manchester, Manchester M13 9PL, England.

Lecturers include: Prof. W. D. Wall ('Constructive Education', 1975); Dame Kathleen Ollerenshaw ('Dilemmas of Manpower Planning', 1976).

C. W. Wardlaw Lectureship

The lectures are financed from the income arising from the investment of a gift presented to Manchester University by Professor Wardlaw, Professor of Botany in the University from 1940 to 1966. This gift was donated from the sum collected by colleagues on the occasion of his retirement.

Awarding body: University of Manchester, Manchester M13 9PL, England.

Lecturers include: Prof. J. Heslop-Harrison ('Mate selection plant-style', 1975).

Warner Memorial Medal

The Textile Institute established this annual medal in 1930 in recognition of valuable services given by the late Sir Frank Warner, K.B.E. (1862–1930) to the Institute. He was its Chairman of Council for many years, and President in 1918 and 1919. The medal is awarded in recognition of outstanding work in textile science and technology, the results of which have been published, and particularly for work published in the Institute's *Journal.*

Awarding body: The Textile Institute, 10 Blackfriars St., Manchester M3 5DR, England.

Recipients include: W. J. Onions (research on yarn irregularity, physics of textile materials and fibre properties, 1973); Wool Research Laboratories of CSIRO, Australia (research on the structure and processing of wool, 1974); J. D. Owen (research into blending properties of yarns and fabrics and their relationship to tactile and aesthetic properties of fabrics, 1975); Prof. G. R. Wray (research in air-jet texturing, machinery for manufacture of pile fabrics and mechanics of weft-knitting, 1976).

Edward Warner Award

A gold medal and a certificate are awarded annually to an individual or institution for outstanding contribution to the safe and orderly development of modern civil air transport. One of the most prestigious awards in international civil aviation, it was founded by the International Civil Aviation Organization Council in 1958 in memory of Dr. Edward Pearson Warner (1894–

1958), the American aviation pioneer and educator in aeronautical engineering and first President of the ICAO Council.

Awarding body: International Civil Aviation Organization, Montreal, P.Q., Canada.

Recipients include: Agence pour la Sécurité de la Navigation Aérienne en Afrique et à Madagascar (1972); Shizuma Matsuo (Japan, posthumously, 1973); Prof. Alex Meyer (Fed. Rep. of Germany, 1974); Charles A. Lindbergh (U.S.A., posthumously, 1975); Corporación Centro-americana de Servicios de Navegación Aérea (1976).

Samuel L. Warner Memorial Award

A medal is awarded annually for outstanding contributions in the design and development of new and improved methods and/or apparatus for sound-on film motion pictures, including any step in the process. The award was established in 1947, and is presented at the SMPTE Annual Conference.

Awarding body: Society of Motion Picture and Television Engineers, 862 Scarsdale Ave., Scarsdale, N.Y. 10583, U.S.A.

Worcester Reed Warner Medal

Worcester Reed Warner, Charter Member and sixteenth President of the American Society of Mechanical Engineers, established this medal by bequest in 1930. It is awarded for outstanding contribution to the permanent literature of engineering. Contributions may be single papers, treatises or books or a series of papers. They are to deal with progressive ideas relative to engineering, scientific and industrial research associated with mechanical engineering; the design and operation of mechanical and associated equipment; industrial engineering or management, organization, operation and the concomitants of each; and other subjects closely associated with the foregoing. To qualify as having permanent value, any paper or treatise should not be less than five years old. Recipients need not be members of the Society. The gold medal is accompanied by an engrossed certificate and an honorarium of $1,000.

Awarding body: American Society of Mechanical Engineers, United Engineering Center, 345 East 47th St., New York, N.Y. 10017, U.S.A.

Recipients include: Burgess H. Jennings (1972); Max Mark Frocht (1973); Victor L. Streeter (1974); Philip G. Hodge, Jr. (1975); Dennis G. Shepherd (1976).

Bertram E. Warren Award

This triennial award was established in 1970 in honour of Professor Bertram E. Warren of the Massachusetts Institute of Technology. It is given for an important recent contribution to the physics of solids or liquids using X-ray, neutron, or electron diffraction techniques; it is not meant to include crystal structure determinations. Work should have been published within the six-year period ending 30 June of the year preceding the award. The winner receives a certificate and $1,000.

Awarding body: American Crystallographic Association, 335 East 45th St., New York, N.Y. 10017, U.S.A.

Recipients include: John D. Axe and Gen Shirane (1970); Ulrich Bonse and Michale Hart (1973); John M. Cowley and Sumio Lijima (1976).

W. H. Warren Medal

This award, now a bronze medal, was first made in 1929 and was known until 1976 as the Warren Memorial Prize. The medal perpetuates the memory of Professor W. H. Warren who was the first President of the Institution of Engineers, Australia. He was also the holder of the first chair in engineering at the University of Sydney from 1883 to 1925. The medal is awarded for the best paper selected by the Board of the College of Civil Engineers (one of the foundation Colleges of the Institution) in the discipline of civil engineering. The award is open to members of the Institution only.

Awarding body: Institution of Engineers, Australia, 11 National Circuit, Barton, A.C.T. 2600, Australia.

Recipients include: B. R. Mutton and N. S. Trahair (1975); J. W. Morgan and V. R. Beck (1976); P. F. Walsh (1977).

Warsaw Siren

This award is made annually by the Polish Journalists Association for the best foreign feature film introduced to the screen in the preceding year. The award consists of a statuette and a diploma.

Awarding body: Polish Journalists Association, ul. Foksal 1, 00-366 Warsaw, Poland.

Wartha Vince Memorial Medal ·

The Hungarian Chemical Society founded this medal in 1955 for outstanding work in chemical engineering by members of the Society, which has been successfully applied in practice during the previous three years. An annual cash prize of 5,000 forints accompanies the medal. It is named in memory of Vince Wartha (1844–1914), a professor at Budapest Technical University who excelled in applied chemical engineering (production of marjolica, wine chemistry, urban water supply, etc.).

Awarding body: Magyar Kémikusok Egyesülete, Budapest VI, Anker-köz 1, Hungary.

Wateler Peace Prize

The prize was founded by J. G. D. Wateler, a Dutch citizen, who died in 1927. He bequeathed his estate to the Carnegie Foundation (which owns and administers the Peace Palace) on condition that the annual revenue should be awarded as a Peace Prize to the person or institution having rendered the most valuable service to the cause of peace or having contributed to the means of preventing war. The prize is given alternately to a Dutch citizen and a foreigner. Its value is currently 40,000 guilders.

Awarding body: Carnegie Foundation, Peace Palace, The Hague, The Netherlands.

Recipients include: Dr. A. H. Boerma (1973); Dr. Henry Kissinger (1974); Drs. Max Kohnstamm (1975).

Water and Environment Group Award
In 1971 the then Industrial Water and Effluents Group (since renamed as above) of the Society of Chemical Industry established an award of a silver medal and a monetary prize of £50 to the author of a paper presented at a meeting of the Group which most advances the technology of water pollution control or water treatment.

Awarding body: Water and Environment Group, Society of Chemical Industry, 14 Belgrave Square, London SW1X 8PS, England.

Alan T. Waterman Award
This award was established in 1975 by Congress to mark the 25th anniversary of the National Science Foundation and to honour Alan T. Waterman, first Director of the Foundation from 1951 to 1963. The award is given to an outstanding young American scientist (normally under 35) in the forefront of his/her field of science. It takes the form of a medal and a grant of up to $50,000 per year for up to three years for research or advanced study in mathematical, physical, medical, biological, engineering, social or other sciences, at any institution.

Awarding body: Alan T. Waterman Award Committee, National Science Foundation, Washington, D.C. 20550, U.S.A.

Recipients include: Dr. Charles Louis Fefferman (mathematics, Fourier analysis, 1976).

Van Waterschoot van der Gracht-penning
This award is made annually by the Royal Geological and Mining Society of the Netherlands. It is in memory of Dr. W. A. J. M. van Waterschoot van der Gracht (1873–1943), a noted geologist and initiator of the Geological Survey of the Netherlands. The award is given for outstanding merit in the field of earth sciences, mining and metallurgy. There is no restriction as to eligibility but candidates should have some link with the pursuit of these sciences in the Netherlands and professional standing of some 20 years.

Awarding body: Koninklijk Nederlands Geologisch Mijnbouwkundig Genootschap (Royal Geological and Mining Society of the Netherlands).

Recipients include: Prof. Dr. L. M. J. U. van Straaten (sedimentology, 1972); Dr. W. H. Zagwijn (tertiary and quaternary geology, 1974); Dr. T. van der Hammen (palynology, 1974); Prof. Th. R. Seldenrath (coal mining, energy resources, 1975); Prof. Dr. F. J. Faber (geology, 1977).

James Wattie New Zealand Book of the Year
The award was established in 1968 by Sir James Wattie, founder, managing director and chairman of Wattie Industries Ltd., and the Book Publishers Association of New Zealand. Since Sir James Wattie's death in 1973, Wattie Industries Ltd. has continued to sponsor the award. It is presented annually in September for all-round excellence in the writing and publication of New Zealand books. These must have been published in the 12 months up to 30 June each year. The competition is open to New Zealand writers, including non-New Zealanders resident in the country. The first prize is N.Z.$1,200, the second prize N.Z.$800 and the third prize N.Z.$500.

Awarding body: Book Publishers Association of New Zealand, Box 31285, Milford, Auckland, New Zealand.

Recipients include: G. Docking (*Two Hundred Years of New Zealand Painting*), M. Shadbolt (*Strangers and Journeys*), W. Ihimaera (*Tangi*), Sir Edmund Hillary (*Nothing Venture, Nothing Win*, 1975); H. Morton (*The Wind Commands*).

Watts Prize
A prize of between £25 and £50 may be awarded annually to a member of the Royal Institution of Naval Architects for proposals to improve crew or passenger accommodation in merchant ships or for the improvement of life-saving apparatus.

Awarding body: Royal Institution of Naval Architects, 10 Upper Belgrave St., London SW1X 8BQ, England.

Watumull Prize
This prize is awarded in even-numbered years for the best work on the history of India originally published in the United States. It carries a cash award of $1,000.

Awarding body: American Historical Association, 400 A St., S.E., Washington, D.C. 20003, U.S.A.

C. A. Weber-Medaille
This medal was established in 1970 by the German Society for Bog and Peat Research in memory of C. A. Weber (1856–1931), the most important scientist in this field in Germany. The prize is awarded at irregular intervals for outstanding achievements in bog and peat research.

Awarding body: Deutsche Gesellschaft für Moor- und Torfkunde, 3000 Hanover 51, Stilleweg 2, Federal Republic of Germany.

Recipients include: Prof. Dr. F. Overbeck, Prof. Dr. W. Baden, Dr. H. Baatz, Berging. Dr. Deilmann.

Alex-Wedding-Preis
This prize is awarded annually by the Academy of Arts of the G.D.R. to an East German author of children's fictional literature, fairy tales, or plays. The prize was founded by the Academy in 1967 in memory of Alex Wedding (Grete Weiskopf), 1905–66, the children's writer.

Awarding body: Akademie der Künste der DDR, 104 Berlin, Hermann-Matern-Strasse 58/59, German Democratic Republic.

Recipients include: Herbert Friedrich (1973); Edith Bergner (1974); Horst Beseler (1975); Fred Rodrian (1976); Peter Brock (1977).

Rudolf Wegscheider Prize for Chemistry

The prize was established in 1929 by the friends and colleagues of Rudolf Wegscheider (1859–1935), professor of chemistry and member of the Austrian Academy of Sciences, in celebration of his 70th birthday. The prize is awarded for an outstanding learned work in the field of physical chemistry. The author must be an Austrian citizen working in Austria, and the work must have appeared in print in the preceding three years. The prize consists of a certificate and a sum of money, and is awarded every two years, in May or June. Full and corresponding members of the Austrian Academy of Sciences, which gives the prize, are not eligible.

Awarding body: Österreichische Akademie der Wissenschaften, 1010 Vienna, Dr.-Ignaz-Seipel-Platz 2, Austria.

Theodore Weicker Memorial Award

This annual award was established by the trustees of the Theodore and Elizabeth Weicker Foundation, to honour Theodore Weicker for his advancement of materia medica and the practice of medicine. A sum of $10,000 and a certificate are awarded to an individual who has made sustained, distinguished contributions in pharmacology. The research may involve work leading to new concepts or knowledge in pharmacology or the development of drugs useful in the treatment of human disease. Studies concerned with means of improving drug therapy or decreasing toxicity of drugs or other chemical substances would also qualify. Candidates must be nominated by a member of ASPET. The award is made on the basis of published reprints, manuscripts ready for publication, and a two-page summary.

Awarding body: American Society for Pharmacology and Experimental Therapeutics, Inc., 9650 Rockville Pike, Bethesda, Md. 20014, U.S.A.

F. C.-Weiskopf-Preis

This prize, which is dedicated to the memory of the novelist F. C. Weiskopf (1900–55), was founded by Grete Weiskopf in 1956. It is awarded twice a year by the F. C. Weiskopf Bequest, affiliated to the Academy of Arts of the German Democratic Republic, in recognition of work which contributes to the maintenance of the purity of the German language and its further development through creative writing. The prize may be awarded to individuals or a group, and consists of a sum of money and a certificate.

Awarding body: Akademie der Künste der DDR, 104 Berlin, Hermann-Matern-Strasse 58/59, German Democratic Republic.

Recipients include: Dr. Eva Schumann (1970); Georg Maurer (posthumously, 1972); Prof. Dr. habil. Wilhelm Schmidt (1974); Thomas Reschke (1975); Eduard Zak (1977).

Arthur M. Wellington Prize

This prize was endowed by *The Engineering News-Record* in 1921 for papers on any form of trans-portation; its scope was broadened in 1946 to include papers on foundations and closely related topics. The award is open to non-members of the ASCE, and consists of a wall plaque and certificate.

Awarding body: American Society of Civil Engineers, 345 East 47th St., New York, N.Y. 10017, U.S.A.

Recipients include: William K. Mackay ('Transportation and Urban Renewal – Experience in the United Kingdom', 1974); Eli Robinsky and Keith E. Bespflug ('Design of Insulated Foundations', 1975); Joel P. Leisch ('New Concepts in Rail–Bus Interchange', 1975); Rodney E. Engelen ('New Institutions for Joint Development', 1976).

George Westinghouse Award

This annual award was established by the Westinghouse Educational Foundation in 1946 to encourage young educators whose past accomplishments give evidence of excellence and effective innovation in the teaching of engineering. The award consists of $1,000 in cash and a certificate. Teachers of any division of subject matter ordinarily taken by engineering students are eligible. Candidates must be under 45 years of age.

Awarding body: American Society for Engineering Education, One Dupont Circle, Washington, D.C. 20036, U.S.A.

Recipients include: Jack P. Holman (1972); Martin D. Bradshaw (1973); Joseph Bordogna (1974); Donald G. Childers (1975); Jerome B. Cohen (1976).

George Westinghouse Medals

To perpetuate the value of the rich contribution to power development made by George Westinghouse, honorary member and 29th President of the American Society of Mechanical Engineers, the Westinghouse Educational Foundation established the gold medal in 1952 and the silver medal in 1971. They are bestowed for eminent achievement or distinguished service in the power field of mechanical engineering. The silver medal is bestowed upon one who has not attained his 41st birthday on 30 June of the year in which the medal is awarded. Considering power in the broad sense, the basis of the awards includes contributions of utilization, application, design, development, research and the organization of such activities in the power field. Candidates are not restricted by profession nor by membership in any engineering society or organization.

Awarding body: American Society of Mechanical Engineers, United Engineering Center, 345 East 47th St., New York, N.Y. 10017, U.S.A.

Recipients include: Gold medallists: Charles W. Elston (1974); John W. Simpson (1976); Silver medallists: Shelby L. Owens (1974); Richard V. Shanklin III (1976).

Wetenschappelijke Prijs Joseph Maisin
(*Joseph Maisin Prize for Science*)

This quinquennial prize is awarded for outstanding work in the natural sciences and medical science. It consists of a cash award of 750,000

Belgian francs. Candidates for the prize must be proposed by three scientists, at least two of whom must be Belgian. The prize is restricted to Dutch speakers; a companion prize, the *Prix Scientifique Joseph Maisin*, is awarded to a French-speaking scientist.

Awarding body: Fonds de la Recherche Scientifique Médicale, 5 rue d'Egmont, B-1050 Brussels, Belgium.

1975 recipient: Prof. Georges Peeters (for his contribution to the study of the mammary gland and lactation in general).

Wetenschappelijke Prijs Ernest-John Solvay
(*Ernest-John Solvay Prize for Science*)

This quinquennial prize is awarded for outstanding work in the human sciences. It is a cash award of 750,000 Belgian francs. Candidates must be proposed by three scientists, at least two of whom must be Belgian. The prize is restricted to Dutch speakers; a companion prize, the *Prix Scientifique Ernest-John Solvay*, is awarded to a French speaker.

Awarding body: Fonds National de la Recherche Scientifique, 5 rue d'Egmont, B-1050 Brussels, Belgium.

Recipients include: Prof. Joseph Nuttin (for his exceptional contribution to the internationalization of psychology and for his theoretical and experimental work on learning and motivation, 1975).

John Price Wetherill Medal

Mr. John Price Wetherill (1843–1906), a consulting engineer and officer of the New Jersey Zinc Company, was a member of the Franklin Institute and of its Board of Managers. In 1917 his family established a fund for the promotion of research to be known as the John Price Wetherill Memorial Fund. In 1925, in accordance with their wishes, the Institute used the fund to establish a silver memorial medal (gold since 1968) for discovery or invention in the physical sciences, or for new and important combinations of principles or methods already known.

Awarding body: The Franklin Institute, Benjamin Franklin Parkway at 20th St., Philadelphia, Pa. 19103, U.S.A.

Recipients include: Donald N. Langenberg, William H. Parker, Barry N. Taylor (establishment of voltage standard using the A. C. Josephson effect and measurement refinement of fundamental physical constants, 1975); Herbert Blades (contributions to polymer technology, 1976); James W. Cronin and Val L. Fitch (contributions to particle physics, 1976).

Wheatley Medal

The Library Association established this annual medal in 1962 in honour of Henry B. Wheatley. It is for an outstanding index first published in the U.K. during the preceding three years.

Awarding body: The Library Association, 7 Ridgmount St., London WC1E 7AE, England.

Recipients include: K. Bodson (Index to *Non-*

ferrous Metals, 1973); L. M. Harrod (Index to *History of the King's Works*, Vol. 6, 1973); C. C. Banwell (Index to *Encyclopaedia of Forms and Precedents*, 1974); M. D. Anderson (Index to *Copy-editing*, 1975); J. A. Vickers (Index to *The Works of John Wesley*, Vol. 2, 1976).

Edith Whetnall Medal and Lecture

A lecturer is appointed every two years to deliver a lecture on a subject connected with the diagnosis, causation, prevention and management of deafness in children. He receives a medal and an honorarium.

Awarding body: The Royal Society of Medicine, 1 Wimpole St., London W1M 8AE, England.

Whitbread Literary Awards

These annual awards 'to encourage good literature, in its many and varied categories, and to provide some reward for the authors' were established by Whitbread Breweries in 1971 and are administered by the Booksellers Association. The rules vary slightly from year to year. Three prizes of £1,500 each are given for books in three categories: best novel; best biography or autobiography; best children's book (sometimes replaced by 'best first book'). Submissions must be made by publishers. Authors must have been domiciled in the U.K. or Ireland for the previous five years, and the books must have been first published in the U.K. or Ireland in the previous 12 months. Presentations take place in November/December at Whitbread's City cellars and the winners also receive an inscribed silver dish or tankard.

Awarding body: Booksellers Association of Great Britain and Ireland, 154 Buckingham Palace Rd., London SW1W 9TZ, England.

Recipients include: Beryl Bainbridge (novel, *Injury Time*), Nigel Nicolson (biography, *Mary Curzon*), Shelagh Macdonald (children's book, *No End to Yesterday*), 1977; Paul Theroux (novel, *Picture Palace*), John Grigg (biography, *Lloyd George: The People's Champion 1902–11*), Philippa Pearce (children's book, *The Battle of Bubble and Squeak*), 1978.

Walt Whitman Award

The Academy of American Poets was founded in 1934 to assist the careers of American poets. Since 1974 is has presented a group of annual awards, sponsored by the Copernicus Society of America, spanning the full range of American poetic accomplishment. The Walt Whitman Award is given to the winner of a competition open to American citizens who have not yet published a book of poems. The author receives a cash award of $1,000, and the Academy undertakes to publish the manuscript.

Awarding body: The Academy of American Poets, 1078 Madison Ave., New York, N.Y. 10028, U.S.A.

Recipients include: Reg Saner ('Climbing into the Roots', 1975).

Eli Whitney Memorial Award

Established in 1957 by the Society of Manufacturing Engineers, a gold medal and an engraved citation are awarded annually for distinguished accomplishments within the broad concept of mass production manufacture. The award is international and nominations are not confined to members of the Society.

Awarding body: Society of Manufacturing Engineers, 20501 Ford Rd., Dearborn, Mich. 48128, U.S.A.

Recipients include: L. V. Whistler, Sr. (S. B. Whistler and Sons, Inc., 1971); William D. Innes (Ford Motor Co., 1973); Alonzo G. Decker, Jr. (Black and Decker Manufacturing Co., 1974); Robert Anderson (Rockwell International, 1975); Henry D. Sharpe, Jr. (Brown and Sharpe Manufacturing Co., 1976).

Ian Whyte Award

The award was established in 1972 by the Scottish National Orchestra to encourage young British composers. The prize of £500 is given by a private donor as a tribute to the late Dr. Ian Whyte's influence on the musical renaissance in Scotland. Ian Whyte (1901–60) was responsible for the founding of the BBC Scottish Symphony Orchestra in 1935 when he was Music Director of BBC Scotland. The award, made every three years, is for a previously unpublished and unperformed work for symphony orchestra not exceeding 30 minutes' duration. As well as the cash prize the award includes five concert performances by the SNO and a BBC radio broadcast. Competitors must be British by birth or have been domiciled in Britain for five years. The upper age limit is 35.

Awarding body: General Administrator, Scottish National Orchestra, 150 Hope St., Glasgow G2 2TH, Scotland.

Recipients: Graham Williams (*Symphony*, 1972); Colin Matthews (*Fourth Sonata*, 1975); Lyell Cresswell (*Salm*, 1978).

Heinrich-Wieland-Preis

This prize is awarded for the advancement of research into the biochemistry and physiology of fats and lipoids and their significance from a clinical and nutritional-physiological standpoint. It was established in 1964 by the Margarine Institute for Good Nutrition, Hamburg, in honour of Prof. Dr. Heinrich Wieland (1877–1957), Nobel prize-winner for chemistry in 1927. The prize is awarded annually, and consists of DM15,000 in cash, a medal and certificate. Scientists of any nationality are eligible; the award is primarily intended for young researchers. The works submitted should be either unpublished, or published during the preceding two years.

Awarding body: Kuratorium für die Verleihung des Heinrich-Wieland-Preises, c/o Prof. Dr. A. Fricker, 7500 Karlsruhe-Grotzingen 41, Ringelberghohl 12, Federal Republic of Germany.

Recipients include: Prof. Dr. Seubert (Fed. Rep. of Germany, 1969); Prof. van Deenen (Netherlands, 1971); Prof. Numa (Japan, 1973); Prof. Brown and Prof. Goldstein (U.S.A., 1974); Prof. Dr. Schweizer and Prof. Dr. Seidel (Fed. Rep. of Germany, 1976).

Norbert Wiener Awards

The International Journal of Cybernetics and General Systems, *Kybernetes*, established in 1978 an annual award consisting of three prizes (U.S.$500, 300 and 200), to be made in respect of essays devoted to a given topic. The competition is organized in honour of the founder of cybernetics, Dr. Norbert Wiener. Entries may be submitted by any individual from any country; papers by a group of authors are not acceptable. The length of the essay must not exceed 3,000 words, and a summary of 100 words must be submitted with the text. The copyright of the three winning essays belongs to *Kybernetes*.

Awarding body: The Editor, *Kybernetes*, c/o College of Technology, Feilden St., Blackburn BB2 1LH, England.

Norbert Wiener Prize

Established in 1967, this prize is awarded jointly by the American Mathematical Society and the Society for Industrial and Applied Mathematics and is endowed by the Department of Mathematics of the Massachusetts Institute of Technology. It is awarded for an outstanding contribution to applied mathematics in the highest and broadest sense. It is a monetary prize of $300 and is awarded every five years.

Awarding body: Society for Industrial and Applied Mathematics, U.S.A.

Recipients include: R. Bellman (1971); P. Lax (1975).

Wihuri International Prize

The Wihuri Foundation for International Prizes, established in 1953 by the Finnish shipowner and industrialist, Antti Wihuri (1884–1962), distributes prizes in recognition of creative work that has specially furthered and developed the cultural and economic progress of mankind. The prizes can be awarded to individuals and associations irrespective of nationality, creed, race or language. The prizes distributed by the Foundation, including the Wihuri-Sibelius Prize (*q.v.*), amount to between 60,000 and 90,000 marks, the amount being subject to alteration according to the funds available. The prizes are awarded on 9 October. At least one international prize must be awarded every third year. Two or, at the most, three simultaneous prizes may be awarded.

Awarding body: Wihuri Foundation for International Prizes, Arkadiankatu 21 B, SF-00100 Helsinki 10, Finland.

Recipients include: Sir John McMichael (U.K., 1968); Lars Ahlfors (U.S.A., 1968); Sir Peter Hirsch (U.K., 1971); Georg Henrik Von Wright (Finland, 1976); Jaakko Hintikka (Finland, 1976).

Wihuri-Sibelius Prize

The Wihuri Foundation for International Prizes was established in 1953 by the Finnish shipowner and industrialist, Antti Wihuri (1884–1962), for the purpose of promoting and sustaining the cultural and economic development of society. The Wihuri-Sibelius Prize, first awarded in 1953 to the Finnish composer, Jean Sibelius (1865–1957), is given to prominent composers who have become internationally known and acknowledged. Composers of any nationality are eligible for the prize, which may be shared. It is awarded on 9 October; however, if the Board of the Foundation so decides, the prize may be withheld. The winner receives a cash prize, the amount being dependent on the funds available from the Foundation, which also awards the Wihuri-International Prize (q.v.).

Awarding body: Wihuri Foundation for International Prizes, Arkadiankatu 21 B, SF-00100 Helsinki 10, Finland.

Recipients include: Olivier Messiaen (France, 1971); Witold Lutoslawski (Poland, 1973); Joonas Kokkonen (Finland, 1973).

Anton Wildgans-Preis der österreichischen Industrie (*Anton Wildgans Prize of Austrian Industry*)

This prize was established in 1962 by the Association of Austrian Industrialists in memory of Anton Wildgans (1881–1932), the Austrian poet. It is awarded annually to an Austrian author who has become prominent as a lyric poet, dramatist, novelist or essayist. The recipient must be young or middle-aged and must be an Austrian citizen writing in German. The prize consists of 50,000 Schillings.

Awarding body: Vereinigung Österreichischer Industrieller, Schwarzenbergplatz 4, Vienna, Austria.

Recipients include: Milo Dor (1972); Barbara Frischmuth (1973); Ernst Hinterberger (1974); Christine Busta (1975); György Sebestyén (1976).

Wildlife Society Group Achievement Award

This annual award was established in 1965 by the Society's Council. It is given to an organization, agency or other group, in recognition of outstanding recent accomplishments in the professional wildlife field. The recipients are presented with a plaque.

Awarding body: The Wildlife Society, 7101 Wisconsin Ave., Suite 611, Washington, D.C., U.S.A.

Recipients include: American Humane Asscn. (1972); Tall Timbers Research Station (1973); Nat. Audubon Society (1974); Wildlife Management Inst. (1975); The Rob and Bessie Welder Wildlife Fndn. (1976).

Harvey W. Wiley Award for the Development of Analytical Methods

This American award is made by the Association of Official Analytical Chemists for an outstanding contribution to the development and establishment of methods of analysis of those materials – foods, vitamins, food additives, colour additives,

pesticides, drugs, cosmetics, plants, feeds, fertilizers, and contaminants of food, water, air, or soil – for which provision is made in *Official Methods of Analysis* of the Association of Official Analytical Chemists. The award consists of $750 with an appropriate scroll, and is presented at the AOAC Annual Meeting in October. It was established in 1957 in honour of Dr. Harvey W. Wiley, Father of the Pure Food Laws, and a Founder of the Association. Nominations may be submitted; nominees need not be members of the Association but, except in unusual cases, should be residents of North America.

Awarding body: Association of Official Analytical Chemists, P.O.B. 540, Benjamin Franklin Station, Washington, D.C. 20044, U.S.A.

Recipients include: Daniel Banes, Ph.D. (development and improvement of techniques and methods for the analysis of complex drugs, 1968); Morton Beroza, Ph.D. (development of gas chromatographic methods for the determination of residues of pesticides and their metabolites at nanogram levels, 1970); C. L. Ogg, Ph.D. (establishing methods for microchemical analysis and tobacco, 1972); William Horwitz, Ph.D. (editor of five editions of *Official Methods of Analysis* and the development of methods of analysis for dairy products, 1975); Walter A. Pons, Jr. (development of analytical methods for the determination of gossypol in cottonseed materials, 1976).

R. H. Wilhelm Award in Chemical Reaction Engineering

This award is sponsored by the Mobil Oil Corporation and presented by the American Institute of Chemical Engineers to an individual (not necessarily a member of the Institute) in recognition of significant and original contributions to chemical reaction engineering. It is usually made annually, and takes the form of a certificate and $1,000.

Awarding body: American Institute of Chemical Engineers, 345 East 47th St., New York, N.Y. 10017, U.S.A.

Wilkins Lecture

A fund was established in 1947 by means of an endowment of £1,000 by Mr. J. D. Griffith Davies, Assistant Secretary of the Royal Society 1937–46, to found a lectureship in the history of science, to be called the Wilkins Lecture after John Wilkins, first Secretary of the Society. In accordance with the wishes of the donor, his gift is associated with the names of Margaret Ann Davies and Elizabeth Kellogg Chase, in whose memory it was made. The Wilkins lecturer is appointed triennially or at such intervals as may be thought fit. A gift of £100 is payable to the lecturer.

Awarding body: Royal Society of London, 6 Carlton House Terrace, London SW1Y 5AG, England.

Lecturers include: Prof. R. V. Jones ('The "Plain Story" of James Watt', 1970); A. R. Hall ('Newton and his Editors', 1973).

F. C. Wilkinson Commemoration Lectureship

In 1951 a fund was raised by members of the dental profession who had studied at or been associated with the Manchester Dental Hospital to commemorate Professor F. C. Wilkinson's tenure of the Chair of Dental Surgery. A trust was formed under which investments totalling £750 were handed to Manchester University to form the Wilkinson Trust Fund to defray the expenses of a lecture.

Awarding body: University of Manchester, Manchester M13 9PL, England.

Lecturers include: J. N. Peacock ('Changing Professional Relations', 1972); Prof. K. P. Liddelow ('Teeth and Tissues in Motion', 1974); Prof. Sir Robert Bradlaw ('Unto their Issue', 1976).

Leonard Willemsprijs

The prize was established in 1961 by the Belgian Royal Academy of Dutch Language and Literature in memory of Leonard Willems (1864–1938), the Flemish philologist. An award of 30,000 Belgian francs is made every two years to a Fleming who has made an outstanding published contribution in the field of Middle Dutch literary studies. Recipients must be Belgian nationals.

Awarding body: Koninklijke Academie voor Nederlandse Taal- en Letterkunde, Koningstraat 18, B-9000 Ghent, Belgium.

Recipients include: H. Vangassen (1963); J. Deschamps (1971); Prof. R. Lievens (1973).

Gwladys and Olwen Williams Lectureship in Medicine

The lectureship was established in 1947 by a gift of £500 to Liverpool University from Dr. Howel P. Williams, in accordance with the wishes of his late mother. The appointment is made every three years by the University Council. The lecturer delivers a lecture or course of lectures related to the study or practice of Medicine. The remuneration is the interest on the sum invested.

Awarding body: The University of Liverpool, P.O.B. 147, Liverpool L69 3BX, England.

Michael Williams Lecture

A lecturer is appointed every two years to deliver a lecture on some topic related to the causes or prevention of cancer. He receives an honorarium.

Awarding body: The Royal Society of Medicine, 1 Wimpole St., London W1M 8AE, England.

Gill Robb Wilson Award

This national award is made annually by the U.S. Air Force Association to an individual or organization for outstanding contributions in the field of arts and letters. It takes the form of a plaque. Instituted in 1948, it was originally named the Arts and Letters Trophy, but was renamed in 1966 in honour of Gill Robb Wilson (1893–1966), aviation writer and editor.

Awarding body: Air Force Association National Awards Committee, 1750 Pennsylvania Ave., N.W., Washington, D.C. 20006, U.S.A.

Recipients include: Hanson W. Baldwin (1972); Capt. Robert J. Hoag (1973); Capt. Tobias van Rossum Daum (1974); Maxine McCaffrey (1975); Michael Collins (1976).

Robert E. Wilson Award in Nuclear Chemical Engineering

This award is presented annually by the Nuclear Engineering Division of the American Institute of Chemical Engineers to a member of the Institute, in recognition of outstanding chemical engineering achievements in the nuclear industry. It consists of a certificate and wall plaque.

Awarding body: Nuclear Engineering Division of the American Institute of Chemical Engineers, 345 East 47th St., New York, N.Y. 10017, U.S.A.

Ludwig-Winkler-Plakette

This award was established in 1966 by the International Society for the History of Pharmacy, marking its fortieth year, together with the family of Dr. Ludwig Winkler (1873–1935) of the University of Innsbruck, who helped to found the Society in 1926 and was its Chief Executive Officer for many years. The award consists of a bronze plaque bearing a portrait of Winkler and is awarded to individuals or organizations who have given special service to the Society. It may be awarded at any appropriate time.

Awarding body: International Society for the History of Pharmacy, Graf-Moltke-Strasse 46, 2800 Bremen, Federal Republic of Germany.

Recipients include: Dr. Werner Luckenbach (Fed. Rep. of Germany, 1967); Prof. Franc Minarik (Yugoslavia, 1968); Dr. Curt Schelenz (Fed. Rep. of Germany, 1968); Philipp Firsching (Fed. Rep. of Germany, 1969); Prof. Hans Kaiser (Fed. Rep. of Germany, 1970).

Winsbury-White Lecture

A lecturer is appointed, not more frequently than every two years, to give a lecture on a medical subject, and receives an honorarium.

Awarding body: The Royal Society of Medicine, 1 Wimpole St., London W1M 8AE, England.

R. W. Wood Prize

The prize was established by the Board of Directors of the Optical Society in 1975 in honour of the many contributions made to optics by R. W. Wood. The prize consists of a cash award of $1,000 and a scroll. It is intended to recognize an outstanding discovery, scientific or technological achievement, or invention in the field of optics. The accomplishment for which the prize is given is measured chiefly by its impact on the field of optics generally, and therefore the contribution is one that opens a new area of research or significantly expands an established one. A five-year grant has been received from the Xerox Corporation in support of the prize.

Awarding body: Optical Society of America, 2000 L St., N.W., Washington, D.C. 20036, U.S.A.

Recipients include: Dr. Emmett R. Leith and Dr. Juris Upatnieks (1975); Dr. Theodore H. Maiman (1976).

World Press Photo of the Year

The award was started in 1956 when the Netherlands national competition for Press Photo of the Year was expanded to include published press photos from all over the world, and the pictures were judged by an international jury. It is an annual event. There are 11 categories of entries, and the best in each receives a Golden Eye Trophy; the second and third best photos in each category receive the Foundation's Gold Medal. The best picture over-all is named Press Photo of the Year; the photographer receives 5,000 Dutch guilders and a return ticket to Amsterdam to attend the prizegiving and the opening of the exhibition of winning photographs. Photographs are not returned (although original colour slides are), and form the basis of travelling exhibitions and World Press Photo Foundation records. A Yearbook containing all prize-winning pictures and a selection of runners-up is published annually.

Awarding body: World Press Photo Holland Foundation, P.O.B. 51333, Weesperzijde 86, Amsterdam, The Netherlands.

Recipients include: Wolfgang Peter Geller (Germany, 1972); Huynh Cong Nick Ut (Vietnam, 1973); Ovie Carter (U.S.A., 1975); Stanley Joseph Forman (U.S.A., 1976).

Wilbur and Orville Wright Memorial Lecture

This lecture is delivered annually by a distinguished figure in aeronautics. It was founded by the Council of the Royal Aeronautical Society in 1912 as the Wilbur Wright Memorial Lecture, in memory of the pioneer aviator. The name of Wilbur's brother Orville was added in 1965.

Awarding body: The Royal Aeronautical Society, 4 Hamilton Place, London W1V 0BQ, England.

Lecturers include: Sir George Edwards (U.K., 1973); Dr. A. H. Flax (U.S.A., 1974); Dr. K. G. Wilkinson (U.K., 1975); Dr. R. C. Seamans (U.S.A., 1976); David S. Lewis (U.S.A., 1978).

Wright Brothers Lectureship in Aeronautics

In 1975 the AIAA changed the name of the Wright Brothers Lecture to the present title. It commemorates the first powered flights made by Orville and Wilbur Wright at Kitty Hawk in 1903, and is intended to emphasize significant advances in aeronautics by recognizing major contributors thereto. It not only honours a particular person but, by means of the lecture, enables the recipient to share his technological gifts with AIAA membership and the public at large. The award consists of a medal and certificate of citation; the lecture is usually presented at the Aircraft Systems and Technology Conference.

Awarding body: American Institute of Aeronautics and Astronautics, 1290 Avenue of the Americas, New York, N.Y. 10019, U.S.A.

Recipients include: J. L. Atwood (1976); Gero Madelung (1977); George B. Litchford (1978).

Wright Brothers Medal

The Aeronautic Engineering Society of Automotive Engineers, Inc. established the medal in 1924, to honour the brothers Orville and Wilbur Wright and to encourage the presentation before the Society of the results of new developments in aeronautics, in the form of engineering papers. The scope of the award was broadened in 1961. The medal is awarded annually to the author of the best paper on aerodynamics, structural theory, research, construction, or operation of aeroplanes or spacecraft, which has been presented at a meeting of the Society or any of its sections during the previous calendar year. If no paper dealing with these subjects is deemed worthy, the medal may be awarded to the best paper on any other aeronautic and/or space subject. Papers are judged primarily for their value as new contributions to knowledge. All papers presented before a Society meeting are automatically considered. Three years must elapse after award of the medal to a given person before he can again be considered eligible.

Awarding body: Society of Automotive Engineers, Inc., 400 Commonwealth Drive, Warrendale, Pa. 15096, U.S.A.

Recipients include: Michael J. Wendl, Gordon G. Grose and V. Ralph Pruitt ('Flight/Propulsion Control Integration Aspects of Energy Management', 1974); J. A. Alic and H. Archang ('Comparison of Fracture and Fatigue Peoperties of Clad 7075-T6 Aluminum in Monolithic and Laminated Forms', 1975).

Wurdigungspreis des Bundesministerium fur Unterricht und Kunst (*Austrian Ministry of Education and Arts Prize*)

The prize is awarded annually to honour creative work in the fields of literature, music, fine arts and cinema. It is non-competitive; a special jury proposes candidates to the Minister. A prize is awarded in each category, and each award is worth 50,000 Schillings.

Awarding body: Bundesministerium für Unterricht und Kunst, 1014 Vienna, Minoritenplatz 5, Austria.

Recipients include: Michael Guttenbrunner (literature), Maria Lassnig (fine arts), 1975.

Wyld Propulsion Award

In 1964 the Propulsion Award and the James H. Wyld Memorial Award, honouring the developer of the regeneratively-cooled rocket engine, were combined to become the James H. Wyld Propulsion Award. The name was changed to its present form in 1975, and the award now is presented for outstanding achievement in the development or application of rocket propulsion systems. The award comprises a medal and certificate of citation, and is usually presented at the Propulsion Conference.

Awarding body: American Institute of Aeronautics and Astronautics, 1290 Avenue of the Americas, New York, N.Y. 10019, U.S.A.

Recipients include: Gerald W. Elverum, Jr. and Norman C. Reuel (1973); Clarence W. Schnare (1974); James Lazar and Roderick Spence (1975).

Y

Yant Award

This is an annual award established in memory of Dr. William P. Yant, first President of the American Industrial Hygiene Association. The award comprises a plaque and a cash prize and is made for outstanding achievement in the science of industrial hygiene. Candidates must be from outside the United States.

Awarding body: American Industrial Hygiene Association, 66 South Miller Road, Akron, Ohio 44313, U.S.A.

Recipients include: Jaroslav Teisinger (Czechoslovakia); C. H. Wyndham (South Africa); Clifford G. Warner (U.K.); Werner Klosterkotter (Fed. Rep. of Germany); Marcus M. Wasserman (Israel).

Ybl Miklós Prize for Architecture

Instituted by the Hungarian Council of Ministers in 1953, the prize is awarded annually by the Minister of Building Construction. It is an honorary distinction, divided into three classes, and given to architects and building engineers for outstanding designs conceived in the spirit of socialist realism, or for the implementation of such projects. It is named after Miklós Ybl (1814–91), the eminent architect whose principal work was the monumental Opera House in Budapest.

Awarding body: Committee for the Ybl Miklós Prize, Ministry of Building Construction, Beloiannisz-utca 2/4, Budapest V, Hungary.

Yorkshire Post Book of the Year

This award was established in 1965 by the *Yorkshire Post* newspaper. Patrons of its Literary Luncheons subscribe to two cash prizes (currently £400 and £250). If the choice for first prize is a work of fiction, the second prize is given for a work of non-fiction, and vice versa. Books should have been published during the preceding year, should not be translations or re-issues, nor of a strictly scientific or technical nature. Presentations are made at a Literary Luncheon.

Awarding body: Yorkshire Post, Literary Luncheons and Book of the Year, c/o Secretary (Richard Douro), P.O.B. 168, Wellington St., Leeds LS1 1RF, U.K.

Recipients include: David Cecil (*The Cecils of Hatfield House,* 1973); Philip Mason (*A Matter of Honour,* 1974); Paul Johnson (*Pope John XXIII,* 1975); Edward Crankshaw (*The Shadow of the Winter Palace,* 1976); Alistair Horne (*A Savage War of Peace – Algeria, 1954–62,* 1977).

Yoshikawa Prize

Two awards, established in 1967, are given annually under this title by the Kodansha publishing company: the Yoshikawa Prize for National Literature, and the Yoshikawa Prize for Culture. The first is given for the best book published in the previous year; it consists of a medal and 1 million yen. The second is awarded for outstanding work in any branch of culture; it consists of a clock and 300,000 yen.

Awarding body: Kodansha Ltd., 2-12-21, Otowa, Bunkyo-ku, Tokyo 112, Japan.

Graham Young Lectureship

A lectureship in Metallurgical Chemistry was instituted in 1899 at the University of Glasgow and endowed in 1908 by the Trustees of Thomas Graham Young. By minutes of 1959 and 1964 the University Court decided to apply the income of the endowment to the foundation of a Visiting Lectureship to be offered annually to a person of distinction in the field of chemistry or engineering or physics.

Awarding body: University of Glasgow, Glasgow G12 8QQ, Scotland.

Lecturers include: Prof. D. H. R. Barton (Prof. of Organic Chemistry, Imperial Coll., London, 1970); Alexander Thom (Emer. Prof. of Engineering Science, Oxford Univ., 1972); Prof. A. B. Pippard (Prof. of Physics, Cambridge Univ., 1974); Prof. Sir William Hawthorne (Churchill Coll., Cambridge, 1975); Prof. Manfred Eigen (Max-Planck-Institut, Fed. Rep. of Germany, 1976).

Thomas Young Medal and Prize

A bronze medal and a prize of £150 are awarded in odd-dated years for distinguished work in optics (including the optical principles existing in branches of physics other than that concerned with the visible region of the spectrum). The award was established in 1961 by the Council of the amalgamated Institute of Physics and Physical Society, to replace the Thomas Young Oration instituted in 1907. Candidates are considered on the recommendation of members of the Institute and of its Awards Committee.

Awarding body: The Institute of Physics, 47 Belgrave Square, London SW1X 8QX, England.

Recipients include: Dennis Gabor (1967); Giuliano Toraldo di Francia (1969); Charles Gorrie Wynne (1971); Walter Thompson Welford (1973); Daniel Joseph Bradley (1975).

Z

Morton Dauwen Zabel Award

Established by a bequest from Morton Dauwen Zabel in 1966, this prize is given each year to an American poet, writer of fiction, or critic, in rotation. The recipients should be writers of progressive, original and experimental tendencies rather than of academic and conservative tendencies. The award is a cash prize of $2,500.

Awarding body: American Academy and Institute of Arts and Letters, 633 West 155th St., New York, N.Y. 10032, U.S.A.

Zagreb World Festival of Animated Films

This festival, founded in 1972, is held every two years in June, and is recognized by the International Federation of Film Producers. Entries must not exceed 30 minutes in length, and must have been completed during the previous three years. The awards take the form of wooden sculptures. The Grand Prix is awarded to the best film of the festival. Prizes are also given to the best films in the following categories: educational films; children's films (not forming part of a series); films forming part of a television series; first films; films lasting less than three minutes; films longer than three minutes. Additional awards may be made for particular aspects of the craft, such as graphics, scenario, music and sound effects.

Awarding body: Svjetskog Festivala Animiranih Filmova Zagreb, Zagreb-Film, 41000 Zagreb, Vlaška ul. 70, Yugoslavia.

Recipients include: Nedeljko Dragić (*Diary*, Yugoslavia), Borivoj Dovniković (*Second Class Passenger*, Yugoslavia), Marcell Jankovics (*Sisyphus*, Hungary), Robert Bloomberg (*Animation Pie*, U.S.A.), Gerald Scarfe (*Long Drawn-Out Trip*, U.K.), 1974.

Sir Basil Zaharoff Lectureship

The lectureship was founded in 1918 by Sir Basil Zaharoff as part of his benefaction for the promotion of French studies at Oxford University. It is directed to be on some subject of French art, archaeology, history, literature, science or sociology. The lecturer is nominated alternately by the Vice-Chancellor of Oxford University and the Vice-Rector of the University of Paris.

Awarding body: University of Oxford, Wellington Square, Oxford OX1 2JD, England.

Lecturers include: Jean-Jacques Mayoux (Prof., Sorbonne Nouvelle, 'L'Humour et l'Absurde:

attitudes anglo-saxonnes, attitudes françaises', 1972–73); Theodore Besterman (Editor, *Studies on Voltaire and the 18th Century*, 'Voltaire on Arts: Unity and Paradox', 1973–74); Michel Butor (writer, 1974–75); R. C. Cobb (Fellow of Worcester Coll., Oxford, 1975–76).

S. H. Zaheer Medal

This medal was established in 1977 by the Indian National Science Academy. It is awarded every three years for outstanding contributions in the field of engineering and technology.

Awarding body: Indian National Science Academy, Bahadur Shah Zafar Marg, New Delhi 110001, India.

G. Zambon Benelux Prize

This award was established in 1974 by INPHAR-ZAM – International Pharmaceuticals Zambon S.A., and named in honour of the company's founder, Dr. G. Zambon. The award of 200,000 Belgian francs is for the encouragement of scientific research into infectious diseases and their treatment. The prize is awarded every two years to the author of the best original contribution to the understanding of the pathogenesis, diagnosis or treatment of infectious diseases. Candidates must be under 40 years old, possess a university degree, and be a national of one of the Benelux countries, although anyone who has studied at a university in one of these countries for at least two years is also eligible. Entries must normally be written in English, German, French or Dutch.

Awarding body: International Pharmaceuticals Zambon S.A., Ave. R. Vandendriessche 18, Bte. 1, 1150 Brussels, Belgium.

Recipients include: Prof. A. Billiau (1974); Dr. G. Cornelis (1976).

Zasłużony Działacz Kultury (*Cultural Merit Award*)

This award is given occasionally by the Polish Ministry of Culture and Art to a Polish citizen for special contributions in the field of Polish culture. The award consists of a badge.

Awarding body: Ministry of Culture and Art, Krakowskie Przedmieście 15/17, 00-071 Warsaw, Poland.

Zelter-Plakette (*Zelter Medal*)

This medal is awarded by the President of the Federal Republic of Germany to choral societies which have promoted choral music and the German folk song. The award was established in 1956. Applications are made through a committee to the regional Minister of Culture, and his recommendation is made to the President through the Minister of the Interior. Foreign choirs are recommended by the German Foreign Office.

Awarding body: Der Bundespräsident, c/o Bundesministerium des Innern, 5300 Bonn 7, Federal Republic of Germany.

John Peter Zenger Award

This award was established in 1954 by the University of Arizona Department of Journalism, and commemorates a colonial American printer who in 1734 was accused and acquitted of seditious libel. It is made for outstanding contributions to the freedom of the press and the people's right to information. Any American is eligible, but it is generally made to a journalist. Nominations are made by previous winners. The award is given annually, and consists of a silver and turquoise plaque, an honorarium of $250 from the Department of Journalism and the same amount from the Arizona Newspapers Association. The recipient is required to deliver an address.

Awarding body: Department of Journalism, University of Arizona, Tucson, Ariz. 85721, U.S.A.

Recipients include: Erwin D. Canham (*Christian Science Monitor*); *New York Times*; Katharine Graham (*Washington Post*); Seymour Hersh (*New York Times*); Don Bolles (posthumous).

Carl-Zerbe-Preis

The prize was established by the German Society for Petroleum Science and Coal Chemistry (DGMK) in 1973 in memory of Carl Zerbe (born 1894), a distinguished petroleum scientist and honorary member of the Society. It is awarded to younger scientists for self-contained projects of outstanding value in disciplines within the Society's scope of activity; the winner is selected by the executive of the Society, and may not be over 35 years of age. The award, normally made annually, consists of a certificate and a sum of money, determined each year. The Society also awards the Carl-Engler-Medaille (*q.v.*).

Awarding body: Deutsche Gesellschaft für Mineralöl- und Kohlechemie e.V., 2000 Hamburg 1, Nordkanalstr. 28, Federal Republic of Germany.

Recipients include: Dr. Ingo Berthold (Esso AG, Hamburg, for work on analysis of hydrocarbons and formulation of new lubricating oils, 1973); Dr. Dieter Severin (Clausthal Univ., for work on hydrocarbons of high boiling temperature, 1974); Dr. Günter Pusch (Deutsche Texaco AG, Weitze, for work on the reactions resulting from partial burning in petroleum storage vessels, by injection of oxygen and water, 1975); Dr. Jens Weitkamp (Karlsruhe Univ., for work on hydrogenizing conversion of hydrocarbons, contributing to the understanding of hydroisomerization and hydrocracking, 1976).

Zibet Prize

This prize was endowed in 1805 by Chr. B. Zibet under the auspices of the Swedish Academy, and is awarded approximately every second year. It is for historical, cultural or literary work with special reference to the reign of King Gustavus III, in whose memory the prize was endowed. It is a monetary prize, currently 5,000 Swedish kronor. It cannot be applied for.

Awarding body: The Swedish Academy, Börshuset, Källargränd 4, S-111 29 Stockholm, Sweden.

Karl-Ziegler-Preis

Established in 1975 by the companies Hoechst Aktiengesellschaft, Frankfurt/Main-Höchst and Chemische Werke Hüls Aktiengesellschaft, the prize is awarded in commemoration of Karl Ziegler (1898–1973), whose work involved in particular the chemistry of organo-metallic compounds and catalysis, and who won the Nobel Prize for Chemistry in 1963. The prize is awarded to German or non-German scientists for outstanding achievements in the chemistry of organo-metallic compounds, preferably in catalysis. The prize, a gold medal and DM20,000, is usually awarded at intervals of several years. It is presented at a general meeting of the Society of German Chemists. The recipient delivers the Karl Ziegler Memorial Lecture, in which he reports on his work.

Awarding body: Gesellschaft Deutscher Chemiker, 6000 Frankfurt (Main) 90, Carl Bosch-Haus, Varrentrappstr. 40–42, Federal Republic of Germany.

Recipients include: Prof. Georg Wittig (Fed. Rep. of Germany, 1975).

Zilveren Anjer (*Silver Carnation*)

The award is given to Dutch nationals of irreproachable patriotic character who in some way have contributed to the cultural life of the Netherlands, or of the Dutch overseas territories. The emblem is the five-leaved rose of the House of Lippe in silver, red-enamelled, inside which is a crowned, stylized silver carnation. The award is presented annually by H.R.H. the Prince of the Netherlands on or around 29 June, his birthday. The funds for the award are found from the bequest of the accumulated salary of the late Thys Taconis, who as a special agent in the second world war was dropped by parachute over Holland, and met his death in the fulfilment of his military service.

Awarding body: Prins Bernhard Fonds, Leidsegracht 3, 1017 NA Amsterdam, The Netherlands.

Recipients include: Dr. A. Horodisch (study and promotion of Dutch books in other countries), Jhr. M. de Jonge (restoration of old buildings in Zutphen), G. Kuipers (publications on the life of the people of Drenthe), 1978.

Zipernovszky Award

This award is made annually by the Hungarian Electrotechnical Association for a paper by a member published during the current year in one of the Association's technical reviews, containing the results of practical or theoretical work in the field of heavy-current electrical engineering. The award consists of a medal and cash prize of 7,000 forints. Instituted in 1912, it commemorates Károly Zipernovszky, distinguished inventor and pioneer in the field of applied electrotechnology.

Awarding body: Magyar Elektrotechnikai Egyesület, 1055 Budapest, Kossuth Lajos tér 6–8, Hungary.

Recipients include: Dr. Pál Ottó Geszti (1952); Dr. Károly Szendy (1958); Dr. György Vajda (1960); Dr. József Lukács (1970); Dr. Ferenc Kövevessi (1975).

Zoological Society of London Silver Medal

The medal was established in 1847, although the present terms of reference have been in force since 1964 only. A silver medal is awarded for contributions to the understanding and appreciation of zoology, including such activities as public education in natural history and wildlife conservation. Any person (other than a serving member of the Council of the Society) is eligible. Recommendations must be submitted by 1 October of the award year, and the winner is announced in the following January or February. Recommendations are requested annually, but the medal is only awarded occasionally.

Awarding body: The Zoological Society of London, Regent's Park, London NW1 4RY, England

Recipients include: David Attenborough (for his wide influence, particularly with young people, in the field of public education, 1965); Aubrey Buxton (for his contribution to the appreciation of natural history, in particular his work in promoting an understanding of wildlife conservation, 1966); James Fisher (for his contribution to the understanding of zoology and to public appreciation of the importance of conservation, 1968); Eric Hosking (for his distinguished work as a bird and animal photographer and his services to public education in zoology and to conservation, 1974); Gerald H. Thompson (for his work as a pioneer and leader of a team making zoological films of great value and high scientific quality, 1975).

Anders and Emma Zorn Prize

This annual prize was established in 1969 by the Swedish Academy to mark the 50th anniversary of the establishment of the Anders and Emma Zorn Bequest, left by the Swedish painter Zorn to fund the Bellman Prize (*q.v.*). The Anders and Emma Zorn Prize is awarded annually to a Swedish writer for a literary work, and consists of a cash prize of 20,000 Swedish kronor. It cannot be applied for.

Awarding body: The Swedish Academy, Börshuset, Källargränd 4, S-111 29, Stockholm, Sweden.

Alphabetical Index

Subject Index

Children's Literature

Civil Engineering

Manufacturing Engineering

Mathematics

Meteorology

Musicology

Natural Sciences

Nature Conservation

Naval Architecture and Marine Engineering

Navigation

Physiology

Plastic Arts

Geographical Index

Argentina
Gran Premio de Honor, 92
Inter-American Association of Writers Prizes, 118
Premio Academia Nacional de la Historia, 197
Premio Alberdi y Sarmiento, 197
Premio Florentino Ameghino, 198
Premio Integración para América Latina, 204
Premio 'Perito F. P. Moreno', 206
Premios de las Salas Nacionales de Exposición, 211

Australia
ANZAAS Medal, 1
'The Age' Book of the Year Award, 3
Alcoa of Australia Award for Architecture, 5
Andrews Lectureship, 13
Angus and Robertson Writers' Fellowships, 14
Australasian Institute of Metals Lecture, 17
Australasian Institute of Metals Silver Medal, 17
Australasian Institute of Mining and Metallurgy Medal, 17
Australasian Institute of Mining and Metallurgy President's Award, 17
Australian Film Awards, 17
Australian Numismatic Society Gold Medal, 18
Awgie Awards, 18
Batchelor, J. E., Award, 23

Book Design Award, 31
Brodie, John A., Medal, 35
Burnet Lecture, 37
Chapman, R. W., Medal, 45
Children's Book of the Year Award, 46
Clarke Medal, 48
Cook, James, Medal, 52
David Memorial Lectureship, 58
Dwyer Memorial Lectureship, 65
Flinders, Matthew, Lecture, 77
Foundation for Australian Literary Studies Award, 79
Franklin, Miles, Literary Award, 79
Gas Turbine Award, 84
Geach, Portia, Memorial Award, 85
Giblin Memorial Lectureship, 86
Gottschalk Medal, 91
Hartnett Award, 103
Johnston, R. M., Memorial Medal, 130
Jolly, Hilary, Award, 130
Julius, George, Medal, 131
Leighton, A. E., Memorial Award, 144
Liversidge Research Lectureship, 148
Logie Award, 149
Lord, Clive, Memorial Medal, 149
Lyle, Thomas Ranken, Medal, 150
Mackie Medal, 154

Uruguay

Venezuela

Yugoslavia